CONTENT

Mechanics' Magazine And Journal Of Science, Arts, And Manufactures, Volume 27

Andrew Ure

Engraved by R. Roffe, from an original Painting by Daniel M.ᶜ Nee.

For the Mechanics Magazine, Vol XXVI.

Published Dec.ʳ 14ᵗʰ 1831, by W. A. Robertson, Peterborough Court.

THE

MECHANICS' MAGAZINE,

MUSEUM,

Register, Journal,

AND

GAZETTE,

APRIL 8—SEPTEMBER 30, 1837

VOL. XXVII.

"Every positive determination in science is susceptible of extension, and of useful application, though the period may be distant. A microscopical observation, or an optical property, which at first sight is only curious and abstract, may thus in time become important to agriculturists and manufacturers."—BIOT.

LONDON:

PUBLISHED FOR THE PROPRIETOR, BY W. A. ROBERTSON,

MECHANICS' MAGAZINE OFFICE, PETERBOROUGH-COURT.

1837.

Engineering

T

1

M48

v27

PRINTED BY W. A. ROBERTSON, 6, PETERBOROUGH-COURT, FLEET-STREET.

REVIEWS AND CRITICAL NOTICES.

EXTRACTS.

NEW PATENTS.

ENGLISH.

Mechanics' Magazine,

MUSEUM, REGISTER, JOURNAL, AND GAZETTE.

No. 713.   SATURDAY, APRIL 8, 1837.   Price 3*d*.

BIRMINGHAM RAILWAY FACADE, EUSTON-SQUARE.

BIRMINGHAM RAILWAY FACADE, EUSTON-SQUARE.

We are happy to see that the Birmingham Railway is so far approaching a completion, that the works of a grand facade for the entrance at the London terminus have been commenced. The view on our front page is from a beautiful lithograph by Cheffins, and if the erection does not disappoint the hopes held out by the design, it will certainly be the grandest elevation of the kind in the metropolis. The architect (Mr. Hardwick) is already favourably known to the public as the designer of Goldsmith's Hall, and this work will add not a little to his reputation.

The erection consists of a Grecian Doric portico in antis, having on each side, in a similar style of architecture, lodges to be used as booking-offices, occupying altogether a frontage of 313 feet. The portico itself is 68 feet wide, the height of the columns 44 feet, and their diameter 8 feet 6 inches. The full height of the portico to the apex of the pediment, is 74 feet. The works are to be executed in Yorkshire freestone, from the Bramley Fall quarries.

In connexion with the engraving, the following particulars will give the architectural reader a clearer idea of the design :—

Grecian Doric Portico in antis.

	Ft.	In.
Diameter of columns	8	6
Height of ditto..................	44	0
Intercolumniation (from centre to centre of columns)	27	6
Ditto in clear	19	0
Total width of portico...........	68	0
Ditto height of ditto from level of pavement in Drummond-street to apex of pediment..........	74	0

Lodges, used as Booking-Offices.

Height ...:.....................	31	0
Width	28	0
Total frontage towards Drummond-st.	313	6

GEOLOGICAL ARGUMENTS IN FAVOUR OF THE ELECTRICAL THEORY.

Sir,—I promised in my last communication to make some remarks on Mr. Mackintosh's position relative to the derivation of the secondary and tertiary strata; I will now, with your permission, fulfil that promise, prefacing my remarks on this head, by making some observations on the letter of your correspondent, " A Country Teacher." I am, Sir, as your correspondent truly says, a perfect believer in the electrical theory, and the *story* of the five moons, I consider to be the most plausible part; but although I consider the theory to be correct as far as the observations of modern times will permit, I at the same time think that better reasons might be adduced in its support, especially in the geological part; and I am really surprized, that the wisdom of the opponents of this theory, has not detected several great mistakes which Mr. M. has made, *not in the theory itself*, but in the deductions he has made from geology in its support.

First, however, let me consider the letter of the teacher. He says, that, by the best authority, the quantity of matter in the moon is, to that in the earth, as 1 to 71. I would ask, on what authority does he base this equation? Has the "Country Teacher," found out that which has so long puzzled the scientific men of this and other countries—is he assured that the moon is a *solid* body, and that its solidity is the same as that of the earth? Is he even assured that the earth itself is a solid body? If he has found the answer to these questions, and can satisfy scientific men as to their propriety, he is certainly entitled to the respect and good wishes of all men. I am inclined to think for my own part that neither the earth, nor any of the planets are solid bodies, and if we are to receive as true the calculations of such an eminent practical astronomer as Sir John Herschel, we must come to the conclusion, that they are of different degrees of solidity and density. He states that the density of Saturn does not much exceed that of a cork ; and if the density of these planets be so different, is not also the density of the moon different from that of the earth? It certainly is in my opinion, and a little calculation with a few equations, would in some manner enable the "Country Teacher" to tell the difference ; and then he will be better enabled to proceed with his equation. M. De la Beche says in the beginning of his researches in theoretical geology, that " the sun and the known planets of our solar system are of different densities ; it therefore follows that the materials of which these bodies are respectively formed are either different, or do not exist under precisely the same conditions in each. Hence a given density is not necessary to the existence of a planet, and consequently, there is no argument à priori against the supposition that the density of a planet, such as the earth, may have changed during the lapse of time." Even allowing the supposition that the moon is a solid body, the equation of the "Country Teacher" itself is wrong. If he were to compute the solid contents of the increased diameter of the earth (18.5564 miles) and the solid contents of the moon (allowing it to be solid) and inform your readers which would contain the most matter, and what was the difference—if he will do this I may perhaps look at his equation again. He seems to be sadly afraid of what may happen to future generations. Let me tell him I am little inclined to think, that any natural phenonema would cease on account of the existence of man, or of any class of animals; earthquakes and storms pay no respect to the presence of man, nor would the fall of a moon. In the last part of the letter he says that the near approach of the moon would cause a second deluge, before the shock took place. If I had tried to bring before your readers, a proof of the fall of a sattellite, I could not have done much better than by endeavouring to prove, that the strata show marks of a repitition of such deluges. Let the "Country Teacher" examine the strata, and he will find there has been a deluge, then a concussion, then again a deluge accompanied with strong currents, such as the return of waters, driven away by the sudden fall of a great body into their basin. The moon on its near approach to the earth would occasion on that part nearest to it extremely high tides or a déluge; then would follow the concussion; then the waters would be driven back with great force by the concussion, and would afterwards endeavour to return as far as possible to their former basin, and eventually, after several fluctuations attain their level.

I have thus far, I hope, treated the opinions of your correspondent with civility and respect, and I hope for the sake of the cause he upholds he will do the same, and not descend to abuse or scurrility in the place of argument, I am not like " a Country Teacher" ashamed of my name,* but I have added it as a supporter of the electrical theory—and I stand as a supporter willing to receive any odium which may occur; not like the " Country Teacher" sheltering himself under an assumed name, ready to retreat if my cause fails, or if it should prove true to come before the world as its supporter.

Mr. Mackintosh says that the difference in composition and appearance of the secondary and tertiary strata, with the primary rocks, are some proof that the matter of these rocks has been obtained from different sources; or that the secondary and tertiary strata, are the matters of which the moons were composed, and he has carried the argument further by dividing them into four periods. Mr. M. happily is not like some of the opponents of this theory, positive and dogmatical in the arguments he has used; and if I may judge by the tenor of his communications, he will pardon me for endeavouring to set him right, especially when he *candidly* acknowledges, that he is not so thoroughly acquainted with geological facts as he should wish to be.

It may be as well to mention that the crust of the globe, is composed nearly, if not altogether, of sixteen commonly called simple substances, which are thus enumerated and classed by M. De la Beche† according to their respective importance-

Simple, not metallic substances.

1. Oxygen.
2. Hydrogen.
3. Nitrogen.
4. Carbon.
5. Sulpher.
6. Chlorine.
7. Fluorine.
8. Phosphorus.

Metallic bases of the alkalies and earths.

1. Silicium.
2. Aluminium.
3. Potassium.
4. Sodium.
5. Magnesium.
6. Calcium.

* How does it appear, that the "Country Teacher" is ashamed of his name? He has adopted, to be sure, an anonymous signature, but what of that? So have hundreds of men whose names are an to our literature.

† De la Beche, Res. Theo. Geol. page 24.

Metals, the oxides of which are neither alkalies nor earths.

1. Iron.
2. Manganese.

If we analize the various rocks and compare the results, we shall not find such a great difference, as we should at first sight be led to imagine: for instance, we will take granite, which has itself such a great variety of composition, as to contain in one case 47 silica, 10 iron oxide, 16 clay or alumina, 11 potash, and 4 magnesia; and clay slate, which to all appearance is decidedly of a different character, contains 49 silica, 23 clay, 11 iron oxide, and 5 potash; so that the difference between them is not so great as we should be led to imagine, if we were to judge only by their outward character and appearance. The graywacké group, again with the conglomerates, sandstones, limestones, clays and sands of the secondary and tertiary strata, are evidently formed from the detritus of those or similar rocks to what I have mentioned. The matter of which the old red sandstone is composed consist of fragments perfectly visible and belonging to the primitive rocks, as granite, primitive slates, quartz, &c., and the matter of this rock resembles very nearly in nature the rocks of the neighbouring mountains; the millstone grit of the coal measures is a rock evidently formed of the detritus of pre-existing rocks; rounded particles of other rocks are distinctly seen in it, and among them felspar. The red marl or the new red sandstone, has also every appearance of being formed of the matter of other masses; and many geologists thinks, that it is formed by a great agitation of the waters, which have washed down the looser and more exposed materials, of these elevated rocks which generally surround it, as the carboniferous limestone, the old red sandstone, slates, greenstones and other rocks. If we examine the coal-field of Somersetshire, we shall find a large tract of red marl, situated in a valley surrounded by the old red sandstone and the carboniferous limestone; it is evident that the red marl, is formed in this case by the action of water on the surrounding hills. I should thus be led to conclude that the secondary and tertiary strata are not directly formed by the deposition of a moon, (although in many cases the matter of the satellite may enter into their composition,) but that they are formed of the

detritus of pre-existing masses, either of the prior rocks of the earth, or of the matter of which the first deposited moons were formed. It may then be reasonably asked me, what would be the condition of the satellite after it had fallen? I dare say some of your readers have seen in frosty weather when the pools of water have been frozen, stones, &c. sticking in the ice, which have been thrown there perhaps by boys to see how strong it was; if not, let any of your readers, or the "Country Teacher" for them, take a stone, and throw it on the ice, and he will find, if the ice be not too thick, or the stone thrown with too great a force, that it will stick in the ice, part being imbedded and part exposed to view, in proportion to the thickness of the ice, or the force by which the stone was thrown. Just so, I think, would be the condition of a moon if it fell to the earth's surface, it would penetrate a considerable way into the earth's crust according to the velocity with which it fell, or the thickness of the earth's solid crust, (for I never can be brought to believe that the earth is of a stoney substance throughout its whole diameter) and form a chain of mountains, such as we see at present existing on the surface of the earth. I could, if your space would allow, show that this is the only reasonable mode of accounting for these high elevations; and that the doctrine of central heat being the only cause is entirely wrong; but I must leave it for the present, wishing the theory success. and hoping the "Country Teacher," with others, will be yet defenders of that which they now oppose.

I remain, Sir,

Yours respectfully,

Joshua Thorne.

March 27th, 1837.

SIR HUMPHRY DAVY, AND———

———————————————

——— (Sed longo intervallo!) ———

——————————————

———————————— John Herapath.

" He lifts up his leg at the noble beasts carcase,
And does—all a dog so diminutive can."

Moore.

Sir,—The readers of the *Mechanics' Magazine*, can scarcely yet have forgotten the very respectable figure which Mr. John Herapath cut in its pages a year or so ago,—how swaggeringly he enacted for a brief space the part of railway censor, (self elected thereto) and how soundly he got thrashed in the end for his pains — what havoc was made of his facts by your acute and intelligent correspondent H.—and what fun of his mathematical pretensions by my erudite and much esteemed friend Iver M'Iver. Never was literary discomfiture more complete —never exposure and disgrace more richly merited. Wordy as the wight is by nature, he had not at last a single word to say for himself; he was literally *beaten dumb*—convicted beyond all further denial of talking prodigious nonsense, and—*something more.* But Mr. John Herapath is like not many persons else in the world (God be thanked !)

"————things like him must sting
And higher beings suffer *   *   *
*   *   *   *   *   *   *
'Tis the reptiles nature."

He may be said, therefore, to act but " after his kind" in seeking no interval of repose from his appointed office in the economy of nature—in darting his fangs as often as opportunity offers, at any of that higher order of beings on whose skirts his lot is cast. When last Mr. John Herapath thrust himself upon the worlds notice, it was as the reviler of Sir John Rennie, and his Brighton line of Railway, for certain alleged faults, the worst of which were afterwards proved to be matter of pure invention. *Now* his censure has taken a higher aim; it is at the bust of Davy—one of the brightest ornaments of modern science, that he spits his venom.

" Though he roar'd pretty well—this the
    puppy allows
*   *   *   *   *   *   *
He vastly prefers his own little bow-wows
To the loftiest war note the lion could
    pour."

Nor is Davy the only " lion" at whom the " puppy" thrusts out his tongue; there is not one of the same noble tribe whom he does not treat with the like " puppy dog" insolence. That there may be no mistake, I shall, with your leave, Mr. Editor, quote Mr. John Herapath's own words.

" It is pretty generally known from a series of letters that appeared in the *Times*

newspaper during the years 1826, 1827, and part of 1828, which ended in *the expulsion* of *the tool* of my opponents, Sir H. Davy from the presidency of the Royal Society, that *I* am in possession of discoveries respecting the principles and laws of Natural Philosophy that have enabled ME to solve problems hitherto defying THE UTMOST EFFORTS of the scientific world, but which principles, &c., owing to the treatment I experienced, *have never been published,* with the exception of a few detached portions."

Sir Humphry Davy *expelled* from the presidency of the Royal Society, in consequence of any letters which ever appeared in the *Times* from Mr. John Herapath, or which could ever possibly proceed from Mr. John Herapath's pen!! *Monstrous supposition—monstrous falsehood!* No man before Mr. John Herapath ever presumed to apply the term *expulsion* to Sir Humphry's *voluntary resignation,* from ill health, of the high office he held—no other man perhaps could be so ungenerous, and so base.

" The tool" too, forsooth " of his opponents. What opponents ? I never knew that he had any within the walls of the Royal Society. I remember to have heard the letters he speaks of laughed at for their measureless impudence and conceit—but that, I am sure, was the utmost notice they ever elicited. He told us then, as he tells us now, that he is " in possession of (but keeps to himself) discoveries respecting the principles and laws of natural philosophy that have enabled him to solve problems hitherto defying the *utmost efforts of the scientific world."* But whose word had we for all this ? Mr. John Herapath's own. And whose word have we now ? Still Mr. John Herapath's own ! I should be glad to know what Mr. John Herapath has ever done for science that should entitle his word to any authority whatever in the scientific world ? What useful discovery has he ever made ? What real help ever given to the march of science ? There is nobody who might not safely assert quite us much as Mr. John Herapath does, if he would only, like Mr. John Herapath, keep the bushel measure, close shut upon the wonderful light which he asserts to be shining beneath. The probability is, that he is as ignorant of the efforts of others in any particular department of philosophy, as he is manifestly incapable of appreciating them with fairness and liberality. Nay, it is quite certain, that such must be the case; for no man with a spark of true philosophy in him could possibly demean himself after the manner of Mr. John Herapath—forever proclaiming himself the profoundest, wisest, cleverest of men, and never at any time giving proof of his being more than an addle-pated, serpent-toothed, vain-glorious braggart.

I am, Sir,
Your constant reader,
PHILO-DAVY.

Camden Hill, 3d April, 1837.

GAS STOVES.

Sir,—I am pleased to observe that my former communication upon this subject inserted in No. 701, has attracted the attention of two of your correspondents, Col. Macerone, in No. 705, and C. H. in No. 706. To the latter I feel obliged for the information he has furnished, and for the attention he has given to the matter.

Before I used a gas stove I had one of the description mentioned by Col. Macerone, which so dried the air as to make the room quite unpleasant, and it was for this reason, with others, I considered gas, if properly managed would be more advantageous; and I think the plan I have now adopted, and which I shall presently state, is preferable to any I have yet seen for the purpose for which I use it; and that the heat obtained is superior to that derived from coals in the usual manner, besides several other material benefits.

I have burnt gas, both in an open and a close stove, in the same apartment, and found the effects of the *former* to be quite in accordance with the statements of C. H., and believe the air in a confined room to be thereby rendered very injurious for respiration. When I wrote to you before, I was using a close stove, and the burnt air was carried off by a pipe about an inch in diameter; but I found the steam produced was so troublesome and disagreeable, that I tried several alterations until I came to the method I now use. I have increased the size of the pipe to three inches and a half in diameter, and find that the steam is thereby entirely got rid of; and though it might at first sight appear that a pipe

of such large dimensions would carry off too much heat, yet this is not the case, for by means of a ventilation at the end of the pipe the draught is decreased so as only to be sufficient to let the gas burn freely.

The following is a rough sketch of my present stove, for which I must apologize, not being an artist.

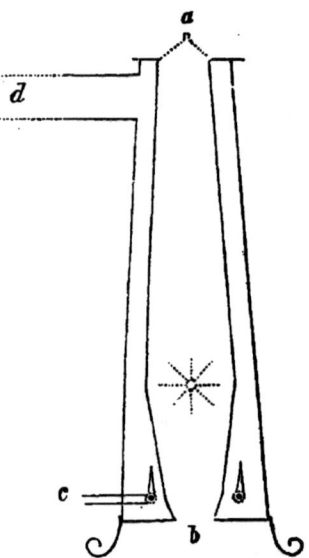

It is 2 feet 5 inches high, and stands on feet 3 inches from the floor, 7 inches square at the bottom, and 5 inches square at the top; mine is made square, but a round one would answer equally as well. It will be seen by the above that it is merely a double cone of iron, made of what is, I believe usually called sheet iron. The two cones are joined together at the top and made *air tight*. The inner cone is made tapering at the bottom, around which the gas burns in a ring, and between the two iron casings, so that no air *from the gas* can possibly enter the apartment, the whole being carried off through the pipe *d*. which is continued out into an open passage : with the former small pipe the gas *flickered* very much, there not being sufficient vent for the air, but with the present pipe (3½ inches) it burns very well; the gas pipe is introduced as marked at *c*.

and rests upon the bottom of the stove, which is made nearly close to the inner cone, so as only to allow enough air to keep the gas burning to enter. It would, however, be better probably to have it quite close round the inner cone and regulate the admission of the air for the gas by a slide or ventilator. At first I had the bottom of the stove *under the gas* open; but I think that by the supply of air being restricted, the iron becomes more heated, and of course warms the room better. The external surface of the stove being heated, of course gives out some warmth to the apartment as well as the pipes, which may be carried all round it, in the same manner as for hot water; but the principal warmth is derived from the air which circulates *up the middle* of the stove from *b.* to *a.* both ends being left *open*, excepting merely a ventilator placed at the top. The bottom of the inner cone should be small, so as not to admit more air than will be heated in its passage up the stove; and a grating might be placed in the middle of the inner cone to prevent the draught being too rapid if the stove be large.

As your correspondent C. H. stated, that no exact information can be given as to the cost and consumption of these stoves, I have made particular observations respecting mine, and will give you that result. The cost of the stove and pipe is under £2; gas ring and fixing about 15s. My room is 9 feet high, 6 wide and 13 feet long. I have a thermometer in it and always keep the temperature, even in the coldest days *between* 55 and 60 deg. (I think there is hardly any other method by which such an even temperature could be obtained, and it is raised or lowered at pleasure by merely turning the stop-cock of the gas pipe.) The gas ring is 4 inches square and contains 40 holes. The gas is *usually* turned about half on. I burn by a three light meter; and from repeated calculations made at various times I find that upon a general average the gas consumed is under *five feet an hour*, so that 100 feet (which is here charged 1s. 2d.) would last upwards of 20 hours. I am thus minute as I have never yet seen any such particulars given, and I imagine they would form sufficient data for any persons who might wish to reckon the expense of gas heating in what I con-

ceive quite an unobjectionable method There are many advantages which I need hardly enumerate—such as, no smoke, no smell, no dust, no trouble in lighting a fire, nor any attention required to keep it alight afterwards; the power of obtaining any required temperature, and maintaining it at an equal height. No chimney necessary, nor any danger from sparks, as the stove may be set any where with perfect safety. I will, however, now conclude for the present, and should further information be required by any of your correspondents, I shall (if in my power) be happy to afford it.

I am, &c.

EVANDER.

17th March, 1837.

<hr>

RIGHTS OF INVENTORS.

Sir,—The plainest truths are usually so overlaid by attendant circumstances, that it is long before they are disentangled; and before they are so disentangled, it seems they cannot be generally understood. How else, Sir, are we to account for the slow, the very slow progress both of the sciences, and the arts which relate to the rights and constitution of society?

One would have thought that no right could possibly be clearer, than that of property arising from production by any effort, whether of hand or head,—that is, whether of labour or invention. The right as arising from labour, was long in establishing itself in organized society; and for want of its establishment innumerable mischiefs scourged all the nations, and the plagues have not yet passed away. The right as arising from invention, seems to be but just now struggling into light and strength.

The design of the patent laws seems hitherto to have been, not to protect justly the inventor, but to extract from inventors the greatest possible number of inventions; the benefit of the public (which public is in the present case a sophistical personification) being the justifying reason. But like other schemes of profit against right, it has signally defeated itself. The classes from whom inventions and improvements would most abundantly, and most efficaciously come, furnish only such as genius and perseverance can thrust by main force through the penury and injustice which imprison them, and of the greater part of these they are robbed. And so I conceive it must be as long as the devisers of patent laws concoct only cunning schemes to keep down the number of patents—to ensure the respectability of patentees—to obtain a proof that the patentee has the means of working out his invention,—or to effect other irrelevant, minor, or mischievous objects; the arguments or pretences of the majority of those who defend the *principle* of the present laws. Would it not have been as reasonable in days of personal danger on the highway, to defend that state of things because it kept poor men from the cost of travelling, and from losing the love of home,—that with safer roads no one would know where to look for his servant, or how to trace a thief; that danger in travelling prevented the sedition which might arise from the two easy intercourse of the labouring classes—that it engendered a bold and martial spirit which was worth more than the wrong it permitted; that the expense of safety made travelling a distinctive gratification of those who alone ought to indulge in it; and by other such arguments—as to defend the principle of the present patent laws by those usually employed? Why should not the law defend inventions as zealously and as jealously as it defends our houses, and our highways? And why may not social effects be anticipated from this new security, given to this most important branch of natural right, as extensive and as conducive to human happiness as those which have followed from the established security of person and of material property?

I am not forgetting that there are other interests to protect besides those of the persons who *have* invented. An uncultivated common may justly be trodden over in any direction, by any human being whatever, though the improvements on the cultivated patch by the side of it, are as justly defended from intrusion. Just so, whatever of science or art has been appropriated by mental labour, is theirs to keep, to sell, or to give away, who have so laboured, (the limitation of the right as to time is another question)—but the infinite remainder is for whoever will use it, and may be appropriated in any part, by whoever will

create a right to it. But in both cases, and especially in that of intellectual property, public and individual justice imperatively require that the appropriated portions should be defined by unhidden landmarks.

The first step, and an indispensable portion of any just and effective system of patent laws, is therefore, the publication of all that has been patented,—condensed, classed, disencumbered of obscuring forms, with correct references to the actual specifications; and so published and deposited, that the working inventor can have free and cheap access, in any part of the kingdom, to this information. To say that the present enrolment and custody of the specifications is, for any purpose of justice towards succeeding inventors, a publication, is a fiction which insults the multitudes it injures. It was with great pleasure I read your advocacy of some such step as this, in your last week's remarks on the Patent Bill, now before Parliament.

I have now, as on a former occasion, to ask pardon for whatever may appear dogmatical in these observations; my design has been to bring the argument into little room. Should, therefore, any of your readers entertain other views, I beg to assure them I shall not be the least grateful of those who may benefit by the discussion of them.

I am, Sir,

Yours with great respect,

J. CHAPMAN.

MR. MACKINNON'S PATENT LAW AMENDMENT BILL.

Sir,—In offering through the means of your journal, a few observations upon the general features of this bill, I do not intend to interfere with the editorial notice of it, given in a late number. I propose rather to allude to the principles of amelioration in our law and practice relative to letters patent for inventions which the bill embodies,—than to discuss its particular clauses. Those principles, as may be gathered from Mr. Mackinnon's speech upon the first reading of his bill—consist in altering the present mode of obtaining the grant, in simplifying the official process, in the abrogation of the government stamp duties, and in lessening of the general expenses of patents for the united empire, and in affording better security to patentees and inventors. The practical difficulties which encompass the combination of these desiderata, in an act of parliament, can only be appreciated by those who possess an intimate knowledge of the evils and imperfections of the existing system of patent grants, and who have actually given their attention to the framing of legislative improvements suited to the requirements of the case. The details of a truly efficient act for the ample security of the inventive talent of the country, can only be founded upon a calm review of the evidence reported by the Committee of Inquiry, upon patent law and practice, appointed by the House of Commons in 1829, aided by a broad and liberal estimation of the close connexion which exists. between our national prosperity, and protection to our national genius employed in the discovery of improvements, in the various branches of art and manufacture.

Now in the examinations before that Committee, the general weight of the evidence, of the most practical and enlightened men, was in favour of the substitution of a commission, or some similar power, for the consideration of petitions and matters relative to the grant of invention patents, in lieu of the cumbrous antiquated machinery of the existing mode. The reports, references, warrants, caveats, oppositions,—the sign manuals, signets, and seals of the present system, were denounced by almost every man examined, who was unconnected with the official duties and emoluments of the present complicated forms. Mr. Mackinnon's bill professes to simplify all this process by the establishment of a permanent commission of scientific and capable men, who shall regulate an improved system under sanction of the Lord Chancellor; and who shall determine, in the first instance, as a court, matters relative to patents for inventions. Certainly, all new details, should under such a commission, be as simple, and inexpensive as they can be rendered, consistently with the great object of public security, and protection to inventors. The commissioners will certainly have no sinecure station allotted them; but still their salaries should be of that moderate amount, that should be deemed but a fair equivalent for the talent and

industry required under this new system. The first clauses in Mr. Mackinnon's bill, should, undoubtedly, have been such as declared the general principles of protection to patent property, and specific ameliorations in that respect,—in which points the bill appears deficient. But when we consider the great difficulties of preparing a bill which should embrace the various necessary improvements—and the failures which have attended the several attempts to legislate upon this " intricate and important subject" since the Committee sat—and when we consider that the Committee found the matters so difficult, that they actually left it in the lurch, and framed no report upon the evidence, as ordered by the House—we cannot but feel obliged to any member, who takes up *the forlorn hope*, and in the face of repeated failure, engages the attention of the legislature to the subject. Mr. Mackinnon's bill is open to all improvements that may be proposed in Committee; he has in his place pledged himself to the support of every efficient amelioration offered; the least that he is entitled to expect in response to this manly pledge, is the support of the public voice to enable him to redeem it by advocating the second reading of the bill,* and presenting to the House sensible and practicable clauses as improvements upon it, so that the great objects which Mr. Mackinnon professes to have in view, may be worked out, and be by the wisdom of Parliament, combined into that practical, rational amelioration of our patent law, which shall eventually bring forth and render available to the national prosperity—the mighty hidden intellectual resources of the inventive talent of this commercial empire.

I am, Sir, your humble servant,
AMICUS PATRIÆ.

20th March, 1837.

SOLUTION OF THE FIRST GEOMETRICAL QUESTION.—BY A WESTMINSTER SCHOLAR. See Vol. xxvi. p. 400.

Problem 1. Given, the base, the vertical angle, and the ratio of the segments

---

* We understand that Messrs. Mackinnon and Baines do not intend to proceed with the bill.—ED. M. M.

of the straight line as divided by the centre of the inscribed circle, and drawn from the vertical angle to the base—to construct the plane triangle.

Let $m\,n$ be the given ratio of the sides, and upon A B, the given base, describe a segment of a circle, A C B, containing an angle equal to the given vertical an-

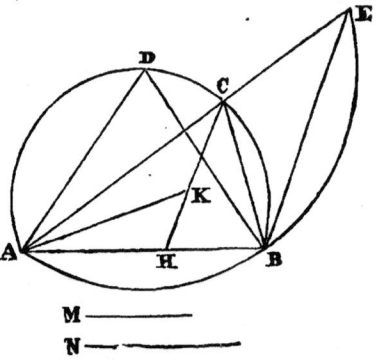

gle. Bisect the arc A C B in D; join D A, D B, and from the centre D, and distance D A or D B; describe the circle A B E, in which place A E, a fourth proportional to $m\,n$ and A B, and let A E meet the circle A D B in C. Join A B, C B, B E; then shall A C B be the triangle required. Bisect the angles A C B, C A B by the straight lines A K C K, and let C K meet the base A B in H. Then K is the centre of the inscribed circle.

Then, because the angle A C B = A D B = twice the angle A E B, also the angle A C B is bisected by the line C H; hence the angle A C H = A E B, consequently, C H is parallel to B E $\therefore$. A B : A E :: A H : A C :: H K : C K; but by construction $m : n :: $ A B : A E; hence H K : K C :: $m : n$. Wherefore, &c.

W. W. D.

Dean's Yard, March 3rd, 1837.

―――

ON ORIGINALITY OF INVENTION.— MR. WIVELL'S FIRE-ESCAPE.

Sir,—Whenever a simple contrivance is made known, and it becomes of importance to the public, there are ever to be found persons to take advantage of the *inventor*, because he has not protected himself by *patent*. I am induced to make this remark, in consequence of some mention of my name in p. 450 of your Magazine (No. 709), in which con-

siderable value is put upon a *pair of wheels* which ascend the front of a house to the *first length* of Mr. Merryweather's ladder: but, how far Mr. M. became the person who first had recourse to *wheels* either for his elevator or the said ladder, must appear in the statement which follows :—

In the early part of the year 1829, I gave some attention to fire-escapes,—not with a view to pirate the work of any man, for at that time I had never seen an escape of any kind. I heard of attempts having been made to ascend a *rope* up to the highest window of a house, which had *failed;* and it occurred to me that an *elevator constructed upon the principles of that which Mr. Merryweather claims to be his invention*, might answer the purpose. Such a machine as this I *first* contrived, and brought into public notice on the 4th of August, 1829. Reporters of newspapers attended its exhibition, and a notice of it appeared in the *Examiner* and others; the *Morning Herald* of the 8th August gave a long and correct account of the machinery and its performance. " Of the *elevator*," it states,—" It consists of a number of hollow wooden tubes, about five or six feet long, and an inch and a half or two inches in diameter, the top of each being lined with copper. These fit into each other, till the whole reaches the third or fourth story of a house. At the top of them are *two iron wheels.* with a projecting iron rod," &c. The above trial took place at the dwelling of Mr. Savage, in Titchfield-street, Oxford Market. The time occupied was four minutes and a half; in that time six persons descended from the window in the roof, four storys high. Now, as Mr. Merryweather's elevator did not appear in public for some months after, and was in every respect like mine, I cannot believe it to be the *invention* of Mr. Merryweather, but a direct copy from the *true original* by myself.

In the spring of 1836, I contrived an escape ladder upon a different plan to any yet offered, at the top of which was a pair of wheels; a model of the same was exhibited at the vestry-room of St. Pancras, at the time I gave a lecture upon the subject of escapes. Shortly after, I was at an exhibition of *Mr. Merryweather's ladder,* which had *no wheels;* but on my observing to the Treasurer of the Committee for fire-escapes in St. Pancras the advantage which would be derived from the application of wheels to the first portion of the series, such wheels were affixed accordingly, and exhibited shortly after.. It appears also that Mr. Baddeley had suggested the same idea to Mr. Merryweather, whose mechanical powers appear to require the united efforts of others to help him through in borrowed robes.

The *Humane Society for Fire-Escapes,* established in March last, was formed through myself, by calling public meetings at my own expence, without the aid of any one of the members who pride themselves as being of the South-West District of St. Pancras Society for Fire-Escapes. The Humane Society has adopted my fire-escape ladders, which I shall at any time be most willing to work in competition with any other which may be *deemed the best.*

I am, Sir, your most obedient,
And very humble servant,
ABRAHAM WIVELL.
Camden Town, March 23, 1837.

WATER FOR FUEL.

Respected Friend,—Twelve years ago I proposed to you, that telegraphic intelligence might be held by the electric shock through a chain of conductors, to any extent; the signals to be given by firing gunpowder at given stations in the line of correspondence. Two years afterwards the experiment was tried, either in consequence of my suggestion or otherwise, between two vessels afloat at some distance from each other; the conductors passed from the first vessel to the mast head, and then to the deck of the second vessel, and thence back to the machine: gunpowder was fired by the electric fluid at both the points mentioned, and the shock returned to the jar, as I supposed it would, without any perceptible loss of time.

Have you the boldness to propose to the public, that *at some future time,* under the forming hand of science, combined with practice, WATER MAY BE USED FOR FUEL? Now, "*let no dog bark;*" I am not going to throw a bowl of water on my kitchen fire!

Water is decomposed by electricity, and in being decomposed, is resolved into gases of a highly inflammable nature. Electricity is brought into action by the revolution of a circular plate of glass with certain accompaniments of easy attainment: a plate of glass of 18 inches diameter will produce more electricity than the human body loves to endure, and will decompose *a little water;* but what is to prevent a steam-engine from turning twenty or a hundred plates of glass of 12 feet diameter? Of water, we know there is enough; of electricity, the store is wholly inexhaustible; and we shall never lack glass while flints may be digged; and kelp (kali in all its forms) continues to grow—and that will grow which is cultivated.

You will perceive that I propose the possibility of using these oxygen and hydrogen gases in aid, or instead of, other fuel, in maritime navigation—and then, the world is an open book.

It has pleased God to give to mankind, his children, little by little, as their capacity could bear it, of the tremendous powers of his natural creation, for their use, at their peril always, to apply or to misapply, his gifts; hence new wonders of science have gradually unfolded, which, to the age gone by, would have appeared impossible and absurd. It is my belief that water is the most combustible of all things that naturally and plentifully occur to us; and whether this hint of mine be received or no, I have no doubt that, in due course of time, the principle referred to will be brought into operation.

I am, respectfully,
EDMUND FRY.

3d Month 27th, 1837, Bishopsgate-street.

AN EXPERIMENTAL ENQUIRY INTO THE MODES OF WARMING AND VENTILATING APARTMENTS. BY ANDREW URE, M.D. F.R.S., ETC.

Read before the Royal Society on the 16th of June, 1836.

⁓ (From the *Architectural Magazine* for April).

THE subjects of warming and ventilating apartments, in reference to the comfort and health of their inmates, have lately excited a great deal of attention. The commissioners delegated by government to inquire into the circumstances of factory labour adverted in their reports to some of the expedients employed for ventilating certain cotton mills ; and, more recently, a select committee of the House of Commons has considered and reported upon the best mode of ventilating and warming the new Houses of Parliament. In an extensive tour which I made, during the two preceding seasons, through England, France, and Belgium, to investigate the applications of chemical and mechanical science to manufactures, I paid particular attention to these subjects, so interesting to science, as well as humanity ; and I have had my mind professionally turned to them by the Directors of the Customs Fund of Life Assurance, on account of the very general state of indisposition and disease prevailing among those of their officers (nearly 200 in number) engaged on duty in the Long Room of the Custom House, London. I now respectfully submit the result of my observations and experiments on these points of public interest to the Royal Society.

The symptoms of disorder experienced by the several gentlemen (about twenty in number), whom I examined out of a great many who were indisposed, were of a very uniform character. The following is the result of my researches :—

A sense of tension or fulness in the head, with occasional flushings of the countenance, throbbing of the temples, and vertigo, followed, not unfrequently, with a confusion of ideas, very disagreeable to officers occupied with important, and sometimes intricase, calculations. A few are affected with unpleasant perspiration on their sides.— The whole of them complain of a remarkable coldness and languor in their extremities, more especially the legs and feet, which has become habitual, denoting languid circulation in these parts, which requires to be counteracted by the application of warm flannels on going to bed. The pulse is, in many cases, more feeble, frequent, sharp, and irritable than it ought to be, according to the natural constitution of the individuals. The sensations in the head occasionally rise to such a height, notwithstanding the most temperate regimen of life, as to require cupping, and at other times depletory remedies. Costiveness, though not a uniform, is yet a prevailing symptom.

The sameness of the above ailments, in upwards of one hundred gentlemen, at very various periods of life, and of various temperaments, indicates clearly sameness in the cause.

The temperature of the air in the Long Room ranged, in the three days of my experimental inquiry, from 62 deg. to 64 deg. of Fahrenheit's scale ; and in the Examiner's Room it was about 60 deg., being kept somewhat lower by the occasional shutting of the hot-air valve, which is here placed under the control of the gentlemen ; whereas that of the Long Room is designed to be regulated in the sunk story, by the fireman of the stove, who seems sufficiently careful to maintain an equable temperature amidst all the vicissitudes of our winter weather. Upon the 7th of January, the temperature of the open air was 50 deg., and on the 11th it was only 35 deg. ; yet, upon both days, the thermometer in the Long Room indicated the same heat of from 62 deg. to 64 deg.

The hot-air discharged from the two cylindrical stove-tunnels into the Long Room was 90 deg. upon the 7th, and at 110 deg. upon the 11th. This air is diluted, however, and disguised by admixture with a column of cold air before it is allowed to escape. The air, on the contrary, which heats the Examiner's Room undergoes no such mollification, and comes forth at once in an ardent blast of fully 170 deg. ; not unlike the simoom of the desert, as described by travellers. Had a similar nuisance, on the greater scale, existed in the Long Room, it could not have been endured by the merchants and other visitors on business ; but the disguise of an evil is a very different thing from its removal. The direct air of the stove, as it enters the Examiner's Room, possesses, in an eminent degree, the disagreeable smell and flavour imparted to air by the action of red-hot iron ; and, in spite of every attention on the part of the fireman to sweep the stove apparatus from time to time, it carries along with it abundance of burned dusty particles.

The leading characteristic of the air in these two rooms is its dryness and disagreeable smell. In the Long Room, upon the 11th, the air indicated, by Daniell's hygrometer, 70 per cent. of dryness, while the external atmosphere was nearly saturated with moisture. The thermometer connected with the dark bulb of that instrument stood at 30 deg. when dew began to be deposited upon it, while the thermometer in the air stood at 64 deg. In the court behind the Custom-house, the external air being at 35 deg., dew was deposited on the dark bulb of the hygrometer by a depression of only 3 deg.; whereas in the Long Room on the same day, a dépression of 34 deg. was required to produce that deposition. Air, in such a dry state, would evaporate 0·44 in. depth of water from a cistern in the course of twenty-four hours, and its influence on the cutaneous exhalents must be proportionally great.

As cast-iron always contains, besides the metal itself, more or less carbon, sulphur, phosphorus, or even arsenic, it is possible that the smell of air passed over it in an incandescent state may be owing to some of these impregnations; for a quantity of noxious effluvia, inappreciably small, is capable of affecting not only the olfactory nerves, but the pulmonary organs. I endeavoured to test the air as it issued from the valve in the Examiner's Room, by presenting to it pieces of white paper moistened with a solution of nitrate of silver, and perceived a slight darkening to take place, as if by sulphurous fumes. White paper, moistened with sulphuretted hydrogen water, was not in the least discoloured. The faint impression on the first test paper may be, probably, ascribed to sulphurous fumes, proceeding from the ignition of the myriads of animal and vegetable matters which continually float in the atmosphere, as may be seen in the sunbeam admitted into a dark chamber : to this cause, likewise, the offensive smell of air, transmitted over red-hot iron, may, in some measure, be attributed, as well as to the hydrogen resulting from the decomposition of aqueous vapour, always present in our atmosphere in abundance; especially close to the banks of the Thames, below London Bridge.

When a column of air sweeps furiously across the burning deserts of Africa and Arabia, constituting the phenomenon called simoom by the natives, the air becomes not only very hot and dry, but highly electrical, as is evinced by lightning and thunder. Dry sands, devoid of vegetation, cannot be conceived to communicate any noxious gas or vapour to the atmosphere, like the malaria of marshes, called miasmata; it is, hence, highly probably that the blast of the simoom owes its deadly malignity, in reference to animal as well as vegetable life, simply to extreme heat, dryness, and electrical disturbance. Similar conditions, though on a smaller scale, exist in what is called the bell, or cockle, apparatus for heating the Long Room and the Examiner's apartment in the Custom-house. In consists of a series of inverted, hollow, flattened pyramids of cast-iron, with an oblong base, rather small in their dimensions, to do their work sufficiently in cold weather when moderately heated. The inside of the pyramids is exposed to the flames of coke furnaces, which heat them frequently to incadescence, while currents of cold air are directed to their exterior surfaces by numerous sheet-iron channels. The incandescence of these pyramids, or bells, as they are vulgarly called, was proved by pieces of paper taking fire when I laid them on the summits. Again, since air becomes electrical when it is rapidly blown upon the surfaces of certain bodies, is occured to me that the air which escapes into the Examiner's Room might be in this predicament. It certainly excites the sensation of a cobweb playing round the head, which is well known to all who are familiar with electrical machines. To determine this point, I presented a condensing gold-leaf electrometer to the said current of hot air, and obtained faint divergence, with negative electricity. The electricity must be impaired in its tension, however, in consequence of the air escaping through an iron grating, and striking against the flat iron valves, both of which will tend to restore the electric equilibrium. The air blast, moreover, by being diffused round the glass of the condenser apparatus, would somewhat mask the appearances. Were it worth while, an apparatus might be readily constructed for determining this point, without any such sources of fallacy. The influence of an atmosphere charged with electricity in exciting headache and confusion of thought in many persons, is universally known.

The fetid burned odour of the stove air, and its excessive avidity for moisture, are of themselves, however, sufficient causes of the general indisposition produced among the gentlemen who are permanently exposed to it in the discharge of their public duties.

From there being nearly a vacuum, as to aqueous vapour, in the said air, while there is nearly a plenum in the external atmosphere round about the Custom-house, the vicissitudes of feeling in those who have occasion to go out and in frequently must be highly detrimental to health. The permanent action of an artificially desiccated air on the animal economy may be stated as follows :—

The living body is continually emitting a

transpirable matter, the quantity of which, in a grown up man, will depend partly on the activity of the cutaneous exhalence, and partly on the relative dryness or moisture of the circumambient medium. Its average amount, in common circumstances, has been estimated at 20 ounces in twenty-four hours.

When plunged in a very dry air, the insensible perspiration will be increased; and, as it is a true evaporation or gasefaction, it will generate cold proportionally to its amount. Those parts of the body which are most insulated in the air, and furthest from the heart, such as the extremities, will feel this refrigerating influence most powerfully. Hence the coldness of the hands and feet, so generally felt by the inmates of the apartment, though its temperature be at or above 60 deg. The brain, being screened by the skull from this evaporating influence, will remain relatively hot, and will get surcharged, besides, with the fluids which are repelled from the extremities by the condensation, or contraction, of the blood-vessels caused by cold. Hence the affections of the head, such as tension, and its dangerous consequences. If sensible perspiration happen, from debility, to break forth from a system previously relaxed, and plunged into dry air, so attractive of vapour, it will be of the kind called a cold clammy sweat on the sides and back, as experienced by many inmates of the Long Room.

Such, in my humble apprehension, is a rationale of the phenomena observed at the Custom-house. Similar effects have resulted from the hot-air stoves of a similar kind in many other situations.

After the most mature physical and medical investigation, I am of opinion that the circumstances above specified cannot act permanently upon human beings without impairing their constitutions, and reducing the value of their lives. The Directors of the Customs Fund are therefore justified in their apprehensions, "'that the mode of heating the Long Room is injurious to the health of persons employed therein, and that it must unduly shorten the duration of life."

It is evident, moreover, that the public service must suffer serious inconvenience in consequence of so many revenue officers, of great experience in business, being constantly exposed to the influence of a cause under which the most perspicacious intellect may become confused, and the most vigorous frame may be frequently disqualified for the discharge of a daily recurring duty. In fact, the absences among the officers of the Long Room in consequence of indisposition must be detrimental to the service, and may, for the most part, be traced to the malaria of the stoves.

For the purpose of producing a comfortable temperature in the air of the rooms occupied by individuals of a sedentary calling, like the in-door officers of his Majesty's Customs, cast-iron pipes, circulating steam a few degrees above the 212th degree of Fahrenheit's scale, should be distributed along the floor, close to the line of desks within which the officers sit. A corresponding range of small orifices should be made in the lower part of the desk partitions, for permitting the free ingress of the warm air around their limbs; and a series of sliding plates should be attached, for regulating these orifices, so as to enable each individual to suit the supply of warmth to his peculiar feelings and constitution. Self-acting register valves should, at the same time, be fixed aloft in the Long Room, which would regulate the discharge of foul air, and maintain a wholesome ventilation in the air below.

Nothing can be more preposterous, in an economical and scientific point of view, than the mode of introducing the hot-air into the Long Room, through two wide vertical tunnels in the line of its centre, whence it rises rapidly to the lofty roof, and can communicate warmth to the inmates, seated near the floor, only by reverberating downwards in a polluted state of mixture, with many cutaneous and pulmonary exhalations. Whereas the great principle of ventilation is, never to present the same portion of air twice over to the human lungs, but to supply them at each fresh inspiration with pure aerial particles, in a genial thermometric and hygrometric condition. Such air should be poured in, rightly prepared, from innumerable orifices in or near the floor, and pass up over the living frames, never to be thrown back upon them, but to be discharged through an equivalent number of orifices in the ceiling, too small to permit a counter current of cold air downwards. By such ceaseless circulation, comfort and health would be permanently secured, at probably one fourth part of the expenditure of fuel now consumed in corrupting the aerial element, and in placing many valuable lives in jeopardy.

In the recent report of the Parliamentary Committee, it is truly surprising that not a syllable is said about the methods of warming and ventilating apartments employed in the factories, although they afford unquestionably the best models for imitation, being the results of innumerable experiments made on a magnificent scale, with all the lights of science, and all the resources of our ablest civil engineers.

The warming is effected by horizontal ranges of cast-iron steam-pipes, properly supported or suspended, so as to give free play to their expansion and contraction from alternations of temperature, as well as to secure the equable distribution of low-pressure steam, and the ready efflux of the water of condensation. There cannot be a single doubt of this system being the only one which can, with safety, certainty, and economy, be used in preparing in one or more antechambers a body of genial air, to be thereafter diffused through the Houses of Parliament and their subordinate committee rooms. The only point which can admit of discussion is, the mode of renewing the atmosphere, or what is commonly called ventilation. In this respect, also, the engineers of the metropolis will find themselves outstripped by those of Manchester, and some other factory districts.

Various schemes were resorted to, at the suggestion of several ingenious projectors, for ventilating the Old House of Lords. Two, at least, of the plans consisted in the erection of a stove furnace in a chamber over that house, and in drawing the air for the supply of that furnace from the apartment below, so as to suck out the foul and hot atmosphere accumulated under its ceiling. The ventilating power of such an apparatus would be proportional to the quantity of fuel consumed, and the rapidity of its combustion; both being dependent, of course, upon the height of the chimney. It is well known that the contrivance was quite inefficient to refresh the air when it was most wanted, namely, when the house was crowded.

The quantity of air discharged in a given time by chimney draughts does not seem to have been hitherto made the subject of very accurate experiments. Whenever a certain volume of air is heated from the freezing to the boiling point of water, it expands into one volume and three eighths; and it therefore tends to rise up with a force equal to the difference between the weight of the volume of the cold air, whose space it now occupies, and its own weight; that is, in the present case, the difference between one and three eighths, and one; or 11 and 8.

Let us suppose a chimney, 50 yards high, to be supplied constantly at the bottom with air heated to 212 deg., while the external atmosphere is 32 deg. Fahr. The tunnel, being full of the hot air, its ascensional force will be obviously the difference between the weights of two columns of air, each 50 yards high, the one at the boiling, and the other at the freezing, temperature of water: the force will, likewise, be the same as that acting in a siphon filled with air, and having one of its arms longer than the other, by the difference between the bulk of the cold and the hot air. This columnar difference

of weight is the sole cause of the movement; and it is well known, both by theory and experiment, that the velocity of discharge through this columnar difference, which, in the present case, is 18¼ yards, would be equal to the velocity which a solid body would acquire in falling freely from that height. But a body falling from the height of 56¼ feet would pass through 60 feet per second, which is the velocity of efflux sought. A small deduction ought to be made from this number, on account of the increased density of the burned air in chimneys, in consequence of the replacement of a portion of its oxygen by carbonic acid.

The density of burned air, as it issues from chimney-tops, compared with that of atmospheric air of the same temperature, may be reckoned as 104¼ to 100. In practice, it will be found convenient to make the calculations as if the air were chemically the same, and to multiply the velocity found by 0·97; which would reduce the above 60 feet to 58·2 feet.

(To be continued.)

COWELL'S WINDOW SASHE SUSPENDERS.

Sir,—In your number of Saturday last, I was much pleased to find that Mr. Cowell's improvement in window sashes has been introduced to your notice.

On the announcement of his plan, I had all the windows of my residence here, as well those of a house in the city, fitted up on his principle, and am so well satisfied, that I wish publicly to bear testimony to its utility; the expense, as you state, is a mere trifle, but the importance of the object it embraces is very great, that of saving human life.

I will only further observe, that my female servant, after shifting them once or twice, manages them with the greatest ease and facility. I mention this, because some of my friends have imagined it to be a much more formidable undertaking for a female than it really is.

I am, Sir, yours respectfully,

J. W. Cox.

9, Gibson-square, Islington,
29th March, 1837.

Dynamometric Check.—A committee of the French Institute, composed of Messieurs Arago, Dulong, and Poncelet, has gone through a series of experiments on the "dynamometric (or power-measuring) check," an instrument invented by Prony, and lately improved by M. de Saint Leger, mining engineer at Rouen, for the purpose of measuring with accuracy the power of steam-engines and the quantity of fuel they consume. A large party of members of the

Institute and the Chamber of Deputies, of professors, engineers, &c. was present at the investigation, which took place on the 10th of March at the machine manufactory of M. Pauwels at Paris. The object of the experiments was to ascertain the practical exactness of the apparatus, and for this purpose a steam-engine of twelve-horse power of M. Pauwels's manufacture was made use of. The result appeared to be perfectly satisfactory, and the scientific world now waits, with some interest, the report of the committee of the Institute. This new invention may, perhaps, supply M. Arago with less disputable grounds for claiming for his countrymen a share in the honour of improving the steam-engine, than he has been able to supply in his two disingenuously national essays on the subject in the French *Annuaire* for 1828 and 1837.

Continental Railways.—A railway between Como and Milan is already begun to be made; another from Milan to Venice has just received the sanction of the Emperor of Austria, according to the German papers; and what is of still more consequence, all the shares have been taken. This project seems the "unkindest cut of all," Venice being, of all places in the world, the classic city of canals, and, one would think, protected by its lagunes, now to be crossed, by a bridge of innumerable arches, from all danger of contact with a railway. After this the new system may be expected to spread to Holland itself, a country whose interest and prosperity are, perhaps, otherwise destined to receive a deadly shock from the progress of an improvement which seems likely to confer incalculable benefits on the rest of Europe, on the Continent, perhaps, more than on ourselves, among whom extended land-carriage is of less importance.

Reverse of Fortune.—A subscription has been opened at Paris for the benefit of Richard Lenoir, once, it is stated, the first manufacturer in France, now an old man of 74, ill and destitute. He once possessed forty manufactories in different parts of France, and employed 10,648 workmen. "My property," he says in his memoirs, the first volume of which has been lately published, "was, on the 22d of April, 1814, about eight millions" of francs (or near £320,000). "On the 24th I was a ruined man." The only cause of this reverse, he states to have been the sudden suppression of the duties on cotton by an ordonnance of that date made by the Count d'Artois, since Charles X., then Lieutenant General.

Ancient Colours.—In the *Courier* Greek newspaper, No. 65, of the date of the 7th of February, an interesting account is given of some archæological researches, recently carried on with much success at Athens. Amongst other discoveries, two old paintings have been found in the Propylæa, fragments of the colours of which have been handed over to the chemist Landerer, for the purpose of investigation. As it is stated, however, that these paintings are on windows, it seems doubtful, though the Greek *Courier* speaks of them as ancient, whether they in reality belong to a higher antiquity than that of the middle ages, in which it is well known that the painters of the Byzantine school, maintained a high reputation all over Europe, which in our own days some German cities have made an attempt to revive. Should this be the case, no

fresh information as to the composition of colours can be expected from their analysis; but if they actually belong to classic antiquity, the investigation will lead to very interesting results.

Preservation of Animal Substances.—M. Gannal, of Paris, has discovered that the substances most efficacious for the preservation of bodies deprived of life are the salts of alumina; and he recommends the acetate of alumina as, of all, the best adapted for this purpose. By means of this substance, a dead body may be preserved for a length of time as effectually as if embalmed in the manner of the ancient Egyptians, and at a very trifling expense. The aluminous fluid may be introduced by the aorta, or still better, by the carotid artery, and any desiccation produced may be counteracted by the simple agency of a layer of varnish. It is anticipated that this discovery, from its simple and economical nature, will produce an important change in all processes to which it is capable of being applied. The preservation of specimens of natural history for museums, may be henceforth effected with a great saving of labour and cost, and the study of anatomy, which could not till now be carried on in summer, and even in winter was attended with serious risk of health, may be pursued in perfect safety, and at all seasons of the year.

The British Museum.—The new regulation of keeping the British Museum open to the public during the holidays has just come into exercise. Easter Monday, the 27th of March, was the first day of its operation, and on that day the number of visitors mounted up to only fifteen short of TWENTY-FOUR THOUSAND! This is, we believe, about four times as great a number as ever visited the Museum in one day before, and the smaller number was hitherto considered as in all probability the greatest that had ever visited the Museum in that space of time. If, after being exposed to such an ordeal as this, the treasures of the collection are found to have suffered no injury or diminution, the slanderers of the English national character in those points, will have been refuted indeed. The present state of things affords a curious contrast to that which existed in 1784, when Hutton, the historian of Birmingham, paid his visit to town. The regulations for procuring a ticket were then so irksome and obscure, that he willingly gave two shillings to a person who was in possession of one for permission to make use of it. He was, with the party of visitors whom he met there, conducted through the rooms in melancholy silence in about thirty minutes, and the party consisted altogether of ten persons. For the petty and annoying ticket system we have now admission "free as air;" the visitors, instead of being "conducted through the rooms," may come, go, or loiter as they please, and "the party" has increased in consequence from ten persons to 24,000.

Coal in France.—Coal mines are worked in 34 of the departments of France, but in most of them only to a very small extent. Four-fifths of the entire production are drawn from the four departments of the Loire, Nord, Saône et Loire, and Aveyron. The number of coal mines is stated to be 209, of which only 140 were worked during the year 1834. The quantity of coal extracted was 1,550,530 tons, the value of which, at 7s. 6d. per ton, amounted to £581,448.

We commence our 27th Vol. with an entirely new type, and on paper of improved quality. The Supplement to the last Volume will be published on the 1st of May.

☞ *British and Foreign Patents taken out with economy and despatch; Specifications, Disclaimers, and Amendments, prepared or revised; Caveats entered; and generally every Branch of Patent Business promptly transacted.*
A complete list of Patents from the earliest period (15 Car. II. 1675,) to the present time may be examined Fee 2s. 6d.; Clients, gratis.

LONDON: Printed and Published by W. A. Robertson, at the Mechanics' Magazine Office, No. 6, Peterborough-court, between 185 and 186, Fleet-street.—Sold by G. W. M. REYNOLDS, Proprietor of the French, English, and American Library, 55, Rue Neuve, Saint Augustin, Paris.

𝔐𝔢𝔠𝔥𝔞𝔫𝔦𝔠𝔰' 𝔐𝔞𝔤𝔞𝔷𝔦𝔫𝔢,

MUSEUM, REGISTER, · JOURNAL, AND GAZETTE.

| No. 714. | SATURDAY, APRIL 15, 1837. | Price 3d. |

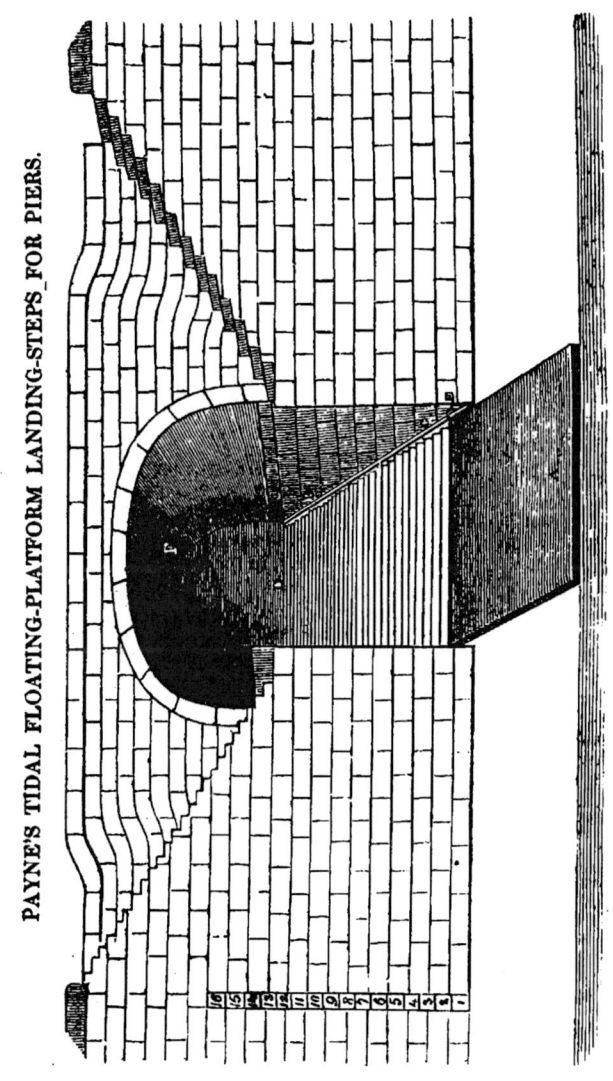

PAYNE'S TIDAL FLOATING-PLATFORM LANDING-STEPS FOR PIERS.

PAYNE'S TIDAL FLOATING-PLATFORM
LANDING-STEPS FOR PIERS.

The river piers for embarking and
landing passengers by steam-boats and
small craft at Liverpool are peculiarly
defective, on account of the great rise
and fall of the tide, which averages about
15 feet, and at low water leaves the piers
altogether dry, compelling the passengers
to walk over mud, or small planks. Some
contrivance for obviating this disadvantage has long been wanted; the corpora-
tion, about ten years ago, awarded two
small sums to different individuals for
models of proposed improvements, and
some members of the modern town council have, more than once, noticed the necessity for some alteration.

The plan required is confined within
very narrow limits; it must not project
into the river when the tide is sufficiently
high to permit vessels to sail close by the
pier, and it must run over the sand and
mud when the water has retired from
the river wall, or the inconvenience now
complained, of will not be obviated.

The inventor of the present plan was
one of those to whom the awards were
made in the year 1826 or 1827, and the
model he then exhibited (an engraving
of which appeared in the *Mechanics'
Magazine* at the time) consisted of a
flight of steps on a number of frame
pieces of iron-work, running on tram-
ways over the sand at low water, and
sliding one within another, like the joints
of a telescope, until entirely out of the
way when the water had risen. But this
contrivance had two objections; one of
which was, its not being of sufficient
strength to allow steamers to beat against
it in rough water; and the other was, the
necessity for the employment of a man at
a windlass, to move the various pieces of
which the machine was composed.

Neither of these objections attach to the
present invention. The steps are all substantial and clear of the river, and the contrivance for projecting a platform over the
sands as the water retires, and withdrawing it as the water advances, depends
solely upon the action of the tide; and
as it consists of a floating machine, it
may be run against by the steamers, at
half and quarter tides, as well as at low
water, without danger or fear of damage.

In the sketch (see front page), A is
the floating platform moving or sliding

on the guide rod B C, at the side of the
flight of steps D, by the ring E. A corresponding rod and ring is of course
placed at the other side of the flight of
steps, but which the perspective of the
view prevents being seen. The platform
is shewn in the position it would be in
at low water, running over the sands to
the water edge. As the tide rises, the
platform would float, and recede, by the
guidance of the rings and rods, into the
archway or recess F, to which at high
water, the inner edge having risen to B,
it would form a floating floor.

The plan has not been drawn to a scale;
but the proportions of the parade, the
river wall, and the sands left dry at low
water in front of it, are near enough to
exhibit the application of the plan either
to the George's or the Prince's pier.

Although this invention was made
more particularly with a view to the
Liverpool piers, it is evident that it is
applicable to any similar erections.

GEO. P. PAYNE.

3, Frederick Place, Hampstead Road,
March, 1837.

MR. MACKINTOSH'S PERPETUAL MO-
TION.

Sir,—The matter at issue between Mr.
Mackintosh and me, is simply this:—
He, in the first place, broached a scheme
for perpetual motion, in a manner evidently calculated to mislead others to
follow up his experiments, whatever his
own conviction of its futility might be;
in the second place, I undertook to shew
that the said scheme was as absurd in
principle, as it was impossible in practice; in the third place, Mr. Mackintosh
asserted that my attempt to do so was a
complete failure, and that he himself
would explain the true cause of the disappointment; and lastly, although invited to prove *my* explanation a failure,
or to publish his own, he has done neither the one nor the other, but has
shifted his ground altogether to the fields
of speculation, whither I never had any
intention of following him.

A word now to Kinclaven. I, in the
civilist manner possible, hinted that even
HE might be caught napping, thereby
giving him credit for all knowledge in
his waking moments; but, impatient,
I suppose, at being aroused from his
doze, he flings back to me my implied

compliment, insinuates that my objection was nothing but hypercriticism, and, merely "to please Nautilus," allows that the expression is *rather* improper; then he corrects the expression in rather a roundabout manner, as if to lead to the conclusion, that to avoid the pedantry of the correction, he had allowed the *rather improper* phrase to pass. Now, let me tell Kinclaven, that there is a term, simple, familiar, and to be found in every primer of geography, which would have exactly and concisely conveyed the intended meaning; the expression should have been, "the distance of polaris from the *solstitial colure*," and *not* "from the tropics of Cancer," nor yet "from the meridian of the first scruple of Cancer." I shall not stop to reckon lines and sentences with Kinclaven. I should no more think of defining *elaborateness* by extent in that way, than I should understand an elaborate picture, to mean one painted on a large surface of canvass.

I am, &c.
NAUTILUS.

MR. JOHN HERAPATH AND HIS " DISCOVERIES."

Sir, — Your correspondent, "Philo-Davy," asks, "What useful discovery Mr. John Herapath has ever made?" I am really surprised at his ignorance. I could cite him a whole century of *discoveries* made by this light of the age; but not to intrude too much on your columns, I will content myself with referring to a few only of the more prominent.

1st. When examined before the Committee on the South Eastern Railway Bill (Session 1836), Mr. Herapath was asked, "Have you been engaged in engineering departments of other railroads?" And this was his answer:— " I am now SUPERINTENDANT GENERAL *of three or four hundred miles of railroads*." I call this a mighty great —discovery! (He never superintended a single mile).

2nd. In the course of the same evidence, Mr. "Superintendant General" Herapath stated to the Committee that he had *discovered* that a man might be an excellent civil engineer without having a practical knowledge either of masonry, or of brickwork, or of carpentry, or of pile-driving,—that is to say, without knowing any thing whatever of his business.

3rd. Before the same Committee, Mr. " Superintendant General " Herapath stated that he had given his attention particularly to speed on railroads, and then proceeded as follows : " I should preface this by an observation to the Committee, that simple as it is, there is an extremely difficult mathematical problem connected with one part of the subject, and it is strange it affects the simplest part. Suppose we give the velocity on a level that an engine will take at thirty miles an hour—if that load is doubled or trebled, there is no branch of science published that would reach to tell us the exact velocity it would take. Having paid attention to philosophical and mathematical subjects, *and having been fortunate enough to make some discoveries, I am able to reach (it) from my own labours.* And it has been the formula I have given (which) has been used by most of the scientific men without acknowledgment." What this wonderful formula is, the witness did not state to the Committee, and the Committee did not care to inquire; but those who are curious in such matters, will see all about it, in the 23rd and 24th volumes of the *Mechanics' Magazine*, where it was shewn that *according to the said formula* a steam-carriage ought to run up hill at the rate of some fourteen hundred miles an hour, and down hill at no rate at all!

4th. Mr. "Superintendant General" Herapath, when before the same Committee, *discovered* that sensible and honourable men may be generally expected to have a very contemptible opinion of shallow and shuffling witnesses. Towards the conclusion of Mr. Herapath's evidence, he was addressed by the respectable Chairman in these memorable words, "*The Committee cannot fail to observe, Sir, that you have never answered one question directly.*"

5th. Mr. " Superintendant General " Herapath made, on the heels of this last *discovery*, another, equally instructive, that there may be causes so bad that even a hired advocate will get at last ashamed of them. Mr. Herapath had volunteered, or had been put forward, to prove that what is called the North Kent line (the one by Dartford, Gravesend,

Rochester, &c.) was unobjectionable in an engineering point of view, *after Colonel Landmann, who planned it, had thrown it up as indefensible;* and when he had done his best in its behalf (been "fooled to the top of his bent"), and had undergone the severe reproof just quoted from the chair, Mr. Rotch, the counsel for the line, is stated in the Minutes of Evidence to have "intimated to the Committee, that, in consequence of Colonel Landmann's resignation, he could not, UPON THIS EVIDENCE," establish the superiority of the North Kent line.

Such, Sir, are some of Mr. John Herapath's "*discoveries.*" Lest " scientific men" should again appropriate to themselves what of right belongs to Mr. "Superintendant General" Herapath, you will perhaps do him the justice of recording them in the *Mechanics' Magazine,* in which case I shall trouble you with a few more of his "discoveries" next week.

I am, Sir, &c.

F. M. MEREDITH.

SOME OF THE ASTRONOMICAL RULES WANTED—SUPPLIED.

Sir,—Nauticus wishes to have the formulæ for the reduction of a certain problem, as given in some of the memoirs of the Astronomical Society, put into familiar rules. I regret that it did not occur to him, that those memoirs may not be within reach of reference to every one; had he given a copy of the formulæ, I should have been most happy in obliging him. But, without having seen these memoirs, allow me to offer an observation upon the problem alluded to. The method for finding correct time, by observing two stars in the same vertical, appears to me to be one extremely ill-calculated for the portable transit instrument, with which Nauticus, rather obscurely, says, he can "observe them in a few moments only." Does he mean with that degree of correctness, or that the observation would consume only that space of time? If the latter, would he not first have to wait for the required position?

The portable transit instrument cannot be shifted in azimuth (in order to follow the stars until in a vertical line) without deranging its level, which, having to be adjusted after every movement, would, I conceive, render the observation nearly impracticable. In the altitude and azimuth instrument, indeed, such a motion is possible; but even with this latter instrument, I doubt that the observation could be taken with any thing like the precision necessary in the nice determination of time, for, as both stars could not be in the field at one and the same time, the position of one must be guessed at, while the other is observed. Allow me, then, to suggest to Nauticus a mode of obtaining the true time, which is peculiarly adapted for the portable transit instrument, and which may, at any time, be performed in the course of an hour or two, without previous knowledge, either of the true meridian or of time nearer than an hour.

From the Nautical Almanack obtain the time of either transit of polaris, some time within an hour of which, point the instrument to the star. Now, if it be even a whole hour from the true transit, still the greatest angular error in azimuth cannot, in these latitudes, exceed half a degree in arc, or two 2 minutes in equatorial time. Next, with the instrument so situated, turn the telescope to a star near the zenith, and, having first levelled with the greatest nicety, observe its transit; then, if the star be precisely in the zenith, the true time is at once obtained, no deviation in azimuth having *there* power to affect it: but, suppose that no ᵥstar can be obtained nearer the zenith than 10 deg., then the error before mentioned of 30 min. in azimuth can only vitiate the result to the extent of 30 sec., or in other words, true time may be obtained within that degree of correctness; if now the telescope be turned again to the pole star, and the instrument be moved in azimuth, until polaris transit correctly, according to the newly found time; then a new position is obtained, which can only err in azimuth to the extent of one second of equatorial time, and which, in the transit of a star within 10 deg. of the zenith as before, will furnish the true time, with an error which need not exceed one quarter of a second; the instrument being, of course, supposed to be, in other respects, in perfect adjustment.

There are other stars nearly as well adapted for the purpose as polaris, but not so easily found: indeed, if it were not for the latter consideration, there is one (*lambda, ursæ minoris*) even preferable in position, it being still nearer to the pole. With respect to the second inquiry of Nauticus, I cannot possibly conceive to what possible use the knowledge required could be turned. The table in the Nautical Almanack of the maximum phase of the moon's libration, with the quadrant of the disk in which to seek it, is given, I apprehend, for no other purpose than as a direction of time and place for the phenomenon ; as for the longitude and latitude of the lunar spots, the terms have long been disused in modern astronomy.

I am, &c.

Your obedient servant,

NAUTILUS.

2nd April, 1837.

AN EXPERIMENTAL ENQUIRY INTO THE MODES OF WARMING AND VENTILATING APARTMENTS. BY ANDREW URE, M.D. F.R.S., ETC.

Read before the Royal Society on the 16th of June, 1836.

(From the *Architectural Magazine* for April).

(Continued from page 15.)

Such are the results of theory ; but they vary considerably from practice, in consequence of the varying lengths and forms of the chimney, which change the velocity of the aerial currents by friction, refrigeration, &c. In high chimneys of wrought iron, like those of steam-boats, the refrigeration is considerable, and causes a diminution of velocity far greater that what occurs in a factory stalk of well-built brickwork. In comparing the numbers resulting from the trials made on chimneys of different materials and of different forms, it has been concluded that the obstruction to the draught of the air, or the deduction to be made from the theoretical velocity of efflux, is directly proportional to the length of the chimneys and to the square of the velocity, and inversely to their diameter. With an ordinary wrought-iron pipe, of from 4 in. to 5 in. diameter, attached to an ordinary stove burning good charcoal, the difference is prodigious between the velocity calculated by the above theoretical rule, and that observed by means of a stop-watch, and the ascent of a puff of smoke from a little tow, dipped in oil of turpentine, thrust quickly into the fire. The chimney being 45 ft. high, the temperature of the atmosphere 68 deg. Fahr., the velocity per second was,—

Trials.	By Theory.	By Experiment.	Mean temperature of Chimney.
1	26·4 feet	5 feet.	190° Fahr.
2	29·4	5·76	214°
3	34·5	6·3	270°

To obtain congruity between calculation

and experiment, several circumstances must be introduced into our formulæ. In the first place, the theoretical velocity must be multiplied by a factor, which is different according as the chimney is made of bricks, pottery, sheet iron, or cast iron. This factor must be multiplied by the square root of the diameter of the chimney (supposed to be round), divided by its length, increased by four times its diameter. Thus, for pottery, its expression is $2·06 \sqrt{\dfrac{D}{L+L'}}$; D being the diameter, and L the length, of the chimney.

A pottery chimney, 33 ft. high, and 7 in. in diameter, when the excess of its mean temperature above that of the atmosphere was 205 deg. Fahr., had a pressure of hot air equal to 11·7 ft,, and a velocity of 7·2 ft. per second. By calculating from the last formula, the same number very nearly is obtained. In none of the experiments did the exceed 12 ft. per second, when the difference of temperature was more than 410 deg. Fahr.

Every different form of chimney would require a special set of experiments to be made for determining the proper factor to be used.

This troublesome operation may be saved by the judicious application of a delicate differential barometer, such as that invented by Dr. Wollaston ; though this instrument does not seem to have been applied by its very ingenious author in measuring the draughts or ventilating powers of furnaces.

If into one leg of this differential siphon, water be put, and fine spermaceti oil into the other, we shall have two liquids, which are to each other in density as the numbers 8 and 7. If proof spirit be employed instead of water, we shall then have the relation of very nearly 20 to 19. I have made experiments on furnace draughts with the instrument in each of these states, and find the water and oil siphon to be sufficiently sensible : for the weaker draughts of common fireplaces the sprits and oil will be preferable barometric fluids.

To the lateral projecting tube of the instrument, as described by Dr. Wollaston, I found it necessary to attach a stopcock, in order to cut off the action of the chimney, while placing the siphon, to allow of its being fixed in a proper state of adjustment, with its junction line of the oil and water at the zero of the scale. Since a slight deviation of the legs of the siphon from the perpendicular changes very considerably the line of the level, this adjustment should be made secure by fixing the horizontal pipe tightly into a round hole bored into the chimney-stalk, or drilled through the furnace door. On gently turning the stopcock, the difference of atmospherical pressure, corresponding to the chimney draught, will be immediately indicated by the ascent of the junction-line of the liquids in the siphon. This modification of apparatus permits the experiment to be readily rectified by again shutting off the draught, when the air will slowly re-enter the siphon ; because the projecting tube of the barometer is thrust into the stopcock, but not hermetically joined ; whereby its junction line is allowed to return to the zero of the scale in the course of a few seconds.

Out of many experiments made with this instrument, I shall content myself with describing a few, very carefully performed at the breweries of Messrs. Truman, Hanbury, and Buxton, and of Sir H. Meux, Bart., and at the machine factory of Messrs. Braithwaite ; in the latter of which I was assisted by Captain Ericsson. In the first trials at the breweries, the end of the stopcock attached to the differential barometer was lapped round with hemp, and made fast into the circular peep-hope of the furnace door of a wort copper, communicating with two upright parallel chimneys, each 18 in. square, and 50 ft. high. The fire was burning with fully its average intensity at the time. The adjustment of the level being perfect, the stopcock orifice was opened, and the junction level of the oil and water rose steadily, and stood at $1\frac{1}{4}$ in., corresponding to $\frac{1.25}{8} = 0.156$ of 1 in. of water, or a column of air 10.7 ft. high. This difference of pressure indicates a velocity of 26 ft. per second. In a second set of experiments, the extremity of the stopcock was inserted into a hole bored through the chimney-stalk of the boiler of a Boulton and Watt steam-engine of twenty horses power. The area of this chimney was exactly 18 in. square at the level of the bored hole, and its summit rose 50 ft. above it. The fire grate was about 10 ft. below that level, On opening the stopcock, the junction line rose $2\frac{1}{4}$ in. This experiment was verified by repetition on different days, with fires burning at their average intensity, and consuming fully 12 lb. of the best coals hourly for each horse's power, or nearly one ton and a third in twelve hours. If we divide the number $2\frac{1}{4}$ by 8, the quotient 0.28 will represent the fractional part of 1 in. of water, supported in the siphon by the unbalanced pressure of the atmosphere in the said chimney ; which corresponds to $19\frac{1}{4}$ ft. of air, and indicates a velocity in the chimney current of 35 ft. per second. The consumption of fuel was much more considerable in the immense grate under the wort copper, than it was under the steam-engine boiler.

In my experiments at Messrs. Braithwaite's factory, the maximum displacement of the junction line was 1 in., when the differential oil and water barometer was placed in direct communication with a chimney 15 in. square, belonging to a steam boiler, and when the fire was made to burn so fiercely, that, on opening the safety-valve of the boiler, the excess of steam beyond the consumption of the engine rushed out with such violence as to fill the whole premises. The pressure of one eight of an inch of water denotes a velocity of draught of 23.4 ft. per second.

The differential barometer was next attached to the suction-chamber of a ventilator fan, used for drawing the air through the fireplace, in the ingenious steam boiler of Messrs. Braithwaite and Ericsson's patent construction. The result was remarkable. Here the draught was so great, that it became necessary to remove the oil, and to employ merely a water siphon. When the speed of the circumference of the revolving vanes was 120 ft. per second, the suction was sufficient to support steadily 2 in. of water. This aqueous column, however, indicates a velocity of only 94 ft. per second, instead of 120. The pressure of air equivalent to this velocity is 224 vertical feet ; equal to a column of water $3\frac{1}{4}$ in. high. But we must consider that the true velocity of the impelling points of the vanes is only seven eighths of the velocity of their tips, or 105 ft. per second. If this circumstance be not taken into account, we should be led to infer that, in an eccentric ventilator of the best centrifugal form, so much air escapes, by inertia, between the vanes and the sides of the box in which they revolve, as to cause a loss of nearly one fourth of velocity in the issuing current. Every principle of physics forbids us to suppose, as some engineers have hastily done, that the siphon pressure indicates only three fourths of the effects of the current upon the atmospheric equilibrium. On this point we shall presently offer some other illustrations.

When the wings of the fan were made to revolve with a velocity of 180 ft. per second, by connecting its rigger band with a larger driving pulley, the difference of water level in the two legs of the siphon amounted to only 3 in. ; an unbalanced pressure, which indicates a velocity of efflux in the air of only 115 ft. per second, and a defalcation of effect, therefore, tantamount to 30 per cent, which is evidently due to the greater effect of inertia at that degree of speed ; the effective velocity of the vanes being taken, as formerly, at seven eighths of that of their extremities.

In a third set of experiments, when the extremities of the vanes revolved with a velocity of 80 ft. per second, the water stood 1 in. higher in the one leg of the siphon than in the other. This difference of level indicates a velocity of 66 ft. per second. Here the loss of velocity, from the inertia and the eddies of the lateral portions

12 inches of water correspond to a velocity of	231 feet per second.
6	163
3	115
2	94
1½	81
1	66
½	47
¼	33
⅟₇ — 1 in. of the water-oil siphon	25
¼	23·4

It has been ascertained, that a power equivalent to one horse, in a steam-engine, will drive, at the rate of 80 ft. per second, a fan the effective surfaces of whose vanes, and whose inhaling conduits, have each an area of 18 in. square, equal to that of the steam-boiler chimney mentioned above. The velocity of air in the chimney produced by a consumption of fuel equivalent to the power of twenty horses, was no more than 35 ft. per second; while that of the fan, as impelled by the power of one horse, was 66 ft. per second. Hence it appears, that the economy of ventilation by the fan is to that by the chimney draught as 66 is to ³⁵⁄₂₀, or as 38 to 1. It is obvious, therefore, that, with one bushel or ton of coals consumed in working a steam-impelled eccentric fan, we can obtain as great a degree of ventilation, or we can displace as great a body of air, as we could with 38 bushels or tons of coals consumed in creating a chimney draught. Economy, cleanliness, and compactness of construction are not, however, the sole advantages which the mechanical system of ventilation possesses over the physical. It is infallible, even under such vicissitudes of wind and weather as would essentially obstruct any chimney-draught ventilation, because it discharges the air with a momentum quite eddy-proof, and it may be increased, diminished, or stopped altogether, in the twinkling of an eye, by the mere shifting of a band from one pulley to another, as is practised upon all spinning-machines. No state of atmosphere without, no humidity of air within, can resist its power. It will expel the air of a crowded room, loaded with the vesicular vapours of perspiration, with equal certainty as the driest and most expansive.

The preference due to the mechanical system may be made popularly plain, by considering how little power could be obtained by applying a chimney current to impel machinery, through the agency of the best-going smoke-jack, or any other analogous construction. It is clear that the consumption of fuel, applied through the medium of steam, which produces the power of twenty horses in the above steam-engine,

of air, is only 6 per cent. upon the effective velocity.

The following table exhibits the velocities of the air corresponding to different altitudes of the differential water barometer:—

would, by the impulsion of an ascending current of air upon any mechanism, barely do the work of half a horse.

In an analogous experiment made at the brewery of Messrs. Truman, Hanbury, and Buxton, the differential barometer being placed in communication, as above described, with the chimney-stalk of the steam-engine boiler, suffered a change of level in the junction line of oil and water of 2¼ in., equivalent, as before, to 0·28 of 1 in. water. The chimney had an area of 16 in. by 18 in. at the point where the lateral tube of the barometer was inserted, and it rose 50 ft. above that point.

About twelve pound of coal were consumed hourly for each horse power, and steam corresponding to the power of fifteen horses, at least, was generated in each boiler. Hence it would appear, that from 180 lb. to 200 lb. of coals were burned hourly to maintain a chimney current of 35 ft. per second, or a discharge of air of 70 cubic feet in that time. This result agrees as nearly with that obtained at Sir Henry Meux's brewery as can be expected in experiments of this nature. The coal employed in the latter establishment is of the excellent Welch quality called Llangennech, which burns without smoke. Were other proprietors of great manufactories to imitate this patriotic example, one of the worst nuisances of London would be abated.

The value of fans to sweeten the atmosphere is beginning to be fully appreciated in the factories, more especially in the power-loom apartments, where several hundred persons are congregated together in a moderate space. The beneficial mode of mounting them, with this view, described in the *Philosophy of Manufactures* has been instrumental in drawing the attention of manufacturers to so simple and efficacious a means of promoting the health of their work-people. In these circumstances, it will appear somewhat surprising that none of the members of the late Parliamentary Committee, nor any of the scientific gentlemen whom they examined, should have made the slightest allusion to mechanical ventilation. This omission will appear the more remarkable, since a celebrated member of the Royal Society, Dr. Desaguliers, one hundred years ago, applied a similar invention, as he says, " to the clearing the House of Commons of foul air." The following paragraph of his memoir deserves peculiar notice, as it shows with what a roundabout of futile expedients the public has been deluded for a century past:—

" In the year 1736," says the doctor, " Sir George Beaumont, and several other members of the House of Commons, observing that the design of cooling the House by the fire machines above described (like the pumping stoves of the Marquis de Chabannes in our day) was frustrated, asked me if I could not find some contrivance to draw the hot and foul air out of the House, by means of some person that should entirely depend upon me; which, when I promised to do, a committee was appointed to order me to make such a machine, which, accordingly, I effected, calling the wheel a centrifugal, or blowing-wheel, and the man that turned it a ventilator. This wheel, though in some things like Papin's Hessian bellows, differs much from it, being more effectual and able to suck out the foul air, or throw in fresh, according as the Speaker pleased to command it; whose order the ventilator awaits to receive every day of the session, the wheel being still in use."

The wheel is described as being 7 ft. in diameter, 1 ft. broad, as taking in air at its centre, and revolving concentrically with its case. It was worked, at least occasionally, from the year 1736 down to the year 1743, when the first edition of the *Experimental Philosophy* of Desaguliers was published.

The machine probably remained in the chamber over the House of Commons, and fell a victim to the fire which lately consumed that time-honoured edifice.

As the ventilating fan of Desaguliers was worked by a man turning a winch, it could not have made more than forty revolutions in a minute, whence the mean speed of the tips of its vanes could not have exceeded 15 ft. in a second. In considering, therefore, the defectiveness of its construction, as well as the small area of its discharge pipe, it was, probably, not misnamed " a philosophical toy" by Sir Jacob Ackworth, then First Lord of the Admiralty, who went down to Woolwich to see its performance in ventilating the hold of His Majesty's ship the Kinsale.

It does not appear that, since the time of Desaguliers, the ventilating fan has been subjected to scientific experiment and examination; for M. Pouillet, a distinguished French philosopher, described last year, in the sixth livraison of his *Portefeuille Industriel*, with high but unmerited commendations, a fan erected at Rouen for blowing a foundary cupola, which, on trial, was quite inefficient in propelling the air, while it shook the floor where it stood with tremendous violence. This fan is of the concentric construction, and must, therefore, expend the chief part of the power applied to drive it, in carrying the air round with its vanes, instead of throwing it off at the discharge-pipe. The English company of machine makers settled at Rouen, to whom it belongs, have been obliged to alter it after the plan now commonly adopted in Lancashire.

The following sketches (*figs.* 1. to 4.) and experimental illustrations will, I hope,

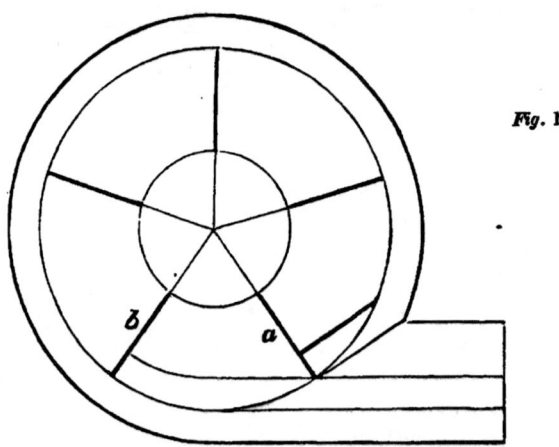

Fig. 1.

throw some light upon the operations of a ventilating fan.

Fig. 1. is intended to show, by the course of the lines traced in it, that in the concentric fan only two leaves out of five are effective, and that very little more than one half of the exit pipe is occupied with the regular current of air produced by the rotation of the leaves. The quantity thrown out by virtue of the pressure under which

the air is kept by the centrifugal force is therefore, very small, being intercepted by the current from the leaf *a*, whose tangent crosses the exit pipe completely, and nearly at a right angle.

Fig. 2 shows that in the eccentric fan *all*

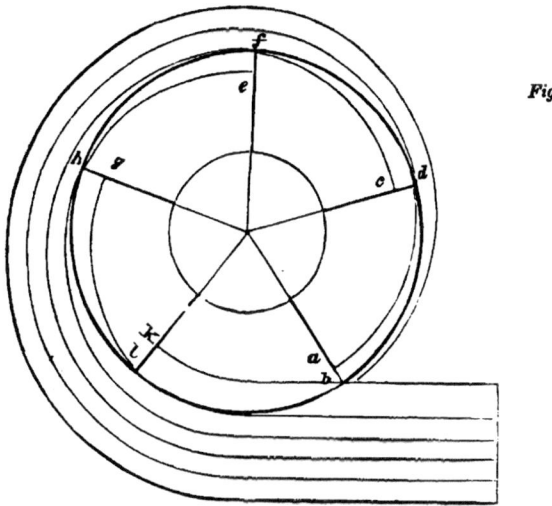

Fig. 2.

the leaves are effective, and that the exit pipe is entirely filled with a current from the impulsion of the vanes, independantly of any pressure by centrifugal force; except as regards its supply of air from the centre, which obviously depends upon the unbalanced pressure of the atmosphere. That the air cannot enter the exit pipe at less speed than the speed at which the points *a*, *c*, *e*, *g*, *k* revolve, would, at first sight, seem to certain; for the sum of the lines *a b*, *c d*, *e f*, *g h*, and *k l*, is equal to the length of the vertical axis of the exit pipe. And, since the points *a*, *c*, *e*, &c. move at a rate of from ⅞ to ⅚ of the extremities of the leaves, the speed will be at least $= \frac{7+8}{120} =$ 105 ft. per second, when the tips move at 120 ft.; whereas, I found 94 ft. per second to be the velocity by experiment. The difference may be ascribed as I have already said to the inertia of the air, the lateral communication, and consequent loss of motion, by the eddies thus produced.

Figs. 3 & 4 (next page) represent the section and plan of a fan, which is considered by my ingenious friend Captain Ericsson, to be of the best construction. The drawing is so plain as to supersede the necessity of a detailed description.

With regard to the quantity of air thrown

out by a fan of this construction, it may be ascertained approximately by multiplying the speed of the points *c*, *e*, *e*, &c. by the sectional area of the exit pipe. The absolute force required to work this fan may be calculated with sufficient accuracy in the following way:—Suppose the extremities of the leaves to move at the rate of 8ç ft. per second, the sectional area of the exit pipe to be square feet; then 2 + 80 = 160 cubic feet; which number multiplied by 60 seconds, gives a product of 9,600 cubic feet of air discharged per minute. This reduced into weight will be $\frac{9600}{13} = 738$ lb., put into motion every minute, at the rate of 80 feet per second. Now in order to acquire a velocity of 80 feet per second, a body must be allowed to fall freely through a space of $\frac{80+80}{64} = 100$ ft.; hence the force required to give to 738 lb. a velocity of 80 ft. per second will be equal to 738 × 100 = 73,800 lb., lifted 1 ft. high. This number, divided by 33,000, will give a quotient equivalent, in pounds, to the impulsive power of 2¼ steam horses for working such a fan.

This calculation agrees well with the result of the trial of a large fan constructed by Captain Ericsson, in the year 1831, at Liverpool, for supporting combustion without a chimney in the furnace of a boiler of 100 horses' power on board the Corsair steam-

boat. The diameter of this fan was 4 ft. 6 in.; area of the exit pipe, 3 square feet;

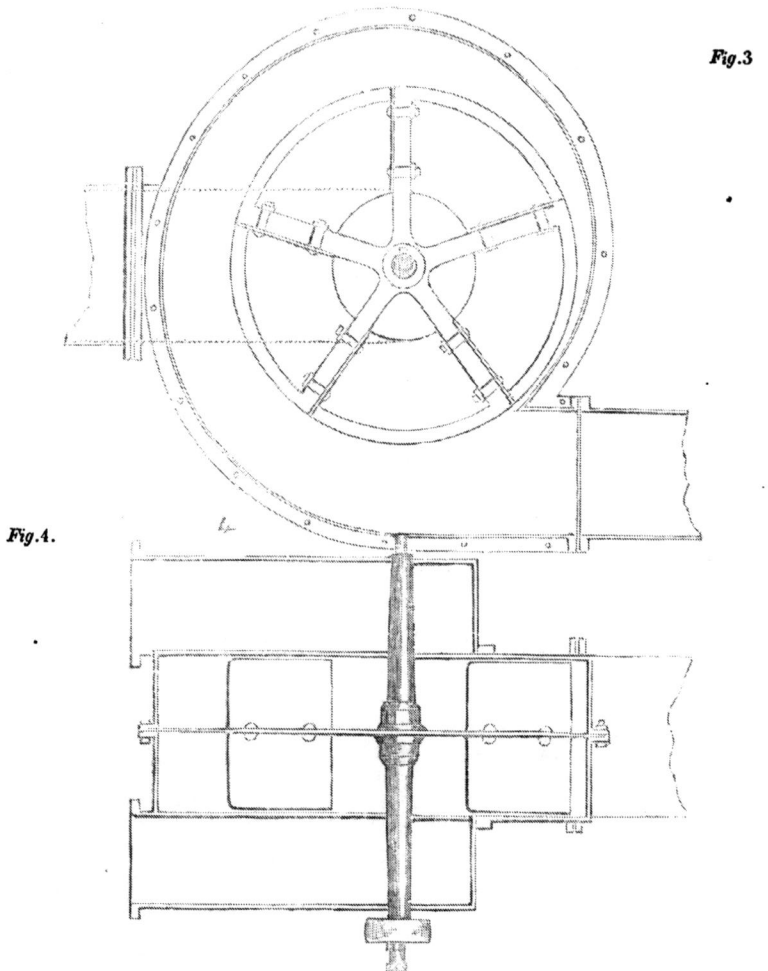

*Fig.*3

*Fig.*4.

effective speed of vanes, 80 feet per second. To work this fan, he constructed a steam-engine, having a 4-in. cylinder, and 10-in. stroke. The result proved that 120 strokes per minute, with steam of 45 lb. pressure to the square inch, were required to produce a speed of 80 ft. in the fan. The engine being of excellent workmanship, from the well-known factory of Messrs, Fawcett and Preston, at Liverpool, and its motion being directly communicated to the fan, we may

fairly conclude that at least 30 lb. to the square inch was the effective pressure of the steam. This number, multiplied by 12, being the area of the piston in square inches, gives a product of 360 lbs. for the moving force; and this product, multiplied by 200 ft. (the speed of the piston), is equivalent to 72,000 lb., lifted 1 ft. high per minute, which represents the power of the engine. The quantity of air = 80 × 30 = 240, multiplied by 60 seconds = 14,400 cubic feet per minute. The temperature of the air, as it entered the fan, was about 300 deg., and was therefore, reduced in specific gravity to about 20 cubic feet to a pound. Hence $\frac{14400}{20} = 720$ lb. weight of air thrown out per minute; which, lifted to a height of 100 ft. (the elevation necessary to produce a velocity of 80 ft. per second), would require a force equal to $720 \times 100 = 72,000$ lb., lifted 1 ft. high, per minute; which quantity exactly coincides with the power of the steam-engine.

It may be worth while to state, though the the fact will be obvious to every practicel eegineer, that, when the exit pipe of the fan was stopped up, and only a little steam admitted into the steam-engine, the fan-leaves moved at an immense speed, the confined mass of air being kept in perpetual rotation; but, whenever the pipe was again opened, so as to admit the stagnant air, the engine was brought nearly to a stand by the weight and inertia opposed to its motion.

(To be concluded in our next.)

SALUBRITY OF RAILWAY TUNNELS. REPORTS ON THE TUNNEL ON THE LEEDS AND SELBY RAILWAY.

Report of Dr. Davy, and Dr. Rothman.

After careful inquiry, and an examination of this Tunnel, we are of opinion that it has no injurious influence on the health of the passengers. We have come to this conclusion from finding:—1st. That the air in the Tunnel at the time of passing is not appreciably vitiated. Chemically examined, its composition appears to be same as that of the atmosphere, even after repeated transits of the locomotive engines.

2nd. That the temperature of the air in the Tunnel, though more uniform than that of the external air, does not vary so much from it as might have been expected. In the warmest weather in which observations have been made, the air of the middle of the Tunnel was only 8 deg. lower than that of the atmosphere, the latter being 70. deg. In February, the greatest difference we found was also 8 deg., the atmosphere then being at 56 deg. We were assured that, during the severest weather of the last winter, the temperature of the Tunnel never fell to the freezing point.

3rd. That the humidity of the air in the Tunnel, judging from the few experiments which we have able to make, will be more uniform than the temperature. That it will generally be somewhat greater than that of the external air, but never sufficiently so to cause the precipitation of aqueous vapour in the carriages, or on the persons of passengers.

4th. That we have not been able to detect, in any part of the Tunnel, traces of acid, or other irritating or noxious effluvia.

The Tunnel, at present, is passed through in darkness, which, though not dangerous, is to many persons unpleasant. This seems to require correction, and it is understood to be in contemplation to attach lamps to the carriages.

The noise made by the engine and train of carriages did not seem to us much greater in the Tunnel than in the open air, nor to form any reasonable ground for complaint. Annexed to this Report is a certificate by Dr. Williamson, a high medical authority in Leeds, generally in accordance with the opinions above expressed. He has even arrived at the conclusion, which we see no reason to doubt, that travelling on the Railway if often beneficial to persons in delicate health, particularly in certain cases of slight pulmonarary disease.

The Tunnel in question is situated very near the terminus of the Railway in the town of Leeds It is 700 yards in length, 17 feet high, and 22 broad. Its direction is nearly east and west. The inclination of the floor is 1 in 300. It has three shafts at irregular distances, which now serve the purpose of ventilation. The westernmost is somewhat the deepest; the depth of this is 23 yards, measured to the floor of the Tunnel. The Tunnel is bricked throughout its whole extent. It is traversed by 20 engines daily, and on an average by 350 passengers. The average time of passing is about a minute and a quarter. The steam is generated by coke of the best quality, under a pressure of 56 lb. with regard to our sensations in passing through the Tunnel, with the windows of the carriage purposely left down, we experienced nothing unpleasant, either from smoke, vapour, or currents of air. The temperature in the carriage was agreeable, and everything felt dry.

We would conclude by observing, that the opinions we have expressed of this Tunnel we hold to be applicable to all other Tunnels, the circumstances of which are similar; and to Tunnels of greater length, if they are higher and have a sufficient number of shafts to secure an adequate ventilation.

JOHN DAVY, M.D. F.R.S.

Assistant Inspector of Army Hospitals.

R. W. ROTHMAN, M.A. & L.M.

Fell. Trin. Coll. Camb.

London. 21st February, 1837.

Dr. Williamson's Report.

In reference to the effects of the transit through the Tunnel of the Leeds and Selby Railroad on the health of passengers, I have to state, that in the whole of my experience, both in private practice and in my official connexion with the infirmary, and with the other Medical Institutions of this town, I have never seen a case in which I could ascribe injurious results to that circumstance. I have, indeed, frequently recommended delicate persons to make excursions on the Railroad for the benefit of their health, and have known very decided advantageous to accrue from such excursions to persons even labouring under the slighter forms of pulmonary irritation.

I conceive that the vapour, smoke, and the gaseous results of combustion can never exist in such proportions as materially to deteriorate the air ; and that there is no degree of humidity or deleterious emanation, peculiar to the Tunnel, which can be appreciably detrimental to animal life.

I believe that persons of irritable bronchial membrane may respire in the air of the Tunnel for a considerable period without feeling the slightest inconvenience or sustaining any injury.

(Signed)   JAMES WILLIAMSON,

Senior Physician of Leeds General Infirmary, and Lecturer on the Practice of Physic in the Leeds Medical School.

Leeds, 19th February, 1837.

ON THE ACTION PRODUCED ON WATER BY HIGHLY HEATED METALS, BY MR. CHARLES TOMLINSON, IN REPLY TO " D."

Sir,—The tone of your correspondent " D" (p. 495), is such as to convince me, that his sole object is the laudable desire to acquire further information respecting the theory of the very curious, and apparently paradoxical phenomena detailed in my letter to you of the 28th Jan. last, and I feel much pleasure in replying to his objections, as, indeed, I shall do, to those of such other of your correspondents, who, I had hoped, would have already investigated the subject for themselves.

I beg to offer to Mr. Baddeley an expression of thanks for affording the assistance of his valuable testimony (p. 510) to the general accuracy of the principal result upon which my theory mainly depends. Mr. Baddeley's pursuits are of a character so eminently practical and useful, that I should be disposed to rely at all times, not only upon his facts, but upon his deductions.

"D." observes, that " we all know that the specific gravity of steam is less than that of air and infinitely less than that of water." But he forgets that the truth of this proposition depends altogether upon its temperature ; at 212 deg. the specific gravity of steam is 0·625, of which 100 cubic inches weigh about nineteen grains :—at 250 deg. the specific gravity of steam is 1.25, of which 100 cubic inches weigh about thirty-nine grains :—at 293 deg. the specific gravity is 2.5 :—at 343 deg. it is 5. and so on, constantly increasing with the temperature while its elasticity is augmented to an enormous extent.

"D." inquires, on what principle can a portion of steam exist beneath the water contained within the white hot platinum crucible, and gives the familiar instance of boiling under ordinary circumstances. Now it must be borne in mind, as Mr. Baddeley well observes, that " if the metal does not much exceed 212 deg. the water *spreads upon and wets* its surface, from which it is rapidly evaporated," but if the heat be intense the water does not spread, but, provided its recipient be concave collects into one globule, which, if the quantity be small, is spherical, and if large, rounded—the circumference being very convex, and in point of form it resembles a globule of mercury in every respect, placed upon a smooth non-metallic surface. In the latter case the repulsion between the mercury and the smooth surface is the cause of the convexity, as in the case of the mercurial surface of the barometer when rising, where the metallic surface is the section of a sphere, whose diameter is that of the barometric tube : but if the mercurial globule be placed upon a smooth surface of a metal such as gold, silver, tin, lead, &c., between which and the mercury there is a decided attraction, then the globule no longer retains its convex and rounded form, but becomes flat, spreads over the surface, and is analagous to water upon a metallic surface heated to 212 deg., or thereabouts.

Here, then, are two cases, which are due to attraction and repulsion :—when the mercury is on a smooth non-metallic surface, chemical affinity is not exerted ; but when on certain metallic surfaces, then it is exerted, and an amalgam is formed. We may apply this analogy to the drops of water contained within the platinum crucible. When the latter is heated to any degree of temperature below about 220 deg., and water dropped into it, calorific attraction is exerted;—the drop of water ceases to be spherical,—it becomes flat, and spreads over the surface of its recipient. When the temperature of the crucible is considerable from incandescense, at a white heat for example, then calorific repulsion is manifestly exerted,—the liquid retains its globular form, and cannot spread, since the slightest tendency to do so is manifestly checked, by the formation of steam at a point of the metal immediately below the globule; and supposing that contact were attained, the effect would be, to resolve the drop of water into steam by one sudden burst, so rapid would be the formation. Now this is exactly what takes places when the source of heat is suddenly removed from under the white-hot platinum crucible containing water, since the crucible parts with its heat by rapid radiation, and in a very few minutes the calorific repulsion is so weakened, that the contact of the globule with the metal is no longer opposed, and a sudden burst of steam is the result. But when the high tempe- of the crucible is maintained, since calorific repulsion holds the drop of water, suspended, as it were, within the crucible, the specific gravity of the drop is greater than the force of the calorific repulsion, and the drop falls in the same manner as a boy's marble falls upon a hard surface, where a minute point of contact only is presented,—a rebound follows; and this is repeated for a considerable time. Now the drop of water is analogous to the marble—it falls to the bottom of the crucible, a minute point only is touched by the hot metal, but contact at this minute point is sufficient to abstract a small portion of the water, which is converted into steam, which, confined with calorific repulsion, is sufficient to cause the ascent of the globule, and its partial suspension in the way I have indicated, while the centre of gravity of the globule, not being exactly over the lowest point of the crucible, and the calorific rays being probably unequal in their repulsive force, the oscillating movements of the drop of

water are perpetuated, and the layer of steam is preserved by repeated accessions, obtained by means of the series of minute contacts with the globule, every time it descends.

I trust, that " D." will now see why it is that the steam has not " the power of darting upwards through the watery globule," in the manner he supposes it should do from the observation of his own tea-kettle. In truth, it often does so, and by dividing the globule, causes it to spit out of the crucible minute drops of water :—but, this happens, however strange it may seem, only when the crucible is at a red, instead of a white, heat, for in the latter case I have never known it to be so. The calorific repulsion by which the compact and globular form of the globule is preserved, prevents the passage of the steam, and affords to the water a certain support, and when the steam is too abundant it glides over the sides, which, as it seems to me, afford the easiest, if not the most direct exit.

The instance adduced by "D." of the Turkish headsman, who could cut off his patient's head without the latter being at all aware of the fact, &c., needs no investigation. I may merely remark, by the way, that the facts quoted of the pistol, the shilling and card, &c. are instances of inertia, and not analagous to the present inquiry. I therefore proceed to the second part of " D.'s" letter.

His remarks on the influence of colour on the action of the drops of water in the white hot crucible, are very ingenious, but not relevant, since it ts obvious, from my experiments, with various fluids, that pure water alone is adapted to the fair estimate of this inquiry. When the water is coloured, the colouring matter acts in two ways; first, it increases the conducting power of the liquid; and, secondly, it is precipitated and decomposed, becomes converted into carbonaceous particles, which act as so many red hot luminous points against which the water impinges, and thus it is that evaporation is accelerated.

I may now conclude this answer, by reminding " D." that heat and light, in consequence of the refined and truly admirable researches of Melloni are now considered to be distinct, and that I have nowhere supposed that the repulsion existing between *water*, limped or coloured, and heated metal, to result from any causes which can be at all referred to electricity.

Yours, &c.

CHARLES TOMLINSON.

Salisbury, 1st April, 1837.

MR. UTTING'S ASTRONOMICAL TABLES.
TO "A SCOTCH DOMINIE."

Sir,—You have made some remarks in No. 709 of the *Mechanics Magazine*, on my paper relative to the observations of Professor Struve, wherein I gave a reference to two sets of observations, purporting to have been made by the professor on the planet Saturn and his ring, and on Jupiter and his satellites. I there represented that there was a difference between the two sets of observations of their $\frac{1}{317}$ part, "with the exception of the fourth satellite only of Jupiter." This remark, relative to the 4th satellite, originated in a misprint in the work from which it was copied; it stands correct in Sir J. Herschell's Astronomy, so that the difference of $\frac{1}{317}$ part, applies to the *whole* set of observations. Now Sir, do you pretend to say, that the two statements are the results of two different series, or distinct sets of observation? No. I defy you to prove it, as it is self-evident that the first set of observations were reduced by their $\frac{1}{317}$ part, and that the results constitute, what are alleged to be his *new results, deduced from a much greater number of observations.*

Whether the professor ever made the above pretensions, or whether the imposition originated with the editors of the works alluded to, is not my concern. My observations on the statements referred to, are indisputable. You next attack my paper on a conjunction of the sun, moon, planets, &c., read before the *Royal Astronomical Society.* Are you aware, that all papers presented to the Society, are first examined by the Secretaries? What an unfortunate circumstance that these gentlemen were not possessed of your profound erudition! Had this been the case, my paper would not have been read, and of course an imposition could not have been palmed upon the members of the Astronomical Society, the Editor of the *Mechanics' Magazine* and its readers.

You enter into a long tirade, about the improbability, or impossibility of a conjunction taking place at all; and, as an example, you propose my taking the tropical revolutions from the best authority, only to the nearest second of time. And yet the period of Saturn, which you, in your supreme wisdom, thought fit to furnish me with, is between four and five hours from the truth, as deduced from the data given by Sir J. Herschell!! Now, admitting a conjunction of the sun, moon, planets, &c. to take place after a long period of time, do you suppose that the periodic times would be *correctly* found from *observations only*, made within one or two centuries? Certainly not; as they are constantly varying from the effects of perturbations, to which their motions are subject.

If the number of revolutions which each planet makes during a supposed conjunction, be ascertained, and from thence their periodic times and secular motions; and if these secular motions accord with those determined from the most correct modern observations, within the limits of the secular variations, to which they are subject; we may conclude, that a conjunction may take place; as no human being can prove anything to the contrary. A long series of observations, will, however, be required, before the periodic times of the planets Saturn and Uranus are obtained to a single second of time. In respect to the latter planet, one revolution has not yet been accomplished since its discovery by Dr. Herschell. If the periodic time of this planet, as stated in Vince's Astronomy (vol. 1, page 125, edit. 1814) be compared with the statement in Pond's translation of Laplace's System of the World (vol. 1, page 252), there will be found a difference of no less than 244 days!! There is also a difference of several hours in the periodic time of Saturn, as stated by some of the most celebrated astronomers of the present day. It is therefore inconsistent to propose taking the periodic time to even seconds or even minutes, and it displays no favourable symptoms of intelligence in that person who expects that the elements of a conjunction can be *rigorously* obtained from observation only.

I shall now proceed to where you ask me "from what authority I deduced the periodic times of the planets given in my first table." To which I answer, that I used my own discretion in selecting those which I presumed to be the most correct.

The data given in Sir J. Herschell's Treatise on Astronomy, are, however, sufficiently correct for your purpose; take the siderial periods from this work, the preeession of the equinoctial points. at 1 deg. 23 min. 30 sec. in a century, compute from thence the *tropical* periods of the planets, and compare them with mine in the *Mechanics' Magazine*, (vol. 26, page 378), and then let me ask you what authority you had for your blundering assertion "that some of my periods are minutes wrong, some, hours, some days," *and last, not least,* "YEA, EVEN MONTHS WRONG! whereas, the greatest difference, which is in the periodic time of the planet Uranus, will be found to amount to but little more than five hours! So much for your knowledge in Arithmetic!

The near approximation of my periods to those given by the best modern astronomers,will, I trust, exonerate me from any imputed intention of imposing on the Members of the Royal Astronomical Society. I observed in my paper sent to the above Society, that the secular motions given in my last table, vary a few seconds from those given *at the present time;* but taking the whole period into account, they might be regulated by the secular variations, to which they are subject, so as to constitute them *the mean secular motions*—but which was inadvertantly omitted in the paper sent to the Editor of the *Mechanics' Magazine.*

I shall now pass to the moon, and agreeable to your order, manufacture a new period for her ladyship!

Deduct the revolutious of the sun, or the earth, which is the same thing, from the revolutions of the moon as given in table 1, and the remainder 3,103,248 is the number of revolutions of the moon from the sun, by which, if the 91,640,740 days be divided, the quotient reduced will be 29 days, 12 hours, 44 minutes, 2.8547 seconds, &c. This is, however, the synodic period of the moon, and not her *tropical* or *solar* period. I might, with as much propriety have inserted the *synodic* period of all the planets, or any other periods that your fancy might dictate! Should you, Sir, have any further communication with the Editor the *Mechanics' Magazine* on the subject of my papers, you will please to have the courtesy to affix your real name and address to your communications, if you expect an answer from me; as if you do not, it will be considered a tacit acknowledgment that you are ashamed of your productions; as we Norfolk *cards*, do not choose to play with your *For-far-shire* (alias For, *far-fetch'd**) *Dominos* in disguise.

I am, Sir, yours, &c.
JAMS UTTING, C. E.
Lynn, April 3rd, 1837.

P.S.—I had a controversy some years since in the *Philosophical Magazine* respecting the *Phillippian Theory of the Universe*, with a correspondent, who, under the signature of *Philo Veritatis,* accused me of hoaxing its readers at the expence of truth. In consequence of which, I gave my name with my next communication. On the receipt of another paper from this individual, *Dr. Tilloch* inserted in his notices to correspondents "that as Mr. Utting's name appeared at his last answer to *Philo Veritatis,* the anonymous reply would not be admitted." The consequence was that we never heard any thing further from this redoubtable champion of the *Phillippian Theory.* (Vide vol. 56.) The above is a corroborative proof, that some persons will write, under an anonymous signature, what they would be ashamed in their own names to claim as their production, and which gives them an unfair advantage. J.U.

IMPROVEMENT IN GAS STOVES.

Sir, Your correspondent Evander in giving a description of his very ingenious and effective gas stove, in No. 713, having done me the honour of mentioning my name, I take the liberty of offering my mede of approbation of his invention, which I think obviates all the objections that can be made to gas warming. All others that I have heard of, allow of the escape of either unconsumed gas into the apartment, or of chemical results, injurious and disagreable.

I am, however, still of opinion that the air of an apartment, heated either by common fuel stove, or by gas, even ac-

---

* Quere. Did not this production *germinate* in a warmer latitude?

cording to Evander's excellent plan, becomes too much dried. Very dry warm air produces a disagreable irritation of the mucous membrane of the nose, and consequently—as the entire lining of the trachea, the bronchæ, and the large air vessels of the lungs, is a continuation of the same membrane—such hot *dry* air may be injurious to the respiring organs. I therefore put it to the ingenious inventor, whether the apparatus might not be improved by the addition of a metallic vessel of water, placed on the top aperture, where now there is the ventilator? The water vessel may still be so placed, as to allow of the abundant escape of the heated current of air. The evaporation of water will be encreased by the encreased action of the gas, and the air to be breathed, will be supplied with sufficient moisture to make it agreeable to the breathing apparatus.

I am, Sir, yours, &c.

F. MACERONI.

P.S. A culinary, or any other vessel, might be made to boil on the top of the cylinder.

MR. MACKINNON'S PATENT LAW BILL.

From the reports of the Parliamentary proceedings of last Wednesday evening (12th April), we extract the following:—

" *Patent for Inventions Bill.*

" Mr. MACKINNON stated that it was his intention to postpone the second reading of this Bill until Wednesday, the 17th May.

" The ATTORNEY-GENERAL wished to know whether it was the intention of the honourable Member to give up the Bill altogether?

" Mr. MACKINNON—had no such intention."

We have been favoured with a note from Mr. Mackinnon, in which he fully confirms the statement made by him in the House.

New Locomotive Invention.—Colonel Prince Jasper Bieloselsky-Bieloselsky, an officer in the Russian service, has just obtained from the Emperor a ten years' privilege for a new invention, which he denominates a *sledge-road*. The novelty of the principle consists in affixing the wheels to the road instead of to the carriage, the effect of which is said to be a great diminution in the labour of draught. The sledges are proposed to be worked by horses, but there seems no reason why, if the principle should really be found to answer, the superior power of steam should not be made use of. The inventor is sanguine in his expectations of the benefit of his discovery, which, among other recommendations, possesses that of economy. The expense of constructing a sledge-road of the length of a Russian verst would, he calculates, at St. Petersburgh, amount to about 10,350 rubles, which is about £645 per English mile. One of his sledges, which are of a peculiar shape, was manufactured by Clarke, of St. Petersburgh, for 220 rubles, or £9. 3s. 4d.

Invention of the Ever-pointed Pencil.—It is not generally known that Mr. John Isaac Hawkins, Civil Engineer, of Hampstead, in the year 1822, invented that useful and now wellknow npocket appendage, the *patent ever-pointed pencil*, and the leads for the same, the right of making which was purchased from him by Gabriel Riddle and Sampson Mordan, under the well-known firm of S. Mordan & Co.

Coal in India.—An extensive bed of coal has recently been discovered in the Saugor district, of a quality superior to any which has ever been found in India. The position of the field is about twelve miles south of the Gurrawarra, at the foot of the hills. " The mere discovery, however," says one of the Indian journals, " is of little importance, unless the government come forward and bring the mineral to the light of day. Here the field for private enterprise is disproportionally large for the few labourers in it ; indeed, we believe we might possess a second Potosi without the smallest diversion of private funds being made to work it. It therefore rests with government to make the discovery useful to themselves and the country, and towards this they have many natural facilities. The distance to Meersapoor is considerable, but the route is open and very accessible for carriages ; indeed, we do not see why a railroad should not be formed at once." It is said that the government are deterred from availing themselves of these facilities by an ill-judged fear of expense.

Improvement in the Manufacture of Sugar.—A new process has been discovered at Strasburg by means of which a white crystallized sugar is produced in twelve hours from beet-root, and which does not require any further refining. This invention is the more curious, as neither any acids or chemical agency is employed in this remarkable operation, and the use of animal blood is entirely dispensed with. It has also the advantage of saving 25 per cent. in the consumption of fuel. The new process is applicable in all the present manufactories of sugar, with the exception of those upon the principle of dessication of the beet-root. The inventor is M. Edward Stolle, who, though not more than 24 years of age, is already highly distinguished for his experiments in chemistry and his works in polite literature.

☞ *British and Foreign Patents taken out with economy and despatch ; Specifications, Disclaimers, and Amendments, prepared or revised ; Caveats entered ; and generally every Branch of Patent Business promptly transacted.*
A complete list of Patents from the earliest period (15 Car. II. 1675,) to the present time may be examined Fee 2s. 6d. ; Clients, gratis.

LONDON : Printed and Published by W. A. Robertson, at the Mechanics' Magazine Office, No. 6, Peterborough-court, between 135 and 136, Fleet-street.—Sold by G. W. M. Reynolds, Proprietor of the French, English, and American Library, 55, Rue Neuve, Saint Augustin, Paris.

𝕸echanics' 𝕸agazine,

MUSEUM, REGISTER, JOURNAL, AND GAZETTE.

| No. 715. | SATURDAY, APRIL 22, 1837. | Price 3d. |

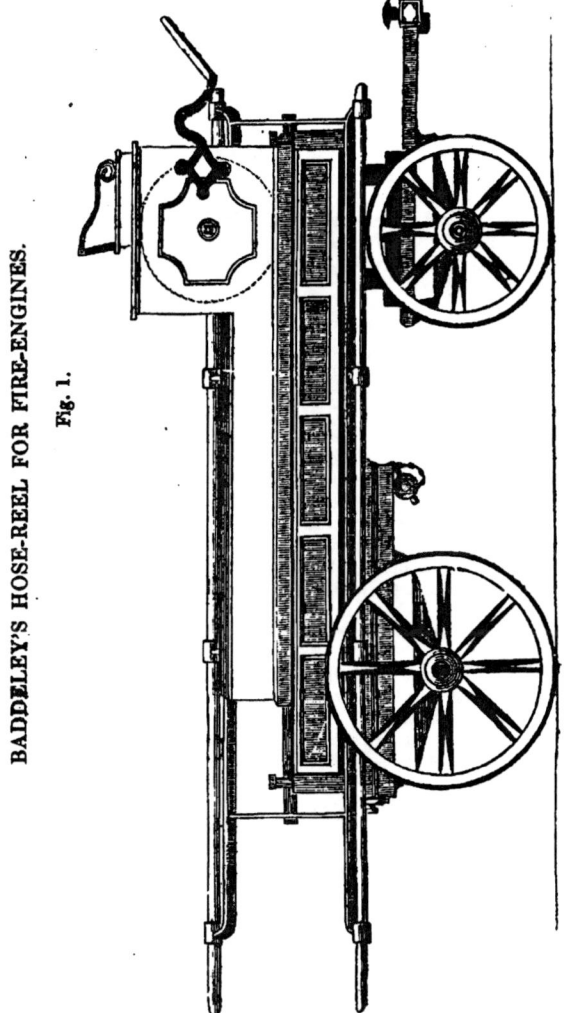

BADDELEY'S HOSE-REEL FOR FIRE-ENGINES.

Fig. 1.

BADDELEY'S HOSE-REEL FOR FIRE-ENGINES.

Sir,—Every contrivance, calculated to save time, and in some measure to supersede skilled labour, is at all times valuable, but especially so when adapted to emergent occasions—as, for instance, when applied to such objects as the extinction of fires.

The present form of fire-engines is so convenient, and so exceeding compact, that it is only in the minor details of its arrangements, that there is any room for the exercise of ingenuity.

In addition to the several minor improvements, which I have from time to time suggested, I have now to submit another, intended to simplify and facilitate the application of this useful machine to its intended purpose.

As fire-engines are now built, the leather hose is stowed away very conveniently in separate lengths (six lengths and a half being the usual compliment,) in the fore part of the engine. In London and some other places, where the firemen, from continual practice, become amazingly expert in the management of all their apparatus, six, seven, eight. or even a still greater number of lengths of hose, are got out and joined up with astonishing rapidity. It sometimes happens, however, even with the most experienced firemen, when short-handed, that some loss of time occurs in performing this necessary operation. When no regular firemen are employed, as in the case of engines belonging to parishes—to public or private establishments, &c., where only one individual is acquainted with, and has himself to perform the several preparatory evolutions, or entrust their performance to strangers altogether unpractised in matters of this sort—the getting out and joining of any considerable quantity of hose is a work of much time and labour.

The drawings herewith sent, exhibit a little invention, which I have termed a *hose-reel;* it is intended to have wound upon it a quantity of leather hose already screwed together, so that on arriving at a fire, the engineer has only to take the branch-pipe in one hand and the end screw of the hose in the other, and run off to any point from which the fire can be successfully opposed; a sufficient length of hose being run out, the next

joint is screwed and attached to the engine, which may immediately commence working. The speed with which an engine can thus be brought to bear upon the flames, at some considerable distance, is very great; one joint has to be unmade and another made, when all that is necessary is performed. Whereas, at present, perhaps five or six lengths would have to be taken out of the engine, carried forward, and as many joints made before the engine could be set to work—to say nothing of the uncertainty as to the quantity required, or of the imperfect manner in which the joints are made when done hastily, amid the confusion which always prevails, and perhaps by persons unaccustomed to the office. By useing the reel all twisting of the hose is effectually obviated—the joints having been previously made are all perfect, and the connecting screws are preserved from much of the injury to which they are at present exposed.

Fig. 1. is a side elevation of a fire-engine of the most approved construction, furnished with the hose-reel, which occupies a space enlarged for the purpose above the cistern and under the driver's seat—the extent and position of the reel being shown by the dotted circle. Fig. 2. is a front representation of the

Fig. 2.

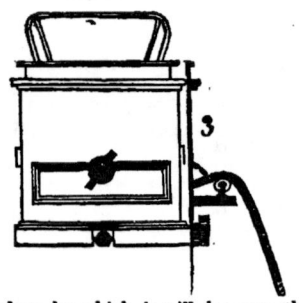

hose-box, by which it will be seen that there is an oblong flap or door, fastened in any convenient manner, with an aperture of such a size as to hold firmly the male screw of the hose. Fig. 3. is a side view of the same, with the hose in the act of being drawn out. A small roller is placed upon the flap for the hose to run in and out upon, the flap being supported horizontally by chains on either side. Fig. 4. shows the construction of the reel; it consists of a hollow spindle *a*, and two circular sides *b b*, of thin sheet iron; the spindle runs

Fig. 4.

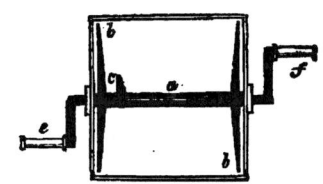

in two brass collars in the sides of the hose-box, and at each end there are two square eyes for the insertion of the handles *e f*, by which the hose is wound upon the reel. In winding up the hose, two men stand, one on either pocket, another one in front guides the hose backwards and forwards from end to end of spindle. The female screw is in the first instance hitched upon the forked notch *c*, which holds it fast, and on turning round the handles the hose is wound upon the reel. There is a pall and ratchet (not shown in the drawing) which prevents the hose from unwinding in travelling, &c. On reaching a fire the ratchet is thrown back, and a sufficient quantity of hose drawn out, which is then disconnected from the remainder and attached to the engine. There is room in the engine for stowing away two or three extra lengths of hose, which, on an extraordinary occasion can be joined to the great length if required; but a reel of sufficient dimensions, to carry hose enough for ordinary purposes, can be obtained without inconveniently extending the shape, or injuring the appearance of the engine.

Yours respectfully,
WM. BADDELEY.
March 23rd, 1837.

LONDON FIRES.—MR. BADDELEY'S REPORTS.—THE INSURANCE SYSTEM.

Sir, — The Annual Fire Reports of your valuable correspondent, Mr. Baddeley, are undoubtedly of the highest interest for the mass of information which they contain, whatever may be thought of the soundness of the inferences sometimes drawn from the facts advanced. Ever since its establishment in 1832, Mr. Baddeley has been a warm partizan of the "London Fire-Engine Establishment," and to such an extent has his enthusiasm in its favour been carried, that, as has heretofore been shewn, he does not hesitate to throw overboard his own objections to the constitution of the Insurance Companies, in order to bear testimony to the superhuman exertions of Mr. Braidwood and the fire-brigade; nor scruple to assert one moment that the Insurance Companies " strain every nerve" for the protection of all sorts of property, although the moment before he had given most exquisite reasons why nothing of the sort could possibly be expected, while human nature is human nature. Nor does he flinch in the least in his last Annual Report, in which, immediately after an appalling account of an almost unprecedented number of extensive and fatal fires, he boldly goes on to observe, —" Having for fourteen years attentively watched the progress of the firemen, under the old state of things, and for four years the results of the united system, I *have no hesitation in most positively asserting*, that both the Insurance Companies and the public generally, are gainers by the change." It is this sweeping assertion which seem to me to call imperatively for a few remarks.

That the Insurance Companies are gainers by the change is doubtless quite correct. Their only object was, to use the words of Mr. Baddeley, to "form a kind of league, with a view to the reduction of their individual expenses;" and this purpose has very probably been effectually served; whether the public have also been " gainers by the change," is a totally different question. And how is it to be decided? All the world knows that the Insurance Companies cannot exist without *some* fires; and that, provided too much insured property be not destroyed, their motto is, "the more the merrier!" It is at least equally plain, that the " public" generally are losers by every fire, and have the most reason to consider themselves " gainers" when fires are few, and the damage done trifling. Well, then, let us take two of Mr. Baddeley's reports, one referring to the last year of the old system, and the other to the year 1836 (in which, we are told, *improvement* has been carried to its highest extent under the new one), and see how far the public have profited by the alteration, by the test, not of opinion only, but of stubborn fact.

The two most important heads are those of "total loss" and "serious damage." There seems to have been some different method of estimating these in the two years, since it can hardly be supposed that, under the inefficient old system, there were only six cases of serious damage (or where the premises were "partly consumed"), while, under the new and much bepraised fire-brigade, there were no less than *one hundred and sixty-four!* It will be the fairest way, therefore, to take these two heads together; the result will still be sufficiently surprising, and tolerably conclusive as to the great "gain" of the public. The number of serious fires, then, in 1832, was *fifty-six* (vide Mr. Baddeley's Report, *Mechanics' Magazine,* vol. xviii. p. 266), and that of the same class, in 1836, no fewer than *one hundred and thirty-seven* (vide Mr. Baddeley's Report, *Mechanics' Magazine,* vol. xxvi. p. 354), shewing a majority *in favour* of the "London Fire-Engine Establishment" of *one hundred and eleven!* That is, the public, in the fourth year of the fire-brigade, obtained a clear gain of 111 serious losses over and above what they experienced in the last year of the "old state of things." If this do not satisfy them, what will?

In "fatal fires," the rate of increase is just 100 per cent. It is hardly fair to lay any of the blame of this on the shoulders of the brigade; but yet it should be borne in mind, that, if the numbers had happened to be the other way, the figures would have been pointed to as proof positive of increased and successful exertion. Since the establishment of the brigade, the number of fires has doubled: this fact, of course, fixes no stigma upon them, although, had the contrary been the case, it would perhaps have been quoted as highly complimentary them. It bears more closely on the question, that since the establishment of the new system, the town has been "frighted from its propriety" by a much larger number of *extensive* conflagrations than it had been accustomed to for many years under the old regime. The two Houses of Parliament form a case in point, and the augmenting length of Mr. Baddeley's successive Annual Reports bears striking testimony to the same effect. It might have been imagined, by the over-sanguine, that, when the fire-brigade came into full operation, Othello's occupation would be gone, and that a yearly report of London fires would be composed of half a column of kitchen-chimney casualties. No such thing,—every year it swells out in size and in importance,—every year fires of the first magnitude come within its ken. In 1832, they were so few, and put out so soon, that they could be dismissed in a couple of lines, with the observation, "that during the last year there were not above half a dozen fires of any considerable magnitude." In 1836, the times were altered; the exertions of the brigade had been so effective as to give full scope for the recorder of calamity, who, so far from suffering for want of material, was hard put to it to find room enough, in the same letter which bore witness to the great gain "the public" had reaped by the change, for the details of "the largest fire that had happened in London for many years," at which "the destruction of property was IMMENSE, —*not more than one fifth of which was insured!*" (Vide Mr. Baddeley's Report, *Mechanics' Magazine,* vol. xxvi. p. 357).

Yet, in the face of all these facts, we are gravely told, that "whatever advantages might have been anticipated from the measure, the experience of the past four years proves that they have been *fully realized!*"—Indeed! did the projectors of the scheme, then, anticipate that among its advantages would be an increase of serious fires to the extent of two hundred per cent., accompanied by a doubling of the number of fatal cases? Did they really lay their plans to bring about a series of conflagrations, destroying property to an almost unparalleled extent? If not, in the name of common sense, what is the intent and meaning of the observation? Tried by the facts furnished by Mr. Baddeley himself, the plan would appear, *as far as the public are concerned,* to be a total failure. It does not follow, from this, that it has not answered the purpose of its projectors;—to wit, divers parties connected with the insurance companies. If the arrangements for extinguishing fires had been sufficiently effective to have put a stop to the London Bridge conflagration at its commencement, what would have been its result? Why, that the insurance companies, at their sole cost, would have saved a hundred pounds worth of their own property, for every four hundred pounds worth belonging to persons, who contribute not one farthing to the expenses of the Fire-engine Establishment! Could it be expected, under such circumstances, that they should go to the expense necessary to the completely efficient equipment of a fire police? Certainly not :—What then was the object aimed at BY THEM in the new system, and which we may suppose to be fully realized? The principal object would appear to be—display. As matters stood, the odds are, at every fire, that the expense gone to by the insurance companies is chiefly for the benefit of other parties, so that it would appear to be hardly worth their while to keep up any preventive establishment at all. The engines, however, are made to do double duty, and the fire-brigade are trained to the service of their employers in more ways than one. If the former arrive too late to put out a fire, at any rate, rumbling as it does, through the streets with streamer flying, and men hollowing, it answers the purpose of an advertising machine most excellently, while the "brigade" sport their peculiar costume, and strikingly novel accoutrements, not so much to awe the " devouring element" as to take the attention of the many-headed monster, and put " the public" in mind of the existence of insurance offices ;—something after the fashion of the Sunday newspapers, with their imposing " brigade" of boardmen, on occasion of any particularly-interesting murder. All these advertising purposes may have been fully answered by the united system, at a far less expense than attended the old-fashioned and more costly mode, when each office employed its own men and machines ;—but that " the public" have as much reason as the companies to be gratified at the " improvement" is not quite so clear. A " good fire" is in itself a sort of advertisement for insurance, and all the accessaries, as far as possible, are turned to account in the same direction. If the public look for a first-rate fire-police, all

property must be insured, or the matter must be taken out of the hands of the insurance companies. It is useless for Mr. Baddeley to go on explaining to us that, under the present system " the uninsured and the insured, as well as the insurers, all equally receive the greatest possible protection," while the first of these classes, at whose risk three-fourths of the whole of the property in the metropolis lies, bear not one farthing of the cost. For what reason should the insurance offices be so benevolently inclined towards parties who hold themselves aloof from them? And if Mr. Baddeley's lately-adopted ideas on this point be correct, wherein lies the force of his remarks, or the folly of the parishioners of St. Olave's for throwing the blame of the damage at the London Bridge fire on " the servants of the insurance companies, who only had one-fifth of the property destroyed lying at their risk?" These worthy gentlemen could hardly expect to be twitted by Mr. Baddeley, of all people in the world, for being simple enough to put faith in his monstrous proposition, that the insured and the uninsured are alike objects of the disinterested anxiety of insurance companies !

I remain, Sir,
Your obedient servant,
AQUARIUS.
London, 4th April, 1837.

ON THE CONSTRUCTION OF THE SEA-GUAGE.

Sir,—That the barometer has been successfully employed in the mensuration of altitudes is known to every one, but that a modification of the same instrument may be adapted to mark the depths to which it is plunged in water, is known only to few, and in this paper, I therefore intend to show how it may be so applied.

It is evident, that the sounding line, in many cases cannot possibly indicate, by the length of line that has been given out, the depth to which the lead has sunk ; for a current may carry it along, without permitting it to sink perpendicularly—and, although the instrument that I am going to describe, is equally liable to be drifted by a current, still in all cases, it will give an indication of the approximate perpendicular depth it has descended, which, of necessity, in a strong current, if it do not reach the bottom, will depend upon the weight that has been attached to the instrument.

As the construction of this instrument depends upon the rate with which air is condensed when subjected to different pressures, it hence becomes me to make some remarks upon this subject. It has been found that the condensation of air is always directly proportional (under low pressures at least) to the compressing force—and the space that any given quantity of air will occupy under different pressures is, inversely or reciprocally proportional to the same pressures. In other words, whatever space a given quantity of air does occupy, under any pressure, it will only occupy half the space, when subjected to double, and ⅓ of the same space, when subjected to triple that pressure.

Let A B C be a bent tube open at both ends, and filled with mercury to the

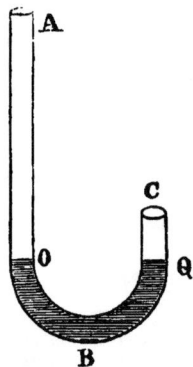

points O and Q. Suppose the tube to be then hermitically sealed or otherwise closed at C, it will be found that a quantity of mercury poured into A O B, sufficient to raise its surface 29·5 inches —supposing that to be the height of the mercury in a common barometer at the instant the experiment is made, above what would *then* be the level of the mercury in C Q,—would compress the confined air ½—and if C Q formerly measured 12 inches, after this addition of mercury, namely, 29·5+12=41.5 inches, the distance of the surface of the mercury from C would only be six inches.

In this case 12 inches more than the equipendevant column of mercury 29·5 inches must be added, because the level is raised 6 inches in C Q, by the addition of an atmosphere, and hence 12 inches of mercury+29·5 are necessary to raise the column in A O B 29·5 inches above this level. Now as the specific gravity of water is to that of mercury nearly as 1 to 13.5, hence 13.5×29·5= 398·25, almost 400 inches—consequently, the pressure of 400 inches of water would condense the air in C Q. one half—800 inches would make it occupy only one third of the space, and so on. The reverse of this problem can easily be solved.

Given the space that air occupies under ordinary circumstances, and the space it occupies when subjected to pressure to discern the intensity of the compressing force

Let P = one atmosphere=29·5 inches of mercury = 400 inches of water x = additional pressure. Then $P + x$ =whole compressing force.

S = volume of uncompressed air,

C = volume of air when compressed. As the volume that air occupies, is, within moderate limits, inversely proportional to the pressure to which it is subjected.

$C:S::P:P+x$, hence $C:S—C::P:x$; or $x = \frac{(S—C)P}{C}$ Let $S = 12$ inches, $C = 11$, then $11:1::$ P (400 inches of water) $: x = C\ 36·36$ in., or the pressure produced by a colum of water measuring 36.36 from the surface of the mercury, (in CQ) would condense the air $\frac{1}{12}$th: or in other words, the surface of the mercury would rise one inch in C Q B by 36·36+2 in. of water's being poured into A O B, or from the instrument's being plunged to that depth in water+the distance of the new surface of the mercury from B, supposing the water had free admission into the leg A O B.—In the same manner it may be calculated, what pressure would raise the surface of the mercury any given height in C Q, supposing the length of C Q was given, or the volume of uncompressed air. As another example, we may take the following: let C Q = 10 inches, and it was required to determine what depth of water would be necessary to condense the air into $\frac{1}{10}$th of its former bulk, or to raise the surface of the water 9 inches, or within one inch of C.

Here $S = 10$ inches, $Q = 1$, hence S

—$Q = 9$, and $P = 400$ inches, a constant quantity, from the formula $x = \frac{(S-Q)P}{Q} = \frac{9 \times 400}{1} = 3,600$ inches or 300 feet. But to give at one view the depth necessary to elevate the surface of the mercury $\frac{1}{10}$th of the whole space, or every inch, supposing C Q to be 10 inches long.

1 inch of elevation requires a depth of	ft.	in.
2 inches	3	8
3 ——	8	4
3 ——	14	3
4 ——	22	2
5 ——	33	4
6 ——	50	0
7 ——	77	9
8 ——	133	4
9 ——	300	0
9½ ——	633	0

To these numbers the elevation of the mercury above the cistern must be added, because the pressure produced by the column of water above the mercury in the tube, is alone manifested by the compressure of the air—in short, 3 ft. 8 in. must be increased by 1 inch and 8 ft. 4 in. by 2: see the numbers in the foregoing table.

From the general law above developed, is deduced the construction of Drs. Hales and Desaguliers' sea-guage. A tube was put into a cistern containing mercury, upon which a film of treacle was spread—and to this the sea-water had access through some holes bored in the top of the cistern. By the pressure produced by the water, the air in the tube was condensed, the mercury necessarily rose, and its height was indicated by the stain left by the treacle. If the tube were 10 inches long, or rather 10 inches above the surface of the mercury in the cistern, it is evident from the above table, that when the air within is compressed, so as only to occupy one half of an inch, the depth will be 634 ft., or nearly one eighth of a mile.

Suppose the tube was 50 inches long, and the air was condensed into $\frac{1}{10}$th part of its original bulk, or to occupy only one half of an inch, the depth necessary to produce this contraction would be 3,300 feet, or ⅚ths of a mile, for ½ : 49½ :: 400 : 39,600 inches = 3,300 feet = ⅚ths of a mile. But since it is reasonable to suppose that the cavities of the ocean bear some proportion to the mountainous parts of the land, and as the summit of Chemborazo is 21,440 feet above the level of the Pacific Ocean, and some peaks of the Himmalaya Chain are supposed to ascend to the enormous altitude of from 21,000 to 27,000 feet, therefore, to express such great depths, another form must be given to the instrument. For this purpose, a globe of metal was attached to the end of the tube, and from the lower end of the globe, a short tube was made to project and enter into the mercury. If the tube above the mercury be 50 inches long, and of such a width, that every inch in length should be a cubic inch of air, and the contents of the globe and tube together be 500 cubic inches, then when the air is compressed into $\frac{1}{100}$ part of its bulk, it is evident that the treacle will not approach nearer to the top of the tube than five inches, — and this condensation, as I have shown, will agree to the depth of 3,300 feet of water. Twice the depth, or 6,600 feet = 1¼ miles nearly, will condense the air into 2½ inches. Again, half that space, or 1¼ inches will indicate a depth of 13,200, or 2½ miles, which, probably, is very nearly the greatest depth of the sea.

Besides ascertaining the depth of the ocean Dr. Hales applied his guage to other purposes, as to ascertain the expansive force of water in the act of freezing. The guage was fixed in the centre of an iron bomb filled with water, and the top of the bomb was then firmly screwed on; when a freezing mixture was applied, the water expanded and compressed the air, thus exhibiting the expansive force of the water by the condensation produced. The guage not being well secured was broken in pieces, but it was computed that a force almost equal to 1,340 atmespheres would be necessary to burst an iron bomb one inch thick. The Florentine Academicians estimated that freezing water would burst a brass ball, whose power of cohesion could sustain 27,720 lbs. weight. A guage somewhat similar, or at least dependant upon the same principle as that which we have described, has lately been re-invented by Mr. Payne, of the Adelaide Gallery. I use the word re-invented, because I am aware that Mr. Payne did not know of Dr. Hales and Desaguliers prior invention. Mr. Payne's guage, I am informed (there is no model of it yet in the Gallery,) has however decidedly the advantage in elegance and the sim—

plicity of its arrangements. It is by means of a bladder that the pressure is communicated to the surface of the mercury in the cistern—the treacle is dispensed with, and hydrogen gas is used instead of atmospherical air. With treacle, the tube must be cleansed after every trial, Mr. Payne's guage requires no such attention, and when atmospheric air is used, the mercury will ultimately become exudated, and hence more sluggish, whereas, hydrogen gas does not act on mercury, and consequently, when this gas is used, the metal will always remain pure.

This method of estimating the depth of the ocean is, however, liable to several objections—and several corrections are absolutely necessary, whereas, to effect these I am doubtful if we possess sufficient *data*. In small depths no correction is required, but in measuring great depths, the temperature of the sub-marine regions would require to be ascertained, and a due allowance to be made—the elasticity of air, according to Hutton (vol. ii. page 258) is increased $\frac{1}{435}$th part, by every degree of heat above 32 deg. Fahr, and water expands $\frac{3}{10000}$th parts with the same increment of temperature. The maximum quantity of water is at 40 deg., and both above and below this temperature it expands. Water itself is not incompressible; its elasticity, and consequently its compressibility is manifested by the reflection of stones from its surfaces in the game of "duck and drake." The experiment of the Florentine Academicians proved directly the opposite of that which they inferred from it. For elasticity always implies compressibility, although a body may be compressible and not elastic. Canton showed that water is condensed by pressure—Zimmerman corroborated his discovery; and the ingenious and indefatigable Mr. Perkins has shown that water, under a force equal to 2,000 atmospheres is diminished $\frac{1}{17}$th part, as indicated by a spiral spring. Hence the greater density of water as we descend, causing the equipendevant column of water to be less than 400 inches, the number which we have assumed to be constant. Shall we then, from Mr. Perkin's experiment, infer that the contraction produced by 1,000 atmospheres is $\frac{1}{14}$th part, and from the supposition if the modulus of elasticity remaining con-

stant, and the condensation being always proportional to the depth, affirm with Leslie " that water would be compressed to half its bulk at a depth of 93 miles."

I mentioned that at low pressures the condensation of air is proportional to the compressing force, but at very high pressures the condensation may follow a very different ratio—a supposition almost rendered certain, because from Mr. Perkins' experiment, it seems that he succeeded in reducing atomspheric air to the state of a limpid liquid by a pressure equal to 1,200 atmospheres.

Δ Λ.

MORE " DISCOVERIES" BY " SUPERINTENDENT GENERAL" JOHN HERAPATH.

Sir,—I beg to thank you for your prompt insertion of the list of " discoveries" which I sent you last week by Mr. ——, I beg his pardon—'' Superintendent General" John Herapath. Encouraged by the favourable reception you have given it, I now send you a small addition to the store.

When our "Superintendent General" was engaged in the honourable task of ridiculing Sir John Rennie's Brighton line, for faults, most of which, as " Philo-Davy" truly observes, proved to be matters of " pure invention," he made the following very remarkable *discoveries*.

1st, That *two miles and a half* of tunnelling according to measurement with a pair of compasses, may, by a mere flourish of a pen, be converted into *seven miles* complete ; *provided only it is an unscrupulous hand which wields the pen.*

2nd, That, when an elevation (such as the Balcombe Down summit) happens to be lower than suits your purpose, you have only to survey it by means of a Herapathian theodolite (a nice article) when it may be raised to any height you please beyond the reality—a " hundred" feet at least, with great ease. " Having been fortunate enough to make some discoveries, I am able to reach THAT from my own labours." A "reach" " THAT" with a vengeance.

3rd, That when it is a bridge or embankment, whose modest elevation is a matter of offence to you (such as Sir John Rennie's embankment across the river Mole,) you have only to heap upon it any quantity of rubbish which lies handy, to give it the desired altitude, be it a hundred or five hundred feet. A lot of dead-born, or condemned letter press will serve the purpose, as well as any thing else; *e. g.*, "My Labours and Discoveries" since A. D. 1800, *single leaf—elephant* paper—the entire impression—authors own copy excepted—or "New Nautical Almanac for the year of Our Lord 0000."

And, 4th, That when you are accused of romancing abominably, to the serious prejudice of another, the fittest course to pursue, is to put a gay face on the grave offence—to plead "guilty," and make a merit of your guilt! As thus: "It may be asked How I came to *depart from my authority*, and to call the tunnels only seven, instead of two and a half miles—THE TRUTH IS, except the inclinations, with which I could not meddle, *I understated every thing.* I took 100 feet from (Query? *added to*) the height of the hills; another, from (Query?—*added to*) the embankments, &c. &c., *lest the public should think I was romancing!!*"

Recommending the new code of morality revealed to the world in the last of these memorable discoveries, to the serious attention of all future aspirants to the honours of the Old Bailey, and their ingenious author to the compassion of a "humane public."

I remain, Sir,

Your obedient servant,

F. M. MEREDITH.

Cambridge, 17th April, 1837.

MR. MACKINTOSH'S FIRST IMPULSE CHALLENGE.

Sir,—Mr. Mackintosh still continues to harp upon his first question. "Demonstrate what produced the first impulse." At first I referred him to his own pastor for a solution of his own proposition; and afterwards I answered the question in the best way I could. In his last letter (No. 712) he informs me that he has actually applied to his own pastor for a solution of the said question, and he (his parson) informed him that he can give him no information about a first impulse: on this head I am not very much surprised. But his pastor also confesses his total ignorance of centrefugal and centrepetal forces, momentum and angular velocity. A pretty gentleman to make a parson of.[*] Well, Mr. M., your own pastor being by his own account such a perfect numskull, you might, peradventure be more successful in applying to some sensible schoolmaster. But really, to be serious, even granting for the sake of argument, that a first impulse was given to the matter (and who can be certain of this, as both may have been co-eternal) to ask for a demonstration of the cause, is, to borrow a favourite expression of your own Mr. M., nothing but "profound nonsense." In support of this assertion I will give you, Mr. M., some written opinions on this subject, by a gentleman, who, of all living men I am sure you have the most elevated opinion and who do you think, Mr. M., the gentleman happens to be? Why no less a personage than your goodly self. In your concluding lecture on physical astronomy delivered at the Hall of Science on Nov. 7th, and reported in the *Mechanics' Magazine*, Nov. 12, you gave utterance to the following rigidly orthodox sentiments:—

"In conclusion Mr. M. remarked, whether this theory was founded on truth or otherwise, by inquiring into its merits our knowledge of the physical world would be extended and improved. So long as our inquiries were conducted with a proper spirit, *and confined to subjects within the human understanding*, the improvement of that understanding must be the result of those inquiries: *there were some things beyond the reach of that understanding*" (the first impulse proposition for one) "and concerning those things, it was *neither needful nor proper that we should inquire.*" (It was for this very reason that I did not attempt to give a demonstration of your celestial problem). "That space was infinite in extent,—that time was infinite in duration, and that the Divine Mind being infinite in its attributes presided over all matter and motion throughout infinitely extended space and time—were propo-

---

[*] In Scotland things are better managed; every student, before he can enter upon his theological course of studies must produce a certificate to the professor of divinity, showing that he has attended, at least one full course of lectures on natural philosophy. The course, at an average, consists of 125 lectures.

sitions in themselves so plain, that they might be regarded as axioms. But they were at the same time propositions upon which we could not reason; because the limited capacity of the human mind could not comprehend infinite quantities. Nor was it *proper that we should attempt to investigate the attributes or essence of the Divine nature.* The modus operandi or manner of connection between the external world and the volitions of the *Deity* being beyond our comprehension, and above our control, *such investigations could lead to no useful result,*" &c.

Could any one believe, that the same Mr. Mackintosh, who promulgated the above very orthodoxical precepts, was the identical Mr. Mackintosh, who jeers me upon my orthodoxy and insists upon me giving a demonstration of a proposition which he knows right well is beyond the reach of the human understanding! I have often had occasion to find fault with Mr. M. for his total disregard of all the rules of consistency; and here again he has given us another specimen of the great progress he has made in the science of equivocation. But how this grand celestial proposition of Mr. M. is to effect the truth of the Newtonian system of the universe, I sincerely believe, that no person on ea.th, except himself can tell us: he is therefore certainly bound to explain himself on this head.

Mr. Mackintosh's remarks on my explanations of his second question (which is to be another nail in the coffin of the Newtonian system) are really childish. He tries to find fault, but in fact he can find none. He tells me that my explanations may be found in every school book: this, perhaps, to a certain extent may be true. But let me tell you, Mr. Mackintosh, had you been conversant with the matter explained in these books, you never would have proposed such an extravagantly absurd question; your own attempt at explanation fully shows this. But, Mr. Editor, as I have no great propensity for writing long letters, and as I find I have much more to say on this subject, I shall reserve the remainder for another letter.

I am, Sir, yours &c.,

KINCLAVEN.

PORTER'S PROGRESS OF THE NATION.

These are piping times for statistical writers. The immense number of thick folios of reports and returns, published of late years by order of the two Houses of Parliament, form an almost inexhaustible magazine for the compilers of plump octavos and thin duodecimos on almost every subject falling within the somewhat ample province of the political economist. M'Culloch's " Statistics of the British Empire," reviewed in our last volume, was a work of the former calibre; that we have now before us* is more modest in its dimensions, although well-nigh as comprehensive in the range of its contents. The present volume, however, comprises only a fourth part of the whole plan. Like Mr. M'Culloch our author derives most of his materials direct from the source to which we have alluded, and, like him, he has been but too willing to take his "brooms" *ready-made* to his hand; or, to borrow another simile, he works up the metal crude as he finds it, without taking the trouble to separate the dross from the ore—a very tedious, and toilsome, process, no doubt, but one which cannot very well be dispensed with. Napoleon Bonaparte, indeed, might be cited as an instance of one great man at least who was perfectly satisfied with statistical information *per se*, without caring a straw for its correctness: but then he required answers on the nail, and did not cage down the information obtained in point, and call on all the world to accept it as the indubitable result of the most profound investigation. Our modern statisticians must expect to find their readers rather more fastidious than so many Napoleons. If all were as indulgent as he, indeed, they might as well shut up shop at once, and leave the field to the writers of *professed* works of fiction,—the only proper successors, perhaps, to Colquhoun and other highly-imaginative *authorities* of the last generation.

That Mr. Porter is aware what " blind leaders" some of the parliamentary returns are likely to prove, if depended

* The Progress of the Nation, in its various Social and Economical Relations, from the beginning of the Nineteenth Century to the present Time. By G. R. Porter, Esq. (Sections I. and II. Population and Production). London: C. Knight & Co. Small 8vo. pp. 358.

upon too absolutely, will be evident from the extract we are about to give. In noticing Mr. M'Culloch's book, we took occasion to remark on some of the glaring fallacies propagated by the Population Census Acts, and to reprobate the system (carried to an extravagant extent in 1831) of introducing a number of minute divisions and ridiculous refinements in the heads devoted to the occupations of the people, which could only be expected to lead to errors innumerable, and cause a vast expenditure of useless trouble. And what says Mr. Porter on the subject? Why, the results are so grossly incongruous, that *he* refuses in this instance to pin his faith on a parliamentary document, and gives his reasons (tolerably convincing ones too) for rejecting *in toto* the information supplied by this portion of the returns, which, thoroughly valueless as they are, must have cost a world of trouble (to say nothing of the expense) in the concoction,—all which might have been spared by a very little reflection on the part of the directing powers of the Census, or even by their bearing in mind the simple axiom, "complexity is the mother of confusion."

"It is perhaps impossible, by any industry or intelligence to compile a schedule of occupations upon which dependance can be placed. The specification now under examination would lead to many erroneous conclusions, in consequence of one branch of a man's trade being frequently given, to the exclusion of others as important. It will sufficiently justify this objection to state a very few of the anomalies which the statement presents. Thus, there are in England, according to this specification, 5,030 coach-makers, and but one coach-spring maker. The whole kingdom is stated to give employment to only three coffin-makers, each of whom would therefore be called upon to provide 300 coffins daily throughout the year. One drug-grinder alone appears, while the druggists whom he is to supply amount in number to 5,423. It cannot be necessary to go farther into this alphabet of trades in order to show, from internal evidence, the little dependence that is to be placed upon it; but having been induced to test the list in some of its particulars by means of another statement which cannot be otherwise than accurate, we here give the result.

"The number of licenses issued by the Commissioners of Excise, upon every one of which a duty is levied, affords as sure an indication as can well be had upon the subject. Some men may carry on a trade for which a license is legally necessary, without taking one from the office; but it may be presumed that nobody will pay for a license who does not pursue the calling for which it qualifies him.

"The following list of the number of excise licenses issued to certain classes of traders in 1831, the year to which the specification of trades relates, is taken from the Official Tables of the Revenue, &c., compiled by the Board of Trade. By its side we have placed the number of persons who, according to the population abstract, follow the several callings mentioned.

Description of dealers.	Number of excise licenses issued.	Number of traders according to the Population Abstract.
Brewers	42,907	5,765
Maltsters	12,716	6,970
Soap-makers	276	20
Spirit-dealers	67,500	4,031
Tea-dealers	89,202	3,456
Tobacco-dealers	150,843	2,224
Wine-dealers	22,553	1,594

"Many licenses for brewing, and for dealing in wine, spirits, and tobacco, are taken out by publicans, but the entire number of this class, including all the keepers of 'beer-shops,' who do not of course take out such licenses, amounts to no more than 61,231. The number of licenses granted to publicans for the sale of spirits or wine, in addition to beer, in 1831, was only 20,638. As regards tea dealers, the discrepancy would not be remedied by confederating under that name all who figure in the specification as grocers, and the number of whom (including the numerous tribe of greengrocers), amounts only to 22,147. A sufficient number of tobacco-dealers to account for the number of licenses will not be got together if all the grocers, tea-dealers, and publicans in the specifications are taken into the account. It must be evident from these facts, that such a specification as this is perfectly useless; and it may be worthy of consideration, whether, in future enumerations of the people, it will be desirable to make any further attempt to obtain this particular kind of information."—P. 65.

To us it appears to be a matter worthy of very little "consideration" whether it is worth while to throw away money, time, and labour once more in getting together a large mass of "perfectly useless" figures. In any such general returns as those of the population, it is evident that the fewer heads introduced the better, because every additional one multiplies the liability to error, and the confusion induced is apt to be contagious; and in *any* returns, the gathering together of " perfectly useless" matter may surely be dispensed with, by the tenderest of consciences.

On another head, Mr. Porter flies out against the voice of authority. All the world knows that divers sapient calculators indulge in the most amazing anticipations as to the effect on the utility of horse-flesh that will be produced by the universal adoption of the railway system. One of the foremost of the tribe, Mr. Alexander Gordon, is for having every farmer shoot his horse forthwith at the stable-door, and dispose of the hide and tallow while there is yet a market for such commodities; and has repeatedly proved, to *his own* satisfaction, that, *when* steam carriages have superseded their four-footed rivals altogether, there will be room enough in the country for sixteen millions more inhabitants, without the least over-crowding; in other words, he maintains that the land now appropriated to growing food for horses is sufficient to maintain that number of human beings, and that steam-locomotion will soon send all the horses in the kingdom about their business. But ideas of this sort are not confined to such personages as Mr. Gordon; they have, in some degree, been promulgated by a body of no less importance than a Committee of the House of Commons. But let us see what Mr. Porter says upon the subject.

" Against the effects of exaggerations proceeding from persons of that class (projectors), the public mind is usually pretty well preserved, but the mischief becomes of a more serious nature when extravagant estimates are advanced and supported by such a body as a Committee of the House of Commons, the members of which are called upon to form a calm and reasonable judgment on the testimony brought before them by interested or over-sanguine parties, while their knowledge of the subjects submitted to their investigation ought to be such as should at least preserve them from the adoption and advocacy of any very glaring absurdities. In the Report lately presented by the Committee appointed to inquire into the subject of railroads, it is gravely stated that the effect of constructing rail-

roads between the principal towns of the kingdom would be to render unnecessary no fewer than a million of horses.* A very slight examination of the documents bearing upon this question, within their reach, would have sufficed to preserve the Committee from regarding so extravagant an assertion. The extent of turnpike roads in Great Britain, as they existed in 1829, amounted to 24,541 miles; and if the whole of those roads were converted into railroads, and the traffic upon every part were fully equal to that already mentioned as the estimate for the Liverpool and Manchester line, the number of horses that would by such means be rendered superfluous would amount to only 785,312. It would be greatly beyond the work to estimate the saving at one-fourth of this number, or less than one-fifth of the million stated in the Committee's report. But much more direct means of testing the accuracy of the Committee's estimate were at hand, furnished by the detailed returns made from the tax-office of the number of horses in respect of which assessed duties were charged in 1832, and which, including that description of farm-horses not wholly used in husbandry upon which the duty is still retained (124,076), amounted to no more than 502,148. However much the railroad system may be extended, it is certain that a very large proportion of these animals must still be kept. Nearly all those employed for pleasure, and for the internal trade of towns, as well as the whole of those used in farms, would be continued."—P. 183.

So much for the value of Parliamentary authority, even when tested exclusively by Parliamentary documents. Nor is this the only instance in which " collective wisdom" has been at fault on similar occasions. The report of the famous Steam-Carriage Committee of 1831 is a standing monument of the simplicity, and capacity of swallow, of our legislators,—and *that* does not by any means stand alone in its glory. To such an extent has the mine been worked, that it appears not improbable that ere long the fact of a dubious speculation having received the approbation of a House of Commons' Committee will be received as *prima facie* evidence of its demerits; even at present, it has no force except with the very *profanum vulgus.*

---

* In some cases where railroads have been opened, it has been found that although the use of horses has been discontinued upon the direct line, the increased traffic has made it necessary to employ, for bringing travellers to the railroad, as great a number of horses as had been displaced.

And yet Mr. Porter's work is composed almost entirely of wholesale extracts from reports issued under the same authority, as that whose futility we have just seen him expose, and from returns of the very same description as that whose "entire uselessness" he has so satisfactorily demonstrated! It is the riches of the present age in such documents which he cites as one of his principal reasons for undertaking to produce it; and, certes, they render its production a matter of little difficulty. Had our author thought it necessary to test all the information they supply as rigidly as that referred to in our extracts (and no less would be required to make it a work on which full reliance could be placed), the result would have been widely different, and his task a far more delicate and difficult one. To present a correct view of the progress of " Population and Production" in Great Britain during the present century, might well be the labour of a life, in spite of all the aid afforded by Parliamentary papers; to compile a sketch of it, as Mr. Porter has done, from a few volumes of those papers, " with all their imperfections on their heads," is, in comparison, the pastime of an hour.

The work opens with a general chapter on population, and the proportions of births, marriages, and deaths,—a mere excerpt from the report on the Census of 1831, with a little assistance from that on the Poor Laws. The second chapter is on " Medical Statistics," the materials for which have been derived from Dr. Hawkins's work on the subject, divers Parliamentary returns, and (strange to relate) original information supplied from various hospitals. The third chapter is that on the "Occupations of the People," drawn of course also from the Population Returns, as to whose accuracy in this particular we have already quoted our author's opinion. Notwithstanding, however, his repudiation of the classification of trades furnished by the returns in question, he makes use of them without compunction on every other point, leaving " time and the curious" to discover whether they are "perfectly" or only comparatively " useless." " Pauperism" is the rich subject which follows, and, as might be expected, the chapter upon it is a mere abridgment of the Poor Law Report,—an almost exhaustless mine for

statistical compilers, a body of men who are too much in the habit of taking things as they find them. It might be supposed that, in a view of the " Progress of the British Nation," whether in prosperity or pauperism, any matter foreign to the subject which might find its way into the few but bulky volumes made use of in the manufacture of the book, would be omitted, especially when compression happened to be an object. It is no such thing, however, in practice. The chapter on " Occupations" is lengthened by a detail of the occupations of the inhabitants of *France;* and in this on " Pauperism" we are treated with pages on pages of detail on " the methods of relieving the poor abroad. This is the less excusable, that it could hardly be for " lack of matter" on this unhappily prolific head in England, that our author felt obliged to take his readers on an excursion to " Norway, Sweden, Denmark, Mecklenburgh, Prussia, Wurtemburg, Bavaria, Berne, France, Holland, and Belgium." The plain truth is, that the Commissioners of Poor-Law Inquiry thought proper to obtain as much information as possible as to the foreign systems of relief, and that Mr. Porter, with the very " erring instinct" of the book-making tribe, has followed his original through the irrelevant as well as the relevant parts, without wasting a thought, during the thoroughly mechanical operation, as to *what* nation it might be whose " progress" he had bound himself to chronicle. So, when he comes to the " Manufacture of Woven Fabrics," he inflicts on the reader a whole chapter on the state of things in that respect in France, Switzerland, Bavaria, Russia, and Prussia! And for what reason? Evidently only because Dr. Bowring's Reports furnished him with the materials ready cut and dry, and he had only to " spurn the narrow bounds" of his self-appointed subject to fill up a chapter with greater ease than if he had confined himself to Manchester and Spitalfields, and so " kept faith" with the reading public.

The first division closes with a chapter on " Emigration," the only original feature in which is a suggestion of Mr. Porter's own, for making Canada a penal settlement! The rest is all the " leather and prunella" of the " Emigration" and " Secondary Punishment" Reports.

Section second, "Production," opens with a general view of the progress of agriculture, chiefly from the Report on Agricultural Distress in 1833, some former Reports of the same nature, and Sir John Sinclair's Statistical Account of Scotland. With the exception of this one chapter, the whole of this part of the volume is dedicated to a view of the manufacturing industry of this country (and partially of some others, as alluded to above), distributed under the heads "Woven Fabrics," "Iron, Steel, and Brass, and Hardware Manufactures," "Machinery," and "Mining." We have left ourselves no room for any extract from this portion, and if such were not the case, we should be at a loss where to find a portion bearing the impress of novelty. The information afforded, and the style and manner of giving it, are so precisely similar to what we have become familiar with in other works of a similar description, that almost any quotation that could be given would have the air of an old acquaintance. Mr. Porter is a regular member of the Useful Knowledge Society school of political economists, and these gentlemen follow each other so closely in all particulars, that it is not a little difficult to distinguish one from the other. So completely is this the case, that we might venture with comparative safety, after having seen what Mr. Porter's first volume is composed of, to prophecy what will be the precise complexion and character of the rest of his projected series,—should they ever appear. As we have already remarked, "Population and Production" comprize only the fourth part of his plan, which is divided into eight sections. The next to come is to be upon "Interchanges," including Internal and External Communications, Currency, and Wages; and this is to be followed by others on the "Public Revenue and Expenditure," "Consumption, "Accumulation," "Moral Progress," and the "Colonies." It would be tedious to review the whole of these beforehand; but let us take that on "Moral Progress" to vaticinate upon. What "constant reader" of the Penny Magazine cannot perceive with what matter this will be made "thick and slab?" How clearly Mr. Porter will prove, from the augmented number of offenders in the prison returns, the vast improvement in the public morals? How

exultingly he will point, at the same time, to the increased number of Sunday scholars as an indubitable proof of the spread of education? How amiably he will explain the wonders of the printing machine, and how imposingly he will trumpet forth the numbers sold of the Useful Knowledge Society's great pennyworth? How pleasingly he will show, with a leetle special pleading, that the increase of gin-palaces and beer-houses has nothing in the world to do with increased drunkenness, while the rise of coffee-shops and reading-rooms has every thing to do with increased sobriety? "All this, and more," the said "constant reader" sees in his mind's eye; and should all these subjects, mixed up with endless columns of figures from gaol returns and similar interesting documents, fail to swell the volume to the proper size, the deficiency will be easily made up with long details on some such matter as "the Penitentiary System of the United States," on which Parliament has presented the world with reports of most alarming bulk, and which has at least as much connexion with the "Progress of the Nation" as many other things which Mr. Porter holds to be quite within his range.

In the meanwhile, this first volume is not to be without honour out of its own country, a translation into French having been just announced in Paris, with additional details as to the "Population and Production" of France.

AN EXPERIMENTAL ENQUIRY INTO THE MODES OF WARMING AND VENTILATING APARTMENTS. BY ANDREW URE, M.D. F.R.S., ETC.

Read before the Royal Society on the 16th of June, 1836.

(From the *Architectural Magazine* for April).

(Concluded from page 27.)

The observations of Saussure, and other scientific travellers in mountainous regions, demonstrate how difficult and painful it is to make muscular exertions in highly rarefied air. Even the slight rarefaction of the atmosphere corresponding to a low state of the barometer at the level of the sea often occasions no little discomfort to persons of delicate frame; while the opposite condition of increased pressure, as indicated by a high barometer, has a bracing effect upon both body and mind. Hence, in ventilating crowded apartments, such as the House of Parliament, instead of having recourse to chimney draughts, as has been hitherto the invariable practice, and which operates by pumping out, exhausting, or attenuating the air (a fact elegantly illustrated by Dr. Wollaston's differential barometer), we ought, upon every sound principle of physiology, rather to increase the density and spring of the atmosphere, by throwing in a continual current of pure air, brought to the proper degree of temperature and moisture in a chamber of preparation. The air, in its ingress and egress, being placed under the control of valves regulated by index-dials, might have its density modified to a very considerable extent, and thus become fitted to supply the lungs of the inmates with an elastic element, eminently conducive to their health, comfort, and activity.

In applying a principle of this kind to ventilate such a noble pile of buildings as the new Houses of Parliament will be, two or more fans of suitable size should be erected in a small apartment on the ground-floor, for the sake of solidity, and near the the centre of the range, for the facility of distribution. These fans should be driven by a small steam-engine, with a boiler heated with coke, on Messrs. Braithwaite's safety plan, emitting no smoke, nor requiring an elevated chimney to disfigure the edifice. From the fans, proper conduits, made of wood, brick, or sheet iron, should be led to the floors of the several chambers to be ventilated. The terminations of these conduits should be furnished with proper valves, for regulating, by a dial-index, connected with a cord or wire (like a common bell-pull), the degree of ventilation required, according to circumstances.

In the state of scientific excellence at which the arts have arrived in this country, especially among the factory engineers, no doubt can exist about the propriety of heating the new Houses of Parliament by means of a series of substantial cast-iron pipes, filled with steam, placed in a sunk area below the level-line of the chambers; from which, as a vast magazine, genial air, of a proper thermometric and hygrometric constitution, could be readily distributed, in any desired quantity, to renovate the atmosphere of every lobby and apartment in the buildings. The same boiler which furnishes steam to the engine would be adequate to furnish a supply to the warming pipes in ordinary weather. In very severe weather, however, an additional steam boiler could be brought into action; the main object being to provide such a body of genial pure air as country gentlemen are accustomed to breate in a fine summer's day on their breezy lawns, but never to be under the necessity of inhaling the mephitic va-

pours emitted by the lungs and skin of themselves and their neighbours, as has been hitherto the established practice in both Houses of Parliament at every interesting debate.

The quantity of steam-pipe surface, at a temperature of 212 deg. Fahr., requisite to heat a certain volume of air in the large apartments of a well-built cotton mill, has been ascertained with perfect precision; and may be estimated, in round numbers, at one superficial foot of pipe for 150 cubic feet of space, to ensure to the air a steady temperature of 62 deg., which is the mean summer warmth of the atmosphere in England. It would be prudent to have at command a great magazine of air for the Parliament, since the consumption of fuel under an economical disposition of apparatus would be utterly insignificant, in comparison of the health and comfort of the legislative bodies of the empire.

For the following estimate of the quantity of cast-iron pipe necessary to maintain a healthy and comfortable temperature during winter in the Long Room in the Custom-house, I am indebted to Mr. Fairbairn of Manchester, whose experience and success as a factory engineer are such as to give confidence to his statement. The above apartment is 190 long, 64 ft. wide, and 46 ft. high, containing fully 20,000 cubic yards of space. Two ranges of cast-iron pipes, 8 in. in diameter, properly distributed upon the floor, close to the bottom of the desk-partitions along the two sides and ends of the room, having arched junction pipes of wrought iron 2 in. in diameter, rising round the entrance doors, will be fully adequate to warm it in the coldest winter weater of this climate. A suitable low-pressure self-feeding steam-boiler, with proper pipes and mountings, would, at the usual factory prices, cost no more than £500. Upon this plan, less than one half of the quantity of fuel would be required, of what is now consumed by the air-roasting furnaces, in generating malaria, discomfort, and disease.

Among the stove-doctors of the present day, none are more dangerous than those who, on pretence of economy and convenience, recommend to keep a large body of coke burning slowly, with a slow circulation of air. An acquaintance with chemical science would teach them that, in the obscure combustion of coke or charcoal, much carbonic oxide is generated, and much fuel consumed, with the production of little heat; and physical science would teach them that, when the chimney draught is languid, the burned air is apt to regurgitate through every seam or crevice, with the imminent risk of causing asphyxia or death to the inmates of apartments so preposterously heated. To obtain the maximum quantity of heat from fuel, its combustion ought to be very vivid, and the caloric thus evolved diffused over the largest possible surface of conducting materials. This principle has been judiciously applied in several French factories. Great care must be taken not to suffer the surfaces to be heated above 240 Fahr. It has been proved that workpeople employed in calico-drying rooms heated by such means become emaciated, wan, and sickly, while they remain perfectly healthy, and even blooming, in rooms of which the air is more highly heated with steam-pipes.

Among the many causes assigned by pathologists for the infirm health of persons who confine themselves much to warm apartments, and seldom venture into the open air, one of the most operative has been altogether overlooked—the rarefactiou, by diminished pressure and heat, of the atmosphere which they breathe.* I find, if

---

* Since the first portion of this paper was put to press, my attention has been called to a memoir of M. Junot, lately published in Paris, concerning the effects of compressed and rarefied air upon the human body. When a person is plunged in condensed air, he breathes with " a new facility;" he feels as if the capacity of his lungs were enlarged; his respirations become ample, and less frequent; at the end of fifteen minutes, he experiences an agreeable warmth in his chest, as if the pulmonary cellules, long strangers to the contact of air, were dilated anew to receive the genial spirit; while the whole animal economy sucks at each inspiration a fresh supply of life and vigour.

The arterial system acts with increased force, while the veins in the surface of the body are depleted, and may be made even to disappear. The functions of the brain are excited, the imagination becomes lively, and the thoughts are "accompanied with a peculiar charm." The movements of the muscular system are rendered, at the same time, freer and more energetic. Digestion becomes more active, but without thirst (la soif est nulle); because the secretory system participates in the increased vigour of the arterial.

In rarefied air, the effects are nearly the reverse of the above: the breathing is constrained, feeble, frequent, ending in dyspnœa, or an asthmatic paroxysm; the pulse is quick, and easily compressed; hæmorrhages often occur, with a tendency to fainting; at length, a defect of vital energy, or apathy, supervenes. The kidneys and salivary glands cease to secrete their respective fluids. M. Junot proceeds to describe the effects of compressed and rarefied air upon different parts of the human body, both in a state of health, and in the cure of diseases, by means of a very ingenious mechanical invention; for an account of which however, I must refer to the memoir itself, in the Archives Générales de Médecine, seconde série, tom. ix. p. 157.

a differential barometer, containing proof spirit in the one leg, and oil in the other, have its horizontal tube thrust into the key-hole of a snug winter parlour, that, on turning the stopcock attached to it, the junction line of the two liquids will rise from half an inch to an inch, according to the tightness of the room, and the force of the fire. By opening the street door a further rise will take place. The pulmonary and sanguiferous systems being, in such circumstances, deprived of their due proportion of chemical aliment and physical support, must languish, and spread exhaustion over the nervous, muscular, and digestive functions. I am persuaded that many of the valetudinarian ailments of the opulent inhabitants of the United Kingdom may be traced to their breathing an air unduly rarefied by chimney draughts. Every well-constructed mansion should have its underground storehouse of temperature, from which a constant supply of genial air could be poured into the several apartments in such quantities as are wanted for comfort, with the effect of increasing rather than diminishing its density. Open fires would, in this case, be used only for enlivening the scene; and, being supplied with abundance of air from the ventilating orifices, could create no appreciable rarefaction.

NOTES AND NOTICES.

Penny Magazines.—We learn, by the latest arrivals from Constantinople, that Sultan Mahmoud is about to establish a Penny Magazine in Turkish, for which he anticipates an extensive sale. We hope that the expectations of the royal speculator in cheap publications may not be disappointed, but that his success may prove sufficient to incline him to publish a Turkish "Penny Encyclopædia" into the bargain. ' Penny Magazine in modern Greek, which was late./ started by the American missionaries at Smyrna, has been discontinued in consequence of the opposition of the Greek Patriarch, who stigmatised some of the articles contained in it as heretical. The influence of the Sultan will probably overrule any objections of a similar kind made to his publication by the mufti, or the Turkish phenomenon will not be likely to be of long duration. The religion of Mahomet is particularly opposed to any representations of men and animals, and wood-cuts of both are in other countries the most frequent ornaments of a penny magazine.

Glass Road.—Among the novelties announced for the approaching season at Tivoli, the Parisian Vauxhall, is a Glass-Road, on which passengers are to travel, at a rate which would carry them over as much space in three minutes as on ordinary roads they could travel in an hour. The invention is probably a first cousin to the Russian mountains, so popular at the same gardens some years ago.

☞ British and Foreign Patents taken out with economy and despatch; Specifications, Disclaimers, and Amendments, prepared or revised; Caveats entered; and generally every Branch of Patent Business promptly transacted.
A complete list of Patents from the earliest period (15 Car. II. 1675,) to the present time may be examined Fee 2s. 6d.; Clients, gratis.

LONDON: Printed and Published by W. A. Robertson, at the Mechanics' Magazine Office, No. 6, Peterborough-court, between 135 and 136, Fleet-street.—Sold by G. W. M. Reynolds, Proprietor of the French, English, and American Library, 55, Rue Neuve, Saint Augustin, Paris.

Mechanics' Magazine,

MUSEUM, REGISTER, JOURNAL, AND GAZETTE.

No. 716.   SATURDAY, APRIL 29, 1837.   Price 3d.

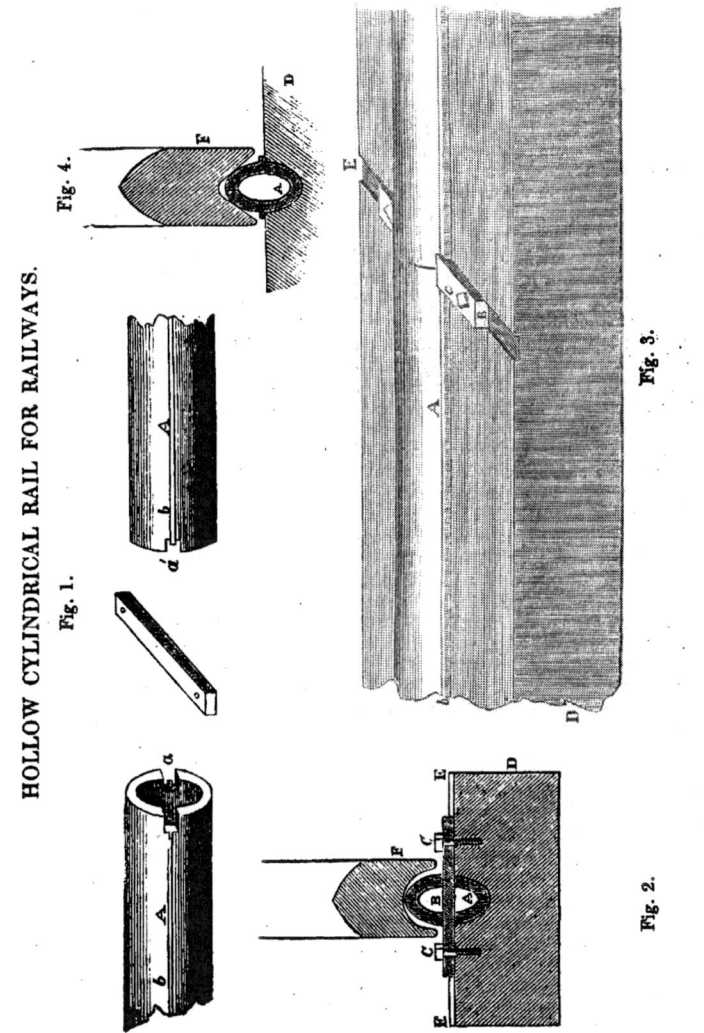

HOLLOW CYLINDRICAL RAIL FOR RAILWAYS.

Fig. 1.

Fig. 2.

Fig. 3.

Fig. 4.

HOLLOW CYLINDROIDAL RAIL FOR RAILWAYS.

Sir,—The following is a description of a new form of rail, in which the strength of the arch is brought into operation—and which I think will be found worthy the attention of railway engineers.

Fig. 1 is a perspective representation of the disjoined ends of two rails A A, with the cross-bar B, which, entering the notches a a, binds them firmly to the longitudinal timbers D.

Fig. 2 is a transverse section of the rail, &c., showing its elliptical shape, with the proposed form of tire (F) for the wheels of the carriages, and the mode of securing the rails—nearly one half being buried in the timbers D.

Fig. 3 is a perspective view of the whole when put together.

The timbers are proposed to be of Kyanized oak, and laid in concrete; the two lines of each track being truly parallel and connected throughout by ties. The longitudinal groove, in which the rails, lie, should be cut out by machinery, a perfect fit being thereby ensured.

The advantages anticipated from this arrangement are—

1st, Greater ease and smoothness of motion to the carriages. Gravity would keep the wheels in a perfectly straight line. By this mode also of connecting the rails and timbers, lateral disconnection of the bearing surfaces would be rendered impossible, and all jolting in consequence avoided. A rib, b b, is proposed to be formed on each side of the rail, for further security, as well as to prevent wet insinuating itself between the rails and timbers. The groove E E, in which the cross bars slide, will also diminish the strain upon the screws c c, caused by the action of the propelling wheels.

(With all deference to the experience of Mr. Vignoles, whose system of continuous timbers I have here adopted, I would ask, if the oft-repeated rapid rolling of a mass of iron, six or eight tons in weight, would not soon loosen rails that are merely nailed or screwed on to their bearings, without at all entering the wood?)

2nd. Greater strength of rail from the same weight of iron. The lower half being firmly bedded in oak, the upper presents an arch to the incumbent pressure.

3rd. A more convenient (and, as above shown, a firmer) method of fixing the rails. In order to remove a rail for repair, it would be merely necessary to withdraw four large screws, and knock out two bars, when it might be lifted out.

4th. Economy in wear. When it has become no longer safe to use a rail in its original position, the simple operation of reversing it would present a new surface as firmly fixed as the first, A bar rail, if formed with this view, would obviously not be held so securely in its second position; it might probably therefore be found advisable, to make the bearing portions of the tube somewhat thicker than the rest.

Should it be objected that the narrow bearing surfaces would induce rapid destruction of the wheels, I reply, that the weight of the engines (the heaviest load, calculating per wheel) might probably be lessened. On the present plan a considerable weight of engine is necessary to give cohesion between the propelling wheels and rails: this I propose to effect by the form of tire represented in fig. 4, which would also give additional safety at high velocities, by diminishing the liability of the train to get off the tracks. (What has become of that beautiful little engine, the "Novelty?" I trust Messrs. Braithwaite have not abandoned the idea of bringing so elegant a construction into use.)

Probably cast-iron might be the cheapest, as it would be the firmest material for hollow rails; but they might be rolled out with a core, in the mode used for gun barrels.

Another advantage of this system, not immediately connected with the subject, has since occurred to me. Various schemes have been proposed for the rapid communication of intelligence between distant places—some of them not a little expensive. Here is a speaking-pipe ready made; for, were such a plan really feasible, some other mode of fixing the rails might be adopted, which would not interrupt the transmission of distant sounds.

J. R.

London, 16 March, 1837.

P.S.—I would add a word on the subject of cost, though having no *practical* knowledge, I can give no very satisfactory account. It appeared to, me that on this plan the rails need not be longer that six feet. If cast then, the greatest addition to the expense would be the additional weight of metal. But as my rails will admit of being turned, when worn, they cannot fairly be compared with others, weight for weight. Perhaps some company might think it worth while to *try* how much substance would be necessary for this form of rail, for without experiment no correct idea can be formed on this point.

ON THE SHRINKAGE AND EXPANSION OF IRON IN THE PROCESS OF CASTING.

Sir,—A short time since I was favored with the loan of the 18th vol. of the *Philosophical Magazine*, on account of its first article, which treats at some length of a subject on which I have before addressed you; (see vols. xvi and xvii, pp. 108 and 61) and although I agree with the author, Mr. David Mushet, as to most of the facts therein described, I differ essentially in the more material point, viz., that of accounting for them.

In his preamble, Mr. M. says, "When the object of experiment is exposed to a heat sufficient to fuse it, it then becomes subject to new laws as a fluid, and exhibits phenomena entirely different. By not taking the change of state, from that of a solid to that of a fluid, into account, some writers have given an *awkward and unsatisfactory account of the laws* which regulate iron in these two different states. Before I proceed to detail some experiments made upon the subject, I shall trace out the different states of shrinkage and expansion, as observed in cast iron. In doing this I shall divide shrinkage into two distinct operations : 1st, Shrinkage, properly so called, when a mass of iron *diminishes or shrinks within itself*, and would actually *displace a smaller quantity of water*, and when *no degree of heat short of fusion would make it occupy its former bulk or volume*."

" 2nd, Contraction, or that diminution of superficial measurement which any body undergoes by evolving its caloric." A unique division this, and very explicit —shrinkage diminishes a mass of iron, making it occupy less space, while contraction, only lessens all its superficial dimensions!

" In casting pieces of ordnance we are enabled to judge of the conjoint effects of shrinkage, contraction, and expansion. We shall suppose that a gun mould of any given length is filled with fluid cast iron, not subject to these laws; then the size and shape of the gun, when cold, would correspond to the dimensions of the mould. But finding that the piece of casting was considerably altered, that it had shrunk interiorly, was diminished in point of length, and had lessened its diameter, we must seek for a solution of these facts, in explanation of the causes respectively."

" First assuming, what shall be hereafter proved by direct experiment, that cast iron occupies less volume when fluid, than when solid; that in the act of the arrangement of the molecules towards consolidation, it occupies a *larger bulk than at any other period ;* and that *when cold, and in proportion to the absence of the heat, so will the volume be diminished.*"

" 1st, then, shrinkage appears to be dependent upon two causes; the gravitation of the fluid metal, and the expansion of the mould. The latter, I conceive, acts a very powerful part : the immense quantity of caloric combined with the iron, is in part easily and almost instantaneously communicated to the iron box; this creates a disposition to expand, in which it is greatly assisted by the great pressure of the fluid iron." I cannot possibly see what this disposition to expand, has to do with this division of his subject; but however the iron box may be *disposed to expand*, sand being a bad conductor, no actual expansion would take place (unless in some extreme cases) while the iron was in a fluid state; and unless the box would resist the pressure of the fluid metal under all circumstances it would be entirely useless. " That portion of the metal in contact with the interior of the mould is the first to lose its fluidity, and is acted upon, and forced to give way, in the same ratio of expansion, before the more subtle and denser fluid." This is downright nonsense, for the face of the casting is formed by the metal losing its fluidity in contact with every part of the mould, and if then forced to give way to the hydrostatic pressure of the more subtle and denser fluid, it must be in cracks and fisures, which of course would render the casting imperfect.

" 2nd Expansion. Of the extent of this operation we may judge from the following facts:—All patterns of castings are made somewhat larger than the piece of goods is wished to be: in common cases $\frac{1}{8}$th of an inch to the foot is allowed, but in many cases the allowance will be $\frac{1}{16}$th of an inch." (A curious fact this to adduce as evidence of Mr M.'s 2nd, or law of expansion.) " In the case of the gun, therefore, the mould would be plus the allowance upon the pattern, what space are gained by beating the pattern to loose it from the sand, and all the extra space acquired by the increased volume of the consolidating iron. These, taken collectively, may amount to $\frac{1}{4}$th or $\frac{5}{16}$ths *of an inch;* and so much less will the *diameter of the gun be found when cold*, to that it would have measured at climax of its expansion." So far we have no proof of this, but a positive statement that it may amount to half an inch in the diameter of the gun; now this expansion, taking place in the same ratio in every direction, must amount to three, or even four inches in its length! Now as cannon are cast in dry sand, I would ask, under such circumstances, what becomes of the iron box? As it cannot be expected to give way in the same ratio of expansion, nothing can prevent its being *burst, by this, Mr. M.'s unaccountable law!*

" 3rd, contraction immediately takes place on the metal ceasing to expand: to its effects are chargeable the reduction of the of the increased diameter of the gun, and which seems merely in consequence of the escape of the caloric."

Thus does this nice observer of the habitudes of metal, continue to heap contradiction on contradiction, not in the *clumsy awkward manner* that some writers would have done, but with a degree of neatness, freedom, and self satisfaction peculiarly his own. He first assumes, what we shall presently examine his proof of, viz., that *cast iron occupies less volume when fluid*, than *when solid;* then, that a trifling loss of caloric produces shrinkage, which *diminishes the mass,* so that *no degree of heat short of fusion* would make it occupy its former bulk or volume. He then says, a further loss of caloric just sufficient to convert the fluid metal into a solid, causes a most startling degree of expansion, varying from a 50th to a 25th of its dimensions: and then again, by the dissipation of the remaining caloric, it not only loses

this immense increase of volume, but also the usual allowance of $\frac{1}{8}$th or $\frac{1}{16}$ths of an inch to the foot on the pattern; at once proving, in my humble opinion, *that the simply evolving its caloric, reduces its volume less by this allowance, plus the loosening the pattern, than when in its fluid state!*

" To prove that cast iron is denser in the fluid state, several pieces of iron may be put into a ladle, and hot fluid iron poured upon them; they will immediately rise to the surface, and expose a considerable portion of their bulk above the surface of the liquid iron. *This buoyancy diminishes;* and as the pieces of metal approach more and more to the state of fusion that exists in the ladle, they gradually sink, till they disappear entirely under the surface; they then rapidly dissolve, and form a part of the fluid iron."

This to me, is any thing but sufficient proof of the superior density of iron in its fluid state, for the known and acknowledged laws of expansion, are directly opposed to the gradually sinking of the solid pieces as they get hotter and hotter: but what a decided contradiction is this to Mr. M.'s great 2nd law; indeed he must have totally forgot it when he stated that the *pieces of solid metal sank and wholly disappeared below the surface of the denser metal, at the very climax of their expansion!* The solution of this phenomena must therefore still continue to *puzzle our judgment*, and perhaps *elude our sagacity* after all.

Now to the proof of his assumption, " That cast iron occupies a greater bulk or volume immediately after it passes into the state of a solid. If a shot mould is carefully separated at a certain period after filling, a metallic crust is formed, more or less thick, which is the natural progress of consolidation, but which is at present an envelope to a considerable portion of fluid contents. In this state the expansion in the shot and mould, is nearly the same; the former is easily extracted from the under and upper parts of the latter. In about two minutes after, however, the expansion of the shot is more rapid than that of the mould, and at this period is difficult to disengage. As the heat is communicated to the mould, its dimensions enlarge, and the extraction of the shot is attended with less violent efforts. The mould is always filled by the shot till cooling has so far taken place as to reduce the shot-mould to its former diameter: beyond this, however, the shot still continues to lessen its bulk, so that when cold, it will be found to have left its mould by nearly $\frac{1}{13}$th part of its diameter."

This proof is of equal value with the rest, depending entirely as it does, on the solitary fact of the shot sticking in the mould at a certain period after casting. Now it appears to me, that the shot, instead of *always filling* the mould, as above asserted, can only be said to do so at two definite periods: first, while every particle of the metal continues fluid; which will only be until the mould carries off so much heat as to reduce the fluid metal in immediate contact with it, to the *state of a solid*, and this operation is attended with a certain amount of contraction, as is fully proved by the shot at this moment freely leaving the mould; and second, at this point expansion proceeds in opposite directions, for the mould begins to expand with the first increment of heat it exhibits, but until this heat is diffused throughout its whole mass, the expansion can only tend to lessen its internal dimensions: the caloric contained by the still fluid part, is at the same time given out, and is freely taken up by the crust with which it is enveloped, causing its expansion as a solid, in a ratio commensurate with its accession of heat. Another proof, if another be still wanting, of the contraction of iron on becoming solid, may be had, by breaking a common shot, when the centre of it will be found spongy, which could not be the case if any expansion had taken place.

I remain, Sir,
Yours respectly,
TREBOR VALENTINE.
Derby, April 6th, 1837.

PAYNES TIDAL FLOATING LANDING STEPS.

Sir,—To my communication of last week, accompanying a drawing of a landing pier with floating platform, you added a description of the engraving, which description is incorrect. In my communication I omitted any explanation, believing the drawing would speak for itself; but I find this was injudicious.

Unfortunately you mistook a *groove* (drawn on the masonry) for an *iron rod:* a much more substantial as well as simple plan is adopted in the model, (now at the Town Hall Liverpool,) and there is neither rod nor ring used. Two iron bolts with friction wheels jutting out from the sides of the platform, nearest the steps, move in two grooves cut in the masonry, six inches from the steps; and as the platform fits the recess within a few inches, the side working in rough water will not have the effect of displacing the bolts, while the action is more free than that of a rod and ring would be, and less liable to get out of order: indeed no part about this landing place can get out of order until the platform be completely worn out, when the expence of a new one would not be worth a thought, if the traffic over it be considerable. These bolts and grooves are shown in the model, from which the only way of withdrawing the platform altogether is by lifting it up perpendicularly instead of horizontally, as it would move in the water.

In the engraving there is an omission of the front barge upon which the platform floats. There are two barges; one towards the water, and the other towards the steps, or, as the nautical term is, *fore and aft*.

I shall feel obliged by your giving a place to this correction.

Yours, &c.
GEO. P. PAYNE.
17th March, 1837.

THE REGENT'S CANAL AND THE BIRMINGHAM RAILROAD.

Sir,—It is certainly a singular thing, that while on the continent, some effort is generally evident to make a canal contribute to ornament as well as utility, in England the consideration of ornament is not only entirely overlooked, but it actually seems the object of the parties connected with canals, to make them as much of a public nuisance as possible.

This observation was forcibly revived in my mind on recently passing over the well-known Regent's-Canal Bridge in the City Road. Most of your readers must be aware that the sheet of water which is crossed by this bridge, is no part of the main body of the canal, but merely an offshoot or "basin," which might, to all appearance, have terminated just as well on the northern as on the southern side of the City Road. The forming of it where it is, and thus carrying the canal under that well-frequented thoroughfare, made it necessary, of course, to build a bridge; the building of the bridge made it necessary to slope the road up to it on one side, and down again on the other; and thus was formed that tremendous hill which, for the last fifteen or sixteen years, has presented itself on the main road from the heart of the City to the west end of London. Really, when one considers the crowds of omnibuses and other vehicles,—Hancock's steam-carriage among the number,—that have been, and are, in the habit of passing along this road, daily conveying an innumerable host of passengers, it does seem strange indeed that this delay, this inconveniance, and this danger of millions should all be occasioned for the paltry object of loading or unloading a few barges a few yards nearer to the city.

This, however, is not the subject of my present complaint. The hill thus formed, however inconvenient and dangerous, had still one recommendation;—it afforded from its height, and from its not being occupied with buildings, a view over the neighbourhood on each side, which might be pronounced agreeable. On the south, for instance, over the wharfs of the basin, were seen rising above the houses, the slender spire of St. Barnebas, and the lofty obelisk, unmistakeable for any other object, which forms the steeple of St. Luke's. This, view, Sir, is now taken away! The passenger who might formerly be tempted to stop a few minutes to survey this variety of objects, is now presented, in lieu of them, with the dreary blank of a dead wall. By the simple expedient of raising the wall of the bridge a few feet, the open scene, over which a breath of fresh air might occasionally be wafted, is now converted into the meanest and gloomiest spot on the whole road from the city to Paddington. As yet, indeed, the northern side of the bridge remains as it was, presenting a view of Islington, with its fields and churches, and in the foreground the canal; but the progress of deterioration, the march of barbarism, is no doubt soon destined to destroy even this last vestige of the agreeable.

What advantage the parties who have effected this improvement propose to reap from it, I am at a loss to know. But it seems, like many other disagreeable things, to be done " upon principle"— as far at least as that inference may be drawn, from the fact that this is by no means the only instance in which it has been done. It will be enough to mention one other case: an American traveller —Slidell, author of " A Year in Spain," mentioned in his travels a couple of years ago, the strikingly-pretty view of a range of villas on the banks of the canal, which was to be had from the bridge near the east gate of the Regent's Park. Since then the same alteration has been effected there, and future Americans who come to enjoy the prospect, will be led to wonder at the gigantic stature of their more fortunate countryman!

It is not, however, in bridges only, that this downward course has been taken. For some years after the canal had been made, the towing-path by the side of it was left open to the public, as some compensation for the innumerable pleasant walks through the fields, which it had deteriorated or destroyed. In a little while, however, the access to the path from the bridges, was in many cases blocked up, so as to render a walk along it less likely to be chosen; and for some time past. this measure has been more and more rigorously adopted. Between Pentonville and Camden Town, a bolder course has been taken; the passengers, who in that very " ill-pierced" region, the disgrace of the Road Commissioners, takes his way by the side of the canal, relying on the " right of way" which he might imagine was secured by the usage of years, is now informed, on arriving at a certain lock, and not before, that it is " no thoroughfare," and directed to walk back about half a mile, reflecting as he goes on the liberality of Canal Companies, and the public spirit of the inhabitants of London. It is almost needless to point out what advantages this peculiar system of exclusion holds out to the suicide, or the murderer anxious to conceal the body of his victim. A path by the side of a canal, open only to a certain extent, is the very thing that suits them; since, while access is not denied to themselves, the public in general is repelled from entering on a road which offers no thoroughfare, and they are thus protected from the likelihood of surprise.

Is this a proper state of things ? Why should the progress of the passenger along the banks of the Regent's Canal be interrupted at all ? Why should not each side of it form a handsome continuous street, as is so frequently the case in Holland, with the water in the middle, and perhaps a row of trees planted on each bank? Why should not the bridges, wherever they occur, be left with merely a dwarf wall at the sides, to allow the free circulation of the air, and the enjoyment of whatever view they may happen to present? Why, in fact, should not a canal in the environs of a great metropolis be made an ornament and embellishment, instead of an eyesore and a nuisance ? " I pause for a reply."

In the meantime, let us hope, that in the numerous railroads now constructing in the neighbourhood of London, the effect of the time which has passed over our heads since the making of the Regent's Canal may be shown, in a superior attention to the public convenience, and a superior degree of architectural taste. The sunk-way of the Birmingham Railroad from Park-street, Camden Town, to its termination near Euston Square, affords an opportunity of a character by no means common. If a line of street be formed on each side of it, with the houses receding to an uniform distance from the road, a scene will be produced of great variety of interest, and entire novelty of effect. If, on the contrary, the ground be abandoned, as is too often the case, to the meaningless and planless caprice of individual builders, we shall in all probability have— here a row of houses fronting it,—there, another backing it, and so on, till the chaotic mass impresses every passenger entering London from Birmingham with the idea, that he is indeed approaching a " rude and inartificial congestion of houses."

In fact, on the conduct of the Railway Companies which are already in operation, depends the question (which, amid all the squabbles about particular buildings, seems not to have attracted one particle of attention from the legislature) *whether the architectural character of London shall be permanently raised, or permantly lowered?*

In the hope that these remarks may not only be found worthy of a place in the pages of the *Mechanics' Magazine*, but that their appearance there may effect some good.

I remain, Sir, yours, &c.

AN INHABITANT OF THE NORTH OF LONDON.

April 18th, 1837.

HUTCHINSON'S PATENT GAS BURNER.

Sir, — The substances which are usually employed in furnishing us with artificial light, such as oil, tallow, wax and coal gas, however excellent they may be in their natural qualities, still require the aid of superior mechanical contrivance, to render the flame which they produce perfectly luminous. A happy combination of chemical knowledge, and mechanical skill is necessary to effect this desirable object. The great diversity of form and variety of arrangement which are exhibited in the lamps-burners, and instruments, used in the process of generating light, testify the attention and study which this important subject is entitled to. Yet it is remarkable, that but few really scientific men have directed their abilities to the investigation of the theory of artificial light— although I believe there is no other branch of what may be called domestic science, administers more extensively to the comfort and social habitudes of civilized man. With the exception of the experimental and philosophical researches of Argand and Count Munster, whose valuable discoveries added largely to the previous information that existed on the subject, I am not aware that any other analytical work upon it, has ever appeared.

The investigations of these individuals, have led to a very accurate knowledge of the philosophy of light generated by artificial means. And upon the principles which were deduced from their experiments, are founded nearly all the best improvements that have been made in the construction of lamps.

The vast amount of money that is annually expended in the procuring combustible materials, ought certainly to be a powerful inducement to scientific men to endeavour to invent such apparatus as will diminish this expenditure; and it appears to me, that a considerable portion of the costly apparatus now in use, might be dispensed with, without lessening the quantity of light given out.

I am of opinion that this object can be accomplished, by constructing a burner, upon the principles which are now generally admitted by chemists, to regulate the admixture of combustible fluids. Ineeed I am persuaded a thorough knowledge of the laws, which govern with such admirable precision the due proportions of inflammable materials, which, when combined, send forth the greatest intensity of light, would lead to considerable improvements in relation to this subject.

It is well known that hydrogen, and also carburetted hydrogen—both gaseous fluids liberated from oil and coal by the application of intense heat, are incapable of yielding either a pure or brilliant light, unless a sufficient quantity of atmospheric air is caused to enter minutely into combination with the ignited gas. Argand was, I believe, the first who discovered the necessity for this combination of the inflammable gases;—and the result of his reflections upon this subject was that happy invention, of the ingenious lamp which bears his name. Previous to this discovery, an enormous waste of illuminating substances was occasioned by the imperfect construction of the lamps then in use.

This celebrated lamp is so generally known, that were it not for the sake of illustration, I should omit describing the principle upon which it is arranged. A metallic cylindrical tube placed in a vertical position, forms the centre of the lamp; another tube is placed outside, and exactly parallel to this; there is thus, between the two tubes, a passage through which the gas or oil rises to the top of the burner, and a constant stream of common air is continually ascending through the inner tube to support the combustion: this process commences at the moment the gas escapes from the small orifices which are situated on the upper surface of the burner. On a circular ledge of brass which encompases the flame, a glass chimney is placed. The effects produced by this contrivance are, a considerable increase to the height of the flame—and an intensity of light, equal to double the quantity emitted by

an ordinary lamp. This fortunate application of atmospheric air, satisfied Argand of the correctness of his theory; he was contented with what he had done, and left the field open to future improvers.

In order the more perfectly to comprehend the nature of Hutchinson's burner, and to show the advantage it undoubtedly possesses over Argand's invention, it is necessary that I should explain in what respects the latter is deficient.

It is obvious to any one who is practically conversant with the nature of artificial light, that a certain definite, or exactly proportioned quantity, of the two gases, oxygen and hydrogen, are indispensible, in order to produce complete combustion. It is settled by the chemists, that the greatest intensity of flame is produced, when the relative proportions of oxygen and hydrogen are— two parts of the latter in weight, to one of the former; any deviation from this principle is found to be detrimental, as it is only when the fluids enter into combination in these exact ratios, that the desired brilliancy can be effected.

Now I cannot imagine, that the ingenuity of man will ever accomplish such a perfect piece of mechanism, as will extract from the atmosphere the precise compliment of oxygen requisite to unite with the volatile gas which escapes from a burner or gas pipes; but it is evident, from the admirable results of both Argand and Hutchinsons' burners, that a progressive approximation has, in this respect, been already attained, inasmuch, as that by the arrangement of their respective burners, a great part of the inflammable air of our atmosphere, is brought into immediate conjunction with the volatile products of decomposed coal and oil.

A series of experiments upon various burners has enabled me to arrive at the conclusion, that Hutchinson's invention has approximated nearer to perfection than any other that I am acquainted with. I think it will be admitted, that in consequence of Argand's burner being a uniform cylinder—*only* the external particles of the column of air which ascends towards the place of combustion, will actually combine with the ignited hydrogen; therefore, the myriads of globules, or those imperceptible atoms of combustible matter, which constitute the centre of this column, are carried (with a velocity peculiar to a cylindrical body of air) beyond the vicinity of the combustion, and thereby escape without having been appropriated.

I am aware that it is the opinion of many gas engineers and chemists, that in order to insure a perfect combustion, the air which ascends through the burner, should be mechanically urged towards the flame with the greatest possible velocity. But this is an erroneous conception; as I am persuaded, that no experiments that were ever instituted could in their results have warranted so unphilosophical a conclusion. Is it not now consistent, even in a theoretical sense, to suppose, that as great a degree of precision is necessary in regulating the velocity of the air, which ascends towards the flame, as is required in proportioning the union of the gases? It must, further, be obvious, that if the velocity is accelerated beyond a certain degree, much of the inflammable materials will pass into the surrounding atmosphere without having been decomposed, or ignited. The injurious effects of too great a flow of air upon flame, may be witnessed by directing a current upon any description of burner; the phenomena presented by this experiment are, a considerable elongation of the violet-coloured or dark portion of the flame; and a consequent diminution of the upper stratum, or that part of the flame which yields the greatest portion of light. Uniform combustion it is also found, is promoted, accelerated, or retarded, by the particular condition of the temperature of the air in the immediate vicinity of the lamp. If the air which is conducted to the place of combustion, be below that degree of rarifaction, which is necessary to produce the perfect separation of the inflammable, from the non-combustible gaseous fluids, that are rushing from the orifices of the burner in such a case, the light will be *reduced* both *in its dimensions and brilliancy*, and a serious waste of material be occasioned. These results, are established by the well known fact, that it requires a much more elevated temperature, to cause production of flame from the union of gases, than even that minute rarifaction of the atmosphere which immediately envelopes metals in a state of perfect fusion. The Davy Lamp will exhibit an apt illustration of the extreme sensitiveness of flame, to the influence of the surrounding air. It will be observed, that the flame of this lamp is instantly detached, and the natural cohesive properties of the inflamed hydrogen broken, at the moment the flame comes into contact with the metallic cylinder by which it is inclosed. The truth developed by this demonstration, I consider to be one of the primary, and indeed one of the most important principles which ought to guide us in the construction of burners.

I shall now give you a description of Hutchinson's burner, and by instituting a comparision between it and Argands, the improvement that has been made, will, I have no doubt, be apparent.

Fig. 1, (see next page) shows the burner complete. Fig. 2, a section down the middle; and fig. 3, a transverse section.

Instead of a perfect cylinder, this burner is formed of two frustums of cones of different dimensions. These cones are united at their perimeters, or smaller extremities. The section B. being therefore reversed. Through the lower frustum, and at its base c., the air which feeds the combustion, is first admitted, and conducted upwards towards the junction of the two cones at b. The diameter of the upper section of the lower cone, being but one half of that of its base; the column of air which entered at c. is concentrated. Immediately this concentrated volume of atmospheric air has passed the junction at b., it is expanded and guided directly to the ignited gas, which issues from the orifices of the burner at d. d.

This gradual contraction and expansion of air, obviates the inconvenient and disagreeable effects produced on the flame, by the unchecked velocity of the stream which rushes through a uniform cylinder, such as that which forms the centre of Argand's lamp. Also the union of the oxygen of the air, with the carburetted hydrogen, is rendered more perfect by this contrivance. This peculiar arrangement (to which is added the hood, fig. 4., which Mr. Hutchinson lays no claim to the invention of) produces an intense, luminous, and brilliant flame.

A series of interesting experiments, which were made at the time this burner was introduced, in order to ascertain the advantages it possessed over others, and

a series of experiments which I made myself upon it, having placed it in juxta-

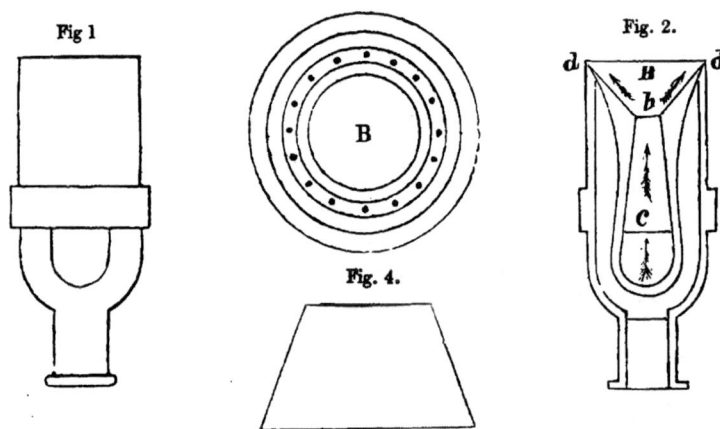

Fig. 3.

Fig 1

B

Fig. 2.

Fig. 4.

position with four of different and various constructions, have convinced me of its superiority over the best burners that I am acquainted with.

I am also happy to observe, that my opinion of its merits is corroborated by its being very generally substituted for the old burners throughout the metropolis, and in conjunction with Mr. Stephen Hutchinson's other great and beneficial improvements in gas machining, it has been introduced into the United States, especially New York.

CLOVIS.

MR. HERAPATH.

Sir,—There is a point beyond which forbearance is a crime. At that point you are considered by the friends of Mr. Herapath to have arrived, in your late unprovoked and unprincipled attacks on the reputation of that profound mathematician, and most amiable and worthy individual. Did all who read, only reflect, as they ought to do, on *what* they read, there would be nothing to apprehend from the worst which the *Mechanics' Magazine*, in its three-penny fury, could say to the prejudice of a gentleman so truly superior to censure as Mr. Herapath. But for one who does so, there are ten who gobble up implicitly what is presented to them in any favourite journal, daily or hebdominal; and hence the common saying, that a lie current and uncontradicted for a week, is as good, for any matter of present effect, as the best truth that ever was promulgated. Lest, therefore, any of your weekly lies respecting Mr. Herapath (for that is the rate at which they are issued) should make an injurious impression anywhere, it is thought fitting not only to give this public contradiction to them, but to give an equally public challenge to you to *prove* (not assert) any thing of which, either as a man of science, or a man of honour, he has any reason to be ashamed. It is hardly expected that you will have the honesty to insert this; but if you do not, there are happily other vehicles through which it shall meet the public eye. Waiting to see whether you do or no, before I go into particulars,

I am, Sir,

Your most obedient servant,

VERITAS.

Chelsea, 23rd April, 1837.

[We insert this letter, spite of its vulgar insolence, as a matter of course; and shall insert "the particulars" with which it is promised to be followed up, (when favoured with them), equally as a matter of course. Mr. Herapath has been charged by certain correspondents of this journal, with saying things of himself and others, which are not true; and he has a right, (which it has never been our practise to deny for an instant, to persons attacked in our pages), to be heard in his defence, by himself, or by any *alter ego* of his acquaintance,—no matter how rude and unbecoming the manner of that defence may be. That there may be no mistake, however, as to the real character of the embroilment in which Mr. Herapath has involved himself, we must add a few words. "Veritas" calls the late attacks upon his friend, "unprovoked and unprincipled," and challenges us " to prove one thing," &c. Now the plain and undeniable fact is, that it is entirely through Mr. Herapath's own attacks on others (Sir Humphry Davy and Sir John Rennie), and through the necessity which resulted of repelling these attacks, that his character, as a man of veracity, has been brought into question. With what propriety, then, can the letter of " Philo-Davy " or Mr. Meredith be called "unprovoked" or "unprincipled"? And why should they, or we, be called upon for proofs, when it is Mr. Herapath on whom the imputation of want of veracity rests, and with whom it lies to clear himself from it, if he can? What Mr. Herapath, or some one for him, has to do, is to prove (by "particulars," not by words,) that Sir Humphry Davy was really expelled from the chair of the Royal Society, in consequence of Mr. Herapath's ridiculous challenge to that Society—that Mr. Herapath was a year ago, or at any other time, "superintendent general of from three to four hundred miles of railway"—and so on to the end of the catalogue of mistakes imputed to him by our different correspondents.—ED. M. M.]

ON HEAT, THE ACTION OF LIGHT AND ATMOSPHERE, AND ON THE DISTRIBUTION OF THE ATMOSPHERE OVER THE EARTH'S SURFACE.

Sir,—In this paper an attempt is made to shew that the effects usually ascribed to the sun's heat, are produced by the combined action of light and air. That the degree of the sun's heat, at any given point is in proportion to the intensity of the light, and the density of the atmosphere at that place, and that the distribution of the atmosphere over the earth's surface, is effected and regulated by the earth's rotation on its axis.

To the effects produced by the burning glass, whether it be the burning of a piece of wood, or the melting of a piece of iron, both light and air contribute. We know that both these agents are present in the operation, and we do not know that any other agent is present; and in the absence of either of them, the burning glass will produce no effect. If a light from a lens which sets substances on fire, be thrown into the same substances in an exhausted receiver, it will produce no heat, no effect. This tends to shew that the effects produced by the burning glass, which are usually ascribed to heat, result from the combined action of light and air. It also tends to shew, that in the pure sun-beam there is no heat, and there are certain natural facts which have the same tendency. The summits of the lofty mountains within the tropics, which, while smitten by the intensest of the sun's rays, are wrapped in everlasting ice, attest that in that ray there is no heat. But then comes the question, why does not the sun's ray in those cases produce its usual effect? In the case of the burning glass the reason is obvious—it is the want of air. In the other case, the reason is the same;—it is the want of sufficient air to enable the light to produce its usual effect. In ascending upwards from the earth's surface, the density of the atmosphere is known gradually to decrease; and it hardly admits of doubt, that the atmosphere about the summits of those mountains, is too highly rarified to enable the sun's ray to produce its usual effect. Those summits, perhaps, transcend, or nearly so, the ocean of atmosphere which rests upon the earth. It is known that the rarefaction of air has a tendency to depress its temperature.

Light and air, in producing the effects attributed to heat, seem to act after this manner: the light being the more subtle fluid, appears to penetrate bodies, and to make way for the admission of air into them; and when the light is sufficiently condensed, the particles composing bodies are thereby separated and set at liberty, and the appearances called combustion and melting are produced. It is, perhaps, unnecessary to say, that light penetrates bodies, since the burning-glass itself furnishes abundant proof of that fact. It is evident that all the convergent rays pass through the glass;

and the expansion of heated bodies seems to be caused by the air which has entered them, and which, when they cool and contract, they give out, or squeeze out; and it is the air so pressed out of cooling bodies, which causes the repulsion steam, and hissing noise perceived when water is thrown upon them. If a piece of red hot iron, or any other red hot body, be plunged into water, the air which has entered it, will be perceived issuing from it in innumerable bubbles. Hence atmospheric air appears to be the most active agent in the melting of metals; aided by intense light, it seems to enter into them, and to be the power which ultimately separates the particles composing them. Moreover, the current of air which agitates boiling water, enters through the metal or substance of the vessel. This, I think, is evident from the following facts :—the air issues from the metal or substance of the vessel, as is plainly perceived by observing a vessel of water put on the fire to boil; it may be caught before it reaches the surface of the water : and if a tin vessel containing water be partly immersed in a vessel of boiling water, the water in the tin vessel may be raised to boiling heat; but it will not boil, because it is protected from the current of air by the vessel which contains it and the water which surrounds the tin.

The distribution of the atmosphere over the earth's surface seems to be effected and regulated by the earth's rotation.

The atmosphere being a fluid resting on the face of the earth, and the earth being a sphere turning with great velocity on its axis, the centrifugal force thence arising will necessarily cause an accumulation of atmosphere at the equator of the earth,* which, under the influence of the same force, will decrease towards the poles ; and the necessary consequence of the accumulation will be, an increased density† at the equator, which will also gradually diminish with the accumulation from thence towards the poles. The sun's light also is most intense at the equator, and within the tropics. Now this distribution of atmosphere and light, supposing the sun's heat to result from the combined action of light and air, and that it is proportioned to the intensity of the light and the density of the atmosphere at any given place, would cause just such a distribution of the sun's heat as is found to exist. It would be greatest, and ascend highest, within the tropics, where the light is most intense, and the atmospheric accumulation and density, are greatest ; and from thence its elevation would decline, and its density decrease towards the poles : and this is the order we find in nature ; there is the greatest heat attaining the highest elevation within the tropics, which from thence gradually declines in elevation, and decreases in intensity towards the poles.

Atmospheric air is susceptible of a great variety of modifications, under some of which it seems to become light, or to give light : of which kind seem to be all artificial lights ; and electric light, and the aurora borealis, probably are but modifications of atmospheric air.‡

W.

RUSSIAN WEIGHTS, AND RUSSIAN EXCHANGE ON LONDON.

Sir,—I send you an article or two from St. Petersburgh. If the mites you receive, or may receive, are not foreign to the design of your valuable and instructive publication, and you may think they may interest any of your numerous readers, you will add them to your repository.

The balance beam by which the weights were ascertained, was made by Mr. Berge, with such accuracy, that when each scale was loaded with 27 pounds avoirdupois,

---

* The waters of the ocean are known to be under the influence of the same force. The centrifugal force of the earth's rotation seems to be the power which obeyed the Almighty fiat, " Let the waters under the heaven be gathered together." This appears to be the power which first established and still maintains the level of the sea.

† Within the tropics, the barometer does not descend more than half as much for every 200 feet of elevation, as it does beyond the tropics; which proves a greater density, and an accumulation of atmosphere.—B ll's Geography, vol. i. p. 70.

‡ Wherever the aurora appears, it is a proof of the rarefaction of the atmosphere at that point, and consequently of its coldness.

and the twentieth part of a grain more in one of the pans (which is the 3,780,000th part of the whole weight), the beam would not remain in an horizontal position.

Concerning the Exchange, notwithstanding it being a subject of contemplation, it may be of use to such persons as may have an idea of establishing themselves in Russia, by letting them know the value of a pound sterling, and how many roubles the working mechanic must earn to be enabled to save a few pounds for *home*.

I am, Sir, your most obedient servant,

BENJAMIN HYNAM.

St. Petersburgh, Feb. 28th, 1837.

Comparative Proportion between the Russian and English Weights.

	lb. Avoirdupois	oz.	dwts. English.
1 Funt, or Russian pound, equals	0	14	$7\frac{1}{8}$
2 Ditto	1	12	$14\frac{1}{4}$
4 Ditto	3	9	$12\frac{1}{2}$
8 Ditto	7	3	$9\frac{1}{16}$
16 Ditto	14	7	$2\frac{1}{8}$
20 Ditto	18	0	$14\frac{5}{8}$
40 Funts, or 1 pond	36	1	$13\frac{1}{4}$

	font.	zol.*	parts.
1 Pound English, avoirdupois, equals	1	10	$31\frac{1}{2}$ Russ.
2 Ditto	2	20	63
3 Ditto	3	30	$94\frac{1}{2}$
4 Ditto	4	41	30
5 Ditto	5	51	$61\frac{1}{2}$
6 Ditto	6	61	93
7 Ditto	7	72	$28\frac{1}{2}$
8 Ditto	8	82	60
9 Ditto	9	92	$91\frac{1}{2}$
10 Ditto	11	7	27

One Russian pound is equal to 1 lb. 1 oz. 3 dwt. $\frac{1}{4}$ gr. Troy.

The smallest weight of Russia is the zolotnick.

3 Zolotnicks is equal to 1 lot.
36 Lots is equal to 1 funt.
40 Funts is equal to 1 pond.
10 Ponds is equal to 1 berkovetz = 3 cwt. 24 lb. English.

RUSSIAN EXCHANGE ON LONDON.

In the year 1695, the exchange on London was at 120 pence per rouble, and in the year 1710, it was at 80 pence. But we find no direct course on London till the year 1763, when a *direct* course was fixed, which has continued ever since. The course of exchange in that year opened at 55. In the year 1803, it was at $37\frac{1}{2}$, since which it has received great fluctuation, and gradually declined, for it was, in 1816, as low as $9\frac{1}{2}$ on London. It is now $10\frac{1}{2}$, and has been so for some years, varying a farthing more or less in the rouble; consequently, a pound sterling in 1755 was equal to about 436 roubles, in 1803, to 768, and is at this moment equal to 2286 roubles.

OBSERVATIONS UPON MR. MACKINNON'S BILL "TO AMEND THE PRACTICE RELATING TO LETTERS PATENT FOR INVENTIONS," ETC.

If from amongst the various subjects which at this moment press on the attention of Parliament, one should be selected for its important bearings upon the great commercial interests of this country—for its nationality—for its prospective beneficial results—and for its claims to be calmly considered without any excitement of that excusable party-feeling which attaches to most matters of public discussion—that subject would be the

* Zolotnick.

relief of the genius and inventive talent of this manufacturing nation from the oppression and difficulties under which it has hitherto laboured, for want of *a systematic code* of patent law, combining simplicity of forms, efficient protection, and reasonable price.

The attention of our statesmen and legislators appears never to have been sufficiently directed to the necessity of treating the subject of patent law and practice as an affair of *national policy,*—both as it regards our internal prosperity and our external commercial relations over the whole globe ; it has never been considered by those who direct the concerns of this country, that the combined rivalry of foreign nations, jealous of our manufacturing superiority, and present commercial pre-eminence, can alone be effectually met by giving vitality and energy to the immense mass of dormant inventive talent throughout this country, which can never be rendered available to its possessors, and to the public, but by a complete remodelling of our antiquated and expensive system of patent law and practice.

The amendment of this system is, I will acknowledge, surrounded with difficulties and perplexities of a peculiar character ; but they are not insurmountable, and the attention of Parliament being once fixed upon the importance of the subject, the wisdom of Parliament can certainly apply the proper remedies.

To appreciate the value that should be attached to the well-intentioned endeavours of any Member who will undertake the almost forlorn hope of patent practice amendment, we need only cursorily advert to the attempts which have preceded the present bill of Mr. Mackinnon upon this difficult point of legislation. In the session of 1829, the honorable House of Commons appointed a Committee of Inquiry into " the Law and Practice of Patents for Inventions," with directions " to report the evidence, *and their observations thereon,* to the House." The Committee was composed of able men from both sides of the House ; they examined witnesses at great length, reported their evidence—but found the subject " *so intricate and difficult,*" that notwithstanding " their earnest recommendation to be reappointed early in the next session," they relinquished the " intricate and difficult" business, and were never reconstituted for the purpose of making that report, which could alone have given an operative result to their previous labours.

The Reform Bill engrossed the attention of Parliament for the two succeeding sessions ; but in that of 1833, Mr. Godson introduced his Patent Law Amendment Bill ;

it was divided into two, for the purpose of separating the more questionable amendments ; the first Bill passed the Commons, the second Bill went through Committee ; they together embraced many important ameliorations, but were defective in detail as a system, or code of patent law and practice. These two Bills were superseded by Lord Brougham's Act, which contains some material improvements, not worded in the best manner (so far as word's are intended to convey precise meaning) ; but Lord Brougham's Act has left all the principal grievances of which men of inventive talent complain perfectly unremedied.   Lord Brougham's acknowledged great talents were not applied to the " intricate and difficult" portions of the subject—the real protection of invention as a matter of personal property *and of personal right*—the abrogation of the useless antiquated forms of passing patents—the complete simplifying of the process as a matter of commercial arrangement affecting the great interests of the country—the substitution of one patent in one " United Kingdom" for three complicated patents ; and, finally, the reduction of the heavy stamp duties and onerous state and chancery fees. Without this reduction, all other improvements are sealed from the great mass of inventors, whose combined talent, industry, and knowledge would add incalculably to the wealth and resources of the empire, and to our means of competing, in every part of the globe, with the increasing efforts of rival powers, who are continually progressing in those combinations of capital, skill, and enterprize, which must eventually have a deep effect upon our future commercial operations.

Mr. Mackinnon's Bill is very far from perfect in many principal points, especially in respect of necessary details for the security of inventors and of the public ; and he has fallen into the error of placing his improvements beyond the reach of men of moderate means; but his Bill contains essential and important ameliorations *in principle;* the forms of taking out patents are materially simplified, and security is afforded from the date of the petition ; the heavy stamp duties are proposed to be repealed, and the numerous classes of fees and emoluments are abrogated by his Bill.[*]

But it is important to impress on the attention of Parliament that the difficulties which are inherent to this intricate subject should secure to the *bonâ fide* endeavours of any legislator who will undertake any thing

---

[*] But *others* substituted, which, we fear, would be equally onerous with those repealed; with this, exception, we cordially subscribe to the sentiments of this judicious and well-timed appeal.—ED. M. M.

like *a systematic* arrangement and amelioration of patent law and practice,—the cordial and effective co-operation of men of every party to amend what is imperfect, and supply what is deficient in this Bill. To prevent its going into Committee because it is defective in its details, would be equally unjust and impolitic; such a course would disappoint the rational expectations and demands of thousands of men of inventive genius, who have been from year to year depending upon the wisdom and justice of the legislature for a *code* of patent law; such a course would be impolitic, by still continuing those restrictions, which exclude from profitable action and reciprocal benefit to the community, the buried treasures of inexhaustible resources of science, talent, skill, and enterprise, which would prove to this country richer mines of wealth than Potosi or Golconda possess. To throw out this Bill upon second reading, would be to discourage every future attempt of individual endeavour to legislate upon this most important and most difficult subject.

Mr. Mackinnon stands pledged to facilitate every proffered improvement upon his Bill; it is but common candour to give him credit for the sincerity of his professions, and but parliamentary justice to allow him to redeem his pledge.

This is not a party question; it is a question of equal policy, justice, and benevolence; the interests of official persons engaged in the present practice of patent-grants are insignificant when put into the balance against the great interests of the country; but fair compensations to all who are entitled to such can easily be arranged under this Bill. The prospective increase to the happiness—the internal improvement—the resources and the external commerce of this great empire, as the result of a good and *available system* of patent protection to the inventive talent of the country, is incalculable. This is, *par eminence,* a question of British policy, of British improvement, and of British interests; and it should be treated with the generous sympathies of *patriotic British legislation.*

JULIUS LUDOLPHUS SCHRODER.

Brixton, 10th April, 1837.

LIST OF ENGLISH PATENTS GRANTED BETWEEN THE 27TH OF MARCH AND THE 25TH OF APRIL, 1837.

Joseph Haley, of Manchester, machine-maker, for "certain improvements in the machinery tools or apparatus for cutting, planing, and turning metals and other substances." March 28; six months.

Joseph Whitworth, of Manchester, engineer, for "certain improvements in machinery tools or apparatus for turning, boring, planing, and cutting metals and other materials." March 28; six months.

Henry Stephens, of Stamford-street, Blackfriar's-road, Surrey, writing-fluid manufacturer, for "certain improvements in ink-stands or ink-holders and pens for writing." March 28; six months.

Michel Berand Lauras, of Lyons, but now residing in Leicester-square, Middlesex, merchant, for "certain improvements in steam-navigation."—April 4; six months.

Henry Booth, of Liverpool, esquire, "for improvements in the construction of locomotive engine boiler furnaces, applicable also to other furnaces." April 4; six month.

William Wynn, of Dean-street, Soho, Middlesex, clock-maker, for "a certain improvement or improvements in apparatus for diminishing the evaporation of vinous, alcoholic, acetic, and other volatile vapours, and for preventing the absorption of noxious effluvia in vinous, spirituous, acetous, and other fluids, such as wines, spirits, malt liquors, cyder, perry, and vinegar."—April 4; six months.

Joseph Amesbury, of Burton Crescent, Middlesex, surgeon, for "certain apparatus for the relief or correction of stiffness, weakness, or distortion in the human spine, chest, or limbs." April 4; six months.

William Weekes, of King Stanley, Gloucester, clothier, for "certain improvements in the dressing or finishing of woollen and other cloths or fabrics requiring such a process." April 4; two months.

Joseph Lincoln Roberts, of Manchester, merchant, for "a certain improvement or certain improvements in looms for weaving," being a communication from a foreigner residing abroad. April 11; six months.

Reuben Bull, of Adam's-street West, Portman-square, Middlesex, ironmonger, for "certain improvements in chimney caps to facilitate the discharge of smoke, and to prevent its return." April 15; six months.

Horatio Nelson Aldrich, of Rhode Island, in the United States of America, but now of Cornhill, London, merchant, for "certain improvements in spinning, twisting, doubling, or otherwise preparing cotton, silk, and other fibrous substances," being a communication from a foreigner residing abroad. April 15; six months.

Henry Stephens, of Charlotte-street, Marylebone, Middlesex, gent., and Ebeneser Nash, of Buross-street, St. George in the East, Middlesex, tallow-chandler, for "certain improvements in manufacing colouring matter, and rendering certain colour or colours applicable to dyeing, staining, and writing." April 15; six months.

David Napier, of the York-road, Lambeth, Surrey, engineer, for "improvements in letter-press printing." April 18; six months.

Thomas Hancock, of Goswell Mews, Goswell-road, Middlesex, water-proof cloth manufacturer, for "an improvement or improvements in the process of rendering cloth and other fabrics partially or entirely impervious to air and water, by means of caoutchouc or India-rubber." April 18; six months.

William Crofts, of New Radford, Nottingham, machine-maker, for "improvements in the manufacture of figured or ornamented bobbin net, or twist lace or other fabrics." April 18; six months.

Edmund Haworth, the younger, of Bolton, Lancaster, gent., (in pursuance of the report of the Judicial Committee of his Majesty's Privy Council,) of the sole use, benefit, and advantage of William Southworth, formerly of Sharples, near Bolton-le-Moors, Lancaster, bleacher, for "certain improvements in certain machinery or apparatus adapted to facilitate the operations of drying calicoes, muslins, linens, or other similar fabrics," for the further term of five years. April 18.

Charles Farina, of Clarendon Place, Maida Vale, Middlesex, gentleman, for "an improved process to be used in obtaining fermentable matter from grain, and in manufacturing the same for various purposes." April 18; six months.

Lemuel Wellman Wright, of Manchester, Lancaster, engineer, for "certain improvements in machinery or apparatus for bleaching or cleaning linens, cottons, or other fabrics, goods, or other fibrous substances." April 20; six months.

William Gratrix, of Springfield-lane, Salford, Lancaster, silk-dyer, for "certain improvements in the process of bleaching or cleansing linens, cotton, and other fibrous substances, and also improvements in the process of discharging colours from the same, either in the raw material or manufactured state." April 22; six months.

John Gottlieb Ulrich, late of Nicholas-lane, London, but now of Red-Lion Street, Whitechapel, Middlesex, chronometer-maker, for "certain improvements in chronometers." April 22; six months.

Sir George Cayley, Bart., of Brompton, near Walton, York, for "certain improvements in the apparatus for propelling carriages on common roads or railways, part of which improvements may be applied to other useful purposes." April 25; six months.

James Pim, jun., of College Green, banker, and Thomas Fleming Bergin, of Westland-row, Dublin, civil engineer, for "an improved means or methods of propulsion on railways." April 25; six months.

Miles Berry, of Chancery-lane, Middlesex, for "certain improvements in machinery or apparatus for making or manufacturing bricks, tiles, and such other articles," being a communication from a foreigner residing abroad. April 27; six months.

Miles Berry, of Chancery-lane, Middlesex, for "certain improvements in machinery or apparatus for making or manufacturing horse-shoes," being a communication from a foreigner residing abroad. April 27; six months.

LIST OF SCOTCH PATENTS GRANTED BETWEEN THE 22ND OF MARCH AND THE 22ND OF APRIL.

Samuel Tonkin Jones, of Manchester, merchant, for "certain improvements in the tanning of hides and skins." March 29.

Charles Brandt, of Upper Belgrave-place, Middlesex, mechanist, for "an improved method of evaporating and cooling fluids." March 31.

Charles Pierre Devaux, of Fenchurch-street, London, merchant, in consequence of a communication from a foreigner residing abroad, for "a new or improved apparatus for preventing the explosion of boilers or generators of steam." April 7.

William Hancock, of Windsor-place, City Road, Middlesex, gent., for "certain improvements in book-binding." April 8.

Richard Burch, of Heywood, Lancaster, mechanist, for "certain improvements in locomotive steam-engines, to be used either upon rail or other roads, which improvements are also applicable to marine and other stationery steam-engines" April 14.

Henry Backhouse, of Walmsley, calico-printer, and Jeremiah Grime, engraver, both of Bury, Lancaster, for "certain improvements in the art of block-printing." April 14.

William Nairne, of Millhaugh, near Methven, Perth, flax-spinner, for "a certain improvement or certain improvements in the machinery of reels used in reeling yarns." April 14.

Bennet Woodcroft, late of Ardwich, Manchester, but now of Mumps, Oldham, gent., for "an improved mode of printing certain colours on calico and other fabrics." April 18.

LIST OF IRISH PATENTS GRANTED IN MARCH, 1837.

Henry Huntley, of Walworth, Surrey, M. D., for "an improvement in the manufacturing of fuel." March 14.

Thomas Henry Russell, of Handsworth, near Birmingham, for "improvements in making or manufacturing welded iron tubes." March 14.

William Sneath, of Ison Green, Nottingham, lace-maker, for "certain improvements in machinery by, and of which improvements, thread-work ornaments of certain kinds, can be formed in net or lace, made by certain machinery commonly called bobbin net machinery, and other fabrics."

NOTES AND NOTICES.

English Manufactures.—The German papers remark. that at every Leipsic fair the quantity of English manufactures offered for sale grows less and less. The editors, are, however, unable to draw so much consolation as they could wish from this interesting fact. The cause of the diminution, is, they observe, an increasing habit in the consumers of the south-eastern parts of Europe, of bargaining for their supplies of English manufactures, particularly twists, at Hamburg, in preference to the time of the fair. The quantity imported, is in their opinion as large as ever.

Errata in our last Number.—In the letter on Mr. Baddeley's Fire Reports, p. 36, lines 16 and 17; the number there quoted ought to be "one hundred and *thirty*-four" instead of "*sixty*-four," and that in line 27 should be "one hundred and *sixty*-seven" instead of "*thirty*-seven." In the Review of Porter's Progress of the Nation: p. 42, col. 2, line 37, for "in point" read "in print;" p. 44, col. 2, line 7, for "regarding" read "hazarding;" same col. line 17, for "beyond the *work*" read "beyond the *mark*."

☞ *British and Foreign Patents taken out with economy and despatch; Specifications, Disclaimers, and Amendments, prepared or revised; Caveats entered; and generally every Branch of Patent Business promptly transacted.*

A complete list of Patents from the earliest period (15 Car. II. 1675,) to the present time may be examined. Fee 2s. 6d.; Clients, gratis.

LONDON: Printed and Published by W. A. Robertson, at the Mechanics' Magazine Office, No. 6, Peterborough-court, between 135 and 136, Fleet-street.—Sold by G. W. M. Reynolds, Proprietor of the French, English, and American Library, 55, Rue Neuve, Saint Augustin, Paris.

Mechanics' Magazine,

MUSEUM, REGISTER, JOURNAL, AND GAZETTE.

No. 717.   SATURDAY, MAY 6, 1837.   Price 3*d.*

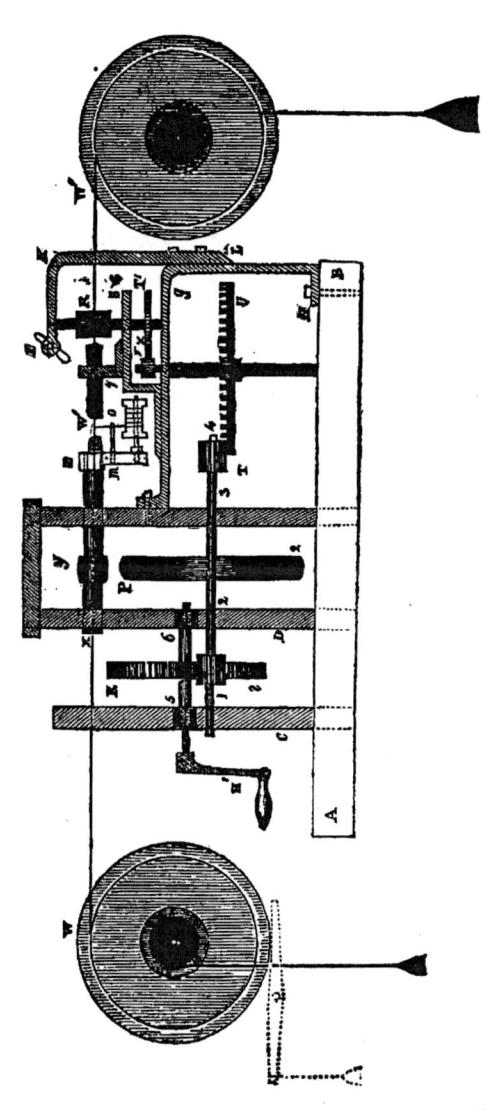

ETTRICK'S MACHINE FOR COVERING COPPER WIRE WITH THREAD.

MACHINE FOR COVERING COPPER
WIRE WITH THREAD, FOR ELEC-
TRO-MAGNETICAL PURPOSES.

Sir,—Being engaged two years since
in making some electro-dynamical instruments, considerable quantities of
copper wire covered with thread were
required, which I found impossible to
be procured in the country without great
delay and considerable expense; I therefore found that it would be advantageous
to give up a few days in the construction of an instrument for that purpose.
The drawing (see front page) is a representation of it, which I would be
obliged by your inserting in the *Mechanics' Magazine,* for the use of those
unfortunates who are in the same situation as myself. That part of the machine on the left hand side, which I call
the "covering part of the machine,"
was finished in the year 1835, by which
part alone several hundred feet of wire
were covered, by simply drawing it
through with the hand, which, though
not so expeditious, nor did it finish the
work so neatly as with the additional
"drawing apparatus," nevertheless, is
all that is absolutely necessary; which is
material to mention, because many persons might be competent, and able to
find time to construct it, who could not
do so for the whole machine. The large
cylinders at the ends are for the purpose
of keeping the wire stretched tight when
it is very fine, as in the case of the
electro-magnetical armature for giving
the shock, where I find that from its
pliableness it gives way under the pressure of the thread.

Description of the Machine.—A. B.,
the base or bottom board, 24 in. long,
6 inches wide, and 2 inches thick.
C D and E, three wooden pillars, the
two D and E having a cross bar at the
top to keep them parallel. X Z, a hollow iron shaft, piece of a gun barrel, one
inch diameter, having shoulders on the
inside of the pillars; upon the end Z
there is an arm Z m fastened for carrying
the pin m upon which the bobbin of
thread (having a brass bush through it,
made to spring by two or three saw cuts
at the ends) turns stiffly. A pin o is
fixed into the arm Z m, having a small
hole at the end o through which the
thread passes, and by which it is kept at
the proper distance from the hollow

shaft. A piece of turned wood having
a small hole through its centre, for keeping the wire in the axis of the hollow
shaft, is driven into the end W' of the
hollow shaft. y is a small wheel rounded
to receive a strap, by which it is driven.
This wheel being small, ten cuts were
made with a triangular file in the manner of a saw, but not so close, lest it
should cut the leather. The *sharp
edges* taking hold of the band, it never
slips upon the wire which it would
otherwise do from the size of the shaft,
and smallness of y. The wheel y, and
consequently the spindle Z X, is driven
by the large wheel P Q fixed upon the
shaft 1 2 3 4. At 1 is a cogged wheel
or pinion, which is driven by the large
wheel R S fixed upon the shaft 5 6,
upon which the handle H' is put, by
which the whole is set in motion. This
constitutes what I term the covering
part of the instrument. I will therefore
now proceed to describe the drawing
apparatus, and then proceed to give the
sizes of the wheels :—F g H, a plate of
iron 1¾ in. wide and ¼th of an inch thick,
bolted to the wooden frame; upon this
iron frame two iron supporters I K L
(one of which only can be seen in a side
view,) are screwed to the frame F g H.
Upon the shaft 1 2 3 4, there is fixed the
pinion 4 which drives the horizontal
wheel T U upon whose axis is fixed
the pinion V. which drives the large
wheel X Y, upon whose shaft is fixed a
brass roller R one inch diameter, somewhat rounded by drawing a coarse file
along the line of the axis. Strictly
speaking this roller is not seen in the
drawing, but another similar one fixed
upon an axis, whose *lower* end works or
rests in the bent piece of iron 7, 8,
and upper one in the piece of iron I K L.
The wire W, X, W', R, W", after passing
through the hollow shaft X W, goes
between the two rollers R being drawn
through by the revolution of the one
fixed on the axis of the wheel X Y. The
two cylinders are drawn together by
a thumb screw at I, so as to lay firm
hold of the wire. I find that it is not
necessary to fix cogged wheels upon the
roller spindles for the purpose of turning
both rollers by the machinery, as the
friction of one roller is amply sufficient
for drawing the wire through. But to
assist the machinery, I have hitherto
wound the wire upon a drum, as at W".

by applying a weight as shown in the drawing, which, being more than what is required for laying the wire upon, the remainder tends to draw the wire through the rollers. The weight upon the drum W is put the contrary way to that on the drum W″, and it therefore tends to prevent the wire passing through the machine, but the weight W″ being the heaviest, the wire is not only drawn through, but kept *stretched tight*, which is absolutely necessary when very fine. The mechanic will immediately see that the roller, or drum W″ might have been turned by a pinion working in the wheel T V, carrying a screw at its opposite end, acting in the ratched circumference of the drum ; but I preferred the weights, because they are more simple, and act better than the self-acting drum, whose diameter is continually altering. Moreover, it will be seen, that had that method been resorted to, the drawing cylinders R would not have been required, but they were considered best, because *any length* of wire can be covered in a single piece, whereas, with the other method, the wire must be removed from the drum when full, which, when thick, very soon takes place. Since this was written, the light weight of the drum W has been removed, and a lever with a weight, has been applied instead of it, which, by the friction of the lever upon the circumference of the drum keeps the wire tight. It is represented by the dotted lines. The drum W″ is fitted with a small cylinder for a *single cord*, as shown in the drawing, or with a pulley for a double cord, as in the common cuckoo clock, a rack being added in either case, for the convenience of winding up the weight. The cylinder, or drum, must have a motion sideways to allow the wire to cover every part of its circumference. As the cylinder for the cord is small, one winding up will be sufficient for several feet of wire when the fall for the weight is considerable, and in mine, with a fall of 14 feet, from 60 to 100 feet ; but I should mention that the machine never acts better than when the cord is simply wound upon the large drum itself. At W′ there is fixed a small hollow cylinder, having small holes at the ends to steady the fine wire, for without such bearance close to the place covering the wire,

the wire would give under the pressure of the thread. The machine would be greatly improved by using two bobbins instead of one, which, if placed directly opposite to each other, as shown in the annexed figure, would not only keep

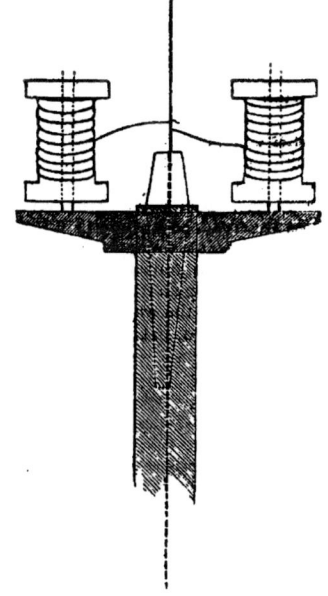

the wire steady, but cover twice as much in a given time as could be done with only one. But in such case one of the wheels must be decreased to half the number of teeth.

Calculation of the speed of the machine. —The wheel R S has 84 cogs and drives a pinion of 28, which gives a velocity of 3. The cylinder, or wheel, P Q is 8 inches diameter, and the small one y 1.3 inch or as 1.3)9.0 (7 nearly. The pinion 4 has 12 leaves, and works in a wheel of 76, or as 12)76(6.34. The pinion v has 18 leaves, and works in the shaft Y Z of 96, ro is as 18)96 (5.34, consequently, the velocity of the shaft Y X to the roller R is as 7×6.34×7.34=237. This machine has covered the wire at the *rate of* 400 *feet* in an hour with the finest cotton colored thread that can be procured.

W. ETTRICK.

Sunderland, 29th March, 1837.

F 2

WAGGON UNLOADER.

Sir,—If you think the following idea practicable, and suitable to the *Mechanics' Magazine*, I should like to see it inserted.

Much inconvenience is often experienced, and even accidents sometimes occur from carts, but more especially waggons, projecting out into the road, while their goods are being unloaded into shops.

In rather wide streets, where two vehicles can pass each other in the remaining portion of the road, this obstruction is not much felt, but in narrow streets, when the waggon stretches across the road, so as only to allow one coach to pass at a time, it becomes quite a nuisance. To obviate this, I thought of the following plan:

At the end of the waggon let there be a sort of platform, in shape, a quarter of

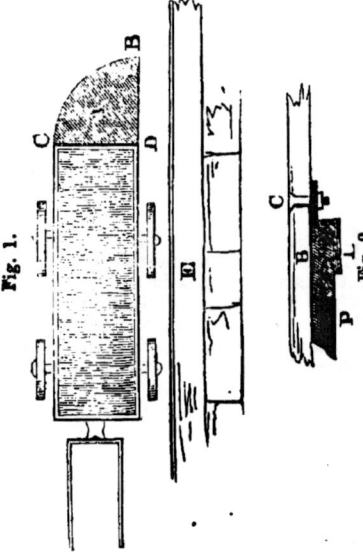

a circle, working on a centre at one side of the waggon; when not used, to slip under the bottom of the waggon, having a narrow ledge of plate iron to support it. The diagram will more clearly show what I mean.

Fig. 1. A is the platform out. B is a leg, in thickness proportioned to the weight it is likely to carry, with a joint similar to those under cart shafts, to put up when not used. At C it will be supported by the ledge, and at D will work upon its hinge or centre. E is the curb of the pavement *along* which the waggon stands, and not projecting from it as is now usual. Fig. 2 will show the way the ledge can be made, B is the bottom of the carriage, C is the screw to fasten up the ledge, L the ledge to support the platform, at P the platform in its place.

I remain, your obedient servant,
V. B.

January 30, 1837.

MECHANICS' INSTITUTIONS OF LIVERPOOL.

The Liverpool Mechanics' Institution, the Theatre attached to which was destroyed by an accidental fire a few weeks ago, is undoubtedly the most splendid establishment of the kind in the kingdom—far outshining its metropolitan prototype. A year or two back it had, in common with most of the provincial Mechanics' Institutions, declined to such an extent that its very existence was threatened, and it was only revivified by the most spirited exertions on the part of several of the most eminent merchants of the " second commercial capital " who subscribed immense sums for the purpose, and thus succeeded,—not in the most legitimate possible manner— in restoring it to its pristine splendour, and, in appearance at least, to its pristine vigour. One of the first measures adopted under the new state of things, was to set about the erection of an extensive and imposing building for the purposes of the Institution, the first stone of which was laid, with all due pomp and ceremony, by no less a personage than Lord Brougham, who, if we recollect aright, took advantage of the opportunity to repeat, for the thousandth time since its complete refutation, his usual puff-direct of Dr. Birkbeck, as the " founder " of the parent establishment in London. The whole cost of the new building is stated at £12,000, and the damage caused by the late fire is estimated at about one-fourth that amount, which is, it is understood, covered by the insurance. A valuable collection of casts, a present from one of the opulent "patrons" of the Liverpool mechanics, was fortunately rescued from the flames. There is another and more modest institution of the kind in Liverpool, the "Mechanics' and Apprentices' Library," which has now been in existence fourteen years, and seems to recovering from the state of depression into which it had fallen, so that it has been determined to continue it as a separate association, instead of uniting with the more wealthy one, as had been proposed. The income, improved as it is, of the Library, is only 100*l.* per annum, a small sum, as the Committee remark in their Report, to be expended in literary recreation by the thousands of workmen composing the industrial population of Liverpool. It should be borne in mind, however, that this Institution owes none of its funds to aristocratic patronage, and confines itself to its direct object, without dazzling the optics of its subscribers by the false glare of lectures on the Belles Lettres, or readings from the drama by gentlemen of the theatre in demi-Thespian costume. Such things have been in Liverpool, as well as other places that could be mentioned.

SIR HUMPHRY DAVY'S PRESIDENCY OF THE ROYAL SOCIETY.

Sir,—In my letter to you of the 3rd April last, I unhesitatingly pronounced the assertion of Mr. Herapath, that his newspaper challenge to the Royal Society which "ended in the expulsion of the tool of his opponents, Sir Humphry Davy, from the presidency" of that body, to be a "*monstrous supposition—monstrous falsehood.*"

Mr. Herapath, in answer to this impeachment of his veracity, has commenced publishing "the correspondence which led to the publications" or newspaper challenges alluded to. But the very words by which this correspondence is introduced to the notice of the public, serve to shew that he has been indeed guilty of the falsehood imputed to him. His first statement was most positive and unqualified, namely, that the letters in question "ended in the *expulsion*" of Sir Humphry Davy from the precedency; but what is his language now?—"Terminated in the expulsion, or *forced re-*

tirement of Sir Humphry Davy." And as if this were not evidence enough of his wish to back out of the charge, the article is thus labelled in his table of contents, "Royal Society and Mr. Herapath; the private correspondence that caused the discussion which ended in *the resignation* of Sir Humphry Davy." Aye, aye, Mr. Herapath, "resignation," "retirement," any thing but "*expulsion :*" that is a charge you now shrink from, and would fain wriggle out of, if you could. But as neither "retirement" nor "resignation" is synonymous with "expulsion," we must leave, if you please,—nay, whether you please or no, —the original phrase, that is, the falsehood sticking in your throat.

Not that there is any foundation for even the present milder version of the story. Far from it. Mr. Herapath and his challenges had, in no shape whatever— whether "expulsion," "retirement," or "resignation," any thing to do with the termination of Sir Humphry Davy's presidential career. I say this with a perfect knowledge of the real facts of the case; and I defy Mr. Herapath to shew, by any thing better than the mere empty suggestions of his own inordinate vanity, that there was the slightest connexion between them.

With respect to "the correspondence," —so much of it at least as is now published,—it proves nothing whatever as to Sir Humphry Davy, whose name is not once mentioned in it from the beginning to the end. No. I. is a letter dated January 23rd, 1800, addressed by Mr. Herapath to Mr. Davies Gilbert, the then President of the Royal Society, in which the writer reminds Mr. Gilbert that he had been introduced to him about eleven years before, and proceeds to say, that he had "since then met with some success in unfolding a principle which seems to him to account *mathematically* (*!!!*) for the laws and phenomena of gaseous bodies, heat, gravitation, &c.," and wished that "a Memoir containing some of the Fundamental Propositions," should be presented to the Royal Society, to have their judgment upon it. No. II. is an answer from Mr. Davies Gilbert, from which it appears that he had no recollection of the introduction alluded to, and did not very much like the scrape-acquaintance style of his unknown correspondent. "I trust," he says, "that an interval of eleven years will apologize for my not recollecting *a name*" (*et preterea nihil ?*); and "I must refer you to the first page of each volume of their (the Society's) transactions for a declaration of their declining, as a body, to give their opinion on any thing submitted to them." No. III. is a letter from Mr. Herapath to Mr. Gilbert, announcing that he had forwarded his Memoir, and trusted to see it inserted in the next volume of the Society's Transactions. No. IV. is Mr. Gilbert's reply, which we shall leave to speak for itself.

"45, Bridge-street, Westminster, June 6, 1820.

"Dear Sir,—I had some time since the pleasure of receiving your very *curious* disquisition on the causes of gravity. *I read it over;* and although I must confess myself not satisfied with the ultimate deduction, yet I was much pleased with the great *ingenuity* displayed throughout the whole: but I entertained strong doubts on the propriety of laying before the Royal Society any thing so abstruse and metaphysical. I therefore desired *two of the best mathematicians in London* to look at the premises, and their opinions have confirmed my doubts. They say that *such a work* should be laid before the public in a separate form. I cannot present it to the Royal Society in opposition to their opinions, and consequently I must wait your directions to dispose of the Treatise in any other manner you may have the goodness to direct.

"Believe me, dear sir,
    "Your very faithful humble servant,
        (Signed)   "DAVIES GILBERT."

No. V. is a letter from Mr. Herapath to Mr. Gilbert, mentioning that he is coming to town, and "will have the pleasure of calling to hear something further respecting the objections of Mr. Gilbert and his friends." To this there is a note appended, in which Mr. Herapath asserts, that he came accordingly to London, and had two interviews with Mr. Gilbert, in the course of which Mr. G. "admitted that it was possible no mathematician could refute the demonstrations, and that the conclusions perfectly corresponded with facts; but observed, "that the principles may be false;" and, "at length confessed, that he had not leisure to read a paper of such length and difficulty;" all which, every one must allow to be exceeding likely, seeing that the only grounds for questioning the accuracy of Mr. Herapath's *recollection* of what really passed, are, that Mr. Gilbert has never been known to be in the habit of talking arrant nonsense, and that there is the letter extant which he wrote to Mr. Herapath just before these interviews, in which he says, that he *did* "*read it* (the Memoir) *over*," and was "*not satisfied*" with the ultimate deduction," &c. No. VI. is a letter from Mr. Herapath to Mr. Gilbert, in which he mentions some experiments he had made, and offers a detail of them by way of "appendage to my Memoir." "I shall have to request," he says, "that you will afterwards have the goodness to inform me, as soon as convenient, whether any obstacles remain to your laying the communication before the Royal Society. Should there be any, I shall have no alternative but to bring it before the public without delay, for my scientific character is so much involved in the fate of this Memoir, that I must either publish it, or be considered by my friends *a mere pretender to science.*" No. VII. is Mr. Gilbert's answer, dated 25th October, 1820, in which he tells his Bristol acquaintance (now, evidently, become 'a pretty considerable bore), "I am not answerable in respect to your paper and the Royal Society"—"There will be elected a new president, and, in fact, a new council, on St. Andrew's Day (30th November)"—"I shall be most ready to put your paper, with the experiments, into the new president's hands," &c. &c. And with this "glad-I-am-done-with-you" valedictory, ends the portion of "the correspondence" now published.

Sir Humphry Davy was the "new president," whose advent was announced by Mr. Gilbert; and it was, I presume, through his treating Mr. Herapath's "Memoir" in the same way as his respected predecessor, that he earned for himself and his memory the honour of Mr. Herapath's abuse. Waiting for such light as the sequel of the correspondence may throw on the matter,

I remain, Sir,
    Your obedient servant,
        PHILO DAVY.

Camden Hill, May 1st, 1837.

THE "SUPERINTENDENT GENERAL" AND HIS "INTENDED" RAILWAYS.

Extract from Mr. Herapath's Evidence before the Committee on the South Eastern Railway.

"You say that you are at present superintendent general of about 300 or 400 miles? Yes.

"State what railroads they are? The Exeter and Salisbury, the Plymouth and and Falmouth lines; another is the Salisbury, Romsay, and Southampton; AND OF COURSE THE DOVER.

"Have any of these been executed? They are, like yours, to be sanctioned by Parliament; *they are lines intended.*

"How long have they been projected; the Exeter one for instance? The exact number of months I cannot tell; some considerable time. I KNOW THEY HAVE GOT THEIR CAPITAL."

Extract from Report of Select Committee of the House of Commons on the Subscription List to the Dover—one of the said "intended" Lines.

"The Committee proceed to notice other circumstances belonging to the signature of some names to the deed which have come out in evidence during their inquiry.

*   *   *   *   *

"John Herapath, of Kensington, editor and proprietor of the *Railway Magazine,* went to the Kent Railway Office, just at the time the deed was about to be lodged; Mr. Hamond, and, he thinks, Mr. Green, Mr. Colin Smith, and Mr. Lancaster, were present. He thinks that Mr. Hamond and Mr. Green asked him to sign the deed. Some one in the office who asked him to sign, observed, that they would take his signature to the deed for 10,000*l.* *He then signed the name of Spenser Herapath, of Kensington, gentleman, who is a son and a minor, as a subscriber, for* 5,000*l.,* *and of his daughter, Maria Herapath, of Kensington, spinster, who is also a minor, as a subscriber for* 5,250*l.* Mr. Lancaster saw this done, and put his initials to the signatures.

"The same John Herapath, in May or June last, signed the name of his son, Captain Alfred Herapath, of Bristol, then a minor, but now of age (at his son's request, as John Herapath states), as a subscriber for 5,250*l.*"

MR. HERAPATH'S LOVE OF TRUTH.— ONE PROOF MORE.

"It is thought fitting to give this public challenge to you to *prove,* not assert, any thing of which, either as a man of science or a man of honour, he (Mr. Herapath) has any reason to be ashamed."—*Veritas, Mech. Mag., April* 29.

In the newspapers of the last month, there appeared the following advertisement:—

"*Eastern Counties Railway from London to Norwich and Yarmouth, by Romford Chelmford, Colchester, and Ipswich.*

"The directors have great pleasure in acquainting the proprietary, that the works OF THE FIRST DIVISION OUT OF LONDON of this

important undertaking are in full progress; that the first call has been so well paid up, that the Board do not anticipate the necessity of making any further call on the shareholders during the present pressure; and that the number of shares now registered amount to 61,225.

"By order of the Board,
J. C. ROBERTSON, SEC.

4, Adelaide Place, London Bridge, April 10, 1837.

In a monthly journal "by John Herapath, Esq.," there is the following commentary on the above advertisement:—

"It is pompously advertised that the works 'of this important undertaking are in *full progress.*" From another quarter, we learn that 500 men are employed. Supposing this to be literally true, it would make, the line being 126 miles long, not quite four men to a mile, if spread over the line,—a very peaceable distance indeed for them. Why, it is hardly a man to three acres of the land the Company proposed to take, and therefore about half enough to keep the weeds down in summer. Not long since, the Birmingham Company employed between 10,000 and 11,000 men on the line alone of 112 miles, and they have now 3,000 on 134 miles. The Eastern Counties have not a twentieth of the former number, or more than one-sixth of the latter on a line fourteen miles longer, and yet publish that the works are 'in *full* progress'!"

The reader will at once detect the *wilful omission,* on which the whole point of this miserable commentary turns, " *First division out of London ;*"—the " works" of that division only are stated in the Company's advertisement to be " *in full progress.*"

Preceding and following the same commentary, there are some personal observations on the Secretary of the Company, which are only here noticed for the purpose of mentioning, that they have been referred to a tribunal which takes them for the present out of the jurisdiction of the press.

BALLOONING.

Sir,—Since the airy flight of Mr. Green and his friends to Germany, public attention has been called to numerous suggestions for rendering practicable the travelling by means of aerostatic machines to any given point, and thus making them really useful; the mere going up and down, and driving before the wind, being as old as the very first experiment fifty years ago; perhaps Mr. Green might be induced to step out of the beaten track, if any practicable scheme could be devised to accomplish this object, and his nerve and experience would greatly assist. If you think there is any thing new or likely to be useful to those who are pursuing this enterprise in the accompanying suggestions, perhaps you will find a corner for them.

I should propose that the balloon be made with flat sides, exactly like a Macin-

Fig. 1.

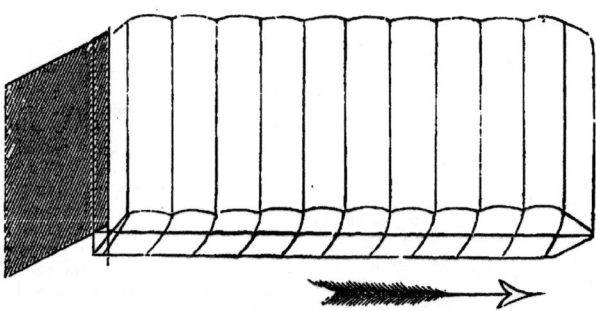

tosh cushion, as in fig. 1; or that it should assume the form of a hollow cylinder, having the same internal structure as the cushion, to prevent the interior of the cy-

Fig. 2.

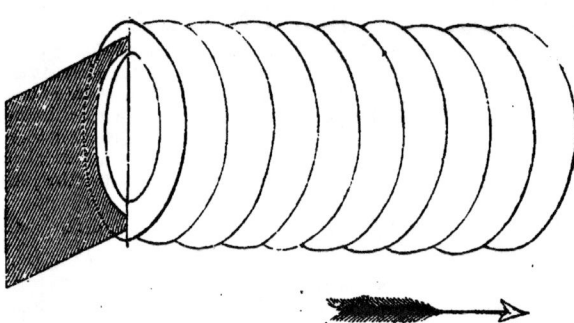

linder from collapsing, as in fig. 2; in other words, the cylinder would have the appearance of one of these cushions sewed together at the two edges, and then inflated. To a balloon of either of these forms, I should attach a large rudder to be acted upon by the persons in the car, or in the cylindrical balloon a man or two might be stationed in its interior to manage the helm; for want of time I omit many things that have occurred to me as to their structure and management, conceiving they would suggest themselves to persons conversant with the subject; contenting myself with attaching a rough sketch of my balloons, and merely stating that my object has been to reduce the resistance in front, and to expose a large surface at the stern, that may be rendered neutral by keeping it in the direction of the balloons course, or turning it in either direction, so as to alter that course; conceiving that the wind striking against a rudder projecting at right angles far beyond the sides of the vessel would have that effect. If desirable, a valve might be added to the cylinder, so as to close the opening altogether when the wind is fair, but I doubt whether this would be found of much use, but in cases of meeting with a sluggish gale, a sail might be hoisted to assist the propulsion.   LANA.

MERRYWEATHER'S PORTABLE FIRE-ESCAPE LADDER. — MR. WIVELL'S CHARGE OF PIRACY REFUTED.

Sir,—In the communication which you have honoured Mr. Wivell by inserting in your last number, he runs full tilt at *" a pair of wheels,"* which Mr. Merryweather employs on his improved escape-ladders ; being well aware that it would be altogether useless to attempt to deny their *utility*, he claims the invention, and endeavours to appropriate to himself all the *merit* of their employment; with how much justice, the following statement will shew.

It was at the memorable conflagration of the two Houses of Parliament, while assisting to raise the escape-ladders which saved the lives of the Earl of Munster and some others, that the idea of employing wheels on the top of *these ladders* first occurred to me, and their use was suggested by the boldness of the architectural projections which then impeded the ascent of the joined ladders. After maturely considering the matter, I sent a drawing and description of a top ladder-joint with wheels, to the Committee of the London Fire Establishment, which plan was subsequently published in your 592nd number for December 13th, 1834. Now, Sir, I would ask, whether Mr. Merryweather would be likely to adopt the wheels from seeing Mr. Wivell's exhibition in the vestry of St. Pancras in

1836, when my published plan was in his possession upwards of fourteen months before ?

At page 10, Mr. Wivell says, " in the early part of the year 1829, I gave some attention to fire-escapes ;" or as he has it in his published lectures, " I entered profoundly into this subject;" at which time, he states, he had never seen an escape of any kind. This, if true, is unaccountably strange, and ignorance of what had been previously done may form an excuse for some portions of Mr. Wivell's subsequent line of conduct. One thing is quite certain, namely, that a little retrospective inquiry would, even at this time, greatly benefit our six-years-old inventor.

It was in consequence of the numerous melancholy loss of lives that occurred in the metropolis during the years 1827 and 1828, that the subject of escape from fire created a great sensation, and was discussed at such length in your ninth and following volumes, as to elicit commendatory notices from the public journals and contemporary periodicals. During the summer of 1828, the first society for preventing loss of life by fire was established; numberless public and private exhibitions of fire-escapes took place, and lectures were delivered on the subject by various able professors. Where Mr. Wivell was all this time, does not appear; but we have his word, that he knew nothing of what was then going forward.

With respect to Mr. Wivell's claims to *originality*, I may just observe, that in 1828, Mr. Glass, in his adaptation of his improved chimney-sweeping apparatus to the purpose of a fire-escape, employed the jointed fishing-rod elevator with a pair of wheels on the top ; precisely the same as Mr. Wivell's *true original* of 1829 ! Mr. Davies employed a similar elevator for his divergent-rope escape, exhibited in January and February, 1829 ! Wheels were also employed on several of the escapes exhibited at a public meeting of the Society before mentioned in February, 1829, especially on the top of a ladder-escape submitted by Mr. Hudson, the founder of the Society !

Mr. Wivell took up the subject of fire-escapes at the beginning of 1829, and states that he suffered the loss of a years' time in the completion of his machines, so that they must have been in an incomplete state when exhibited in August; the fact is, that Mr. Glass, Mr. Davies, Mr. Wivell, and Mr. Merryweather, were nearly contemporary, and their apparatus was in some respects similar. Mr. Merryweather's closely resembled that of Mr. Glass, while Mr. Wivell's was most like Mr. Davies's. In the two last named machines, dependence was placed upon some person being at the window above, to take hold of the escape and attach it to some suitable object, while the escapes of Messrs. Glass and Merryweather had the merit of being independent of any previous provision, or of any personal effort from the parties in danger. All these, and several other similar contrivances, however, have been consigned to he tomb of all the Capulets, by the introduction of improved machines, infinitely adapted to the objects in view.

I can readily believe, that each of the parties I have named are entitled to originality of invention; that all of them produced their respective contrivances without any knowledge of what the others were doing. Were I, however, to adopt the uncharitable and ungenerous language of Mr. Wivell, I should be compelled to say that *his escape* was a " direct copy" of Mr. Davies's " *true original.*"

Mr. Wivell has a most undoubted right " to do what he likes with his own," even to the extent of paying a good round sum for permission to introduce his fire-escape into the last new pantomine, or of adopting any other equally expensive and unlikely mode of giving all due publicity to his efforts. He may rest assured, however, that this sort of notoriety will never compensate for want of merit in the machine, nor will he in any way forward his own interests by endeavouring to depreciate the merits of more successful rivals.

After what has been stated in this communnication, perhaps Mr. Wivell will see the great impropriety of talking about " mechanical powers that require the united help of others," and will in future scrupulously avoid all mention of " borrowed robes." With respect to the former, he might take a useful lesson; as for the latter, he comes so late into the field, that the tables will be inevitably turned against him whenever he talks about *piracy.*

I would also recommend him to understand the exact nature of his own inventions, and endeavour to make himself acquainted with the true production of others, and not again commit himself by saying, as he has done in the case of Merryweather's elevator, it is " in every respect like mine," when such is not the case.

Should Mr. Wivell disregard these friendly hints, and reject this useful advice, he may expect to continue lamenting the loss of time and money, and frequently find himself repeating his singular exclamation, " I am at a loss to guess why my exertions for the welfare of the public have hitherto received no patronage!"

I am, sir, yours respectfully,
WM. BADDELEY.

April 11, 1837.

THE PENNY CYCLOPÆDIA.
LETTERS B AND C.

Never surely was anything more unhappily named than the " Penny Cyclopædia." Hardly had it emerged into notice, before, by regularly publishing a double number every week, its price was raised to twopence, and from twopence it soon rose in the same way to threepence. Even the penny plea that might, until then have been in a manner maintained, that by charging no more than a penny for each sheet, some right to the title was still made good, was at the same time utterly knocked on the head by a measure which gives a strong idea of the good faith and liberal commercial spirit of the Useful Knowledge Society. The singular measure was now adopted (for what reason we could never learn,) of publishing the parts at a quicker rate· than the numbers, so that those who chose to take the work weekly, instead of monthly, had a fair prospect of finding themselves in the middle, about the time the purchasers of parts arrived at the end. By this very ingenious arrangement the general body of the readers was of course driven to prefer the parts, and here, a new principle, a great favorite of the Society's came into action. In each twelvepenny part of the *Penny* Cyclopædia, only eleven sheets of letter press were given, the additional penny thus levied on its purchasers, being stated to be due for the four pages of brown-paper cover occupied with advertisements for Rowland's Macassar

Oil, Harvey's Anti-Drastic Aperient Pills, &c. &c. The purchasers might have replied indeed, that by taking a shillingsworth, instead of a pennyworth at once, they considered that they occasioned to the parties who published, a saving of time and trouble, much more than equivalent to the cost of a wrapper filled up with advertisements of every description that offered; and the simple fact of no other firm's making such a charge, but that of Brougham, Charles Knight and Co., sufficiently proves the correctness of the view. However just these deductions might be, the letter-press deduction was made, and the title of Penny Cyclopædia rendered more absurd than ever. Shortly afterwards the price of the parts was raised to eighteen-pence, and only sixteen sheets of letter-press given, the purchaser being thus mulcted of another penny, on account forsooth of the cost of sewing. Nay, there seems some intention of carrying the system still further, but in a still more stealthy way. In part 50, for March, price 1s. 6d., only fourteen sheets were given, and it was stated in the wrapper that the next part would contain eighteen, to make up for the deficiency. In part 51, for April, we find, however, only sixteen sheets, the usual number, and neither in the wrapper nor anywhere else do we see a word of apology. It may be said, that in making this strict inquisition after pennies, we are " cutting too close"— that the work is still cheap at eighteen-pence, for sixteen, or even for fourteen sheets. We feel no disposition to deny this; but we do feel in common with the world in general, a great indisposition to have our money wrested from us " by any indirection." After the flourish of trumpets that was made about publishing a cyclopædia for only a penny a sheet, an absolute penny and nothing but a penny—with the penny principle indelibly branded, as it were, into the work by means of its very title, after this, the extraction of one additional farthing from the pockets of the purchaser, is neither more or less than a breach of contract. Besides, we must remember that " every little makes a mickle." If we take the number of purchasers of the Penny Cyclopædia at only 15,000 (or about a twelfth of what has been stated as the number of supporters of its kindred magazine) this alone will make the overcharge of twopence per monthly part amount to the respectable sum of *fifteen hundred pounds a year*, to not one farthing of which has the Society any right.

There is another point in which the original principle has also been lost sight of. The extent of the work as first projected was to be eight volumes. At the time the letter A was concluded, we pointed out, that if continued upon the same scale, the Cyclopædia must at least occupy forty. The scale increased instead of decreasing, and while A had *only* taken up two volumes and about two fifths, to B the editors gave two and three quarters. By this time, however, the publisher had probably begun to intimate the necessity of " pulling up" a little. In an " advertisement" prefixed to volume the sixth, it is acknowledged that the continuance of the support of the publication had obtained, must depend upon its being completed within a reasonable period, and in a moderate number of volumes. This advertisement will serve as a convenient text for our further remarks. It proceeds thus :—

" It has been the constant endeavour of the editor, and the gentlemen who contribute to the Encyclopædia, to render the articles as concise as was compatible with preserving their value, and experience will now enable them to effect this object more completely than has already been done."

Nothing can seem more ludicrous to a reader of the Cyclopædia, than this attempt on the part of its writers to claim the merit of conciseness, the very last to which they have any pretensions. To say nothing of the article on " Antelopes" in forty-four columns, for which some apology was offered, or that on " Boroughs" in sixty (containing about as much as a common octavo volume,), for which there was none,—considering these two as exceptions, which do not effect the general character of the work, it is notorious that all the articles on so extensive a subject as natural history, always have been, and continue to be, of a most disproportionate length. The notices of quadrupeds are commonly eked out with lengthy extracts from the most modern writers, who have described them; entertaining enough assuredly, but still out of place, " pleasant but wrong." By this means the article "Bison" is made to occupy thirteen columns, the article "Bear" no less than three and twenty, and so on in proportion. With shells, insects, fossils, &c. the case is worse; the superintendent of that department has not only the fault of being lengthy, but the crime of being tedious; his researches are of the dullest, dryest and dreariest description, of no interest whatever to any but a confirmed naturalist, and possessing no claim whatever to appearance in a cyclopædia of general information. The "value" of these articles would be considerably increased by shortening them nineteen-twentieths. And in addition to these established encroachers upon the space of the Cyclopædia, there is a third, a minute biographer of Scotch lawyers, whose articles are quite unsusceptible of any improvement, but ought never by any chance to appear in the Encyclopædia at all. To resume.

"Added to this, many of the articles already published, are necessarily of greater length than those which are to come; for advantage has been taken in most cases to explain the general principles of a subject on the first notice of a word connected with it; and in many instances it has been considered advisable to give under one head, or title such a general view of a subject as will render it sufficient in many subsequent heads or titles to refer to the general article."

This assertion unfortunately happens not to be correct, for the general method of the Penny Cyclopædia is not to assemble a number of articles under one head, but to distribute one into several. Under the title "Architecture," for instance, we in most Cyclopædias find the whole subject treated of; in this, we are, after a few general observations occupying two pages and a quarter, or about one fifth of the space allotted to an account of the "Bear," referred to *seventeen separate articles* to come, of which at the time this advertisement was published, only one had appeared, and that one of the least consequence. In like manner the article "Bridges" is remarkable, for shortness—occupying only five columns—while that on "Blackfriars Bridge" in particular, takes up three and a quarter, and similar articles on "London," "Southwark" and we know not how

many other bridges may of course be expected to follow. The account of the university, under the head of "Cambridge," is hardly more than a page in length; but hitherto there has been a separate article on each hall, and each college, both there and at Oxford. We need not weary the patience of the reader with more instances. These are, we should think, quite enough to show that the assertion thus positively made, on a subject of which, assuredly the committee ought to be cognizant, is altogether groundless. We proceed.

"Without any material alteration of the present scale as regards the length of the more important articles, the committee feel assured that *somewhat more than a fourth of the whole Cyclopædia is now published,* and they therefore propose that the work shall be completed in eighteen volumes of the present size, and they pledge themselves that it shall not exceed twenty volumes."

The vagueness of language in this passage is remarkable. "Without any *material* alteration, as regards the length of *the more important* articles." It is evident enough, that the writer of the advertisement feels, what he is loth to acknowledge, that the assertion he is just about to make is too, rather too glaring to be received. The committee may indeed decide very comfortably among themselves, that a Cyclopædia which has arrived at the letters Buy, or not quite got through the second letter of the Alphabet, may be fairly considered as having discharged one quarter of its duties, which are to perform the circuit of the whole twenty-six, but it is more than questionable if the public will subscribe to the correctness of such an opinion, based as it is, upon statements like those we have just examined. The real purport of the "advertisement" appears to be this, that the "committee" did at length become sensible of what every body else had discovered before them, that the Cyclopædia was being conducted on a plan of the most immoderate dimensions, and that they resolved thereupon to contract the scale, though still unwilling frankly to acknowledge their mistake. Untaught by their previous experience of the danger of making pledges in the dark, they determined likewise, in the spirit of an Irishman who makes a vow against the " liquor" to tie themselves down to a definite number of volumes, in order, as it were, to take security to themselves against their own irresolution.

And what (to quit the advertisement and return to our original inquiry,) has been the result of all this. The letter C was begun with these protestations of reform; it has now been brought to an end, and it will be found on examination to occupy two volumes and nearly 190 pages, the space occupied by the letter A being two volumes and 220. The first three letters of the alphabet have thus each taken up on an average about two volumes and a half, and the remainder are calculated by " the committee" to require no more than about half a volume each. The calculation is evidently absurd. It is plain that their plan of curtailment has failed, and that either the second pledge must be abandoned like the first, or that the latter part of the Cyclopædia must be " scamped."

And what has led to the failure of the attempt to confine the work in moderate bounds? The editor (if there an editor) has evidently not yielded to his fate without an effort on his part. The geographical articles of the earlier volumes of the Cyclopædia were universally allowed to possess particular excellence. They are now reduced to the level of their brethren in other works of the kind, by apparently, an unceremonious use of the editorial scalping-knife, if, indeed, the original contributor of the chief portion of this department have not retired altogether. The inferiority is unquestionable. One of these articles, for example, affords an excellent instance of a defect which is observable in many other parts of the Cyclopædia. It is that on " Candy," in Ceylon. After a short and dull account of the town, we have a paragraph devoted to its history, in which we are informed, that in the beginning of 1803, a British force entered the Candian territory and took Candy, but on the following June, the garrison, then in a sickly state, was attacked by a native force, and obliged to capitulate. All these disasters of 1803 are related with sufficient minuteness, and we are then left to suppose, that since that time the Candians have " ruled the roast" in Candy. Not a hint is given of what is in fact the case, that in 1819, sixteen years after, the English, at the invitation

of the Candians themselves, again entered their territory, dethroned their king, took possession of his territories, and have ever since retained them; that several improvements have been effected there by Sir Wilmot Horton, and that the formerly barbarous inhabitants have now some tincture of civilization. In this article in fact, the writer has omitted precisely what was most interesting, and it would be well for the Cyclopædia if this were the only instance of the kind. Unfortunately, this rather considerable defect is constantly recurring. Under the head of " Cape of Good Hope," for instance, in the same part with Candy, we are told of that colony's being settled by the Dutch; but we do not hear a word of its now being in possession of the English! Still in the same part, in the article on " Canterbury," we hear nothing of its having been, for upwards of three hundred years, the principal place of pilgrimage in England, and in that capacity renowned all over Europe. Again, in the same part, under the head " Carolina, South," which professes to contain a history of that state, we find nothing of the agitation on the question of nullification, which constitutes the most interesting part of the recent history of the United States. We could go on enumerating more instances of this kind, but four of this magnitude in one part are probably enough.

The articles on Biography are now, as they always have been, inferior to those on Geography, and in much the same proportion. The lives of foreigners are often written with the most incredible carelessness. Thus, in that of Henry, Count von Bruhl, the Saxon minister, his character is quoted, as given by Frederick the Great. who is about as good an authority on that subject as Bonaparte on the character of Lord Castlereagh. " Bruhl," we are afterwards told, " involved Saxony in a war against Frederick II., who made the whole Saxon army prisoners in the camp of Pirna, while the King and Bruhl escaped into Poland. After the peace they returned to Dresden, where Augustus soon after died." To say nothing of the omission of all dates in this statement, it may be remarked, that the struggle in which Bruhl is stated to have involved Saxony, was commenced by Frederick the Great without any declaration of war, and that this contest, which from the statement of the writer in the Cyclopædia, would appear to be nothing but an insignificant scuffle between Prussia and Saxony, was in truth the Seven Years War, not only carried on between these two powers, but by Austria, Russia, Denmark, Sweden, Spain, France and England, and fought with desperate energy in all quarters of the world, with results which still materially affect the the destinies of Europe, America and Asia. So much for this enlightened historian with his " Bruhl involved Saxony in a war." The literary information is often as imperfect as the political. We are told of Bürger the German poet, that " his Leonora has been translated into English—Bürgers Leonora by Wm. Robert Spencer, fol. London, 1796." We beg to inform the biographer that Bürger's Leonora, or rather as it is usually written Lenora, has been eight times translated into English; one of the said translations having been the first production of an obscure Edinburgh lawyer, who afterwards attained some notoriety by writing " Religious discourses," and pamphlets on the banking system—one Walter Scott. This life of Bürger is remarkable for other omissions, which are not here worth particularizing. Our own poets fare little better. In the short and scanty notice of Bloomfield, there is no mention of his " May Day with the Muses." The lives of Crabbe, of Coleridge, &c. are written with a strange abruptness and disagreeable vagueness of statement, which afford a model of what a short biographical sketch ought not to be.

The principle of curtailment however, has been carried still further than this. These omissions are small ones, even taken all together, compared with one gigantic gap in the articles of the letter C. There is no notice whatever on the important subject of " CARPENTRY." As, when the Cyclopædia was first announced, it was recommended as especially calculated from its cheapness, and the style in which it was to be written, for the patronage of the mechanic and the artisan, it is needless to add any comment.

In spite of all this, the letter C has still, as we have already remarked, attained to a length altogether disproportionate with the intended extent of the

work. This is easily explained. Whatever other biographies have been shorn of their fair proportions, the biographies of Scotch lawyers, whether advocates or writers to the signet, have been as yet protected from the sacrilegeous hand of mutilation; however the descriptions of lands and cities may have been docked, those of " Cryptaceous Mollusks," " Culicides," " Cephalopoda," and so forth, still flourish in their original luxuriance. The articles on natural history, are in fact the consuming canker of the work. Without actual inspection a reader can hardly form an idea of their ludicrous minuteness. We must for the sake of illustration, quote one specimen; the following is the description of " Mactra" a genus of " Fossil Amphidesmata," belonging to the family of " Conchacea," under which latter head we find it:—

" Animal oval, somewhat thick, with the borders of the mantle thick and simple, furnished posteriorly with two tubes, but little elongated and united; branchial lamina small and nearly equal; foot oval, trenchant, very long, angular. Shell transverse, inequilateral subtrigonal, sometimes a little gaping at the sides; urnbones protuberent; hinge with one cardinal tooth, folded into the the shape of the letter V, the point being nearest the umbo and the branches diverging from it; posterior to this, and very close to it, is a very thin sharp tooth : sometimes the branches of the folding tooth are separated at the base, forming two diverging teeth; ligamental pit immediately behind the angular tooth, and projecting within the shell. Lateral teeth, two on each side in one valve, one on each side in the other, diverging from the umbones, and very near the margin, thin, mostly elongated. and the inner ones more prominent than the outer, but in some species very short, in the thicker species perpendicularly striated. Muscular impressions two, lateral distant; pallial impression with a small sinus. Ligament consisting of two portions (as usual) one, by far the larger, internal; the other external. In some species the umbones are separated, and the ligament forms a deep pit extending both within and without to the point of the beaks; of this *Mactra Spengleri* is an example."

We dare say our readers will excuse our quoting the scientific divisions of this genus into *Mactra gigantea, Mactra trigonella*, and so forth, including one which might seem to bear some covert reference to the minute naturalists of the Cyclopædia, *Mactra stultorum.* We are confident likewise, that they will require no further explanation of the causes why a Cyclopædia, which thinks it necessary to treat in this style of every fossil shell in existence, should appear disposed to prolong its continuance to the " crack of doom."

To conclude : if there be really a committee to whom the destinies of the Penny Cyclopædia are confided, the best thing they can do, would seem to be to send their writers of natural history about their proper business of compiling separate cyclopædias of oryctology, and all the rest of the ologies, for oryctologists and all the rest of the ologists. They might then give a greater extension to their articles on history, biography, geography, and above all, *on the applied sciences* and the *useful arts*, and might thus, possibly, without allowing the latter part of the work to present too glaring a contrast to the former, (except in the natural history, the change in which would be hailed by their readers in general with the extreme of pleasure) complete the undertaking, not in twenty, but in thirty volumes.

This the committee might do, but, as before intimated, there seems good reasons for doubting if there be any committee that troubles itself about the matter. The list of committee-men which appears on the cover, is a very clumsy farce. Under the head of " Madrid," we have found for the last year or two the name of " *Signor* A. Munoz de Sotomayer," who most assuredly, if he feel any interest in the credit of the concern, would have written off before now to inform these learned Thebans, that though Signor is certainly the Italian term for " Mr"—the Spanish equivalent is " Senor." Again, under the head of " Calcutta," Lord William Bentick is still regularly put down as a member of the " Local Committee," though one would think it notorious to every one who wields a pen, that he has long been succeeded in his office of Governor General, by Lord Auckland, has returned to Europe, and now sits in Parliament as M. P. for Glasgow. A list drawn up in such a state as this, of course proves nothing, but that the parties mentioned cannot by any possibility act as committee-men, whatever use they may allow to be made of their names.

ON THE HEIGHT ATTAINABLE BY BALLOONS. BY MR. CHARLES GREEN.

(From the *Times.*)

Sir,—A paragraph has lately appeared in several of the newspapers, professing to be a calculation of some scientific gentlemen, that if the great Vauxhall balloon were to be fully inflated with pure hydrogen gas it might be made to attain an elevation of 15 miles, or, in other words, about three times the altitude of the highest mountain in the world.

With all due deference to these scientific gentlemen, such a calculation is quite erroneous ; and, without wishing to indulge in the marvellous (which persons on subjects of this description are more or less inclined to), permit me to state the result of my own experiments and observations, as fully proved by the barometer when applied by me to aerostation. If the balloon on leaving the earth have the mercury in the tube of the barometer standing at 30 inches, the mercury will, at an elevation of one mile, have fallen below 25 inches ; at two miles below 21 in. ; at three miles below 17 inches ; and at four, below 14 inches. It is therefore evident that the atmospheric pressure on the mercury at an altitude of a little more than three miles and a half is reduced from 30 inches to 15 inches, thereby showing a reduction of one half of the whole atmospheric pressure : | the consequence of which is, that the gas in the balloon during its ascent to this elevation would have gradually expanded and occupy nearly double the space of that which it did on the earth's surface ; it then follows in regard to the Vauxhall balloon, which contains 70,000 cubic feet when fully inflated on leaving the earth, that after having attained the above elevation of 3½ miles, one half of the gas must have been allowed from time to time to escape by means of the valves, so as to allow for this gradual expansion of gas, and likewise to prevent the balloon from bursting ; the effect of which loss of gas is, that the original ascending power of the machine has been by this time reduced to one half, and in order to prevent the balloon from decending, the aeronaut has been obliged to part with one half of his ballast and weight that he had originally taken with him.

It is therefore obvious that no advantage (except in the balloon's appearance) is gained by the aeronaut in having the machine fully distended on its first leaving the earth, and that if his only object be to attain a great altitude, it is better to ascend in the first instance with the balloon only half inflated, by means of which the trouble to the aeronaut of having to part with gas and ballast is thereby saved and, indeed, even in a pecuniary point of view, there would be a saving of one half the expense for gas, which would not exceed 120*l.*, inasmuch as the cost of generating 70,000 cubic feet of pure hydrogen gas would amount to 240*l.* The legitimate induction from the foregoing facts amounts to this, that the Vauxhall balloon cannot be made (by one person only to ascend with it) to attain a greater elevation than 10 miles, on account of the great expansibility of the gas at that altitude, arising from the extreme diminution of atmospheric pressure, as it would at that height occupy by its expansion six times the space or volume of that which it did on the earth's surface ; consequently, there would then be left in the balloon 12,000 cubic feet, which, although at that height it would be quite sufficient to fully distend it, would be no more than sufficient to support the weight of the balloon, netting, car, appendage, and aeronaut.

In the above calculations, no allowance has been made for atmospheric temperature, which is continually varying, according to the seasons and other local circumstances, but still not sufficient to make any material alteration worth notice.

                              CHARLES GREEN.
April, 1837.

NOTES AND NOTICES.

Steam Navigation of the Atlantic.—Every thing promises that it will not be long ere the Atlantic is ploughed as regularly by steamers as it is now by sailing vessels; indeed, all things considered, the strangest thing about the matter is, that the object should not have been effected many years ago. Steam boats, of a peculiar construction, are now building at New York for the Packet service, between that port and Liverpool ; and another is constructing at Blackwall for an English company, who do not, however, anticipate that they shall be able to commence operations before the Spring of of 1838. Meanwhile a steamer plies regularly between London and Jamaica. It has, we believe, performed the trip several times, although the fact has attracted very little attention. Of the vast utility of the improvement no doubt can be entertained, especially at the very moment when, notwithstanding the anxiety of the mercantile world ofr American intelligence, the sailing packets have been detained by contrary winds, in sight of the English shores, a longer period than might have sufficed for the whole voyage. One ship, during the recent easterly winds, it is said, was detained in soundings no less than thirty-five days ; the trip from Liverpool to New York has often been effected in thirteen.

Fine Arts—The Napoleon Medal.—The French medal machine engravers have just produced a new specimen of their art, on the same scale as their well-known portrait of Louis Philippe. The head of Napoleon occupies the centre, and this is surrounded by a series of medallions of his most celebrated marshals ; most of whose faces, by the way, bear considerable resemblance to those of the monkey tribe, especially that of Marshal Ney. The whole has evidently been very elaborately executed, but the effect, upon the whole, is not equal to that of some of their former productions. We think Mr. Bate would find no difficulty in surpassing it, and hope it will not be long before he enters the " field in force." In such matters, delays are dangerous, as he has had pretty good reason for knowing.

Cheap Travelling.—Such is the extent to which competition is carried among the owners of the Northern steamers, that is possible to perform the voyage from London to Edinburgh, four hundred miles *by land*, for no more than *seven shillings!* This is effected by making Hull a half-way-house, the lowest fare to which, from London, is *two shillings* only !

The March of Science anticipated.—From Sir Robert Walpole's Private Correspondence we extract the following morceau.—" My present and sole occupation is planting, in which I have made great progress. The deliberation with which trees grow is extremely inconvenient to my natural impatience. I lament living in so barbarous an age, when we are come to so little perfection in gardening. I am persuaded that 150 years hence it will be as common to remove oaks 150 years old as it is now to transplant tulip roots. I have even begun a treatise or panegyric on the great discoveries made by posterity in all arts and sciences, wherein I shall particularly descant on the great and cheap convenience of making trout rivers. I shall talk of a secret for roasting a wild boar and a whole pack of hounds alive, without hurting them, so that the whole chase may be brought up to table ; and for this secret, the Duke of Newcastle's grandson, if he happen to have a son, is to give a hundred thousand pounds. Then the delightfulness of having whole groves of humming birds, tame tigers taught to fetch and carry, pocket spying glasses to see all that is doing in China, with a thousand other toys, which we now look upon as impracticable, and which pert posterity would laugh in one's face for staring at, while they are offering rewards for perfecting discoveries, of the principles of which we have not the least conception." With respect to Walpole's first idea, his prophecy has been fulfilled to the letter. Sir James Stuart, of Allanton, some time ago, invented a method of transplanting grown trees. Allanton, in Lanarkshire, a naked and unadorned estate, was, in a few years, by its proprietor's ingenuity, converted into a delightful, well wooded, country residence !

☞ *British and Foreign Patents taken out with economy and despatch ; Specifications, Disclaimers, and Amendments, prepared or revised ; Caveats entered ; and generally every Branch of Patent Business promptly transacted.*
A complete list of Patents from the earliest period (15 *Car. II.* 1675,) *to the present time may be examined. Fee* 2s. 6d. ; *Clients, gratis.*

LONDON : Printed and Published by W. A. Robertson, at the Mechanics' Magazine Office, No. 6, Peterborough-court, between 185 and 186, Fleet-street.—Sold by G. W. M. Reynolds, Proprietor of the French, English, and American Library, 55, Rue Neuve, Saint Augustin, Paris.

𝔐𝔢𝔠𝔥𝔞𝔫𝔦𝔠𝔰' 𝔐𝔞𝔤𝔞𝔷𝔦𝔫𝔢,

MUSEUM, REGISTER, JOURNAL, AND GAZETTE.

| No. 718. | SATURDAY, MAY 13, 1837. | Price 3*d*. |

Fig. 1.   Fig. 2.

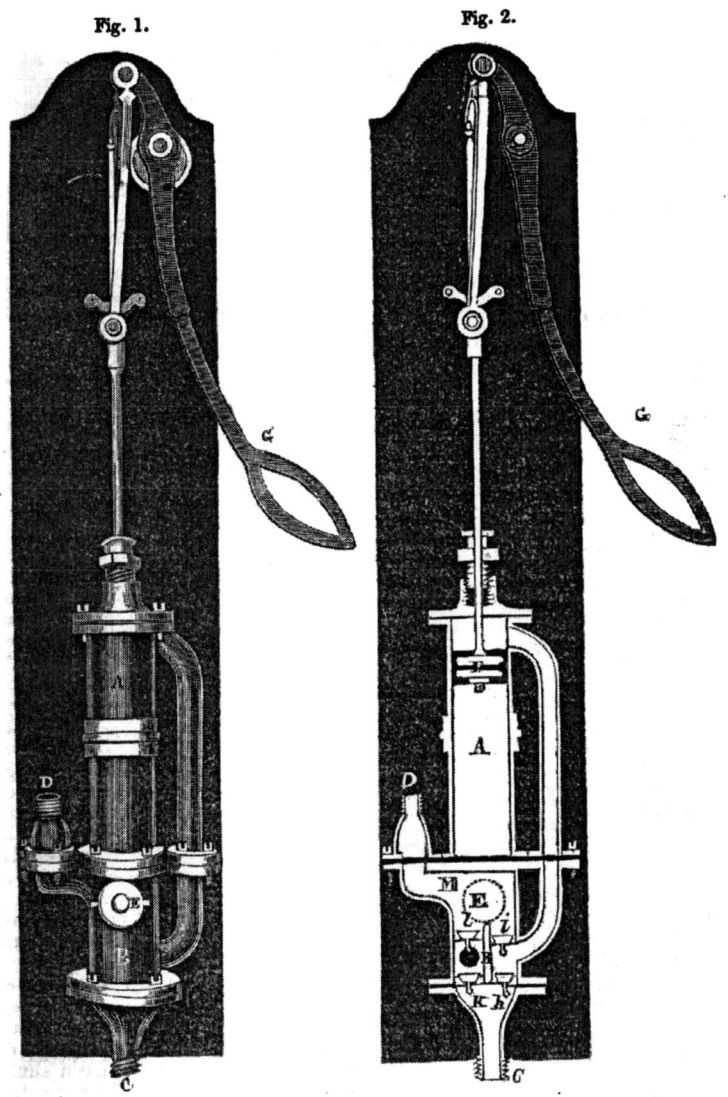

LAMBERT'S PATENT DOUBLE ACTION PUMP.

Sir,—When calling the attention of your numerous readers to the peculiar advantages offered by the form of a pump called after its inventor, M. de la Hire, which has a double action, I observed, that " we have but few instances of its adoption, and considering its advantages it is surprising that it is not more frequently put into practice."*

Although *a model* of this pump nearly always forms part of the apparatus of an hydraulic lecture table, I never knew of the existence of more than one full-sized pump of this description, which, I believe is, to this day, to be seen in the shop-window of a plumber, nearly opposite the church at Newington, Butts. I am induced to suppose, that the somewhat inconvenient and difficult form of construction adopted by M. de la Hire, has had much to do with keeping back this invention from general use, and I am rather confirmed in this opinion, from the circumstance of a more recently invented pump on a similar principle, having already come into very extensive employment.

The accompanying drawings (see front page) represent a patent double-action pump, manufactured by Messrs. Lambert and son, New Cut, Blackfriars Road, in which all the advantages sought to be obtained by M. de la Hire are fully realized, in combination with convenience and even elegance of construction.

Fig. 1 is a front view of Messrs. Lambert's pump; A is the working barrel; B the valve and delivery chamber; C the feed-pipe, and D one of the delivery pipes. There is a second exit at E, furnished with a screwed nosel, and closed with a cap. Fig. 2 exhibits the internal disposition of all the working parts; A, as before, being the barrel—B the valve chamber, etc. F is the metallic piston with cupped leathers. The piston-rod works in an air-tight manner through a stuffing-box at the top of the barrel, its upper end traversing in a guide, and connected by slings to the handle G.

The action of the pump is as follows : on raising the handle G the piston F is depressed, and a vacuum formed in the upper part of the working barrel, in consequence of which, the water, urged

by atmospheric pressure, rushes up the feed pipe from the well, etc., passes through the valve h, and fills the void left by the downward motion of the piston. On reaching the bottom of the barrel, the motion is reversed ; the piston ascends, driving before it the water contained in the upper portion of the cylinder, which passing down the pipe through which it entered, raises the valve i and enters the chamber M. At the same time, the ascent of the piston causes the water to raise the valve k, and pass through another pipe at the back, communicating with the lower part of the barrel. At the next descent of the piston this water comes back again, and raising the valve l, enters the delivery chamber M ; so that the whole contents of the cylinder are expelled both in the up and down strokes of the pump.

In this engine, which differs but little in appearance or expense from the common lifting force-pump, twice the quantity of water is delivered in any given number of strokes, consequently there is only half the wear. The labour, friction and liability to derangement, as compared with the work performed, are greatly diminished ; at the same time, the screwed nosel E affords the opportunity of applying any length of leather-hose and a branch-pipe which furnishes a very powerful and efficient domestic fire engine. The ascending service-pipe is attached to the orifice D, with a stop-cock at any convenient distance above the joint, for shutting off the communication in that direction whenever the hose is employed. Although the stream is continuous without the introduction of an air-vessel, yet when the pump is intended to be frequently employed in this way, it is better to be equipped with that appendage, the stream being more uniform and capable of being directed with much greater precision. A cylindrical air-vessel with hemispherical ends, should be attached at D, and the ascending service-pipe led off from the top of it.

Mr. Lambert has just applied a small pump of similar construction to the purposes of a water-closet, with considerable success ; on raising the handle, the basin is emptied, at the same instant a jet of water rushes in and effects the perfect cleansing ; on depressing the handle, the basin shuts, and a second discharge of water enters

* Vol. 13, page 281.

and remains in the basin till it is again emptied. By means of this arrangement an elevated cistern of water above the closet is dispensed with, an advantage, in many situations of first-rate importance. The water being raised by the party using the closet, is used in the exact quantity and at the precise time it is required, thereby most effectually preventing both loss of labour and waste of water.

In all cases where water has to be raised in large quantities, or to considerable heights, this pump will be found admirably adapted for the purpose, as well as being an excellent stationary fire-engine for manufactories, theatres, mansions, &c.

I remain Sir,

Yours respectfully,

WM. BADDELEY.

March 15, 1837.

GEOLOGICAL ARGUMENTS IN FAVOUR OF MACKINTOSH'S THEORY OF THE UNIVERSE.

Sir,—I said in my last letter that the deposition of a moon was the only reasonable mode of accounting for the varied elevations of strata, and that the doctrine of central heat being the only cause, is wrong; and if I do not intrude too much, I will occupy a part of your pages with remarks on this head. That the strata has undergone considerable alterations, both in position and character, since its first deposit or formation, is a fact which cannot be disputed, and it has received the sanction of all geologists, who, however, disagree as to the causes of the varied arrangement of different beds, as also of their contortions and elevations. The strata all over the world present an appearance of having at one period been subjected to a violent turmoil, accompanied with great pressure; and geologists have canvassed many a theory in vain to account for these effects, the causes for which combined, have never yet been found. If we for a moment reject the pressure, and confine ourselves to invent a theory which shall only account for the fractures and elevations, we may, as many geologists fancy they have done, soon bring to light causes actually sufficient to explain these phenomena ; but if the contortions of some

of the strata, occasioned as they are by violent pressure, be taken into account, the best of the yet invented theories is at fault. The theories of Werner and of Hutton have in a great measure given way to others of a more modern school. The Huttonian idea that there were alternate periods of disturbance and repose, or paroxysmal convulsions at particular periods, though supported, and in a great measure revived, by a Playfair—with the Wernerian, that all the materials of the globe were once held in solution by water, have in most instances given way to theories of a medium character; most geologists of the present day attributing all the effects we now see to causes at present in operation. But are we to suppose that things were always as they are at present, or that in past ages no more causes were in operation than there are now ? Are we to have now, when society so prides itself on the increased scientific attainments of its members, the same trouble in introducing to the world a theory which accounts for the irregularities of the strata by the deposition of a satellite, as men of the past age had in shewing that the world was more than 6,000 years old, or that its temperature was formerly much greater than what it now is ? Are the theories of a Cuvier, a De la Beche, a Lyell, a Buckland, a Ure, or a Penn, as perfect as it is possible for man to make them ; or have they their defects, and must they consequently give way to those of more matured growth, founded on the experience of these theories, and all the new and important facts which are every day being brought to light ? I think as others gave place to these, so these in their turn must give place to such as may follow after; their known defects eradicated, and a new theory founded which future generations must criticise and add new features to, occasioned by the development of new facts.

That a resisting medium exists in space is now rendered extremely probable, and may be proved more especially by observations on comets, whose tails are often curved, bending towards the region the comet has left; and also, as Sir J. Herschell expresses it, that the periods are constantly diminishing; or, in other words, the mean distance from the sun, or the major axis of the ellipse, dwindling, by slow but regular degrees.

G 2

If it be true that there is a resisting medium, it follows that all the planets, with their attendant satellites, must eventually fall into the sun, or that their orbits will slowly but gradually decrease, and, consequently, there must be some change in their relative heat. Now, if the sun be the source of heat, it follows that the nearer the earth, or any of the planets, are to it, the warmer they will be: but geology teaches us the reverse of this; it teaches that the earth in every part was hotter than it at present is, even in the tropics; for it would be impossible for the fossil animals and plants which are now found in the coldest regions, to have grown with such luxuriance in situations which now will not even produce grass, and scarcely moss, unless a much greater amount of heat had existed than there does at present. Then, if the planets do approach the sun on account of the resisting medium, and they at the same time get colder, it follows that they possessed more innate heat, and that the strata were less both in number and thickness; or that they were better conductors of heat than they are at the present time; and it is to this innate heat that geologists have attributed most of the geological phenomena. However some of your readers may laugh at the idea of a resisting medium, and the consequent approach of the planets to the sun, as well as the satellites to their primaries, I know I am supported by most astronomers, and the greater number of scientific men, who are capable of judging; and, being thus supported, it does not become me, in a paper like the present, to reiterate opinions so well known and so generally received.

I have previously intimated, that modern geologists attributed all the phenomena by which the more ancient con-

tinents were broken up, and some parts sunk in the sea, while others were upheaved in some cases to considerable altitudes, to irruptive powers; and that this was endeavoured to be proved by a reference to volcanic agency, and the eruptions of melted matter, as basalt, &c. I acknowledge, that this may be the cause of many phenomena in which the mass has only undergone an alteration in altitude—(as was the case in Chili on Tuesday, November the 19th, 1822, when, according to the observations of Mrs. Maria Graham, the alteration of the level at Valpariso was about three feet, and at Quintero, about four feet; she also thought, after comparing several ancient lines of beach, that the coast had risen to the height of fifty feet);—but to say that the same cause produced those very immense inequalities of the earth's surface (compared to the rise of the land in Chili, which is one of the greatest alterations of level which history records), as those ranges of mountains called the Andes, the Himalayan Alps, &c., is, in my opinion, totally wrong; and, as a proof that the eruptive force is unable of itself to produce many of the phenomena we see, I shall refer your readers, first, to the contortions of various strata observed in mountainous countries, as in the Alps, and in this kingdom, in some parts of Scotland and Cornwall, in which last cases, it is the primary slates that are so contorted; and secondly, to the coral islands and reefs, which geologists say offer proofs of the elevations of the submarine strata by eruptive submarine forces. In the first place, we will see in what manner the eruptive force could by any possible means have contorted the strata, and that your readers may have some idea of the manner in which some of the strata are so contorted, the accompanying diagram will

Ruchorn.   Blatti.   Riga.

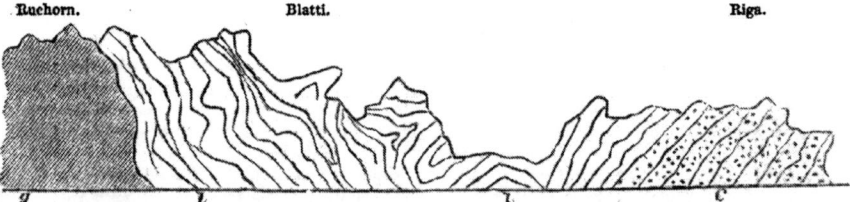

in some manner instruct them. It is a section of the Alps from the Hospice of St. Gothard to the Riga, *g* being gneiss,

l l, limestone, and *c*, a conglomerate; it is from Dr. Lusser, and not at all exaggerated, for in the Alps themselves better sections might be found, in which the causes which fractured and contorted them must have been immensely powerful, and the intensity of a modern earthquake be insignificant when compared to them. If the position of the strata in the above diagram be examined, it is evident that there must have been a powerful lateral pressure; and Sir James Hall has shewn, that to produce contortion by lateral pressure, there *must* be resistance both above and beneath, one of which must yield in a small degree; but in this case the contorted limestone *l l* experiences no resistance from above; and M. De la Beche, in reasoning upon this fact, says, that geologists are quite at a loss to know how this and like contortions were produced without a superincumbent pressure. In endeavouring to explain the cause by which this pressure was removed, he says, " that an immense volume of matter must have indeed been taken away, as the great masses of conglomerate and sandstone on the flanks of the chain, abundantly testify, but how far the amount of this mass would be sufficient for the effects required is not apparent." Now, Sir, it seems to me absurd to think, that if these strata were deposited in or near this position in nearly horizontal beds, as in the first place they must have been, that a !ateral pressure was exerted at *g* or *c*, or by the gneiss and the conglomerate upon the limestone *l l*, and that the required superincumbent pressure should have entirely fled so as not to leave one vestage remaining. Can the doctrine of central heat apply in this case? What power removed the immense mass of rock which must have covered the limestone, and by its weight and consequent pressure contorted the limestone? Would it not, if such an immense mass of rock had existed, (which to produce the pressure it undoubtedly must), have left some trace behind it; can we suppose that every particle has been swept away, and in some cases near the junction, deposited beneath it? For my own part, I cannot suppose such was the case, and I am obliged to look to other sources for information; and at present I have nothing which solves the enigma so well as the fall of a satellite.

I asked in my first letter why the situations at present occupied by great masses of mountains might not be the places where the satellites have been deposited? The phenomena of contortion goes further to prove, that satellites have been deposited, and that these were the places of deposit: the same, and even a greater, amount of pressure is required here to account for the contortion, than was required to flatten the heads and break the teeth of the *crocodilus priscus*, and a pressure would be obtained by the fall of a satellite, fully sufficient to accomplish either of these purposes: and the concussion of two such bodies would very much fracture, the strata and produce contortions of which we have no adequate idea. And, lastly, how is it that the conglomerate, a rock of posterior formation should be tossed over, and plunged beneath the limestone, and appear to support that which once supported it, and from which, the author I have mentioned supposes it has been derived, being part of that which was the superincumbent strata from which the pressure was derived? If any of your readers can account for these phenomena better, than by the deposition of a satellite, let them do so as soon as possible, for if Mr. Mackintosh's theory is wrong, the sooner they refute the arguments I have adduced from geology in its support the better. I am afraid, Sir, I have already been too tedious, and I must defer the second part, relative to the coral islands, till another opportunity.

In the mean time, I remain,

Sir, yours respectfully,

JOSHUA THORN.

April 15th, 1837.

ON THE IDENTITY OF LIGHT, HEAT, AND ELECTRICITY.

Sir,—I am not at present prepared to continue in the direct line I chalked out for myself in my former letter (*Mechanics' Magazine*, 10th December last) on electricity. In the mean time, perhaps, a few loose observations developing some new views of light, or the cause of colour, may not be unacceptable. The agents we call electricity, light, and caloric (considered as bodies) are distinguished from others by the supposed negative quality of imponderability. Many of their effects seem to indicate the identity of all or some of them, or at least a fluid commixture of them. Now, besides imponderability, caloric has two other qualities or capacities, conductibility and radiation, each of which we might from analogy expect to find both in light and electricity. We might indeed find light to be radiant—electricity, to be conductible; but who ever heard of conductible light or of radiant electricity? Attached to the pursuit of analogies, and to Newton's rule, not to admit more causes than are necessary to explain natural appearances, I was led to inquire whether electricity were not conductible light—light, radiant electricity. Whether we develope electricity by friction, or by chemical decomposition, or by the influence of the magnet, it may be made to evolve radiant light. A single, and by no means large, galvanic pair will effect this. Even a penny and a piece of zinc in the mouth, produce the sensation of light in the closed eye, and seem to evidence light as well as electricity to be a constituent of the human body. We can scarcely perform an experiment with electricity, without its connexion with light forcing itself on our notice. How very intimate that connexion appears by every experiment in vacuo! When we discharge electricity over dry chalk, paper, &c., light is emitted for several minutes after from its path. Mr. Hawksbee, by rapid rotation, and with his hand for a rubber, excited an exhausted globe, the rubbing part covered with a considerable thickness of sealing-wax, and the figure of his hand was distinctly seen through that otherwise opaque substance. We even call one of the grandest effects of electricity by the significant name *lightning*. The production of light when electricity passes suddenly through air has been attributed to the compression of the latter by its collapse after the passage of the spark. It may with equal reason be attributed to the air compressing the stream of electricity, and forcing the light out of that. The appearance of the spark in a (comparative) vacuum, seems an answer to both suppositions. Its rapid motion would, one would think, be sufficient to cause undulations in all the surrounding light-causing fluid of other bodies, and thus produce the sensation of light in the eye. It seems to me by no means improbable,

that if the instantaneous light-producer were furnished with an insulating piston, rod, and stand, electricity might be produced in considerable quantity by the compression. That electricity (as well as light and caloric) exists in large quantities in air, is shewn by a point affixed on the insulated rubber of the electrifying machine. There are very strong indications of the existence of all three in union with every particle of ponderable matter. Sir Isaac Newton believed in the existence of a fluid at the surfaces of bodies. Franklin proved the existence of electricity there, as to glass, and we can prove heat to be there by friction; and by peculiar management of surfaces, we produce the refraction of light and Newton's coloured rings. These rings I know are attributed to thin plates of air, water, &c. : are they not more properly referrable mediately only to those substances, but immediately to their envelopes of caloric and light, or electricity? I think experiments sufficient to determine some yet unknown effects of electricity on light, would readily suggest themselves to an inquisitive mind. The passage of galvanic, or even machine, electricity in lines transverse, parallel, and perpendicular to the rays of white homogeneous and polarized light, and through substances while causing diffraction, would, I think, develope some phenomena leading to the elucidation of the subject.

It appears to be a nearly universal rule, that the non-conductors of electricity are permeable to radiant light, and generally the more so in proportion to their non-conducting power; and the converse holds good as to conductors and opaque bodies. About the only exceptions in the class of conductors, are acids and water, and substances on which they confer the conducting power; and it may possibly be their fluidity alone which gives them the power of conduction; and very probably so in the case of water, for a spheriod of its ice made quite dry, has in fact been excited like any other electric. Non-conduction and fluidity united in oils seem, however, to militate against this supposition. A cat's skin is the most electrical substance we know of, with which the sensitiveness of her eye to light is a remarkable coincidence.

Light is evolved on the formation of some crystals; and Mr. Crosse has formed crystals by means of electricity.

Mrs. Somerville by light magnetized needles, and, on the other hand, magneto-electricity produces light.

Further consideration has led me to the reception of a very strong impression, that neither electricity, nor any other single substance, forms what we understand by the term light, or the cause of colour; but that what we call colour arises from the undulations of combinations of electricity and caloric. Electricity, as far as we know, is essentially concerned in chemical changes, and the non-luminous rays, at the violet end of the spectrum, have chemical properties. The non-luminous rays at the other end of the spectrum have calorific properties, and intermediately we have seven colours. What is more reasonable than to suppose those colours arise from combinations in different proportions of the principles that are developed at the two extremes? If so, it may be said, why did Newton still find each colour homogenous after a new refraction of it? To which I answer—we find electricity in combination, and that in definite proportions with other matter, as Dr. Faraday has shewn. I suppose that latent heat is generally believed to be so too by those who think it material. Then why may not electricity and caloric be united in a similar manner, and in different but, definite propositions, and so strongly combined, that refraction, or the power of ordinary attraction developed at the surfaces of bodies, may be incapable of separating them, or changing them from a latent into a free state?

These views are singularly confirmed by the circumstance of there being *several* complementary pairs of colours in the spectrum, any pair of which will produce by combination, white light; the excess of electricity or caloric in one colour, apparently answering to and making up for the deficiency in its complementary colour.

The very curious phenomena of polarisation seem to accord very much with the above views as to luminous and non-luminous rays. May not the points of non-reflection be where the calorific side or pole only, or the chemical side, or pole only of the compound particle of light is towards the eye, when according

to the above supposition as to the composition of colour, no vision could be produced. In no optical works within my reach can I find recorded any attempt to reproduce the light apparently destroyed by falling on the analysing plate. It by no means follows, the motion of the ray is destroyed in such case, although it cannot be seen on account of the dark side, or pole being presented to the eye. It may possibly be capable of being again reflected, so as to present one of its luminous sides to the eye.—I have not met with any account of experiments made to ascertain whether the non-luminous rays be polarised, as well as the luminous—experiments well worth the trouble of philosophers possessing the requisite time and means. If these non-luminious rays be found not to be polarised, it will add to the probability of polarisation arising from a compound nature in the atoms of luminous rays. I am not aware, either that any attempt has been made to recombine the non-luminous rays of the two kinds for the purpose of ascertaining whether their coincidence produced colour. If colour be a chemical combination in *definite* proportions of electricity and caloric, the two sets of non-luminous rays, must, in order to produce colour unite in the same (?) manner which I scarcely suppose they would.

Electricity appears to have an attraction for other matter much stronger than caloric has, and in this it coincides with the relative developments of chemical (or electrical) and calorific rays in the prismatic spectrum; and of light and caloric in the ordinary instances of heating. In the first case, the chemical (or electrical) rays are more refracted than the calorific, apparently from their greater attractive power for the matter or imponderable envelope, or constituent of the refracting body. In the second case (by heating iron for instance), we have first non-luminious calorific rays; with a greater heat opposed to the attractive power of the substance, we obtain red, the least refrangible colour; and with a still greater heat, we have also the more refrangible colours combined in white light. Electricity, from its greater attractive power for its own particles, and those of other substances appears to require a greater atomic action than caloric, to give it the undulatory intensity

required to elicit the more refrangible
rays, in which I suppose it to predominate in quantity over the caloric. That these
two imponderable substances have a strong
affinity, appears by the great development
of heat in a galvanic circuit, as though
the electricity dragged the caloric along
with it. Some experiments of de la Rive
on the loss of intensity of a galvanic current passing through several metallic
plates seem to favour this view. In
thermo-electricity, developed as in M.
Becquerel's experiment on a single
metal, the electricity and caloric move in
the same direction (from the hot part to
the cooling part) as though, in this case,
the caloric dragged along the electricity
towards its own place of radiation.

CORPUSCULUM.

22d April, 1837.

HINTS TO THE PERPETUAL MOTION
DISPUTANTS.

Sir,—In adverting to a correspondence
which has occupied a considerable portion of the *Mechanics' Magazine* for some-
time past, I do so merely to remark upon a
peculiar feature which has all along been
prominent, but which, of late, has made
that correspondence disagreeable to *many*
of your readers.

In order to ascertain the result of a
proposition, it is proper that a fair hearing be allowed of the arguments on every
side; but when personal dispute, and ex-
pressions of obvious illnature are introduced, the interest of the discussion is
lost.

Of several subjects which have of late
been remarkable for a prevailing tincture
of dispute, the one of " Perpetual Motion" is prominent. In the contending
communications the reader is continually
led away from the matter at issue by
repetitions, dissentions, and quotations
entirely devoid of information, and in
every respect unworthy of being recorded; these are occasionally " summed up"
as in the communication by *Nautilus* in
your last number, and much valuable
space is thus devoted to that which is of
no interest to the general reader.

It is now a long time since Mr. Mackintosh described in your pages the instrument which he at one time supposed
might produce a *perpetual motion;* but,
if I recollect rightly, he at the same time
expressed his doubts that such an effect

would ever be caused. The subject of
perpetual motion is always curious, and
in the present instance was (amusing if
it was not) instructive. I tried the experiment at the time, with an instrument
made according to Mr. Mackintosh's
description, and you were pleased to give
to your readers my brief report of the
result. I do not personally know either
of the parties interested, and it is with
due consideration I say, what will be
allowed by every impartial reader, that
Nautilus is unjust, when he asserts that
Mr. Mackintosh " broached a scheme
for perpetual motion in a manner evidently calculated to mislead others to
follow up his experiments, whatever his
own conviction of its futility might be,"
The learned disputants should rather
" broach" something new than tire your
readers so long with a series of communications which ought rather to be post
letters, than papers for the instruction
and entertainment of your readers. The
proper summation of the whole is—an
absurd discussion, intended to make out
an absurdity.

I am, Sir,
Your obedient servant,
R. MUNRO.

17th April, 1837.

MERRYWEATHER'S FIRE-ESCAPE—MR.
WIVELL'S CLAIM TO PRIORITY OF
INVENTION EXAMINED.

Sir,—Since I addressed my last communication to you on this subject, I
have obtained such a clue to the *age* of
Mr. Merryweather's fire-escape, as will
completely refute Mr. Wivell's charge
of *piracy.* Mr. Merryweather's apparatus was made in December 1828, and
the first *public exhibition* took place in
the Regent's Park on Monday, June 15,
1829. The following paragraph appeared
in the " British Traveller" of Friday,
June 19, 1829, and was copied into Bell's
Weekly Messenger, and some other
papers of the following Sunday.

" *Fire Escape.*—On Monday evening an
experiment was tried in the Regent's Park,
of a fire-escape on a new construction. The
machinery is both portable and simple; a
purchase is effected from the outside of the
house, entirely unconnected with the inside,
or the agency of any person within. By
this purchase, a light machine or cradle, is
passed up to the window of the first, second

ór third flóòr of the house ;—the person escaping gets into the machine, which is immediately lowered down by means of lines and pullies, worked by four persons. There are two different methods (both of which are capable of being used simultaneously) of affixing the machinery to the windows, one of which required two minutes, and the other only one minute elapsed in fixing the purchase and lowering down the machine. The invention, we learn, is by Mr. Merryweather, managing clerk to Messrs. Hadley and Co., Long Acre. Mr. Merryweather went up and descended from the second-floor window (a distance of 32 feet from the pavement) several times, as also did one of the workmen."

Now as Mr. Wivell's first exhibition (upon his own showing) did not take place till August—*two months afterwards* —his charge of piracy falls to the ground —or rather reverts upon himself; Mr. Merryweather's escape being unquestionably the "TRUE ORIGINAL."

As I said before, however, neither of these escapes are now worth a pinch of snuff, compared with the highly improved apparatus of the present day.

I am, Sir, yours respectfully,
WM. BADDELEY.

London, April 22, 1837.

P.S.—It is perfectly true, as observed by Mr. Utting at page 31, "that some persons will write, under an anonymous signature, what they would be ashamed in their own names to claim as their production, and which gives them an unfair advantage." To *Aquarius*, therefore, whose tissue of misconceptions and misrepresentations appears in this day's number, I offer no reply. "The *stranger* must first show that he is good knight, and of honorable lineage. The Temple sendeth not forth her champions against *nameless men.*"

[We beg to refer Mr. Baddeley, Mr. Utting, and others who object to anonymous correspondence, to some remarks of our own upon the subject in our 19th volume, pp. 249, and 366, and of our esteemed correspondent, Mr. Rutter, p. 414.—ED. M. M.]

SOANE'S MUSEUM.

This institution has recently been opened to the public, so far as is consistent with the views and arrangements of its founder. Persons who wish to procure admission have to leave their names and addresses at the Museum, specifying at the same time the day on which they wish to view it; and on, or before that day, they will receive, by post, a ticket of admission drawn up as follows :—

"SIR JOHN SOANE'S MUSEUM,
"13, Lincoln's Inn Inn Fields.
"Admission Ticket for Mr.   on the
or   of   1837.
"The parties mentioned in this card are to sign their names individually in the book kept for the purpose at the Museum, and only the persons named can be admitted upon its production.
"Parties will be conducted over the Museum according to regulations placed in the rooms for general convenience.
"Dated
"By direction of the Trustees.
"GEORGE BAILEY, *Curator*.
"The Museum will be open during the months of April, May and June.
"The Trustees request it may be understood, that from a desire to give early admission to the Museum, they have adopted the present regulations as a temporary measure, until the catalogues of the works of art and library are completed.
"(No admittance in wet or dirty weather)."

The method of admission to the Museum is more liberal than that in practice at some other similar establishments, since here a perfect stranger may present himself at the door, and apply for a ticket; while, at the Royal Asiatic Society, for instance, it is necessary to procure the introduction of a member, and at the East India Company's Museum, that of one of the Directors. Some of the other regulations, however, appear unnecessarily strict. It is troublesome to be obliged to specify on first applying for a ticket the name of every person who will be of the party, since it is very well known, that arrangements of that kind are in most cases left to the "last moment," and are peculiarly liable to the influence of the chapter of accidents. In other museums the name of one individual only is required, and is generally considered a sufficient guarantee for the respectability of those who accompany him. The obligation of naming the day is open to a similar objection.

A choice of two is indeed given in the ticket of admission, but this is certainly not enough, especially as in our inconstant climate it may often happen that the weather of both will come under the category of " wet or dirty." There is no very obvious reason why the ticket should not admit for any day of the season in which it is issued. On the card of admission there is no mention of restriction with regard to days of the week or hours of the day, but we believe that Thursday and Friday, and from ten till four, are the only days and hours on which the Museum is open.

The first room the visitor enters is the Library, a large and handsome apartment fitted up in a style of equal elegance and luxury. Here he enters his name in the book of visitors, and may, if he pleases, consult for information the work of Sir John Soane on the museum. The chief curiosities of this room are the portrait of the late owner, by Sir Thomas Laurence, a painting by Sir Joshua Reynolds, of which, as usual, the colours are faded, some Etruscan vases, from the collection of Sir H. Englefield, of no particular beauty, some painted glass in the windows, and a French timepiece, intended to point out the days of the week as well as hours of the day, but which, like other curiosities of that description does not go. On the ceiling are paintings by Howard, an artist whose imagination seems steeped in classic elegance. These articles thus enumerated do not carry with them a very imposing sound, but the visitor leaves the library with the conviction that he has seen as elegant and interesting an apartment as he can well imagine.

In the passage through which the visitor now passes to the Painting Room, a number of interesting articles and curiosities are assembled, but in so confined a space, that to survey them at all is awkward and difficult, and in company with a party impossible. In the painting room the eye is first greeted by three splendid productions of Canaletti, which are, as might be expected, views of Venice, and by the four original pictures of Hogarth's Election, which are inferior in execution to the " Marriage-à-la-Mode" at the National Gallery, and in an inferior state of preservation. When these have been surveyed, the custodian draws forward the pictures hitherto shown, and thus exhibits behind them the series of Hogarth's Rake's Progress, as well as several other paintings of interest. The same process on the other side of the apartment reveals to view one half of the room called " the Monk's Parlour," which is on the floor below.

We have not room to go through the remainder of the museum with equal minuteness, but these two apartments may be considered as forming a fair specimen of the whole. In some there is a collection of elegantly arranged and not over-crowded objects, which seem assembled by the hand of taste, in others the number of articles is rather too great for the space at disposal, and though ingenuity has been exerted in placing them aright, the effect produced is not so pleasing. The character of elegance has been lost, and that of grandeur, has from the smallness of the dimensions been unattainable. Of the remaining curiosities, few will be found of such general interest as the two small portraits of Bonaparte over one of the mantlepieces; one, taken by an obscure Italian artist, soon after his first battles, and executed much in the style in which portraits may now be had done about town for two or three shillings; and the other, a beautiful miniature by Isabey, taken when he was in the plenitude of his pride and power; one presents a slovenly, down-looking slender youth; the other the stout, imperious, overbearing man of middle age. Between them is a magnificent pistol, which has had a strange succession of possessors—first, a Turkish bey, next Peter the Great, then the Emperor Alexander, the Emperor Napoleon, Sir John Soane, and now the British public. In a singular gallery at the back of the house, the chief ornament is formed by the Alabaster Sarcofagus, brought by Belzoni from Egypt. We must, however, restrain ourselves from adding more; suffice it to say, that there are all kinds of articles, of all classes and grades, scattered all about the house, including a number of beautifully executed drawings of Sir John Soane's architectural plans, which are of very various degrees of merit; paintings and drawings, from the genuine comedy of Hogarth and the imaginative beauty of Howard, to the meaningless extravagance of Mortimer; models of both ancient and modern buildings, and trumpery old

French prints, such as the death of Rousseau, &c. wholly unworthy of the room they occupy on the walls.

We in fact on a recent view missed but two curiosities which we had been taught to expect from the catalogue. One, the article on Sir John Soane's architectural capabilities cut out from the Champion newspaper, and framed and glazed as a memento of his persevering resentment against its author, we were glad to see had been removed; but we were much disappointed to find that the autograph of Tasso's Jerusalem Delivered was not visible. We were told that the reason for this was, that the library was not yet open, but this we conceived to be no reason at all. That book is surely an *exceptional* one, as the French say, and ought to be laid on the table with the other curiosities.

The visitors are not *conducted* through the rooms in the manner the ticket of admission might lead one to expect. There is a "custodian" in almost every room, and the privilege of loitering is generally allowed, which is the greatest of all privileges on such occasions. The party of visitors when we were there was nine or ten in number.

THEORY OF COMBUSTION, RARE-FACTION, &c.

Sir,—In a paper signed "W." in your last week's number respecting the influence which light and the atmospheric air exert in the phenomena of combustion, rarefaction, &c., the writer arrives at very wonderful clonclusions, and draws from his observations extremely ingenious inferences, but unpossessed of the slightest foundation.

"W." states that light and atmospheric air (which is composed 21 parts oxygen gas, 79 parts nitrogen gas, and about $\frac{1}{1000}$th part of carbonic acid gas by measure) are the essential cause and influence of combustion. The following simple experiment will prove the fallacy of his assertion; place in a dark room a glass jar of oxygen gas, and through its cap insert the negative and positive wires of a voltaic battery, connect them by a fine wire of copper, or iron, &c., then set the battery in action, and the metal will become ignited, and combustion proceed in a most brilliant manner, which will continue as long as the metal, or oxygen lasts, without the presence of solar light or atmospheric air in the jar, either before or after the experiment. I may further insert the rationale of combustion in the open atmosphere, for simple, and well known as it is, there still may be a few of your readers who know so little of the influence which the unerring laws of nature exert over every particle of matter around us, as to be led astray by the whimsical method in which "W." and some other writers account for the various phenomena enumerated.

Combustion, like every other chemical process, can be explained by means of the laws of chemical affinity. The combustible material, whatever it may be, when raised to a certain temperature by the application of a light, a burning glass, &c., having greater affinity for the oxygen of the atmosphere, than oxygen has for caloric, the base of the oxygen gas unites with the combustible, and becomes fixed and condensed—at the same time giving out its light and caloric, which were essential to its former existence as a gas.

This is proved by the analytical examination of the resulting compound, when the oxygen gas and the combustible may be separated from each other, and exhibited in a separate state, being perfectly free from the slightest trace of nitrogen or carbonic acid, the other constituents of our atmosphere. Were the views of your correspondent correct, it would be impossible for chemists to ascertain the composition of any substance in nature, for every attempt to examine its constituents separately, by means of heat would fail, in consequence of an immense and unappreciable quantity of air condensed within it.

"W." says, "If a light from a lens which sets substances on fire, be thrown on the same substances in an exhausted receiver, it will produce no heat, no effect." This is erroneous, he could never have seen the experiment tried; the substance, if reducible by heat, will liquify or evaporate readier in a vacuum than in the open air; but combustion will not take place, simply because no oxygen is present.

Respecting the fact of the mountain summits being crowned with ice in the midst of summer,—the following explanation seems most accordant with natural laws as now understood. The atmospheric air is not heated by the simple passage of the solar rays through it, for they give out their heat only when impinged upon opaque or solid substances, as the earth, &c., and the heat after being received, is gradually released by them, and diffused through the surrounding atmosphere; hence, the higher we ascend the less opaque substance will there be to conduct the heat, and consequently, the colder will be the air; and although the sun's intensest rays may be darted on a body of ice existing at a great elevation, the atmosphere will subtract the caloric from it as fast as it is received, assisted also by its high state of rarefaction which always accelerates the evaporation or distribution of heat, or any other fluid.

"W." states, "it is known that the rarefaction of air has a tendency to depress its temperature:" then, of course, with the greater facility will it absorb from the ice the caloric which it is receiving; for the colder and more rarefied the air, the readier passage will it afford for the transit of caloric through its medium.

His explanation of the cause of the bubbling appearance of boiling water is scarcely worth refuting; its fallacy must be evident to every one. A letter appeared in your Journal some weeks since, containing the very same ideas upon the subject, which were perfectly disproved by your correspondents "G S" and Trebor Valentine (See Nos. 704 and 5), who gave correct explanations of the phenomena.

"Atmospheric air is susceptible of a great variety of modifications:" most certainly it is; but not such as the worthy writer deduces; the electric light, for instance, cannot be one, for the rarer the medium through which it passes, the greater is the intensity of its light; and in an exhausted receiver, its appearance is brilliant and intense; whereas the reverse would take place if the atmospheric air was the illuminating agent.

I am, Sir, your obedient servant.

A. Y.

May 3rd, 1837.

___

ON THE VELOCITY OF A RIVER'S CURRENT,

(From the *Franklin Journal* for February.)

It has been often questioned whether the current of a river be equable from its surface to its bottom. Some suppose that the velocity of the current is greatest at the surface; others, that it is greatest near the bottom. The most general, and, I think, the most correct opinion, is, that the velo-

city of the current of a river, or stream, is greatest at the surface, and diminishes at every point from the surface towards the bottom, and that at the bottom there is no, or scarcely any, current.

While I resided at Harrisburg, in the summer of 1811, a gentleman and myself made the following experiment:

A machine or instrument like that represented in the annexed figure was made by a

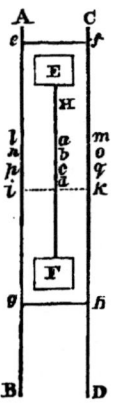

cabinet maker. A B and C D are two sticks, an inch square, and about five feet in length, connected at the distance of about seven inches from each other, by the cross pieces *e f* and *g h*. E and F are two thin boards, exactly five inches square, (we called them fans,) connected by a stick G H, an inch square; the whole length from the top of E to the bottom of F being exactly three feet.

i k is a pin passing through A B, and C D, and G H, being fast to G H at *d*, but turning freely in the holes through which it passes in A B and C D.

Holes were also made in the three sticks, A B, C D, and G H, at *l a m*, at *n b o*, and at *p c q*, the holes being exactly an inch apart, for the purpose of moving the pin *i k* (when required) from the centre of G H, one inch, or two inches, or three inches, above the centre.

We went in a skiff to the middle of the river between Harrisburg and Maclay's island, and anchored the skiff at a place where the river was about five feet in depth, and the velocity of the current, according to our estimation, about four miles per hour. The instrument was set in the river perpendicularly, B D being on the ground at the bottom, the side of the instrument being to the current, so that the current should strike the fans E and F. The fan E was about two inches beneath the surface of the river, and the fan F three feet lower in the water.

The frame A C, B D, was held steadily in a perpendicular position, and the stick G H, connecting the fans E and F, was suffered to turn on the pin *i k*, as it should be forced by the current of the river. The upper end of the stick G H, and the fan E, immediately inclined down the stream, and the lower end of the stick and the fan F inclined up the river ; so that the stick G H formed an angle of perhaps thirty degrees with the frame A B C D, which was held perpendicularly.

The pin *i k* was then inserted through the holes at *p c q*, and afterwards at *n b o*. The fan E was still pressed by the current down the stream, though to a less and less distance as the pin was moved from *d* to *c*, and then from *c* to *b*. At length the pin was inserted at *l a m*, being three inches above *d* the centre of the stick G H. Upon setting the frame carefully in the current, the stick remaided nearly perpendicular, but still the fan E was pressed a little down the stream, and forward of the upright frame A B C D. The pin *i k* was always fastened to the stick G H, when it passed through the holes at *d c b*, or *a*, and permitted to turn freely in the holes through which it passed in A B, and C D.

As the stick G H was just twenty-six inches in length, and as the fans were each five inches square, from the centre of E to the centre of F was thirty-one inches ; and when the pin was placed at *l a m*, it was three inches above the centre, giving to the fan E a lever of 12¼ inches, and to the fan F a lever of 18¼ inches, measuring from the pivot point *a* to the centre of each fan. The velocity of the current near the surface at E being, to its velocity at F, (thirty-one inches lower down in the water) in the proportion of 18¼ to 12¼.

It would be interesting to repeat the experiment under different circumstances ; for example, in currents of two, and in currents of six, or more miles per hour ; in rivers of three, and in rivers of ten, or more feet in depth, and with the lower fan (as F) as near as could be to the bottom.

The reason of the current of rivers or streams being greatest at the surface, and diminishing gradually to the bottom, seems to be manifest. It is on the principle of bodies falling or sliding down inclined planes. The application of the principle is more obscure and difficult in the case of the river, on account of the falling or sliding body being a liquid, instead of a solid body.

It is on the same principle that the velocity of the current of a river increases, in proportion as it is swelled and raised higher and higher by rains and floods.

E.

ON THE VELOCITY OF FLOATING BODIES ALONG THE CURRENT OF A RIVER.

(From the *Franklin Journal* for February).

When I lived in Harrisburg, I often heard raftmen and boatmen say that rafts, loaded boats, and arks, floated faster than the current of the Susquehanna. They said that when a rise occurred in the river, in consequence of a heavy rain above any particular point, say Sunbury or Wilkesbarre, if a boat or raft started with the flood, it would soon go beyond the flood, and get into shallow water, and that, for this reason, it was their practice never to start till the rise, or flood, had preceded them about twenty-four hours.

They also said that a heavy boat, or raft, floated faster than a light one, and that, by fastening two or more rafts together their speed was increased.

The facts seemed propable, independant of the direct testimony of the boatmen, and to be accounted for on the principle of falling bodies, and bodies sliding down inclined planes, acquiring velocity in their progress, the acquisition of velocity being in proportion to the inclination of the plane, and the weight of the decending body.

To ascertain the fact that a loaded boat floated faster than the current, the following experiment was made in the summer 1811, by several scientific gentlemen, with myself.

A common water wheel was made, about sixteen inches in diameter, and fastened *to the end* of a stick or shaft, about two feet in length. We entered a skiff, and went to a rapid part of the river, where the currant, for the distance below us of one hundred yards and upwards, was even, and of the rapidity, as we estimated it, of five miles per hour. The skiff was anchored ; I sat in the middle of it, hanging the water wheel over the side of the skiff, so that the wheel dipped an inch, or more, in the water. The shaft rested on the side of the skiff, and I held it loosely in my hands, allowing it to turn round freely, as the currant gave motion to the wheel.

While the skiff remained at anchor, the force of the currant made the wheel turn pretty quickly upwards, or against the stream.

The rope that held the skiff to the stone that served for an anchor was cut, and the skiff was allowed to float down the river The skiff gradually but rapidly increased in the velocity of its motion, and the motion of the water wheel turning upwards, or against the the current, proportionably diminished in velocity. After the skiff floated not more (as well as I can remember at this time) than four or five rods, the motion of the wheel on its axis, or shaft, ceased altogether, and it began to turn on its axis down the stream, slowly at first, but quickly increasing. And after the skiff had floated not more (I think) than fourteen or fifteen rods from the place where it had been anchored, the water wheel turned downwards, or with the current, as often as once round in the distance of a rod or less.

It is evident that while the wheel turned up the stream, the current of the river went faster than the skiff, or ran past it ; and when the wheel turned down the stream, the motion of the skiff was more rapid than that of the current. We expected this result in a certain degree, but all of us were surprised that the floating skiff should so soon acquire a velocity greater than that of the current of the river.

It would be interesting to repeat this experiment under change of circumstances. For instance—

1. In a slower, and in a more rapid, current.

2. In a boat heavily, and one lightly, loaded.

3. In a flat bottomed, and in a sharp keeled, boat.

4. On rafts of different sizes.

Also, to ascertain whether any difference would arise from having the load lie in the bottom of the boat, such as a quantity of pig metal, or having the load consist of men standing up in the boat.

Times and distances should, of course, be accurately noted. E.

PORK ESTABLISHMENT OF MEXICO.

There exists in Mexico a very fine race of hogs, which are regarded as an important article of commerce, and the care which is taken of these animals so far surpasses that which I have seen elsewhere, I think it may be very useful to our farmers, brewers, and distillers, to be made acquainted with the principal details.

The buildings of these establishments include a house for the manager and the workmen, a shop, a slaughter house, a place for singeing, rooms and vessels for the fat and lard, (articles which often supply, in Mexico, the place of butter) other rooms where black pudding is made and sold to the poor, and a soap manufactory, in which all the offals are used. The stables, which contain about 800 hogs, are behind these buildings. They consist of out-houses, well made, thirty feet deep, with overhanging roofs. The entrance is by a low vault, in front of which is an open space twenty-four feet wide. extending the whole length of the yard. In the centre of this, is a stone aqueduct, through which flows clear water from a well or spring, the hogs being allowed to pass their snouts only into the stream, through openings in the wall,

which prevents their soiling the beverage. It is the only liquid they are allowed to take. They are fed with Indian corn, slightly moistened, and spread upon the floor. The pens and the space on which the animals walk are kept in great cleanliness.

The hogs are in the immediate charge of a number of Indians, attached to the establishment, and who often give them a cold bath, for it is thought that cleanliness contributes to that prodigious increase of fat which constitutes their principal value. It is the business also of these care takers to keep them in good humour. Two persons are employed from morning to night in adjusting their quarrels, and in singing to induce them to sleep. These persons are chosen on account of the strength of their lungs and abilities to charm the ears of their amiable associates, which is deemed an affair of no inconsiderable merit !

The proprietor of one of these establishments assured us that the expense of it amounted to 300,000 francs, and that the sales rose to 10,000 a-week ; the luxury of his equipage indicated, in fact, the possessor of a large fortune.—*Jour. Conn. Usuelles*, Juin, 1836.

RECENT AMERICAN PATENTS.

(Selected from the *Franklin Journal* for December.)

IMPROVEMENT IN THE ART OF TANNING; *Henry C. Locher, Lancaster, Pennsylvania, Administrator of Henry Locher, deceased, March 18.*—" A general communication with every vat intended to be used, is made by means of trunks, or tubes, placed on the outside, and about six inches from the top of the vat, and made level so that the water may be sent with equal ease in any direction through them ; a perpendicular trunk or tube, is placed in one corner of each vat, extending from the top, to within about four inches of the bottom ; small tubes are branched off from the main, or horizontal trunk, or tube, and inserted into each of the perpendicular trunks, or tubes, and also into the opposite ends of the vats called handlers, and into the reservoir; other small tubes are made to connect the several perpendicular trunks, or tubes, with the adjoining vats, of those generally termed leaches, so that the liquor or juice of the bark may be transferred, or driven from one vat to another, in any direction. The perpendicular trunks, or tubes, may, to save room in the vats, be placed on the outside, with communication at the bottom.

This plan enables the tanner to multiply the liquors or juices, in the vats termed leaches, to any degree of strength, and at the same time to exchange strong for weak, without mixing scarcely any, and without labour more than drawing the plugs out of the tubes necessary to be opened, and turning the water from the hydrant, or pump, on one or more of the leaches, thus as many as you please will exchange, and the leaches successively recruit in strength. This is done on the philosophical principles of the lighter bodies rising to the top. As for example, to drive the strong liquor out of the vat, cause a light and steady stream of water to fall on the bark in the vat, or on a board laid on top of the liquor, and as soon as the liquor rises to the tube, in the perpendicular trunk, it escapes by that tube, and is let into any other vat that is opened to receive it, and its place is supplied by the water; if the reverse is wanted, let the liquor into the perpendicular trunk, it sinks to, and spreads over the bottom of the vat, and raises the water to the top, where it escapes by the small tube.

False bottoms are useful in this operation, as they prevent the trunks or tubes from being stopped, or clogged, and they receive the settlings."

A MODE OF CONVEYING RAFTS, BOATS, &c., OVER DAMS AND SHOALS; *Stephen Underwood, New Hampshire, March* 19.— Two inclined plane railways are to be erected, one on each side of the dam, or other obstruction, over which a boat &c., is to be carried; these are to extend into the stream, so that the load can be floated on to a car, constructed to run upon the planes. The planes are to terminate, at their upper ends, at the distance of from thirty to sixty feet from each other, or equal to that of the car upon which the boat or raft is to be carried. This space is occupied by a vibrating railway or bridge, which tilts on a centre, and will form a continuous plane with either of the sections, accordingly as it is tilted towards the one or the other. A windlass, turned by water, or other power, receives a rope, or chain, by which the car can be raised, or lowered, upon the planes. When a load is to ascend, the bridge is tilted towards the plane up which it is to be drawn, and it is hauled upon it; the bridge is then tilted towards the descending plane, and the load si lowered into the water.

There is a contrivance on the car, by an arrangement of eccentric rollers, by which the level of the load can be changed, so that it shall stand horizontally in ascending and descending.

The claim is confined exclusively " to that part of the apparatus employed, which is denominated the *vibrating railway*, which is intended to receive the load at the summit of the inclined plane, and to be adapted by its vibrating motion to the plane of either,

for the purpose, and in the manner set forth."

This plan has been carried into successful operation; large rafts of timber being conveyed, by its means, down rivers where the passage was previously attended with extreme difficulty, and where it could not, sometimes, be effected.

IMPROVEMENT IN THE PROCESS OF TANNING HIDES AND SKINS; *Laban Emery, New York, March,* 19.—The patentee directs the hides, or skins, to be prepared for tanning in the usual manner, and adds, that " my improvement or invention then consists in the application to the bark liquor, of nitre, or alum, or epsom, or Rochelle, salts, or other neutral salts, either separately or together, mixed in with the liquor, in the proportion of about four pounds to four dozen skins, more or less ; and also bearing some proportion to the strength of the liquor. Every time the bark liquor is renewed, a like quantity of such neutral salt may be added, or not, as may be thought proper; or as the process of tanning may be required to be hastened. Either of the said articles may be used separately, or together, in the process of tanning morocco, as well as every other description of tanning."

PRESERVING MILK FOR USE ON VOYAGES, &c.; *John Lewis Granger, New York, March* 19.—Fresh milk is to be put into bottles, and these are to be closed, in the manner of corking, with some porous substance, which will allow air to pass through it ; the bottles are then to be put into a vessel of cold water, and the whole gradually heated to the boiling point, after which the porous stopper is to be covered with wax.

The claim is " to the evolving of gas, and suffering it to escape from the milk, and immediately afterwards excluding the atmospheric air from commingling therewith, by the method substantially as described."

We apprehend that the theory above intimated, namely, that the gas contained in milk is the cause of its spontaneous decomposition, is not founded in fact ; were this the case, an exhausted receiver would as effectually effect the object in view, as the boiling heat, and this process would not be " substantially as described." There is a chemical change produced in milk by boiling, by which its liability to further reaction is very much diminished, and which would not be produced by the mere expulsion of gas. This theoretical point, we are aware, has nothing to do with the validity of the claim, although we have thought proper to give it a passing notice ; we have also something to say about the novelty of the process. In the celebrated report published by the French Government in 1810, on Mr. Appert's mode of preserving all kinds of animal and vegetable substances, milk is mentioned as having been preserved by boiling and corking closely; it was concentrated in the boiling by allowing a portion of its watery particles to evaporate; the process was, we think, substantially the same with the above, the principle of which was perfectly well known.

DISSOLVING CAOUTCHOUC, OR INDIA RUBBER; *Patrick Mackie, New York, March 23.*—"What I claim as new, and of my invention, is the use of oil of tar, or spirits of tar alone, and also the use of oil and spirits of tar mixed with the prepared sulphate of zinc, as a solvent for dissolving India-rubber."

We could turn to patents for the use of the same liquid, in the employment of which, therefore, there is not any thing new. The spirit from coal tar has been extensively used in England, and is well known here, but its odour is extremely offensive. The spirit from common tar is principally oil of turpentine, with empyreumatic matter, which does not improve it.

SPARK CATCHERS, FOR LOCOMOTIVE STEAM ENGINES; *William Schultz, Philadelphia, March 31.*—There is to be a swell in the smoke pipe, which will give to it the force of two funnels joined together at their rims; and across this wide junction there is to be wire gauze stretched, the enlargement being intended to prevent any obstruction in the draught. The pipe for waste steam is to perforate the sheet of wire gauze, which is secured to it by a flanch. Flues, which may be opened when the engine is at rest, are to pass on the outside of the conical enlargements, allowing a free draught; these are to be closed by valves, when the engine is in motion.

CLAIM. "What I claim is, the whole arrangement, as hereinbefore described, without any connection with any other machine heretofore constructed for the same purposes."*

[A spark arrester precisely similar to this, invented by Mr. Grey, of the Temple, was described in the last volume of our Magazine, p. 375.—ED. M. M.]

NOTES AND NOTICES.

Short and Long Railways.—"It is a great, though I believe very common, mistake to imagine that steam power can be employed for short distances to full advantage. The briefer the course which a river has to run, the less its average bulk of water—the oftener it is subject to floods, the oftener to be dried up: so in a like manner, the shorter the distance of a railway, the less the average weight transported upon it, the more liable it is, to have too much traffic and too little. I have travelled on the London and Greenwich Railway when there were three hundred passengers in the train of a forty horse engine, and I have travelled on it when we did not exceed a dozen. What a vast disproportion was here between the power expended and the results obtained! In the one case, there was but a fair profit earned; in the other, a heavy loss sustained. Yet to mend matters is impossible; the forty horse engine must be kept in readiness and be set to work whatever may be the number of passengers,—be it five or five hundred. The case is the same on the Dublin and Kingstown, a similar line to the Greenwich. I have it from the best authority, that in consequence of the great disproportion between the carrying establishment which the Directors of this Railway are obliged to keep up, and the daily average amount of business done, full nine tenths of their steam power is completely wasted. (Yet, even with this enormous loss, the concern pays well. Of what sort of speculation, save a railway, can as much be said?) The converse of the proposition I have here laid down holds of course equally true, namely, that the longer the line of the railway, the more numerous its tributaries, the larger the population whose wants it has to supply, the greater will be the certainty of an average weight equal to the power of the engines employed; and therefore it is, that great as our gain may be from completing the two terminal sections of our line, the gain will be much greater, even as regard these sections themselves from completing the whole. A twenty horse engine having to traverse daily the whole way from London to Yarmouth, or from Yarmouth to London, will always be much surer of a full weight every time, than if it had but the distance between London and Chelmsford, or between Yarmouth and Norwich, to accomplish."—*Letter to H. N. Ward, Esq. on the Progress and Prospects of the Eastern Counties Railway Company; by J. C. Robertson, Secretary.*

Strength of Paper.—Mr. Cowper, at a lecture which he delivered lately at the Society of Arts, produced a sheet of quarto post writing paper, the ends of which he had pasted together, thus forming an endless web; into this web he inserted two rods of wood, to one of which was attached a half hundred weight, and taking the other in his hands, he raised the weight. The same sheet, he observed, had lifted a man off the ground who weighed 150 lbs. A bank note, he also mentioned, would lift 18 lbs.

Steel Letter-press Engraving.—A young artist of Vienna, named von Sieglünder, has, we are informed by the German papers, recently discovered a process by which he can execute engravings in the style of copperplate, which can, nevertheless, be printed with letter-press in the same manner as wood-cuts. This invention may prove of some importance. The Hamburgh Correspondent tells us with as much solemnity as it speaks of the invention, that Mr. Ficker, Professor of Asthetics, at the High School of Vienna, has already given it the name of *Chalcoxylography.*

☞ *British and Foreign Patents taken out with economy and despatch; Specifications, Disclaimers, and Amendments, prepared or revised; Caveats entered; and generally every Branch of Patent Business promptly transacted.*
A complete list of Patents from the earliest period (15 Car. II. 1675,) to the present time may be examined. Fee 2s. 6d.; Clients, gratis.

LONDON: Printed and Published for the Proprietor, by W. A. Robertson, at the Mechanics' Magazine Office, No. 6, Peterborough-court, between 135 and 136, Fleet-street.—Sold by G. W. M. Reynolds, Proprietor of the French, English, and American Library, 55, Rue Neuve, Saint Augustin, Paris.

Mechanics' Magazine,

MUSEUM, REGISTER, JOURNAL, AND GAZETTE.

| No. 719. | SATURDAY, MAY 20, 1837. | Price 3d. |

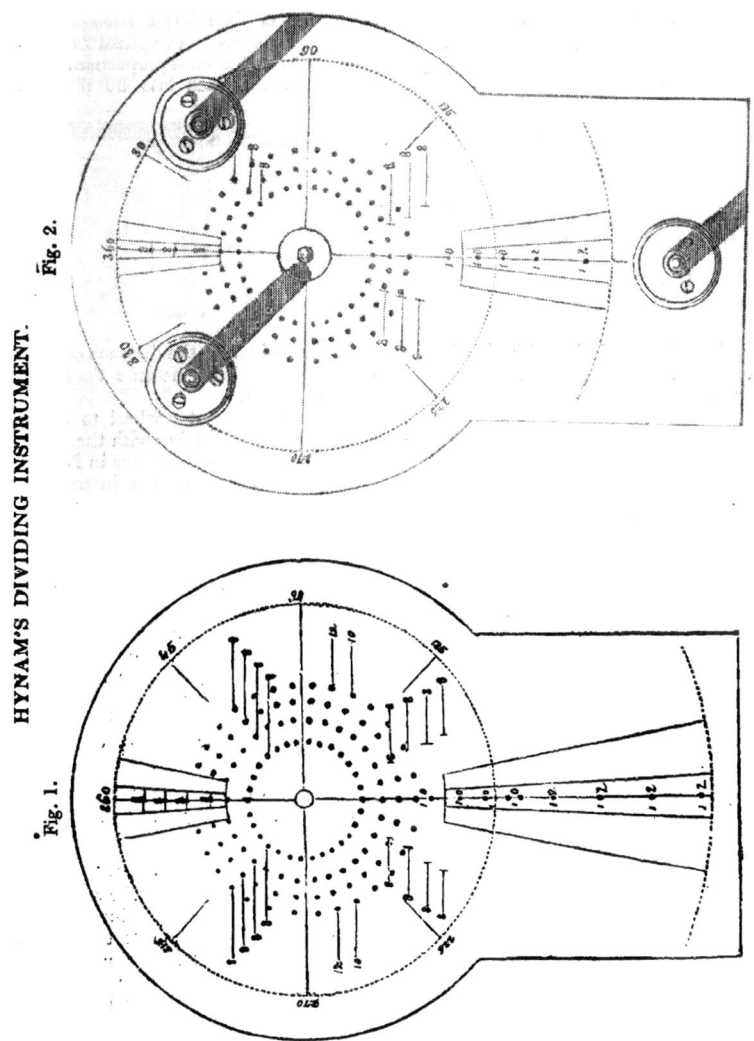

HYNAM'S DIVIDING INSTRUMENT.

Fig. 2.

Fig. 1.

HYNAM'S DIVIDING INSTRUMENT.

Sir,—I send you a drawing and description of a machine in my line of business, made by my late father, Mr. Robert Hynam, If you are inclined to add it to the mighty store of knowledge contained in your invaluable 25 volumes I have in my possession, it is perfectly at your service.

I am, Gentlemen, your

Most obedient servant,

BENJAMIN HYNAM.

St. Petersburg.

Description of an Instrument for marking off the distances of the centres of Swing Wheels and Pallets, the distance of the Pallets from each other, and their slope and plain of action.

Fig. 1 is a front view of the dividing instrument, and fig. 2 a reversed view (see front page). Fig. 4 is a profile or edge view.

The brass plate has a circle divided into 360 divisions   A segment of a circle divided in the same proportion. Four circles divided, each into 30 divisions

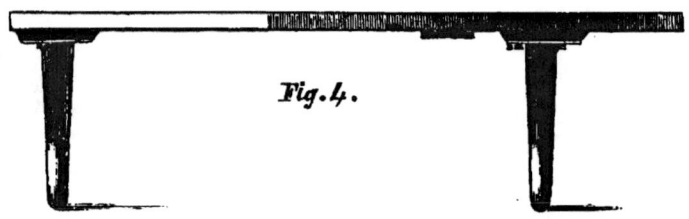

Fig. 4.

(teeth). A central line with the figures 8. 10. 12. The figures 8. 8. 8. 8. are used in the recoiling scapement. The figures 10. 10. 10. 10. and 12. 12. 12. 12. are the distances the pallets must be from each other when they scape over different sized wheels, and different numbers of teeth. The lines drawn from the centre of the instrument describing the angles 3 and 10 upon the segment of the circle, are to determine the plane or slope of action of the pallets for the dead beat and the length of each pellet.

To use the Instrument.—Suppose your swing wheel of the size of the smallest divided circle, place your dividers in the centre, and extend them until they reach the first number 10 in the central line, that distance is the true geometrical distance from the centre of the swing wheel hole, to the centre hole of the pallets, when the pallets scape over 10 teeth—the 2d 3d and 4th circles are different sized wheels—for the 2d 3d or 4th circle or wheel, you must extend the compasses or dividers from the centre to the other numbers 10. 10. '10., each number increases in distance from the centre.

If your pallets scape over 12 teeth, the same rule must be observed as usual with the number 10; only with this difference, the dividers must be extended to the numbers 12. 12. 12., according to the size of your wheel.

Having obtained the distance of your centres, proceed to measure the length of your pallets.

Suppose you want a wheel to escape over 10 teeth, beginning with the smallest wheel : place your dividers in No. 10, nearest the centre of the instrument, extend them until they reach the smallest circle, No. 10 or 5, divisions (teeth) from the central line; this distance is the right length of your pallets. To determine the distance from the point of the ascending pallet to the point or edge of the descending pallet.; place your dividers in the 5th division of either side the central line, and measure across the divided circle to five divisions on the other side the central line, it will give you the distance the edges of the pallets must be from each other.

To determine the slope or plain of action, and the length of the Pallets from the delivering edge to the head.

Place the centre of the pallets (axis) into the centre of the instrument, bring the delivering edge to the central line, then the slope or plain of action of the pallets must reach the next line from the central line, the head of your pallets must reach the second line from the central line, and so on with the others. It must be observed, that the last mentioned measure is of little signification, whether longer or shorter than laid down in the instrument; the length laid down appears pleasing to the eye. The thickness of pallets should be very near half the space between the teeth of the swing wheel.

The recoiling scapement must be taken off the same manner as that already described, with this difference, you take all the measures from the numbers 8. 8 8. 8., the inclined lines drawn from 8. 8. 8. 8., and the lines marked thus, are the inclinations of the recoiling pallets or plains of action.

The recoil is arbitary with clock-makers, the less recoil, the less friction; consequently, the less recoil has the preference.

Fig. 3 is a diagram illustrative of the action of the instrument.

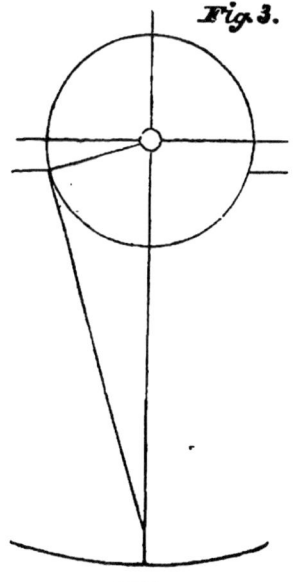

Fig. 3.

MACKINTOSH'S ELECTRICAL THEORY —APPROXIMATION OF THE EARTH TO THE SUN—POSTSCRIPT TO NAUTILUS.

Sir,—Mr. Mackintosh in his explanation of his second question, compares the motion of the earth in its orbit, to that of a carriage moving up and down an undulating railway. He states, No. 712, " The earths, path or orbit, would be truly represented by a line of railway, consisting of one long line of undulation, so that the carriage would be continually accelerated in descending towards the *perigee* (perihelion I presume he means) or lowest point of the line, and exactly in the same ratio retarded in ascending towards the *apogee* (aphelion he means) or highest point *Therefore we perceive that by the undulation of the earth in her orbit nothing is either gained or lost to the velocity,*" &c.

Let us contrast this up hill and down hill motion of the earth or celestial undulating system, with that part of the electrical theory in which Mr. Mackintosh demonstrates—I beg his pardon—asserts—that the earth, and all the other planets belonging to our unfortunate system are continually posting on towards the sun (or the roasting system, so named by " An Old Correspondent"). In No. 681, Mr. M. states, " If he (Kinclaven) will examine it more attentively (the roasting system he means) he will perceive that so far from the momentum of the planets being extinguished (and Kinclaven never said they would) they are supposed to be accelerated, because it is assumed that they move in spiral orbits, which (the orbits being elliptic) is the same in effect as if they were rolled down an undulating inclined plane. This assumption derives support from several considerations, as well as from the established fact of the moons secular acceleration." Here we have another precious specimen of Mr. M.'s consistency. How is it possible to believe in a system, the one half of which contradicts the other? However, I will allow that this new up hill and down hill, or celestial undulating system of the universe is far more feasible than the roasting, or burying, or drowning systems (see a " Country Teacher's" article, No. 311,) which would necessarily result from the first assumed principles of the electrical theory.

Will Mr. M. be pleased to tell us what great circle of the celestial sphere represents, under this new system of his, the horizontal plane, and how many feet per mile the alternate rises and falls of the earths orbit make with the said celestial horizontal plane? My motive for asking this question is, that Iver M'Iver demonstrated that the railway theroms invented by General Herapath, could not apply in any terrestial case

H 2

perhaps they might with with some modifications be applied in determining the velocities, &c. of the planets on the principles of the new celestial railway system of the universe. Modifications, I say, would, no doubt, be necessary; because, if the fall should turn out 22 feet per mile exactly, General Herapath's theorem produces an infinite velocity; and then, good bye to the centripetal force of the sun. Again, if the fall should be more than 22 feet per mile, the velocity, by the General's theorem, would be negative; that is, the earth would not budge one inch down hill, but would always be inclined to run up hill; of course, when the earth arrived at her aphelion, she would come to a dead stand still. I need hardly state, Mr. Editor, that Mr. Mackintosh's second question, which I answered in No. 710, is the same in substance as the one he put to your ingenious correspondents, Nautilus, and Trebor Valentine.

Mr. M. compares himself with Galileo, and your humble servant, Kinclaven, to one of the Seven Cardinals of the Inquisition, who tried and condemned Galileo to the flames, for his heresies, and he alleges that, if I (Kinclaven), had the same power, I would torture him with the *rack, wooden shoes, warming pans, &c. &c.*—Sentimental Fudge!

Mr. M. then puts his second question under the following practical form, which he requests me to solve for him: Question. " Suppose a carriage has a velocity imparted to it?" &c. See No. 712, page 502.

Had Mr. M. been conversant with a few of the first articles of the First Book of the Principia (and surely he ought to have been so, before he undertook the Herculean task of overturning the Newtonian system) he would have found directions for finding the primitive impulse the body must receive; or in the case of the body moving in the circumference of a circle, had he been acquainted with the first principles of Dynamics, which is contained in every " School Book" that treats on that subject, he might have discovered an easy method of solving his own question. I shall give him a formula for it; which, although not contained in any book that I have ever seen, still the principles from which the formula is deduced is to be found in thousands of school books. The formula for the primary impulse, is simply this : $.078051 \sqrt{m} =$ primitive velocity in miles per second : and m the number of miles the revolving body is from the earths centre, and if we assume $.078051$ $\sqrt{m} = n$, then $\dfrac{.10472m}{n} =$ number of minutes the body will take to revolve round the earth. This formula is not confined to a height of 30 feet (as proposed in the question); it will answer without any sensible error, although the body were to revolve at a height exceeding that of any mountain on the earth. In numbers, suppose $m = 3980$ miles, then $.078051 \sqrt{m} = 4.943$ miles per second for the primitive velocity : and $\dfrac{.10472m}{n}$

$$= \dfrac{.10472 \times 3980}{4.943} = 86 \text{ minutes } 26 \text{ se-}$$

conds is the time the body would take to revolve round the earth. The same question might be solved from principles deduced from Keplers Laws.

I have still left the "Country Teacher" a good many pickings if he should choose to reply to that part of Mr. M.'s last letter which applies to himself.

Yours, &c.

KINCLAVEN.

April 26, 1837.

P. S.—I really must say, that your correspondent Nautilus is one of the most fastidious gentlemen I have ever had to deal with in my lucubrations in the *Mechanics' Magazine.* In correcting an expression which " O. N." (who has since proved himself to be an able mathematician) copied from Leadbetter's astronomy, I stated it ought to be " the difference of longitude between the Pole Star and the first scruple of Cancer (see No. 705, page 367). Nautilus has since found out a more concise expression, which he states " is to be found in every primer of geography, which would have exactly and concisely conveyed the same meaning. The expression should have been " The distance of polaris from the *solstitial colure,*" &c. (see No. 714, page 19). I beg leave to inform Nautilus, that I decidedly differ with him in opinion; the distance between polaris and the solstitial colure is surely not an arch of the ecliptic upon which celestial longitude is reckoned. An infinite number of great circles (and small ones too) might be drawn through polaris to intersect the solstitial colure; which of all these great circles are we to use? Why, none of them. Could you, Nautilus, describe a great circle that would coincide with a portion of the ecliptic, and pass through polaris? I should think not. There is a small error in my last article, which, Mr. Editor, I would wish you to correct (lest I should hear of it again). No. 718, page 41, col. 2, for " a first impulse was given to the matter," read "a first impulse was given to matter."

K.

MR. BADDELEY'S FIRE REPORTS—ANONYMOUS CORRESPONDENCE.

Sir,—I have been not a little surprised at the reason assigned by Mr. Baddeley for his determination to give no reply to my last letter on the Fire Insurance System. The perusal of the remaks on anonymous correspondence to which you request his attention, will probably work some change in his opinions on the subject;—opinions which he must certainly have taken up at a *still more recent period*, than those he has of late chosen to advance as to the indiscriminating beneficence of the Insurance Companies.

It is difficult to see in what consists the force of the objection to anonymous correspondence in a periodical,—at any rate where facts are not concerned. Now, as it happens, all the facts that are alluded to in the letter in question, rest on very good authority,—no less than that of Mr. William Baddeley himself; so that he will hardly take an exception on that score. As to the conclusions drawn from them, the readers of the *Mechanics' Magazine* will most likely allow them to pass quite as current with the signature of "Aquarius" attached, as if they were graced with the name and local habitation of "John Smith" or "William Jones." If Mr. Baddeley pleases, he may suppose either of these names to figure at the end of the communication, which has excited his ire, and fall to work with a good conscience accordingly. To the uninitiated it appears a matter of very small consequence, whether a paper confined to reasoning alone be sent forth to the world with or without a name. "William Baddeley" itself, is "*vox et præterea nihil*" to the vast majority of

the readers of the *Mechanics' Magazine;* that is to say, the weight which it carries is due, not to the fact of its being a real name, but to the merits of the many preceding articles which have proceeded from the same source: had Mr. B. always written under the signatnre of "X. Y. Z.," by this time, with ninety-nine readers out of every hundred, "X.Y.Z." would have excited as much influence as "William Baddeley" in his own proper person.

But how long has this antipathy to anonymous correspondence existed? Not long, certainly, as the pages of your last volume will bear witness, filled, as several of them are, with replies, by Mr. Baddeley, to the letters of " P. R." and " Fire-Fury" on this very question of Fire Insurance (Vide vol. xxvi. pp. 157, 158, 159, 227, 228. 229, 261, 262, 263). Changed are the times, indeed, since our worthy friend rushed with such ardour to the combat *with a pair of anonymous antagonists*—that he headed his letter with the quotation—

" Lay on, Macduff,"

evidently with a covert allusion to the succeeding line—

"And damn'd be he that first cries, Hold !—enough !"

of which your readers will be apt enough, *now*, to make an awkward application. " The Temple sendeth not forth her champions against *nameless men*," quoth Mr. Baddeley; but what would be thought of the knight who should cover his retreat from the lists by such a plea, immediately after encountering two masked assailants, in whose case it was never even dreamt of?

I remain, Sir,

Very respectfully yours,

AQUARIUS.

17th May, 1837.

PICTURE-BUYING SOCIETIES.

Amid the numerous schemes for joint-stock companies, which sprung into being some years ago in England, there was none, so far as we know, that had for its object the encouragement of art; that invention was reserved for Germany. Among our Teutonic neighbours they have now for some years been popular; they have recently been introduced at Liverpool, and two schemes are now on foot for the establishment of similar companies in London. In each, the annual subscription is a guinea, and in each the equivalent which the subscribers are to receive is to be the annual chance of acquiring a work of art; but in other respects the plans are different. In one society, which bears the name of the "Art-Union," the prizes are to be of different sums of money, which those who gain them are to lay out on any modern productions of painting or sculpture which they may themselves select from the exhibitions of the Royal Academy, the Society of Painters in water-colours, &c. In the other, the "Society for the Encouragement of British Art," the prizes are to consist of paintings, &c. previously chosen by a select committee appointed by the main body of the subscribers. It is alleged that the latter plan will secure a better employment of the patronage of the society than can be possible when it is distributed by individual hands. The scheme is, however, open to so many objections, that we cannot but anticipate that the Art Union will attract in a far greater degree the patronage of the public. A person who gains one of the great prizes of the Encouragement Society, may often be more puzzled than the poor Vicar of Wakefield, where to put it, and the very proposal of selecting by a committee, shows that it is intended that the "fortunate holder" shall occasionally be saddled with something not much to his taste. Etty's picture of the Syrens in the present exhibition of the Academy is, we suppose, to be considered a specimen of "high art," but how many persons in this, or any other metropolis would like to have it hung up in their best parlour? It strikes us, in fact, that the plan of the Encouragement Society is best suited for the convenience of artists, and that of the Art Union for the convenience of the public, and that as the power is in the hands of the latter, the result may be expected to be conformable. One feature is absent from the plans of the two Societies, which might, we think, be advantageously added to both. The British Institution has done itself immortal honour by presenting some fine pictures to the National Gallery. Might not the Art Union lay by an annual sum, and its rival annually devote its best picture, to the augmentation of the same collection? This would enable the subscriber of a guinea to participate in a patriotic gratification hitherto reserved exclusively for the rich and great. These presents would be the more appropriate, as being in many instance the production of British artists.

SOLUTION OF A CAMBRIDGE STUDENT'S 2ND GEOMETRICAL PROBLEM (PROPOSED IN NO. 706).—BY O. N.

Problem. Given the base, the vertical angle, and the rectangle contained by the sides, to construct the plane triangles upon principles not extending beyond the 3rd Book of Euclid.

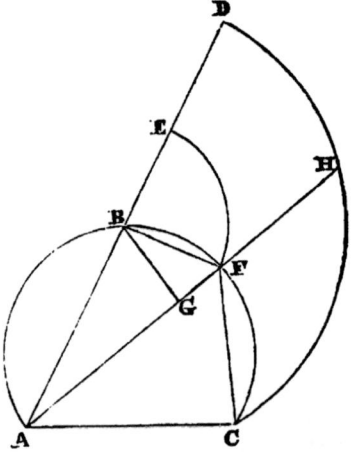

Upon the given base, A C, describe a segment of a circle A B C containing an angle equal to the given angle. Bisect the arc A B C in B, and from the centre B, distance A B or B C, describe the semicircle A C D, and draw the diameter A C D, which divide in E; so that the rectangle contained by A E, E D may be equal to the given rectangle contained by the sides of the required triangle; from the centre B, and distance B E, describe an arc meeting the circle A B C in F. Join A F, F C, then shall A F C be the triangle required.

Produce A F to meet the circle A C D in H, and draw B G perpendicular to A E. Join C E and B F. Then $A F . F H + G F^2 = A G^2$; adding $B G^2$ to both then $A F, F H + B G^2 = B G^2 + A G^2 = A$

F. F G + B F² (or B E²). But B G² + A G² = A B² = A E. E D + B C² therefore A F. F H + B E² = A E. E D + B E². Hence A F. F H = A E. E D. But F H = F C.* Therefore A F. F C = A E. E D = to the given rectangle. Therefore, &c.　W. W. D.

O. N.

P.S.—Your astronomical correspondent, Nautilus, commenced his first essay in the *Mechanics' Magazine* to the tune of " Cropies lie down." But I am much afraid (unless he pays a little more attention to his lucubrations) his last dance will be to the tune of " Roslin Castle"(the 'Dead March'). His geographical primer (No. 714, page 19) is downright nonsense, and I trust Kinclaven will tell him so. He informs Nauticus (No. 714, page 20) that if he will put him in possession of certain formulæ as given in some of the memoirs of the Astronomical Society, that he (Nautilus) will solve the question, that he (Nauticus) proposed in No. 711. Now I beg leave to inform Nautilus, that although he was put in possession of the formulæ he will never solve Nauticus's question. The reason why, I shall leave him to find out. Instead of Nauticus's question, I beg leave to propose one of the same kind, which will be found to be possible, and which I request may be solved in such a way that any one acquainted with spherical trigonometry may understand the solution.

On Feb. 1st, 1837: In lat. 55..58 north, and longitude 3..13 west, the stars Procyon and Capella, when east of the meridian, were both observed to be in the same azimuth circle. Question. To determine the apparent time of observation ?

THE FRENCH SCIENTIFIC ANNUAL.

In our recent notice of Dr. Thomson's " British Annual," it was incidentally mentioned that it originated from a suggestion that the "Annuaire" of the French Board of Longitude might not be unwelcome to the English public in an English dress. The original work itself is now before us,* and presents, in many particulars, a strong contrast to its follower and imitator, and, in not a few instances, its copyist. For one thing, there is a vast difference in size and price. Dr. Thomson's book was rather a consumptive 18mo., neatly done up in the prevalent fashion of cloth-binding, and charged, if we recollect rightly, at the genteel sum of four or five shillings. The " Annuaire" is a substantial tome, presenting its readers with pretty nearly three hundred and fifty pages of " closely-printed letter-press," (to say nothing of a bookseller's catalogue of fifty or sixty pages more, stitched in along with it); rather shabbily sewed in paper covers, to be sure—but, to make up for that, vended to the reading public at the low charge of " one franc,"—to wit, *ten-pence* of the good and lawful money of Great Britain! Surely, this must satisfy the most ardent admirer of cheapness, and reduce the whole body of the Useful Knowledge Society to despair; it fairly outdoes all their out-doings. The fact is, we suppose, that our over-channel friends have the assistance of the government purse in getting up and sending forth their lucubrations,—a consideration which at once " plucks out the heart of the mystery," and relieves Dr. Thompson and his worthy publisher from all suspicion of an heinous attempt to extort an undue amount of cash from the pockets of such as the lieges as might be inclined to patronize a home-bred " Annuaire." In England, every thing is allowed to stand (or fall) on its own bottom; in France, hardly any establishment seems able to exist without the " support" of the government,—except the gaminghouses, which probably form one of the sources from whence the " Bureau des Longitudes" derives the funds which enable them to produce their Annual at ten-pence. If Dr. Thomson were awarded a decent per-centage on the winnings and losings at Crockford's, he would doubtless engage to undersell even his Parisian rivals. But it will perhaps take some time to persuade John Bull that " rowley-powley" may be made a prolific parent of astronomical calcula-

---

* This important property of the circle was first demonstrated by Kinclaven, in vol. xvi, page 63 of the *Mechanics' Magazine*.

* Annuaire pour l'an 1837, présenté au Roi par le Bureau des Longitudes. Prix, 1 franc. Paris, 1836. Bachelier. 18mo., pp. 343.

tions, or "blind hookey" the munificent founder of an observatory!

But a truce with digressions. The "Annuaire" commences with a very full calendar for 1837, which is followed by a vast variety of tables of the same complexion as those in its English imitator; indeed, they are in a great measure the originals of those contained in the latter work, many of which, from their nature, contrast so strongly with the very exclusively-national tone of its title. The tables of old and new weights and measures, in particular, are excessively minute and elaborate. The chief statistical details introduced, relate to the consumption of Paris in 1835, and what the French call the "movement of the population" for the same year, i. e. the "births, marriages, and deaths." With these are mingled an infinity of tables on a vast variety of subjects; among others, on the "Decimal Monies of France," the "Weight and Diameter of Coins," "English Measures compared with French," "Linear Foreign Measures compared with French," "Laws of Mortality in France and England," "Latitudes of the principal Places in France," "Heights of Mountains," and a host of similar matters. The calendar and these tables occupy the first two hundred and twenty pages; and the remainder of the work—no less than a hundred and twenty pages more,—is occupied by "Scientific Notices," a head which is this year confined to a single article, on a subject by no means destitute of interest to the English reader; it is the production of M. Arago, the distinguished member of the Institute, whose name has been well known in this country since the publication of his voyage round the world with Captain Freycinet, and is entitled, "An Historical Notice on Steam-Engines."

M. Arago's chief object, in this rather lengthy paper, is to put in a claim, on the part of his countrymen, to a share—(not to mince the matter, to a principal share)—in the invention of the steam-engine; and, joined to this, is an ever-appearing desire to prove that all the English writers on the subject have endeavoured, with one accord, to suppress the evidence in favour of the French claims, and, at whatever risk, to deck their own countrymen in the laurels torn from the brows of their neighbours. The result, in both instances, is—failure. After all the facts adduced, M. Arago is constrained to allow, that "Newcomen's, or the atmospheric engine, was the first which rendered any real service to industry," and to leave the name of WATT unchallenged on its "proud pre-eminence;" while his sweeping charge against the whole body of English scientific historians needs only the quotation of his own words to refute it. Will it ¡be believed, that, after indulging in page after page of wholesale animadversion on that excessive self-love which, according to him, has led every Englishman who has touched upon the topic to disguise and distort the truth for the "honour and glory" of his own countrymen,—after preparing his readers to expect, from his own gallant and Gallic arm, the complete demolition of the whole national fortress of lies and deceit,—after magnifying to the utmost the amazing labour and research expended by himself in getting at the root of the matter, under the mass of fraud and falsehood with which British vanity had overlaid it,—will it be believed, after all this, that his long-winded exordium concludes with the sneaking acknowledgment which follows?

"I ought to observe, before concluding this preamble, that a remarkable work has recently appeared in England itself, entitled, 'A Descriptive History of the Steam-Engine, by Robert Stuart,' in which all the trials made to turn the vapour of water to account as a mechanical agent, are appreciated with great discernment, and, which is much more rare, with an entire freedom from national prejudice; with a few exceptions, the opinions of Mr. Stuart on the relative merit of the various engineers who have borne a part in the creation of that wonderful machine, are perfectly conformable to those which I had formed from the perusal of the original authorities; a concurrence so flattering to me, that I gladly hasten to avail myself of it. I will even add, that if my Notice had not been in a great measure prepared when I became acquainted with Mr. Stuart's history, I should probably have contented myself with inserting here a simple analysis of his work; the object I propose to myself would, by that means, have been equally attained."

Did ever author before show himself up in so ridiculous a false position as this? The Irishman who turned his back upon himself, was but a type of M. Arago; even *he* would have thought it going a trifle too far to bring forward a truth-telling Cretan, by way of proof, that "all the Cretans are liars." Nor is this all. Further on, when M. Arago has set all his proofs in favour of his countryman, Papin, before the reader, with a very grandiloquent summing up of his merits, he very quietly observes, in a note, " Messrs. Stuart, and Partington have explicitly acknowledged all these titles of Papin to the gratitude of mechanicians." So then, after all his tirade, as to the influence of national prejudice in pro-curing the denial of Papin's claims on all hands, from the peer to the peasant, in England, it turns out, on his own showing, that the writers of the only two distinct histories of the steam-en-gine, which our literature possessed, at the time his paper was written,—actually render the very fullest measure of jus-tice to the merits of French invention ;—that very measure of justice, to the full, which it is the professed object of his paper to seek, and, *if possible*, obtain.

The whole affair, so far, gives rise to a vehement suspicion, that M. Arago, who is so apt to suspect others, has been guilty of a literary larceny himself. He wishes it to be believed, that his paper is the result of a series of elaborate re-searches made by himself in order to free the question from the mystification in which British ingenuity, spurred on by British vanity, had enveloped it; and that he did not meet with Stuart's work, by which all his labours would have been forestalled, until after his own task was completed. Believe it who will! To us the story appears in the highest degree incredible. Stuart's History was published three or four years before M. Arago took the matter in hand, and must naturally have been one of the first works to which he had recourse: if not, how extensive must have been his research,—how complete his reference to British authorities! The book once in hand, the rest of the task was easy. It consisted only in abridging its contents, and interspersing the hash with savoury morsels of abuse of the whole generation of the author's countrymen, for sup-pressing the very facts which were thus being turned to account against them! This is " quartering upon the enemy"

with a vengeance ; a highly refined im-provement on the art of adding insult to injury.

The facts which M. Arago has thus retailed to the pupils of the Ecole Poly-technique, are certainly of such a nature, as satisfactorily to establish the claim of Papin to a highly honourable station among the earlier inventors of the steam-engine. Indeed, as is observed by Mr. Elijah Galloway *another Englishman*, in *his* history, " it is to be regretted that he discontinued his experiments, as they would have probably led him to the dis-covery of the atmospheric engine." That discovery was reserved for our country-man, Newcomen, who, as we have already seen, is allowed by M. Arago, himself, to have produced the first working steam-engine ever made; notwithstanding this admission, however, it goes sadly against the grain, to allow the shadow of a shade of merit to be his due. M. Arago shows all the expertness of a practical tactician in throwing a cold blanket over his pre-tensions. While divers wood-cuts are devoted to the elucidation of Papin's con-trivance, the far more elaborate and com-plicated one of Newcomen is left to shift for itself with dry words alone, and, in those words, his production is never alluded to, but as a *modification*, an *im-provement*, of Papin's machine, and *the latter* is always pointed to as " the at-mospheric engine." Newcomen's engine, as soon as it appeared, effected a com-plete revolution in the draining of mines, and that too, in Papin's lifetime, and under Papin's observation, without his ever claiming the invention as his own; yet M. Arago delights himself by turning such nicely-rounded phrases as " *the at-mospheric engine of Papin, thus improved by Newcomen* attracted universal atten-tion," and so on, with the evident view of impressing on the mind of the cursory reader the idea that Newcomen's engine, on its first appearance, was generally recognized as the invention of Papin, " new-revived" only by the mechanician whose name it has always borne, from its first introduction to this day. This is a trifling with fact, quite unworthy of a professed searcher after the plain truth: a sort of *finesse*, which the advocate of a sound cause would hardly feel obliged to resort to.

The same *modus operandi*, is carried into effect in another quarter, where it is still more glaringly absurd. Savery's ingenious machine is actually described under the character of an amelioration of the hot-water fountain of De Caus. It would be only a few steps further to describe a regular Boulton and Watt as an improvement on the tea-kettle,—for "is there not *steam* in both, look you?" De Caus's machine (as every English reader knows) consists merely in a boiler with a pipe at the top, to let out the water in a jet when sufficiently heated to produce steam. It is a mere philosophical toy. M. Arago takes the trouble to give a diagram of this simple contrivance (a little altered from his original, by the way) and when he comes to Savery's engine, exhausts all his ingenuity in describing its numerous and complicated parts, without the assistance of any graphic illustration beyond the view of De Caus's toy, of which he takes it for granted, that Savery's engine is a mere copy. The reader will easily guess what hard work this must be: it is, in sooth, a very serio-comic exhibition to see M. Arago labouring to prove that Savery *only* added another boiler here, a receiver there, a pipe of communication in a third place, a few valves where they were evidently required, and besides these trifles, *a new principle never dreamed of by De Caus,*—that of condensation,—and, by this *simple process,* succeeded in tearing the laurels of invention from the deserving brows of his illustrious countryman! — And, yet the perpetrator of this tomfoolery is a gentleman, who is never tired of lauding his own impartiality, and interspersing his lucubrations with exclamations of surprise at the extent, to which *English* writers have been carried by the blindness of national predilection!—Burns's verse,

" Oh ! wad some power the giftie gie us
    To see oursells as ithers see us !"

may well be applied to M. Arago. There is scarcely a line of his elaborate essay which does not bear testimony to the thoroughly *French* bias of its author; nor, perhaps, a matter of fact which is not more or less distorted to suit his view of the question.

The claims of the Marquis of Worcester to the invention of the steam-engine are not worth supporting; indeed, it is a matter of surprise that they should ever have been seriously put forth, es-

pecially as we have only his word (the word of a daily inventor of impossibilities) and a description so vague, that it would require more ingenuity to decipher its meaning than to invent the whole machine anew;—to prove that he ever discovered any machine of the kind. In all probability, if it ever *was* made, it was not a much rarer approach to the modern steam-engine than the "simple" apparatus of De Caus. These two may be pitted against each other, without much loss of national credit on either side; unless, indeed, the odds be given to the Frenchman, on the ground that he *did* describe his machine, while the Marquis wisely kept his secret (if any) to himself : a measure which, it might be thought, would have been sufficient to quash any claim to the honour of the invention on his behalf, were his reputation for veracity ten times higher than it stands at present.

The claims of Papin are of a far higher order; so much so, that the trickery of M. Arago, perfectly in place as it was when the bolstering-up of De Caus was the object, might well have been spared (as unfortunately it has not been) in blazoning forth the merits of "the inventor of the atmospheric engine!" If M. Arago had confined himself to translating from his English authority, Stuart, he would probably have done more credit both to himself and to his country, which must needs share in some degree in the disgrace, especially when it is considered that this miserable effusion of spleen and malignity we have been exposing, has arrived at the honour of a *second edition* in a work of the national character of the "*Annuaire du Bureau des Longitudes.*"

Besides attempting to prove Papin the inventor of Newcomen's engine, M. Arago advances for him a claim to the title of the father of steam-navigation, which he supports with considerable success. We shall quote the passage in which this is done, as it possesses not a little interest, and a greater portion of novelty than now-a-days falls to the share of most dissertations on so hackneyed a theme. It may be as well to caution the reader, that M. Arago (a member of the Institute!) does not hold himself responsible for the fidelity of his extracts, a single moment after he has escaped from the trammels of "inverted commas,"—and not always while he is within them. This is a remark of some importance, inasmuch as, in quoting diagrams, he considers himself at liberty to introduce what alterations he pleases,—a privilege which (without hinting a word to his readers) he turns to some account. There are no diagrams in the following extract, but there is a parenthesis, in which "the atmospheric steam-engine" is familiarly mentioned as having been invented long before the date of Newcomen; this it may be as well to observe, is an addition of M. Arago's, and *not* a part of the original text of Papin. It presents an instance in point, of the *catching* style of the whole production:

"The application of steam-engines to navigation is, of all inventions of the mechanicians of modern times, the one which, in some countries,—America, for instance, seems to have led to the most important results. The honour of priority in the invention has, consequently, been very strongly contested. From the first, France has been quite out of the question; the contending parties have been only the English and the North Americans. The latter attribute the first application to Fulton, while the English produce the much earlier writings of Jonathan Hulls and Patrick Miller to sustain their cause. The argument is conclusive, as against Fulton: but may there not exist still older works than that of Jonathan Hulls, in which all· his ideas may have been forestalled?—Let the reader decide whether my researches on this point have been fruitless.

"The work of Jonathan Hulls is dated 1737. It contains—1. The figure and description of two paddle-wheels placed at the stern of the boat; 2, the proposal to turn the axis of the wheels by the aid of Newcomen's engine, then well known, but employed only, according to Hull's own expression, 'to raise water by fire.'

"The work of Patrick Miller appeared at Edinburgh in 1787. It also contains a description of paddle-wheels * * * * *

"This is the oldest matter, and the most in point, that the English critics have been able to bring forward in the discussions they have maintained with their American antagonists. I shall now in my turn furnish my quota of information.

"The work of Papin, from which I have before quoted, his ' Recueil' of 1695, contains *textually* the following (pages 57, 58, 59, 60):—

" ' It would take up too much space to describe here in what manner this invention (that of the atmospheric steam-engine) might be applied to the drawing of water from mines, *the throwing of bombs*, and *rowing*

against the wind. But I cannot help remarking how preferable this method would be to that ' of galley-slaves, for making quick progress at sea.' Some remarks follow on animal movers, which, observes our author, occupy a considerable space, and consume a great deal, even when they are not at work. He remarks that his pipes (or cylinders) could be less embarrassing, 'but,' says he, ' as they could not conveniently work oars of the usual construction, it would be necessary to employ revolving oars.' Papin relates that he had seen such oars attached to an axle in a boat of Prince Rupert's, and turned by horses. We shall soon see how he manages to transform the up-and-down movement of his piston into a rotatory one: ' The piston-rods must be furnished with teeth, in order to turn little toothed wheels, fixed to the axle of the oars.' But as a piston does not work with any effect at the lower part of its stroke, he proposed, in order that the rotary motion might be continuous, to employ several cylinders, the pistons of which should work in opposite directions, one beginning to ascend when another had arrived at the end of its stroke, and so on.' But, ' perhaps it may be objected,' adds Papin, ' that the teeth on the piston-rods, fitting into the teeth of the wheels, would, in going up and down, give opposite motions to the axle; that the ascending pistons would hinder the motion of the descending ones, and *vice-versa*.' But this objection is easily got rid of; for it is a very common thing with clockmakers to' fix toothed wheels on arbors or axles, in such a manner that, when propelled one way, they cause the axle to turn with them; but that, when moved the other way, they can turn freely without giving any motion to the axles, which may thus have a movement diametrically opposite to that of the wheels. The greatest desideratum of all, therefore, is simply the setting up of a factory for making with facility pipes of sufficient lightness and strength, and of equal dimensions from one end to the other,' &c.

" It appears then, that Papin proposed, in a printed work, to propel ships by the aid of the steam-engine, 42 years before Jonathan Hulls, who is regarded in England as the inventor."—p. 285.

Nor is our author satisfied with affirming a Frenchman to have been the theoretical inventor of steam-navigation; he will have it also, that his fellow countrymen were the first to reduce the idea to practice, although, even he cannot contend that they were the first to succeed in the attempt; and that, after all, seems the honour best worth the fighting for.

" In speaking of steam-engines in general, I have endeavoured to assign their a share of merit to the inventors properly so called, and to the engineers who have first reduced their ideas to practice. If we follow the same method in this instance, we shall find :—

" That M. Perier, in 1775, was the first to construct a steam-boat (a work by M. Ducrest, printed in 1777, contains an account of the experiments, at which the author was present : the date is thus authentically established).

" That trials on a larger scale were made in 1778 ; at Baume-les-Dames, by the Marquis de Jouffroy.

" That in 1781, M. de Jouffroy, passing from experiment to practice, actually established on the Saone a large boat of the same kind, which was not less than 46 metres long by 4½ metres wide.

" That the then Ministry referred to the Academy of Sciences, in 1783, the account of the successful results arrived at by this vessel, in order to decide whether M. de Jouffroy was entitled to the exclusive privilege which he sought.* (Messrs. Borda and Perier were named commissioners.)

" That the trials made in England by Mr. Miller, Lord Stanhope, and Mr. Symington, are of a much later date (the first belong to the year 1791, those of Lord Stanhope to 1795, and the experiment made by Symington, on a Scotch canal, to 1801).

" That, as the attempts of Messrs. Livingston and Fulton, at Paris, date only from 1803, they afford them still more slender claims to the invention, especially as Fulton had acquired, in England, a detailed acquaintance with the trials of Messrs. Miller and Symington, and as many of his own countrymen, Mr. Fitch among others, had engaged in public experiments with the same object from the year 1786. Let us never forget to add that the first steam-boat which was not given up after it had been tried— that the first which was ever applied to the transport of men and merchandize, was that constructed by Fulton at New York, in 1807, and which performed the voyage from that city to Albany. In England, the first steam-vessel which was ever seen in action to supply the wants of travellers and traffic, dates only from 1812."—p. 290.

On this we shall only remark, that this synopsis affords but little ground for the belief that M. Arago's researches have been so extensive and so profound as he would wish us to believe. He tells us

* The boat tried at Lyons contained two separate steam-engines. The events of the French revolution forced M. Jouffroy to emigrate, and frustrated all his attempts.

enough, indeed, of M. Perier and M. de Jouffroy (Frenchmen both), but his information on the whole question is lamentably deficient. Is it possible, we feel compelled to ask, that he can have prosecuted *any* researches beyond the sphere of France, without having met, for instance, with some mention of the earlier experiments of Symington, or at least a whisper of the name of " Bell of Helensburgh ?"

———

STEAM-ENGINE INQUIRIES.

Sir,—The insertion of the following inquiries in your interesting and valuable Magazine, and a satisfactory reply from one of your able correspondents, will much oblige

Your obedient servant,
W.

A person has recently purchased a five-horse power high pressure steam-engine, and with it a wrought-iron plate dome boiler, three-eighths of an inch thick, containing, to the water line, from 250 to 300 gallons, and the diameter of which boiler, at the water line, is two feet six inches ; and, being a second-hand engine, and the boiler having been used to work it, he is satisfied of its competency as relates to strength and capability of generating a sufficiency of steam for the purpose. But certain considerations induce him to wish to substitute for this small boiler another made of copper, three-sixteenths of an inch in thickness, containing 800 gallons of water to the water line, and the diameter of which at such line is five feet, and the dome to which is as proportionate in height, &c. as that of the small boiler.

The inquiry, therefore, is, that as it is proposed to throw precisely the same work upon the engine in using the large boiler, as would be, if using the small boiler, whether or not the substitution can be safely made, as relates to risk of bursting the large boiler, in consequence of its lesser thickness, &c.

The inquirer will not only be glad to know the fact in relation to the difference in the thickness of the metal, the size, and of the tenuity of each metal of which the two boilers are composed ; but he will feel much obliged by a demonstration by calculation (not algebraic) relative to the respective (probable) capabilities of the two boilers, having reference to the difference in their size and thickness only.

If not deemed too intrusive on the columns of the *Mechanics' Magazine*, and the kindness of some correspondent, the inquirer would feel obliged also if furnished with a formula by which to calculate the proper thickness of copper or sheet-iron in the construction of a boiler for a high or low pressure engine of any given horse power, based upon the size of the boiler, or the area of the evaporating surface, or any other point which should be the condition, or one of the conditions, of the computation.

Brighton, May 6, 1836.

A FEW WORDS OF RETROSPECTIVE CRITICISM.—MR. WILLIAMS IN REPLY TO O. N.

Sir,—Your Magazine has just been shewn me, in which I perceive I have been unhandsomely treated by a writer signing " O. N."; will you indulge me with leave to offer a few remarks in reply.

In December last, by the kind intention of my respected friend, Mr. Richard Evans, a few figures in the shape of calculation appeared as my production in your Magazine. In February, you inserted an explantion how that they appeared by accident, being intended only for private and momentary curiosity,—were hastily put together; the result was an error ;—its correction you obligingly inserted with the explanation.

Your correspondent " O. N." commented on both these letters with rather more acrimony than intelligence. In speaking of the first, he says (at p. 185 of December last), " *his method of solution is perfectly false.*" Pointing out the error was very commendable; but he imputed it to the wrong quarter; he attacked the method when he should have attacked the calculator. His language in italics is therefore very objectionable, and did not come well from him who was at the same time doing a sort of penance for errors of his own ; it was offering *one* error to atone for *another;* but what astonished me most, was the singular modesty of this writer, who, while himself was using *part* of the method to find the difference of longitude, &c. declared the *whole* to be perfectly false. The other part, under the zodiacal sign, I would suppose he had not been accustomed to, and which must have misled him in his remark ; he seemed not aware, that multiplying the differeuce of longitude by the cos. mid. lat. would have reduced it to the departure, and so would have produced a correct answer.

In March Magazine, p. 475, he tacitly admits his first judgment to be wrong, yet speaks of some errors of 50 and 60 per cent.; this is captious, and belongs to some other question not in dispute ; for I had given no opinion on the comparative merits of the different methods, therefore his remark was uncalled for, futile, and pedantic. It was sufficient that the method I adopted answered

the question in hand. The advantage of art lies in choosing the readiest way to obtain an end according to the data given ; were the latitudes high, or more especially, if the difference of latitude were great, I certainly would have used spherics ; but in Mr. Green's trip, the distance would be found without it ; and, besides, *distance* does not contribute to produce the error "O.N." speaks of, any further than it affects the difference of latitude, for as far as regards Mercator and mid. lat., the error in the difference of longitude varies as $\frac{\text{mer. diff. lat.}}{\text{prop. diff. lat.}}$ exceeds $\frac{\text{rad.}}{\text{cos. mid. lat.}}$, in which *distance* is not considered. But I cannot, perhaps, do better than by referring to Robertson's Mathematical Elements, edited by Wales ; this work is a magazine of mathematical information.

I observe a little thing by " O. N." on interest, at p. 474 of March last ; he would have done well if at the same time he had referred the reader to the same problem, with a solution less complicated, in Ward's celebrated Mathematician's Guide, published much above a century ago; or to Keith's well known Treatise of Arithmetic, or to any other work on the subject ; for if silent on books where these things are to be found, the discerning reader will soon perceive the jackdaw in pigeon's feathers.

Replying to an anonymous writer is contending with a person sheltered behind a disguised name; but, perhaps, were we more acquainted, we might be better friends: however, I shall only add that

I remain, Sir,
Yours obliged
JOSEPH WILLIAMS.

Swansea Savings' Bank, 9th May, 1837.

MANUFACTURE OF INDIA-RUBBER WEB IN PARIS.

(From the *Franklin Journal* for January.)

Gentlemen,—The general employment of gum elastic web, induces me to send you for publication, a brief notice of the processes for its manufacture, indulging the idea, that it may prove of sufficient interest to amuse, or perhaps instruct, some of the many readers of the Journal who are seeking for information.

Circumstances, which need not be related, enabled me to see in detail all that is noted in the following pages, at the manufactory, at Saint Denis, near Paris, which, if I am not mistaken, is the only establishment in France and which has a branch in London, both of which are usually kept impenetrably secret. The fabric was commenced at Vienna, but much improved and extended in the manufactory at St. Denis, in which there are about 1500 of the machines for plaiting the thread around the filaments of gum, and all the other departments in correspondent proportion.

No pledge was given, nor will any breach of confidence result from the publication of these notes, which were written immediately after the visit to the establishment in 1834.

Such as they are, they are at your service with the best wishes of

Your obedient servant,

FRANKLIN PEALE.

Philadelphia, February, 1837.

1st Operation.—The gum elastic is provided in the usual form of bottles. The first operation is to divide these bottles into two equal parts; they are then placed in piles fo six or eight in height and of an indefinate number in extent upon a plank, and another plank is placed upon them, when the two are drawn together by wooden screws and nuts. They remain in this state a sufficient time to render them flat, or to take out in a great measure the original curvature of the bottles.

2nd Operation.—The first machine contains a circular knife which revolves rapidly, its diameter being about 8 inches. At the side of its edge is an advancing carriage or slide, which receives its movement by means of a screw from the shaft of the knife. Upon this slide is attached the gum, a hole being made in its centre to receive a screw, which serves as a pivot upon which it may turn; it is held down by a nut that is screwed upon it, and the edges are held down by springs placed near to the knife, but not so strong as to prevent its turning under them. A box under the table contains water, in which the knife runs, and a box above it encloses the blade, and prevents the water from being thrown into the face of the workman. When the machine is started, the gum advances and is turned round by hand, whilst the knife cuts off the irregular circumference, until a continous slip comes off, which the workman takes hold off and draws away, the carriage advancing and the knife cutting until the gum is exhausted. The operation resembles the cutting of leather strings out of circular pieces of that material in the manner practiced in the olden time by shoemakers.

3rd Operation.—These slips pass into a bucket of water, from which they are taken and examined through their whole length by a woman, who removes the defective parts and joins together the ends of the slips, by cutting them off in a sloping direction and making a nick near the extremities, with a pair of sissors, in the manner indicated at fig. 1. These ends are then placed together, and

Fig. 3.

Fig. 1.

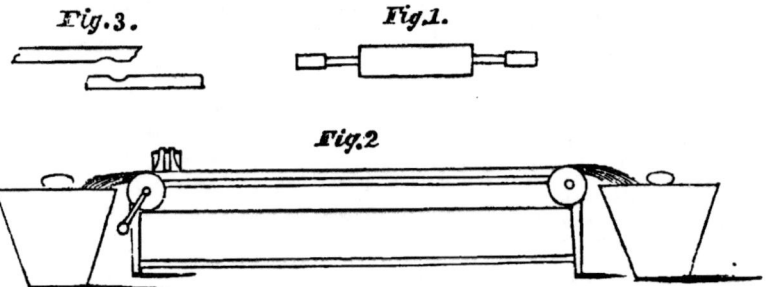

Fig. 2.

hammered with some force upon an anvil, by which means they are made to adhere with considerable tenacity.

4th Operation.—These slips thus joined pass to another engine, which resembles in almost all respects the slitting mills of iron works, of a size proportionate to the material upon which they operate. The slip, always contained in water, is guided into this cutting mill, which has five or six blades according to the width of the slip, and is kept in its place and prevented ftom turning by a slight spring. After passing between the cutters it is drawn off by two rollers, between which it passes, and from thence into the

hands of the attendant, who passes the slip, thus divided into threads, into water.

5th Operation.—The filaments then pass into the hands of females, who examine them through their whole extent, remove the imperfect parts, and join the extremities as before.

6th Operation.—The next machine is important, having for its object to remove the elasticity of the gum, or in other words, to stretch the filaments to their utmost extent. It consists of a reel of eighteen or twenty inches in diameter, revolving with considerable rapidity. Between the attendant and the reel is a wheel with several grooves of different diameters, revolving with a movement slow compared to that of the reel, and which has a transverse movement from the right to the left side, thus serving as a guide to the filament, and preventing it from overlapping upon the reel. This latter wheel was evidently intended to give an equal tension to the gum as it was wound upon the reel; but I observed that the filament was simply held by the hand, and the wheel only used as a guide, sufficient practice on the part of the workmxn giving to the motion every desirable regularity. The slips are left upon these reels to dry and harden for a period varying from three to six weeks.

7th Operation.—They are then wound upon bobbins by the usual means of a wheel and spindle, by a woman, care being taken to retain the tension.

8th Operation—The next operation is the plaiting of silk, cotton, thread, or other material, around the filament of gum, previously coloured or white, according to the objects into which it is subsequently to be manufactured. This is performed by an extremely ingenious machine, the construction of which it would be impossible to illustrate without drawings; the machines are manufactured, and for sale in Paris, by Blanchin, No. 98, Rue Faubourg, St. Martin. They have the important quality of stopping if a thread breaks or is exhausted.

9th Operation.—The machine last alluded to draws the filament off the bobbins upon which it was previously wound, and after plaiting around it, winds it again upon others, which, when filled, are conveyed to the looms, and there placed in frames, with a strap and counter weight to give the necessary tension, and in sufficient number to form the warp of the web, which of course varies in width according to the object to which it is destined. The looms were usually simple and moved by hand; but there are also looms capable of weaving six webs or more at the same time, the shuttles of which are furnished with racks, by means of which they are carried through the chain.

The plaited filament is combined with silk or other matter, and filled with different materials, according to the object of the manufacturer, and in this respect, all the variety of the weaver's art may be exercised.

All the operations thus far noticed have been performed by machinery, driven by a steam-engine, with the exception of the looms, which it appears to me are not necessarily excepted. In most of them the gum has been deprived of its elasticity; the last operation consists in restoring this quality. This is effected by taking advantage of that well known though extraordinary character which gum elastic possesses, of shrinking by the application of heat.

10th Operation.—The machine to effect this is a long table covered with coarse cloth or felting in several thicknesses; at each end is a shaft passing from one side to the other, upon which are pullies; a strap passes over these pullies, connecting the two ends of the table by a band, which has upon it a crotch. One of the shafts is furnished with a handle to give motion to the whole. These will be best illustrated by a sketch (fig. 2); a heavy square smooth iron, heated to a convenient degree, is drawn by means of these straps from end to end; three or four webs are laid upon the table at one time; their extremities on the right are held by weights, whilst a light block lies upon them at the other extremity, keeping them flat, but not preventing their advancing as they shrink by the application of the heat of the iron; inclined planes near the ends lift off the weight at the close of the operation. The iron is of the form indicated at fig. 3, with wooden handles for convenient management. Baskets at one end, and boxes at the other, receive and supply the web.

The web shrinks in length as the heated iron passes over it, to about two-thirds of the previous length, and has all its original elasticity restored. This operation closes the process, the web being subsequently prepared for sale by being made into rolls and properly packed.

IRISH PATENTS GRANTED IN THE MONTH OF APRIL, 1837.

John Baillie, of Suffolk-street, Southwark, Surrey, engineer, and John Patterson, of Trinity-square, London, gent., for improvements in propelling vessels and other floating bodies by means of steam and other power. April 3.

Miles Berry, of Chancery-lane, Middlesex, mechanical draftsman, for improvement or improvements in power-looms for weaving. April 18.

Miles Berry, of Chancery-lane, Middlesex, for improvement or improvements in making or constructing of meters or apparatus for measuring gas, water, and other fluids. April 18.

Henry Backhouse, of Walmersley, calico-printer, and Jeremiah Graves, engineer, both of Bury, Lancaster, for improvements in the art of block-printing. April 19.

James Pim, jun., of College Green, Dublin, banker, and Thomas Fleming Bergin, of Westland-row, Dublin, civil engineer, for an improved mode or method of propulsion on railways. April 25.

NOTES AND NOTICES.

Railway in Holstein.—Some interest has been felt in the question, whether the Danish government would sanction the making of a railway over the neck of land which, connecting the peninsula of Jutland with the continent of Germany, separates the waters of the North Sea from those of the

Baltic. The advantages to commerce in general of such a line are very obvious; but it is equally so, that all the traffic diverted into this channel from the circuitous track by the Cattegat will be withdrawn from the seas of Denmark, and freed from the onerous taxes of the Sound, which form no inconsiderable portion of the revenue of the Danish government. The decision has now been made, and it is in favour of the railway. The ground is ordered to be levelled at the expense of government, from Altona to Kiel, and likewise from Altona to Neustadt, preparatory to the construction of two lines of road, which, however, it is not the intention of the government to execute itself, but throw open to the competition of companies, or individual capital.

Paris and Brussels Railway.—The railway which has long been projected for uniting the capitals of France and Belgium, at length bids fair to be commenced in good earnest. The king of the French has just granted to Mr. John Cockerell, the celebrated English iron-master of Liege, the "concession" of the railway for fifty years. The French government is to advance 25 per cent. of the cost on the distance from Paris to the Belgian frontier; and Mr. Cockerill is to be entitled to all tolls and profits for the first half century, when, it is to be presumed, the works will become the property of the nation, The only condition with which the grant is accompanied, is, that the toll for the French portion of the railroad shall never exceed *fifteen* francs, or 12s. 6d. The terms of the concession were not agreed to until after the "high contracting parties," Louis Philippe on one side, and Mr. Cockerill on the other, had had several personal interviews. The latter must be allowed to possess a most adventurous spirit; he was a severe sufferer by the revolution at Brussels in 1830; and yet, it seems, is not deterred from adventuring his capital on a soil like that of France, which in fifty years may experience, probably, half as many revolutions.

Silk-worm Rearing Apparatus.—At the recent annual meeting of the French Central Agricultural Society, the report on the attempts of M. Camille Beauvais to introduce the rearing of silk-worms into the north of France excited the greatest share of attention. After several years spent in experiments, he has at length succeeded, by the aid of the system of ventilation of M. Darcet, in overcoming the principal difficulty,—the obtaining an equable temperature, and a constant succession of fresh air for the breeding-rooms; the result is, an increase of 31 per cent. in the produce of the cocoons. If the improvement could be universally introduced, therefore, the production of France would soon be equal to its consumption; but M. Darcet's apparatus is not applicable to every locality. The great bulk of the silk produced in France is made in places not specially-set apart for silk-worms; the object occupies, during the six weeks devoted to its rearing, a part of the dwelling of the family, among both rich and poor, sometimes barns or out-houses, in which the open coal-fire keep up the requisite heat, and at the same time assist in the ventilation. It often happens, that the breeding succeeds better in an open barn than in closer situations, on account of the air being oftener changed : where such is the

case, the apparatus of M. Darcet will hardly come into use, although in the end it is probable that the system of M. Camille Beauvais will be brought to bear. According to the glowing anticipations of the Agricultural Society, this system, combined with the information which one of M. Beauvais' pupils has sailed to China, "the land of silk," expressly to obtain, and with the light to be thrown on the subject by a Chinese work which M. Stanislaus Julien is about to translate, will sooner or later relieve France from the heavy burden of seventy-five millions of francs which she is now obliged to pay to Italy and Turkey for the importation of an article so necessary to her most important manufactures.

North London Cemetery.—The works of the Highgate Cemetery, adjoining the conspicuously situated new church, are now in full activity. The locality is certainly one of the finest that could have been selected so near to the metropolis,—it commands views of great extent and beauty. This is the cemetery whose projection we noticed some time ago; the actual execution of the plan, however, has only just commenced. Notwithstanding its contiguity to the church, the establishment is to be provided with a chapel of its own, though, apparently, one of the smallest possible dimensions.

Beet-root Sugar.—The cultivation of the beetroot sugar manufacture progresses rapidly in France. The gross produce of "indiginous sugar" in 1835, was of the value of thirty millions of francs; in 1836, it amounted to forty-eight millions. The manufacture is now carried on in 431 communes, in which were 542 establishments already in full activity, and no less than thirty-nine building. If France can only get ships and commerce, she seems inclined to do without colonies at all, at least at the breakfast-table, where "chicorée" is often the substitute for coffee, and beet-sugar the only sweetener.

Iron Trinkets.—A beautiful and delicate specimen of sand-casting, from the foundry of Messrs. Harvey & Co., at Hayle, attracted, as it merited, general attention. Chains of a similar kind, it is well known, form a staple article of manufacture at Berlin, where they are usually constructed by *casting* the rosettes first, and then uniting them by *wrought-iron* links. The mode of formation of that exhibited by Messrs. Harvey & Co. was peculiar; the rosettes were first cast, each separately, and then the small adjoining links were afterwards *cast*, each in its present position, probably the first specimen of a similar process ever attempted.—*Fourth Annual Exhibition of the Royal Cornwall Polytechnic Society.*

True Meridian.—The Royal Cornwall Polytechnic Society announces, in their (fourth) annual report for the last year, that they are making preparations to supply "a desideratum long wanted by the accurate determination of the true meridian." The spire of St. Keven's church has been fixed on as the southern extremity of the line; and it is intended to erect a granite pillar in a field to the westward of Beacon Hill, to make its other extremity near Falmouth. This will give a base line of about 40,000 feet, and it is hoped that it will be continued through the country to the Bristol Channel.

☞ *British and Foreign Patents taken out with economy and despatch; Specifications, Disclaimers, and Amendments, prepared or revised; Caveats entered; and generally every Branch of Patent Business promptly transacted.*
A complete list of Patents from the earliest period (15 Car. II. 1675,) to the present time may be examined. Fee 2s. 6d.; Clients, gratis.

LONDON: Printed and Published for the Proprietor, by W. A. Robertson, at the Mechanics' Magazine Office, No. 6, Peterborough-court, between 135 and 136, Fleet-street.—Sold by G. W. M. Reynolds, Proprietor of the French, English, and American Library, 55, Rue Neuve, Saint Augustin, Paris.

𝔐𝔢𝔠𝔥𝔞𝔫𝔦𝔠𝔰' 𝔐𝔞𝔤𝔞𝔷𝔦𝔫𝔢,

MUSEUM, REGISTER, JOURNAL, AND GAZETTE.

| No. 720. | SATURDAY, MAY 27, 1837. | Price 3d. |

WINDMILL-PUMP IN THE ISLINGTON NEW CATTLE MARKET.

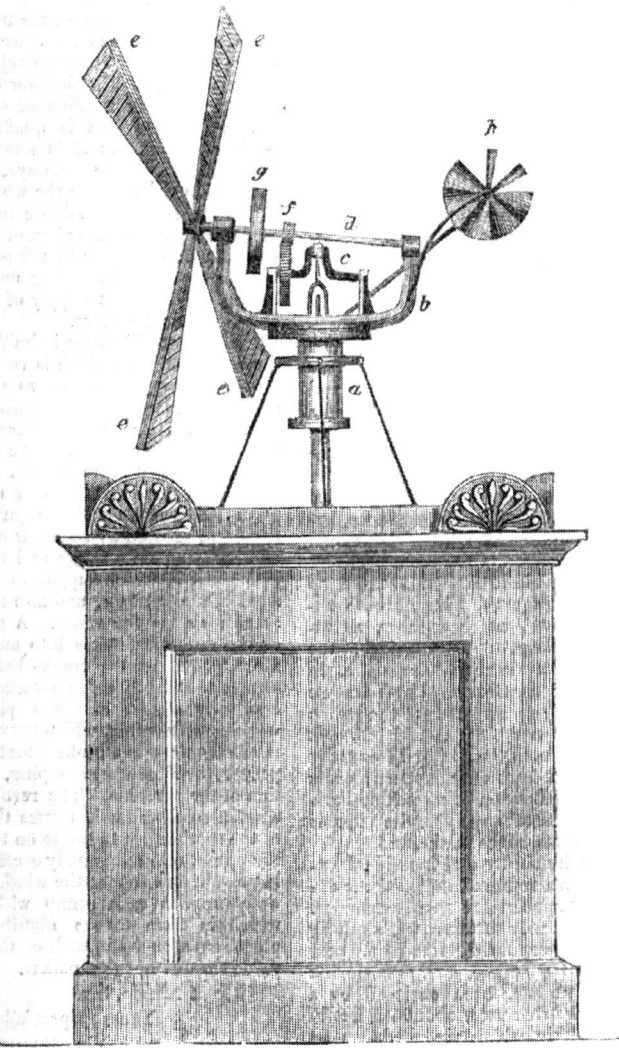

WINDMILL-PUMP IN THE ISLINGTON NEW CATTLE MARKET.

Sir,—Who is there amongst us that has not heard of Smithfield· (or, as it is commonly called by its frequenters, *Smif-feld*), the scene of many a matchless deed in England's chequered history ? It was here, in former times, that tilt, and tournament, and pageants, delighted the flower of the nobility of all Europe. It was here, the rebel Tyler fell by the hand of London's loyal mayor. It was on this spot, accursed bigotry led men to inflict tortures upon their fellow-men, because they were not all disposed to address the UNIVERSAL FATHER in precisely the same manner. It is here that riot and debauchery hold their annual revels, sacred to Saint Bartholomew. These, and a thousand other notable events, have combined to render Smithfield a place of great celebrity. It has, however, acquired the greatest and most unenviable notoriety from its *beastly* Monday and Friday markets, which are continually productive of scenes disgraceful to those who wear " the human form."

The bare idea of cattle-markets and slaughter-houses in the very heart of a crowded and populous city, is revolting, to say little of the personal inconvenience and dangers which are the necessary and inevitable consequences. The removal of this most intolerable nuisance has long been desired by a large majority of the citizens; but the few (comparatively speaking) whose interests are mixed up with its continuance, have hitherto opposed, with too much success, all attempts at reform. " The removal of the market was a matter of mammon, in which, even the fear of unwholesome meats and the preservation of the public health, were not duly considered. It was a question of *finance*, and humanity was but a feather in the balance; while the taunt, of London being behind Paris in the means of supplying its citizens with food, was borne in silence."

Private humanity and individual enterprize have removed many of the obstacles that appeared to oppose a change. An area of nearly fifteen acres, abutting on the Lower Road, Islington, near Ball's Pond Turnpike, has, as is already generally known, been enclosed by a substantial brick wall, about ten feet in height, within which are sheds on all the four sides. Each side is eight hundred feet long, and the span of the roofing to the sheds is twenty-five feet. The roofs rest on the enclosing walls outward, and on substantial piers within. These sheds are divided into pens or stalls, with yards or lairs before them in which the cattle may range. A road goes round on each side of the market, within the lairs before the stalls ; and within this road are other yards or lairs, for cattle also, but these are without sheds. The remainder of the inner area is formed into pens for sheep. The centre of the inner area, a circle of 150 feet diameter, is intended for a sort of exchange for the meeting of salesmen, &c. The inner area is quadrated by roads crossing it at right angles, in a line with the entrance gateways. Drains and sewers run through the whole area, and there is much to admire in the arrangements and mechanism of the various fittings, especially in the mode that has been adopted for raising and distributing an abundant supply of that necessary element—water.

This is effected by two windmill-pumps, the construction of which is very ingenious, and the plan is such as might be adopted in many situations with peculiar advantage. The accompanying sketch will give a tolerable idea of the mechanism of these useful engines. In the centre of a stone building of a quadrangular form, is erected the pump a of cast iron, secured by strong iron braces, and carrying on a flange at its top, an iron frame b, which supports the crankshaft of the pump, c, and also the vane-axle d; $e\,e$ are the vanes. A pinion f, on the vane-axle, takes into and drives a spur wheel on the crank-shaft of the pump, the piston being attached to the crank by slings, and the piston-rod working in a guide, which preserves its parallellism : g is a brake-wheel for impeding, or altogether stopping, the motion of the machine. The revolution of a set of small vanes h, causes the whole of the mechanism to rotate on the top of the pump, and continually occasions the large vanes $e\,e$ to face the wind. A good well supplies each pump with water, which is from thence distributed by pipes into troughs in each of the cattle-yards throughout the market.

I remain, Sir,

Yours respectfully,

WM. BADDELEY.

April 17, 1837.

SEQUEL TO A VOICE FROM THE SHOPBOARD.

Sir,—Your correspondent, J. R. Croft, having conceived and brought forth an invention, seems prepared to go his whole length in absurdity, rather than see the offspring of his brain treated as an abortion. With a parental fondness for his bantling, far more creditable to his feelings as a philanthropist than to his judgment as a mechanic, he sets up his dogmatical opinion in its favour, against the united experience of a whole class, whose knowledge of the convenience or inconveniences, attending a particular mode of performing a certain kind of work, must qualify them much better to estimate its real merits, as designed for their use, than its fabricator.

Mr. C. says he leaves to me "the physiological discussion of the subject." If this is intended as a sarcasm, because I offered a hint in my last paper, which implied a smattering of this subject, I am willing to receive one of those reproofs, to which my unconscious ostentation might have exposed me; but as the nature of the question necessarily led to the principles of the science, I trust the reader will consider my allusion to it as a venial offence. If, however, your correspondent is serious, in conceding this ground of the controversy to me, he virtually yields the point contended for; since, if he cannot prove that any law of physiology is violated by the posture of sitting he complains of, he cannot plead the necessity of a change, nor establish the advantage of any other mode proposed. On the contrary, I have my own practical knowledge, as well as that of many others, to show that no physical evil results from it, and that no expedient can answer the purpose so well, as that in common use.

Mr. C. tells us, he "proposes nothing but sitting on a stool, in an ordinary manner." But does he conceive that this kind of sitting for tailors has never before been tried and abandoned? Are we to suppose, that as soon as the male sex began to sew together their own garments, they erected a *shopboard*, on which to sit cross legged? Is it not far more natural to conjecture that the plan J. R. C. recommends was the *original* one, and that the present mode was a subsequent improvement, suggested and adopted in consequence of the inconvenience and tediousness of the other?

In consequence of my alluding to instances of benefit, instead of injury, resulting from the common posture, Mr. Croft is seized with a paroxysm of squeamish incredulity, and proceeds with a string of interrogatories, which no doubt he concludes to be a poser to "the tailor;" but which, in truth, is nothing more than a refinement upon the logical shifts often resorted to by way of evading the force of an opponent's arguments. "Do surgeons," he asks, "recommend the posture used in the trade to cure distortions?" To this, I reply that whether they do or not, is nothing at all to the purpose; and if Mr. C. has made up his mind to doubt every thing given as a fact in physiology, till it is sanctioned by the *imprimatur* of the "Royal College," his faith must often be staggered at some of the most obvious truths. I see no reason why we should presume the surgery to be the repository of all remedial knowledge; or why, even supposing the remedy in question to be amongst its stores, we should expect surgeons to recommend their patients of deformed legs to turn tailors for a cure, any more than they should advise those with awkward gaits, knock-knees, and turned out toes, to enter the lists at the Horse Guards, because it is known that the military drilling exercise tends to correct such defects; especially if the subjects of them should be of the more *delicate* sex!

I am next asked, "Do painters and sculptors seek their living models amongst the fraternity of tailors?" Oh! there's the rub! This happy home thrust, thinks he, will throw him off his shopboard, from whence his "voice" will no more be heard! I am, however, yet speakable, and have to say of this species of reasoning, that it shows him to be hard driven for sophisms. Your correspondent, presents to me something which he calls a new working board for a tailor, I endeavoured to prove the superiority of the old shopboard; but unless I can demonstrate that it has the effect of producing models of animal perfection as a turner's lathe would throw off handsome pillars and table legs, I am to be considered refuted! This is a new mode of foiling an antagonist.

I am not aware that any artist would

object to a tailor for his model, provided he were a good specimen of nature's handy work, in the symmetry and proportion of make; but probably Mr. C. thinks that she handles tailors in their formation, as if they were to be mere ninnies of humanity, and the oddities of her workmanship—the *fag ends* and *shreds* of her mouldings—in a word, fragments of men as they are proverbially called. I have no great wish to become special pleader for my fellow knights of the thimble (and for myself, my *puny frame* is against me); but if this be his opinion of the whole fraternity, I would just observe, that I have been much deceived by appearances, if I have not seen amongst them many a piece of human organisation bearing the strongest resemblance to what both painter and sculptor—yes, and even the *Colonel* of a regiment, would denominate " *a fine fellow.*" Since writing thus far, I have taken the opportunity of asking a member of the Royal Academy (a gentleman intimately known to the Editor of the *Mechanics' Magazine*), if it was a rule of the profession to select their models by the trade or calling they follow, and whether a tailor was exceptionable on that ground? And he tells me he is not aware of such rule. But even if this were the case, it would not at all invalidate my arguments against the utility of your correspondent's invention. It is sufficient for me to prove that the present method was more advantageous, which I consider I have fully done.

Your correspondent, in conclusion, although no tailor, with all the confidence of one of the most experienced in the trade, holds out his invention as a cure for all the evils he has imagined ascribable to the present manner of sitting, grounding his opinion of its merits on a solitary instance of trial in its crude state of formation. I do not mean to insinuate that there is any fiction in this; for I am willing to believe, that Mr. C. has been grossly deceived, partly from his own deficiency in the ability to investigate and distinguish causes; and partly from some interested or improper motives of his patient, misleading him. It is to be noticed that not a word is said respecting the nature or seat of the disease affecting him. It is probable that a bad knee, such as the white swelling, would hinder a man from sitting in the usual

manner, or by his so sitting, increase the complaint; but there is no proof that it could be the first *cause* of it: and if this was the disorder of the person alluded to, the conclusions founded on it, in all probability, are erroneous.

I have now finally done with the subject, leaving to your correspondent the last word in favour of his plan, if he choose to take it, and to the impartial reader to decide between us; at any rate, he will do no harm, if he does no good, by his project.*

R. MILLS.

Chard, April 16.

<hr/>

ARCHITECTURAL DEPARTMENT OF THE EXHIBITION OF THE ROYAL ACADEMY. — RAILWAY ARCHITECTURE.

The annual exhibition of the Royal Academy is not interesting to the lovers of the fine arts alone. Any one who takes an interest in the progress of public improvement in general, should never miss paying a visit to the room set apart for the display of architectural models and designs. In it he will always find collected an ample store of materials of the very best and most authentic description for forming an idea of what is going on in the way of great public and private works—a branch of information, which not only affords the most captivating intellectual amusement, but a never-failing supply of topics for general conversation.

In the exhibition of the present year, the railways now in course of construction, take, as might be expected, a very conspicuous place among the attractions of this attracting apartment. It is one of the most striking indications of the growth of architectural taste among us, that even in the great enterprises of utility, that utility is now required to be set off with splendour. Who ever thought of looking for elegance in the bridges over canals, or the warehouses at the side of them—Who looks for it in vain in

<hr/>

* The writer takes this opportunity of mentioning that he has an article of his own invention, which he has used for years, to facilitate the operation of cutting a coat, which, to a master of very extensive business, would prove a considerable saving of time. It consists of a piece of brass, in shape of a right angled triangle, graduated on mathematical principles; and is applicable to any system of cutting, for the purpose of finding the relative distances of the essential points of fitting, in any size, to the strictest nicety of practical measurement.

the entrances or in the terminations of railways? The last generation seemed contented to sink in public magnificence below the level of the Dutch—while the present seems to aspire to rivalry with the Romans. We find in this room (No. 1106), "the principal entrance of the London station of the London and Birmingham Railway, now erecting near Euston Square;" and (No. 1023), "the principal entrance of the station at Birmingham, now building," both from the design of Mr. Philip Hardwick. The former, the readers of the *Mechanics' Magazine* must be already familiar with from the engraving of it which appeared in No. 713, the first of the present volume—it has been, we believe, universally admired for its simple grandeur. Its *pendant* at Birmingham is of a plainer and more usual character—less severe in its details, and less striking, but still well worthy of the great undertaking it is intended to adorn. No. 1007, is a view of the Brent Viaduct at Hanwell, being part of the great Western Railway, from the design, and under the superintendence of J. K. Brunel. The arches are truly gigantic; their form is stern and massive; the whole is of a colossal grandeur, which reminds one of the most impressive works of the Romans. There can hardly be a greater contrast to this frowning line of arches than the "interior view of the arcade beneath the viaduct" of the projected Westminster and Greenwich Railway by Mr. J. D. Paine, in which ornament and elegance seem to have been the objects chiefly attended to. We believe that this project is not likely to be put in execution, but the failure must certainly not be attributed to any deficiency in setting off its advantages on the part of Mr. Paine. One seldom sees a more captivating sketch than his "birds-eye view of the railway taken from above the summit of the Duke of York's Column" (No. 1868), which, with its companion, has been lithographed, and has formed, for some months, an attractive ornament of the print-shop windows. This print will still preserve its value, even if the railway never be executed, since its winding line of arches forms a very inconspicuous portion of the picture, and when they are overlooked, which they easily may be, either with or without intending it, there still remains an ex-

cellent view of the metropolis taken from one of its most commanding points. Mr. Paine exhibits likewise the "Terminus of the St. Petersburgh and Zarskogeselo (Isarskoe selo) Railway from the drawings sent to St. Petersburgh, April, 1836" (No. 992). This is an elegant edifice of the Grecian style of architecture, but as it strikes us, more like a small temple, or a commemorative monument than the terminus of a railway, which, we consider ought, of ancient buildings most to resemble the triumphal arch. It should be evident on the first view, that it must be an entrance, and nothing else, and this characteristic is certainly not the most prominent one in Mr. Paine's drawing. It is better brought out in the "design for an entrance to a railway," by H. D'Oyley (No. 1082), and the "design for the principal entrance to a railroad," by N. T. Randall (No. 1045). Neither of these are, we believe, to be executed, though the latter has considerable merit, and both are certainly superior to the "design for the termination of the London Grand Junction Railway at Skinner-street in the city of London, a sketch submitted to the City Lands Committee and Committee of the House of Commons," by Smith and Barnes (No. 1035). It might perhaps be considered appropriate to give somewhat of a gloomy and prison like aspect to a building intended to be so close a neighbour of Newgate and Giltspur-street Compter, but as the situation of the Grand Junction City Terminus has now been shifted to a less melancholy vicinity, we hope the ideas of the directors have been elevated to a more cheerful "elevation." We can hardly congratulate Messrs. Smith and Barnes, on their other effort which "shows the proposed alteration in the north-west entrance to Greenwich Park, submitted to the Princess Sophia for her approval, as Ranger of the Park, by the Kent Railway Company" (No. 1097). The only interesting feature in this view is the new church which stands there already.

While the number of designs for railways gives proof how well the convenience of the public is being cared for, it is satisfactory to perceive that its instruction is equally kept in view in the progress of improvement. The drawings of new libraries, museums, &c. are this year more numerous than usual. The "Perspective View of the New Literary and Scientific Institution now erecting at Islington, from the Designs, and under the direction, of Gough and Roumien," (No. 1138), exhibits a neat and handsome villa, more like a "genteel residence," perhaps, than a public building. The architects must, we suppose, have encountered the whole weight of the competitive system, since designs were invited to be sent in, by the very unusual method of large posting bills. We hope the infant institution will find no cause to regret expending its funds in building at so early a stage of its career; and we are glad to find that another establishment of the same description, the oldest of its class in London, at length holds out a promise of showing a more attractive exterior. The "Proposed new Front for the Royal Institution of Great Britain, by L. Vulliamy" (No. 1119), exhibits, it is true, an aspect both of tameness and sameness; but its range of tall columns from one end of the edifice to the other, will be infinitely preferable to the pierced wall of brick, which now absolutely forms a disgrace instead of an ornament to Albemarle-street. "The Principal Front of a proposed Provincial Literary and Scientific Institution" (No. 999), is, we observe, the production of Mr. W. M. Brookes, the architect of the best building of the kind the metropolis possesses, the London Institution in Finsbury Circus; but he does not appear to have succeeded in this so well as in his former attempt. In striving to be classical, he has, we think, been too severe, and the edifice wears an aspect of gloom not suited to its character. We should like to have been told in the catalogue, to what provincial town the proposed institution belongs, a piece of information which we cannot conceive the motive for withholding. Mr. Brookes exhibits likewise a "design submitted for the Fitzwilliam Museum, Cambridge," (No. 1068); but this is completely eclipsed by "One of the four Designs selected by the University of Cambridge for the Fitzwilliam Museum, by E. Lapidge," (No. 1096). This beautiful plan has, for the present, it appears, been laid aside, but we hope not for ever; it is of that class of excellence which it would really do honour even to the me-

tropolis to execute, and a fine building is but too much wanted to efface the disgrace of some of our late erections. The University has been unusually fortunate, however, on this occasion; the "view of the front towards Trumpington-street, of the Fitzwilliam Museum, building at Cambridge, by G. Basevi, jun." (No. 1069), is, in our opinion, though not equal to that of Mr. Lapidge, one of the finest works of recent architecture. "The London Amphitheatre, Designs for a National Building to concentrate the Scientific Institutions of the Metropolis, by J. Goldicutt," (No. 1098), is, of course, a mere castle in the air. We somehow omitted to notice "the Façade for a New Gallery of Practical Science about to be erected in Regent-street, by J. Thomson, (No. 1109).

In general improvements, the exhibition of this year, presents us with about the ordinary quantity; but one of them at least is of more than ordinary quality. "The View of Grey-street, Newcastle-upon-Tyne, as it will appear from Blackett-street, when completed, with the monument to Earl Grey, now in progress," by B. Green, (No. 1102), is the view of a street which will have very few rivals in the metropolis itself, and none, we, suppose, in any provincial town. It is one of the numerous progeny of Regent-street, and fully worthy of its renowned progenitor. The "General View of Bournemouth, Christchurch Hants, a new Marine Neighbourhood on the Estate of Sir G. W. T. Jervis, Bart. M. P., the Hotel, Baths, and a portion of the the Villas now erecting, the Church, and other extensive Buildings in contemplation," exhibits a sight which, however unusual in former days, is becoming common in this age of improvement—a whole *townlet* built solely with a view to the luxurious and the picturesque. We do not think, however, that the architect, Mr. Ferrey, has been very fortunate in the arrangement of his houses; in this view they look too scattered to belong to one another, and too close to have the advantages of being alone. We shall mention but one other design, the "Principal Entrance to the London Cemetery Company's Northern Station at Highgate, by S. Geary," (No. 1107). This is a handsome edifice, but as the style is Grecian, it is to be hoped that it will not stand too near Mr. Vulliamy's new Gothic church on the top of the hill.

In addition to the designs and models, the architectural room contains a few busts, among which will be found that of Mr. Perkins, the well-known civil engineer and inventor of the steam-gun, by C. A. Rivers, (No. 1156). Its striking resemblance to the portrait given in our 15th volume, is a guarantee for the accuracy of both. In the Sculpture-room is a fine marble statue of Dr. Dalton, of Manchester, by Sir Francis Chantrey, (No. 1162). It represents him in a sitting posture, engaged in meditation. The painting (No. 356) in the Middle-room, is a portrait, by J. Moore, of " Dr. Church, the eminent Mechanician," who would have been more eminent by this time if his steam-carriage had been found to answer.

We cannot quit the subject of the Royal Academy's exhibition without expressing our great disappointment at the want of space, so glaringly evident in its new locality. We are told at the end of the catalogue, that, " in consequence of the great number of works of art sent for exhibition this year, it has been found impossible to assign places to many of those which had been accepted." Many as those sent and accepted may, however, have been, the number shown is very little over what it has constantly been of late years ; and yet these are, as of old, hung all along the walls from the floor to the ceiling, so that at least half the number cannot be seen in a satisfactory way. We thought this system was to be " reformed altogether," and we can conceive no greater barbarism than this " wilful murder" of the works of many deserving artists (except, indeed, the plan adopted in Paris, where one row of paintings is hung in front of another, and, to mend the matter, the productions thus hid are the best works of the great old masters that France can boast of possessing). Why is not the range of apartments on the ground floor made use of for the purposes of the exhibition ? The Council Room of Somerset House was turned to account, and the same plan might surely be adopted here, though we own, that had the arrangements been properly attended to, such expedients would not have been necessary in Trafalgar-square.

Another improvement of easier accomplishment must suggest itself to every one who looks over the catalogue. Why is not some method adopted of giving a notion of the size of the pictures, and why it is not mentioned whether a portrait is a whole, or a half, or a three-quarter length? This information would be equally useful to the future inquirer into the history of art, and to the visitor standing in the exhibition room.

OBSERVATIONS ON THE APPLICATION OF EXPANSIVE STEAM.—BY J. S. ENYS, ESQ.[*]

It is the object of the annexed calculations, which have been deduced from the tables published in the Report of the preceding year,[†] to point out the importance of ascertaining the quantity of water converted into steam, of the pressure per square foot or square inch in the cylinder, on closing the steam apertures, as a basis for the connection of practical and scientific knowledge; and I trust the two premiums given by Mr. John Taylor, and awarded by this Society, relative to the quantity of water evaporated per bushel of coal, (94lbs.) will excite that attention in this county, which is due to this subject.

The first table has ben drawn up in reference to the premiums offered by H. H. Price, Esq., for the application of the expansive action of steam, in steam vessels ; and in it the quantity of coal required, is assumed to be proportional to the grains of water evaporated : its columns are calculated for fresh water; the corrections required for salt water, and the quantity blown off to preserve that within the boiler at a given saturation, should be applied to sea going vessels: the propriety of adapting data founded on the steam pressure on the closing of the valve, combined with the capacity of the cylinder, instead of the common method of the load per inch on the safety, is more necessary in this county where no uniform rule prevails, either as to the proportional size of steam valves, or the pressure of steam used, than in those cases in which the low pressure engine is employed.

The coal affords no fixed points, since it varies as much as 30 ℈ cent in effect, and boilers, even in similar engines, differ much

* From Report of the Royal Cornwall Polytechnic Society for 1836. Fourth year. We are glad to observe the increasing prosperity and usefulness of this most excellent institution.—ED. M. M.
† See Mechanics' Magazine, vol. xxv. p. 4.

in their evaporating powers, with similar coal.

When the quantity of steam due to the ascertained evaporation of cubic feet of water in the boiler, and the quantity consumed in the cylinder, (allowing for waste) both taken at the pressure in the cylinder on closing the steam valve, are found to coincide, a fixed point, (conveniently represented in lbs. 1 foot high, or as efficiency if required) becomes known, which is as important for a criterion of the relative merit of boilers, as for comparison either with the neat power of the engines; or, if the machinery worked is included, of the neat work done.

The advantage of using the same denomination for the area of the cylinder, and the length of the stroke is obvious; and the cubic foot is preferable to the cubic inch,

as the unit of capacity, both from its coincidence with that of height, and from the incomprehensible numbers which calculations would require, if made in cubic inches; for instance, 90 inch cylinder, 10 foot stroke, contain 764.404 cubic inches, and condenses perhaps 6 or 7 millions inches of steam, although of some lbs. below atmospheric strength per minute.

An estimate is annexed of the gross power due to the evaporation of one cubic foot of water in the cylinder, at a pressure of 33 lbs. per square inch, or 4752 lbs. per square foot, expanded 4 times. The efficiency of a bushel of coal, (94lbs.) is readily known by the number of cubic feet of water which can be evaporated p bushel in each boiler; which may be taken at about 14 cubic feet, for the best boilers in this county.

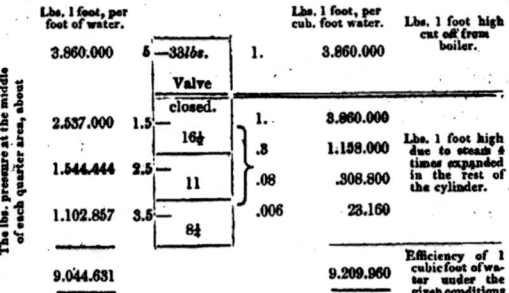

In the efficiency derived from the common theory, no allowance is made for diminution of temperature and deficiency of

water on expansion, and perhaps in practice the other method is nearer the truth.

Cut off at	Per sq. inch.	Per square foot.	Efficiency.	Bushel of coal without expansion.	Advantages of expansion	Bushel of coal. with expansion.
4-11	26	3744	3.776.000	51,780.000	1.89	98,642,200
1-4	35	4752	3.860.000 ×14	54.040.000	2.386	128.939.440
1-6	37	5328	3.890.000	54.460.000	2.79	151.943.400

Pumping engines often use steam expanded 4 times, and seem to obtain advantages equivalent to the theory, in consequence of the inertia of the water, main rods, heavy beams, balance bobs, &c., at the commencement, which once in motion, tends to its continuance to the end of the stroke, even after the load exceeds the power.

Whatever objections to the employment of steam exceeding 2¼ lbs. per square inch are insurmountable, the application of its expanding force is much limited: its action against an uniform resistance also limits expansion to 2 or at most 3 volumes; and in consequence, the steam pressure necessary to produce a mean equal to that obtained in a low pressure engine, is scarcely high enough to create sufficient apprehension of danger to prevent its introduction.

It may be observed, that in engines working at full pressure, the power supplied by the boiler, and that exerted in the cylinder coincide, allowance being made for the effects of the common excentric, if used in closing the steam apertures, but in expansion engines, the power from the boiler is less than that exerted in the cylinder by the amount due to the force of the steam expanding during the rest of the stroke, after the valve is closed: but this advantage can only be gained either by the expense of a larger cylinder, or the danger of higher steam.

Two stamping engines have been erected

by Mr. James Sims; one at the Charlestown mines, the other at Wheal Kitty, expressly arranged for expansion; a plan probably suggested by the improved duty which attended his introduction of it, in an old double acting engine at Poldice; it has also been tried at Binner Downs: the cylinders are 32 inches in diameter, stroke 9 feet; consequently, the ratio of length to diameter 3:37 is greater than usual; the cogged wheels introduced to diminish the revolutions of the barrel as compared with the crank, have been omitted.

This gearing was probably adopted, in the first instance in the conversion of a whim engine of power insufficient for stamping, and the plan has been followed, though more freedom is allowed in the dimensions of cylinders in those places where an engine's merits are judged by a reference to work done per bushel of coal, instead of horse power; these engines are single acting. with a heavy balance connecting rod, and two fly wheels, and use steam about 22lbs. ℔ square inch, on the safety valve, or about 36lbs. pressure, expanded 2 or 3 times in the cylinder. The stamps about 70, are arranged in equal numbers on each side, and are lifted by a barrel directly attached to the crank—their average lift is 9 inches, 3 inches out of the 12 to which they are set to rise being allowed for the ore beneath them—their weight can be ascertained and checked at any time for calculations for duty,

The average performance has been :

			Duty.	
Sim's ⎰ Charlestown mines, 12 months ⎱	.... ⎰	45,677,347 ⎱	Lbs. 1 ft.
engines ⎰ Wheal Kitty...... 6 ditto	to Dec. 1836	50,606,042	high per
Ballaswidden............ 12 ditto		18,685,273	bushel of
Wheal Vor............ 6 ditto	....	21,326,144	coal.

An improvement amounting to a saving of 50 or 60 per cent of coal.

The average at Wheal Kitty includes the December report of 36 millions, the highest was 55 millions.

Comparative estimate of the steam required per month, and of the cubic feet of steam which can be produced by a month's consumption of coal.

Cylinder 396 cubic feet............... ⎱ with expansion 4 times.
Steam at each stroke 99 cubic feet...... ⎰

Steam 2¼ atmosphere, 808 Volume for 1 of water.

	Consumption of coal.
277,080 stroke	2,734 Bushels used
99 cubic feet	14 Water in feet evapo-
	[rated per bushel
27,430,920 steam in the cylinder	38,276
2,743,092 waste 10 per cent	808 volume
30,174,012 cubic feet of steam.	30,927,808 cubic feet of steam.

Tables referring to a Steam Vessel of 90 horse power engines, or two 45s, chiefly taken from No. 2 and 3 of the tables of last year, without any allowances for expansion.

Steam cut off in the cylinder.	Cubic feet required for each stroke in the cylinder.	Steam pressure in lbs. per square inch on closing the valve.	Ditto in lbs. per square foot.	Lbs. 1 foot high while the valve is open.	Lbs. in the remainder of the cylinder after it is closed.	Lbs. in feet high in the cylinder.	Grains of water per cubic foot of steam.	Grains of water per stroke.	Cubic feet of steam per minute, 25 revolutions. 2 cylinders.	Cubic feet of water per minute.	Ditto ditto per hour.
30	16	2304	69120	....	69120	275	8250	3000	1.18	113
20	17.⅘	2520	50400	20412	70812	301	6020	2000	1.37	82
15	19	2736	41040	28440	69480	326	4890	1500	1:11	66
10	23	3312	33120	36365	69485	387	3870	1000	.883	53
7.5	23	3312	24840	34428	58268	387	2902	750	.664	40
7.5	27	3888	29160	40415	69575	449	3367	750	.77	46
1	2	3	4	5	6	7	8	9	10	11	12

This table is intended as an approximate illustration of the action of two double acting engines on the crank shaft, and is obtained by multiplying the statical pressure of the steam remaining after *four-tenths* of the gross power is deducted at 12 points in the cylinder, by the leverage of the crank at the same points.

The different columns represent the up and down strokes of the engines separately from one revolution.

The average pressure, or 9·6lbs., multiplied by the mean of the crank leverage, is about 759, or 1518, for both engines.

Full Pressure Steam.					Steam cut off at ½					Steam cut off at ⅓				
Right.		Left.			Right.		Left.			Right.		Left.		
up	down	up	down		up	down	up	down		up	down	up	down	
383			956	1339	443			1106	1549	503			1181	1684
634			929	1063	734			1074	1808		833		855	1686
779			878	1657	901			920	1821	1023			637	1660
878			779	1657	1009			712	1721	1145			454	1599
929			634	1563	1074			507	1581	1219			294	1513
956			383	1339	1106			230	1336	1242			130	1372
956	383			1339	1106		443		1549	1181		503		1684
929	634			1563	1074		734		1808	853		833		1686
878	779			1657	920		901		1821	637		1023		1660
779	878			1657	712		1009		1721	454		1145		1599
634	929			1563	507		1074		1581	294		1219		1513
383	956			1339	230		1106		1336	130		1242		1372
	383	956		1339		443	1106		1549		503	1181		1684
	643	929		1563		734	1074		1808		833	853		1686
	779	878		1657		901	920		1821		1023	637		1660
	878	779		1657		1009	712		1721		1145	454		1599
	929	634		1563		1074	507		1581		1219	294		1513
	956	383		1339		1106	230		1336		1242	130		1372
	956		383	1339		1106		443	1549		1181		503	1684
	929		634	1563		1074		734	1808		853		833	1686
	878		779	1657		920		901	1821		637		1023	1660
	779		878	1657		712		1009	1721		454		1145	1599
	634		929	1563		507		1074	1581		294		1219	1513
	383		956	1339		230		1106	1336		130		1242	1372

It should be observed, that efficiency has been here considered as statical power, or the pressure that would be exerted provided the piston was stationary at each point; the nearest approximation to which is the supposition of a motion of the piston, so slow, that the force required to produce that motion, is almost unappreciable; and if gross power or efficiency ℘ square inch, is made unity, then the difference between statical pressure and the dynamic pressure on the piston due to its velocity, friction, resistances of the uncondensed steam, &c., &c., may be represented as decimals, the remainder being net power usually expressed by Engineers as horse power; but the steam pressure in the boiler becomes unity, plus the force required to produce motion, and in the steam pipes and valves.

RESTORATION OF THE AMERICAN PATENT OFFICE.

(From the *Franklin Journal* for January.)

Mr. Ruggle's Report to the Senate.

The special Committee appointed to examine and report the extent of the loss sustained by the burning of the Patent Office, and to consider whether any, and what, measures ought to be adopted to repair the loss, and to establish such evidence of property in patented inventions as the destruction of the records and drawings may have rendered necessary for its security, submit the following report:—

In examining the subject referred to them, the committee have been deeply impressed with the loss the country has sustained in the destruction, by the fire of the 15th December, of the records, originals, drawings, models, &c. belonging to the Patent Office. They not only embraced the whole history of American invention for nearly half a century, but were the muniments of property of vast amount, secured by law to a great number of individuals, both citizens and foreigners, the protection and security of which must now become seriously difficult and precarious.

Every thing belonging to the office was destroyed—nothing was saved. There were one hundred and sixty-eight large folio volumes of records, and twenty-six large portfolios, containing nine thousand drawings; many of which were beautifully executed and very valuable; there were also all the original descriptions and specifications of inventions, in all about ten thousand, besides caveats, and many other documents and papers.

There were also two hundred and thirty volumes of books belonging to the Patent Office library, the cost of which was 1,000 dollars. Some of these were procured prior to the passage of the act of July 4, 1836, making an appropriation of 1,500 dollars for purchasing a library of scientific works. Others were procured subsequently, for which 320 dollars of that appropriation was expended.

The model-cases, press and seals, desks, book-cases, and other furniture and effects belonging to the office, were estimated at 6,600 dollars.

The Patent Office contained also the largest and most interesting collection of models in the world. It was an object of just pride to every American able to appreciate its value as an item in the estimate of national character, or the advantages and benefits derivable from high improvements in the useful arts—a pride which must now stand rebuked by the improvidence which exposed so many memorials and evidences of the superiority of American genius to the destruction which has overtaken them.

The number of models was about seven thousand. Many of them displayed great talent, ingenuity, and mechanical science. The American inventions pertaining to the spinning of cotton and wool, and the manufacture of fabrics, in many respects exceed those of any other nation, and reduced so much the expense of manufacture, that the British manufacturers were reluctantly obliged, at the expense of a little national pride, to lay aside their own machinery and adopt our improvements, to prevent our underselling them even in their home market. In this department were the inventions of Browne, Thorpe, Danfort, Couilliard, Calvert, and some others. The beautiful operative model of Wilkinson's machine for manufacturing weaver's reeds by one operation was considered one of the most ingenious mechanical combinations ever invented. Of this character was Whittemore's celebrated machine for making wool cards. There were several models of valuable improvements in shearing and napping cloth, patented to Swift, Stowel, Dewey, Parsons, Daniels, and others.

In another department were several models of machines for manufacturing cut and wrought nails. The machinery for this purpose, which has reduced so much the price of that important article, was of purely American origin, and was invented by Briggs, Perkins, Reed, Odiorne, and several others.

The models of improvements in grist-mills, saw-mills, water-wheels, &c. were numerous.

The application of steam power to the driving of all kinds of machinery for propelling boats, locomotives, mills, and factories, has brought out a great number of American inventions and improvements, displaying a degree of talent, ingenuity, and science highly creditable to our country. Some of the models in this department were very valuable. America claims the honour (contested, indeed, by England) of the first successful attempt to apply the power of steam to the propelling of vessels. The name of Fulton is associated with one of the noblest efforts of genius and science. It has often been regretted that no model was preserved of his steam-boat, which was the first to demonstrate the practicability of making steam subservient to the purposes of useful navigation. There was, however, deposited in the Patent Office a volume of drawings elegantly executed by his own hand, delineating the various parts of the machinery he employed, and embracing three beautiful representations of his steamer making its first triumphant struggle against the opposing current of the Hudson. The steamer was represented passing through the Highlands, and at two or three other interesting points on the river, with a beautiful sketching of the surrounding scenery, smiling as it were at the victory which science and art had at last achieved over the power of the winds and the waters, and at the opening era of steam navigation, the benefits of which have since been so widely diffused. It contained also an account of his experiments on the resistance of fluids, and various estimates of the power required to propel vessels of various tonnage and form through the water at a greater or less speed. This volume, which should have been preserved among our choicest archives, shared the fate of every thing else in the office. What sum would be too great to be expended in replacing it?

The department of agriculture contained a great number of models of highly useful improvements in the implements of husbandry. The number of inventions which had for their object the advancement of the agricultural interests, was about fifteen hundred; those which pertained to navigation were little short of a thousand. The inventions and improvements in factory machinery, and in the various manufactures, were upwards of two thousand. In the common mechanical trades there were as many more. It were vain to attempt to enumerate or classify them within the reasonable space of a report of committee. There was no art or pursuit to which ingenuity and invention had not lent their aid.

. That this great national repository should have received so little consideration heretofore as to be left so long exposed to conflagration, which has at last swept every vestige of it from existence, cannot be too deeply deplored. But the reproach does not rest at the door of the present Congress. The act passed at its first session, reorganizing the office, containing many important provisions for its management, and the appropriation for erecting a fire-proof building, for the accommodation and preservation of the records, models, &c., which is now under construction, attest the interest inspired by, and the attention devoted to it, though, unfortunately, too late to rescue it from destruction.

That the benefit of such an institution is limited to the mechanic arts and manufactures, or that it is confined to any particular section of the Union, is an erroneous idea. Its influence is felt in every branch of national industry, and no one section of the country can justly be said to derive less advantage from it than another. The idea is equally erroneous that such institutions are established for the benefit of patentees only. The advancement of great national interests is the first object of the patent laws of all nations where they exist. The specifications, models, and drawings, are required that, after the patent-term shall have expired, the public may have the benefit of a disclosure of the invention, so full and intelligible that any one can apply its principles to practical use, or make them the foundation of further improvements.

It is a still more erroneous idea that no drawings or models of new inventions are of use to the public, unless the machinery they represent is susceptible of a practical application to the use designed. Mechanical science, like all others, is matured and perfected by degrees, and by calling to its aid the investigations and ingenuity of various minds. Most inventions are but the foundation of progressive improvements. It is necessary to know what has been done, in order to know what remains to be accomplished. Every age avails itself of the experience and discoveries of that which has preceded it ; were it otherwise, knowledge would be stationary, and every generation, instead of being wiser than others gone by, would be employed in learning over again what had been acquired before. The drawings and models of even those inventions which are imperfect, or incapable of producing the desired effect, serve to show how far

others have progressed, and either furnish hints for the full accomplishment of the design, or as beacons to enable others to avoid fruitless labour and expense. Whoever would attempt to improve the arts, must begin where others have left off ; hence, the model rooms of the Patent Office were constantly visited by men of genius and science from all sections of the country, and from Europe, where they were able to discover at once how far American invention had gone, and where they frequently derived important hints from inventions and contrivances of apparently but little value.

They would seem, also, to be almost indispensable in deciding upon new applications for patents, to enable the proper officers to judge of the originality of the invention, and to prevent the issuing of interfering patents. It often requires a very close examination of the principles of a machine, and a careful comparison of models and drawings, to discover how far they interfere with previous inventions. The provisions interdicting the granting of patents for what is not new and original, is the most valuable feature of the act of July last. But it will be impossible for the Commissioner to administer the law in that particular, according to its intent, without models and drawings of inventions previously patented. The consequence would be in effect, the restoration of a great portion of the evils of the former system in multiplying conflicting rights, leading to much perplexity and expensive litigation. Much of the ground travelled over in the last forty years would have to be travelled over again, before the point could be reached at which we had arrived prior to the late conflagration.

The Committee therefore believe that it is important to the interests of the country, as well as to the security of individual rights, that measures be immediately adopted to replace, as far as practicable, the records, drawings, and models which have been destroyed. After much inquiry and consideration, the Committee are satisfied that, notwithstanding the apprehensions and anxiety so generally entertained, a restoration is practicable to a very gratifying extent. The first step must be to procure, for the purpose of being copied and recorded anew, the original patents. In most instances, descriptions and specifications of the inventions, and in perhaps a sixth or eighth part of the cases, drawings also have been annexed to the patents when granted. Drawings have been attached only when referred to in the specifications. The whole number of patents is a little upwards of ten thousand. It is believed that from six to seven thousand may be obtained for record. Many of the deficient drawings may be obtained from patentees, or may be supplied by the assistance of those whose familiar knowledge of the inventions will enable them, aided by the specifications, to deliniate them with accuracy. Many copies heretofore certified from the record to be used as evidence in the courts, will supply others.

Of the models, such as were trifling and unimportant, containing no new principle or combination of mechanism, and not useful for any of the purposes before alluded to, it will not be necessary to replace. The whole number of models was about seven thousand. It is the opinion of the Commissioner, and others most conversant with the subject, that three thousand of the most important can be replaced, which will form a very interesting and valuable collection, less numerous, indeed, but more select, and scarcely less useful than that which has been destroyed. Some of these would be replaced by voluntary contribution. But the greater portion of them, even of those whose restoration would be most desirable, the Committee are satisfied, can only be had by means in the hands of the Government. If it were in the power of the Government to compel the patentees to replace the models and drawings lost by its improvidence, it would be an onerous and unjust tax upon those who, by their ingenuity, and at their own expense, built up an institution which, in its connexion with manufactures, with agriculture, and even commerce itself, has done much to advance the prosperity of the country. They have paid into the Treasury 116,907,73 dollars more than has been required to meet the expenses of the office, including the salaries of the officers employed in it; and the Committee cannot hesitate in recommending the appropriation of that balance to carry into effect the provisions of the bill which is herewith submitted.

The sentiment is not an uncommon one, that the tax upon patents is both unwise in policy and unjust in principle. Inventors are public benefactors, contributing to the promotion and improvement of all branches of national industry, and, in most instances, without any adequate remuneration. Who has done more to enrich the South, nay, indirectly, the whole country, than Whitney? And what was his reward? Let the South answer. Evans and Fulton, with genius and talents never, while they lived, appreciated to their worth, died overwhelmed by embarrassments. Whittemore, it is true, was more fortunate; but it was said that he availed himself of the mechanical genius of another who lived and died in poverty and obscurity.

It has not been the policy of our Govern-

ment to draw a revenue from patentees. The duty imposed was intended only to meet the ordinary expenses of issuing patents. Many believe that even that should not be exacted. It is levying a contribution upon science and ingenuity, which cost the nation nothing, while they confer upon it important benefits.

The measures to be adopted in selecting and obtaining the models and many of the drawings, are matters of detail involving such a variety of circumstances and considerations, that it is impossible to make provision for them by law. That properly belongs, and should be intrusted, to a temporary board of Commissioners. The sum required to replace the three thousand models, which would include all whose preservation would be most desirable, is estimated by the Commissioners at 100,000 dollars. The expense of transcribing and recording descriptions, specifications, drawings, and assignments, is estimated at 53,000 dollars. A judicious and economical expenditure of these sums, it is believed, will restore the records and models to the full extent contemplated by the provisions of the bill submitted. By the statement from the Treasury Department (marked E), it appears that the balance of the patent fund on the 31st December last, was 156,907 dollars 73 cents, including moneys received for patents and copies prior to the act of July, 1836, which, though not expressly embraced by the terms of that act, properly belong to that fund. This balance will cover the expenditures above proposed of 153,000, together with 3,100 dollars for record-books, desks, and other office furniture, as per estimate D, and leave a balance of 807 dollars 73 cents.

With such a restoration, and the addition of the specimens of fabrics and manufactures of various kinds which are in preparation in a number of the manufactories and workshops of the country, to be deposited in rooms in the new building, pursuant to the act of July last, we shall soon have less reason than is now apprehended throughout the country, to deplore the destruction of this great national repository. In two or three years the number of models will be scarcely less, and their character and value in the aggregate greatly improved.

It appears by the Commissioner that an additional examining clerk, and also another copying clerk, are necessary to keep up the increasing business of the office. The new duties assigned to the examining clerk make it a very responsible and laborious office. It is his business to make himself fully acquainted with the principles of the invention for which a patent is sought, and to make a thorough investigation of all that has been before known or invented either in Europe or America, on the particular subject presented for his examination. He must ascertain how far the invention interferes in any of its parts with other previous inventions, or things previously in use. He must point out and describe the extent of such collision and interference, that the applicant may have the benefit of the information in so shaping or restricting his claim of originality as not to trespass upon the rights of others. The applicant should also be referred to the sources of this information, that he may be able to satisfy himself on the particular points of interference. This frequently leads to a lengthy correspondence, before the applicant can be persuaded that his invention, or some rejected part of it, is not new. He often employs skilful and persevering council to urge and enforce by argument new views of the principles of his invention, who sometimes brings to his aid much mechanical astuteness. The examiner must also see that the specification accords with the drawing, and that the model is in conformity with both.

An efficient and just discharge of these duties, it is obvious, requires extensive scientific attainments, and a general knowledge of the arts, manufactures, and the mechanism used in every branch of business in which improvements are sought to be patented, and of the principles embraced in the ten thousand inventions patented in the United States, and of the thirty thousand patented in Europe. He must moreover possess a familiar knowledge of the statute and common law on the subject, and the judicial decisions both in England and our own country, in patent cases. This service is important, as it is often difficult and laborious. Here is the first check upon attempts to palm off old inventions for new, or to interfere with the rights of others previously acquired. This is also the source whence the honest and meritorious inventor may look for aid and direction in so framing his specification as that he may be able to sustain his patent when issued, and find security and protection against expensive and fruitless litigation.

Suitable qualifications for these duties are rare, and cannot be obtained without such compensation as they readily command in other employment. It will, undoubtedly, be wise in the Government to affix such salary to this office as will secure the best talent and qualifications. Although an appeal is allowed by law, yet if a high character is given to it, this will be the best, as it is the most appropriate, tribunal, for judging of these subjects, and its decisions

commanding respect and confidence, there will be but little inclination to take exceptions to its judgment. Thus will be cut off a fruitful source of law-suits, and our court calenders will cease to be crowded with cases arising out of the interfering rights of patentees. Meritorious inventors will be secure in their rights, and the public relieved from imposition and embarrassment. These are among the first of the objects and merits of the act of last session. It appears that about one-third of all the specifications are found, on examination, to contain no new principle, and that three-fourths of the residue are either too broad in their claims of originality, or are otherwise irregular or defective, and are required to be set right at the office or sent back by the Commissioner for correction.

Under existing circumstances, without written, pictorial, or model-record of any kind, it is apparent that the business of the office must either stand still, or proceed under very great embarrassment, which can be relieved only by the early action of Congress on the subject.

[A bill here follows for the consideration of Congress, embodying the suggestions in the foregoing Report].

ESTIMATE OF THE WATER DISCHARGED BY A RIVER[*]

(From the *Franklin Journal* for February.)

If the currents of rivers diminish from the surface towards the bottom, and be very slow at the bottom, the quantity of water discharged by rivers into the ocean is much less than has been usually imagined. Dr. Halley, in his theory of the origin of springs, probably estimates much too largely the quantity of water poured into the ocean by all the rivers of the world.

When the dam at Fairmount, near Philadelphia, was erected across the Schuylkill, it was stated in some of the newspapers, that some gentlemen wished to ascertain the quantity of water that flowed in the river in a given time. For this purpose, the newspapers said that the breadth and depth of the river at Fairmount were measured, and that to obtain the velocity of the motion of the water in the river, four or five gentlemen entered a boat, and floated a certain distance on the river, noting the time required to pass a given distance, after the boat had acquired its *natural velocity and motion*, as it was called.

If the newspaper account was correct, it would seem that two great errors entered into the calculation.

First. The current diminished in velocity

---

[*] See No. 718, p. 93.

from the surface to the bottom, the current in the bottom of rivers being very slight, unless in places where the descent in the bottom or bed, is considerable, as at rapids or ripples.

Second. The boat loaded with four or five men floated much faster than the fastest part of the current of the river—faster than the current at the surface. E.

LIST OF ENGLISH PATENTS GRANTED BETWEEN THE 27TH APRIL AND THE 25TH MAY, 1837.

Henry William Craufurd, of No. 5, John-street, Berkeley Square, commander in the Royal Navy, for an improvement in coating or covering iron and copper, for the prevention of oxydation, being a communication from a foreigner residing abroad. April 29 ; six months.

Alexander Dixon and James Dixon, of Cleckheaton, near Leeds, York, manufacturing chemists, for improvements in dyeing, by the application of materials not hitherto so used. April 29 ; six months.

Joseph Barker, of Regent-street, Lambeth, artist, for certain improvements in the construction or making of umbrellas and parasols. April 29 ; six months.

Jean Baptiste Mollerat, of No. 27, Leicester Square, manufacturing chemist, for an improvement or improvements in the manufacture of gas for illumination. May 2 ; six months.

John Heathcoat, of Tiverton, Devon, lace manufacturer, for a new or improved method or methods of manufacturing, producing, forming or fashioning ornaments or ornamented work or figures, upon, or applicable to gauze, muslin, and net, and divers kinds of cloth, stuff, or woven textures, and also certain machinery, tools, implements, or apparatus to be used in manufacturing, producing, forming, fashioning, and applying such ornaments or ornamented work. May 4 ; six months.

Thomas Wells Ingrand, of Birmingham, Warwick, horn button manufacturer, for improvements in the manufacture of certain descriptions of buttons, and in the tools used to manufacture the same ; being a communication from a foreigner residing abroad. May 4 ; six months.

Thomas Baylis, of Tamworth, Stafford, civil engineer, for certain improvements in heating and evaporating fluids, being a communication from a foreigner residing abroad. May 6 ; six months.

Henry Ross, of Leicester, worsted manufacturer, for improvements applicable to the combing of wool and goat hair. May 6 ; six months.

George Hayman, of St. Sidwell-street, Exeter, coach builder, for improvements in two-wheel carriages. May 6 ; six months.

William Angus Robertson, of Peterborough-court, Fleet-street, gentleman, for certain new or improved machinery for, or methods of, sculpturing, cutting, shaping, moulding, and otherwise figuring and working marble, stone, alabaster, and other substances suitable for sculpture ; and for taking copies of the works produced thereby, or of similar works produced by the ordinary means ; and also an improved process or method of taking casts of the living human face or figure, or other form, being a communication from a foreigner residing abroad. May 6 ; six months.

Thomas Bell, of South Shields, Durham, manufacturing chemist, for improvements in the manufacture of sulphate of soda, which improvements, or parts thereof, are applicable to other purposes. May 8 ; six months.

William Nairne, flax-spinner, Millhaugh, near Methven, Perth, for a certain improvement or certain improvements in the machinery of reels used in reeling yarns, being a communication from a foreigner residing abroad. May 8 ; six months.

Peter Steinkeller, of the London Zinc Works, Wenlock Road, gentleman, for certain plates or tiles made of zinc or other proper metal or mixtures of metals, applicable to roofs or other parts of buildings, being a communication from a foreigner residing abroad. May 8 ; two months.

John Spurgin, of Guildford-street, Russel Square, doctor of Medicine, for an improvement in the mode or means of propelling vessels through water, and part of which means may be applied to other useful purposes, May 8 ; six months.

John Hague, of Castle-street, Wellclose Square, engineer, for certain improvements on wheels for carriages. May 10 ; six months.

James Boydell, junior, of Dee Cottage, near Hawarden, Flint, esq., for improvements in propelling carriages. May 11 ; six months.

William Bell, of Edinburgh, esq., for improvements in heating and evaporating fluids. May 11 ; six months.

Edward Austin, of Warwick-place, Bedford Row, for improvements in raising sunken vessels and other bodies. May 12 ; six months.

Pierre Barthelemy Guinibers Debac, of Brixton, Surrey civil engineer, for improvements applicable to rail roads. May 13 ; six months.

William Rhodes, gent., and Robert Hamingway, mechanic, both of Earls Heaton, near Dewsbury, York, for improvements applicable to machinery for carding and piercing wool, in process of manufacture in woollen mills. May 22 ; six months.

George Nelson, of Leamington Priors, Warwick, gent., for a certain new or improved process or processes, by the use of which, the qualities of a certain gelatinous substance, or certain gelatinous substances, called isinglass, may be improved. May 22 ; six months.

Samuel and William Smith, of Luddenden Foot near Halifax, York, worsted spinners, for improvements in machinery for combing or clearing sheeps wool and goats hair. May 23 ; six months.

Elijah Leak, of Hanley, Stafford, engineer and lathe maker, for certain improvements in the construction of shutters and sashes for windows of buildings, which improvements are also applicable to hot-houses or conservatories, carriages, and other purposes, and in the of fitting or using the same. May 23 ; six months.

Charles Pierre Devaux, of Fenchurch-street, merchant, for a new or improved apparatus for preventing the explosion of boilers or generators of steam ; being a communication from a foreigner abroad. May 23 ; six months.

Charles Joseph Freeman, of Frederick-place, Surrey, for an improvement, or improvements in the machinery or apparatus, called rolls for rolling iron or other metals, applicable to rails for roads and bars of various shapes for other purposes. May 25 ; six months.

LIST OF SCOTCH PATENTS GRANTED FROM THE 22ND APRIL TO 23RD OF MAY 1837.

George Crane, of Yniscedwyn, iron works, near Swansea, iron master, for an improvement in the manufacture of iron. April, 26.

Nathaniel Partridge, of Elm Cottage, near Stroud, Glouster, gentleman, for a certain improvement, or improvements in mixing and preparing oil paints, whereby a saving of ingredients commonly used will be effected. April 27.

James Hardy, of Wednesbury, Stafford, gentle-

· man, for certain improvements in the manufacture of iron into cylindrical, conical, and other forms suited for axletrees, shafts and other purposes. April 27.

Christopher Nichels, of Guilford-street, Lambeth, Surrey, gentleman, partly in consequence of a communication made to him by a certain foreigner resident abroad, and partly by his own invention, for improvements in preparing and manufacturing caoutchouc, applicable to various purposes. April 29.

William Coles, of Charing Cross, Middlesex, Esq. for certain improvements applicable to locomotive carriages. April 29.

Moses Poole, Lincolns Inn, Middlesex, gentleman, in consequence of a communication made to him by a certain foreigner residing abroad, for improvements in making fermented liquors. May 10.

Joseph Bunnett, of Newington Causeway, Southwark, window blind maker, for certain improvements in window shutters, which improvements may also be applied to other useful purposes. May 12.

John Samuel Dawes, of Birmingham, Warwick, iron master, for certain improvements in smelting the ores or oxides of iron, copper, tin, lead, zinc and other metals, and in remelting or refining the said metals. May 16.

Joseph Amesbury, of Burton Crescent, Middlesex, surgeon, for certain apparatus for the relief, or correction of stiffness, weakness or distortion in the human spine, chest or limbs. May 20.

John Gordon Campbell, of Glasgow, merchant, and John Gibson of the same city, throwster, for a new or improved process or manufacture of silk, and silk in combination with certain other fibrous substances. May 20.

Henry William Craufurd, of John-street, Berkeley Square, Middlesex, commander in the Royal Navy, for an improvement in the coating or covering iron and copper, for the prevention of oxydation. May 22.

NOTES AND NOTICES.

· *Rival Burners—Mr. Hutchinson's and Messrs. Kilby and Bacon's.*—Sir, in your Number of 29th April last, I observe an article on the advantages of a gas burner, there called " Hutchinson's burner," from the name of the supposed inventor. It is not my intention to call in question the merits of that burner, but simply to enter a protest against either the title or merit being ascribed to a quarter where neither may be found due. With this view, it is proper to inform Clovis, and the readers of your valuable periodical, who may not be aware of the fact, that a patent was, in the year 1829, taken out by Messrs. Kilby and Bacon for an improved gasburner, of which it is contended that Hutchinson's patent is a mere colorable evasion. On this burner (manufactured by Messrs. E. and W. Dixon, of Walsall) there are some justly commendatory remarks, founded on experiments, made by your correspondent Mr. Rutter, of Lymington, in your Number of 28th February, 1835. I have myself obtained some of these burners from Mr. Vardy, 145 High Holborn, one of the agents for sale, and

have tried them, both with the old burners and with Hutchinson's alleged invention. Hutchinson's so called burners, seem to me in nowise to differ in *principle* from the older patent, and so far as they differ in practical operation, they are, according to my experiments, inferior. But it would be idle to discuss, and prejudge a question at this moment pending in the courts of justice. When a competent tribunal shall have decided whether Mr. Hutchinson is really intitled to rank as an inventor, or as (in this instance) a mere imitator and appropriater of the inventive talent of others, I shall beg your insertion of some additional observations and corrections of Clovis's statements on the subject of gas-burners, which will not, I think, be wholly devoid of interest. At present I refrain from further remarks, lest I should appear in the light of an advocate of debated claims. JUSTUS.—London, May 15, 1837.

A Steam Tug belonging to the Symington Steam Towing Company, was launched on Wednesday last (May 24), after having been very appropriately named, at the suggestion of a punning member of the Company, the " *Drag-on.*" The boat is of a very peculiar shape and construction, and designed, (by her builder, Mr. Ritchie,) particularly with a view to dragging a load in her rear. She is to be fitted with a pair of Mr. Symington's paddle wheels, and also with his patent boiler; the principal features of this latter invention are, that one boiler will answer the purpose of two, on board a vessel.—and the prevention of priming.

· *Valuable Acid for Engravers.*—M. Deleschamps has written to the *Académie des Sciences* that he has accomplished the solution of the following problem, for every kind of biting acids employed in engraving. *To obtain a clean and deep line, without sensibly enlarging the furrow in ordinary engraving, and without eating away the sides of the subject in engraving in relief.* He uses a composition of acetate of silver, and hydrate of nitrous ether. Immediately after the contact, the acetate is precipitated into the lower part of the furrow, where it produces a rapid and energetic action. The upper parts of the furrow are occupied by the nitrous ether, and preserved by its presence.

· *New Surveying Instruments.*—M. Lalanne, engineer of the *Ponts et Chausées*, in France, has laid before the *Académie des Sciences* three instruments for topographical surveying, which, if they accomplish all that the inventor promises, correctly and with facility, will be eagerly sought after. To the immense number of surveyors, who are about to commence operations in every part of the United Kingdom, under the numerous railroad acts which have passed this session, such instruments would be invaluable. They are, 1st, a Levelling Instrument, or Carriage, which it is only necessary to run over the ground, the levels of which are desired, and the section is at once obtained; 2nd, a Drawing Instrument, which lays down the plan of the ground; and can be mounted on the carriage of the Levelling Instrument; 3rd, a Power-measuring Instrument, or Dynamometer, which exhibits the effort exerted on every point of the line passed over.

☞ *British and Foreign Patents taken out with economy and despatch; Specifications, Disclaimers, and Amendments, prepared or revised; Caveats entered; and generally every Branch of Patent Business promptly transacted.*

A complete list of Patents from the earliest period (15 Car. II. 1675,) to the present time may be examined. Fee 2s. 6d.; Clients, gratis.

LONDON: Printed and Published for the Proprietor, by W. A. Robertson, at the Mechanics' Magazine Office, No. 6, Peterborough-court, between 135 and 136, Fleet-street.—Sold by G. W. M. Reynolds, Proprietor of the French, English, and American Library, 55, Rue Neuve, Saint Augustin, Paris.

Mechanics' Magazine,

MUSEUM, REGISTER, JOURNAL, AND GAZETTE.

| No. 721. | SATURDAY, JUNE 3, 1837. | Price 3d. |

DEAKIN'S IMPROVED BLAST-FURNACE FOR SMELTING IRON-ORE, &c.

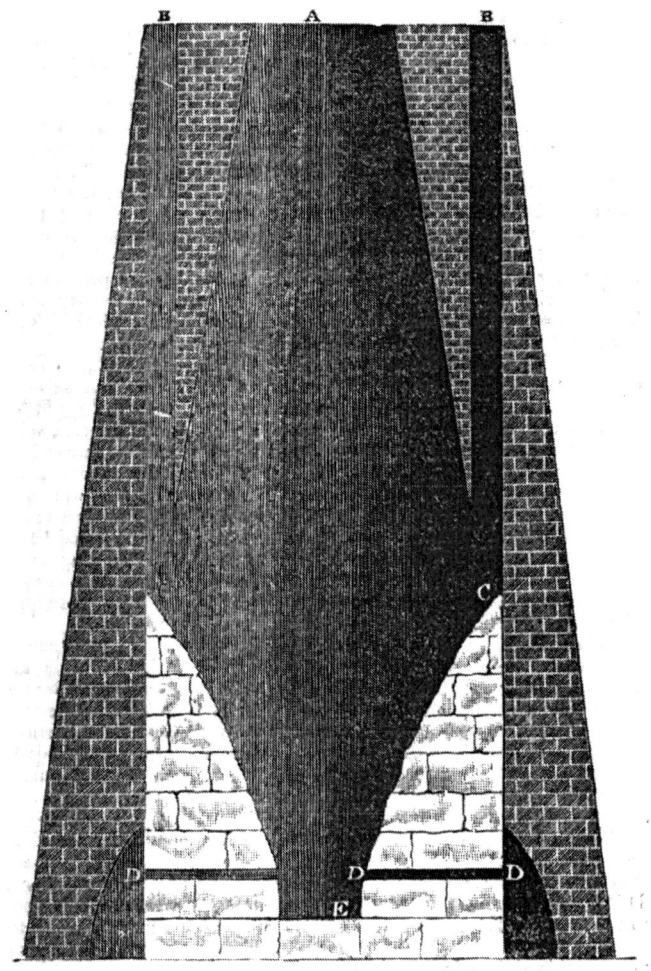

DEAKIN'S IMPROVED BLAST FURNACE FOR SMELTING IRON ORE, ETC.

Sir,—I send you a new plan of a blast furnace, for smelting iron-stone, ore, &c.

In the present method of filling blast furnaces, the whole of the materials for making iron, namely, coal or coke. mine, limestone, &c., are put into the furnace at A. On my improved plan, the mine and limestone, will, at first, still be put in there; but when the furnace works in a certain state, a part of the mine will be put into it at B B; and also the greater part of the fuel used for smelting the iron will be put into the furnace at B B, which are flues or pipes from 2 to 3 feet in width, brought up from the bosses of the furnaces at C C. If pipes are used they may be carried up on the outside of the stack of the furnaces, and may be applied to any blast furnace now in work at a small expense. When this plan is adopted on a furnace being repaired, or newly built, the chimney flue should be carried up in the furnace stack. The coal, or coke being put into the furnace mixed with limestone, mine, scroffula, and rubbish, however free, such coal or coke may itself be, when put in, as at present at A, it must become impregnated with the filth that accompanies it, as soon as the heat begins to act; and it is, moreover, consumed before it comes down to the bosses at C C, and consequently, the power of the fuel is destroyed, before it arrives at the part of the furnace where it is wanted to smelt the mine; but by putting the fuel into the furnace at B B, it will meet the blast in the proper place, free from impurities, and in full strength to melt the materials above it. Better iron will thus be made, with a smaller quantity of fuel, than is done by the present method of filling blast furnaces.

Description of the Engraving.—A is the present feeding place of blast furnaces. B B are the pipes or passages through which I propose that the greatest part of the fuel should be put in. There must be a damper on the top of these passages. C C are the bosses of the furnace. D D D the tweers, where the blast goes into the furnace. E is the hearth of the furnace.

Your giving this a place in your excellent Magazine, will oblige your obedient servant,

THOMAS DEAKIN.

Blaenavon Iron Works,
April 19, 1837.

CAPTAIN ERICSSON'S NEW PROPELLER.

The American packet ship "Toronto" of 630 tons burthen, and drawing 14 feet 6 inches water, was on Saturday last towed down the Thames at the rate of full 4½ knots an hour *against* wind and tide by an experimental steam-boat, called the "Francis B. Ogden," (after Mr. Ogden, the able and intelligent Consul of the United States, at Liverpool,) fitted with the new propelling apparatus lately invented and patented by Capt. Ericsson. The "Francis B. Ogden" measures 45 feet in length, 8 feet beam, and draws 2 feet 3 inches water without the keel. The propelling apparatus is placed at the stern, and works entirely under the water. It consists of a peculiar application of the old, and well-known principle of the water screw, by which a great propelling power is concentrated in a small space. Of the degree of power concentrated, no better proof can be adduced, than the fact, that the speed of 4½ knots against wind and tide, was produced by an apparatus, measuring only 5 feet 2 inches in diameter, and 2 feet 2 inches wide, and worked by a high pressure engine having two cylinders of 14 inches stroke, and 12 inches diameter; and which, during the experiment, made only 60 strokes per minute, and showed a pressure of not more than 50 lbs. to the square inch.

The new propelling apparatus consists of two short cylinders made of thin wrought iron, and supported by arms of a peculiar form, which are placed entirely under the water at the stern, and made to revolve in contrary directions round a common centre. To the outer periphery of each cylinder, there is attached a series of spiral planes or plates, which may, we understand, be placed at any desired angle, according to the effect sought to be obtained, whether it be great speed, or great propelling power.

The apparatus may be made to ship and unship at pleasure; the engine that works it may also be loco-moveable, so as to be worked upon deck, and on any part of the deck; and in these two peculiarities, we are inclined to think the chief advantage of this new step in steam navigation will be found to consist. Sailing vessels may, by this means, command all the aid that steam can give them, without divesting themselves of any of their peculiar fitness for long sea voyages, or undergoing any change in their original construction.

We subjoin a copy with which we were favoured of the certificate given by the pilot and mate of the "Toronto" of the performance of the "Francis B. Ogden" on this occasion.

Packet Ship Toronto, in the Thames,
28th May, 1837.

We feel pleasure in certifying that your experimental steam boat, the "Francis B. Ogden" has this morning towed our ship at the rate of 4½ knots an hour, through the water and against the tide.
(Signed)   E. NASULT, Pilot.
           H. R. HOVEY, Mate.
To Captain Ericsson.

THE NEW SCHOOL OF DESIGN.

The "School of Design" recommended to be established by the late Parliamentary Committee on the Arts and Manufactures, and for which fifteen hundred pounds were voted by the House of Commons, is to commence operations on the 1st of June, at Somerset House, where the rooms just vacated by the Royal Academy have been appropriated to the purpose. It is to be under the direction of a committee, composed of the President and Vice-President of the Board of Trade, several of our most distinguished artists, a few amateurs of some pretension to " taste," and two or three rather aristocratic representatives of the manufacturing interests. The members of the latter class already appointed are, Mr. Alderman Copeland, who may be regarded as the representative for the Potteries; Mr. Morrison, the M. P. for Ipswich, who, albeit, himself no manufacturer, is to be taken as the delegate, we suppose, from the silk and fancy trade, in virtue of his dealing in such articles,—and Mr. Thompson, the eminent calico-printer, of Clitheroe, in Lancashire. Among the artists, Chantrey and Eastlake, are the most conspicuous; and Mr. Hope, the son of the author of Anastasius, represents the wealthy patrons of art. The director of the establishment is Mr. Papworth, the architect,

who, it will be recollected, was examined before the Parliamentary Committee; as, however, the course of instruction is to comprise " light and shade, colouring and composition," it is to be presumed, that Mr. P. will be assisted by artists more conversant with those branches, than mere architects usually are. It may not be too uncharitable to suppose, that some of the *other* witnesses before the committee,—men who strained a point or two to prove the glaring want of a " School of Design" in this benighted country,—will appear again as officer-bearers in the new institution.

The strangest feature of the whole we have yet to notice. The cry before the committee was for an establishment in which "art" should be *cheaply* dispensed to the working classes; and the Parliamentary grant was supposed to be made for carrying such an object into effect. Notwithstanding all this, it is one of the regulations of the new " school" that each pupil shall pay at the rate of *four shillings per week*. This is a sum which, as the directors ought to be aware, is far beyond the means of the working artizan. If the rule be persisted in, it requires no conjuror to predict that the supposed advantages of the scheme will vanish into thin air. The idea of most of the witnesses who recommended such an establishment seemed to be, that, if any payment were required, one guinea per annum ought to be the maximum: the rate now fixed amounts to nearly *ten* guineas per annum; a sum which most mechanics would look upon as fully sufficient to procure them the advantages of the instruction sought, without the assistance of a single farthing from the public purse, —and at the same time, one which it is absolutely impossible to spare from their scanty earnings. The hours of attendance, also, are at present so fixed, as to consult anything but the convenience of the working man; viz. from ten o'clock to four daily. We are informed, however, that preparations are making for opening an evening school, and at *that*, perhaps, the insuperable barrier of the four shillings per week may be removed. Until that is the case, the " School of Design" will be *open to the labouring classes* in name alone,—and will constitute a mere mockery of the expected boon. It were as well indeed, that the working man should, according to the principle laid down at the foundation of the London Mechanic's Institution, disdain to receive instruction on any other terms than *paying* for it;—but it is rather too bad to tempt his independence, by talking roundly of furnishing him with *gratuitous* instruction in the fine arts, and after all, to charge him ten guineas a year by way of a trifling acknowledgment!

MR. MACKINTOSH'S ELECTRICAL THEORY.

Sir,—I am somewhat apprehensive that the remark of your correspondent, Mr. Munro, is correct with respect to the prolonged discussion which has taken place in your pages upon the "Electrical Theory." I shall therefore, in the present communication, so far at least as my own lucubrations are concerned, endeavour to draw that discussion to a close. I am the more determined to adopt this course, seeing the line of argument, if argument it may be called, which is followed by your able, but uncandid correspondent, Kinclaven. My object in this controversy has been to draw his refutation from his own lips. I have done so as far as the *supposed primitive impulse* was concerned. He gave that up at last—when the point could be no longer evaded. I therefore very naturally imagined that we should hear no more about a "primitive impulse." But Kinclaven knows very well that his mechanical system could not be set a-going without this first push; we therefore find in his last, that he again lugs in this old servant, and actually presents me with a formula, for which I never asked him, to enable me to determine the necessary force of the primitive impulse! It will be quite time enough to take the formula into consideration, when Kinclaven has brought forward some proof, that the planets ever did receive the impulse of which he speaks. Kinclaven says, "had Mr. M. been conversant with a few of the first articles of the First Book of the Principia, he would have found directions for finding the primitive impulse." Singularly enough, another learned gentleman, who is manfully attacking the electrical theory in a different quarter, has these words,— "If Mr. M. had ever read the Principia, he would have known that Newton says nothing whatever about a primitive impulse; that it forms no part of the Newtonian system." When these profound philosophers can agree between themselves, I will answer them upon this point.

Again, Kinclaven says, "In the case of a body moving in the circumference of a circle, had he been acquainted with the first principles of Dynamics, he might have discovered a method of solving his own question." Well, let us see.

In the accompanying diagram: Let a body, A, be acted on by two forces at the

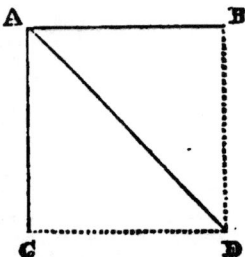

same instant, one of which, acting alone, would cause it to move uniformly over the line A B in a given time, and the other acting alone, would cause it to move over the line A C at right angles to A B, in the same time; then the moving body will describe the diagonal line A B, and at the end of the given time, will have arrived at the point D.

Now I presume that Kinclaven does not require to be told, that any two sides of a triangle, are greater than the third side; and therefore, I suppose he will admit that the line A D, which the body under the action of the two forces has described, is not quite so long as the two lines A B and A C taken together. How is this, Kinclaven? I will tell you. A portion of the *momentum*, which would have carried the body over the line A B, has been destroyed by the force acting in the direction A C, and a portion of the *momentum*, which would have carried the body over the line A C, has been destroyed by the force acting in the direction A B; therefore, the joint effect which is represented by the line A D, is less than that which is due to both forces, because, in consequence of the two forces interfering with each other, a portion of the *momentum* of each has been destroyed.

Now, Kinclaven, suppose we draw a circle round this diagram thus—are the conditions changed by this addition?

Let A represent the sun, and B the

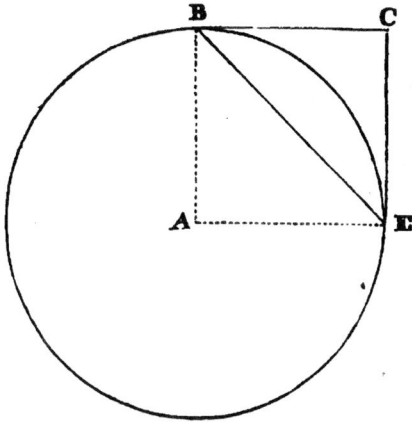

earth; then the line of attraction acts in the direction B A; let the force with which B is attracted towards A be equal to 1, and let the primitive impulse in the direction B C, be given to the body B, by which a *momentum* is imparted, also equal to 1. Now, for the sake of simplicity, we will suppose, that after the first instant the attractive force ceases to act upon the moving body till it arrives at the point E, then the body has simply received two impulses at right angles to each other, and as in the former case, the body will describe the diagonal line B E, and at the end of a given time will come to a state of rest at the point E; because, by the opposition of the two forces the *momentum* has been annihilated. We now find that the force of attraction, which we supposed to be suspended till the body had arrived at the point E, is equal to 1, as at first, and will ever remain so, whilst the *momentum* is equal to 0, and therefore, another primitive impulse is required to prevent the body B from falling directly upon the body A. Gravity, or attraction is a real force; *momentum is no force.* Momentum may be, and is destroyed by force; gravity, or attraction cannot be destroyed by any force. If the planets moved in perfect circles this effect would be more apparent, but their conditions are not altered by their moving in undulating orbits. In con-

sequence of the undulation of the earth in her orbit, the effect upon the momentum is continually varying, but the entire effect is precisely the same as if the orbit were a perfect circle. Now, Kinclaven, if the earth's orbit were a perfect circle, would the momentum derived from the supposed primitive impulse remain for ever undiminished, notwithstanding that gravity (acting at right angles to the momentum as in the diagrams which accompany this letter,) is constantly tending to its annihilation? This is the question which I have put to Kinclaven, which he has not yet answered, and which I defy him to answer in a fair and candid manner, without upsetting his whole system.

. Kinclaven must not suppose that my objections to the system which he upholds are confined to these; I could very readily introduce a few more to his notice. The following may serve as a specimen, although, it is one upon which I do not place any very great importance —We are told, that—

Space is a vacuum; and that—

Light is a fluid issuing from the sun, and filling the whole solar system.

That is; space is a vacuum filled with a fluid. Now this from the lips of an Irishman would be considered a very capital bull, but as it forms a part of the Newtonian system, it is to be received as sublime philosophy.

I shall not take up your valuable pages in replying to Kinclaven's last; as it appears to me that his observations are wholly beside the argument. I deny that the planets ever did receive the mechanical impulse of which he treats. and therefore I do not at present require his formula.

In conclusion, I beg to thank your several correspondents who have favoured us with their remarks upon the electrical theory—Kinclaven amongst the rest; I honour him for his indomitable spirit; right or wrong, he is determined he will not be beaten. Not forgetting the "fastidious" Nautilus. By the bye, if Nautilus should at any time think of coming to London, let me recommend to him to put the *bottle of crusted port* to which he formerly alluded, in his portmanteau, that its contents may be discussed. I have no doubt that Kinclaven will as as willingly take a part in such discussion, as he has done in that upon electrical theory.

Yours respectfully,
T. SIMMONS MACKINTOSH.

GRIFFIN'S ELECTROMETER.

Sir,—I believe no adequate means have have hitherto been discovered of measuring with any degree of precision the absolute quantity (without reference to intensity) of electricity contained in a charged battery. I have turned my attention to the subject, and long since formed the leading idea of the Electrometer of absolute quantities, about to be described. It is founded upon the generally admitted fact, that the quantity of electricity communicated to one coating of a battery is equalled within a very minute proportion by the quantity given off by the other coating. This latter quantity being measured, will therefore furnish a pretty accurate measure of the former. To effect this, the battery must be insulated, and its outer coating suffered to give off its electricity to a self-discharging jar. In the process of charging the battery, *whatever be the intensity of the electricity contained in it,* for every absolute quantity communicated to one coating, a similar quantity will be parted with by the other, and assuming this quantity to be just sufficient to discharge the self-discharging jar, so as to dis-

charge itself the number of times that jar does so discharge itself, will be a direct measure of the absolute contents of the battery.

I do not pretend to describe a perfect instrument, but only to give the leading principles of it, with such minor suggestions as occur to me. The meter jar should discharge itself at a very low intensity, that the electricity intended to pass into it, may not be dissipated, by passing slowly from one of its coatings to the other, or from the emitted side of the battery into the air.

For the same reasons the coatings of the jar should be far apart, and the emitted side of the battery should be free from all points and roughness. The jar should, in consequence of its discharging itself at a low intensity, be large enough to give sparks at sufficiently long intervals of time, to be easily counted when a large machine is used. The discharging knobs should be of a metal the least liable to be acted upon by sparks, and should be inclosed in a glass tube to exclude the dust and damp; and if the tube, and jar also, be air tight, it would perhaps be better, in order to prevent the discharge being affected by changes in the density and dampness of the air.

The communication of the battery with the prime conductor should be quite perfect, the electricity never passing by sparks. The generation of the electricity should also be regular, to prevent irregular and extraordinary undulation of the fluid communicated to the recipient coating of the battery, and causing correspondent undulations of that passing from the constant coating through the meter. A means should also be very carefully devised of forming a standard meter, to represent unity, a standard that could be readily and exactly imitated at any time or place. This would perhaps, best effected by using a plate of air at a certain medium temperature and dryness, coated by two circular plates of metal of a certain diameter (one being insulated in the most simple and perfect manner) and discharging themselves by two spherical balls, also of a certain diameter. These balls and the plates being being also at certain distances apart.

Such a standard being once formed and preserved in a public institution, all other meters otherwise constructed, might be regulated by it, by having their discharging balls set by a micrometer screw, to discharge with the same, or any multiple or aliquot quantity of electricity.

To compare this standard electrometer, with others, a coating of each of two exactly similar plates of air might be made to communicate, one with a prime conductor; the other two coatings to communicate, one with the standard electrometer, and the other with the one to be regulated by it. One of the balls of the latter should be moved till it be discharged at the same instant as the standard meter; or (if it cannot be made to do so) till it is uncertain which will discharge first. Between every trial, the electricity to be, of course, completely discharged. The whole apparatus, should also, during the operation, be placed at a distance from the machine and from every other substance capable of interfering by induction.

Unless every part of the battery coatings be very far apart, I doubt if this electrometer would do with high intensities, as the electricity would pass over the uncoated part of the battery, from the recipient to the emitted coating, and add to the absolute quantity of fluid passing through the meter; but this source of error might, I think, be obviated by a ring of coating passing round the battery jars near the outer coating, and communicating with a row of points, suspended by silk, at a distance from the battery. If the rings communicated with the earth, they might occasion damage by a spontaneous discharge through the meter.

I have thought that a balance with knobs might be usefully placed between the discharging knobs, and made to move an index; but the beam must be a very delicate one; and the probabilities of inaccuracy from friction and other causes seem to more than counterbalance the trouble of counting the sparks.

My situation does not enable me to make accurate experiments, and the only one I have tried is, in comparing the sparks that passed while charging a jar with those that did so while discharging it gradually by a point. When that jar, was not highly charged, and every care used, the number of sparks out and in were equal.

The following sketch of my own instrument, such as it is, may serve to illustrate :—

A is the meter jar.

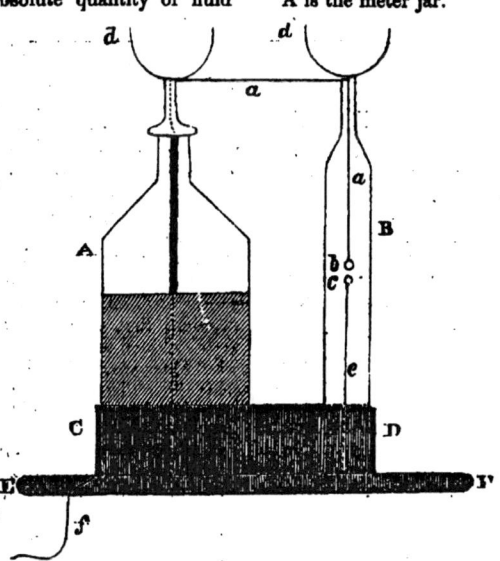

B an Eau de Cologne bottle, air tight. C D a metallic sole to receive the bottoms of A and B, and fastened to E F. E F a platform to keep all steady.

a a a metallic communication from the meter jar to the ball *b*.

b the knob of the jar.

c is the discharging knob communicating by the brass tube *e* through the bottom of the bottle with the metallic sole, and the coating of the jar.

d d are two removable metallic forks, on which is laid the charging jar, when one only is used, as the readiest mode of insulation.

f is a wire going to the rubber to ensure perfect freedom of motion for the fluid.

A jar with two necks, would perhaps be better, and be more simple, one neck to communicate with the prime conductor, and the other to receive the tube containing the discharging knobs.

CHARLES GRIFFIN.

April 22, 1837.

FIRES IN PARIS.

Sir,—Through the kindness of a friend, I am enabled to hand for insertion in your Magazine the following particulars of the Parisian fires for the last six years. The present report is issued by the Commandant of the Sapeur-Pompiers, or military firemen of Paris, who are noted for their numerical strength, and for the excellent state of discipline in which they are constantly maintained, as well as for their general success in dealing with conflagrations.

They are, however, nearly as much inferior to the firemen of London in respect to their machinery and equipments, as they are superior in point of numbers and training.

I remain, Sir,
Yours respectfully,
WM. BADDELEY.

A List of Fires of every description which took place in Paris during the Years 1831 *to* 1836, *both included, and the principal Casualties attending them.*

Anno Domine.	Number of Fires.	Fires in Chimnies.	Total.	PERSONAL ACCIDENTS.							
				Suffocated.		Hurt.		Burned.		Deaths.	
				Firemen.	Populace.	Firemen.	Populace.	Firemen.	Populace.	Firemen.	Populace.
1831	122	693	815	..	..	3	..	..	5	..	..
1832	153	1134	1287	..	..	2	..	..	5	..	..
1833	151	931	1082	..	..	4	7	..	9	..	..
1834	190	1124	1314	8	..	5	1	..	3	..	1
1835	213	1348	1561	1	3	10	2	2	13	1	10
1836	191	1352	1543	..	6	7	8	..	13	..	14
	1020	6582	7602	9	9	31	18	2	48	1	25

The small number of firemen killed and wounded, is attributable to the expertness acquired by the men in their daily drills.

GREGORY'S LEVER FOR FIRE-ESCAPES AND SCALING-LADDER JOINTS.

Sir,—The accompanying sketch is illustrative of an apparatus that has been designed for the purposes of either making or breaking the joints of the portable fire-escape-ladders, on the principle of the military scaling ladders, which have been already very fully described in your pages.

This apparatus is the invention of Mr. John Gregory, of fire-escape celebrity, many of whose ingenious contrivances for various humane purposes have been recorded in your past volumes. The present apparatus consists of a cross-rail and two cheeks of wood, with a lever or handle, by means of which the series of ladders may be joined up, or disjointed with great facility; there are two iron stirrups at the ends of the cross-rail *a a*, which hold it firmly upon the round of the ladder; a strong iron hook *b*, pendant from the axis *c*, goes under the ladder-round, and prevents upward motion. If a joint is to be tightened, the apparatus is placed on the top step of the lower-most ladder, with the lever *d, above* the bottom step of the upper ladder, and the handle pushed upwards. On the

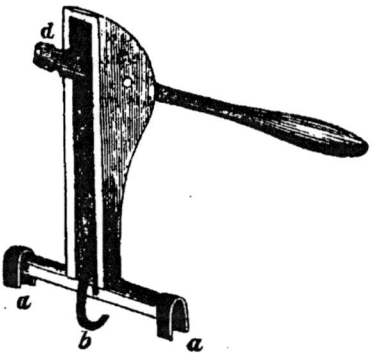

contrary, if the joint is to be undone, the end of the lever *d* is placed *beneath* the round, and the handle pulled downwards, which instantly raises and unships the ladders.

After being joined up for several hours in the wet, these ladders are very apt to set fast, and the joints are separated with difficulty; to obviate the inconvenience arising from this cause, the present apparatus was designed, and from practical experience I can state that it fully answers its intended purpose.

I remain, Sir,

Yours respectfully,

WM. BADDELEY.

Wellington-street, Blackfriars Road,
May 20, 1837.

DR. MORRISON'S CHINESE LIBRARY.

There is no other Asiatic nation from which Europeans can ever expect to learn half so much in practical science and the useful arts, as the Chinese. The means of information on these subjects accumulate every year more and more in our hands, and a most important addition has very recently been made to their number. At a meeting of the proprietors of the University College, (or, to use its former appellation, the London University), on May the 20th, it was stated that the destination of the late Dr. Morrison's Chinese library had been at length decided, and that it was to be added to the library of that establishment (which, it does not appear to be generally known, is already rich in Chinese books presented by the late Jeremy Bentham and Dr. Gregory). The history of this collection is most singular, and it is hard to decide whether it reflects most credit, or discredit, on the English nation. It was originally formed by Dr. Morrison in China, and on his temporary return to England, twelve or thirteen years ago, thrown open by him to the public, in connection with an establishment called the "Language Institution," in which he taught Chinese gratuitously to all who gave a pledge to devote themselves to missionary labours in China. The institution drooped, and on his second departure for Asia, died a natural death; the books were transferred to the premises of the Church Missionary Society, first in Austin Friars, and then in Bloomfield-street, and there they have remained till now, packed up in boxes, and made no use of whatever. An offer to purchase the library was, it appears, made by the Royal College at Paris, which, it is said, Dr. Morrison rejected "with indignation," being anxious that the stores he had collected should be made subservient to the purpose of promoting the study of Chinese in his native country. "Indignation" is not the right word;—there was nothing improper in the offer of the French, who, on the contrary, did themselves honour by the desire they shewed to obtain the means of extending knowledge; while Dr. Morrison did himself still more, by his noble perseverance in a wish to benefit and enlighten his countrymen, at a time when their apathy might well have made him *indignant.* In 1834, Dr. Morrison died; his family was left in some degree unprovided for; to raise a fund for their support, an attempt was made to dispose of the library to some of our great public institutions, and this attempt was unsuccessful. The Trustees of the British Museum were at that time, at the suggestion of the Chancellor of the Exchequer, expending £750 on the purchase of a single volume—a curious ancient copy of the Bible; but neither Trustees nor Chancellor could be brought to sanction the expenditure of £2,000 for the purchase of a library of several thousand volumes, rich, there is no doubt, in curious information, and superior to any thing else of the same kind in Europe. It is well that while we are forced to blush for the incomprehensible niggardliness of our public institutions, we have it in our power to record an act of the most generous and enlightened public spirit, on the part of individuals. When the authorities of the Museum had declined the acquisition, a subscription was raised, chiefly among the personal friends of Dr. Morrison, for the purpose of purchasing the library, and of presenting it to some public institution of the metropolis, which would undertake to establish a professorship of Chinese. It is on the condition of appointing a professor of that language for the term of five years at least, at the rate of £60 a-year, that the library has become the property of the London University. From this short statement of the history of this library, it is evident that a debt of gratitude is owing to the memory of the late Dr. Morrison, not only from all Chinese students in England, but all to whom the honour of their country is dear. There is also another and a living name to which, perhaps, even greater respect is due. The learned translator of the Laws of China presented his own library of Chinese works, consisting of nearly a thousand volumes, to the Royal Asiatic Society. As a Trustee of the British Museum, he urged his brother Trustees, earnestly, but in vain, to the purchase of Dr. Morrison's collection, though conscious that it eclipsed the glory of his own; and when they refused, he, as a trustee of Dr. Morrison's collection, inrolled and liberally contributed to the subscription which has led to its being placed in a public establishment. For all this we are indebted to Sir George Staunton.

ON THE PHENOMENA ATTENDING THE EVAPORATION OF WATER BY HIGHLY HEATED METALS, AND INFERENCES AS TO THE PROPAGATION OF STEAM UNDER PRESSURE.

Sir,—It is a well known fact, that metals gradually heated above 212° will evaporate small quantities of water, more and more rapidly, until a temperature is attained (varying with different metals, and under different circumstances, from about 300° to 500°), at which the rapidity of evaporation is at a maximum; after this the water is repelled and separated from the surface of the metal, and the evaporation is retarded; and a continued increase of the temperature further delays the dispersion of the water.

The investigation of this subject is of considerable importance, inasmuch as the boilers of locomotive engines are frequently heated to temperatures sufficient to produce these effects on small quantities of water, under the natural pressure of the atmosphere. It is also a matter of interesting conjecture, whether the phenomena in question would interfere with the propagation of steam under such pressures as would render the boiling point of the water, and consequently the heat of the boiler, equal to the temperature of repulsion in an open vessel. With reference to these considerations, I am induced to suggest the following explanations of the phenomena.

In the process of ebullition, every globule of steam formed at the heating surface, must, *pro tempore,* displace therefrom an equivalent bulk of water, and the more rapidly the globules are formed, at the greater number of points will the water be displaced. Hence, therefore, if the heat be communicated to the water with such rapidity, as to effect the *simultaneous* production of steam at *every* point of the evaporating surface, steam must also necessarily exist at every point between such surface and the water. Thus, then, I conceive, that owing to the rapidity with which vapour is formed at the under surface of the water, a stratum of steam is maintained between it and the metal.

Heated metals exert no such repulsion on solid bodies, however light they may be; neither do metals, at temperatures sufficient to produce the effect on water, repel other liquids whose boiling points exceed that of water. A considerable excess in the heat of the metal above the temperature at which ebullition, or the production of steam commences, is in all cases essential to the effect, from which it is manifest that the phenomenon is at all events in some way or other attributable to the formation of vapour; and I think the effect cannot be ascribed to this cause in any other way than that I have mentioned.

I shall now endeavour to show how this rapid production of steam at the heating surface, to which I attribute the separation between the water and the metal, is to be reconciled with the fact of the dispersion of the water being at the same time retarded.

So long as the water remains in contact with the metal, the steam formed at the heating surface ascends through the water, and in its progress diffuses the redundant heat which it acquires by contact with the heated metal; and thus vapour is produced not only at the surface of the metal, but also throughout the mass of the water; but as soon as the water is uplifted from the metal, the heated steam is enabled to escape from the space intervening between the water and the metal, without passing through the water, whereupon the evaporation which had previously proceeded, as well at the heating surface, as also throughout the body of the water, becomes confined to the heating surface, and the dispersion of the water is therefore necessarily retarded.

When a lump of red-hot metal is partially immersed in a vessel of hot* water, the separation which takes place between the water and the metal enables the steam formed at the heating surface to escape without passing through the water. Under these circumstances, I find by experiment, that the evaporation does not arrive at its maximum, until the metal has parted with the most of its caloric, and has come into contact with the water.

But when the heated metal is *wholly submerged* in the water, in which case the steam formed at the surface of the metal is compelled to ascend through the water, then the evaporation, instead of increasing as the temperature subsides, is most rapid when the metal is hottest, and gradually diminishes as the metal cools.

As to the evaporation being further retarded by the continued increase of the temperature after the separation has taken place, this, I think, is owing to the interposing stratum of steam being expanded by the increased heat, and the water being thereby removed to a greater distance from the heated metal.

The non-appearance of vapour when water is thrown upon very intensely heated metal, has induced some people to suppose that no steam is actually produced. The fact, however, is, that the water is always more or less rapidly evaporated; but the steam produced being heated by its contact with the metal greatly above the temperature necessary to maintain it in the state of steam, is dissipated in the atmosphere before it becomes sufficiently cooled to suffer any condensation, and be thereby rendered visible.

From these observations, the following inferences may be drawn:—

1st. That the separation between the water and the evaporating surface cannot take place in the boiler of a steam-engine, until the temperature of the boiler exceed the boiling point of the water, however that boiling point may be rendered by pressure.

2nd. That since pressure would diminish the volume of the steam formed at the heating surface, it would also render a more rapid evaporation, and a greater excess in the temperature of the metal above the boiling point of the water, requisite to produce the effect.

3rd. That although the separation between the water and the boiler, would doubtless impair the efficiency of the fuel, that is to say, would render the rapidity of the evaporation less than commensurate with the intensity of the fire—yet the evaporation would not be actually *diminished* by increasing the heat, unless such a separation were established between the sides and bottom of the boiler as would permit the escape of the steam without passing through the water.

* Hot water must be used, otherwise the steam will be condensed as fast as it is propagated.

I do not wish it to be understood that I claim originality for all the suggestions contained in this letter. Many persons, among others, your scientific correspondent, Mr. Tomlinson, attribute the separation between the water and the metal, either wholly or in part, to the intervention of a stratum of steam; but I am not aware that the *existence* of such a stratum has received the explanation I have given it.

I shall be glad if any of your correspondents, who have paid attention to the subject, will point out the objections which may exist to the explanations I have offered for the phenomena in question, and to the inferences I have deduced therefrom.

W. G. A.

REPORT FROM THE COMMITTEE ON THE LONDON AND BRIGHTON RAILWAY BILLS.

Lord George Lennox reported from the Committee to whom the several bills for making a railway from London to Brighton were severally referred, and to whom several petitions against such lines were referred, and who were instructed by the House to make a special Report " of the engineering particulars of each of the four competing lines, to enable the House to determine which to send back, for the purpose of having the landowners heard and clauses settled." That, in compliance with such instruction, they have agreed to the following Report :—

The first, second, third, and fourth resolutions required by the standing orders of the House, do not relate to engineering particulars.

Fifth Resolution.

Stephenson's Line.—That the line proposed by Mr. Stephenson is a complete and integral line from the junction with the Southampton railway at Wimbledon to the Depôt in the parish of Hove, with a further extention of 44 yards into the parish of Brighton.

The Direct Line.—The line proposed by Sir John Rennie and Mr. Rastrick is a complete and integral line from its junction with the Croydon railway, near Croydon, to Church-street, Brighton, near the centre of the town.

South-Eastern Line.—The South-Eastern Brighton, Lewes, and Newhaven Railway, is a complete and integral line from its junction with the Dover Railway at Oxted, 19 miles south of London, to near Dorset Gardens, Brighton.

Gibbs's Line.—The line proposed by Mr. Gibbs is a complete and integral line from its junction with the Croydon Railway to North-street, Brighton.

Sixth Resolution.

That there is no competing line of railroad now before the Committee, except those above stated.

Seventh Resolution.

Stephenson's Line.—That there is no plane on Stephenson's line proposed to be worked by assistant engines, either stationary or locomotive ; nor any such plane on that part of the Southampton line adopted in connection with this line.

The Direct Line.—There is no inclined plane on the direct line between Croydon and Brighton, or on its branches ; but there is one on the Croydon railway proposed to be worked by an assistant locomotive engine, the length of which plane is 2 miles 48 chains, and the gradient is 1 in 100.

South-Eastern Line.—There are no planes intended to be worked by assistant engines, stationery or locomotive, on this line ; but it also adopts the Croydon Railway as its outlet, on which is the plane above stated.

Gibbs's Line.—There are planes on this line which will be required to be worked, either by assistant engines, stationary or locomotive ; but this line also adopts the plane on the Croydon Railway above described.

Eighth Resolution.

That there are no peculiar engineering difficulties on either of the proposed lines.

The total amount of earthwork upon each of the lines is as follows :—

	Cubic Yards.
Stephenson's Line ..	6,023,000
The Direct Line	9,250,295
Branch to Shoreham .	495,920
———— Lewes	1,070,642
———— Newhaven .	1,129,294
	————11,946,151

	Cubic Yards.
South-Eastern Line..	8,893,890
Branch to Lewes	251,538
	1,571,074
	————10,716,505
Gibbs's Line	8,496,444

The largest embankments upon the lines are as follow ; and these, being the greatest works, afford a measure of the time necessary for the execution of each line :—

	Cubic Yards.
Stephenson's Line ..	660,000
The Direct Line	948,503
South-Eastern Line..	1,533,906
Gibbs's Line	924,592

Ninth Resolution.

Stephenson's Line.—That there are two tunnels on Stephenson's line, viz. one at Epsom Common 500 yards long through London Clay. The other tunnel is at Dorking, which is 572 yards long ; the soil is indurated sand and sandstone; the breadth of both tunnels is 23 feet, and the height 27 feet.

The strata through which these tunnels pass have been mentioned; the clay is not a peculiarly favourable or unfavourable soil, and the indurated sand and sandstone are favourable.

The tunnels will not require ventilation except from the apertures.

The Direct Line.—That there are two tunnels on the main line, one at Balcombe 470 yards in length, and the other at Clayton 850 yards in length. These two tunnels are of the respective height of 30 feet, and of the respective width of 24 feet; the strata through which they pass are exceedingly favourable, and from the shortness of the tunnels they will ventilate themselves.

There is a tunnel on the Lewes branch of 875 yards long, of the height of 20 feet, and of the width of 16 feet. An archway on the Newhaven branch 120 yards long, of the height of 50 feet, and of the width of 16 feet. The strata through which they pass are exceedingly favourable, and they will ventilate themselves.

South-Eastern Line.—There are five tunnels on the main line, of the respective lengths of 640 yards, 880 yards, 200 yards, 200, and 570 yards. There is also a tunnel on the Newhaven branch of 150 yards; these tunnels are proposed to be 25 feet wide, and 30 feet high. The strata through which they pass are peculiarly favourable. The three longest tunnels are to be ventilated by shafts.

There are also two tunnels on that part of the South-Eastern Dover line which is adopted as the outlet for this line, viz. one at Riddlesdown of 807 yards, and one of 2 miles 312 yards at Oxted.

Gibbs's Line.—There are two tunnels on this line, one at Mertsham of 1364 yards in length; the tunnel is double; each passage is proposed to be 27 feet 6 inches high, and 15 feet wide, and will be ventilated by two shafts; the stratum through which it passes is favourable. The other tunnel is at Horsham, 924 yards long, 24 feet wide, and 25 feet high; no ventilation is required. The stratum through which it passes is neither favourable nor otherwise.

Tenth Resolution.

Stephenson's Line.—The gradients on Stephenson's line are favourable, the prevailing gradient being one in 330, or 16 feet a mile. There is no curve of less than a mile radius, except the following, namely, one on that part of the Southampton Railway, used by Stephenson's line, of half a mile radius, and another at the depôt of the Southampton Railway, of a quarter of a mile radius, and one near the depôt at Brighton, of three quarters of a mile radius.

The Direct Line.—The gradients on the main line and branches are favourable, the steepest gradient being 1 in 264, or 20 feet per mile; the smallest radius of a curve on the main line is one mile, except at the depôt at Brighton, where there is one of three quarters of a mile radius. There are two curves on the Lewes branch, of three quarters of a mile radius, and one of a quarter of a mile radius, where it joins the main line. There is also a curve on the Shoreham branch, of a quarter of a mile radius, where it joins the main line.

South-Eastern Line.—The gradients and curves on the main line are favourable, the steepest gradient being 1 in 264, or 20 feet per mile; the smallest radius of a curve is one mile. The steepest gradient on the Lewes branch is 1 in 228, or 22 feet in a mile. On the Newhaven branch the steepest gradient is 1 in 203, or 26 feet in a mile. The smallest radius of a curve three quarters of a mile.

Gibbs's Line.—The gradients and curves on this line are favourable, the steepest gradient being 1 in 230, or 16 feet per mile. The smallest radius of a curve is one mile, except near the depôt at Brighton, where there is one of three quarters of a mile radius.

Eleventh Resolution.

Stephenson's Line.—The length of Stephenson's line, from the junction with the Southampton Railway to its terminus at Brighton, is 49 miles 1452 yards; from Nine Elms, Vauxhall, to the junction with Stephenson's line, is 5 miles 660 yards. The total distance from Nine Elms to Brighton is 55 miles, 352 yards.

The Direct Line.—The length of the main line from its junction with the Croydon Railway is 41 miles, 59 chains; and from its terminus at London-bridge to its terminus at Church-street, Brighton, 50 miles, 62 chains. The length of the branch to Lewes is 7 miles; the length of the branch to Newhaven is 6 miles, 75 chains; the length of the branch to Shoreham is 5 miles, 68 chains.

South-Eastern Line.—The length of the main line to Brighton is 32 miles and 3 chains; and from the point of junction at Oxted to London-bridge, is 20 miles; making the total length 52 miles, 3 chains. The length of the branch to Lewes is 2 miles, 67 chains. The length of the branch to Newhaven is 6 miles, 41 chains.

Gibbs's Line.—The length of the line to be constructed is 47 miles, 56½ chains, and the whole distance from London-bridge to the terminus at North-street, Brighton, is 56 miles, 77½ miles.

Twelfth Resolution.

Stephenson's Line.—That Stephenson's

line is a fit line in an engineering point of view.

The Direct Line.—That the proposed main line and branches are fit lines of railway in an engineering point of view.

South-Eastern Line.—That the line is well fitted, in an engineering point of view, for the purposes intended.

Gibbs's Line.—That this line does not appear well fitted, in an engineering point of view, for the purposes intended.

Thirteenth Resolution.

None of the proposed lines of railway pass on a level any turnpike or highway.

Fourteenth Resolution.

Stephenson's Line..—The amount of the estimate of the cost of this line is £1,000,000, including the land, and £10 per cent. for contingencies; which is adequate, and appears to be supported by evidence.

The Direct Line.—The amount of the estimate of the cost of the main line is £897,073, and of the branches £302,833, including the land, and £10 per cent. for contingencies; which is adequate, and appears to be supported by evidence.

South-Eastern Line.—The amount of the estimate of the cost of this line and branches is £1,200,000, including the land, and £10 per cent. for contingencies; which is adequate, and appears to be supported by evidence.

Gibbs's Line.—The amount of the estimate of the cost of this line as deposited in the Private Bill Office, is £950,000; but the cost, as proved in evidence, is as follows, viz. :—

For the works on the line .. £770,335
For land 193,466
                         ————————
                         £963,801

This does not include the usual £10 per cent. for contingencies, amounting to £77,033; the estimate is therefore inadequate, and is not supported by evidence.

Fifteenth Resolution.

Stephenson's Line.—That the estimated charge of the annual expenses of Stephenson's line when completed is £40 per cent. on the gross annual income.

The Direct Line.—That the estimated annual expenses of this line is £50 per cent. on the gross income. The engineer of the Direct line stated that he considered it prudent to estimate the annual expense of all railways at £50 per cent. upon the gross income, and therefore estimated the annual expense of the Direct line at that sum.

South-Eastern Line.—The annual outgoings of the proposed South-Eastern line, in rates, taxes, agency, management, collection of tolls, carriages, and maintenance, is estimated at £500 per mile.

Gibbs's Line.—The estimated charge of the annual expenses of this railroad, when completed, is £40 per cent. on the gross annual income.

Sixteenth and Seventeenth Resolutions.

These resolutions do not relate to engineering particulars.

Eighteenth Resolution.

Stephenson's Line.—That the engineers examined in support of Stephenson's line were Messrs. Robert Stephenson, George Parker Bidder, Charles Vignoles, John Dixon, Peter Sinclair, I. K. Brunel, and Thomas Grainger.

The Direct Line.—The engineers examined in support of this line were Joseph Locke, William Chadwell Milne, John U. Rastrick, and Dr. Lardner.

South-Eastern Line.—The engineers examined in favour of this line were Messrs. Provis, Storey, Sopwith, M'Neill, and Cubitt.

Gibbs's Line.—The engineers examined in support of Gibbs's line were Messrs. Joseph Gibbs Samuel Hughes, and F. Giles, junior.

Nineteenth Resolution.

This resolution does not relate to engineering particulars.

Twentieth Resolution.

That it appears desirable to your Committee that the House should be informed that they came to the following resolutions, previous to receiving the instructions from the House of the 9th May instant :—

25th April, 1837.—Resolved, As it appears from the evidence adduced before the Committee that the termini of Stephenson's line of railway, both at London and Brighton, are inconvenient to the public; that the line is circuitous and several miles longer than others now under consideration; and that it does not afford facilities of communication with the harbour of Newhaven, the town of Lewes, and the eastern parts of Surrey and Sussex, this Committee cannot recommend the House to sanction it.

3rd May.—Resolved, That the engineering case of the Direct line of railway, proposed by Sir J. Rennie and Mr. Rastrick, has been made out to the satisfaction of this Committee, and this Committee recommend that line to the House for its adoption.

Resolved, This Committee, having adopted the Direct line, proposed by Sir J. Rennie and Mr. Rastrick, cannot recommend the House to adopt the South Eastern line.

Resolved, That the engineering merits of Mr. Gibbs's line of railway are not such as to sanction this Committee in recommending it to the House for adoption.

That your Committee had also, previous to the 9th May, proceeded to hear the cases of the landowners on the Direct line

That the principal reasons that guided your Committee in recommending to the

House the adoption of the Direct line in preference to either of the others, were, That it is shorter than any of the other lines, and can be travelled at less expense to the public. That the termini are central and convenient to the public. That it interferes with but very little ornamental property. That the nature of the soil through which it passes is favourable for the execution of the works. That it connects the ports of Shoreham and Newhaven, and the county town of Lewes, with Brighton and the metropolis. That it runs through the centre of the counties of Surrey and Sussex, and affords great facilities of communication both east and west. That it is supported by a great majority of the town of Brighton ; and, That there is no appreciable difference between the gradients of the Direct and any of the other lines.

Your Committee, in conclusion, beg to observe, that they adopt the Direct line of railway upon a careful consideration of the whole of the evidence upon various lines before them, and having reconsidered the subject, they feel no hesitation in recommending the House to send back the Direct line for the purpose of having the landowners' cases proceeded with, and the clauses settled.

INSTANCES OF SPONTANEOUS COMBUSTION, DETAILED IN. A PAPER READ BEFORE THE ROYAL IRISH ACADEMY.—BY M. SCANLAN, ESQ.

[We insert the following article at the request of an old correspondent, who thinks it may help to throw some light on the circumstances of the late fire at the St. Catherine's Docks.—ED. M. M.]

In the beginning of last March a fire broke out in the extensive turpentine distillery on Sir John Rogerson's quay, belonging to Mr. John Fish Murphy, which is separated from my chemical factory by Windmill Lane. The fire, which was speedily got under, was confined to a heap of what is termed, by turpentine distillers, chip cake, and, from the circumstances under which it occurred, could not be attributed to any other cause than the act of an incendiary, or to the spontaneous ignition of this chip cake.

As spontaneous combustion of this substance had never occurred before in Mr. Murphy's distillery, nor that of his father, an extensive distiller of turpentine, for many years, at Stratford in Essex, I at first doubted that the fire could have originated in this way ; howeuer, on inquiry, I found his mode of working had been, on this particular occasion, different from that usually employed in his distillery, and, experiments which he kindly permitted me to make, have since

proved beyond doubt that combustion did take place spontaneously.

Raw turpentine, as it comes from America, in barrels, includes a considerable quantity of impurity, consisting of chips of wood, leaves, and leaf stalks.* It was hitherto the practice, in Mr. Murphy's distillery, as it is in England, to heat the raw turpentine up to temperature of about 180°, as I found by plunging a thermometer into one of his large copper pans, and to strain the turpentine, thus liquified, from the impurities, previously to introducing it into the still, where it is submitted to distillation in the usual way, with portion of a water, yielding turpentine oil, which distills over along with the water and rosin which remains behind in the still. The chips, when separated by a wire strainer, still retain a quantity of adhering turpentine worth saving, and with this view, are transferred to a large close vat, where they are exposed for some time to the action of steam furnished by a boiler kept for this purpose, as well as for steaming the empty barrels, in order to remove any turpentine that may adhere to them. Still, however, the chips are a good deal imbued with resinous matter, and in this state form a loose porous mass, which the turpentine distillers call chip cake, a material which is used by the poor in the neighbourhood as fuel.

As long as the process I have just described was pursued, which is the London mode, and that which produces the best rosin, no accident occurred from fire in Mr. Murphy's premises, although I have frequently seen immense heaps of this chip cake collected together in his yard ; but, on making trial of a different plan, namely— that practised by a Dublin distiller, Mr. Price of Lincoln Lane, the accident in question occurred.

On this occasion, the raw turpentine together with its impurities, was put directly into the still, along with the proper quantity of water, and the boiling rosin at the end of the operation, strained from the chips.

The chip cake resulting from a single operation thus conducted was laid in a heap outside the still house, at three o'clock in the afternoon, and at midnight was observed to be in flames.

In the first mentioned process it is obvious the chips were never exposed to a

* The following extract from the letter of a French turpentine merchant, will account for the presence of these foreign bodies. To obtain the turpentine " the fir timber is chopped about a man's height down its side with an axe, not hand deep and, afterwards higher up. The turpentine or rosin pat is scraped up from the foot of the tree. That which is on the side wound, when scraped off, is white, and called gulley pat, of which the burning incense is made. It does not yield so much turpentine spirit as the pat."

higher degree of temperature than 212°; but in the latter, especially when it is the object of the manufacturer to make amber rosin, the temperature to which they are exposed is much higher.

The first experiment I made was on the 16th March; I found the temperature of the boiling rosin, in the still, to be 250° when the turpentine oil and water had been distilled off, the fire just drawn from under the still, and when the liquid rosin was in the act of being strained from the chips which were introduced into the still with the turpentine.

I had the whole of the chip cake resulting from this distillation carried into my own yard, upon a wire screen, and left in the open air, with a view of watching its progress.

The temperature increased gradually in the centre of the heap, although externally it became quite cold and brittle. In four hours, in fact, a thermometer thrust into centre of the *porous* mass indicated a temperature of 400°; a good deal of vapour was now given off, and the adhering rosin in the heated parts began to acquire a high colour; the smell could be perceived at a considerable distance from my premises; it was a mixed smell of pitch and rosin.

The chip cake, in this experiment, was first exposed to the air at one o'clock in the afternoon, and though it rained during the night, at half-past eleven the following morning it burst into a flame.

In a second experiment, I placed the chip cake in an open tar barrel, having three holes bored in the bottom, about two inches diameter each, and it did not take fire till the expiration of thirty-six hours; but the temperature of the mass was lowered by removal from the wire strainer to the barrel, and besides, I am of opinion the limited access of air retarded the combustion.

In a third trial which I made, combustion took place in five hours; but in this experiment the temperature of the boiling rosin drawn from the still was 260°, and the chip cake was laid, as in the first experiment, on the wire screen; the wind, too, was very high. The screen, in this case, was raised a few inches from the ground, in order to let the rosin, as it melted, drip away, which it did in abundance.

It appeared to me as if the porous mass became slowly red hot, in the centre, like a pyrophorous, and as if the vapour and gaseous matter arising from the decomposed rosin which lay immediately beneath, were inflamed on coming in contact with it. I was standing by when it suddenly burst into flame, and I thought, at the time, had the melted rozin been permitted to drop into water, or had it fallen to such a distance as not to be kept liquid by the radiant heat from the red hot mass above, that there would have been no flame, but silent combustion.

I have since learned from Mr. Price, in whose distillery it has always been the practice to put the unstrained turpentine into the still, that he was well aware of the fact, which it is the object of this paper to record, from a fire having occurred several years ago on his premises, when in the possession of his predecessor, Mr. James Price, and that, ever since, they cool down the chip cake, immediately on removal from the still, with water, and afterwards use it as fuel under the still.

An instance of spontaneous combustion occurred with my friend Mr. Philip Coffey, of the Dock Distillery, which is worth relating while on this subject.

He had made a quantity of the mixture used in theatres for producing red light, a powder consisting of nitrate of strontion, sulphur, chlorate of potash, and sulphuret of antimony with a little lamp black. A paper parcel of this " red fire," of about a pound or two by weight, was left by him on a shelf in a store-room where there was no fire nor candle lights, the following day, while reading in an adjoining room, he perceived a smell as if some of this powder were burning, and, on examination, he found it had ignited spontaneously on the shelf and was actually consumed.   M. SCANLAN.

Dublin, 25th June, 1835.

NOTES AND NOTICES.

The Euphrates Expedition.—The survivors of the unfortunate Euphrates Expedition have just arrived in England, with the exception of the leader, Colonel Chesney, who remains in India, still cherishing the idea of establishing steam-communication by the Euphrates route, notwithstanding the disasters and delay he experienced, would seem to be conclusive as to its impracticability as a good working line.

The Fine Arts in the City.—The execution of the Equestrian Statue of the Duke of Wellington, for which upwards of seven thousand pounds have been subscribed by the citizens of London, it has been determined shall be entrusted to Sir Francis Chautrey, although such is the number of commissions confided to him, that it is expected *twelve years* will elapse before the statue can be cast and ready for erection.

☞ *British and Foreign Patents taken out with economy and despatch; Specifications, Disclaimers, and Amendments, prepared or revised; Caveats entered; and generally every Branch of Patent Business promptly transacted.*

A complete list of Patents from the earliest period (15 Car. II. 1675,) to the present time may be examined. Fee 2s. 6d.; Clients, gratis.

LONDON: Printed and Published for the Proprietor, by W. A. Robertson, at the Mechanics' Magazine Office, No. 6, Peterborough-court, between 135 and 136, Fleet-street.—Sold by G. W. M. Reynolds, Proprietor of the French, English, and American Library, 55, Rue Neuve, Saint Augustin, Paris.

Mechanics' Magazine,

MUSEUM, REGISTER, JOURNAL, AND GAZETTE.

| No. 722. | SATURDAY, JUNE 10, 1837. | Price 3d. |

CROFT'S HEARSE AND MOURNING COACH COMBINED.

Fig. 1.

Fig. 2.

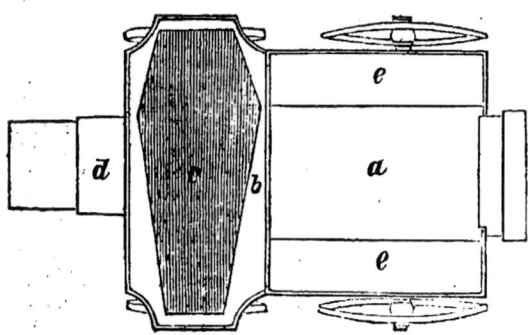

CROFT'S HEARSE AND MOURNING COACH COMBINED.

Sir,—I have often thought when passing those mournful—but unavoidable processions, formed by relatives and friends, following the corpse of some valued human being to the tomb, that their feelings might be spared the anxious gaze of the curious, and might have some means, by which, like their richer neighbours, they could shed the tear of regret separated from the "busy hum of men," at that time so little suited to their feelings. The exposure too, in severe weather, of females has often caused severe illness, and sometimes death, from colds caught on such occasions; and although the custom of females attending funerals is falling into disuse, yet sometimes the feelings of a fond wife, or affectionate mother, will break through the bonds of fashion.

The middle classes of society are as intelligent, and as sensitive, as their richer brethren; but cannot, in many instances, afford the usual expense of carriage funerals, but still would often be willing to pay half that expense; and I believe, were the vehicles I propose adopted, the object might be affected at less than half the expense, double bearers' fees being deducted. I do not think it would injure the interest of those already engaged in the undertaking trade, but would very likely be a source of profit to those speculating in its adoption, as it is very probable there would then be *more carriage funerals.*

The increasing wish to bury in cemetries a short distance from town, is often a cause of fatigue, and in some instances the distance prevents many from using them at all, a vehicle of some kind being absolutely necessary; now if the double-bodied omnibus hearse after described were adopted, the funerals in these more reasonable repositories of the dead would become more numerous.

The drawing (see front page) represents a vehicle like an omnibus, with the part behind the driver's box appropriated to the coffin; the part behind that forming a mourning coach capable of containing eight persons. If the partition be made tight, no offensive smell would be experienced; the corpse, too, would precede the mourners, as is usual, and the part containing the coffin being

over the lower wheel, and passing transversly across the coach, every facility would be afforded for depositing or removing the corpse from the hearse to the shoulders of the bearers; and by passing on well oiled rollers, all grating noise offending the ear would be prevented. The mourners would descend in the way usual in an omnibus.

Description of the Engravings.—Fig. 1, a side view of the vehicle; and fig. 2, a plan: *a,* the department of the vehicle for mourners; *b,* the part containing the coffin, *c;* *d,* the driver's box. The body is represented as 5 feet by 5 feet 2 inches wide; the part containing the coffin, as 6 feet 2 inches, by 3 feet wide, being the full width of the nobs of the wheels; *e e,* the mourner's seats.

J. R. CROFT.

19, Moscow Road, Bayswater.

MR. UTTING'S ASTRONOMICAL TABLES.

Sir,—I beg leave to make a few remarks upon Mr. Utting's last letter, (No. 714.) He still continues to assert, that Professor Struve is an imposter. (For no milder name does he deserve, if he has been guilty of such contemptible fraud as Mr. U. imputes to him)—that he has gulled the astronomical world by giving them a second pretended set of observations on Saturn and his ring, and on Jupiter and his satellites, which he obtained from his first set of observations by a mere reduction of the $\frac{1}{317}$ part. So says Mr. Utting; and he calls upon me to prove to the contrary. Now I should rather think that it is Mr. Utting that should make good the truth his assertion, and prove to us that no imperfections in the instruments could have produced the results stated by the professor in the two sets of observations. The Nautical Almanac for the present year, in noticing a similar subject, makes the following remarks; "Different *telescopes give different results,* and care should be taken to have recourse to those corresponding observations which have been made under circumstances the most similar, and particularly with telescopes of the same quality and power," &c. If there be any truth in this quotation, I think it will go a great way to account for the small differences between the professor's two sets of observations. And poor Sir John Herschell too (according to Mr. U.'s statements) has been hoaxed into a belief that the two sets of observations were honestly obtained in the way stated by the professor; for if he had had any doubts upon the subject he surely never would have given them a place in his astronomy. But has Mr. Utting himself had so much experience in astronomical observations, as could warrant him in supposing that the readers of the *Mechanics' Magazine*, are to take for granted his unsupported assertions?

Mr. Utting at my request has been so condescending as to manufacture a synodical period for the moon,, from his 1st table (vol. xxvi., page 378). This period he makes to be 29 days, 12 hours, 44 minutes, 2.8547 seconds = 29.5305886 mean solar days; and according to the said table her periodical revolution round the earth is performed in 27.3215823 mean solar days. Well, allowing all this to be correct, we have sufficient data to test the accuracy of Mr. Utting's length of a mean tropical year, from the well known astronomical theorem

$$T = \frac{PS}{S - P}$$

where P and S are the periodical and synodical periods of the moon, and T the tropical period of the earth. Hence

$$T = \frac{27.3215823 \times 29.5305886}{2.2090063}$$

= 365.24223892 mean solar days = 365 days 5 hours 48 minutes 49.4427 seconds[*] —differing from that given by Mr. Utting in his first table by .4426 parts of a second in one tropical year. Although this is but a small error for one year, still in 250904 solar years it would amount to 1 day 6 hours 50 minutes 50 seconds, which would be perfectly fatal to any thing like a conjunction. between the sun and moon; leaving altogether out of the question the secular equation of the moon.

Having now, Mr. Editor, shown (and I trust satisfactorily) that Mr. Utting's conjunction of the sun and moon at the end of 250904 solar years is a pure matter of moonshine, I shall now, with your leave proceed to show that the planet

Venus, and the Sun at the end of the above period, are still farther from either a superior or inferior conjunction, than that of the sun and moon. Still taking the leading data from Mr. U.'s first table.

The tropical periods of the earth and Venus from table first are, 365.2422440 and 224.6955699; to each of these periods, if we add .0141551 and .0051800 the respective differences between the tropical and periodical revolutions of each produced by the precession of their respective equinoxes, we obtain their periodical periods 365.2563991 and 224.7007499. Call these numbers P and P', and let S be the synodical period of Venus; then from another well established astronomical theorem we have

$$S = \frac{PP'}{P - P'} = \frac{365.2563911 \times 224.7007499}{140.5556492}$$

= 583.9209400 that is, the synodical period of Venus is, 583 days 22 hours 6 minutes 9.216 seconds. Now, according to Mr. Utting's statement 91640740 mean solar days is the grand cycle of conjunction of all the planets; hence 91640740 ÷ 583.92094 ought to quote a whole number; but it does not, for it produces the unfortunate number 156940.321, that is, in 91640740 mean solar days, Venus will make 156940.321 mean synodical revolutions, and consequently, will at the end of that period be nearly as far as possible from either a superior or inferior conjunction. Upon trial, I find that the planet Mercury is also out of the path of a conjunction. I might, lastly, proceed to inquire how the superior planets, Mars, Jupiter, &c. are situated at the termination of Mr. Utting's grand cycle, but as the calculations for these planets are fully as fatiguing as those of the inferior planets, I shall reserve this for another communication; and I will then make some particular observations upon the astronomical remarks of Mr. Utting's last letter, and endeavour to show Mr. Utting the radical error he has fallen into, in his attempt to find out the period of conjunction of all the planets.

I am, Mr. Editor,

Yours with respect,

A SCOTCH DOMINIE.

Forfarshire, May 14, 1837.

---

[*] The mean equinoctial or tropical year is assumed in the Nautical Almanac from the authority of Bessel (*Conn. des Tems*) to be 365 days 5 hours 48 minutes 47.6 seconds.—N. A. 1837.

HYDRAULIC WEIGHING MACHINES.

Sir,—In the hope of standing excused for troubling you with the following observations, I venture to make them.

In Part XVIII. of the Engineers' and Mechanics's Encyclopædia, which has just now come to my hands through my bookseller, I find, under the head "Weighing-machines, &c." the following statement and figure:—

"Weighing machines have been described by us under the article "Balance," in which article, however, we have omitted a notice of the annexed singular but simple and useful contrivance, the invention of Mr. Hawkins, of Fleet-street. It is called the Hydraulic Weighing-machine, and is chiefly designed for domestic use. *a*, in the annexed figure, denotes a cylindrical vessel made of tin, and japanned, and partly filled with water; *b* is another

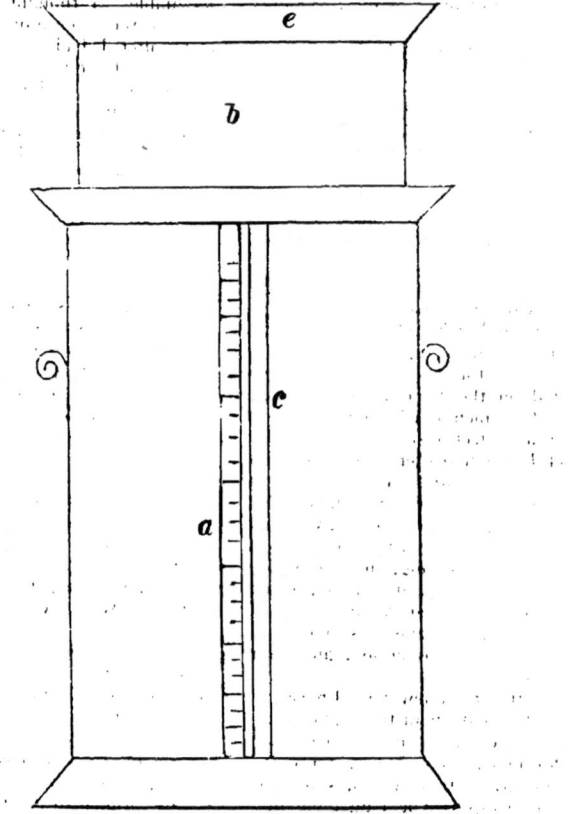

cylinder of the same kind, but of less diameter, resting upon or floating in the water contained in *a*; *a* is a graduated scale, with a glass tube running up the middle, fixed to the exterior cylinder; the bottom of this tube opens into the lower part of the cylinder, therefore the water always stands at the same level in both : *e* is a dish or scale, for holding the article to be weighed, the pressure on which causes the internal cylinder to sink lower, and raise the water higher between the two vessels, the level of which is indicated by the tube, and the weight at such level exhibited on the scale. There is of course a liability to change, by a portion of the water evaporating; but, by leaving a weight in the scale when not in use, and pouring in of a small quantity of water occasionally, to bring it to the level of the mark on the scale, an adjustment is easily made."

In the first part of the Gallery of Practical Science, just published, which fell into my hands the other day, there is allusion to a weighing machine constructed on the principle of the one before described.

With the exception of the two publications just alluded to, I never saw any thing which could lead me to suppose that such a machine was in existence; and yet I have seen many works on subjects, in illustration of which, a description of such a machine might have been given. Whether any allusion has been made in your valuable publication, I cannot tell, because (though now a subscriber to it) I have not yet seen the earlier volumes, in which such would probably appear. Presuming that no satisfactory information there exists, I continue my observations.

On the 2nd of March, 1835, I sent a model of a weighing machine to the Secretary of the Society of Arts, constructed on the same principle as the one before mentioned, but somewhat nearer a perfect instrument, of which model I will hereafter give you a description and figure. The result of my communication to the Secretary, without troubling you with details, was, that I received, on the 3rd April, 1835, a note from him, stating, that the Society did not consider that my endeavours were entitled to their reward, but that they considered themselves obliged to me for my good intention, and exertions, &c.

Till within these few days, I have little troubled myself about the application of the principle applied in my model; and, but for a claim being set up for its application by another person, should not now have trespassed, as I am doing, upon your valuable attention.

I need scarcely observe, Sir, that the principle applied in Mr. Hawkins' machine, is that upon which the hydrostatic bellows and hydrostatic press are constructed; its application almost follows from a proper consideration of the hydrostatic bellows, as usually exhibited in books; for, in them, we see weights supported by the pressure of a column of air; a little thought shows us that a greater number of weights would require the pressure of a longer column of air, and that the substitution of water would at once relieve us from any difficulty we might have in lengthening the column of air.

Now, Sir, if there was any merit due to the first applier of this principle, (and I dont think there was a great deal), I certainly considered my claim to it, indisputable. I thought so little of the value of the application, that, for three years after I had constructed various models, and one large machine for a particular purpose, I did not think of publishing my application. With the nearer approach to perfection in my model, as compared with Mr. Hawkins' machine, I considered the application of the principle to a weighing machine attended with many objections, and, though many improvements have since suggested themselves to me, I am still of a somewhat similar opinion. A weighing machine constructed upon this principle is, nevertheless, with all its disadvantages, a pretty toy, and, where no great degree of accuracy is desirable, may be convenient. The great points of deduction from the utility of such a machine are, the cohesion and friction of the materials and matter employed in its construction. When the thought first struck me of making such a machine, I determined upon testing (sceptical I think I was) the principle by two tin cylinders, one without a top, the other in the form of a drum; this was, if we except the tube and scale, Mr. Hawkins' machine: these instruments of tin, I believe, I have even now somewhere in my possession. When I had completed my model, and compared it with the bent lever balance, I could not but confess the inferiority of my production, and I cannot now obliterate my then received impressions. When I made my model, I chose the square form, instead of the cylindrical; there existed, in my mind, an idea that it was more easy to be so constructed by those whom I was obliged to employ; its form was that of a short square pillar, with a base and capital; its construction I will now more particularly describe.

I used a mahogany casing, and a mahogany cover; within the mahogany casing, I placed a brass casing; to the bottom of the brass casing, which fitted extremely close to the mahogany casing, there was added two thick pieces of brass, in each of which was drilled a hole, in which a rod might play, and in the bottom of which brass casing there was inserted a brass tube, which communicated with a glass tube sunk in the outside of the mahogany casing, against which glass tube there was a graduated scale, like that in Mr. Hawkins' machine, and for the same purpose. Across the top of the mahogany and brass casings, was fixed a brass bar, through which also were drilled two holes, for the purpose of allowing two rods to play in them. Within the brass casing, I placed a very light brass box, fitting very loosely in the brass casing; through this brass box, were placed two tabular rods, which

rods played upwards and downwards in the holes before mentioned. Upon the top of the brass box, were four small tabular supports for the mahogany cover, and, upon these supports, of course, the mahogany cover was placed; the cover being somewhat larger than the mahogany casing. My great object in the construction of my model was, to obviate, as much as possible, any unnecessary contact of its parts, and to make it steady and convenient for use; and I think I succeeded. The sides of the cover were so deep, that they concealed the top of the mahogany cases under all circumstances, except when the cover was removed. Having thus described my model in words, I will endeavour to render my description more plain by the following figure :—

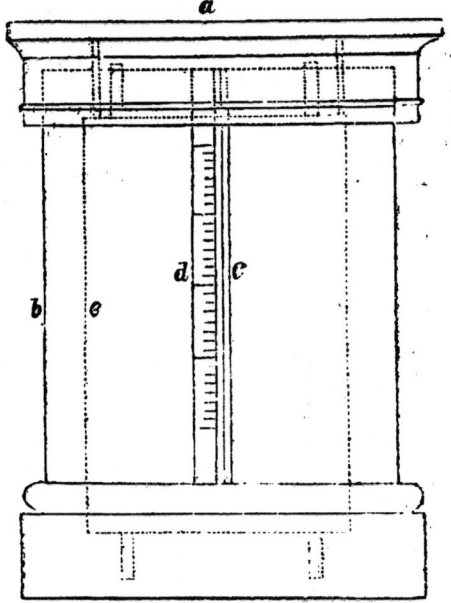

a is the mahogany cover; b, the mahogany casing; c, the glass tube in the mahogany casing; d, the graduated scale, by the side of the glass tube; e, a part of the brass box as it would appear if one could see through the mahogany and brass casings. The other dotted lines show parts of the interior of the machine as they would appear if the casings were transparent.

I conceive that my model has advantages over Mr Hawkins' machine in point of steadiness, of there being less friction between the parts, and in its greater convenience. Mr. Hawkins' interior cylinder, for want of guides, must continually be pressing against some part of his exterior cylinder, both at top and bottom; and this quality must render the inaccuracy of its indications comparatively very great.

From my want of connexion with the scientific world, I have no means of ascertaing whether the first application of the principle of my model has been made by Mr. Hawkins or me; yet, having a desire to be informed on this point, I have made bold to trespass thus long upon your attention, in the hope that you, or some one of your intelligent correspondents, will be able to give me the information I seek.

Making every apology for taking up so much of your valuable time,

I have to subscribe myself,

Sir,

Your humble subscriber,

J. P. H.

18th April, 1837.

P.S. I had almost forgotten to observe, that the instrument described in the Gallery of Practical Science, is, for all the purposes of a weighing machine, practically useless; because, either the parts must be ground together more beautifully than man can do, or than he ever will try to do, or, there must be friction something similar to that between the piston and cylinder of a steam-engine.

BERNHARDT'S WARMING AND VENTILATING PROCESS— APPLICATION TO HOME CULTIVATION OF SILK, MENAGERIES, ETC.

Sir,—In the *Mechanics' Magazine* of Saturday last (May 20), I observe a notice of a " Silk Worm Rearing Apparatus" in the north of France, and as a very evident increase in the quantity of silk produced, is shown to be owing to the improved mode of ventilation, I beg leave to offer a few remarks, with the view to induce the British public to compete with their continental neighbours in the home production of silk, and which they will be enabled very successfully to do, by adopting the mode of warming and ventilation invented by Mr. F. A Bernhardt, architect from Saxony (now resident in this country), and which I look upon as one of the most valuable discoveries of modern times.*

The French are a spirited people, and leave nothing untried, to naturalize the valuable productions of other climates,

to their own soil,—a trait well worthy of imitation.

It is no secret that silk worms require a warm and equable temperature, together with a good ventilation, and the fact of an increase of nearly one-third in the quantity of silk, consequent on M. D'Arcet's improvement, is conclusive on this point. The subject is one, perhaps, as interesting to us, as to our French neighbours, since we have at present to draw our supplies, in great part, from the same sources; and as there is not much difference in temperature between the north of France, and many of the southern parts of this island, there does not seem any reason to doubt, but that silk might be quite as successfully produced with us as in France. In Italy the worms are fed on the leaves of the white mulberry tree; but it has been found they thrive equally well on those of the red. I believe the climate of England is favourable to the growth of either sort, and that the white mulberry is only not cultivated here, because its fruit (hitherto the sole object with us) is so very insipid and inferior to the red. In what way the improved mode of ventilation in France is effected, does not appear; but Mr. Bernhardt's discovery bids fair to rival the atmosphere and climate of Italy itself, in all cases where warmth, equableness of temperature, freedom from draughts, and good ventilation are required. The discovery might not only be made available for the rearing of silk worms on a large scale, but it is equally applicable to the preservation of the lives of the valuable zoological specimens in this country—natives of warmer climates, multitudes of which are annually lost for want of an atmosphere approximating to their own; nor should the most important of all objects be omitted, the restoration to health of consumptive patients, who, by means of Mr. Bernhardt's invention (instead of being sent abroad as a forlorn hope, to die uncared for in a land of strangers, as heretofore,) may now continue to reside in their own country, with restored health, surrounded by their families and friends, amidst all the endearments of social life, and with all, and more than all, the advantages of the climate of Italy or Madeira.

The subject of warming and ventilation on *scientific* and *unalterable* data,

---

* For a notice of this method, see *Mechanics' Magazine*, vol. xxiii, p. 165.

has occupied the attention of the ablest chemists and mechanicians for a very long period; but that it has baffled all the learning and ingenuity bestowed upon it, is proved by the failure of the thousand and one schemes put in operation to attain it. Every fresh experiment tried, is like groping in the dark; for the result can never be foretold with any degree of certainty. This is not the case with Mr. Bernhardt's invention, his theory is perfect—his plan simple—the result invariable and certain: and since we, as Englishmen, cannot " lay

the flattering unction to our soul," of having made the discovery, still we ought, as wise men, to receive with gratitude the benefits which the skill and research of intelligent foreigners may confer upon us, without feelings of envy or jealousy. For were not the art of printing, the compass, and a thousand other useful inventions discovered by foreigners?

I have the honour to be, Sir,
Yours &c.
THOMAS GRIFFIN.
Cheltenham, 22d May, 1837.

IMPROVED CARRIER FOR TURNERS.

Sir,—The *carrier*, is an indispensable appendage to a turning-lathe; as usually constructed, however, they are somewhat objectionable, the single prong having too much play against the driver. The use of *two prongs*, instead of a single one, as shown in the accompanying sketch, fig. 1, gives a convenient steadi-

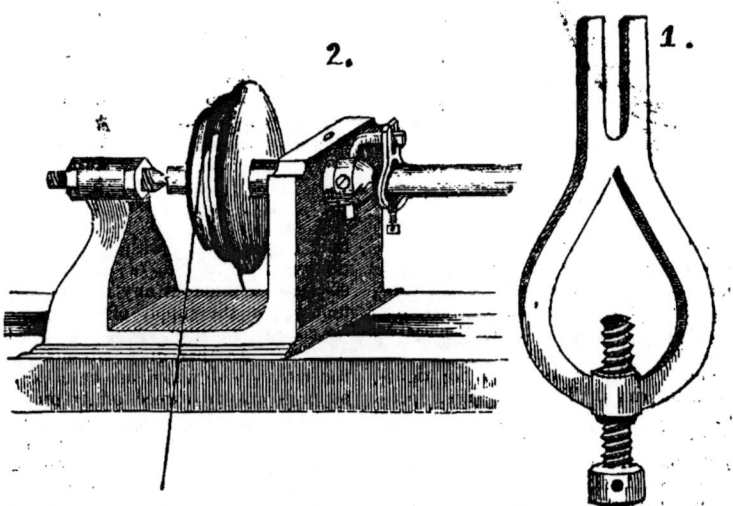

ness to the work not usually attainable. Fig. 2. shows the lathe-head with a rod of metal placed for turning, to which the carrier is affixed; the tongue of the driver being brought down between the prongs or chaps of the carrier and the setting-screw tightened, the work is firmly held, having no play, but turning only with the mandril.

I think it probable that this contrivance may have been employed before,

and from its extreme simplicity and palpable utility, it most likely has, but I have inquired of a great number of intelligent workmen without being able to learn of any persons having seen one in this form, and it may, by possibility, be as new as it is really useful.

I remain, Sir,
Yours respectfully,
WM. BADDELEY.
London, May 9, 1837.

Sir,—The accompanying drawings exhibit a design for a new stand-cock with three water-ways, which I some time since submitted to "the proper authorities," and which offers several important advantages over those in ordinary use. Fig. 1. is the stand-cock complete, consisting of a brass socket *a*, hard soldered on

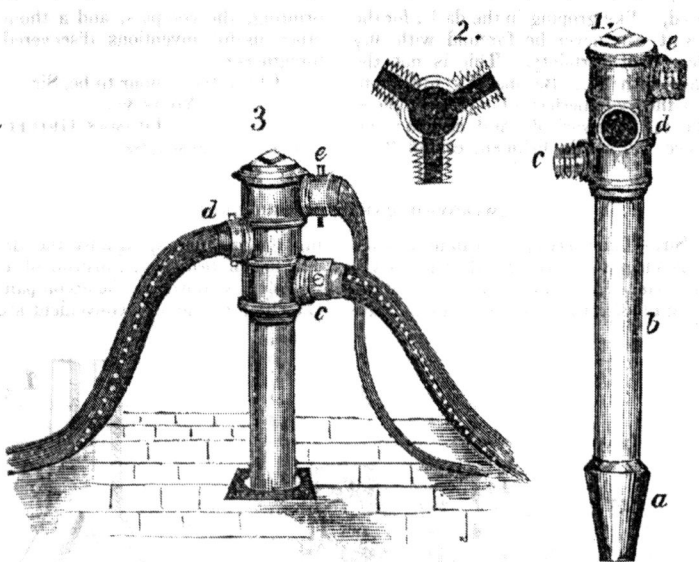

to a stout copper tube *b*, furnished with a brass head-piece turned truly cylindrical, upon which revolve in a water-tight manner three rings carrying the screwed nosels *c d* and *e*. The head-piece is finished solid, with a cap and washer on a square shoulder, and a nut for tightening the rings. There are three openings in the cylinder at equal distances on its circumference, at heights corresponding with the situation of the screwed nosels. Fig. 2. shews the situation of the water-ways, viewed perpendicularly, with the screws so set as to be all open. Fig. 3. represents one of these stand-cocks in use; lengths of leather hose are attached to the three nosels *c, d*, and *e*; *c* and *d* being open, while *e* has been shut by turning it round about one-sixth of a revolution. Among the numerous advantages attending the employment of this apparatus, are the following, viz.; the utmost possible freedom of water-way, with the power of delivering one, two, or three distinct streams of water at any required distances, for the supply of fire-engines, for cooling ruins, or for watering roads, &c. &c. Another great advantage is, the facility with which one or all of the supplies can be turned off or on, entirely independently of each other. This instrument affords the opportunity of working three engines most advantageously from a plug, when the supply of water is sluggish, by attaching the suction pipe of the engines to the nosels, upon the plan introduced, and so successfully employed, by the late Mr. S. Buston, as described at page 31 of your 8th volume.

I remain, Sir,
Yours respectfully,
WM. BADDELEY.

Wellington-street, Blackfriar's Road,
May 9th, 1837.

MR. CROSSE'S EXPERIMENTS.

Sir,—I have been considerably interested in perusing the various accounts of Mr. Crosse's apparatus and experiments, which have recently appeared in yours, as well as the scientific publications; but more especially so on reading the account given by Mr. C. himself, in p. 384 of your last volume. The thought has struck me, that if Mr. C.'s second experiment were varied, by substituting *a gentle stream of electricity*, obtained from the common electrical machine, instead of the electricity from the voltaic battery, the insects would be produced in much less time, *perhaps in a few hours*. Not having my apparatus with me, where I am at present residing, I have not been able to put this to the test of experiment. Even if it were the case, I should not be much surprised, as we very well know, that by the agency of the electrical machine, insects may be produced in rain or other stagnant water, in a few hours, which before was apparently free from animalculæ. I am of opinion also, that if experiments were tried on various fluids in the same manner, a great many new and remarkable facts would be brought to light.

I have been persuaded to commit the few above remarks to paper, hoping that some of the intelligent readers of your Magazine, who have more time than I have at present, to devote to such subjects, will be induced to follow out my imperfect suggestions.

Yours, &c.

I. F.

Near Sheffield, May 19, 1837.

P. S.—Perhaps all the readers of your Magazine are not acquainted with the way in which the silicate of potass, used by Mr. Crosse, is prepared, I therefore subjoin the following :—

Formula for the Preparation of Silicate of Potass.—Mix intimately 100 grains of fine sand, and 300 of pure carbonate of potass; fuse the mixture in a hessian crucible capable of containing three times as much. The silica and potass combine and produce glass. Pour out the glass on an earthern or iron plate, and dissolve it in water, the large quantity of alkali present rendering it perfectly soluble in this fluid.

I. F.

SPOTS ON OBJECT GLASSES.

Sir,—I am anxious through the channel of your excellent publication, to obtain from some practical optician information on a subject, which I confess has puzzled me. I have an acromatic telescope, the object glass 2¾ in. aperture, which has been made about 20 years; and before it came into my possession, I believe it had rarely been used, but was kept in the box, secluded from light, though in a place free from damp. I perceive on the *plano-side* of the *flint* piece of the object glass, a series of light brown spots, or perhaps more properly speaking, *stains* have appeared, and though they do not affect the qualities of the glass, which is a remarkably fine one, still in some degree they must deteriorate, and I begin to fear, will ultimately injure it. I have a glass by Dolland, of a smaller construction; on the flint piece of the object glass, and same side as the other, a brown stain or spot, has likewise appeared; this glass also has been for a long period secluded from the light, and I strongly suspect that such exclusion is the cause of the mischief; if so, it is most important, that those possessing good telescopes, should be apprised of the circumstance. I hope some one of your numerous readers acquainted with the subject will kindly communicate his opinion as to the cause of the evil I have stated, and if there is a possibility of its removal. I have tried the most powerful acids without effect, and intend to give the strongest alkalies a trial; I shall also keep the glass constantly exposed to the light, though, I confess, with little expectation of success. It may be suggested, that if the flint piece is polished again, the spots will be taken out, but this is a very hazardous experiment on a fine glass; and as the greatest difficulty exists to get one of a *fine* description, I am unwilling to incur the risk. It is singular that the spots invariably appear on the side next the eye-tube of the telescope, and never on the concave side, next the crown-glass piece. I must observe, the spots I speak of are totally distinct from the spray-lichen, which sometimes is seen *between* the two glasses of an acromatic, particularly one which has been used much at sea.

Whilst on the subject, may I be permitted to inquire if any account has been published of the experiments made some time since to ascertain the component part of a flint glass, possessing all the qualities requisite for the telescope, and which failed. If they are not published, they ought to be, to enable others to avoid what proved abortive; for I think at some future time a glass will be discovered, which *singly* will possess all the peculiarities of the compound pieces of flint and crown. With apologies for thus trespassing on your valuable space,

I am, Sir, your obedient servant,

W. G. E.

STEAM NAVIGATION OF THE ATLANTIC.
BENNET'S STEAM AND AIR ENGINE.

(From the Liverpool Journal).

In an article in the Edinburgh Review, attributed to Dr. Lardner, on the prospects of crossing the Atlantic in vessels propelled by steam, an opinion is expressed by this eminent mechanic that it is possible to effect such voyages with tolerable regularity from the west coast of Ireland, but not possible to effect them with any certainty, if possible to effect them at all, from the west coast of England. The calculations of Dr. Lardner were made on a basis simply experimental. He proceeded on proved results; and taking the performances of the best working steam boats in existence, as the extreme point of perfection in their construction, to be arrived at by existing shipbuilders and engineers, he demonstrated pretty satisfactorily that the number of tons of coal required to propel a vessel for 3200 miles would exceed her tonnage, or at least, approach so nearly to it, as to leave no stock for contingencies, and thus take away all certainty as to the results. This conclusion was the most favourable one, being independent of the minor considerations of the alteration of the water line from the consumption of fuel, the choking up of the boiler, and possible accidents to boilers and machinery. The Doctor, however, it must be observed, entirely omits the consideration of the possibility of effecting the voyage by means of high-pressure engines. Engines on this principle are found in Cornwall, where they are in use on a very large scale, to be more economical of fuel than those of the low pressure principle, and they are commonly used on the American waters for steam boats.* They present

the advantage of greater economy of fuel, of cost of construction, and of space. In this country there is a feeling against them, from the liability of the boilers to explosion; but that is no objection to employing them in the conveyance of the mails, and of valuable parcels, nor would American passengers be deterred by any such apprehensions.

This project, which has always been felt to be of considerable importance, possesses at present a more than ordinary interest. The delay of advices between Europe and America is now certain to produce the most serious embarrassments, and very often the ruin of individuals, and scarcely any sacrifice would be too great to effect their regular interchange. Of this the commercial community on both sides of the Atlantic, are fully sensible, and there can be no doubt that any feasible proposal would meet with ample encouragement.

Dr. Lardner, we have observed, founds his calculations on the data afforded by existing steam vessels, and we are by no means disposed to disagree with him in his conclusions. But the question still remains open whether an improvement in the steam engine itself may not make it adequate to the desired purpose. This seems to be the view taken at present by our enterprising brethren on the other side of the Atlantic, who are, at the least, our equals, both in mechanical invention and naval architecture.

The steam engine, as left by Watt and applied to nautical purposes by Fulton* and and Bell, has experienced little or no real improvement. The attempts to improve, may be divided generally into five sections.

Firstly, to improve the the working parts of the engine itself. These, we believe, may hitherto be described as vain attempts. The attempts to construct engines directly rotary have all failed, and hopelessly failed, and the reciprocating engine stands nearly, or altogether, as left by its great inventor. In marine engines the position and bearings of the beam and parallel motion have been a little altered, but the principle remains the same.

Secondly, to improve the mode by which water is acted on for purposes of propulsion. Innumerable have been the patents and projects for the improvement of paddle wheels; many of them conceived in ignorance of the true motion of the floats, which is a parabola, and not a circle; most of them in inexperience of the force and violence of waves. We believe that Dr. Lardner is right in treating all inventions for feathering the paddles as worse than useless in rough weather and that the old and common construc-

---

* The writer here confounds high pressure *boilers*, with high pressure *engines*. The Cornwall engines are on the condensing or low pressure principle; the boilers only are high pressure.—ED. M. M.

* Or rather, *Symington.*—ED. M. M.

tion of the undershot mill wheel is in every respect the best.*

Thirdly, to improve the construction of the boilers ; that is, to alter them so as to get, *cæteris paribus*, more heat with less expenditure of fuel, or in less space, Excepting in cases where tubular boilers are applicable, (which they possibly might be at sea, with high pressure engines and condensing apparatus to replace the water, so as to avoid the choking up from salt,) the construction of boilers has, we believe remained much the same for the last thirty years, and is likely to remain so. Mr. Perkins's "steam generator." seems a failure ; Mr. Braithwaite's plan of injecting air is so, decidedly.†

Fourthly, to improve the material of combustion, There we remain stationary. Coal is still considered the best fuel. Much misapprehension has arisen from confounding light with heat, and bulk with weight. Coal, if good, combines more calorific power in the same volume than any known available substance, besides being the most abundant of combustibles. All attempts to substitute the oils and resins have hitherto failed, either from price, bulk of stowage, or action upon the metals. Wood is only available for short voyages.

Fifthly, to use some fluid other than water to be transferred in vapour from the boiler to the piston. Alcohol and essential oils form elastic gases at a lower temperature than water ; but independant of other sufficiently obvious objections, the speculators in this department entirely overlooked the volumes of the gases.

These are the leading points on which the steam engine has been supposed capable of improvement, but in which, for many years, little or no real improvement has been effected. We pass over the innumerable trifling adaptations, some of real, more of doubtful utility ; but in all material points the steam engine remains as left by Mr. Watt, who not merely possessed that natural talent which

---

* The respectable authority of Dr. Lardner, notwithstanding, we hold the value of feathering paddles, in rough weather, to be established beyond all doubt. The French mail courier packet, which has been running for several years past, between Dover and Calais, always beats the English boats in rough weather, because she has feathering paddles, and they have not.—Ed. M. M.

† Mr. Braithwaite's plan, which is not only to inject air, but to draw it through (by an exhauster at the end of the funnel) cannot be said to have failed so "decidedly," since it is now actually to be seen in daily operation, at numerous places, in and about the metropolis. We may instance Currie's distillery, Fairle, Anderson, and Co.'s sugar refinery, Sturtevant's soap manufactory, the Greenwich Hospital brewery, &c. In some applications of it, we believe it has failed, but owing to accidental circumstances, and not to any fallacy in the principle.—Ed. M. M.

many people think the only thing essential to a mechanic, but was profoundly versed in statics, chemistry, and mathematics, and employed them all, in completing this most wonderful of human inventions.

We are promised, however, from the other side of the Atlantic, an improvement which certainly Watt never dreamt of. It is one undeniably bold and original, and one which we should be slow to pronounce impracticable, though it does seem a little wild. It comes within none of the categories above mentioned; except, perhaps, partially, the second and fifth. It consists in carrying on combustion under pressure, and delivering the elastic gases generated in the furnace, along with the steam into the cylinder. In a locomotive engine on our railroad, the steam, after it is taken from the cylinder, is let into the chimney to assist the draft ; but here the chimney is taken into the cylinder to assist the steam, and condensed air is injected from behind. In fact the cylinder is worked on the high pressure principle, by heated, and, consequently, expanded air passing directly through the furnace. On this principle they are building, at New York, an engine of the computed power of three hundred and sixty-five horses.

We give below Mr. Bennett's account of his engine. Mr. B. is evidently an imperfectly educated man, ignorant of chemical and mechanical science. We had to read his communication two or three times over before, to use the common phrase, we could make "either end or side of it," but flatter ourselves that we now perfectly understand his meaning. The confusion arises, in a great measure, from his calling his furnace a "steam generator" and "a boiler," which it is not; and speaking of all the elastic gases as "steam." We shall endeavour to explain his meaning to our readers.

He takes an upright drum or cylinder, three feet and a half diameter and nine feet and a half diameter and nine feet high. This is his furnace, and he cases it with a cylinder four feet in diameter and twelve high, This is of wood, because we persume wood is a bad conductor of heat. He closes both at top and bottom, and fills the space between the cylinders with water. By what mechanical means he makes the wood to resist the high pressure of which he speaks, he does not tell us, nor can we readily conceive, nor how he gets the fuel into, nor the ashes out of, the cylinder. But there he says, he has, and we see no reason to disbelieve him, the furnace inside filled with burning fuel, and the water outside, all tight, excepting when they discharge steam and vapour together into an eduction pipe, common to both, which takes steam and vapour together at a high state of elasticity into the cylinder, to work a piston in the common manner. He feeds the inner cylinder, or furnace, with air, by means of a forcing pump or blowing cylinder, and he finds that it requires a volume of air one fourth of that which is given out in a state of rarefaction for working purposes.

The principle is exceedingly simple, and, if we are not far mistaken, perfectly original. Most pre-eminently in mechanics, great efforts spring from causes unperceived by the multitude. When Watt was maturing his great invention, no politician foresaw that great mechanical revolution, which gave this country the productive power of many hundreds of thousands of men and horses, and which, to use the favourite phrase of those who wasted its first fruits in deeds of blood and rapine, enabled us, " single-handed, to wage war with the world." It may be some such revolution is now brooding.

It would be rash to say what will be the result. We fear that, whatever be the intrinsic merits of the discovery, it will require much time and experience to perfect, before it is adequate to such a Herculean task as propelling a vessel across the Atlantic. Its obvious merits, if practicable, are economy of space, economy of construction, and economy of fuel, in relation to the amount of elastic gas sent to the working part of the engine. Not a particle of heat is wasted. The most obvious disadvantage is that experienced at first, the production of resins and other results of imperfect combustion, which choke up the tubes and cylinder ; but this, he says, he has overcome. This we rather doubt, and fear that acids will be generated which will have a very injurious action on the metal. It remains, also, to be ascertained what power will be absorbed by the forcing pumps, what, under those circumstances, by friction in the cylinder, or what wasted by leakage; for, if the vapours do act on the metal, or if they are sent into the cylinder at such a temperature as to decompose the oil used to lubricate the cylinder, either objection will be fatal. It is also to be ascertained how far this engine is liable to the objection to which Messrs. Braithwaite and Ericsson's was obnoxious—that the injection of air into the furnace rapidly oxydized the metal of the boiler.

Altogether, we are inclined to think favourably of this experiment, and, though we scarcely expect that Capt. Cobb will be the first to achieve the adventure of bridging the Atlantic by steam, we are disposed to hope that Mr. Bennett's attempt may eventually succeed, and, if so, shall be proud of the honour of having first introduced it to the notice of the British public.

(From the New York American).

" The fine vessel designed for a steam-packet between this port and Liverpool, under the auspices of Captain Cobb, which has been some time in construction, was launched last week, and is now preparing to receive her machinery. Under these circumstances, we have thought it would interest our readers to see a description of the new sort of engine by which she is to be propelled. It is the invention of Mr. Bennett, of Ithaca, in this State, to whom we are indebted for the description we annex. We have examined a small model of the engine—now at the rooms of the American Institute in Broadway, and, so far as an eye and judgment unskilled in mechanics may be trusted, the advantages of this engine in producing combustion, in applying all the heat of the fuel, and in the extraordinary economy thereof, appear to be striking and manifest.

" *Mr. Bennett's Narrative.*

" As a laudable interest has been excited in the public mind by the engine now making for the steam-packet built by our enterprising citizen, Captain N. Cobb, and his associate, and, as many false conjectures concerning the enterprise have agitated the public, and as success depends upon the steam generator intended for the said packet, the inventor deems it due to the public to give a brief history and a description of it.

" In the year 1819, while experimenting for the improvement of the steam-engine, my attention was arrested by the great loss of heat, under the circumstances in which steam is generally produced, and the idea of my generator suggested itself to my mind at that time. I continued to theorize until the winter of 1824-25, when I constructed a boiler to test the principle ; and, in March, 1825, made the first experiment in R. L. Cadrey's carriage-shop, Ithaca, Tompkins county, New York.

" It was to me a very flattering one. I used a blacksmith's bellows to supply the fire with air, and from the volume of steam generated with this apparatus, I concluded there was about eight times as much steam propuced as air forced into the fire, but had no means of measuring the steam, it being simply blown off into the air. I immediately built an engine to ascertain the proportion of air blown into the fire, and the steam generated, knowing that success hung upon that point.

" As I before stated, I presumed there was as much as eight times the quantity of steam and air (which mingled together in the operation) as there was air blown into the fire ; accordingly, I built the bellows of one-eighth the capacity of the steam-engine.

In attempting to put it into operation, I found the bellows was too small, as the steam would not keep up ; consequently, I substituted another, one of larger dimensions, and found by that there was about four times the quantity of steam as air, which much reduced my former calculation.

"As the apparatus I then had was rude and imperfect, the boiler being only twenty inches diameter and thirty inches long, and the furnace that contained all the fuel used was enclosed in this scanty allowance, I was unable to make a perfectly satisfactory experiment ; but believing enough was shown to warrant the construction of as good an engine as could be built at Ithaca, the place of my residence, where the facilities of building were extremely limited, no engine at that time having been built within one hundred and sixty miles, I employed two ingenious coppersmiths, Messrs. Gee and Thomas Walker, to make all the copper and sheet-iron work. The generator was composed of two cylinders of seven feet long; the inner one (of copper) two feet diameter, the outer one (of wood) two feet and a half diameter; the inner cylinder containing the fuel, and the space between the inner and the outer cylinder contained water. My steam cylinder was copper, sixteen inches diameter, two feet stroke—bellows nearly half the capacity— the whole on the beam-engine plan, calculated to make forty-five double strokes per minute.

"In the month of September, 1825, every thing being ready for trial, I filled the furnace with wood, started the engine, and regulated its speed to forty-five strokes per minute ; and ran regularly for three hours, without any more fuel than was first put into the furnace. Perceiving that tar, or matter nearly resembling it, was discharged with the steam, and that after repeated trials, if the water in the boiler was the least deficient, the tar became so hard that the engine would stop, I laid it by until the year 1834, when I made another experiment, and succeeded in wholly burning up the tar and smoke, and thus rendered the steam pure.

"In 1835, I contracted with Messrs. Cook and Conrad, of Ithaca, steam-engine builders, for an engine, composed of two steam cylinders, each two feet diameter, and two foot stroke, with boiler thirty-two inches diameter and four feet long; which contained all the water and fuel. It was completed in October of the same year. On putting the engine into operation, I found that the boiler was too small the blast blew the fuel off from the grates—they occupying a space only seventeen inches square ; but as it was, it would, under favourable circumstances, work the engine at seventy-five re-

volutions per minute. I immediately set about making a new boiler, eight feet high, three feet diameter, outer cylinder ; the inner cylinder, six feet high and two and a half diameter, which contained the fuel. When completed, I found that it answered every purpose intended. It would furnish steam in abundance, so that the engine would make ninety revolutions per minute, while, at the same time, large quantities of steam were blowing off at the safety-valve, say about one-third of the whole quantity made. At this time the engine was doing no labour, but moving itself. I then put the engine on a lake canal boat of seventy-five feet keel, and fourteen and a half feet beam, and which obtained its full breadth of beam ten feet from the stern—built for burthen and not for speed.

"I made trials upon the Cayuga Lake, and her speed was eleven miles per hour when in order, though it was all but impossible to keep her so. The engine was built to sustain forty-five pounds to the inch, but when in order, it would rise to sixty ; then, invariably, something would fail. Twice the shafts broke, which were six and a half inches in diameter, and perfectly sound. I found the engine wholly insufficient, and laid it by in the mean time, I disposed of some part of the patent right, a portion of which has since changed hands, at the rate of 1,280,000 dollars for the whole patent. Subsequently, I became associated with several gentlemen, and made a contract with P. A. Sabbaton, esq., of New York, to build an engine of 350 horse power, and entered into an arrangement with Captain N. Cobb, to put it on board his Liverpool steam-packet.

"The engine is called a ' double steam-engine,' having two steam cylinders of thirty-five inches diameter, six feet stroke ; two blowing cylinders of just half the capacity; which are worked by the engine, and the air is conducted to a boiler, whose outer cylindrical case is four feet in diameter, and twelve feet high; the furnace, or inner case, and a half feet diameter and nine feet high—the fuel introduced into it down the chimney, and it is so constructed, that not one particle of heat generated by combustion can escape, but must absolutely pass into the water, together with all the gases generated by combustion, and become as powerful an agent as the steam itself, passing through the steam cylinders with it.

"The engine used on Cayuga Lake, as near as I could ascertain, burnt one cord of wood in eighteen hours. The engine for the Liverpool packet is of six times the capacity, consequently will burn one cord in three hours. It takes about 225 feet of air to burn one pound of dry wood or coal, and the engine will blow into the furnace, when it is making 35 revolutions per minute, 2,625 feet of air in the same time. I would have it borne in mind, that no air whatever gets into the furnace when the engine is in operation, but what is forced in by the blowing cylinders ; hence, invariably it takes at least 35 revolutions to burn 12 pounds of fuel, which, with a 20-foot paddle-wheel (which is the size of onrs), will move the boat 1,750 feet, or will take 36 pounds to propel the boat one mile."

DAVENPORT AND COOK'S ELECTRO-MAGNETIC ENGINE.

(From the Saratoga Sentinel).

In company with Dr. Steel and several other gentlemen, we called upon Messrs. Davenport and Cook, of this village, on Saturday, with a view of examining the electro-magnetic engine invented by the senior partner.

The ingenuity, yet simplicity of its construction, the rapidity of its motion, together with the grandeur of the thought that we are witnessing the operation of machinery propelled by that subtle and all pervading principle—electricity, combine to render it the most interesting exhibition we have ever witnessed.

Although we shall say something on the subject, it is perhaps impossible to describe this machine by words alone, so as to give more than a faint idea of it to the reader.

It consists of a stationary magnetic circle, formed of disconnected segments. These segments are permanently charged magnets, the repelling poles of which are placed contiguous to each other. Within the circle stands the motive wheel, having the projecting galvanic magnets, which revolve as near the circle as they can be brought without actual contact. The galvanic magnets are charged by a battery, and when so charged, magnetic attraction and repulsion are brought into requisition in giving motion to the wheel —the poles of the galvanic magnets being changed more than a thousand times per minute.

Having in its construction but one wheel, revolving with no friction except from its own shaft, and from the wires connecting it with the galvanic battery, the latter of which can scarcely be said to impede the motion in any degree, the durability of this engine must be almost without limit.

There is no danger to be apprehended from fire or explosion; and we understand it is the opinion of scientific gentlemen who have examined it, that the expense of running this machine will not amount to one-fourth as much as that of a steam-engine of the same power.

From the time when the Greek philosopher supposed the magnet possessed a soul, its mysterious power has been regarded with increasing interest and attention to the present day. In addition to its utility in the compass, thousands have laboured in vain attempts, to obtain through its agency a rotary motion. So intense has been the application of some to this subject, that in the attempt they have even lost that elevating attribute of our species, reason. It was reserved for Mr. Davenport to succeed where so many had failed.

He commenced his labours more three years ago, and prosecuted them under the most discouraging and unfavourable circumstances—sustained by a constitutional perseverance and a clear conviction of ultimate success. He obtained the first rotary motion in July, 1834 ; since which time he has devoted his whole attention to improvements in his machine. During this period, it has passed through five different modifications, and is now brought to such a state of simplicity and perfection (having apparently the fewest possible number of parts) that the proprietors consider no further important alterations desirable, except in the due proportions of the different magnets, in which they are daily improving.

We were shown a model in which the motive wheel was 5¼ inches diameter, which elevated a weight of *twelve pounds*. And to illustrate the facilities for increasing the power of this engine, another model was exhibited to us with a motive wheel of eleven inches in diameter, which elevated a weight of *eighty-eight pounds*. Although these models have been for some time in progress, and we have occasionally been permitted to examine them, we have waited till the present period, when the practicability of obtaining a rapid and unlimited increase of power seems to be placed beyond a doubt, before expressing an opinion, or calling the public attention to the subject.

If this engine answers the expectations of the inventor, (and we believe no one can assign a *reason* why it should not, it is destined to produce the greatest revolution in the commercial and mechanical interests which the world has ever witnessed. We may consider the period as commencing when machinery in general will be propelled by power concentrated upon the plan of this engine ; when the vessels of all commercial nations will be guided to their point of destination and urged forward in their course by the same agent, triumphantly contending against winds and tides, with the silent sublimity of unseen but irresistible power.

The prophetic ken of science is happily exhibited by Dr. Lardner, in his treatise on the Steam Engine. His far seeing genius seems to have anticipated the invention of which we are speaking. "Philosophy," said he, "already directs her finger at sources of inexhaustible power in the phenomena of electricity and magnetism, and many causes combine to justify the expectation that we are on the eve of mechanical discoveries still greater than any which have yet appeared ; and that the steam-engine itself, with the gigantic powers conferred upon it by the immortal Watt, will dwindle into insignificance in comparison with the hidden powers of nature still to be revealed, and that the day will come when that machine, which is now extending the blessing of civilization to the most remote skirts of the globe, will cease to have existence except in the page of history."

NOTES AND NOTICES.

Perpetual Motion again !—By the *Georgia* (American) *Messenger*, we learn that a Dr. Stringfellow, of Macon, has actually discovered the long-sought, and never-before-found perpetual motion. The editor thus partially describes it :—" The machine is very simple, the whole consisting of a very few pieces, yet comprising the most ingenious and the most perfect principles of mechanism. It is comprised within a square frame of about eighteen inches, and the parts consist only of two perpendicular spindles, and two horizontal cog-wheels, a trundle-head, three small suspension chains, a spiral spring and weight, and a small inclined plain."—*Weekly Chronicle.*

A Sinecurist against his Will.—Most of the Professorships at the London University (now " University College") have turned out anything but profitable to their holders, who receive no remuneration beyond the " fees" payable from those students who choose to attend their lectures. Mr. M'Culloch, the Professor of Political Economy, it appears, cannot boast of a single pupil, and several of the other Professors are understood to be pretty nearly, if not quite, in the same predicament.

Preventing Acidity in Malt Liquors. We understand that Mr. David Booth, of Charlotte-street, Bloomsberry, the author of the Treatises on Brewing, published by the Society for the Diffusion of Useful Knowledge, has discovered the means of preventing *acidity* in malt liquors; Mr. Booth is ready to communicate instructions on the subject, upon certain terms which may be learnt on application to him.

Improved Percussion Tubes for Cannon.—At a late meeting of the Society of Arts, the silver medal was awarded to Mr. J. Marsh for his improved percussion tube for cannon. Mr. M. had previously received a pecuniary reward from the Board of Ordnance. All percussion tubes which have hitherto been tried have been abandoned in consequence of the danger which resulted from the pieces of metal which contained the fulminating powder, upon explosion, injuring the faces, &c. of the gunners. Mr. M. has obviated this objection, by substituting for the metal, a crow, or other small quill, from the fragments of which no danger can result. Mr. M. has also made a great improvement in the composition of the fulminating powder, by adding to the sulphate of antimony and chlorate of potass, a certain proportion of powdered glass, by which addition, in consequence of the greater attrition of the particles, the explosion is rendered much more instantaneous than with the ordinary composition. Some experiments were tried in the presence of the Committee with the improved, and the metal percussion tubes ; it singularly happened, that on exploding one of the latter, a piece of the metal struck the chairman in the face : on exploding, Mr. Marsh's, the fulminating tube was found to be split only, and no ill effects could consequently arise from its use: a cartridge at a distance of two feet from the point of the percussion tube was exploded, so that it would answer for guns of any thickness. On board his Majesty's exercising ship, Excellent, at Portsmouth, 9000 rounds have been fired by this tube without a single miss. The Board of Ordnance, have in consequence given orders to fit 1,000 guns with percussion locks

Stevenson's Patent Safety Paper.—It is now generally known that certain chemical fluids will obliterate ink from every description of paper hitherto in use. The " Safety Paper," it is stated by its inventor, will prevent the possibility of any alteration in the writing, as it cannot be expunged without immediate detection,—the properties of this Paper being, that when subjected to the action of the chemical fluid used for the purpose of fraud, its colour changes, and becomes deeply stained, according to the nature of the chemical agent employed ; the act of forgery or fraud is thereby defeated.

Penny Cyclopædia.—In the part of the Penny Cyclopædia which has appeared since the notice of it in our 717th Number, the errors in the list of the committee pointed out in that article have been corrected. Lord William Bentinck no longer flourishes at Calcutta, and " A Munoz de Sotomayor" of Madrid, no longer rejoices in the Italian prefix of " Signor." We regret to observe, however, that the latter gentleman's name, now appears without any prefix or affix soever, a piece of neglect, which, as the Spaniards are not the humblest nation on earth, may very probably, occasion the loss of the " Señor's" valuable services. The two missing sheets of letter press, which are spoken of in the same article, have since been supplied, and their not having been so before, seems to be attributable to mere negligence.

Dr. Morrison's Chinese Library.—By an error of the press, the number of volumes of Chinese works in Sir George Staunton's library, presented to the Royal Asiatic Society, was stated (col. 1, page 138) to amount to " nearly one thousand" only. It should have been " nearly *three* thousand." The offer to purchase Dr. Morrison's library, mentioned in the same article, was made, it appears, by the French Institute, which possesses for its librarian, the most active and industrious Chinese scholar now in Europe, M. Stanislas Julien.

☞ *British and Foreign Patents taken out with economy and despatch ; Specifications, Disclaimers, and Amendments, prepared or revised ; Caveats entered ; and generally every Branch of Patent Business promptly transacted.*
A complete list of Patents from the earliest period (15 Car. II. 1675,) to the present time may be examined. Fee 2s. 6d. ; Clients, gratis.

LONDON: Printed and Published for the Proprietor, by W. A. Robertson, at the Mechanics' Magazine Office, No. 6, Peterborough-court, between 135 and 136, Fleet-street.—Sold by G. W. M. Reynolds, Proprietor of the French, English, and American Library, 55, Rue Neuve, Saint Augustin, Paris.

Mechanics' Magazine,

MUSEUM, REGISTER, JOURNAL, AND GAZETTE.

No. 723. SATURDAY, JUNE 17, 1837. Price 3d.

MR. WIVELL'S FIRE-ESCAPE.

MR. WIVELL'S FIRE ESCAPE—REPLY TO MR. BADDELEY.

Sir,—In reference to Mr. Baddeley's answer to my letter of the 22nd of April, I beg leave to throw back his imputation of being ungenerous, uncharitable, or of ever having attempted to depreciate the merits of others, either directly or indirectly, to benefit myself.

I have inspected the volumes of your Magazine, to which Mr. Baddeley has referred me, for the account of elevators, supposed to have been adopted previous to the year 1829, but I can find no account of any one in which wheels are used; five years after, there is a confession that Mr. Baddeley had *availed himself of my plan*—the very gist of my complaint. Since no better proof, therefore, can be brought against my claim to originality of invention, I will quit the subject for one of more general interest, namely, the adoption and regulation of the public fire-escapes, intended to be distributed through every parish of the metropolis.

Three different fire-escapes of the most simple construction have been stationed in a few districts. Two of these escapes, Merryweathers' and Fords', have already been fully described in your Magazine, and which, with the one of which I now offer a suitable illustration, are so much approved of, as to be patronised by the Humane Society, formed expressly as guardians of our lives, at a time when we are the least prepared to assist ourselves.

As a designer of numerous escapes, I shall not assume the *critic*, in relation to the inventions of others; although the combined qualities of the whole, would, doubtless, form an interesting subject of discussion.

The first consideration, in regard to escaping from a house on fire is, the *time* by which escapes ought to be at the place of the fire, so as to save the lives of persons, who may be in either of the upper floors of a house. A fire commencing in a parlour, or drawing-room, is the most perilous, inasmuch as the retreat of the inhabitants from above becomes impeded, even from the obstruction of smoke alone; and the fire soon making its way through the windows, without the timely aid of escapes, death to the inmates is inevitable. In this view of the case, it becomes one of the most important points to ascertain the *progress of fire*, in the most usual instances, against *time*. Should there appear upon an average, that under the above circumstances the greater number of lives have been lost during the first *fifteen minutes*, it must therefore appear that escapes ought not to be stationed further apart than a quarter of a mile; and that they should be as free from *locks* and *chains* as possible, substituting bolts, placed so high as to be out of the reach of boys. I apprehend, that in case of a fire commencing midway between the stations of the two escapes, at this distance ten minutes would pass in the fetching and adjusting of the escape, so that inhabitants would have five minutes for their retreat.

There can be no objection to the escapes being under locks, &c. during the day, as they are then rarely wanted, but the confining of escapes by night, when fires most frequently occur, I hold to be extremely injudicious, and, having a great tendency to defeat the very purpose for which the escapes are intended. In the event of escapes being placed at a greater distance than a quarter of a mile apart, it then becomes absolutely necessary that an *alarm bell* should be placed in the centre of whatever distance may be agreed upon, to which any person might apply his hand; and a specific sum should be given to the party who should be the first to take an escape to any house on fire.

The attaching of fire escapes to fire engines is injudicious, the firemen have quite sufficient to attend to in working their engine, and endeavouring to extinguish the conflagration. A set of active and able men should be appointed solely to conduct the escapes; this is absolutely necessary to complete so worthy an undertaking, as that adopted by the *Humane Society*, to which, with many others, I have endeavoured to give my best service and support; at the same time hoping that every benevolent person will join to ensure such a formidable establishment, as will exhibit the humanity of the British nation,

I am, Sir,
Your most obedient
And humble servant,
ABRM. WIVELL.

Description of the Engraving of Mr. Wivell's Fire Escape.—The machine is formed of four ladders,—the shortest of which, is intended for the area and drawing-room; the next, a double ladder for the room above, and the fourth, which acts upon the last, reaches to the attic.

A, one side of the double ladder with a trough of sacking under it, through which a female is about to descend from the second floor window, and a child is emerging, at the foot of the ladder.

B, the other side of the double ladder, forming an ordinary ladder, from which the fourth ladder C, springs, being jointed by pivots at D. When the apparatus is not in use, it is folded down, and lies along the ladder B. E. is the short ladder detached from the escape, which may be used to reach the drawing-rooms, or area, of a house, and which, when the apparatus is not in use, lies along the trough ladder A. F is a metal shield to cover the window beneath the top of the trough ladder, to prevent any flame which might be issuing from it, injuring the canvass trough, or persons on the ladder. G, the lever, by pressing upon which, the escape is elevated. H, a belt attached to a rope, one end of which is fastened to the top of the ladder C.

The escape, it will be seen, travels upon a pair of wheels, and with the assistance of three or four men, can be made to go at the rate of six miles an hour. The only preparation to raise it is, for three men to bear their weight upon the lever G at the *base* of the double ladder,—when it will rise on the instant, and in a few seconds it may be wheeled against the house, under the sill of the window above the drawing-room. A rope is next pulled, which acts on the lever of the top ladder C, which instantly springs to the window of the attic; while a similar application to raise the *iron shield* F, will cause it to be suspended over the parlour or drawing-room window, by which means, the fire from such windows is prevented from doing damage to the escape, and allows more time for persons to make their exit in safety. One minute is all that is required to accomplish all this; and it will be seen upon examination of the *drawing*, that access is given to three distinct floors at the same time; the inmates of the house can with ease descend through the trough from eight to ten in

a minute, which has frequently been practically proved.

The belt H may be carried by a fireman or other person into a room, buckled round the inmate, who may, perhaps, from stupefaction or fright, be unable to help himself, and who may be thus protected from a fall in going down the ladder; or else let down the trough on reaching as low as the second floor.

The following *letter* is a correct statement of what took place on the night of the fire in Compton-street, April 3, 1837, which appeared in the *Morning Herald* of the 5th of the same month.

" Mr. EDITOR,—In the report of the dreadful fire that occurred last night in Compton-street, Soho, no mention is made of the arrival of the Fire Escape belonging to the Society for the Protection of Life from Fire; and although happily not required, I conceive it will be a gratification to the subscribers and the public to be made acquainted with the circumstance; and although its station was in Robert-street, Regent's-park, it arrived in seventeen minutes at the fire, from the time it quitted Robert-street. During the raging of the fire, an alarm was given that another fire had taken place in White Lion-street, arising from the burning embers falling on the house; the Machine instantly proceeded to the spot, and was attached to the floor window, when two of the affrighted inmates immediately descended into the street; thereby fully demonstrating the utility of Fire Escapes, if thickly planted throughout the metropolis, which, by the assistance of a generous public, the society hope speedily to accomplish. Your immediate insertion of the above will greatly oblige, your obedient servant,

" W. SPRING,
" Secretary to the Society,
" 48, Great-Portland-street, Portland-place."

THE SOCIETY FOR THE PROTECTION OF LIFE FROM FIRE.

Sir,—Your correspondent, Mr. Baddeley has given a very proper check to Mr. Wivell, in his attempt to deck himself in borrowed plumes; but there is one part of his letter that I am somewhat surprised has not been adverted to by Mr. Baddeley,—I refer to the statement of Mr. Wivell, that the Humane Society have adopted his fire-escape ladders.

The facts are simply these:—In the spring of 1836, in consequence of the establishment of a Fire Association in the south western district of St. Pancras, Mr. Wivell attempted the formation of a similar society, on a more extended scale, for the purpose of bringing out with proper eclat, his own inventions. It so happened, however, that the individuals who were solicited to come forward upon this occasion, were not disposed to form a society for the purpose of furthering the views of any particular inventor, and Mr. Wivell's name was at a very early period struck out of the printed prospectuses. The society was ultimately formed at a public meeting held in the London Coffee House, Ludgate Hill, on the 22d March, 1836,—not called by Mr. Wivell, nor held at his expense.

The new society having declined the several escapes submitted to them by Mr. Wivell, as the St. Pancras Association had done previously, he set about collecting subscriptions on his own account, and succeeded in forming a local association in his own neighbourhood, for the purpose of working his own escape. The Society for the Protection of Life from Fire, not choosing, I suppose, to have any competitor, at length bought up Mr. Wivell's machine and his subscribers in one lot, giving £32 for the apparatus, and £18 for one years' rent of its station. In this way, then, and in this way only, has Mr. Wivell's ladder-escape been *adopted* by the Society. Whether they have acted either justly, or wisely, in thus expending £50 of their subscriber's money, may be a matter of opinion; for my own part, I think they have acted imprudently.

I have now before me the first "Annual Report" of the society in question, from which I expected to have learned all the particulars relating to these transactions; but in this I have been disappointed. The Report contains, the prospectus of the Society; a short and imperfect account of the first annual meeting; letters addressed to the Society, explanatory of the conduct of some policemen; a list of subscribers, and that is all!

Not a word is to be found about the numerous escapes submitted to the Society's inspection, nor of the particular qualifications, and points of superiority, of those that have been selected; as to any particulars of *receipt and expenditure*, the members are left as ignorant as if such things had never been.

As your intelligent correspondent, Mr. Baddeley, is a member of the above Society, perhaps he can explain the circumstances which have led to the appearance of this meagre report, and inform us if any reason can be given for the concealment of the financial operations of the Society.

I remain your obedient servant,

H. JENKINS.

London, May 18, 1837.

EXTRACTS FROM THE FIRST ANNUAL REPORT OF THE SOCIETY FOR THE PROTECTION OF LIFE FROM FIRE.

The Report of this Society is, as our correspondent, Mr. Jenkins, observes, extremely meagre; but the following passages are deserving further publicity than the circulation of the Report itself amongst the members will give them:

" Your Committee have now to report that several situations have been selected, some of which are already provided with fire-escapes, and the others are in a state of great forwardness. The stations are as follows; viz. Robert-street, Regent's Park; Great Portland-street; Regent's-street; Adelaide Place, near St. Martin's Church; Strand; and Holborn.

" In order to prevent delay in bringing fire-escapes to the place of danger, the police are supplied with keys made to correspond, so that the key in possession of a policeman will open the lock of *every* fire-escape. And it is also intended to leave a key with the nearest publican and baker, as the publican retires to rest when the baker is about to rise."

" Your Committee have to state, that, to induce scientific men to turn their attention to the invention of fire-escapes, they purpose offering rewards for the best constructed machine for that purpose; likewise to reward the first person, who, on the alarm of fire, shall bring a fire-escape to the scene of danger.

" In conclusion, they now forcibly appeal to the feelings of every individual throughout the metropolis, as they value their own lives, and the lives of their dearest relatives and friends, to come forward, and afford them that prompt and liberal support which shall enable them to carry out to the utmost extent the plans of this Society, instituted for the *sole* purpose of the " *Protection of Life from Fire*."

DESCRIPTION OF A LARGE SYPHON
EMPLOYED IN THE FOUNDRY AT
CASSIPORE TO CONVEY WATER FROM
A DISTANCE TO THE STEAM ENGINE.

*Extract of a Letter from Major Hutchin-
son, of the Engineers, F. R. S.*

I observe in the *Mechanics' Magazine* for February, 1836, a description of
of an "Easy Method of filling Syphon
Tubes, by Wm. Foster, Esq.," in which
the author observes—

" The application of the syphon upon a
large scale for the purpose of drawing water
from distant places, may not be new ; but I
do not remember to have seen it in this or
any other country before I tried the experiment."

The accompanying little sketch of one
we laid in the foundry-yard here in 1833,
may be interesting to you, or to the readers
of the *Mechanics' Magazine.* I had been
authorized to make a deep cut from the
well to the *tank,* and to construct an
arched tunnel from one to the other; but
as this, from the great depth required,
would have been an expensive undertaking, it was determined to cast lead pipes
in the foundry, for the construction of a
syphon, and to try if it could not be
made to answer, before we made the
tunnel. I confess I was afraid we should
not succeed, as we had never attempted
the casting of pipes. However, it has
fully succeeded. At first I had thought
of filling with water in the mode described by Mr. Foster ; but the idea of connecting the point *a* of the syphon with
the pump of the engine, has at once removed every difficulty ; and by another
little pipe, a little of the overflow of cold
water being carried into the tunnel *b,* the
pipe and the tunnels, *b* and *d,* are kept covered with water, by which much trouble
from any little leakage of air is avoided.
You will observe, the bore of our pipe is
five inches. The one mentioned by Mr.
Foster is only three quarters of an inch.

Description of the Engraving.

The total length of the syphon is.. 247 feet.
Depth of well...................... 29
Length of syphon in the well 22

From the top of the syphon at *a,* a
small pipe goes to the pump of the engine (having a stop-cock); thus, a few
strokes of the engine removes the air in
the syphon, and the water flows. The
tunnel *b* and *d,* can be kept sufficiently
full of water to overflow the syphon,

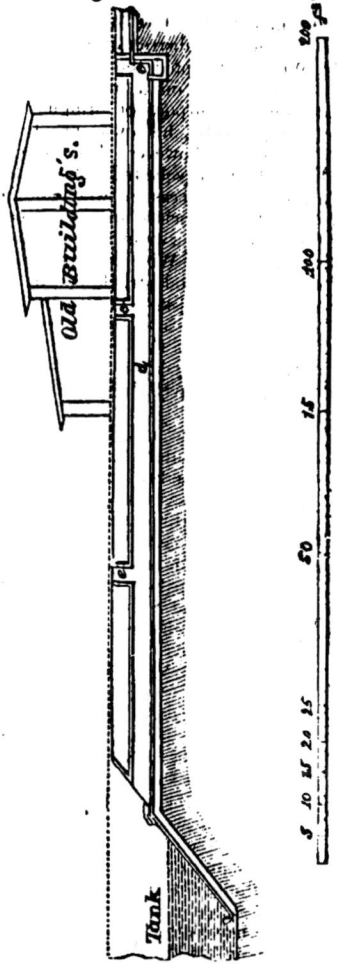

which prevents it from drawing air. The
old buildings rendered it necessary to
carry the syphon underneath them, in an
arched tunnel (*d*): *c* is the cess pool;
e e, air holes. The pipe is in convenient
lengths of 9 feet, of 5 inches bore, and
half an inch thick, with 1½ inch flanges.

MR. LOUDON'S " SUBURBAN
GARDENER."[*]

The most indefatigible, and, perhaps,
most practically useful, of all living

[*] No. I., price 1s., to be completed in from ten
to fifteen numbers.

writers, is our excellent contemporary, of many Magazine and Encyclopædia celebrity, Mr. Loudon. Of his numerous works, there is not one, which has not supplied some obvious and urgent want, nor one which has not been productive of a world of good. We hardly expected that he could have done more for the "divine art" of gardening, than he has done already by his Gardeners' Magazine, his Gardening Encyclopædia, and his Cottage, Farm, and Villa Encyclopædia; but of a character quite distinct, yet nearly akin to all these, and likely to be nearly quite as useful, is the new work, the first number of which we have now before us. The "Suburban Gardener" is for the millions who professionally (if we may use the term) have no connection with the cultivation of the soil, who know little or nothing of gardening, but have a lively sense of the beauties of nature, and delight in making their little boxes out of town, as rural-like, and ornamental as possible. For these, Mr. Loudon treats of the choice of a situation for a suburban or country house, and grounds, on a small scale, touching not only on such permanent considerations as soil, aspect, water, &c., but entering fully into the various accidental and artificial circumstances, by which situations, indisputably good in themselves, are often most materially affected; such as—state of society in the neighbourhood, vicinage of markets, churches, &c. For these, also, he discusses the sort of house they should build, and how build it; the most elegant and ornamental way of fitting it up, &c. Here the first number of the work before us stops; but in the dozen or so, by which it is to be followed *and completed*, we are promised most ample information respecting the laying out, planting, cultivating, and keeping up of the garden and grounds attached to the house so chosen and erected; not forgetting a few words, by the way, on those very convenient, if not necessary, appendages, a dairy and poultry-yard. Mr. Loudon, in short, proposes "to concentrate" here, for the benefit of the suburban population of the country, "all the knowledge on rural subjects which he possesses," which every body who knows any thing of Mr. Loudon, or of the useful literature of the times, must know to be nearly unrivalled. To wish such a work success were wholly superfluous; it requires only to have its existence and objects, made known, to command instantly a most extensive circulation, not only in our own country, but wherever there are cities and towns to 'flee from, and rural retreats to be cultivated and prized.

ARCANA OF SCIENCE FOR 1837.

This work has now been in existence sufficiently long to take its station as an established periodical : the Tenth Annual Volume is now before us.* Although specially devoted to the recording of novelty, there is nothing of novelty in the form and arrangement of the volume itself. The matter it contains is ranged under precisely the same heads, and in precisely the same fashion, as in its nine predecessors. The motto " Let well alone" has been scrupulously—too scrupulously, adhered to by the editor. He can hardly be blamed for his unwillingness to deviate, in any great degree, from a plan which experience must by this time have shown to be in the main satisfactory, but still we think a few *little* improvements, of the complexion hinted at in our notices of his volumes of former years, might have been ventured on without much fear of *deteriorating* the character of the work, and not without hope of adding another to the list of " useful improvements" which it is the business of its pages to chronicle for general information.

The principal articles under the head " Mechanical and General Science" are, as has been usual for some time, devoted to the very extensive subject of " Railways:"amongst them are tolerably minute descriptions of the "London and Birmingham," the " Dublin and Kingstown," and the "London and Greenwich" Railways, besides Dr. Lardner's paper, read before the Royal Society, on the "Theory of Railroads." The doctor is also laid under contribution on the question as to the practicability of steam navigation between England and America, and India. Even on the worthy doctor's own showing, we think

* Arcana of Science and Art ; or, an Annual Register of useful inventions and improvements, discoveries and new facts in mechanics, chemistry, natural history, and social economy. With several engravings. Tenth Year. London, 1837, Limbird, 12mo. pp. 317.

he is much more decided in his adverse opinions, as to the plan for a direct steam voyage across the Atlantic, than the facts of the cases will warrant: it was going too far, at any rate, to talk about "a voyage to the Moon" as being in the same category, and, if we mistake not, the doctor would not now be sorry if the unlucky expression were forthwith forgotten. As matters are progressing, it is by no means unlikely, that the "impossible" thing itself may actually be done before the doctor has had time enough to explain away his *ex cathedra* condemnation. A task which he is apparently not disinclined to attempt.

The progress of the Thames Tunnel during the past year is duly reported; as well as the proceedings of the British Association at their Bristol meeting, of which, however, there is only room enough for a small sketch. The construction of Mr. Rowland Hill's rotary printing machine is given in pretty full detail, upon what principle we are at a loss to guess, since, if every patent of equal importance were to receive as much attention, the Arcana would require to be in fifty yearly volumes, instead of one. It is too late, however, now to complain of this want of homogeneous character; the book must be taken as it is—" a thing of shreds and patches," and the reader will only have himself to blame, if, after consulting its pages, he imagines himself to be acquainted with *all* the " discoveries and improvements" of the by-gone year.

A great portion of the contents of this division has, as usual, been derived from the columns of the *Mechanics' Magazine:* a circumstance which may well account for the difficulty of selecting any extract by way of specimen, which our readers would not recognize as an old acquaintance. Fortunately, the next head, "Chemistry," supplies us at the outset with a very interesting paper, which is as "good as MS.," and well worthy of being transferred to our pages: especially as it may be taken as an illustration of the views of our correspondent, Colonel Maceroni, on the subject of the light-houses of the Euxine. Who shall dare to predict a stop to the march of *enlightenment*, when a British scientific journal adds to the stores of practical philosophy by a communication from the very capital of the Turks,—the centre (once) of uncivilization?

" It may be well to state, as introductory to the following letter; that Mr. W. H. Barlow has been a resident for some time in Constantinople, for the purpose of constructing a brass foundry and boring-apparatus, upon a large scale, with a view of remodelling the Turkish artillery; and that on the return of Namik Pasha from this country, (who had examined with a scrutinizing eye many of our manufacturing and scientific establishments), Halil Pasha, the Sultan's son-in law, sent for Mr. Barlow, and spoke to him on the subject of restoring some dilapitated light-houses in the Black Sea, and requested to know if he was acquainted with a very remarkable light, which was known in England under the name of Drummond's lamp. He was answered that he knew of it generally, and that if he could find find any description of it in any of his books, he would furnish him with the particulars. Fortunately, on referring to an ingenious American physician, Dr. Zohrab, who had studied at Edinburgh, he fell upon a number of the Nautical Gazette, in which an account was given of the light; and on the ground of the information thus obtained, the experiments detailed in the following letter were undertaken.

' *Constantinople,* Jan. 6, 1836.

' I have already informed you of my first experiments on Drummond's light, and the astonishment it produced in the Turks when it first shone forth in all its brilliancy. ' *Mashallah allah! gunez boo!'** was heard on all sides; and I must acknowledge that my astonishment and delight were no less when I first found my attempts successful, in which Dr. Zohrab equally participated; neither of us having ever seen it in England. I promised you that on my return from examining and reporting on the state of the light-houses in the Black Sea, I would give you a detailed account of my proceedings, a promise which I now propose to redeem, as far as the extent of a letter will permit.

' When Halil Pasha first mentioned the Drummond's light, having searched my own library in vain for any description, I applied to Dr. Zohrab, who, having studied in Edinburgh, and being in the habit of reading English works, I thought might possess the desired information; and, fortunately, he had a number of the Nautical Gazette, in which was given several particulars of the light, with drawings; and, as we were reading of its beauties, a sudden thought struck us of trying to make it. I set to work that night, and made a drawing of the simplest apparatus I could conceive capable of producing the desired effect, which was as follows: In Fig. 1, A and B are two bladders, one

---

* Good heavens! it is the sun!" (Reviewer')

containing oxygen, the other hydrogen. C is the mixing-box, to which they are attached

Fig. 1.

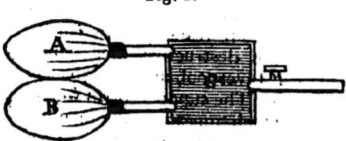

by being firmly tied upon the two projecting pipes. In this box were placed about thirty pieces of wire gauze, which, by the bye, we were sadly at a loss to obtain, till we accidentally fell upon two wire-gauze masks which had been used at the last carnival; these were instantly cut up and arranged in the mixing-box, at the upper end of which we attached the small pipe and stop-cock, as in the the figure. The stop-cock belonged to an apparatus of Dr. Zohrab's, and the small pipe was made by an ingenious American at Galata. Thus prepared, we filled the bladders with the proper gases (after only one unsuccessful attempt), and a piece of lime placed on a lump of clay, was put before the jet; a board was then placed on the bladders, with a weight on it. We then lighted the jet, and, to our inexpressible joy, a light instantly burst forth, so intense, that it was impossible to look directly at it. This being accomplished, and our apparatus appearing safe, I determined to exhibit the light itself to the Pasha, instead of the drawing of it which I had promised him. The astonishment and approbation were, as I have stated, very great, and I was immediately dispatched to the Black Sea, to examine and report on the state of the light-houses. On my return, I was requested to make a larger and more complete apparatus, in which I have succeeded the full extent of my expectation; this light burns for an hour. But I must here first mention a circumstance attending our first exhibition: after this was over, Dr. Zohrab and myself removed our apparatus, and there being still some gas in the bladders, we lighted it again for our own amusement in my drawing office, when it exploded with great violence while I was pressing the bladders with my hands. You remember the explosion of my gases in my little room at Rushgrove Cottage, but that was nothing; this was so sharp, that I lost the sensibility of my right ear for nearly a month, and the explosion forced pieces of the bladders quite through the cloth of my trowsers; and yet, excepting my ear, I escaped without injury.' "

Mr. Barlow goes on to describe his enlarged apparatus at some length, and winds up by observing :—

" The difficulties we encountered, and the extraordinary shifts we were put to, would be very amusing to you, but they are too long for a letter; suffice it to say, that, in the end, the experiment succeeded beyond our most sanguine expectation. The Pasha was delighted with its performance, and has taken the apparatus to his palace. I have since exhibited to him coal-gas light, which I manage much easier, and have drawn out my estimates for this light, and oil; but no doubt the latter will be preferred, and I soon expect to be at work in putting in proper repair the lighthouses of Fanaraki. I am anxiously waiting your further description of Beale's light, which I will also show to the Pasha, who takes great interest in all these matters."

Success to the worthy Pasha!—say we, —and may the streets of Constantinople speedily be lighted with gas! without which preliminary we are afraid Beale's light, whose great merit is that it turns to account the hitherto useless residuum from the retorts,—will be no great acquisition to Mr. Barlow's patron.

There are a great variety of interesting articles, besides this, in the " Chemical Science" department, and also not a few which hardly deserve the room they occupy—the account of " Donium, a new metal found in *Davidsonite*" among the number:—such matters are of moment only to the parties concerned; the "amber immortalization" of whose names is the object in view: it is needless to say that the discovery of this " new metal" is of the smallest conceivable importance. In the " Natural History" division, we have another specimen of the same ridiculous humbug, still more ludicrous. A Mr. Wetherell proposes to call an undescribed cockle shell by the name of his friend Mr. Sowerby, while Mr. Sowerby, not to be outdone in generosity, insists upon it that a species of voluta, slightly differing from those already known, shall be styled *Voluta Wetherelli*," " as a just tribute" to the author of the paper, namely, " the perpetuator of the glorious name of Sowerby!!" " One good turn deserves another," is an old saying, which these worthy naturalists evidently hold in high esteem : but their mutual clawings might just as well be left in their original obscurity,—the interests of science in general would suffer but little in consequence, and more room would be gained in the " Arcana" for really valuable matter.

FIRE AT ST. KATHARINE'S DOCKS— SPONTANEOUS COMBUSTION.

Sir,—The article on spontaneous combustion by M. Scanlan, Esq., which is inserted at page 143 of your 721st Number, does not happen to throw any light upon the circumstances attending the origin of the fire in the St. Katharine's Docks, on the 24th May last, yet I am sure that most of your readers will feel as much obliged to your " Old Correspondent," at whose request the paper was inserted, as I do myself. The nature of spontaneous combustion—or rather the numerous circumstances which give rise to it—are at present so imperfectly known, that thanks are due to all those persons, who will investigate and record the facts attending each occurrence, as far as they may be ascertained. Vegetable decomposition is a prolific source of accident, and the late fire in St. Katharine's Docks appears to have arisen from this cause. A quantity of empty rice bags, known among rag merchants and paper manufacturers by the name of Gunny-bagging, was lying in a heap, on one of the quays in the dock, which, having become heated, burst into flames about half-past ten o'clock of the night stated ; the fire consumed the bagging, and extended to a large stack of barrel-staves that was lying on the quay ; having burned through a window, the flames entered the cooperage, attacked the joists and flooring, and was preying upon a quantity of staves on the first floor of the building, when the firemen and engines reached the spot. The firemen were very prompt in their attendance, and by dint of great exertion in the midst of a most annoying smother, they soon succeeded in stopping the spread of the fire.

Much alarm was naturally excited, by the breaking out of a fire in this place ; the most experienced engineers who have inspected the buildings of these docks, having given it as their unanimous opinion, that if a fire once gets fairly hold of the warehouses, the whole edifice will inevitably be destroyed. The docks being continually crowded with merchandise, generally of the most combustible description—the buildings most intimately connected throughout, and of the most unapproachable description as to dimensions, height, &c., renders it most probable, that a large fire raging in these docks could not be checked by any ordinary efforts.

I cannot omit this opportunity of referring to the apparatus, which I contrived about four years ago, in consequence of the destructive fires which took place at Liverpool, and described in an article on "The suppression of waterside fires" which appeared in your nineteenth volume, page 184. This apparatus was designed for the purpose of securing a prompt and efficient supply of water to fire-engines, in situations corresponding to that of the docks in question. The want of some provision of this kind was much felt at the recent conflagration, and may be more severely felt at some future time, if not provided in the interim. Perhaps the gentlemen who have the superintendance of these matters, will see the propriety of immediately adopting the protection afforded by this simple means, before an extremity arises.

The spontaneous ignition of hemp, cotton, lampblack, and damp rags when collected in a mass, are by no means rare occurrences—the process being fermentation, heating, and ultimately ignition ; the same accident occurs more frequently with hay when stacked before sufficiently dry, as agriculturists know to their cost. There are some chemical actions that are confined to the mineral kingdom which produce the same ill effects, as the spontaneous ignition of coals, owing to the presence of iron pyrites, the admixture of sulphur and iron filings, &c. &c. ; but the accidents from vegetable matters are the most frequent, as they have been the most disastrous in their effects upon society.

I remain, Sir,
Yours respectfully.
WM. BADDELEY.

June 5, 1837.

PATENTS AND COPYRIGHTS.

A bill was passed last Session by Parliament for the protection of patents, and another is now before it for the protection of copyrights. The one enables patentees to secure, for an enormous sum, the right to their inventions for the space of fourteen years, and, in very particular cases, on receiving particular permission, and paying particular fees, to get that space extended:—the other provides, that on a simple registry of new publications, with no further formality and expense than are absolutely necessary, the copyright of a work shall be secured till sixty years after the author's death, no matter when that event may take place; so that, in some cases, as that of the poet Crabbe, for instance, the right may be prolonged for considerably upwards of a century. The law for the patents was passed not without difficulty, and held out somewhat in the light of a boon;—the bare proposition for the law of copyright has been received with enthusiasm, and the speech of its proposer, replete with reproach to the legislature, for not having adopted some similar measure before, has been almost drowned by the legislature itself, with thunders of applause.

Why is this great, this enormous difference to be made between the protection accorded to the genius of the author, and that of the inventor? " Hath not an *inventor* eyes, hath not an *inventor* hands, organs, senses, affections, passions? —Is he not fed with the same food, hurt with the same *dishonesties*, subject to the same *discouragements*, healed by the same means as an author is." An author, it is said, occasionally confers inappreciable benefits on the public. So does an inventor. An author is sometimes deprived of the due reward of his labours, by his works not being properly valued, on their first appearance. Of how many an inventor may the same be said? An author—but it is needless to pursue the parallel further,—the difficulty would be to point out a difference worth mentioning.

Yet so it is, that while patentees are apparently left to struggle unpitied with all the ills that flesh is heir to, Mr. Serjeant Talfourd not only proposes, with apparently every chance of success, to confer on authors,—already in comparison so highly favoured,—a number of still additional favours, but maintains, that even then, they will be hardly treated. In his opinion, the right to literary property ought never to terminate, and we ought still to be paying copyright for the works of Shakspeare. By the same rule we should still be handing over a valuable consideration to the descendants of Capt. Savery. But in affirming such a proposition as this, is

not the Serjeant blinded by his habit of seeing things in general with the eyes of a lawyer?—are not his views in reality narrow, at the very moment when he most supposes them enlarged? What is there in the law of property, and its descent, so sacred and all-embracing, that it should in justice be applied to even the productions of intellect itself? The political economists justify the perpetual transference of land and wealth from father to son, on the plea that the public is benefitted by their being in the possession of an individual, since he is likely, from motives of private interest, to manage them best, while, if in the hands of the public, they would only be the sources of strife and confusion. This state of things is decidedly reversed in the case of literary property, as well as patents;—the interest of the public is evidently best consulted by its being in the hands of the public, and the attempt to continue it in the possession of individuals, would lead to those very evils, which in other cases, are guarded against by that very measure. How are the works of Shakspeare, for instance, to descend? If by the laws of personal property, his different plays would by this time have been assigned to as many different persons, nay, perhaps would have been split into separate acts and scenes! On great and general principles, the law of inheritance, especially as it stands in this country, is open to many objections. The chief argument for it, is its convenience; now in regard to the productions of intellect, it has not that argument to plead. The effect of it, as regards them, would probably be bad in the extreme. We should not see the posterity of Milton and Addison, but the posterity of Tonson and Curll, riding in their carriages.

Relinquishing, however, what he considers the high ground of principle, Mr. Serjeant Talfourd descends to that of expediency. The present law is, that an author may dispose of his copyright for the term of twenty-eight years, at the end of which it reverts, if he be dead, to the public; if he be alive, to himself. It is proposed, in lieu of this, that the term assignable shall extend to sixty years after the author's death; the chief object being, it is said, to benefit his children. In proof of the insufficiency of the present term, and the injustice of the present law, the Serjeant in his speech adduces several instances, which are, it may fairly be presumed, the strongest he could offer. He speaks of a descendant of Milton, being reduced to take a benefit at the theatre, from the charity of Garrick; but this is by no means a case in point. That circumstance did not take place till much more than sixty years after Milton's death, and, according to Serjeant Talfourd's previous statements, the copyright of Paradise Lost was sold in perpetuity, the state of the law at that time allowing it—so that nothing remains but to blame the improvidence of Milton. He mentions the case of Burns—a name which it seems rather singular to find brought forward on an occasion like this. "As to any remuneration," writes Burns to Thomson, in the well-known correspondence, "you may think my songs either above or below price, for they shall absolutely be the one or the other. In the honest enthusiasm with which I embark in your undertaking, to talk of money, wages, fee, hire, &c. would be downright prostitution of soul." It is true, that the ideas of Burns in this respect were very unreasonable, but perhaps those of the Serjeant are hardly less so, in a different way. He complains that the public are now luxuriating in the works of Burns at a cheap rate, because the copyright is expired, without considering the loss sustained by his descendants. It is generally understood that the publication of those works was successful in no ordinary degree, in effecting the object for which they were given to the world, of raising a fund for the support of his family. Such being the case, his admirers are surely at liberty to congratulate themselves, that at length, after they have for twenty-eight years, been compelled to purchase a dear and bad edition of his works, sent out under the sanction of his family, by one who showed too little appreciation of his genius, and too little respect for his character, those works are now offered in all the forms of elegance and cheapness, to the Scottish peasantry *(for whom he wrote, and by whom he most wished to be read,)* and edited by biographers and critics, of feelings and powers far superior to those of Dr. Currie. The name of Coleridge is likewise made use of. It is said that the copyright of his works having ter-

minated on his decease, his children are now left without an inheritance. Under the proposed act their situation would certainly have been no better, and their father's would have been worse. Coleridge sold the copyright of his works to the booksellers at a time when it was of little value; they would retain it under the new law for nearly sixty years to come —while, under the old one it reverted to him at the expiration of the twenty-eight years, and he was thus in the decline of life enabled to derive profit from his productions himself. The last name which the Serjeant adduces, is that of Sir Walter Scott. Surely the prices that he received for his works are an ample proof, that under the old law, there was good reward for successful literary exertion. The unfortunate circumstances in which he left his family were the result of imprudent speculations, quite unconnected with literary merit, and which certainly do no honour to his name. Were Lord Wellington unfortunately to sacrifice his interest in Strathfieldsaye, to a fruitless attempt to support the cause of Don Carlos, or to reckless speculation in the funds, his Grace's consequent embarrassments, might as well be quoted as a proof of the ingratitude of the nation. Had Sir Walter Scott lived another year, he, like Coleridge, would have derived the benefit of the falling in of some of his earlier copyrights, and the operation of the old act would have shown its benefits in another conspicuous instance.

Such then are the strong cases for the new law. Many of them seem to tell quite as much for the old one. That of Coleridge points out how useful it may be to protect an author from his own improvidence. That of Burns points out how an author's family, may not prove the best guardians of his fame. In fact, this latter consideration is by no means an unimportant one. Twenty-eight years after an author's death, is now the longest period that a copyright can by possibility extend to. At that time many of his friends and acquaintance in general, remain alive; and if in the meanwhile his fame has continued extending, there is an opportunity of their coming forward, and throwing light on his works and character; in which case, some editor ten times more enthusiastic, and more discriminating than any selected by his family, might undertake the task of doing justice to his memory. Under the new law the long period of sixty years after the author's death, will have extinguished all an author's contemporaries, before his works become the property of his admirers. Had such been the rule in times past, we should have been deprived of some of the best and most entertaining works in our literature. Southey's edition of Cowper, miserably maimed, as it is, by the withholding of the letters which are still copyright, would be forced to yield the field altogether to that of Grimshaw. Croker's Boswell would be an impossibity. Should we be able to get a copy of Boswell's Life of Johnson at all? His son was ashamed of the work that gave his father immortality, and would, had it been in his power, have suppressed, what has justly been called, the most entertaining book in the English language.

THE "RUBY" STEAMER.

Sir,—I beg to transmit you the following account of a new steamer, the "Ruby," now running on the Thames, as there appears to me many things about her especially worth the notice of the readers of your valuable journal.

The "Ruby" has been built expressly for the Diamond Gravesend Steam Packet Company, with a view to great speed and ample accommodation; both of which have been obtained in a remarkable degree, as the results have proved. This vessel is 160 feet long between the perpendiculars, and 19 feet beam. She draws with all her machinery, coals, and 200 passengers on board, 5 feet water, and is propelled by two engines of 50 horses' power each. Her speed through still water, the result of various trials, at the mile ground in Long Reach, is 13¼ miles per hour, which is greater than has been obtained by any vessel in the kingdom, by nearly half a mile. She has successively beaten every vessel she has competed with, whatever their power may be. On several occasions she has made the passage from Gravesend to London, with the tide, but including all stoppages, in one hour and forty minutes. Her accommodations are of the most perfect description; she has a ladies cabin 14 feet long, a saloon 32 feet, and a fore cabin 32 feet, each most elegantly fitted up, with every convenience for the traveller, or the man of pleasure.

This vessel was constructed by the Messrs. Wallis of Blackwall, from the designs of Mr. O. Lang, jun., of Woolwich Yard, son of the eminent builder of that name, and is, I understand, built upon quite a novel principle. On the whole, she does great justice to the public spirit of the directors of the Diamond Steam Packet Company, as they may truly boast of having the most commodious and the fastest steamer afloat; and I imagine a trip in this vessel will be equally gratifying to the man of pleasure, and the man of science. One proof of her extraordinary speed, is the fact, that against a strong wind and ebb tide, she has run the distance from Gravesend to the Victualling Office Deptford, in two hours, and she is now making four trips a day, to and from Gravesend.

I am, Sir,

Your most obedient servant,

NAUTICUS.

FIRES IN PARIS—MR. BADDELEY'S FIRE REPORTS.

Sir,—The table relating to the Parisian fires for the last six years, in your last, for which we are indebted to the indefatigable Mr. Baddeley, seems to require a few explanatory notes to render it perfectly clear. For instance,—what is to be understood by the term "suffocated" which heads one of the columns? Most *English* readers, at any rate, would take it for granted that the persons returned as "suffocated," were, *ipso facto* dead, did not the last column, that of deaths, forbid the supposition—only one fireman being returned in the latter, while no less than nine are reported as "suffocated." The *Sapeurs Pompiers* of Paris are evidently of the same breed as the "boys" of Donnybrook Fair, who are all the more lively for being "kilt" now and then.

Again, what is meant by "populace?" Is the designation intended to comprehend the mob only—the lookers-on,— or it is a sweeping term for the whole of society who are *not* firemen, the inhabitants of the burning premises, included? "Populace" refers only to the former class; but then there are only two distinctive heads, and it can hardly be supposed, either, that no inhabitants received injury, or that they should not be included in the return; indeed it is not improbable that this second head may refer to them only, as the mob can hardly have occasion to incur any danger in a city, where we are told all the arrangements for extinguishing fires are in such apple-pie order, and where, above all, there is a numerous corps devoted to the especial service. Any way, circumstances considered, the term "populace" is of so indeterminate a signification as to render the column in question useless. Perhaps Mr. Baddeley will favour the readers of the *Mechanics' Magazine* with the original French word, which would probably go far to clear up the matter.

Mr. Baddeley informs us that " the small number of firemen killed and wounded is attributable to the expertness acquired by the men in their daily drills." The number, however, appears to be anything but small, amounting, as it does, to forty-three. As far as can be gathered from Mr. Baddeley's reports of London fires, this would seem to be much greater than our own ratio, notwithstanding the number of fires in London is usually three or four times greater than in Paris. I do not recollect reading of a single fireman being killed during the last six years, and only of two or three being hurt. True, the numbers of the firemen here and in Paris may be vastly disproportionate,—but neither the table nor Mr. Baddeley's letter affords any precise data on that subject.

While this topic is yet in hands, allow me to call Mr. Baddeley's attention to a paragraph in your sixteenth volume, relating to the comparative efficiency of the old and new systems of extinguishing fires in London. I venture to call this gentleman's attention to the passage, because it is not the production of an " anonymous" writer, but carries all the weight which the appending of the name of the author ought to give it. It is as follows:—" About four or five years back, there were fifty fire-engines belonging to the different insurance companies, stationed in different parts of the metropolis; the present number is only thirty-eight and the reduction in the number of firemen, has been in proportion. Some of the oldest insurance companies have formed a sort of union, or alliance, by which they mutually agree to aid and assist each other, thereby reducing the number of engines and firemen necessary to be kept by each. Thus, the co-operative system *works exceedingly well for the insurance companies, but is not equally advantageous for the public, seeing that the chance of prompt and effectual assistance, in case of accident, will always be in proportion to the number of men and engines that are distributed over the metropolis.*" (*Mec. Mag.* vol. xvi., page 311.)

These remarks are on the face of them so clear and convincing, that they seem of themselves sufficient to settle the question: but when it is added, that they proceed from a gentleman well known for his intimate acquaintance with the subject, as well as for the deep deliberation, with which his opinions upon it are formed, who shall venture to controvert them? To sum up all in a word, the letter from which they are extracted bears the signature of " WM. BADDELEY."

I remain, Sir,

Yours most respectfully,

AQUARIUS.

Wednesday, 7th June, 1837.

EXPLOSION OF THE BOILER OF THE "UNION" STEAM PACKET, AT HULL.

We have received numerous communications, offering suggestions as to the cause of the explosion of the boiler of the " Union" steam packet at Hull. On referring, however, to the Report of the experiments made by the Committee of the Franklin Institute on the causes of steam boiler explosions (for which see *Mechanics' Magazine*, Nos. 666, 667, 668, 670, 671, 672, 698, 699 & 705), we do not find any probable cause mentioned that has not been anticipated, and examined into, by the committee—with two exceptions, which we subjoin. We beg to call the particular attention of our readers to the recommendations of the Franklin Committee, with a view to meet the dangers in question (see our 26th vol., p. 235); in fact, the report altogether ought to be studied by every one having the responsibility of the direction of a steam engine, and human life in his care. When the coroner's inquest at Hull has closed, we shall give an abstract of the evidence, as far as relates to the explosion.

Sir,—Allow me to contribute my mite in explanation of the catastrophe which has unfortunately occurred at Hull. It appears to be the opinion of most, that the explosion arose from the generation of hydrogen gas in the boiler. Now, from my experience on this head, I do not hesitate to express my conviction that such was not the case; and the capital experiments lately made in America (and recorded in your Periodical,) fully confirm such opinion. To what cause then are we to attribute the effect—one undoubtedly of the most *violent* and *sudden* nature? I submit that it may be explained thus:—That the water in the boiler had become so low as to expose a large flue surface to be unduly heated. That, either by design or accident, the safety-valve was not then in action. Now, we have a quantity of water ready to foam by violent ebullition the instant the pressure was relieved; and this being effected, perhaps by the safety-valve opening, or by a partial rent in the boiler, the water would boil up and lightly cover the flue surfaces, which, either having been heated to, or if above, quickly reduced to, the temperature of most rapid vaporisation, about 400° to 500°, so vast an accumulation of steam, would *instantly* occur, that no safety valve, nor indeed any thing short of the most open exit, could save the boiler from immediate destruction.

I am, Sir,
Your most obedient servant,
THOMAS HOWARD.
London, 15th June, 1837.

———

Sir,—Is the chloride of sodium, or common salt (left after the vaporization of the sea-water in the boiler) decomposed by the great heat arising from an insufficient quantity of water in the boiler? In case it is, will not the chlorine mix with the hydrogen and oxygen arising from the decomposition of the steam (occasioned by an insufficient quantity of water also), and form an explosive mixture, which the heat of the boiler may be sufficient to explode; and does not the iron of the boiler assist in the separation of the chlorine? May I beg the favour of your calling the attention of your scientific readers to the subject, as I think a sufficient number

of accidents by the bursting of steam-engine boilers have already occurred to justify an inquiry into the causes of their bursting, beyond what may happen through inattention or negligence.

I am, Sir,
Your obedient servant,
H. P. J.
London, 12th June. 1837.

———

COPPER BOILERS.

Has any such explosion ever occurred in a copper boiler? And if not, does not the fact of the safety of these boilers afford obvious ground for legislative enactment, irrespective of any scientific controversy upon the causes of explosion in iron boilers.

These appear still involved in much doubt; the prevailing opinion of engineers appears to be, that the expansive power of steam—particularly of low pressure steam, is totally inadequate to account for the terrific violence of such explosions as that of the Hull steamer, and that in such cases the steam must have been decomposed by contact with some part of the iron boiler at a red heat. Formerly, hydrogen gas used to be obtained for the inflation of balloons, by passing steam through a red-hot iron tube, charged with iron wire or nails to facilitate the process, the oxygen combining with the heated iron, and the hydrogen being evolved in the form of gas. This is a familiar illustration of the well-known fact, that steam is liable to be decomposed into its constituent gases by contact with iron at a high temperature; and the impossibility of obtaining hydrogen gas by passing steam through heated copper tubes, seems to be equally demonstrative of the safety in this respect of copper boilers for steam engines.

By the evidence given at the coroner's inquest at Hull, it is proved that the boiler was properly filled with water, and that the fire-flues were, therefore, covered by it; but it is generally supposed that the steam generated upon the surface of the boiler plates, may sometimes prevent the actual contact of the water, at particular parts, for a considerable time, and allow of those parts becoming hot enough to decompose the steam. But whatever may be the prevailing theory by which the violent explosion of iron boilers is explained by engineers, if the fact be, as I apprehend it is, that such explosions as that at Hull, never occur in the case of copper boilers, does not the public safety require that these should be universally adopted, or at least, that they should be so in all marine engines?—*Correspondent of the True Sun.*

COCHRAN'S MANY-CHAMBERED GUN.*

(From the *American Railroad Journal*).

The chambers, or receptacles for the charge, are in the periphery of a cylinder of about four inches in diameter, and seven-eighths of an inch thick, which revolves horizontally on a pivot, bringing each chamber alternately in a line with the barrel; on the under side, and about equidistant from the periphery, and centre of the cylinder, is placed a small cone to receive the percussion cap. There is a cone to each charge, having a communication with the powder. When the cylinder is charged, each having *nine* charges, the caps are put upon the cones, and then the cylinder is put in its place, and secured there by a spring. When in its place, each chamber, or charge, points in a different direction, and each cap is per-fectly protected from explosion, except the one communicating with the chamber in a line with the barrel, and after discharging which, no further explosion can take place without moving a spring, which permits the cylinder to make the *one-ninth* of a revolution, thereby bringing another chamber, or charge, in a line with the barrel. A person familiar with the use of this, having extra cylinders in his belt, can easily make thirty shots in a minute, as he would only remove it from his face three times, to make thirty-six shots.

The great facility with which it can be discharged, is not, as will be perceived on reading Capt. Gordon's letter, its highest recommendation. The certainty of explosion, even after long exposure in damp weather, is of the first importance, a quality which it appears to possess in an eminent degree.

The accompanying drawings show the

positions of the cylinder, in which is represented the chambers and the cones for the caps.

A number of certificates of the performances of the rifle follow, from which we select the following :—

Cochrane's Gun tested in a Battle with the Seminoles, in Florida, by Captain Gordon.

New York, March 17, 1837.

Sir,—Having had very ample opportunities of testing the very great superiority of your " many-chambered" gun, it affords me great pleasure to state, for the public information, that I consider it far superior to any other now in use. Its peculiar adaptation to the purposes of war, gives it just and strong claims to the patronage of the general government. I do not hesitate to declare it as my firm and decided opinion, that one hundred men, armed with your gun, would be equal, in point of efficacy, in battle, to one thousand armed with any other. Its superiority for hunting purposes is equally great, and cannot fail to secure for it the public favour.

The astonishing capability of your gun to resist dampness, or injury of its charge, when loaded, I consider of the greatest importance. A very strking and satisfactory instance of this manifested itself in the late battle with the Seminoles, on Lake Monroe. Your gun had at the time been loaded at least two weeks—had been taken out on one or more excursions, and exposed to the dampness of the atmosphere, which in that country is very great, and such other causes as had made it necessary to discharge and re-load all or most of the other arms similarly exposed ; yet, under these circumstances, without re-loading, yours went off in every instance (the whole round of chambers), as if recently charged. The simplicity of the machinery, and the great power with which it throws its balls, will justly enhance its estimation with all who will take the trouble to examine and make trial of them.

In conclusion, I will repeat, that I have no hesitation in giving it as my firm conviction, that your's is by far the most efficient fire-arm ever offered to the public, and every way worthy of confidence and patronage.

I am, Sir,

Very respectfully,

Your most obedient

Humble servant,

W. GORDON.

Capt. U. S. Dragoons.

To Mr. John Cochran, New York.

* See *Mechanics' Magazine*, vol. xxvi. p. 412.

NOTES AND NOTICES.

Travellers see strange Things.—"One day, in going down Broadway, New York, the carriage in which I was stopped for some time, in consequence of an immense procession on the side-walk having attracted the attention of all the drivers within sight. The marching gentlemen proceeded on their way with an easy air of gentility. Banners were interposed at intervals; and, on examining these, I could scarcely believe my eyes. They told me that this was a procession of the journeymen mechanics of New York. Surely, never were such dandy mechanics seen,—with sleek coats, glossy hats, gay watch-guards, and doe-skin gloves! I rejoice to have seen this sight." Miss Martineau, from whose new work on America the above is extracted, might have been gratified without going so far from home. Can she possibly be ignorant, that her description is, to a Londoner, that of something which (at this time of year) is continually passing before his eyes? There are only two alterations wanted to make the likeness complete. In England, the processionists are generally not content with the side-walks, but usurp the carriage-way for the nonce, and they also contrive to have at least *one* band of music.

Beet-root Sugar in America.—The cultivation of beet-root for sugar is about to be extended to the New World. Deputies from the United States have already arrived in France to be initiated in the arcana of the process; and it is expected that if, on their return, the plant should be found suitable to the soil and climate of the more northern states, a great blow will be dealt at the slavery of the south. It ought to be added, that, at the very moment of their arrival, the beet-growers of France were in apprehension of total destruction, in consequence of a measure having been introduced by the ministry, which would have the effect of bringing colonial production in fair competition with that of the mother-country. The measure has since been modified to suit the views of the now numerous class of beet-root cultivators; and, taken altogether, the circumstance augurs but ill for the success of the American speculation.

Paris and Brussels Railway.—The inhabitants of St. Quintin have taken the alarm at the concession granted to Mr. Cockerill for a railway from Paris to Brussels. The line proposed by that gentleman, it appears, will pass at some distance from St. Quintin, whose citizens allege that the circumstance will be fatal to the manufactures of the place, deprived, as it will be, of the facilities of communication enjoyed by other localities. They have sent in strongly drawn addresses to the powers that be, praying for the restoration of the line to its old station, through St. Quintin, as a matter of vital importance to their interests. As their town produces the same sort of fabrics as Manchester, they insinuate that English influence has been at work to procure the alteration, and are fortified in their idea by the circumstance of Mr. Cockerell's being an Englishman, and also by the fact that the new line will be far more convenient for effecting a railroad communication between London and Paris

than the old one. "If the measure be persevered in," they observe, "the total ruin of St. Quintin and its manufactures, will be the result, and this will form *the greatest sacrifice which has yet been offered on the altar of alliance with England !*"

New Waggon Steam Drag.—Mr. Boydell, of Dee Cottage, near Chester, has invented a locomotive engine, which, when fixed to heavy waggons, &c., will propel them on common roads at a very rapid rate. It was exhibited on Tuesday, and elicited the strongest approbation from many scientific and practical men who witnessed the trial, and minutely examined the machinery. It is applicable to ploughs, which it propels with great ease and velocity.—*Chester Courant.*

Patent Spring Folding Hat.—A new hat has lately been introduced into London from Edinburgh, to which it was imported from Paris, which is composed of a skeleton of highly tempered steel springs, extended by an internal metallic ring. It is covered with felt or silk, and may be formed into any fashionable shape, may be compressed into a very small compass, and instantly restored to its original form. *Open* and placed on the head, it resembles other hats, and is equally pleasant to wear; *shut*, it is reduced to the thickness of an inch and a half, when it may be carried under the arm, put between the coat and the vest, like a portfolio, and will only occupy the room of a shirt in a portmanteau. Its exceedingly simple mechanism may be adapted to various forms, while its durability is declared to be equal to that of any other hat: thus, for the convenience of travelling and attending crowded assemblies, this invention must be very useful. When the hat is to be put on, the metallic ring, which is covered with the lining, is pushed towards the inside of the hat; then the edges of the ring slide along the springs, forcing them and the outside covering to its proper form, in which, by means of a notch in the ring, it remains extended. When it is wished to compress the hat, two of the springs must be pressed with the thumb, which make the crown come down, and reduce the hat to its compressed state.

Waste Lands.—An apparatus has been invented, and secured by patent, by which bog and marsh lands may be drained with the greatest facility, and at an extremely small cost (compared with every other known method). At a period such as the present, when the means of finding employment and food for the Irish poor (the majority, unfortunately, of the Irish population) are occupying so large a share of the public attention, an invention which offers, like this, a method of speedily converting millions of now useless acres into fertile, arable land, can scarcely be too highly appreciated. We have seen a report which was made to a public board, by a gentleman deputed to witness a trial lately made of the apparatus, in which its practical efficiency is attested in the strongest terms. The inventor, who is desirous of obtaining the co-operation of some monied individual, in bringing the invention into use, may be immediately communicated with, by addressing a note to him, to the care of our publisher.

☞ *British and Foreign Patents taken out with economy and despatch; Specifications, Disclaimers, and Amendments, prepared or revised; Caveats entered; and generally every Branch of Patent Business promptly transacted.*

A complete list of Patents from the earliest period (15 Car. II. 1675,) *to the present time may be examined. Fee 2s. 6d.; Clients, gratis.*

LONDON: Printed and Published for the Proprietor, by W. A. Robertson, at the Mechanics' Magazine Office, No. 6, Peterborough-court, between 135 and 136, Fleet-street.—Sold by G. W. M. Reynolds, Proprietor of the French, English, and American Library, 55, Rue Neuve, Saint Augustin, Paris.

Mechanics' Magazine,

MUSEUM, REGISTER, JOURNAL, AND GAZETTE.

No. 724.　　　　SATURDAY, JUNE 24, 1837.　　　　Price 3*d*.

BUNNETT'S REVOLVING IRON SAFETY SHUTTERS.

Fig. 1.　　　　　　　　　Fig. 2.

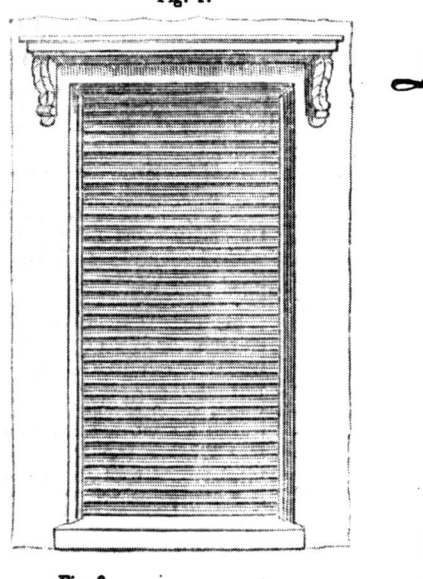

Fig. 3.　　　　　　　　　Fig. 4.

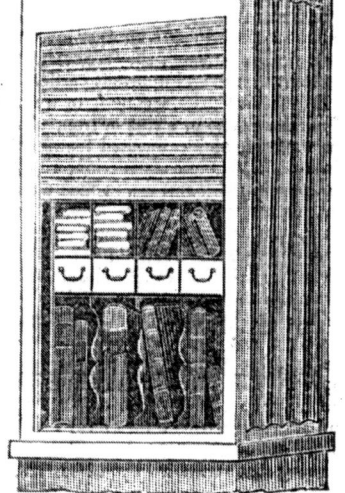

BUNNETT'S REVOLVING IRON SAFETY SHUTTERS.

Sir,—There is scarcely any thing more desirable in populous towns and cities, than a ready and convenient method of securely closing the houses and shops of the inhabitants. The modes that have been devised for effecting this purpose are very various; but up to a comparatively recent period, most of the plans in common use were more or less inconvenient—many of them excessively clumsy, both as regarded the material and the manner of its application. The trouble of putting up every night, and taking down every morning, from ten to twenty heavy wooden shutters, together with the difficulty of finding a suitable place for stowing them away in the day-time, were among the most prominent evils entailed upon shopkeepers by the old-fashioned methods.

The cellar was very often the only eligible place of depository, from whence the shutters were drawn out across the foot-pavement of an evening, to the great and grievous annoyance of the pedestrians, with which the thoroughfares are at that time crowded.

Sundry remedies have been proposed for these evils, and of several improved shutters that have appeared, the most recent, and, in my humble opinion, the best, are Bunnett's Revolving Iron Safety Shutters, for which his Majesty's royal letters patent were obtained in June last. Although these shutters bear a slight resemblance to another invention for a similar purpose, they are essentially different in a most important particular.

Bunnett's shutters consist of a series of narrow plates or strips of iron, placed horizontally, and connected together by hinges of a simple construction, rivetted on to their under surface, in such a manner, that the iron plates overlap each other, and entirely conceal the hinges from external observation; considerable advantage arises from this circumstance, inasmuch as the hinges cannot be seen on the outside of a building; they are therefore not liable to be cut, nor can the knuckle-pins of the hinges be removed. The pieces of metal to form the hinges are struck out of plate iron, and afterwards bent up into the required form; each hinge being held to the strip forming the shutter by three rivets.

The knuckles of each hinge being bent in opposite directions, allows the strips of iron to overlap each other; at the same time, the combined shutter is capable of bending over and winding round the roller, to which the first set of hinges is fastened. This arrangement entirely obviates the necessity for cutting away any portion of the substance of the shutter itself.

Fig. 1, is a front view of a window closed with one of Bunnet's patent shutters, which has a light and elegant appearance, closely resembling a Venetian blind, the resemblance being greatly increased when they are painted (as they should be) green.

Fig. 2, is a section of the closed shutter and window frame, by which the method adopted for opening and closing these shutters will be rendered intelligible. An iron roller with a toothed wheel at one end, is fixed in suitable bearings on each side at the top of the window; a worm, or endless screw on the top of a vertical shaft, takes into this toothed wheel, while the lower end of the shaft carries a small bevelled wheel, working into another similar wheel placed at right angles with it. The axle of the last bevelled wheel is squared off for receiving the handle, the turning round of which raises or lowers the shutter.

The compact form of these shutters requires no deviation from the present mode of building, but that of placing the lintel over the window a few inches higher than usual, to admit the shutter when rolled up, as it is shewn in fig. 3, which is an interval view of the sashes and frame, with the shutter out of use.

Fig. 4, represents an iron fire-proof safe, for the protection of books, deeds, manuscripts, &c. The sides and other parts of the outer safe are formed of patent corrugated iron, leaving an air space between that and the inner safe, for the purpose of rendering them fireproof. If desired, it can be covered with an ornamental casing of thin woodwork, so as to combine a neat and elegant appearance with great security and facility of extensive arrangement, the contents being instantly secured from curiosity or theft by the application of a good patent lock.

The same principle may also be advantageously resorted to in fitting up valuable libraries; it is equally well adapted to the front of glass cases, &c. containing jewellery, or other valuables. As a temporary partition, for the division and protection of shops, the iron shutters will be found superior to every other contrivance.

The ends of the shutter slide up and down in two metal grooves, one on each side of the window-frame; there are two steady-pins in the window sill, which fit into corresponding holes in the lowest bar of the shutter; on the inside of this bar, one or more square holes are made for the reception of self-acting spring bolts, which catch the shutter on its descent, and most effectually prevent its being raised by any force either internal or external, until they are withdrawn. These bolts may be replaced by locks, where the shutters are not to be opened but in the presence of the owner.

Among many other advantages offered by this ingenious invention, the following are some of the most striking :—Perfect security in all situations against both fire and thieves; the simplicity of construction, and the nature of the materials employed, which ensure their continuance in good and efficient working order; the short space of time required to open or close them (a few seconds), and the ease with which it is accomplished, enabling even females or children to manage them without any liability to accident. They are equally adapted to the house of business or private residence, the absence of inside shutters allowing the windows to be finished in any way that taste or necessity may dictate.

In the mansions of the nobility and gentry, where many windows remain closed a considerable part of the year, the protection of the sashes and frames from the effects of the weather, sun, &c. will be an object of consideration, independently of the security afforded against the attacks of robbers, or of riotous assemblage.

Another most important advantage would be gained by fixing these shutters to fire-places generally, so as to fall in front of the stove when fires are left, or extinguished for the night, and thereby preventing those accidents which frequently arise for want of such a provision. In the event of the chimney taking fire, the shutter would enclose the falling particles of ignited soot, and by stopping the draft, extinguish the fire, thereby removing the cause of danger.

Although the first year of Mr. Bunnett's patent is not yet expired, his shutters have already come into very extensive employment; two, of a large size, have been put up lately at Mr. Riddle's patent ever-pointed pencil manufactory, in Blackfriars Road.

I remain, Sir,

Yours respectfully,

WM. BADDELEY.

May 25, 1837.

MR. SHIRES' ORRERY.

Sir,—The following is an account of the much admired scientific orrery discovered by William Shires, early in the year 1836, which one of the Royal Society has of late got scent of, and attempted to pirate; but from his imperfect knowledge of it, his solution is incomplete. That it is Mr. Shires's discovery, is well known to the Secretary of the Western Institution. Newton's *Principia*, though the most valuable of all known works, has been void of a reason for his impulsive force given to planets, and drawn into orbits by the attraction of central bodies. But since they all move in a like manner, and with velocities inversely as the square roots of their distances from their centres of motion, this gave rise to the following solution, viz., that there is a fluid about the fixed star Regulus, and the sun, like unto a line about two pullies, and extending in a plane, which gives a diurnal rotation to the sun, and annual motions to primary planets about him; which fluid received by the sun, is imparted to the primary planets, that give diurnal motions to the primaries, and revolve moons about them. No such fluid, however, is imparted from dark bodies, and hence moons have no such diurnal rotations as primaries have. By following out the above theory, all planetary motion may be easily accounted for. The inclination of the axes of planets to their orbits, will be found to arise from a magnetic effect.

The Orrery.—Let R represent the fixed star regulus; S, the sun; P, the primary planet; m, the moon; m A, the moon's orbit; and B D, the orbit of P; and let the lines about them be strings representing the fluid. Then the rotation of R will turn all parts of the system in a like direction, shewing the motions

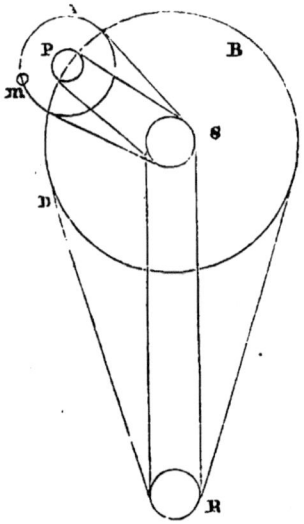

in all our systems, viz., solar and lunar to arise from the rotation of R. All which holds good by dynamics, which solution has been tried by your humble servant,

WILLIAM SHIRES,
Teacher of Mathematics.

MR. MACKINTOSH'S ELECTRICAL THEORY.

Sir,—Mr. Mackintosh tells me, No. 712, that I have made a furious attack upon Mr. Thorne's geological observations, without offering one geological argument in support of my opinions, &c. I must here inform Mr. Mackintosh, that I brought astronomical facts to bear against his geological suppositions, as I considered it would be better to reason from well established facts than to oppose guess work with guess work arguments; for I still hold, that the arguments that he or his supporter, Mr. Joshua Thorne, have brought forward in support of the story of the five moons, are all derived from the science of guess work.

Mr. M. informs us, that his electrical theory of the universe has received the commendations of several eminent professors, among whom is Professor Faraday; and that his general views have been adopted by more than one professor in the University of Cambridge. Professor Faraday, in his own department of science, has, perhaps, no superior. But with regard to his astronomical or geological attainments, I have never heard that he was famed for either. Indeed, the Professor is sometimes rather rash in giving opinions upon subjects that he has not duly considered. I might refer to some of the Numbers of the *Mechanics' Magazine* to bear me out in this assertion; and with regard to the opinions of *one* or *two* of the professors of Cambridge, I dare say *three* or *four* of them might be found that know as much about the subject, as their great grandmothers did, aye, and would have no objections to see the bust of Newton kicked down and that of Mr. Mackintosh put in its place. But, Mr. Editor, the only part of the electrical theory of the universe which I have yet interfered with, is, that the earth, at one period, must have been attended by five moons, four of which, at the same or different periods, have been precipitated upon the earth. Now, I will ask Mr. Mackintosh, does Professor Faraday, or any of his Cambridge supporters, believe in this part of his system? If they do so, I dare say they will find no difficulty in admitting the truth of all the rest of his system. In that case, I would advise Mr. M. to attend at Liverpool at the next meeting of the British Association, and lay the whole subject before that learned body. This would be the most effectual method of bringing the whole matter to a final issue. I shall now, Mr. Editor, with your leave, address a few words to your geological correspondent, Mr. Joshua Thorne.

Mr. Thorne asks me upon what authority I found my assertion, that the quantity of matter in the moon is to that in the earth as 1 to 71, and from what equation (!) I derive my authority? Had this question of Mr. Thorne's been put before Newton wrote his *Principia*, it no doubt would have been a poser. But at the present time, aye, and for 100 years back, the principles of this equation (as Mr. Thorne styles it) are as well known to every student in physical astronomy, as that the three angles of every plane triangle are equal to two right angles is known to every one that has attentively read the First Book of Euclid. From this question of Mr. Thorne's, it is pretty certain that his head is not over-burdened with physical astronomy. " Again," adds Mr. Thorne, " is he (a Country Teacher) assured that the moon is a solid body, and that its solidity (density he should have said) is the same as that of the earth ? or is he assured that the earth itself is a solid body?" This second question of Mr. Thorne's has no pretentions to originality. It has lately been much discussed by some of our ablest philosophers and mathematicians; and some of them contend, that our earth is of a cavernous structure, as the mean density of the whole mass is only about five times that of water, or double that of its exterior crust, if the general materials were the same. Then, according to the laws of compression, the condensation towards the central parts would cause the general density of the whole mass to be much greater than what observations have determined it to be. It is therefore inferred, that our planet, to a great extent, must be of a cavernous structure. But be that as it may, by knowing the mean density and magnitude of the earth, we can determine the absolute weight of the general mass; and the same can be done with respect to the moon. When I calculated (No. 712) that in the event of a collision of the earth and moon, and that if all the matter in the moon were equally scattered over the whole surface of the earth, the present surface of our planet would be buried 18½ miles by the matter contained in the moon—I might also have added,— and the mean weight of that covering will be equal to the mean density of the general mass contained in the earth; or that every square foot of surface on the earth would sustain a pressure of 13,627 tons. True it is, I made the calculation upon the supposition that the moon is a solid body; but suppose it is cavernous, and that the dimensions of the hollow parts are equal or greater than those of the solid parts—what then ? It would diminish the depth of the covering; but its weight would remain the same, that is, every square foot of surface would have to sustain a load of 13,627 tons.*

Mr. Thorne states, "allowing the supposition that the moon is a solid body, the equation (!) of the Country Teacher is wrong. If he were to compute the solid contents of the increased diameter of the earth (18.5564 miles), and the solid contents of the moon (allowing it be solid), and inform your readers which would contain the most matter, and what was the difference—if he will do this, I may, perhaps, (wonderful condescension), look at his equation (!) again."

The above quotation puts criticism to the blush. To calculate the solid contents of a mathematical line is a problem which I am sure was never thought of before by mortal man. Again, he says 18·5564 miles is the increased diameter of the earth. Now, I should think that it requires very little knowledge of arithmetic to discover that 37·1128 miles will be the increased diameter of the earth. If Mr. Thorne cannot understand my solution, that is not my fault. Sure I am, Mr. Editor, none of your able mathematical contributors can dispute its accuracy. I might with very little trouble shew Mr. Thorne, from some of the observations he has made in his letter about solidity and density, &c., that he ought to have studied the subject a little more attentively, before he promulgated the strange opinions he has formed concerning these matters. Mr. Thorne asks me to take a stone, and throw it on the ice, and I will find, if the ice be not too thick, or the stone thrown with too great force, that it will stick in the ice, part being imbedded and part exposed to view, in proportion to the thickness of the ice, or the force by which the stone was thrown. " Just so, I think, would be the condition of a moon, if it fell to the earth's surface," &c. I thank Mr. Thorne for this hint, for I find it will furnish me with materials fully more fatal to the moon-dropping system, than any that I have yet adduced. But this, and some other observations, I will make the subject of another communication.

I am,

Mr. Editor,

Yours, &c.

A COUNTRY TEACHER.

May 25, 1837.

---

* One mile = 5280 feet; hence 5280 × 18·5 × 5 = 488400000 ounces avoirdupois = 13627 tons 4 cwt.

GEOLOGICAL EVIDENCES OF MR. MACKINTOSH'S · ELECTRICAL THEORY.

Sir,—In my last I alluded to the cause of the contortion of the strata of the earth, and promised a reference to the state, and the observed phenomena, of the coral islands. I will now first consider their nature and condition, and then trace the cause of the alterations of the relative levels of the land and sea, to the magnetic influence, as well as those changes produced by the precession of the equinoxes.

Many of the islands to the south of the equator, and between New Holland and the west coast of America are decidedly of the coral formation, produced by the tribe of molluscous insects, called polyparies. It is well known that these insects cannot build their stupendous edifices above the level of the sea; and as many of the islands do rise considerably above its level, it becomes philosophers to enquire into the probable cause of the elevation. The coral rocks round Tongataboo are ten feet above high water mark, while the island itself rises from sixty to seventy feet higher. At Eora, coral rocks have been observed 300 feet above the sea; and in the most inland and elevated parts of Owhyhee, coral is also observed. Now the causes, which have been hitherto assigned for these effects, are volcanic agency and the existence of central heat producing expansion, and a consequent upraising of the strata. The idea that the sea has sunk in that part of the globe, has been ridiculed as being an extravagant hypothesis.

It is true, that there are many active volcanoes at present existing in this part of the world, as, for instance, those of Owhyhee, (including that remarkable one of Monte Roa) Tanna and Amboyna of the New Hebrides, the Marian isles, and several groupes to the north of the Marians, whose names indicate their nature as Volcanic island, Sulphur island, &c. One would suppose that such a number of volcanoes would be sufficient to ensure a stability to the surrounding isles, and serve as outlets to any quantity of matter which might be expanded in the interior of the earth. In the department Calvados, in France, madrepore edifices exist of immense extent and thickness, high above the level of the sea; now, if the islands of the Pacific Ocean were elevated by the influence of volcanoes, or by central heat,—so also it must be allowed was the department of Calvados. But if there is such a continual rise of the land, immense abysses must be formed in the interior of the globe; and if the earth still goes on upheaving and expanding, the abyss will be fully sufficient to contain the chaotic ocean of Werner.

This is the present condition of the coral islands, and now we will trace the cause of their change. Though central heat and volcanic agency may disrupt the strata, and alter the condition of the earth's surface; still I think they have not been the cause in all cases; and we may, in the case of the coral islands, find a simple and more gradual, but equally effective, cause. It is the leading feature of the theory I am advocating to attribute the *state*, as well as the motions, of the planets to electrical causes, of which magnetism and galvanism may be styled modifications. The phenomena of magnetic influence have hitherto been but badly understood, and most discoveries relative to it are of very modern date. Since the discovery of the variation by Columbus, 1492, and the dip by Norman in 1576, Descartes with Halley, Leonard Euler, &c., endeavoured to fix the position of the magnetic poles, but they have in a great measure failed, owing to their not being fully acquainted with the nature of the variation. The position of the magnetic poles has now been determined for some time, both by theory and observation; and the revolutions of the magnetic poles seem to be the causes of various elevations and depressions of the waters, which will account for many geological phenomena. It appears from the numerous accounts of inundations which history records, that while the magnetic points approach the meridian of any place, the sea seems to gain upon the land, and when the magnetic point recedes from the meridian of any place, the contrary is the case. Since the year 1657, the magnetic points have been approaching the meridian of Greenwich; and if we peruse historical records, we shall find that the waters have risen under that meridian. The continual increase of the waters of the Baltic Sea and the German Ocean would warrant this conclusion; so that while the two magnetic points are approaching the meridians of Dover or Vineta, (as they do at present) the waters will be found to rise in those places. But what the sea gains on this side of the globe, it must lose on some other, for it would be improbable, nay, impossible, for the sea to rise in every part at once; and we accordingly find, if we look to those parts from whose meridian the magnetic point is receding, that the coasts bear evident marks, either of elevation of the land or of a depression of the waters. In the Pacific Ocean there is a space from whence both magnetic points have now a retrograde motion, and in this space the waters continue to fall. Captain Cook after describing the elevations and situations of various islands, with their appended coral rocks, says, speaking of the peninsula of Cape Denbigh, " It appears that this peninsula must once have been an island, for there are evident marks of the sea having once flowed over it, and even now it appears to be kept out by a bank of sand, stones and wood, thrown up by the waves. By this bank it was evident that the land was here encroaching on the sea, and it was easy to trace its gradual formation." Now here is a case on the authority of an acute observer where the land was gradually encroaching on the sea; and the peninsula referred to is similarly situated to the volcanic isles I have before mentioned,—and the sea retires in both the instances. In two cases so nearly alike we are justified in coming to the conclusion, that they are the result of the same cause; and if Captain Cook was right in his observations, we may conclude, that the sea is, at present, gradually retiring from the Pacific Ocean, and the land is being elevated above the sea level by the depression of the waters, and not by a central expansive power, or a volcanic agency.

Then, if the question be asked, why the waters rise in this part and fall in others? it is plainly and simply answered by a reference to the powers of electricity. The same powers, and the same laws, which guide the planets in their courses, guide also the floods and tides of this earth; and although magnetism, as a science in its infancy, is not fully understood, we have every reason to believe its nature to be the same as electricity or galvanism. The fact that the waters rise at any particular place, when

the magnetic point approaches its meridian, cannot be controverted; and to what else are we to attribute that rise but to that magnetic or electrical influence?

I have in my several letters collected what I consider to be undisputed facts. I have referred your readers to the rapidity of various convulsions, to the enormous pressure exerted at the time of such convulsions, and to the contortion of the strata; and in the present letter, referred what has been heretofore attributed to sudden upheavings to the depression of the waters occasioned by electric action. In my former letters, my object was to shew that the power exerted by the fall of a satellite was a fit and fair representative of the cause which has produced the phenomena referred to; and in the present letter, that electricity is the cause of the water rising and decomposing the hardest rocks, whereby their particles are carried to the lowest level they can find, to be formed into fresh beds of sandstone, replete with the remains of the more recent animal and vegetable life.

I will again hint to your correspondent, the "Country Teacher," the fallacy of his equation. If he will turn to page 360, No. 681, of the *Mechanics' Magazine*, he will find an extract from Dr. Wilkinson, who says, that the mass of the earth is to the mass of the moon as 1 to 49.22. But the "Country Teacher" says, it is as 1 to 71. So here are two mathematicians, who have come to quite a different conclusion on the same point; and I will not take upon me to decide which is right.

I was revolving in my mind, a short time ago, the probability of the comets eventually becoming planets, when it occurred to me that they might have a transparent nucleus. Most astronomers, who have examined cometary bodies, say they have no nucleus; because stars of the smallest magnitude can be seen through them, though Sir J. Herschell says, that in some a small nucleus may be observed. I was led to this consideration, by referring to the liquefaction of gases by pressure. Now, if the comets are composed of something resembling the matter of the earth, I conceive those particles in the interior would undergo a considerable pressure, and consequently be liquified. I think this idea might be carried out much farther, and I thus prematurely refer it to the consideration of your readers, hoping some use may be made of it, perhaps by Mr. Mackintosh, or some other person, in support of the electrical theory.

I remain, Sir,
Yours respectfully,
JOSHUA THORNE.
May 27, 1837.

THE MARQUIS OF WORCESTER AND DE CAUS.

Sir,—Perceiving, among some very just remarks made by you on the " British Annual" and the " Annuaire par le Bureau des Longitudes," a few allusions to De Caus and the Marquis of Worcester, relative to their claims to the invention of the steam engine; the following additional observations on the same subject may not, I trust, be unacceptable to your readers.

The work of De Caus is assigned to the year 1624, but from a careful examination of several copies of the original French edition, I have, I think, collected evidence sufficient to prove, that it was not published for some years afterwards. On applying for the opinion of several friends eminently versed in bibliography, I was unanimously informed that it was not printed on the continent, but in England; and with respect to its date, it varied from 1640 to 1650. Many copies have the plain title " *Nouvelle invention de lever l'eau plus haut que sa source, avec quelques machines mouvantes par le moyen de l'eau, et un discours de la conduit d'icelle. Par Isaac de Caus, ingenieur et architecte, Natif de Dieppe,*" and some have an ornamented border with the same title, but one which is in my possession, and two more that I have seen, have ornamented borders, and the same title at the bottom, " *Imprime à Londre l'an* 1644." The contents of most of those title-pages, which have the border, vary a little in their orthography, but some are entirely altered; another copy in my possession is thus entitled ; " *Instructions mathematiques pour la jeune Noblesse, ou Bref traite de Geometrie Arithmetique perspective Fortification.*" Now the only method, in which I can account for this, is, that the work was printed in London a very few years before 1644, and obtained these different

title-pages from some convenience of the bookseller.

The translation of De Caus's work was not published till 1659, and therefore some, believing Worcester's assertion, that his self-styled inventions "were set down in the year 1655," have inferred that he has not taken any hints from it, but from what has been said above, it is very evident that abundant opportunity was afforded for his complete perusal of it, and many examples of inventions, similar in character, might be mentioned.

Some of the French scientific journals of the present day are endeavouring to show that the name of De Caus ought to be substituted for that of the Marquis of Worcester, as giving the first suggestions of the steam engine; but, on a careful and impartial examination of the claims, which each possesses, no one will, I think, be induced to grant either the slightest pretence to the right of having given a suggestion of any one principle in common with those of the steam engines of the present day.

I remain yours,
J. O. H.

HYDRAULIC WEIGHING MACHINES.

Sir,—In your Magazine of this day I find a communication signed " I. P. H.," seeking information respecting hydraulic weighing machines. I am the inventor of that made public by the firm of Hawkins and Co., and can satisfy " I. P. H." that my machine is not only the original, but the best of the two. On referring to my books, I find I commenced selling them in January, 1825,—just ten years before " I. P. H." sent his to the Society of Arts. As " I. P. H." very justly observes, friction is the difficulty in making them act—and what will he say, when I tell him that my machines have an upright rod or axis, fixed to the bottom of the outside cylinder passing up the centre of the floating cylinder, so inclosed in tubes, that it never gets wet, only touching two rings well oiled ? Consequently, the exterior and interior cylinders never come in contact, or cause friction ; besides, the slightest impulse makes the floating cylinder revolve on its axis, and by this means it is sure to indicate correctly. I have no hesitation in saying, that my one axis or rod working in oil, must be very superior to "I. P. H.'s" two rods working in water; and that being the only fault he found in my machine, I trust he is satisfied on that head. I must take the liberty of setting your correspondent right as to the principle of the machine. It has nothing to do with either the hydrostatic bellows or hydrostatic press, but merely the well-known rule, that a floating body displaces exactly its weight of water; and in the weighing machine, as the water cannot escape it runs up the sides; the pressure of the column of water thereby formed floating the cylinder.

I am, Sir, a subscriber to your Magazine from its commencement, and your obedient servant,

ROBERT WISS,

38, Charing Cross, 10th June, 1837.

THE PATENT STYLOXYNON

Sir,—From the great personal convenience I have myself experienced, in the use of the ingenious little instrument of which a sketch accompanies this communication, I feel assured that I shall be rendering an important service to all such of your numerous readers as are draughtsmen, by introducing it to their notice through the medium of your pages. The drawing, which is the full size, represents Messrs. Cooper and Eckstein's patent pencil pointer, which they have appropriately termed the *Styloxynon*; it consists of two sharp files neatly and firmly set together at right angles in a small block of rosewood.

The instrument thus formed, speedily produces a most delicate point to Black Lead, Slate, or Chalk Pencils, and will be found generally useful for renewing the points of various other articles that are in common use.

A point as fine as that of a needle, may be given to good H H or H H H pencils,

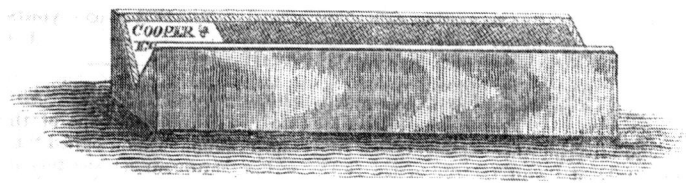

by means of the Styloxynon, and this instrument will be found an invaluable addition to the drawing table of Architectural and Mechanical draughtsmen in particular, as well as for artists generally. The mode of using it is merely to rub the pencil carefully backward and forward with the point slightly depressed in the angular groove, turning the pencil round at the same time between the finger and thumb, when a most exquisite point will be produced, which by occasional recourse to the Styloxynon may be maintained at pleasure.

When a new pencil is first used it should be roughly pointed with a knife before employing the Styloxynon.

I remain, Sir,

Yours respectfully,

WM. BADDELEY.

Wellington Street, Blackfriars Road
May 31st 1837.

EXPLOSIONS IN COAL MINES—THE LATE ACCIDENT AT THE WALLSEND COLLIERY.

Sir,—While every one, at the present day, is willing to place a high value on our abundant supply of coal fuel, few seem to consider that it is solely obtainable by bodily labour of the severest kind, *and constant risk of life*. That severe bodily labour, should be inseparable from the miner's avocations, may, from its nature reasonably be concluded, but that a constant risk of life must necessarily be added, is, I trust and hope, without any proper foundation. I am led to this belief, from some practical knowledge of coal mining operations, and a careful perusal of the volume published by the late Parliamentary Committee, on accidents in mines—entitled, " Report and Minutes of Evidence, &c." This work appears to me a most valuable document, taken altogether as a fair exposition of the present state of coal mining in Great Britain. The Report is not, perhaps, in itself of so decisive a character as the evidence warrants, yet, as it removes a great stumbling block in the way of a safer mode of working coal mines—the mistaken notion that the Davy Lamp is a sufficient protection against the ignition of an inflammable atmosphere, it ought to be received by the miner with great thankfulness, notwithstanding its many defects in other matters. I must, however, add, and I do so with regret, that this volume, though of two years' date, is, at present, little better than a sealed book to those whom its contents most affect, and that too, not from its *price alone*. That there should be in any quarter a disinclination to give publicity to that which might prevent the frequent destruction of their fellow creatures, under the most terrific forms of death, is much to be deplored and condemned. Happily, while a publication like yours exists—devoted to the just interests of the working classes, that cannot long be hid from them, by which they might be benefitted.

Having prefaced so far, I shall proceed to the point, to which I most particularly wish to draw the attention of your readers, whether practical or theoretical miners. It appears that the Committee, in despite of their powers, found it no easy task to get the return of the persons destroyed in coal mines, during the last twenty years, from the coroners of the coal districts. And after all, they state, that they have reason to believe such returns fall far short of the full number. However, notwithstanding this, they have been able to arrive at one important fact, namely, that taking eighteen years before, and eighteen years since the introduction of the Davy Lamp, the violent deaths in coal mines, during the latter period, have been nearly one-fourth more. Against this adverse position of the Lamp, are placed the circumstances of more coal being raised, and mines of a more fiery kind being in constant work. This,

however, is not, I contend, a proper way of meeting the point at issue, which is,—ought, or ought not, the Davy Lamp to be trusted? For, if it be, as long affirmed, safe in an inflammable atmosphere, what has the working now of mines, of a more fiery nature than were before worked, to do with the matter? It was given to work fiery mines ; and it is absurd to say that it is ever used in any other—its want of light makes it an article of necessity, not of choice, in this respect. That it must be considered as a faulty instrument, and, that even while its parts are perfect, it will not resist the passage of flame, cannot be denied; and that it will not, as fully proved, do so, ought to be fully known to the thousands who still are allowed, nay, forced, to look to its protection in their perilous labour. And, if taken as a partial protection, it is imperative that those, whose lives are placed in imminent danger, if its powers be exceeded, should know how far that protection extends—for there is great uncertainty in its protection, even in its most common uses. Thus, it should never be *heated beyond dull redness ;* never exposed to a current of explosive air. How human care can always guard against either contingency, remains to be found. It has never yet been able to do so. Or how have so many destructive accidents happened? The tale is no longer to be told, that they arise from the neglect of the victims. The late dreadful one at the Wallsend Colliery is a case in point. All the Lamps were found, after that accident, in a state as perfect as hands could make them. Let the coal owners, the coal viewers, and the coal workers reflect on this particular case. This, amongst many, is one that tells those, who profess a belief in the safety of the Davy Lamp, that they are upholding a most destructive fallacy—and those, who still trust in its protection, that they lean on a broken staff.

There are many other matters connected with this subject, which I would willingly notice, and will do so shortly, if you consider my present communication worthy of insertion. In the meantime, I wish to impress on the minds of all interested in this subject, and all the human race, that a better protection against explosion in coal mines than the Davy Lamp is required, and ought to be diligently sought,—but with this reservation, that, as coal mines are not opened by their owners for amusement or philanthropy, whatever would materially lessen the gains of this pursuit must be considered impracticable.

Your constant reader, &c.

CARBON.

May 30, 1837.

SELF-REGISTERING SURVEYING INSTRUMENT.

Sir,—I observe in your last Number a notice of a new French surveying instrument, which lays down on paper a section of the country, over which it is made to travel. Be it known, however, for the honour of England, that in 1826 a very ingenious instrument, designed for precisely the same purpose, was submitted to the Society of Arts by Mr. George Edwards, of Lynn, who was rewarded for it with their gold medal. The inventor called it a Klinograph. Its principle is this : paper being fixed on a drawing board, a small dotting wheel is made to travel along it, by means of a rotatory motion, communicated from one of the carriage wheels. The dotting wheel is also made to assume various angles with the horizontal line, according to the inclination of the road, by an ingenious train of mechanism connecting it with a heavy pendulum. By the combination of these two motions, a section of the ground is dotted on the paper. It will be observed, however, that the wheel depends for its forward motion, as well as for the correct delineation of slopes, upon the hold it takes of the paper. Is not this an objection ?

I remain, Sir,

Your obedient servant,

J. R.*

London, 29th May, 1837.

OCEAN STEAM NAVIGATION.

An article in the Nautical Magazine, for March, furnishes the following notice of preparations, which are making in reference to the establishment of regular steam packet comunications between this country and the United States. The boats, it will be seen, are to be of extraordinary dimensions, with machinery of corresponding power.

There are two vessels at present building to run direct from Bristol and London to New York. The great Western Ship Com-

* We shall be obliged to our correspondent, if he will favour us with a description of the machine referred to in the postscript to his letter.—ED. M. M.

pany's vessel is building at Bristol, and is of the following dimensions and power :—

Length between perpendiculars	216 feet.
Beam	35 —
Depth in hold	22 —

The engines are 400 horse power, having cylinders 73 inches diameter, and 7 feet stroke.

This noble vessel is expected to be ready in the course of the approaching summer, and will most probably make her first voyage in August next. She is intended to carry twenty-five days' fuel — a quantity sufficient to ensure the regular performance of the voyage in all weathers.

The British and American Steam Navigation Company, whose head quarters are in London, have contracted with Messrs. Curling, Young, and Co., of Limehouse, for a vessel of 1,795 tons, builders' measurement, and of the following dimensions and power:

Length between perpendiculars	235 feet.
Beam	40 —
Depth	27 —

to have engines of 460 horse power, having cylinders 76 inches in diameter, and 7 feet stroke. The engines are fitted to work either with or without Hall's condenser, at the option of the engineer. This magnificent vessel, the largest steam vessel ever yet propelled, will have capacity for twenty-five days' fuel, 800 tons of measurement goods, and 500 passengers.

We sincerely wish both the Bristol vessel and the London one all manner of success ; and when we reflect on the immense intercourse between this country, the United States, and Canada,—sixty thousand people having landed at New York from the 1st January to the 1st September, and twenty-seven in Quebec last year,—the increase that will naturally take place when the passage is shortened to fifteen days, instead of thirty-seven, the present average passage of the New York passage ships, we do not think that any, out of the numerous plans before the public, hold out stronger inducement to the capitalist than such undertakings.

It is difficult to estimate the national benefit that will accrue to both countries by the establishment of steam communication between them—the one with an overflowing population, the other with inexhaustible reserves of fertile lands,—the one the greatest manufacturing, the other the most extensive producing, country in the world,—both talking the same language, and allied by blood, religion, and feeling, with one another. Thus much, we may affirm, that it will greatly improve both countries, and render perpetual the peace. that now so happily exists between them.

MEMOIR ON THE CALCINATION OF COKE.
Abridged from Report, by Messrs. Perdonnet and
 Leon Coste, in the *Annales des Mines.*

Coke is obtained in England by two distinct processes; in the open air, and by means of ovens constructed for the purpose. The former is the method usually adopted, the latter being applied almost exclusively to the small coal or slack. In the vicinity of Dudley, in Staffordshire, all the coke is made in the open air; the process consists in forming a small conical chimney, with bricks placed in such a manner as to leave spaces between them; these openings are larger in the lower than in the upper courses; the usual height is about four feet six inches, surmounted by a cylinder of one foot. The coal is then disposed around the chimney, the largest lumps being placed first to form the base of a cone, after which more is thrown on the heap, until the top is above the level of the brick work; the whole surface is then covered with slack, with the exception of the lowest part of the heap, to about one foot high; the fire is then lighted in the chimney; at a certain period of the operation, the remaining part is also covered with slack, and when the carbonization is judged to be complete, the fire is extinguished, by throwing on a sufficient quantity of water and dispersing the materials of the heap.

The dimensions of the coke heaps vary considerably; they are most commonly fourteen or sixteen feet in diameter, and contain about twelve ton of coals. From the time of lighting the pile, the operation is completed in seven days, three for the calcination and four for the extinction and subsequent cooling of the mass.

It would appear that a method so simple as this would be invariable in the results; nevertheless, the contrary is the fact, much depending on the attention and judgment of the burner or superintendant. A ton of coal usually yields twelve cwt. of coke, or sixty per cent., sometimes ten cwt. or fifty per cent. from the same materials. In South Wales, both methods are practised; but the coke is not calcined with so much attention as in Staffordshire; the process differs in the heap being made in the form of a long bank four to six feet in breadth, and about three feet high, the large coals in the middle, and the fire being lighted either at one end or at several parts of the heap. At Pontypool and Abergaveny, the coke is calcined in the open air; the coal in some parts of this district bears a resemblance to charcoal; in converting it into coke, great care is taken to preserve this entire; the operation is completed in five days. In the neighbourhood of Merthyr Tidvill, the process is conducted in the open air, and al-

though very little care seems to be given to its progress, yet a considerable quantity of coke is produced, the coke being generally dry and giving but little smoke. At Plymouth works, six tons of coal yield five tons of coke; at Dowlay, 720 lbs. of coal yield from 450 to 500 lbs. of coke; at Pen-y-Darran, the operation lasts only three days, the increase in bulk being also very considerable, three tons of coals producing twelve barrows of coke, each containing seventeen cubic feet, or above one fourth part more than previous to calcination.

At Neath Abbey, the carbonization is more rapid than in any other place, it being finished in nine hours, producing rather less than sixty per cent. of coke. In Scotland, calcination in the open is generally adopted; formerly, the heaps were burned without much attention being paid to their progress; but the Staffordshire mode has been used latterly with great advantage, the heaps, consisting of eighteen tons of coal, well covered with slack, being kept burning three or four days, and four or five days more being allowed for the cooling of the mass; the loss in weight is about fifty per cent.; the old method occupied only five days, but the loss amounted to from sixty to sixty-six per cent. The coke is of very unequal quality, some parts being very heavy, and others light and porous. In Yorkshire, the coal is arranged in long banks, six feet wide by two and a half high, with square vertical chimnies eight or nine inches in diameter, formed with large coals, at about the distance of six feet from each other throughout the length; the loss is about fifty per cent. in weight.

Calcination in ovens is considered to produce a heavier coke than the open calcination; the process varies but little, being in all cases performed in ovens of a circular or oval form, with a low arch surmounted with a small chimney; the furnace has two doors or openings opposite to each other, sliding in a groove and raised by a lever; they are usually of cast-iron, the dimension of the furnace about twelve feet by six; height of the arch in the centre, five feet, at the door, twenty-one inches; the chimney rises three feet externally, and about nine inches in diameter. At Neath Abbey, the furnaces are smaller; the chimney is eighteen inches externally, and only one door; but in this case, a hole is made in the opposite side to facilitate the clearing out of the coke. From the small coal carbonized in this manner, the produce is about sixty per cent., while the same quantity of coal in the open air yields but fifty per cent., the coke from the furnace being so much more dense. At Swansea, by the same process, the produce is about fifty-four per cent.

In the vicinity of Glasgow, a circular oven with one door is in use; the diameter is nine feet, height of the arch, six feet. The coke is drawn out every twenty-four hours; the ordinary charge, one ton and a half of coal, rising about two and a half feet in the oven; the loss is from fifty to sixty per cent. On Saturdays, the charge is increased to two tons, and is not withdrawn until the Monday. At the Lymington works, near Newcastle-upon-Tyne, all the coke is made in ovens; the usual charge is one chaldron of about two and a half tons; the operation lasts forty-eight hours, and the average loss is thirty-nine per cent. The coke is screened to the diameter of about one inch, for smelting in the high furnace, the smaller portion being employed in roasting the ores. At Bradford, in Yorkshire, the method is similar to Newcastle; but the furnaces are smaller, the charge being only about one ton; the loss is about forty per cent. It is difficult to decide to which process a preference ought to be given; the loss is less in the ovens, but they require more space, more attendants, and more expense, while the open carbonization is considered to yield coke better adapted for smelting in the high furnace.

ABSTRACT OF THE EVIDENCE AT THE INQUEST RELATING TO THE EXPLOSION OF THE BOILER OF THE "UNION" STEAM PACKET AT HULL.

Israel Myers was on board about twenty minutes when he heard a crackling noise, like the sound of a few sticks breaking. Did not recollect seeing anything particular until he turned himself round and was surprised to perceive the vessel sinking. Heard a noise like the escape of steam, through what might be the safety-valve,—heard a heavy weight drop off, and saw somebody do something at the valve,—thinks it was the captain who went to the valve; this was about five minutes before the explosion.

William Lewis, of Wellington-street, who was lying ill in bed, from the wounds received at the explosion — deposed to the following effect:—I went on board the "Union" into the engine-house. I observed the fire doors, four in number, to be open. I tried the "gage-taps," which are placed in the boiler to ascertain the height of the water. The first emitted nothing but pure steam. There was no peculiar colour or smell about that steam. The second let out water. When I had turned it, I could not get it stopped; after one effort I desisted, being afraid of scalding myself. The engineer, Joseph Gamble, came down immediately after me. I said to him, "Joe, what's the matter with this

tap?" He said, "It's rather slack," and stopped it immediately. I am certain it was water which came out of the second tap, it flowed so strong—I dare say, for a minute and a half. Boilers are considered safe when there is water in the lowest tap and steam in the two top ones; the use of these taps is to keep the water between the top tap and the bottom one. There was no index to the "Union's" boiler that I am aware of. I do not know whether the vessel was upon an even keel or not; she appeared to me to be so when I went on board. I could not be certain whether the boiler rested perpendicularly in the vessel or not. The vessel was what is called "tender," and about a fortnight ago, I ordered some boards to be placed between the funnels and the boiler to preserve the boiler in its proper place. To prevent the water passing from one side of the boiler to the other, in case of the vessel rolling, a board was placed across the middle of the boiler. [These facts were elicited to ascertain whether the trial of the gage taps would give a true indication of the height of the water. It appeared they would perfectly do so.] When the engineer had stopped the tap, I was looking round to see how the fires burned. The boy was raking a fire; the engineer said to him, "Let that fire alone," and ran up stairs. I was then going towards the ladder, and was about two feet from the boiler, when I received a blow, which drove me towards the ladder and stunned me. I remember no more until I found myself upon deck in the midst of other sufferers. I did not notice the safety valve before the accident. I do not know the weight usually placed upon it. I did not hear any noise like the breaking of a stay in a boiler, or the falling of anything on the deck. I do not know what is the 'calculated weight' of the safety valve of the vessel. The explosion took place within two minutes of my trying the gage tap. From the trial of the taps, I should consider the boiler quite safe.

James Vernon, of Dock-street, steam-engine manufacturer, deposed—I have seen the boiler of the "Union" in that vessel; before the explosion I thought it a very secure boiler; I have seen a portion of it since its explosion; there was nothing in its appearance to induce me to think it to have been imperfect for some time. I am positive no working steam pressure could have caused the explosion; the boiler was capable of bearing a pressure of 10lbs. per square inch with perfect safety; I never knew what was the working pressure of that engine; I should not think a boiler like that capable of being burst by steam; I have seen boilers after they have been burst by steam; they are generally rent, as though this table were rent, and the moment the steam has escaped, the power is gone. I never saw pieces detached ; they are always rent in the weakest part; I do not consider the "Union's" boiler has been rent in the weakest part; I should hesitate in saying what has caused this explosion—it depends upon a theory not well understood; there has been some extraordinary power employed in this explosion ; there would be a better chance of ascertaining what was the cause of the explosion, if the parts of the boiler were minutely examined by scientific men in company. He was of opinion that atmospheric air could not descend through the safety-valve, when open, if the interior of the boiler were full of gas, because there would be a greater pressure outwards than inwards ; but he thought the gas might ignite itself.

John Barrett, boiler-maker—I know the boiler of the "Union ;" it was a very good strong boiler, made of good materials, and good workmanship, and quite fit for all ordinary purposes of a marine boiler—1 mean as to strength and durability ; I have seen it since it exploded ; I entertain the same opinion of it as before ; not a single rivet has given way ; it is the solid material which has given way—the material is of good quality. I have seen steam boilers which have been burst by steam, and I have seen steam boilers burst by what I consider other causes. The explosion of steam caused a rent five inches long by a quarter of an inch wide, and no more. I suppose the explosion in question was occasioned by two small a supply of water being in the boiler, which being exhausted, the tops of the flues became bare, and the fire continuing to act upon them they became red hot; and then the steam is decomposed, and the quantity of steam generated keeps decreasing and the act of decomposition increasing ; this process would go on till the whole mass becomes gas ; the top of the flues continuing hot, the gas would become more and more rarified till ignition took place. I cannot determine whether it would ignite without coming in contact with atmospheric air ; I think it would. A boiler burst by this means always exhibits marks of extreme violence, and of powers incalculable, the tops of such boilers being rent in separable pieces. I am decidedly of opinion that the explosion of the "Union" boiler has arisen from the causes I have explained, arising from their being too little water in the boiler. [The safety-valve was produced, and identified by Mr. Overton (the maker). It did not appear to have been altered since he made it.]

Thomas John Pearsall, late professor of chemistry in the medical school, had a general knowledge of steam engines and boilers, and their properties. Had examined the portions of the "Union's" boiler, which

were lying on the quay shortly after the explosion, and was of opinion that the bursting of that boiler was entirely owing to steam ; he was of opinion that hydrogen gas could not be disengaged from the oxygen of water inside a boiler, and more particularly a marine boiler, in sufficient quantity to cause an explosion. The expansive power of steam alone, he conceived to be sufficient to produce all the effects which he ever knew or heard of being produced by explosions of boilers. If the explosion in question were not caused by a deficiency of water in the boiler he could not account for it, and would say it was a fact demanding the consideration of the very highest intellect. From all he had heard of the explosion of low pressure boilers from whatever cause—and he spoke it after consideration—he had come to the firm conviction that they all arose either from carelessness, ignorance, or wilfulness on the part of the makers of the boilers, or those who had to attend them.

John Malam had been quite familiar with steam engines from his childhood. He attributed the explosion to hydrogen gas, disengaged from the water in the boiler by a deficiency of that element and the overheating of the flues. The presence of atmospheric air in the boiler, which was necessary to effect combustion and explosion, he accounted for by supposing it to have entered with the water, or to have been present before the introduction of the water into the boiler, and for the expulsion of which an air-pump was necessary—he knew not whether one had been used on this occasion. Steam, he believed, never could have caused such an explosion as this—the power of gas was more than a thousand times that of steam.

Richard Holme also attributed the explosion to gas. The gage taps were very fallacious tests of the height of water in a boiler, and more so in marine than land boilers, because when there was a great quantity of steam in the boiler, on the opening of one of these taps the steam would rush to it, carrying with it a great body of water, and giving a discharge at the tap which would indicate the presence of much water inside, when, in fact, it was very low, owing to the water being saturated with saline and other matter. He preferred glass gages, which are in much use—they are on board all the London and Scotch packets from this port, the *Railway* and *Hirondelle* also possess them, but he preferred, above every other method yet known, floats, of sufficient expansion, placed inside the boiler, with indexes in one or both cabins, and a plate with an inscription calling the attention of passengers to them, so that any person might observe the deficiency when it arose and give notice to the captain. The use of floats had long been known, but their connexion with a dial in the cabin was a new idea, perfectly practicable, and which had occurred to him in consequence of the present explosion. It might have occurred to other persons, but he knew not that it had. He had several times been down in the engine-house of the "Union" along with Gamble, the engineer, when she was on the Grimsby station a few weeks ago, and he always saw him remarkably attentive to his business, and formed such an opinion of his character that he would most readily trust him.

Joseph Iredale, fire mender of the "Union." The boiler was filled to a proper height, on the morning of the explosion; he helped to fill it, and tried both the taps; they both ran; he knew nothing of the safety-valve.

William Mail—Made the four planks fixed up in the boiler—they are not burned in any part; if the flue had been red-hot, the end which was against the chimney would have been charred. The board was fixed up to prevent the water from running too fast from side to side; was not fixed in water-tight.

Thomas Longman fitted up these boards between seven and eight weeks ago. Confirmed the evidence of last witness as to their not being charred.

William Watson was formerly engineer of the "Union." The required an unusual quantity of water to get up steam for a vessel of her size; there were two gage taps on each side when he left the vessel. Gamble put two more on each side, about 3 inches above the top of the others. Would have considered the boiler safe if water had issued from the tap which was at the top in his time, that is, from the middle tap at the time of the explosion. Never saw a "sign of leak" in the boiler, which was a good one. Had there been 7 inches of water above the flues, and the pressure not greater than 6 or 7 lbs. per square inch, does not think the explosion could have occurred. The method of making safety-valves used by witness, is allowing 1 circular inch for every inch in the diameter of the cylinder. An engine of 15 horse power would require 14 or 12 circular inches in the safety-valve. If there had been no safety-valve, but an open space equal to the diameter of the safety-valve, does not think that circumstance could have prevented the explosion.

James Overton re-examined. The safety-valve of the "Union" was 4 inches diameter, giving 12¼ inches area; in the steam exhaustion pipes 1 inch area is allowed for every horse power; the safety-valve is a discretionary-matter, calculated to relieve the overstraining of the boiler; the engines could

not work five minutes with it open. Had examined the flues and found some appearance of their having been red-hot; the wood might not have been burned from being surrounded with water. Never saw nor heard of a safety-valve made the size of the steam pipe; considered the safety-valve of the "Union" quite large enough. There was but one safety-valve to her boiler.

Joseph Vernon had examined the bottom of the boiler, and saw no signs of its having been heated to redness.

Thomas Thompson, engineer, took to pieces the safety-valve of the "Union" after the explosion. Found the spindle below the lid bent, and also the spindle above the lid, which goes through the weight and stuffing-box, and to which the lever is attached. Both injuries might have been done by, or since the explosion. There was a considerable quantity of packing in the stuffing-box, so hard as to be difficult to remove, this would cause additional friction in the spindle, which would act as an additional weight and prevent the escape of steam.

James Overton said the safety-valve was made to work without stuffing.

John Williamson, a waterman, had heard a noise similar to a trunk falling. Captain Waterland, on being sent for came on board, spoke to the engineer, and went to the safety-valve, and lifted it up when steam escaped.

T. J. Pearsall, was of opinion that the explosion could not have taken place if the boiler had been sufficiently supplied with water, unless the safety-valve had been fastened down or obstructed. Considered the immediate cause of the explosion to have been the expansive power of steam; was most decidedly of opinion that it did not arise from gas, because water is not decomposed unless the surface of the iron be in a metallic state, as in a new boiler. The gas produced from the water of the Humber, or the ocean would not be inflammable of itself, nor without the presence of oxygen. Did not know that water could be resolved under any circumstance into its two elements by heat alone. Would say, that if hydrogen were in the boiler, and oxygen to gain access, the hydrogen would escape by the same entrance; might escape without being perceived. Did not think that there would be sufficient oxygen present in the water to cause an explosion by mixing with the hydrogen. Had the explosion been caused by gas there must have been a vivid flash accompanying it.

W. A. Barrett thought the other two flues might have been red-hot, and not the centre one on which the board was placed, as the heat must traverse the whole six before reaching that.

Dr. Charles Wallich considered greatly

condensed steam to have been the cause of the explosion; did not think sufficient gas could have been formed in the boiler to cause it. If the flues had been red-hot, and water suddenly dashed over them, a volume of steam would have been raised sufficient to cause explosion, if the safety-valve had been closed or too small. The noise previous to the explosion might be accounted for by the escape of steam through the waste-pipe under the surface of the water. The opening of the safety-valve might cause such an ebullition of water, as would make it rise to the gage-tap.

J. Vernon attributed the explosion to the generation of steam faster than it could escape by the safety-valve. Did not think it arose from want of water in the boiler; nor that the flues had been red-hot. Considered if there was water between the flues, and the flues much heated, and part of the boiler red-hot, it would be dangerous to open the safety-valve, as it would cause the water to rise over the heated parts; in his opinion this had caused the bursting.

John Wakefield, engineer, was of opinion that the explosion had arisen from the safety-valve being too small; instead of an area of 16 inches, it should have been about 60. Never knew of an explosion from a red-hot boiler.

T. Rowbottom, practical engineer, was of opinion that the explosion had arisen from the safety-valve not working freely, or from want of sufficient water in the boiler; both causes might have been combined. Packing would not impede the action of the spindle if it were kept in good order, if new put in, and not too much screwed down. If the boiler had been weak, it would not have burst with so much violence. If the safety-valve had been free, and emitting steam, the explosion could not have taken place. If the water were low in the boiler, the pressure of the steam would increase more rapidly. Considered gage-taps very fallacious; preferred floats. When there has been too little water in the boiler, had heard a loud crackling noise, and sometimes one resembling a weight falling. Did not think a boiler could burst with even a very small safety-valve; should think a 4 inch valve safe for the size of a boiler like that of the "Union."

Joseph Ireland, fireman of the "Union," had tried the water gage taps five or ten minutes before the explosion, and never came out. The stuffing was put in on the Monday previous to the accident; the valve seemed to work as well after that as before; only put one square weight on the safety-valve; they put on two, when the vessel was going.

The Jury, after an absence of forty-five minutes, returned a verdict of *manslaughter against the engineer, Joseph Gamble;* accompanying the verdict with an expression of their feeling as to the necessity of legislative interference to determine the best mode of preventing the recurrence of such frightful catastrophes.

NOTES AND NOTICES.

A New Fire Proof Dress.—A Signor Sebastiano Botturi, from Brescia, in Italy, on Thursday exhibited a fire-proof dress, in which he enveloped himself, and passed through a small cottage or shed, erected for the occasion, in the grounds of Cremorne-house, and set on fire for the purpose of proving the incombustibility of his invention. The shed was constructed of thin wood and spars, and crammed with straw and dry chips. The experiment was advertised to take place at half-past three, but it was half-past five before the shed could be prevailed upon to blaze with sufficient fury for the proof of his salamander-like qualifications. The Signor, when clothed in his fire-proof habiliments, bore some resemblance to a Polar bear on his hind legs; his head was covered with a curious kind of gear, something like a conical cap; it had two glass eyes, or rather windows, which glared without speculation on the company. There was also a snout or chimney for the purpose of respiration. This last apparatus made the whole a most grotesque exhibition. The dress was plastered with a sort of compound resembling a mixture of grease and mortar; but, as this is the secret of the contrivance, it is impossible to describe what it really was. As soon as the flames had sufficiently seized on the shed, the Signor boldly entered at one end, and made his exit at another, repeating this feat several times without injury. It cannot be said that the experiment was sufficient to prove either that the dress can be rendered of general utility, or that it would actually enable its wearer to resist the heat and fire of a house in a state of conflagration. The shed was much too small, and the stay of the Signor within it much too short, to prove its perfect efficacy. As it was, it was rather a matter of joke than anything else, and was so absurdly arranged, that it proved nothing at all.—*Times.*

The Supplement to Volume xxvi. containing Title, Table of Contents, and Index, with a Portrait of his late Majesty, William IV., executed by Bates' Patent Medallic Engraving Machine, will be published on the 1st of July next. Also, Volume xxvi., price 8s. 6d.

☞ *British and Foreign Patents taken out with economy and despatch; Specifications, Disclaimers, and Amendments, prepared or revised; Caveats entered; and generally every Branch of Patent Business promptly transacted.*

A complete list of Patents from the earliest period (15 Car. II. 1675,) to the present time may be examined. Fee 2s. 6d.; Clients, gratis.

LONDON: Printed and Published for the Proprietor, by W. A. Robertson, at the Mechanics' Magazine Office, No. 6, Peterborough-court, between 135 and 136, Fleet-street.—Sold by G. W. M. Reynolds, Proprietor of the French, English, and American Library, 55, Rue Neuve, Saint Augustin, Paris.

The Chesselden Medal.

Royal Academy Medal.

Mechanics' Magazine,
MUSEUM, REGISTER, JOURNAL, AND GAZETTE.

No. 725.   SATURDAY, JULY 1, 1837.   Price 3d.

LORD WILLOUGHBY'S MACHINE FOR PRESSING PEAT.

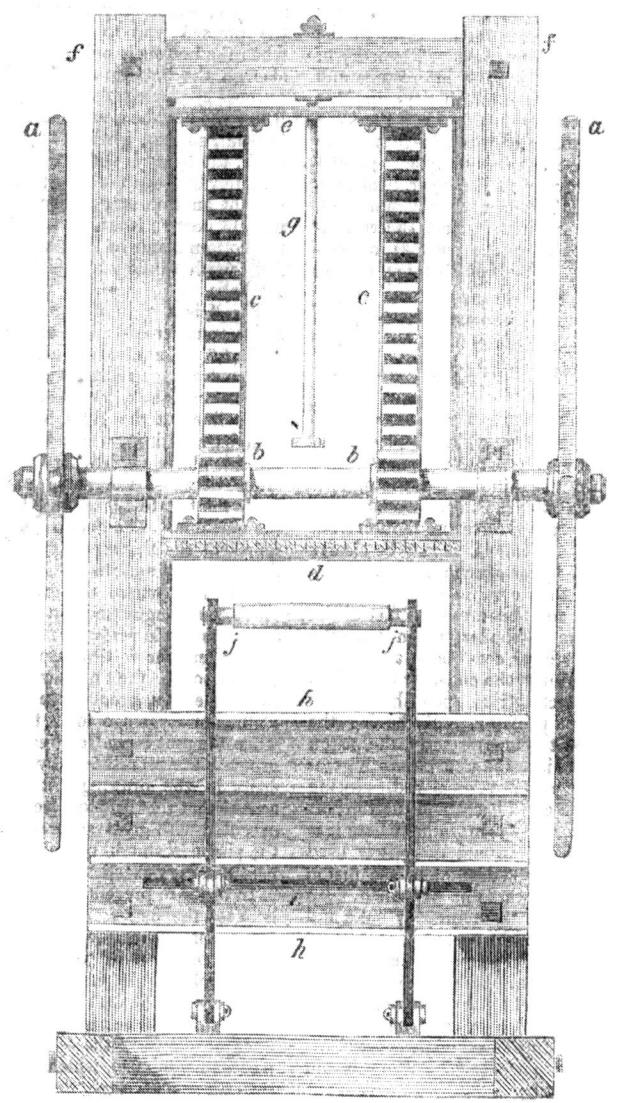

Fig. 1.

DESCRIPTION OF AN IMPROVED MA-
CHINE FOR PRESSING PEAT MOSS
FOR FUEL, — INVENTED BY THE
RIGHT HON. LORD WILLOUGHBY
D' ERESBY.

Sir,—I have the honour of enclosing
you a drawing and description of a machine, constructed by my directions, for
the purpose of compressing peat, in the
hope that you may consider it worthy of
being noticed in your interesting and
useful Magazine. I find that the machine
answers perfectly on about half the sorts
of peat usually consumed—that is to
say, on those of a fibrous quality; and I
am still carrying on the experiment on a
large scale. The peat, when compressed,
has been used with perfect success, instead of coal, for the purpose of calcining lime, for the smith's forge, as well
as for ordinary fuel.

I have the honour to remain,
Sir, your faithful and obedient servant,
WILLOUGHBY D' ERESBY.

London, June 20, 1837.

Fig. 1 (see front page) represents a front
view of the machine; a a are two levers, on
the axes of which are two pinions, b b, and
c c are two racks, into which the pinions
work. d, is a self-cleansing piston for pressing the peat; it receives its motion from
the racks and pinions, as may be clearly
understood by the drawing. e is a cross
bar, to which the racks c c, are secured
at the top, and they are made fast to the
piston d in a similar manner at the
bottom. Both the cross bar e, and piston
d, are grooved in the ends, for the reception of projecting ribs upon the sides of
the upright posts f f. By having the
grooves to fit the ribs exactly, the piston
is conducted into the peat-box with great
precision. g is a vertical rod, passing
through the cross bar e, and the top part
of the frame of the machine, where it is
secured by a screw and nut; it is used
for regulating the descent of the piston
d, as will afterwards be explained. h h
is a cast iron plate, secured by bolts and
nuts to the upright posts f f, and there
is another, in every respect the same, on
the opposite side. These two plates, together with the upright posts f f, form
the peat-box; i represents its bottom,
and j j a double lever, of the second order, for the purpose of pulling it out
when required.

Fig. 2 is a side view of the machine,
having the same letters to denote similar
parts. In this view of the machine, the
action of the lever j, to move the sliding
bottom i, is perfectly clear. It will be
seen in the drawing that the bottom i
projects beyond the back plate h, to some
distance; in this projection there is an
aperture, sufficiently large to admit of
the pressed peat to pass through it,
when the bottom is pulled out. There is
also on the bottom a stop at i, for the
purpose of placing the aperture directly
below the peat-box, and there is another
in front, so that, when the machine is at
work, the lever j, slides the bottom alternately between the two stops. k k represent an iron stay for supporting the
upright post f; it is shown broken off at
the bottom frame of the machine, as the
full length would exceed the limits of
the page.

Fig. 3 is a plan of the peat-box, h h,
and a transverse section of the upright
posts f f. The interior dark shaded part
on the drawing, represents the capacity
of the peat-box, and the subdivided
white lines at the sides, represent vertical bars of iron, which are riveted to
the side plates h h, leaving a very narrow
space between the bars, which reach
from the top to the sliding bottom i of
the machine. The dotted parallel lines
represent the thickness of the metal, of
the plates h h, and the additional breadth
which is shown in the drawing, represents the flanges thereon. The plates
are to be made perfectly flat on the surface, where the vertical bars are riveted
to; opposite the narrow spaces between the bars, grooves are cut into the
plates, for a passage to let the water off,
when the peat is under pressure. These
grooves are represented by dark shaded
spots in the drawing; it is quite essential that this part of the machine be
executed with great accuracy, and, that
the piston d should fit and slide into the
peat-box very exactly.

In order to prevent the fine interstices
between the bars from clogging up with
small fibres from the peat, the piston d
is so contrived as to obviate all difficulties of this kind. It will be seen in
the drawing, Fig. 1, that it is formed of
two plates, between which short parallel
lines are drawn, these lines represent
pieces of thin steel, which work into the
interstices each time the piston d des-

cends and rises out of the peat-box. On the ends of the pieces alluded to, for keeping the interstices clean, there are pieces of iron brazed securely, and they

Fig. 2.

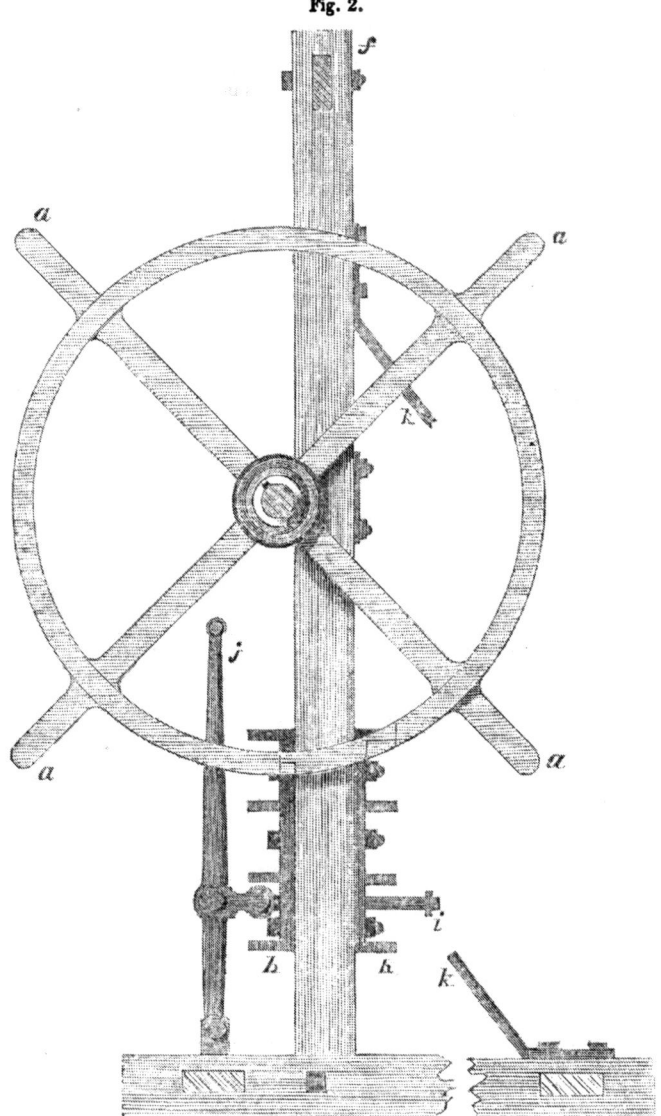

are formed to suit the grooves in the plates *h h*. The grooves are therefore kept clean also.

When the machine is to be used, the peat which is to be compressed, should be first cut into a shape as nearly as poseible to the form of the peat-box; and when it is placed therein, the piston d is

made to descend by the power of two men upon the levers a a, until it be suf-

Fig. 3.

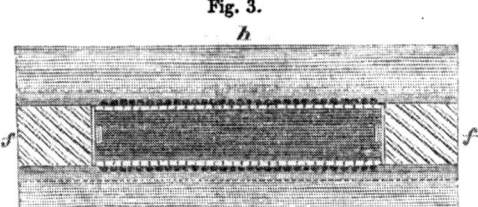

ficiently compressed. After which, the sliding bottom i is withdrawn; and the piston d made to descend until the cross bar e, comes in contact with the head of the vertical rod g; at which time, the

compressed peat will be entirely forced out. It is then to be carried away to be dried. The piston d may then again be raised, and the sliding bottom replaced, and the former operation repeated.

SERGEANT TALFOURD'S COPYRIGHT BILL.*

The observations on Sergeant Talfourd's proposed new Copyright Act, which appeared in our 723d Number, were founded on the report of his speech in the newspapers. An authorised version of that speech has now been published, which shows that the account in the newspapers was remarkably correct. We should therefore have been under no necessity of offering any further remarks on the subject, but that in the Preface prefixed to this "official" publication, we find a quantity of new matter, quite as important as any in the remainder of the pamphlet. The Sergeant informs us that these particulars were "omitted in the speech, from a desire not to intrude too long on the patience of the House of Commons"; but we must own, that this hardly appears to us a sufficient reason, for passing over in total silence some of the most essential points in the whole bill. Had he really been anxious to spare the patience of his colleagues, there are numerous flights of eloquence in his oration—such as the eulogium on Coleridge, and that on Wordsworth,—which we are confident no one would have missed.

The first of these additional points, is as follows,:—"The extension of the term of property, which is the chief object of the bill, can only operate on subsisting copyrights; as all works which according to the prevailing construction of the law belong to the public, are beyond the power of the legislature to reclaim for their action. But it is proposed that *wherever copyright still subsists*, whether by reason of the continuance of the author's life, or, though he is dead, by reason of the subsisting term of twenty-eight years, in part unexpired, *the extension should operate*". It is proposed, in other words, that this act should have a retrospective effect, to the disadvantage of the public, whose duties Mr. Sergeant Talfourd is very anxious to enforce, but of whose rights he appears to have no notion. What adequate motive can be assigned for breaking through the general rules of enlightened legislation in this instance, it is not easy to conceive? The proposal for extending the time of copyright in future is supported by the argument, that as authors will derive an additional reward, they will be animated to additional exertion, but the works it is thus proposed to protect have already been completed; if the argument have any force at all, they have been "finished off" in the inferior style, which the inferior degree of protection has led to; and as they belong to the old system altogether, it is

---

* A Speech delivered by Thomas Noon Talfourd, Serjeant at Law, in the House of Commons, on Tuesday, 18th May, 1837, on moving for leave to bring in a Bill to consolidate the law relating to Copyright, and to extend the Term of its duration. London. Edward Moxon, Dover-street, 1837.

only that, to which they can properly be subjected. The Preface continues:—
" When such subsisting copyright has been assigned, it is not proposed to give the benefit of the extension to the assignee, who is only entitled in justice to that for which he contracted and paid, but to the representatives of the author, as portion of his personal estate. In order however to secure to the publisher the full benefit of his contract, it is proposed that he should have the right of disposing of any copies of the work which he may have in hand, at the time when his right shall cease, and that of the representatives of the author shall take effect in possession". It is easy to see that this provision will lead to some curious manœuvring on the part of the publishers. It was formerly their policy to have as few copies as possible of a work on hand at the time when a copyright expired, from a dread of the formidable competition, which instantly rushed into the market; it will now be as obviously their interest to print a large edition immediately before the property goes out of their hands.

" In proposing," it is continued, " to declare the law that foreigners or their assignees should have the benefit of copyright in this country, on registering their books at Stationers' Hall, in the form prescribed, it is not intended to give the Act an operation retrospective, so as to affect works, which, having been published abroad, have been already reprinted here, and are now in the English market, but to apply it only to works hereafter to be published, and which shall be registered within a stated period after their publication abroad. Thus, if a foreign author shall so long neglect to claim his rights here as to give cause for belief that he does not propose to avail himself of its benefits, he shall not be entitled to complain of any one, who may here avail himself of his labours." This condition is much the same as that of the proposed new American copyright Act, with the important exception, that the foreign author will there be compelled to publish an American edition to establish his right. In neither law do we find any thing to determine what is to be done, with respect to translations. If they be left as free and fetterless as before, while the price of the original is artificially kept up, the new regulation

is likely to be of advantage to English literature, by inducing the translation of a greater number of works.

We now come to the most singular provision of all :—" As one object of this Act is to secure to the descendants of authors, who may produce works of permanent attraction, the benefit of their works beyond the subsisting term, it seems desirable to provide against the assignment of that remote contingency, at a period when the probability of its arising may be wholly incapable of estimate, and when the pressure of necessity may induce them to make assignments for small sums. It will therefore be proposed to provide, that no assignment, *by an author, of copyright, shall be valid for a greater term than that, which he now enjoys—that of twenty-eight years, or for his life*." This is plain enough, at all events; we would, however, suggest one alteration in the wording. Instead of, " as *one* object of this Act," it should run, " as *the* object of this Act is to secure to the *descendants* of authors the benefit of their works." Till we came to this passage, we thought that Sergeant Talfourd had lost sight of the interest of the public in his anxiety for that of authors; but here it is evident that he can regard the sufferings of authors without any extravagant sympathy; it is only their descendants who excite his commiseration; had it been Milton himself, who was reduced to take a benefit at the theatre, he would not have been shocked;—it is the circumstance that his great grand-daughter came to want, which arouses his sympathy. Napoleon used to talk of the advantages he should have enjoyed if he had been his own grand-son, and a similar complaint will be by no means uncommon in the mouths of authors, if this bill should ever become law. It is true,'that some provision was called for, to prevent the irrevocable alienation of a copyright, before either the author or publisher could be well apprised of its value; a suggestion to that effect was thrown out in our previous remarks; but this is far from saying that any provision at all like the present was wanted. By enacting that no author should have the power of disposing of the additional term of his copyright till five years after the publication of his work, all the protection, which is wanted, would be effectually given; by enacting that an author shall, under no circumstances, be entitled to control his own property, in the same manner that others control it, he is at once injured and insulted,—he is treated as a madman or an idiot. How requisite it may be for him to possess this control, it needs but a scanty examination into the records of genius to shew; nay, at the very moment when it is proposed to deprive him of the power of relieving his necessities, it is assigned as a cause for so doing that the pressure of necessity "may be great." It cannot, however, be needful to waste more words in exposing the absurdity of this proposal; the other portions of the bill may very possibly be made the law of the land, but this is assuredly too monstrous to pass.

The next provision, which is mentioned, seems to us the best in the whole bill; but Sergeant Talfourd appears to bring it forward most unwillingly. "It has been sometimes suggested," he remarks, "as an objection to the existence of property in copyright, that an author or his family may perversely withhold their works from the public. This objection seems somewhat fantastical; but it is proposed to disarm such perverseness of feeling in the authors or their descendants, by a proviso, that in case no edition of a work shall appear for a specified time, any one shall be, after notice of such intention left with the last publisher, or at the last place of its publication, and advertized in the London Gazette, be at liberty" (it is thus printed in the original) "to treat the copyright as abandoned, and publish it for his own benefit." Why the objection should be styled fantastical and chimerical, we do not know; the slightest acquaintance with literary history is sufficient to shew, that it is just the reverse. Did not Coleridge suppress several of his earlier poems? Has not Moore done all in his power to prevent the republication of some of his? Did not Byron buy up and destroy the copies of his "English Bards and Scotch Reviewers"? Was not the Lord Chancellor applied to, on the part of the Poet Laureate, for an injunction against his own "Wat Tyler"? Nay, "last *and* least," did not a certain learned Sergeant very recently exhibit this strange "perverseness of feeling," by coquetting in a very "fantastical" manner with the pub-

lic, respecting the publication of a certain tragedy? This instance, at least, ought to be familiar to Mr. Sergeant Talfourd.

This is the last of the new provisions mentioned in the preface, and the only one in the whole bill, that seems intended for the benefit of the public. We were in hopes of finding at least one other,—to provide for some method of "taxing" the price of new works, as used formerly to be done in foreign countries, when a copyright was granted. A limit is proposed to be fixed to the profits of railway companies; why are authors and publishers to be allowed to demand what sums they please? When they find they have a giant's strength, they are too apt to use it like a giant. There is such a thing, not only in theory, but in practice, as laying too heavy a tax on an author's admirers. In the height of Walter Scott's popularity, there was no other way of obtaining an early copy of a new poem, than by purchasing it in the inconvenient form of a ponderous quarto; it generally a few months afterwards, appeared in an octavo shape; but in one instance, Sir Walter, finding it desirable to force the sale of an unsaleable periodical, with which he was connected, "the Edinburgh Annual Register," inserted one of his poems in one of the yearly volumes, and drove all such of his adversaries as had not bought the quarto to buy a cartload of old news, along with the Vision of Don Roderick. Is all this justified by the comprehensive maxim, that a man may do what he likes with his own? Since the copyright of Sir Walter's poems has drawn near the term of extinction, his publishers have thought fit to issue them in editions, not only so cheap, that they suit the pocket, but so small, that they may be put into it. His novels are copyright still, and the consequence is, that they are still not only dear, but ill got up. What a torrent of Elzevir editions of Waverly there would be, if it were now public property. At present, there is not one edition of it in one volume, the most usual and convenient number for a standard novel,—not one edition in Elzevir, the most usual and convenient size. And this is to remain so for the next sixty years!

Sergeant Talfourd might provide a remedy for these evils in the literary tribunal, which, though he makes no proposal for it in the present bill, he is anxious to see established for the decision of literary cases (and his arguments for which, by the bye, would answer equally well in regard to every other profession). It would provide itself, if a project were adopted for a copyright law, of which we shall now proceed to state the outlines, but without the forlornest hope of ever seeing it tried.

Let an author be empowered to sell the copyright of his work to a particular publisher, for the space of five years only; a term, at the end of which, nine-tenths of the works now published are completely forgotten. Let it then become public property, in the same way that a play, on being published, becomes public property since Mr. Bulwer's act. As a manager now has the right to act any play he chooses, on paying a certain sum to the author, for each night of representation, so let any printer have the right to print any work on paying a certain sum to the author, for each copy he issues. The main, perhaps the only, objection to the plan, would be the necessity of establishing some excise regulations with regard to printing offices, for the prevention of fraud.

The great recommendation, of course, would be, that of every work of reputation we should have cheap and elegant editions ; that such of them as required comment and illustration (and now, when the copyrights expire, it is speedily found that very few of them do not) would receive it at an earlier period, and that the works of living authors would be much more extensively diffused than they are, while their interests would, it is hoped, be advanced in an equal proportion to their fame.

After all, however, we are afraid that no copyright Act, however favourable to authors, will exercise a perceptible beneficial influence on literature. Our own at present is frivolous, and it is assigned as a cause that our authors are ill protected. If this be really the cause, in what sort of a state ought that of Germany to be ? It is, however, in the very country where piracy is most prevalent, that solid literature is most flourishing. Unhappily, no Act of Parliament can reform the taste of the public.

STEAM BOILER EXPLOSIONS.

Sir,—The appalling accident, which lately happened to the Hull steam-boat,

is of such a nature as to call loudly for the interference of the legislature to prevent similar calamities. I have had a few opportunities of being a steam-boat passenger, and have frequently conversed with those entrusted with their management. The result has been, that I only wonder how so few mishaps take place, seeing the very little mechanical knowledge necessary for being dubbed a steam boat *Engineer*. That, it may not be imagined I am dealing only in generals, I shall furnish a few particulars, which I dare say will be easily credited by those, who have given attention to the subject, and easily ascertained not to be improbable, by such as may seek farther to satisfy themselves.

It is not an unusual occurrence in the smaller class of steam-boats, that a fireman or stoker is entrusted with the engine on the sudden dismissal, or unlooked for absence, of the party who had previously officiated. And were he questioned as to his fitness, he would in most instances give utterance to the greatest absurdities. And that, too, with all the presumption attendant on ignorance.

I was once on board of a steam-boat, where the safety-valve was loaded considerably beyond the pressure the constructor had calculated his boiler could sustain ; at that time I was not aware of the danger we were in—these very boilers having since given way under a far less pressure.

There was a small high-pressure boat, which ran occasionally, some time ago. The boiler burst and killed the engineer, who only that morning had been saying he " would make her speak French," alluding to his intention of urging up the steam for a race.

I have heard an engineer boast of having not only loaded the valve with all the weight he possessed, but even of adding a hammer not of the lightest description. " Give her the hammer" is a slang phrase on board of some steamboats, when it is wished to increase the rate of speed.

Although it might be deemed incredible that any one would sit on the lever of a loaded safety-valve to preclude the escape of steam, yet even this has been done. To such lengths will ignorance and rashness extend !

Many dreadful steam-boat accidents

have occurred in America, owing, it is said, to the use of high-pressure marine engines. This may be one cause certainly, but the public ought to be aware, that even the lowest pressure steam engine can be converted into a high pressure one, and that too, of the most dangerous kind, being inferior in strength, and possessing more material to scatter, destruction.

Having thus, noticed some of the evils which exist, I would propose as the most likely means of abating, if not altogether removing, them, that no man be entrusted with the care of a steam engine, until he has not only undergone an examination, but obtained a certificate of his competency, from a Board of Engineers capable of judging of his qualification.

Your giving this a place in your valuable periodical will be esteemed a favor by

AN ADMIRER OF IMPROVEMENT.

London. June 17, 1837.

GAS LIGHT BURNERS—HUTCHISON'S, AND BACON AND KILBY'S.

Sir,—A correspondent under the signature of Justus, whose letter appeared in your Journal of the 27th ult., complains with some degree of asperity, that Mr. Hutchison, in laying claim to the invention of a burner described in the *Mechanics' Magazine* for April last, "unjustly avails himself of the inventive talent of others;" also representing that the burner in question is "a colourable evasion of one patented in 1829, by Messrs. Bacon and Kilby. Justus asserts that Hutchison's burner is the *same in principle* as Bacon and Kilby's; but that the result of certain experiments has led him to the conclusion that it is *inferior*, when brought into practice. This very confident assertion, however, is wholly unaccompanied by proofs, either in the shape of calculation or data of any description. Justus, it is true, mentions, that the case is now before one of our courts of law, awaiting the decision of a competent tribunal,—that he therefore refrains from making any farther remarks, "least he should be looked upon as an advocate for disputed claims." That is to say, he wishes to be thought an entirely disinterested and unprejudging party, and yet, in the same breath he

denounces both Mr. H. and his burner, not in subdued or qualified language, but in terms of unlimited condemnation!

As Justus has merely favoured the public with the address of the agent appointed for the sale of the burner, which he has taken under his special protection, without accompanying his advertisement with any particulars illustrative of its principles or peculiar mode of action, you will, perhaps, Sir, permit me to lay before the intelligent readers of the *Mechanics' Magazine* the following diagrams.

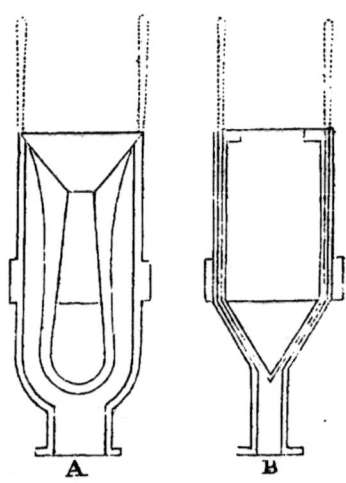

A   B

" Here are the counterfeit representations (*not*) of two brothers," but burners. A. is Hutchinson's, B. Bacon and Kilby's.

These burners are plainly very different in the principle of their construction; and in their practical results, they disagree still more widely. I have now before me the burner patented in 1829 by Bacon and Kilby. It is (as shown in the diagram,) neither more nor less than an Argand—with the addition of a *ring* brazed upon its upper surface. This ring constitutes what its talented inventors are pleased to designate an *improvement*,—and for which they secured a patent right in the year 1829. Eight long years have since passed away, but they have done so little for this burner, that at the present moment, even the most experienced inspectors, belonging to our first gas establishments, are unacquainted with it. Its merits, if it ever possessed any, are yet to be discovered—hitherto they have remained in profound and undisturbed obscurity. As Justus has kindly promised at a future time to favour Clovis with corrections of his remarks upon gas burners. I shall, with his leave, take time by the "forelock," and proceed to make a few experimental observations upon that celebrated unknown improvement, for whose unrecognized merits Justus would wish it to be supposed he is a most disinterested advocate.

The great improvement Argand effected by introducing a cylindrical tube into his lamp, causing thereby a distribution of atmospheric air to all parts of the circular flame, has justly been considered the most important advantage, that has ever been attained in the production of artificial light.

Now this principle of arrangement, which I believe has never been controverted—cannot have been sufficiently understood by Bacon and Kilby: otherwise they could not have committed the absurd blunder of *interposing* between the flame and the necessary supply of air —*a broad circular ring*—which, instead of conducting the atmosphere gradually* towards the place of combustion, positively acts as a barrier to their uniform junction. The supply of pure oxygen, which flame requires for its support, and which, under ordinary circumstances, it absorbs from the surrounding air, is also, by this unscientific mode of construction, in a considerable degree withheld. The truth of this may be satisfactorily demonstrated by attaching Hutchison's and Bacon and Kilby's burners to a tube charged with gas, and igniting the streams of gas, when it will be seen - that the flame from Hutchison's burner will measure 3½ *inches* in length, while that of Bacon and Kilby's measures only 2¼ *inches*. This must be a matter of the most serious importance to persons, who burn gas by meter, and of still greater consequence to gas establishments. If the experiment be still further pursued, it will be found, that upon reducing the pressure, Hutchison's will yield a bright and luminous light—while, at the same point

of diminished pressure, that of the other patentees is so feeble and attenuated, as to be scarcely perceptible.

In support of the patent of 1829, Justus alludes to the commendating remarks of Mr. Rutter, which appeared in No. 603 of the *Mechanics' Magazine*. That gentleman, from his practical experience and general intelligence on subjects of this nature, is no doubt perfectly qualified to give a correct opinion on the merits of the burner. I was, therefore, induced to refer to his observations on this particular point. I find, however, that Mr. Rutter's eulogy does not *apply* to the patented invention of Bacon and Kilby; he does not even particularise the form of its construction, nor the principle of its action. In fact, there is no trace nor vestige of their burner to be discovered throughout Mr. Rutter's remarks upon this subject. That gentleman's observations are limited to a few (certainly well-merited) sentences in favour of an *adjunct* to a burner—which adjunct is a brass cone—technically called "The Gallery Cone"—sometimes perforated at its base with circular orifices or openings, and so constructed as to render it convenient to be added to a burner, or dispensed with at pleasure. It is no more a burner, however, than the glass chimney. In my description of Hutchison's patent in No. 716, I distinctly alluded to this *cone*, and at the same time, renounced on his part all claim to this invention. I also as distinctly declare, and am prepared with evidence to prove the truth of this declaration, that neither Bacon nor Kilby, Messrs. Dixon nor Justus have had any hand or part in the invention of this undoubtedly clever and valuable improvement.

The improvement Mr. Rutter speaks of, and which Justus is so anxious the world should believe is the invention of his friends', has been applied to Argand's oil lamps, and also gas burners for at least twenty years. The patent article of Bacon and Co. bears no resemblance whatever to the invention Mr. Rutter very properly commended.

The effects produced upon artificial light by this decided improvement, and those that result from the use of this burner, are different. The cone occasions additional brilliancy, intensity, and almost unalterable steadiness in the

---

* This is one of the effects produced by Hutchison's conical burner.

flame. The reverse of these desirable qualities necessarily result from the principle of construction, which characterises Bacon and Kilby's burner; indeed, they are the inevitable consequences. Let, for instance, the draught of air passing through the tube be accelerated; the abrupt projection of the ring over the orifice will check the uniform progress of the air: the impulse given by this check, or rather shock, will be instantly communicated to the flame.

Justus is evidently led astray by a very common error in the case of disputed patents. He imagines, that it is the *principle* of an invention that is entitled to the protection of an exclusive right. Through ignorant legislation, discrepancies have undoubtedly entered into the composition of our patent laws, which are perpetually leading to ruinous litigation But, assuredly, the law in reference to the subject now in contest is distinct, clear, and explicit. Principle cannot be monopolized,—it is form alone that can be protected. The principle in all burners is the same; a body of common air is required to produce perfect combustion; therefore, an original and hitherto unknown means of applying this air to the flame of a lamp or burner *is* entitled to special protection.

I am not sorry to hear that the matter is to be investigated by one of our courts. The decision, I have no doubt, will establish another instance (if such were wanting) of that absurd enthusiasm, which leads inexperienced persons to expend and waste money upon crude, useless, and imaginary inventions.

Your obedient servant,

CLOVIS.

FLOATING BRIDGE BETWEEN STAINBOUL AND ITS SUBURBS, GALATA, TOPANA, ETC.

Sir,—The above is a rough and hasty sketch of a floating bridge lately thrown across the Golden Horn; connecting the city of Stainboul with its suburbs, Galata, Topana, Pera, &c.; and which, from its novelty of construction, you may perhaps deem worthy of a place in your valuable pages.

The whole is formed of wood, and floated on rafts; it is divided into compartments, which are capable of being easily removed, to allow ships to pass through; the Turkish Navy being laid up for the winter in that part of the Golden Horn above the bridge. There are two arches for the passage of Caüchs; and a series of anchors and cables confine it; the total length is four hundred and seven yards, and the width about twelve; three arubas could pass abreast.

A long system of harassing quarantine with Constantinople in consequence of plague, will be, I think, a sufficient excuse for the rudeness of my epistolary materials.

I am, dear Sir, yours truly,

HENRY D. CUNNINGHAM.

Therapia, on the Bosphorus,
March, 1837.

EXTINGUISHING FIRES ON BOARD STEAM VESSELS.

Sir,—Reflecting on the melancholy loss of life, occasioned by the burning of the Ben Sherrod, American steamer, I am induced to offer a few remarks, which may lead to the prevention of similar accidents.

The destructive effects of fire on shore, cannot, in many instances, be arrested from the want of a proper supply of water; but at sea, this want can never be experienced. A large supply could be obtained in the vessel by the mere turning of a cock; and by the addition of a force-pump to the engine and a few inexpensive furnishings, those on board would have the means of deluging any part, where fire either existed or threatened to commence. Besides, in using such an auxiliary as the steam engine, there would be this advantage, that it would continue to work while steam was supplied, without being injured by a very great increase of heat.

There is yet another purpose, for which the steam engine can be applied in a case of emergency—the connecting it with the common pumps when the vessel has either sprung a leak, or has shipped an unusual quantity of water.   There is nothing novel in this; but, at all events, it affords an additional instance of the security, conferred by the use of the steam engine in navigation.

I remain, Sir,

Your obedient servant,

WILLIAM SYMINGTON.

Dean-street, Commercial Road, June 21, 1837.

MR. WIVELL'S ESCAPE.—FIRE IN COMPTON STREET, &c.

Sir,—I really must again check Mr. Wivell, in his unbecoming endeavour to appropriate to himself all the merit of an invention, to which he has not the slightest claim. I have already noticed Mr. John Hudson's employment of wheels on the top of his ladder escape of 1828 (as described in the Register of Arts for February 1829) and also the elevators of others, exhibited before Mr. Wivell had turned his attention to the subject; when Mr. Wivell asserts, therefore, that I have confessed to having availed myself of *his plan*, he states that which is incorrect,

I have no hesitation in giving Mr. Wivell all the merit due to him, on account of his escape described at page 163 of your last number; in which there is more originality, and far more ingenuity, than in any of his previous contrivances. The mode of transporting the apparatus from place to place on *three wheels* (not two as stated in the description) and detaching the fore-carriage on reaching the fire—together with the novel mode of elevating the ladders, is very ingeniously managed.

The principal objections to this machine, however, are; its original cost; the difficulty of finding and the expence of providing suitable stations; its complexity, which precludes the efficient working of it by persons not well practised in its use; and finally, the utter impossibility of applying it in many situations where

a fire-escape may become needful. In all these points, Mr. Wivell's apparatus falls behind those of Mr. Ford and Mr. Merryweather; it is, in fact, a practical contradiction to the character given by Mr. Wivell himself in his lectures, as necessary to constitute a useful and efficient fire-escape.

As the injudicious communication of Mr. Spring, secretary to the Society, to the Morning Herald newspaper, relative to a fire in Compton Street, Soho, has been brought forward in your pages, I think it but right to add the following particulars, to the "correct statement" already published.

I was called from my then residence in Wilderness Row, Goswell Street, on the night of April 3rd, by the light of a violent conflagration, that was raging, apparently in the direction of Piccadilly; I started off on foot, and on reaching the fire in Compton-Street, I found the west end engines of the London fire-establishment in full and efficient operation: the engines from Farringdon-street, Watling street and other eastern stations, had just reached the spot, and were in the act of being placed.   By the time I had been on the ground about twenty minutes, the firemen had succeeded in stopping the further spread of the fire in the premises adjoining, to which it had communicated, and the force of the engines was being concentrated upon the main body of the fire, when Mr. Wivell's Fire-escape arrived (as it is said)—"in seventeen minutes from Robert street"!   The fire had by this time been burning about *three quarters of an hour*, the floors and roof had fallen in, and the outer wall was expected every moment to give way; notwithstanding this, the ladders were raised to the second and third floor windows, amid a shower of falling sparks, with occasionaily some remaining portions of the roof &c.   It was altogether a fool-hardy exhibition, exposing the machine and the lives of those, who worked it to imminent danger, without the possibility of any good result. I may also observe that the reckless manner, in which the machine was wheeled along the foot-pavement through the dense crowd, on its arrival, was most disgraceful: some persons were hurt, and I heard one gentleman threaten to punish the parties who conducted it.

At the *crisis* of a large fire, the time is

sadly out of joint for all such *exhibitions*, as they not only add greatly to the confusion incident to the scene, but divert the attention of the police from their proper duty, and impede the well directed efforts of the firemen.

By a singular coincidence, Mr. Wivell's description of his fire-escape, and some curious points in its history by Mr. Jenkins, appear in the same number; the latter gentleman's remarks upon the conduct of " the Society " requiring farther notice, I shall take an early opportunity of returning to the subject, In the mean time, I would wish to say, that I am aware of no reason for concealing the financial transactions of the Society ; on the contrary, there is every reason for giving them the utmost possible publicity.

I remain, Sir,

Yours respectfully,

WM. BADDELEY.

June, 21st, 1837.

NOTICE OF THE ELECTRO-MAGNETIC MACHINE OF MR. THOMAS DAVENPORT, OF BRANDON, NEAR RUTLAND, VERMONT.

(From the *American Journal of Science and Arts* for April, 1837.)

Many years have passed since motion was first produced by galvanic power. The dry columns of De Luc and Zamboni caused the vibration of delicate pendulums and the ringing of small bells, for long periods of time, even several years without intermission.

In 1819-20, Professor Oersted, of Copenhagen, discovered, that magnetism was evolved between the poles of a galvanic battery. Professor Sweigger, of Halle, Germany, by his galvanic multiplier, succeeded in rendering the power manifest, when the galvanic battery was nothing more than two small wires, one of copper and the other of zinc, immersed in as much acidulated water as was contained in a wine glass. The power thus envolved was made to pass through many convolutions of insulated wire, and was thus augmented so as to deflect the magnetic needle sometimes even 90°. Professor Moll, of Utretcht, by winding insulated wire around soft iron, imparted to it prodigious magnetic power, so that a horse shoe bar, thus provided, and connected with a galvanic battery, would lift over one hundred pounds. About the same time, Mr. Joseph Henry, of Albany, now Professor Henry, of Princeton College, by a new method of winding the wire, obtained an almost incredible magnetic

force, lifting six or seven hundred pounds, with a pint or two of liquid and a battery of corresponding size ; nor did he desist, until, a short time after, he lifted thousands of pounds, by a battery of larger size, but still very small, (1830.)

This gentleman was not slow to apply his skill to the generation of motion and a successful attempt of his is recorded in this Journal, Vol, xx. p. 340. A power was thus applied to the movement of a machine, by a beam suspended in the centre, which performed regular vibrations in the manner of a beam of a steam engine. This is the original application from which have sprung, or at least to which have succeeded, several similar attempts both in this country and in Europe. A galvanic machine was reported to the British Association in 1835, by Mr. M'Gauly, of Ireland, and he has renewed his statements of successful experiments at the late meeting at Bristol. Mr. Sturgeon, of Woolwich, England, also reports a galvanic machine, as being in use on his premises for pumping water, and for other mechanical purposes.*

But I believe that Mr. Davenport, named at the head of his notice, has been more successful than any other person in the discovery† of a galvanic machine of great simplicity and efficiency. During the last two or three years, much have been said of this dicovery in the newspapers, and it is probable, that in a future number of this Journal, drawings, and an accurate description of the machine may be given. Having been recently invited to examine a working model, in two varieties of form, and to report the result, I shall now attempt nothing more than a general description, such as may render intelligible the account I am to give.

1. *The Rotary Machine, composed of revolving electro magnets, with fixed permanent magnets.*

This machine was brought to New-Haven March 16, 1837, by Mr. Israel Slade, of Troy, N. Y., and by him set in motion for my examination. The moving part is composed of two iron bars placed horizontally, and crossing each other at right angles. They are both five and half inches long, and they are terminated at each end by a segment of a circle made of soft iron ; these segments are each three inches long in the chord line, and their position, as they are suspended upon the ends of the iron bars is horizontal.

The iron cross is sustained by a vertical axis, standing with its pivot in a socket, and admitting of easy rotation. The iron cross

---

* Sturgeon's Annals of Electricity, Magnetism, etc. No. 1., Vol. I. October, 1836.

† Mr. Davenport appears to have been strictly the inventor of a method of applying galvanism to produce rotary motion.

bars are wound with copper wire, covered by cotton, and they are made to form , at pleasure, a proper connection with a small circular battery, made of concentric cylinders of copper and zinc, which can be immersed in a quart of acidulated water. Two semicircles of strongly magnitized steel form an entire circle, interrupted only at the two opposite poles, within this circle, which lies horizontally ; the galvanized iron cross moves in such a manner that its iron segments revolve parallel and very near to the magnetic circle, and in the same plane. Its axis at its upper end, is fitted by a horizontal cog-wheel to another and larger vertical wheel, to whose horizontal axis, weight is attached and raised by the winding of a rope. As soon as the small battery, destined to generate the power, is properly connected with the machine, and duly excited by diluted acid, the motion begins, by the horizontal movement of the iron cross, with its circular segments of flangers. By the galvanic connection, these crosses and their connected segments are magnetized, acquiring north and south polarity at their opposite ends, and being thus subjected to the attracting and repelling force of the circular fixed magnets, a rapid horizontal movement is produced, at the rate of two hundred to three hundred revolutions in a minute, when the small battery was used, and over six hundred with a calorimotor of large size. The rope was wound up with a weight of fourteen pounds attached, and twenty-eight pounds were lifted from the floor. The movment is instantly stopped by breaking the connexion with the battery, and then reversed by simply interchanging the connexion of the wires of the battery with those of the machine when it becomes equally rapid in the opposite direction.

The machine, as a philosophical instrument, operates with beautiful and surprising effect, and no reason can be discovered why the motion may not be indefinitely continued. It is easy to cause a very gradual flow of the impaired or exhausted acid liquid from, and of fresh acidulated water into, the recepticle of the battery, and whenever the metal of the latter is too much corroded to be any longer efficient, another battery may be instantly substituted, and that even before the connexion of the old battery is broken. As to the the energy of the power, it becomes at once a most interesting inquiry, whether it admits of indefinite increase? To this inquiry it may be replied, that provided the magnetism of both the revolving cross and of the fixed circle can be indefinitely increased, then no reason appears why the energy of the power cannot also be indefinitely increased. Now, as magnets of the common kind, usually called permanent magnets, find their limits

within, at most, the power of lifting a few hundred pounds, it is obvious that the revolving galvanic magnet must, in its efficiency, be limited, by its relation to the fixed magnet. But it is an important fact, discovered by experience, that the latter is soon impaired in its power by the influence of the revolving galvanic magnet which is easily made to surpass it in energy, and thus, as it were to overpower it. It is obvious therefore that the fixed magnet, as well as the revolving, ought to be magnetized by galvanism, and then there is every reason to believe that the relative equality of the two, and of course their relative energy, may be permanently supported, and even carried to an extent much greater than has been hitherto attained.

2. *Rotating Machine, composed entirely of electro-magnets, both in its fixed and revolving members.*

A machine of this construction has been, this day March 22, 1837, exhibited to me by Mr. Thomas Davenport himself, who came from New-York to New-haven for that purpose.

It is the same machine that has been already described, except that the exterior fixed circle is now composed entirely of electro-magnets.

The entire apparatus is therefore constructed of soft unmagnetic iron, which, being properly wound with insulated copper wire, is magnetised in an instant, by the power of a very small battery.

The machine is, indeed, the identical one used before, except that the exterior circle of permanent magnets is removed, and in its place is arranged a circle of soft iron, divided into two portions to form the poles.

These semicircles are made of hoop iron, one inch in width, and one-eighth of an inch in thickness. They are wound with copper wire insulated by cotton—covering about ten inches in length on each semicircle, and returning upon itself, by a double winding, so as to form two layers of wire, making on both semicircles about one thousand five hundred inches.

The iron was not wound over the entire length, of one of the steel semicircles ; but both ends were left projecting, and being turned inward, were made to conform to the bend of the other part, as in the annexed figure,

which is intended to represent one of them ; each end that is turned inward and not wound is about one-third of the length of the semicircle. These semicircles' being thus fitted up, so as to become, at pleasure, galvanic magnets, were placed in the same machine that has been already described, and occupied the same place that the permanent steel magnets did before. The conducting wires were so arranged, that the same current that charged the magnets of the motive wheel, charged the stationary ones, placed around it, only one battery being used. It should be observed that the stationary galvanic magnets thus substituted for the permanent steel ones, were only about half the weight of the steel magnets. This modification of the galvanic magnet, is not of course the best form for efficiency ; this was used merely to try the principle, and this construction may be superseded by a different and more efficient one.

But with this arrangement, and notwithstanding the imperfection of the mechanism of the machine—when the battery, requiring about one quart of diluted acid to immerse it, was attached, it lifted 16 lbs., very rapidly, and when the weight was removed, it performed more than 600 evolutions per minute.

So sensible was the machine to the magnetic power, that the immersion of the battery one inch into the acidulated water , was sufficient to give it rapid motion, which attained its maximum, when the battery was entirely immersed. It appeared to me that the machine had more energy with the electro magnets, than with those that were permanent for with the smallest battery whose diameter was three inches and a half ; its height five inches and a half, and the number of concentric cylinders three of copper and three of zinc, the instrument manifested as great power as it had done with the largest batteries, and even with a large calorimoter, when it was used with a permanent instead of a galvanic magnet. With the small battery and with none but electro or galvanic magnets, it revolved with so much energy as to produce a brisk breeze, and powerfully to shake a large table on which the apparatus stood.

Although the magnetization of both the stationary and revolving magnets was imparted by one and the same battery, the magnetic power was not immediately destroyed by breaking the connexion between the battery and the stationary magnet ; for, when this was done, the machine still performed its revolutions with great, although diminished energy ; in practice this might be important, as it would give time to make changes in the apparatus, without stopping the movement of the machine.

It has been stated by Dr. Ritchie, in a late number (Jan. 1837) of the Lond. and Edinb. Phil. Magazine, that electro-magnets do not attract at so great a distance as permanent ones, and therefore are not well adapted for producing motion. On this point Mr.

Davenport made the following experiment, of which I was not a witness, but to which I give full credit, as it was reported to me by Mr. Slade, in a letter dated New York, March 24, 1837.

Mr. Davenport suspended a piece of soft iron with a long piece of twine and brought one pole of a highly charged steel magnet within the attracting distance, that is, the distance at which the iron was attracted to the magnet ; by measurement it was found that the steel magnet attracted the iron one inch and one-fourth. A galvanic magnet was next used of the same lifting power, and consequently of much less weight ; the attracting distance of this magnet was found to be one inch and three-fourths, showing a material gain in favor of the galvanic magnet.—Mr. Slade inquires, " has Mr. Ritchie's magnet been so constructed as to give a favorable trial to this principle ?" [*] Mr. Davenport informs me that each increase in the number of wires has been attended with an increase of power.

Conclusions.

1. It appears then, from the facts stated above, that electro-magnetism is quite adequate to the generation of rotary motion.

2. That it is not necessary to employ permanent magnets in any part of the construction, and that electro-magnets are far preferable, not only for the moving but for the stationary parts of the machine.

3. That the power generated by electromagnetism may be indefinitely prolonged, since, for exhausted acids, and corroded metals, fresh acids and batteries, kept always in readiness, may be substituted, even without stopping the movement.

4. That the power may be increased beyond any limit hitherto attained, and probably beyond any which can be *with certainty* assigned,—since, by increasing all the members of the apparatus, due reference being had to the relative proportionate weight, size, and form of the fixed and moveable parts—to the length of the insulated wires and the manner of winding them—and to the proper size and construction of the battery, as well as to the nature and strength of the acid or other exciting agent, and the manner of connecting the battery with the machine, it would appear certain, that the power must be increased in some ratio which experience must ascertain.

5. As electro-magnetism has been experimentally proved to be sufficient to raise and sustain several thousands of pounds, no reason can be discovered why, when the acting surfaces are, by skilful mechanism, brought as near as possible, without

---

[*] This question I am not able to answer, as I have not seen any account of the apparatus or of the experiment, but only of the result.

contact, the continued exertion of the power should not generate a continued rotary movement, of a degree of energy inferior indeed to that exerted in actual contact, but still nearly approximating to it.

6. As the power can be generated cheaply and certainly—as it can be continued indefinitely, as it has been very greatly increased by very simple means—as we have no knowledge of its limit, and may therefore presume on an indefinite augmentation of its energy, it is much to be desired that the investigation should be prosecuted with zeal, *aided by correct scientific knowledge*, by *mechanical skill*, and by *ample funds*. It may therefore be reasonably hoped, that science and art, the handmaids of discovery, will both receive from this interesting research, a liberal reward.

ON THE PROCESS OF CARBONIZATION, OR MANUFACTURE OF CHARCOAL, AT GOERSDORF, IN SAXONY.

(From the *Quarterly Mining Review*.)

It having been suggested by M. Boult, that a superior charcoal might be produced, by filling the interstices of the pile with small charcoal, the refuse of former burnings, an experiment was made, which, after being several times repeated, gave the following results : 1st, an increase of produce, amounting to not less than four per cent., above that yielded by the ordinary process ; 2nd, a much smaller quantity of dust and small coal; 3rd, scarcely any smoke ; 4th, charcoal of a very equal and superior quality.

A pile prepared for carbonization at Goersdorf contained in general about thirty *schragen* (318 cubic yards) of pine trees split in quarters, which yielded, including the small coal, from eighty-nine to ninety-two per cent. in bulk of charcoal. It was considered desirable to ascertain, whether by increasing the size of the pile, a more considerable product would be obtained. A pile containing forty-nine schragen (about 520 cubic yards,) of cleft pine wood, gave in an experiment, during which the weather proved favourable, 89.94 per cent. of charcoal (including the small,) very sonorous, and of very good quality. A second trial of 69½ schragen (740 cubic yards,) of similar wood produced only 87.98 per cent., but the weather in this instance was unfavourable.

This experiment was repeated with seventy-one schragen (750 cubic yards,) the weather continuing fine throughout the process ; the produce amounted to 94.87 per cent.; equal in quality to the former results. The average results of the adoption of this process at Goersdorf, will appear from the following table of the produce, from the commencement to the date of the latest improvements.

	Produce per cent.		Total produce per cent.
	Large.	Small.	
1821............	74.94	3.91	78.85
1822............	76.24	4.76	81.—
1823............	76.44	5.25	81.69
1824............	77.95	4.09	82.04
1825............	86.31	4.35	90.66
1826............	86.31	3.62	89.93
1827............	87.53	4.20	91.73

The increase observable in the produce of 1825, is to be attributed, principally to the care with which the operations were conducted; but it must be also remarked, that the removal of the pipe for collecting the acid formed in the process of carbonization, may also have contributed beneficially to the results. M. Karsten in his *Voyage Metallurgique*, states, that in Carinthia, the carbonization of pine wood is performed in large stacks, containing 20,000 cubic feet, and without the trees being previously split, yet the produce in bulk is computed at from seventy-one to eighty-six per cent. It is obvious, that there exists no analogy between these results and those obtained from the brushwood and billets of oak, beach, &c., by the common process of carbonization, which seldom yields more than from thirty-five to forty-five per cent.; it is, therefore, only necessary to call public attention to the fact, and it may naturally be expected that, in the present state of practical science, a subject of so much importance in metallurgy will be duly investigated.

LIST OF ENGLISH PATENTS GRANTED BETWEEN THE 24TH MAY AND THE 22D JUNE, 1837.

James Partridge Blake, of Little Queen-street, Middlesex, Engineer, for certain improvements in machinery or apparatus for hulling, cleansing, preparing or dressing paddy or rough rice, hulling, dressing and preparing oats, and such other grain, part or parts of which are applicable to other purposes; being a communication from a foreigner residing abroad. May 30; six months.

Joseph Woollams, of Wells, Somerset, gent., for certain improved means of obtaining power and motion from known sources. May 30; six months.

Francis William Gerish, of East-road, City-road, Middlesex, smith and ironmonger, for improvements in the apparatus for closing doors, gates and shutters. May 30; six months.

Richard Oke Millett, of Peupalls, Hayle, Cornwall, gent., for improvements in instruments for extracting teeth. June 1; six months.

Edward Schmidt Swaine, formerly of Bucklersbury, London, but now of Leeds, in pursuance of the Report of the Judicial Committee of His Majesty's Privy Council, for a method of producing and preserving artificial mineral waters, and for machinery to effect the same. For seven years, from the 9th day of October, 1837, the day of the expiration of the former letters patent. June 6.

Joseph Choild Daniell, of Limpley Stoke, Wilts, gent., for certain improvements applicable to stone masonry. June 6; six months.

Miles Berry, of Chancery-lane, Middlesex, mechanical draftsman, for a certain improvement or certain improvements in obtaining motive power for propelling or working machinery, being a communication from a foreigner residing abroad. June 6; six months.

John Kirkham, of Aldenham Terrace, St. Pancras Road, Middlesex, engineer, for an improved mode of removing the carbonaceous incrustation from the internal surfaces of retorts employed in the process of distilling coal for generating gas. June 8; six months.

John George Bodmer, of Bolton le-Moors, Lancaster, for certain improvements in machinery for spinning and doubling cotton, wool, silk, flax, and other fibrous materials. June 12; six months.

Godfrey Woone, of Berkeley-street, Piccadilly, Middlesex, gent., for an improved method of forming plates with raised surfaces thereon, for printing impressions on different substances. June 12; six months.

William Fothergill Cooke, of Breeds-place, Hastings, Sussex, Esquire, and Charles Wheatstone, of Hanover Square, Middlesex, Esquire, for improvements in giving signals and sounding alarums at distant places, by means of electric currents transmitted through metallic circuits. Six months.

Richard Roe, of Everton, near Bawtry, York, gent., for a certain improvement or certain improvements in machinery or apparatus for making bricks, tiles, and other articles made from earthy materials. June 17; six months.

James Leonard Clement Thomas, of Covent-garden, Middlesex, Esquire, for an improvement applicable to steam engines and steam generators, having for its object economy of fuel; being a communication from a foreigner residing abroad. June 17; six months.

William Nicholson, of Manchester, Lancaster, engineer, for certain improvements in the construction and arrangement of preparation and spinning machinery; being a communication from a foreigner residing abroad. June 17; six months.

James Buckingham, of Great Randolph-street, Camden Town, Middlesex, engineer, for certain improved combinations of machinery, to be applied as mechanical agents in a great variety of situations, in which tooth gear and other mechanism have been hitherto employed. June 17; six months.

Theophilus John Nash, of John-street, Downshirehill, Hampstead, letter-maker, and John Ross, of Wyld-street, Lincoln's-inn-fields, Middlesex, brassworker, for a method of manufacturing in metals, wood, and other substances and materials, letters, figures, and other devices, having a flat surface, presenting by the aid of colours the appearance of projection and domed letters, figures, and other devices made from the same materials without seam or joint. June 19; two months.

William Yetts, of Yarmouth, merchant, for an improved mode of caulking ships and other vessels. June 19; two months.

LIST OF SCOTCH PATENTS GRANTED FROM THE 21ST MAY TO 21ST JUNE, 1837.

William Henry Crauford, of John-street, Berkeley Square, Commander in the Royal Navy, for an improvement in the coating or covering iron and copper for the prevention of oxydation. May 22.

Charles Guynemer, of Manchester-street, Manchester Square, Professor of singing, for certain improvements in piano-fortes, communicated to him by a foreigner residing abroad. May 24.

William Bridges Adams, of Porchester Terrace, Bayswater, coach-maker, for certain improvements in the construction of wheels and in wheel carriages. June 2.

William Gossage, of Stoke Prior, Worcester, chemist, for certain improved apparatus for decomposing common salt, and for condensing and making use of the gaseous product of such decomposition; also

certain improvements in the mode of conducting these processes. June 2.

John Joseph Charles Sheridan, of Ironmonger-lane, London, chemist, for certain improvements in the several processes of saccharine, vinous, and acetous fermentation. June 6.

Pierre Barthemy Guinebert Debac, of Brixton, Surrey, for improvements applicable to rail-roads. June 12.

Joel Livesey, of Bury, Lancaster, cotton spinner, for certain improvements in machinery used for spinning, preparing and doubling cotton and other fibrous substances. June 21.

NOTES AND NOTICES.

Meteorology.—A trial, we understand, has lately been made by Mr. Murphy, already favourably known to the public as the author of some works on meteorology, of principles discovered by him for calculating in advance the approaching changes of the weather in the construction of weather tables, which he prepared so far as the commencement of March for the succeeding months of April and May just past, in which the daily state of the weather throughout, or during sixty-one days consecutively, was set down; and the result has been, that, not only in the general outline of the changes which during this interval took place, but in by far the greater number of the details, his calculations have been verified, so as to place beyond doubt the correctness of the principles of calculation resorted to by him. So exact, indeed, in some instances, did the changes of the weather correspond with the predictions, that in more than one case, as we understand, when at or immediately preceding the change the barometer was at fault, the calculation proved correct. We understand this is not the first time these principles have been tested; as in a letter from Mr. Murphy, which was published in the Agriculturist of the 20th of October, 1836, the tremendous storm of wind and rain which occurred the 13th Nov. following, was distinctly pointed out by him, as noticed in an article which appeared in the Morning Post of the 3rd of December, 1836, &c. In reference to the weather tables for April and May alluded to, as besides one enclosed to Viscount Melbourne in March last, accompanied with a letter from Dr. Birkbeck, President of the Meteorological Society, recommending Mr. Murphy to the patronage of government, several copies of them were supplied to others; thus many can attest as to their general correctness.—*Times.*

New Coach Wheel Retarder.—The new mails have a piece of machinery attached to the hind part of the mail, for the purpose of locking the wheels down steep hills without the guard getting down; or in case of the horses running away down a hill, of stopping the mail instantly. The contrivance is very simple, and is done by the pressure of two pieces of wood against the wheels; the connecting rod going to the top of the coach is turned by a screw, and the effect on the wheel is immediate.—*Times.* This is an importation from France, where the diligences have for a long time been fitted with a precisely similar contrivance. It is worked by the "conducteur" in the cabriolet, with a winch handle. Almost every cart and waggon in France has some contrivance for retarding the wheels, which, although rendered more necessary there than here, in consequence of the road levelling system not being so extensively adopted in France as in England, yet in some districts of our country the plan would be useful.

The Supplement to Vol. xxvi., containing Title, Contents, Index, etc., Medallic Portrait of his late Majesty, and Wyon's Cheselden Medal, engraved by Freebairn by Bates' patent machine, is published, price 6d.

☞ *British and Foreign Patents taken out with economy and despatch; Specifications, Disclaimers, and Amendments, prepared or revised; Caveats entered; and generally every Branch of Patent Business promptly transacted.*

LONDON: Printed and Published for the Proprietor, by W. A. Robertson, at the Mechanics' Magazine Office, No. 6, Peterborough-court, between 135 and 136, Fleet-street.—Sold by G. W. M. Reynolds, Proprietor of the French, English, and American Library, 55, Rue Neuve, Saint Augustin, Paris.

Mechanics' Magazine,
MUSEUM, REGISTER, JOURNAL, AND GAZETTE.

No. 726. SATURDAY, JULY 8, 1837. Price 3d.

BALANCE LOCKS FOR CANALS AND RIVERS.

Fig. 1.

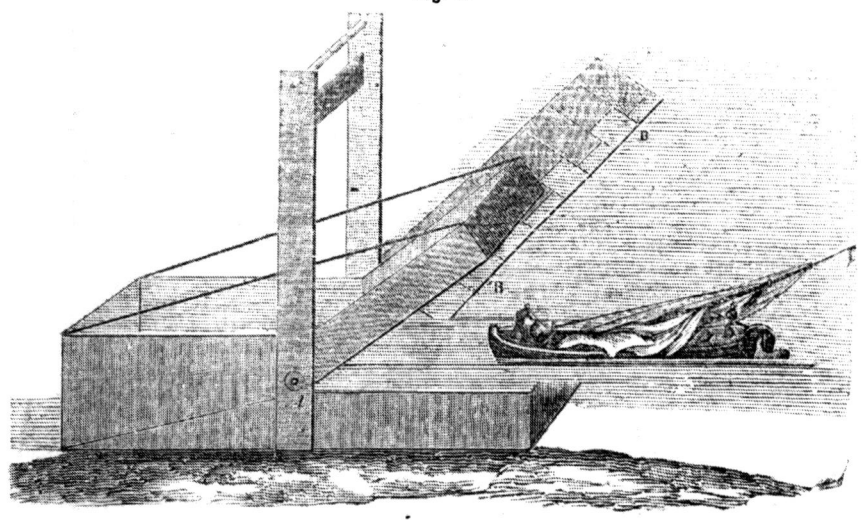

Fig. 2.

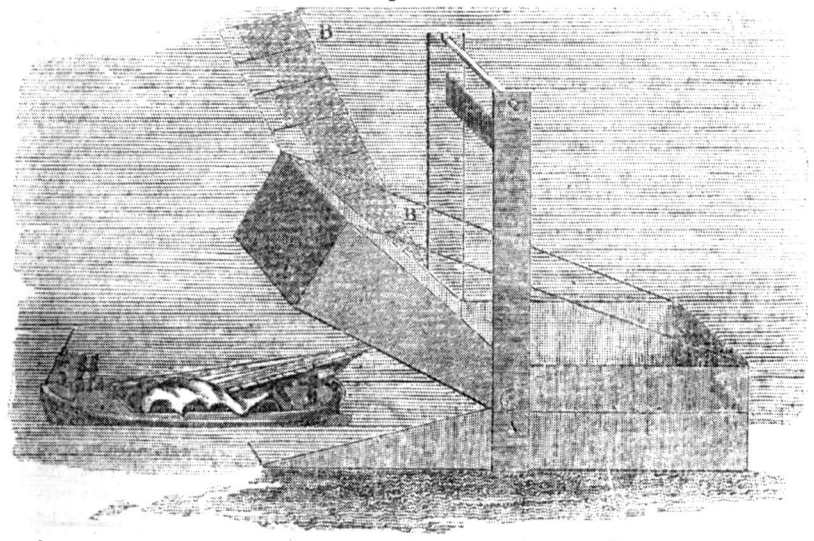

BALANCE LOCK FOR CANALS AND RIVERS.

Sir, — The accompanying drawings exhibit two views of a balance lock for rivers or canals : Fig. 1 represents a barge sailing down a river and entering the lock : Fig. 2 represents the barge sailing out after the lock has been turned over. A A the centre on which the moving part of the lock turns, and upon which it may be balanced to a nicety. B B is a weir of sluices across the river, to slide so as to leave always an opening at bottom; a current is thus produced at the *bottom* of the river or stream, which would continually scour, and prevent depositions of soil taking place. Cast iron I think is the fittest material for making these locks and weirs, but they may be made of wood, or wrought iron, or any other material that is of sufficient strength. If locks of this description should be found to answer it would expedite very much the transit on canals, as a boat might pass the lock in a minute.

I am, Sir,
Your obedient Servant,
ROBERT HARDY.

Iron Foundry Worcester. June 7th 1837.

THE GLOBULE MICROSCOPE.

Sir,—I have at different times made many experiments in the construction of magnifying glasses, particularly on glass spherules ; and I have lately made a microscope on this principle, of surprising magnifying power, for the following description of which, I beg to solicit a place in the *Mechanics' Magazine.*

The instrument consists of two tubes, one sliding within the other, each about 6 inches long ; and has two glasses, an object glass and an eye glass. The object glass is a small globule, about $\frac{1}{10}$th part of an inch in diameter, fixed at one end ; the eye-glass is a convex lens of about 2 inches focus, fixed at the other end, and with an eye-piece, or tube of a conical form, through which the eye looks upon the glass, rather more than 2 inches long. At the other end there is a small tube, about 1 inch long, with an aperture of about $\frac{1}{4}$th part of an inch in diameter, through which the light passes to the object glass; the microscope may be used either with or without this appendage ; but, by using it, the direct rays fall upon the object, while the others are excluded, and the object appears clearer; perhaps a thick lens might send more light on the object.

In using this instrument, the object should be placed upon the object glass so as to touch it; and the tube may be drawn out to any length ; the farther it is out, the more the object is magnified. The object must touch the glass in all situations, and not be shifted when the tube is altered. By day light the glass is of no use, as the object cannot be seen. It may be seen best at some distance from the light of a good candle or lamp ; I have tried many schemes to make the object appear clear in high magnifying powers ; but there appears to be a deficiency for want of light, which is remedied in some respects, by the small tube, which only admits the direct rays. Perhaps some of your correspondents, who may be disposed to try experiments of this kind, may find out some more efficient means, as the instrument may be made at a small expense by almost any one. Its chief use is for objects that cannot be seen by the naked eye. The hair of a person's head will appear about 3 inches broad through the glass, and its transparency may be also seen pretty clearly. Its magnifying power is thus found $10 \div \frac{1}{32} = \frac{4}{1} \times \frac{4}{1} = 320$, then $320 \times 3\frac{1}{2} = 1120$ and $1120^2 = 1254400$ the power, the tube being considered 10 in. long. The power may be increased to any extent by lengthening the tube, or making use of a smaller globule for the object glass.

I have tried many ways to make these globules. At first I fixed a slender wire round the end of a longish bit of glass, and holding the wire by the other end, introduced the glass into a strong heat of the fire, when it was soon melted into a globule, having a neck. But after this I found out a better method, as follows: I got a piece of tin plate, about 16 or 18 inches long, and 1 inch broad, and chalked one end of it well; I then broke a bit of good window glass (which is better than the whiter sort,) into many little bits, and laid them upon the chalked end of the tin, holding it by the other end, and introduced it into a strong open heat of the fire ; and presently every bit of glass was melted into a globule perfectly round ; in this way they may be made from the $\frac{1}{10}$th to the $\frac{1}{100}$th part of an inch in diameter. No bellows need be used in the operation. One of these globules, if put in a case, would of itself make a powerful microscope, the least magnifying the most.

I am, Sir, yours, &c.

THOMAS COOKE.

Draycott, near Derby

RETROSPECTIVE CRITICISM—NAUTILUS IN REPLY TO MR. MUNRO, KINCLAVEN, ETC.

Sir,—If I were to allow the several notices, with which I was honoured in your last monthly part, to remain unanswered, I fear it might be supposed, at least by the writers themselves, that I had fulfilled the prophecy of O. N., whose clumsy facetiousness evinces a sad falling off from the humility, with which he was so properly impressed by a former exposure of his absurdities. To begin, then, with Mr. Munro, who, at page 88, complains of the annoyance felt by himself and others, from the discussion of the perpetual motion question: surely, if he wished the subject to be dropped, it was *not* the most wise mode of attaining such an end, to make an accusation, which could not be suffered to pass without reply. I can easily imagine, that it must be disagreeable to Mr. Munro, to have a subject alluded to, that can only remind him of time lost, and labour thrown away; but he, of all men, should have been the last to accuse me of injustice, seeing that he himself is a living refutation of the charge; and a *recorded* instance of the truth of my observations. Every line in the original communication of Mr. Mackintosh would justify the inference I drew from it, but I shall be content with referring to one sentence, because it is the last, and consequently, not weakened by any subsequent remark.— "However, if any of the readers of the *Mechanics' Magazine* should feel disposed to try what can be done by adding the ratchet; I hope, I have stated the principle plain enough, to enable them to proceed." Vol. xxvi, p. 150. And, *accordingly*, Mr. Munro *did* proceed, " to try what could , be done with the ratchet"—a piece of unprofitable labour which he might have saved, had he waited for the very discussion, of which he now so unreasonably complains.

Kinclaven, who favours me with a postscript at page 100, claims my attention next; had he been content with calling me fastidious, had he even stopped at the uncandid, and palpably untrue, insinuation, that it was, "since," his own correction had appeared, I found out mine, he should have retained undisturbed possession of the last word, of which he seems so desirous; but, when his anxiety to prove me in error, betrays him into a gross mistake, it becomes my duty to correct him.

In the diagram, let S T be the ecliptic, P T, P S, two great circles at right angles

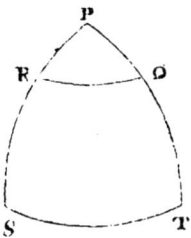

thereto; one of which is the solstitial colure, the other passes through polaris at R. The planes of these two circles make a certain angle, which may be measured, indifferently, either upon S T, or upon its parallel R Q; but Kinclaven thinks *not*, and he actually asserts that the segment R Q is *not* a measure of the segment S T, or in other words, that the angle S P T, is *not* equal to the angle R P Q! Do I misrepresent Kinclaven? here are his words, " The distance between polaris and the solstitial colure is surely not an arch of the ecliptic, upon which celestial longitude is reckoned. An infinite number of great circles (and small ones two) might be drawn through polaris to intersect the solstitial colure which of all these great circles are we to use? why, *none* of them!" Now the original blunder consisted in using the expression " *distance* of polaris from the *tropic of cancer*, which last is one of the armilliary circles." Surely, then, the shortest and plainest mode of correcting the mistake, was to substitute *another* armilliary circle for the erroneous one, and so change the expression to " *distance* of polaris from the solstitial colure." You must pardon all this repetition; it is forced from me, by the uncandid and

P 2

unhandsome partipacity of Kinclaven himself.

Lastly comes the doughty O. N., at page 103, who must needs have a try whether he, too, cannot wield the weapon, from which he has, himself, suffered so keenly. In lending his powerful aid to Kinclaven's view of the segments, he calls the geographical primer "all nonsense," thereby affording a clue to what had otherwise been unaccountable, namely his own profound ignorance of its commonest precepts. He then proceeds to misrepresent the whole drift of my letter to Nauticus, whose question, respecting two stars in the same vertical, he pronounces, with his usual acuteness, to be impossible of solution, and as an improvement, proposes one himself in lieu of it. Now, not only is the solution of the question of Nauticus perfectly possible, but it is infinitely a more appropriate, and more practical, position, than that proposed by O. N., copied by him, doubtless, from some old navigation book, with the intention of holding over the solution, until he can offer it as an atonement for his next blunder; that I am not wrong about the navigation book, let me offer one little proof. In O. N.'s unmerciful correction of the balloon calculation at page 186 of your last volume, he had occasion to refer to a table of *meridional parts;* which table, has generally at the head of each column the initials, "M.P." or "Mer. P.;" now, O. N., fancying that these initials meant, not *Meridional Parts,* but *Mercator's Principles,* and unwilling that he should lose the benefit of his acuteness, claps down, at full length (lest the slightest abbreviation might injure the effect,) "3617 *Mercator's Principles.*" But to return, in thumbing over the said navigation book, O. N. has found out, that the longitude, is one of the elements in similar questions; and seeing that Nauticus omitted longitude, in stating *his* question, he of course thought that the question itself, must be impossible; but, in the first place, the longitude is not absolutely a necessary datum in this particular question, which, strictly speaking, is the determination of the star's distance from the meridian; and in the second place, even though it were, still, none being expressed, the obvious inference is, that, Zero, is understood; even if it were not corroborated by the given latitude being that of London. But perhaps the best proof of the possibility of solving the question will be to work it, as follows: premising that the formula used are deduced from the commonest problems in spherical trigonometry.

	R. A.	Polar Dis.	
1st Feb. 1837 ; Stars, Polaris,	1. 0. 42	1° 33′ 18″	Latitude 51° 30′
γ Dracs. .	17.52.48	38. 39. 42	

Let A = Diff. of AR

P = Polar dis. lower star

P′ = Polar dis. upper star

L = Latitude

Δ = Hour angle of upper star.

Then, $\text{Tan. } x^1 = \text{Cos. A. Tan. P}$

$\text{Cotan. } x^2 = \text{Tan. A. sin. } x^1. \text{ Cosin. P}$

$\text{Cosin. } x^3 = \frac{\sin (x^1 + P')}{\text{Tan P. Tan L. Cosin. } x^2}$

$\Delta = x^2 \mp x^3$

P = 38. 29. 42 .... Tan 9.900528,

A = 106. 58. 30....Tan.. 0.515339..... Cosin.... 9.465315

x^1 = 13. 4. 19....Sin..9.354443.... Tan 9.365843

P^1 = 1. 33. 18....Cosin.9.999840..... Tan.... 8.433714

$x + P'$ = 14. 37. 37....Cosec 0.597697.... Tan.L.... 0.999397

x^2 = 18. 49. 35... Cotan 0.467319..... Cosin ... 9.976138

x^3 = 99. 8. 55................. Cosin ... 8.509237,

　　　　　　　　　　　　　　　　h. m. s.

Δ = 69. 19. 20 = 4. 37. 17

　　　　　　AR Polaris 1. 0. 42

　　　　　　　　　　　　　　　h. m. s.

Observed sidereal time 5. 37. 59 = 8. 50. 36 Greenwich Mean Time.

I remain, Mr. Editor, your very obedient servant,

　　　　　　　　　　　　　　　　　　NAUTILUS.

STEAM BOILER EXPLOSIONS.

Sir,—Much discussion has taken place upon the sudden disruption or bursting of steam-engine boilers, but as yet no sufficient reason therefor has been assigned. In this manufacturing country, where the steam engine constitutes the principal motive power of our machinery, and where its use is every day called forth, it is a matter of regret that no sufficiently extensive, and methodically conducted, investigation into the causes and means of prevention of such accidents has been instituted. I have been led to these remarks by hearing of the late disaster at the Dowlais ironworks, in Glamorganshire, where it appears a boiler about 40 feet long, and about 6 feet diameter, exploded and scattered its fragments to a considerable distance, killing some, and injuring others, besides doing damage to the amount of nearly one thousand pounds. The cause assigned, there, it is said, "by those best enabled to judge," was, "owing to some thin worn-out plates giving way at the bottom of the boiler." But was there not some other cause? Had not some other and greater power than steam been generated within the boiler? Do not these accidents arise by having the boiler *nearly empty*, and thereby overheating the plates—reducing their strength—decomposing the small quantity of water within, and resolving the same into its component *gases*, which suddenly expanding with strong elastic force burst the boiler? I give this as a conjecture of my own.* In this place four explosions have taken place; three being boilers used in the colliery winding engines. In the first instance, the boiler was thrown from its seat, and carried some distance. In the next, a boiler from 16 to 18 feet diameter was thrown from its seat, capsized, and prevented going farther, from being thrown against the engine-house. Another of the same size was elevated to the height of its stack, or chimney, about 60 feet, and fell about the same distance from its seat. I am inclined to think that "weak and thin plates" are not the cause of explosion, for how often do we find *old* boilers to *tear* and *burst*, letting out the water without *exploding?* In support of this, I give the following fact: A few months ago an oblong boiler with rounded ends and semicircular top about 20 feet long, 9 feet wide, and 9 feet deep was put in good repair. Half of the bottom was made anew, of good 4th in. plates. The engine worked occasionally for about two months,—until one morning about five o'clock, when it exploded —but was not elevated from its seat; the bottom, which had been curved inwardly, or raised in an arch over the fire, about 18 inches in height, was thrust downwards—the arch being completely inverted and broken; several of the new plates, otherwise uninjured and *unworn*, were drawn apart, as if they had been strained by some strong lateral force applied to their edges, which produced several rents in the direction of their lengths. Now this boiler must have given way under a very powerful pressure. And, observe, these plates were not thin nor worn—nor was the weight on the safety-valve increased. Where, then, are we to look for the cause? I call upon the man of scientific practice to investigate this subject, the importance of which demands the immediate co-operation of every one concerned in engines. The honour of the profession of the engineer—of the country—the calls of humanity—the preservation of life and property,—all unite to demand an elucidation of the cause, and provide methods for its prevention. It is well said, that "the knowledge of a disease is half its cure."

This I commit to you, Mr. Editor, for insertion in the *Mechanics' Magazine*, and I trust it will elicit the attention of your talented readers and contributors.

I am, Sir,

Yours respectfully,

Y. Z.

Old Park, May 27, 1837.

P.S.—A co-relative point required to be known, is the proper weight per square inch on the safety-valve of Boulton and Watt's double powered steam-engine, which, probably some of your friends will be so kind as to supply, as many engines, have their valves very randomly loaded—from 3, and 4, to 6 and 7 lb per square inch and upwards.

---

* We have no doubt our correspondent firmly believes this theory to be *quite* his own, but our well-informed readers need not be told that it is by no means new.—Ed. M. M.

EXPLOSIONS IN COAL MINES—CORONERS' INQUESTS.

Sir,—When I addressed my last letter to you on accidents in mines, it was my intention to confine the observations which might immediately follow, to the Report and the Minutes of Evidence printed by order of the late Parliamentary Committee. The doing so, I considered would be the best mode I could take of rendering those documents, what they have not yet been, and which they are especially capable of being—useful to the coal miner. The announcement, however, in the Merthyr Guardian of last week, of the explosion of a coal pit in its neighbourhood, induces me to deviate from my intended course, that I may take for my present subject, a matter seriously connected with that, and all explosive accidents—namely, the verdict of the Coroner's Inquest. The history of the event referred to, like the history of the hundreds of other explosive accidents, which have preceded it, is brief and sad—the cause, the use of unsafe lights—the consequences, the destruction of human life, and the destitution of widows and fatherless children. All this is however sepulchred, as usual, from public view and sympathy, by the verdict of the Coroner's Inquest, which acquits from any blame, those on whom much seems to rest. Thus, ignorantly and mischievously attributing to Providence, that which is clearly traceable to man's neglect. I should not, Sir, make such strong observations on this particular matter, were it not necessary to mark with its proper name, every part of a system, which holds, in the union of its operations, every thing in higher estimation than human life. Such, I fearlessly assert, is the apparent basis on which the present, and long pursued, system of working coal mines, is founded. In reference to this particular accident, it may fairly be asked of the mine owners, why they suffered unprotected lights to be used in that pit? This question should have been put seriously to them by the Coroner. Had it, they could not have escaped just and severe censure, for exposing the lives of these workmen to an awful, unnecessary, and in this instance, fatal risk. Surely that must be considered indefencible, which common prudence might have avoided.

And that a risk of this kind might always be avoided, must be conceded, when it is known that every operation necessarily connected with coal mining can be efficiently conducted with protected lights. It may, and naturally will be demanded, why then do the coal owners suffer naked lights to be used? The answer is this—is it a money consideration. The collier, at the present rate of wages, could not earn sufficient to supply himself and his family with their pittance of course food, if he were confined to the use of the safety lamp. This he can generally manage to do with a naked light. Consequently, the preventing, as humanity dictates, the use of unprotected lights, is opposed to the pecuniary interest of the coal owners; inasmuch as the same price must then be paid to the working collier for the obtaining a less quantity of coal. It is therefore altogether a *money question*, whether explosions in coal mines shall continue or not? Whether hundreds of industrious and honest men shall, or not, be annually sacrificed, and numerous families reduced to beggary and misery, to feed to repletion an inordinate appetite for gain, on the part of the coal owner. This is a question for Coroner's inquests to determine. Were they to return verdicts as they ought, of culpable homicide against the mine proprietors, where unprotected lights were used, the evil now complained of, would, as a remedy could be found, soon end. I shall, Sir, close this letter, by referring to a matter which has not even the money excuse;—the loss of life annually occasioned by the present mode of lowering and raising the workmen in coal pits, which is, in the great mining districts, one of the most insecure that human ingenuity and barbarity could possibly devise. This is a subject also worthy of the attention of a Coroner's inquest.

Your obedient servant,
CARBON.

4th July, 1837.

MR. UTTING'S ASTRONOMICAL TABLES.

Sir,—Mr. Utting, C. E., tells me in his letter (No. 704), that if I will take the sidereal periods of the planets from Sir John Herschell's Astronomy, and the precession of the equinoxial points at 1° 23' 30" in a century, and compute from these the tropical periods of all the planets (Mr. Utting wishes to put me upon short allowance in respect of data), and compare them with his in the *Mechanics' Magazine*, vol. xxvi. p. 378; "Then," adds Mr. Utting, "let me ask you (a Scotch Dominie) what authority you had for your blundering assertions," &c.

I have never seen Sir John Herschell's Astronomy; but I have no doubt that the mean sidereal periods of the planets are all (as far as is known) correctly given; but I will inform Mr. Utting, that had I been disposed to calculate the grand period of conjunction of all the planets, I never would have put myself to the trouble of converting the mean time of the sidereal revolutions into mean tropical periods. I should have at once converted the mean sidereal revolutions into mean synodical periods. Thus, suppose S S^1, S^2 S^3, &c. to be the mean synodical periods expressed, say to the nearest second of time, and let G be the grand period of conjunction of all the planets expressed in the same denomination. Then, taking for granted that there has, or will be, a time when all the planets were, or may be, in conjunction, then G must be such a number as to be exactly divisible by all the synodical periods, S, S^1, S^2, S^3, &c., or $\frac{G}{S}$, $\frac{G}{S^1}$, $\frac{G}{S^2}$, &c. must all be whole numbers, To those, who delight in the luxury of long arithmetical calculations, this question involves no difficulty. Well, suppose G is determined to the nearest second of time, what would be the probability that this calculated value of G should be an exact number of mean tropical years (which Mr. Utting states to be 250904 solar years)? Why, it would be in the ratio of 1 to the number of seconds in a tropical year minus 1, or as 1 to 31556928.

Mr. Utting's great object has been to manufacture a period consisting of an exact number of mean tropical years, which number of tropical years should be a multiple (or very nearly so) of all the mean tropical periods given in his first table. In this attempt he has shown considerable arithmetical skill; but he has completely overlooked the principal requisite, namely, that the grand period of conjunction of all the planets must be a multiple of all their synodical periods. True it is, if Mr. Utting is allowed to manufacture synodical periods, in the way that he has done for the moon (see No. 714), in that case his grand period of conjunction will be a multiple (or very nearly so) of all their synodical periods; but in my last letter (No. 722) I have shown in two cases that this new method, that Mr. Utting has discovered, of manufacturing synodical periods is not *exactly consistent with truth*, and this I will more fully shew presently.

Having in my last letter shown that Mr. Utting's grand period is not true in respect of the moon, nor of the inferior planets Mercury and Venus, I shall now proceed to shew that Jupiter is also out of the line of a conjunction at the end of Mr. Utting's grand period of conjunction.

From Table 1st, the tropical period of Jupiter is 4330·64733098, and adding 1·94897652, the difference between a tropical and periodical period, produced by the precession of the equinoxial points of Jupiter, we obtain 4332·5963075 days for the sidereal or periodic period of Jupiter, and the periodic period of the earth is 365·2563991 (see No. 722). Call these periods P and P^1, and let S be the synodical period of Jupiter, then in the case of a superior planet, we have the well known astronomical theorem, $S = P^1 + \frac{P^2}{P - P^1}$, that is, $S = 365·2563991 + \frac{(365·2563991)^2}{3967·3399084} = 398·8840292 = 398$ days 21 hours 13 minutes 0·123 seconds. Hence, 91640740 ÷ 398·8840292 ought to be a whole number, but it produces the unfortunate number 229742·81.

In the same way, it might be shown that, instead of all the planets being in conjunction at the end of 250904 mean solar years (allowing there had been a general conjunction at the beginning of that period), there will not be a single one of them in conjunction with the sun; or, in fact, they will all be farther from a general conjunction than they are at the present minute I am now writing.

The radical error Mr. Utting has fallen into, is in his method of manufacturing a synodical period. Thus, suppose we were to calculate the synodical period of Venus according to Mr. Utting's rule—

From the tropical revolution of Venus, Table 1st, &c.,... } 407844

Subtract the tropical revolution of the earth................ } 250904

Remains.............. 156940

Hence, 91640740 ÷ 156940 = 583·922136 days; this period, we calculated, in No. 722, from Mr. Utting's own tropical periods, to be 583.920940 days, the error will in no case be great for a single synodical revolution, but for a period of 250904 mean solar years, the error will accumulate to such a quantity, as to prevent any thing like a conjunction. In short, Mr. Utting has confounded tropical periods with periodical revolutions : this will more clearly appear by computing the synodical period of Venus, independant of the number 91640740. The tropical periods of the earth and Venus from Table 1st are 365·2422440, and 224·6955699. Respectively call these numbers T and T¹, then say S =

$$\frac{T \cdot T^1}{T - T^1} = \frac{365 \cdot 242240 \times 224 \cdot 6955699}{140 \cdot 5466741} =$$

583·922136 days, the same as by Mr. Utting's rule. But the true value of S ought to have been computed from the theorem $S = \frac{P \cdot P^1}{P - P^1}$, where P and P¹ are the periodical revolutions.

I trust I have now, Mr. Editor, fully established what I asserted in my first letter, and I hope Mr. Utting will allow that it is just as possible for a Scotch Dominie to know a little of astronomy as an English engineer. In the tedious multiplications and divisions, &c., I may perhaps have made some slight slips. In principles, I trust I have made none, but if I should, I will feel much obliged to any of your able mathematical contributors to point them out.

Yours with respect,
A SCOTCH DOMINIE.

Forfarshire, June 5th, 1837.

COWHOUSE OR STABLE FOR EXERCISING ANIMALS, AND MAKING USE OF THE POWER EXERTED IN SUCH EXERCISE.

Sir,—On looking over a portfolio of designs and drawings this morning, I found the inclosed plan for a cowhouse, in which the beasts could be exercised and their labour applied to the purposes of churning, chopping their food, washing, cleaning the place out, and so forth.

The design may be said to be copied from the horse ferry-boats which ply on the Mississippi, in which we may often see a number of horses harnessed in their stalls, and pushing the floor from under their feet. In this plan the cows are not represented fastened or harnessed, as that in a great degree will depend upon the fancy of the owner. The common pails, or yoke of Germany, or collar and traces, would answer for them to push against; the labor should be light for heavy cows giving milk. The plan I believe is good, and is worthy trial by some of your London dairy-men, who are unable to bring their cows out for exercise.

Though the plan may not answer in its present form, yet a hope may be entertained, that, with a few modifications, it may be found beneficial and useful in particular situations.

Truly yours
E. C. TALEBOIS.
Liverpool. December 23rd. 1836.

Description of the Engraving.

AA, level platform, on which the cows stand and walk. B B, upright shaft, turning on the iron block M; to this A A is firmly secured by the braces L L L L. C C C C, chains from the iron collar c c to the ground, supporting the roof, D k and D k, to which the rods E E E, E E E are attached, which support the frames G G H H and G G H H. FF braces part of G G H H, and which are firmly set in the ground. I, iron weather-cock, fixed in top of B B; K C C K, open space to admit light and allow bad air to escape. M iron block for B B. to turn in. N N rollers (plain or toothed) on which the stage A A is partly supported. When the cattle walk, the stage A A moves on these, and if any power be required to cut or chop food, or pump water &c. it would be taken from one or more of them; churning &c. might also be performed by one of them, towards which the milk house and dairy should be erected; 3 is the smallest number for these rollers N N, and would probably be the best. O O O O are the props to support the centres of the pulleys N and N. These should be very securely fastened. p, shaft from the roller N, from which power might be taken.

Note.—When a very great force was required, the centre post B B could be

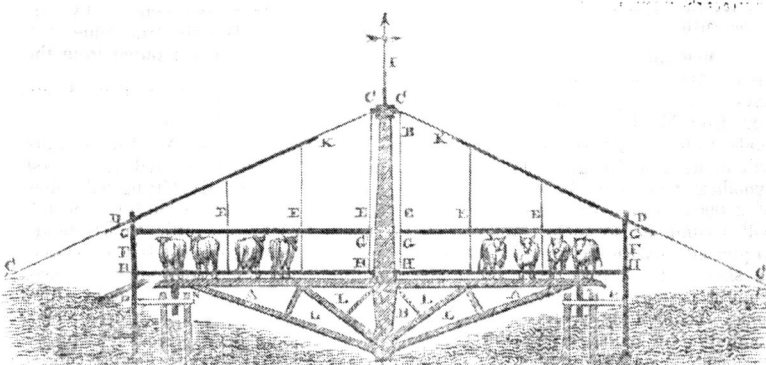

used as a capstan, the rope to be wound on it in the same way.

It is to be observed, that the cattle never move out of their places, the ground only on which they stand moving from them when they walk; and brushes &c. being properly fixed in the frame G.G. H.H. all the filth is carried to the outside of the circular platform where it falls over.

DOUBLE ACTING MOVEABLE SET SQUARE.

Sir,—From the favourable manner, in which you have received my communications, I trust you will excuse the trifle I send on the present occasion; it is a drawing of a double acting moveable set square,* which I continually use in drawing angular lines parallel to each other, or lines at right angles to them, or of any angle required. I have found it so very useful in isometrical drawings of machinery, or plans not at right angles to each other, that I should feel myself wanting to draftsmen if I failed to communicate my invention to them. It not only unites the capabilities of the common set square and angle, but is much lighter, and used with more ease, and from both sides being capable of being drawn by, it is used with more facility. It consists

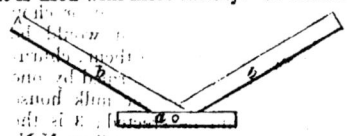

of three pieces of ivory or bone, and is in form like a T square. The rule is in two parts, the lower one being the 24th part of an inch thick, and the upper one the 12th part of an inch thick. The third, or head piece, is $\frac{7}{15}$ths of an inch thick. The two pieces are rivetted to the head so stiffly as not to move with ordinary pressure in drawing. The accompanying drawing, represents the instrument as set to draw isometrically; *a* is the head (which has a recess, in it to allow the rule, to pass under) and *b b* the two rules; *o* is the rivet. At the different edges of the rules, are marked the various scales of eighths, sixteenths, &c.

I am, Sir,

J. R. CROFT.

Bayswater, March 13, 1837.

THE FIRE INSURANCE SYSTEM.— REPLY TO AQUARIUS.

Sir,—There is a perversity of meaning, and a continual misstatement of facts, in the communications on Fire-extinction signed "Aquarius," well calculated to provoke eternal discussion, were the subject (in that shape) worth the extended space it would occupy in your pages, or of sufficient interest to your readers

* The name, it must be confessed, is rather objectionable; but I have no better to propose.

generally, to warrant such an appropriation.

With respect to the paragraph in your
16th. volume—written by me five years
and a half ago—which "Aquarius" has
tauntingly brought forward at page 173,
and erronously stated to refer "to the
comparative efficiency of the *Old* and *New*
systems of extinguishing Fires in London "—it is only necessary for me to
state, that by referring to the 16th. and
following Volumes of your Magazine,
where all the changes that have taken
place in these matters from time to time
have been faithfully chronicled, (by WM.
BADDELEY) your readers will at once
perceive, that the paragraph in question,
referred merely to a Reduction in the
number of firemen and engines in London, that had taken place under the *Old
System !* The New System, (that is, the
United London Fire establishment, under
one superintendent, with the men continually on duty, day and night) was not
at that time formed—or even thought
of ! This explanation converts the whole
of "Aquarius's" fanfarronade into arrant
nonsense, and it may be taken as a fair
specimen of the carelessness too often
evinced, in the getting up of "anonymous" communications.

"Aquarius" expresses himself sadly
annoyed that he is unable to provoke
the discussion he desires; the fact is, Mr.
Editor, I am now rather differently cir-
cumstanced, to what I was when I held
myself ready to answer "all comers".
After enduring the fatigues of business
fourteen hours per day, I find I have not
much energy, and but little leisure left;
I trust therefore, I may be permitted to
employ the times taken from my brief intervals of repose, upon such subjects as
I think most acceptable to your readers.
The claims of anonymous correspondents to attention and reply must always
greatly depend upon the manner as well
as the matter of their communications,—
wherever courtesy is due, I hope I shall
never be found wanting.

It is now "ten years ago" since I made
the subject of "fire extinction" peculiarly my own in your pages, and it is well
known that I have never, at any period,
had the slightest personal interest in the
matter.

With regard to "Aquarius," one thrust
of my pen would pierce the flimsy arras
behind which he has concealed himself—

let out his *watery* humour,—and at once
explain the cause of his pertinacious attacks ; but I do not choose to dispel his
misty disguise at present.   Suffice it to
say, he is a gentleman preeminently qualified to amuse and to instruct; as a writer he has shown himself possesssed of
great power, and I can only regret that
he should have condescended to employ
talents of the very first order, in so discreditable a line of argument as that,
which he has been pursuing for some
time past.

Once more I have the honor to subscribe myself yours respectfully,
                        WM. BADDELEY.
June 20, 1837.

SYMINGTON'S PATENT BOILER.

Mr. Symington has lately patented a
new boiler, particularly applicable to
marine engines, the advantages of which
are—the prevention of "priming," and
that a large heating surface is obtained
from one fire only.   As it is well known
that a more perfect combustion takes
place when the fuel is collected into one
burning mass, and consequently more
heat given out in proportion to the quantity of fuel consumed, than when, in the
usual way, it is divided into two or more
smaller fires—it is calculated that a considerable saving of fuel (the great desideratum in steam navigation) will thus be
effected.

In the plan, Fig. 1. A is the furnace
B B the centre flue, which is divided
into two equal divisions, by the vertical
tubes 1 2 3 by means of which vertical
tubes, the flame from the furnace is
bisected, thereby causing it to pass in
equal portions along the return flues C
C, making its final exit into the chimney
by the upright flues E E.   G G is
the interior of the boiler.   The vertical
tubes 1 2 3 in addition to their more
immediate and direct intention, that of
dividing the flame into two equal portions, and directing each portion into
its respective side-flue, will cause a very
rapid formation of steam, as each tube
contains a column of water, every part of
which is exposed to a most intense heat.

Fig. 2 is a cross section of the boiler,
taken through the steam chest; A A is
the boiler; B B the steam chest; *a*, the
steamway from the boiler to the steam-
chest; *c* a cap to cover the steamway to
prevent the water from the boiler being

Fig. 1.

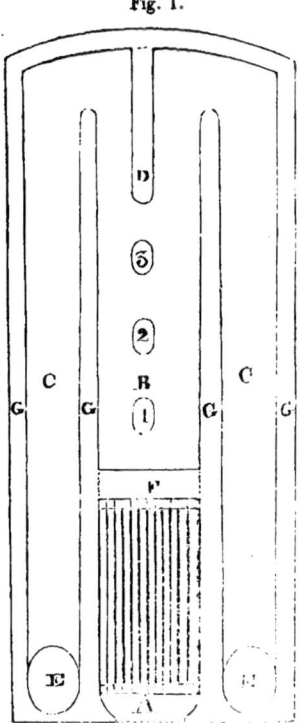

Fig. 2.

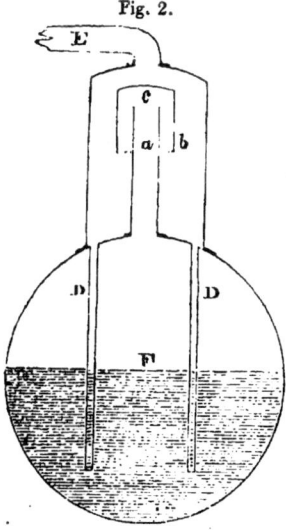

carried along the steam pipe E, into the working cylinder, which effect is techinally called " priming" ; D D return tubes, through which the water, that has been arrested in its progress, is returned into the boiler; F is the water level.

The description of the different parts renders any farther remarks upon this portion of Mr. Symington's improvement unnecessary. Those engineers, who may have been annoyed by "priming" will at once perceive, and appreciate, the utility of the means here adopted to obviate this most vexatious evil. A boiler upon this plan has been placed in the Symington Towing Company's new tug the *Dragon*, from which very favourable results are anticipated.

REPORT OF THE MILITARY ENGINEER ON THE BRIGHTON RAILWAYS.

The following is the report of the Military Engineer, appointed in pursuance of an Address of the House of Commons to his late Majesty, on the several lines of Brighton Railway:—

In obedience to your orders of the 2d and 9th of June, 1837, directing me to report in conformity with the instructions from Her Majesty's Principal Secretary of State for the Home Department, on the following proposed lines of railway between London and Brighton, viz. Sir J. Rennie's, or the Direct Line, Mr. Stephenson's, Mr. Gibbs's, and the South Eastern, I have the honour to state, that I have carefully read over the evidence given before the committee, as well as their report, and attentively compared the several plans and sections submitted to me; that I have also taken a general survey of the sites of the different lines, examining more attentively those portions where works of importance are proposed, and have no hesitation in stating, that the line proposed by Mr. Stephenson, considered in an engineering point of view alone, is preferable to either of the others. Availing himself of the vallies of the rivers Mole and Adur, he avoids the heavy cuttings necessarily consequent on forcing a passage through the chalk ridges known as the North and South Downs ; and, with the exception of two short tunnels, one at Epsom, and the other at Dorking, arrives at Brighton, *viâ* Shoreham, having only such ordinary difficulties to contend against as are necessarily consequent on undertakings of a similar nature and extent.

As, however, there is but one point for consideration of a main line of railroad, I will now proceed to consider the respective merits of the several lines with reference to the second resolution of the House of Commons.

On referring to the map and the population returns, it will be seen that the country passed through, or approached by either of the lines, as well as on the coast, within reach of railroad communication by branches, containing neither manufactoring nor mineral districts, the town presents only the usual traffic of an agricultural population, and are, as compared with Brighton, of minor importance. It appears to me, therefore, that after attending to one principal point in the construction of any main line, viz.' that its London terminus be central,'—that route between London and Brighton which best unites engineering facilities with convenient termini should be prefered. I will then consider the termini of the various lines with reference to the accommodation they afford to the metropolis at one end, and the town of Brighton at the other. Each of the proposed lines avails itself of a terminus already constructed, or for which an act of Parliament has been obtained. Mr. Stephenson adopts the terminus of the London and Southampton Railway at Nine Elms, a little above Vauxhall-bridge with a depôt on the banks of the Thames, branching from this line at Wimbledon-common, five miles and a half from the terminus. The Direct line and Gibbs's adopt the Greenwich Railway terminus at London-bridge and avail themselves of railway communication, already sanctioned and now constructing as far as Croydon. The South Eastern also has its terminus at London bridge, and, in addition to the Croydon, avails itself of 12 miles of the Dover Railroad, branching off at Oxted.

Taking the Middlesex side of Blackfriars-bridge as a centre, and describing circles with the several radii of one, one and a half, and two miles, thus including within the last an area of upwards of 12 miles bearing the densest population in the world, it will be found, that, whilst the terminus of London-bridge is within the smallest of these circles, that, of Nine Elms is without the largest ; under these circumstances it may be fairly inferred, that Stephenson's London terminus is not so conveniently situated as that of the other lines, particulary for an extensive passenger traffic, as that of any line connecting Brighton with the metropolis is almost sure to prove.

The Greenwich Railroad being already constructed on a viaduct of sufficient width only for two lines of rails, I doubted whether it would be capable of affording sufficient accommodation for the increased traffic proposed to be thrown upon it, more particularly, as on this line the trains start every quarter of an our. On inquiry, I found

that the Greenwich Railway Company possessed sufficient ground on each side to enable them to widen the viaduct so as to meet any probable increase of traffic, and that a plan and estimate had been framed for this purpose, ready to be carried into effect as soon as possible.

There is still, however, an objection of some importance to any new line adopting either this or the Southampton terminus,— the necessity of limiting the distance between its rails to that of the lines already laid down.

At Brighton, Stephenson's line, as in London, stops at the western extremity of the town, at Chalybeate-street; this is inconvenient for passengers ; and, besides, as one of the advantages proposed in connecting Shoreham with Brighton, is, that the latter may obtain coal at a cheaper rate than at present, it is important that that article should be brought as far into town as possible. Gibbs's line, entering nearly at the same point as Stephenson's, extends its terminus farther into the town, and is well situated with respect to Brighton. The South-Eastern, on the other hand, enters Brighton at the north-eastern part of the town, at Carlton Hill, and nearly as much to the eastward as Stephenson's is to the westward, and cannot, therefore, without great additional expense, get a branch to Shoreham. This remark applies equally to Stephenson's and Gibbs's lines, with reference to the Lewes and Newhaven branches ; and, lastly, the Direct line enters at the north-western part of the town, having a depôt for goods abutting on Trafalgar-street, and a passenger terminus on Church-street, 35 feet above its level, to which an inclined plane from Church-street gives an access for carriages. This appears to be the most central terminus of the four, and that which affords the greatest accommodation to the town of Brighton. And here, too, after alluding to the Brighton termini of the different lines, I must refer to the peculiar character of the property of that place, for I conceive that the second resolution of the House of Commons, by opening the whole question, has rendered it necessary that I should do so. This town owes its present importance to the proximity of the sea, at that place, to the metropolis, and large sums have been expended there for the accommodation of its numerous visitors. A railroad touching the coast before it reaches Brighton might transfer the advantage of position so another place, and sooner or later prove injurious to the property at Brighton; thereby causing a large capital to have been wasted without any corresponding national advantage ; and in this point of view, Stephenson's and Gibbs's line are both objectionable

ble ; not, however, to the extent they would have been had the situation of Shoreham, with respect to the sea, been better.

The termini of the lines having been considered, their relative facility of construction and subsequent expense of working must be noticed. It will appear that Stephenson's and the Direct line in the heavy traffic are nearly on a par, the former having the advantage by thirteen chains only ; that the South-Eastern is next, and Gibbs's line the last ; and that in the passenger traffic, the direct line has the advantage of them all the South-Eastern, Stephenson's, and Gibbs's being the order in which the remainder follow, the South-Eastern and Stephenson's appearing nearly equal. It should also be borne in mind, that, in comparing the Direct line with Stephenson's, about two and a half miles ought to be added to the length of the latter, to make his termini as central as those of the former. It must, however, be observed, that the equivalent horizontal distances are only a comparative measure of the time, in which two lines can be passed over when the tractive power applied is on each line equal ; the maximum velocity, as yet obtained, may be given to a train on a gradient of 20 feet in a mile, as well as on a gradient of 16 feet, by using larger engines ; this would, however, occasion additional expense ; but it is necessary that it should be remembered, since it shows the advantage of reducing the actual distance when passenger trains are to be very much considered. The Direct line gives branches to Lewes, Shoreham, and Newhaven, the two latter being extremely valuable to Brighton by placing it between ports, with a certain and rapid conveyance to each.

The Shoreham branch of the Direct line appears to me incomplete in not communicating with the wharfs like that to Newhaven. Stephenson's and Gibbs's lines give a communication with Shoreham, liable to the same objections as that of the Direct line, and in a greater degree, and altogether exclude Lewes and the port of Newhaven. The South-Eastern gives a communication with Lewes and Newhaven, but excludes Shoreham, and has therefore a corresponding disadvantage in this respect to Stephenson's. Had this line, however, adopted the terminus of the Direct line in Brighton with the addition of its branch to Shoreham, and been able to select a better route from Oxted, it would, from having the smaller quantity of railroad to construct, have been the most desirable. On the other hand, had Stephenson's line more central termini, and, instead of making the coast at Shoreham, proceeded direct to Brighton, it would have had strong claims to consideration, and, if there were no other

lines already constructed south from London, deserve a preference over all the others. Gibbs's line appears to unite the principal objection to the Direct line, viz., the extensive cutting at Merstham, with that of Stephenson's line in going round by Shoreham ; and though it preserves a better gradient than the Direct line, yet, from its circuitous route, works to less advantage than any of the others.

Taking, then, into consideration the great advantages of the termini of the Direct line, — that it affords by its branches greater facilities of approach to the other towns on the coast within reasonable distance, avoiding unnecessary intersection of the country ; and that it is, on the whole, the best working line, with the least length of railroad to support ; for, though the South-Eastern has less to construct, yet each must support, in proportion to its traffic, whatever length of line it travels over, and also, that the Croydon Railway offers greater advantages than the Southampton Railway in the construction of a main southern trunk line ; it only remains to be seen what are the difficulties of construction it has to contend with, and whether they are such as can be recommended to be undertaken, to insure between London and Brighton a line possessing the advantages which it would appear this does over its competitors. On referring to the section, there appear to be three summits to be crossed, viz., Merstham, Balcombe, and Clayton. The former of these, the greatest work on the line, consists of a cutting through chalk of more than three miles in length, varying from 50 to upwards of 100 feet in depth, and which it is proposed to open out with slopes of one-sixth. As the prejudice against tunnelling is rapidly giving way, I should imagine that this mode would be resorted to on a considerable portion of this extensive excavation, as it appears to me beyond the point at which open cutting is more advantageous than tunnelling, especially in so favourable a soil. The greater part of the chalk obtained from this cutting must be run out on the adjoining land, not being required for embankment. The next excavation of importance is at Handcross-hill, near Balcombe, at the twenty-third mile, where a tunnel of 470 yards in length is proposed through favourable soil ; and the third at Clayton-hill, at the thirty-sixth mile, where a tunnel of 800 yards is proposed ; both of which, I think, may with advantage be increased in length, for the reason previously stated. At the southern extremity of the latter tunnel, there is a considerable length of open cutting ; the whole of Clayton hill is, like Merstham, a chalk formation.

Of the embankments on the line, one at the thirteenth mile, one across the river and valley of the Ouse at the twenty-sixth, and those between the thirtieth and thirty-fifth miles, are the principal; but of this description of work, the most objectionable in the construction, though there is less than of excavation, yet there are many short deep vallies to be crossed by embankment, and which, owing to the excavations being concentrated in two or three places, instead of being spread over the line, must be formed from side cuttings. After getting through Clayton-hill, the line runs nearly parallel to, and to the westward, of the turnpike-road to Brighton, to its terminus in Church-street, on a viaduct from its depôt in Trafalgar-street.

It will then appear, though the embankments are extensive, that on this line the amount of excavation through chalk forms the principal item of expense; and, from the conflicting evidence given before the Committee of the House of Commons, for the Direct and Gibbs's line, relative to the properties of chalk, and the best mode of excavating through it, and on which the correctness of the estimate for the former in a great measure depends, I thought it necessary to inspect, with great attention, the quarries of Merstham and Clayton, as well as one near Lewes, which is as deep as any of the proposed cuttings, and which has not been worked for ten years. In none of these quarries could I see any thing to induce me to adopt the plan proposed by the Direct line at Merstham and Clayton, viz., vertical cutting, or with a slope of one-sixth; on the contrary, I was convinced that, in excavations through every description of chalk, more or less of debris would be found to accumulate, even were the sides not subjected, as in the present instance they would be, to a constant vibratory motion from the traffic, in addition to the action of the wet and frost; and that, in order to afford security to the public, tunnelling, or, if open cutting, benching, of slopes of one to one, as proposed by Mr. Gibbs, ought to be resorted to.

In comparing these objections in an engineering point of view with the advantages the Direct line possesses, I am of opinion the latter are not too dearly purchased, and that it is the best line between London and Brighton. In giving this opinion, however, I beg distinctly to state that I do not pledge myself to the estimate; I think in all probability it would be found inadequate. I may be permitted to remark with respect to estimates generally, that were they fairly and impartially framed, which experience has shown is not the case at present, they would, with other information arranged in

a tabular form, enable even unprofessional men, with the assistance of a good map, to decide between two or more proposed methods of obtaining the same object.

Having proceeded thus far prior to receiving the plan of a joint line agreed to by the Committee of the four Brighton Railway Companies, I shall now, in obedience to your orders of the 22nd inst., proceed to report on it, in conformity with the instructions contained in the letter from her Majesty's Principal Secretary for the Home Department.

It is proposed in this joint line that there should be two termini in London; one at London-bridge, and the other at Nine Elms, near Vauxhall; also two lines going south, one through the valley of the Mole, and the other through the Mertsham Pass, meeting at or near Capel; and from thence there should be one line to Brighton, *via* Shoreham, adopting at Brighton the terminus and branches of the Direct line.

It is thus intended to construct between London and Brighton nearly seventy miles of railroad, independent also of using upwards of fourteen miles of railway constructed, and this, too, through a country possessing neither manufactories nor minerals, and with no town on the line, excepting Croydon, of more than 5,000 inhabitants; and which, therefore, must principally look for support from the towns of its termini, only fifty miles apart.

In the present uncertain state of the return which railways will make for the capital expended, and the absence of any great national advantages proposed to be obtained, I cannot think it advisable to venture on so great an outlay of capital, or that the traffic is such between London and Brighton as to demand it.

The company proposing, therefore, as a part of their plan, to come from Croydon through the Mertsham Pass to Earl's Wood Common, the distance from thence to Brighton (twenty-nine miles) by the Direct line, is all that is required to be constructed to render the communication complete between the two great termini; whereas, in the proposed joint line, nearly seventy, instead of about forty-two, miles of railroad will have to be constructed and maintained, as well as a second terminus and depôt, without any additional traffic except what may be afforded by the towns on the line.

Under these circumstances, it appears to me, that continuing the route proposed by the Direct line from Earl's Wood Common to Brighton is better for the interests of the company, and affords to the public all the accommodation required.

I therefore adhere to the opinion already

given in favour of the Direct line. I have the honour to be, Sir, your most obedient humble servant,

ROBERT ALDERSON, Capt. Roy. Eng.
London, June 27.

OPENING OF THE GRAND JUNCTION RAILWAY BETWEEN BIRMINGHAM AND LIVERPOOL AND MANCHESTER.
(From the *Morning Herald* Report.)

On the 4th inst. this railway was partially opened for the conveyance of passengers. It commences in Curzon-street, Birmingham, at the station adjoining that of the London and Birmingham railway, and passes near Wednesbury, Walsall, Dudley, Bolston, Wolverhampton, Stafford, Stone, Eccleshall, Newcastle, the Potteries, Nantwich, Middlewick, &c., to Warrington, terminating at Newton on the Liverpool and Manchester railway (midway). The distance from Birmingham to Newton is eighty-two and a half miles. From Newton, whence the train started at two minutes before seven in the morning, it arrived at the first stopping place, Warrington, distant 19½ miles, in 27 minutes. On leaving Warrington, a most delightful line of country was presented to the eye, while to the engineer the works forming the railway itself, were an object of admiration. The bridge of the river Mersey and embankments on either side, was the first object that attracted attention. The railway next passes through some deep cuttings on an ascent to Preston Brook. The cutting then becomes deeper, owing to the line running under the Duke of Bridgewater's canal. The view from the viaduct over the Weare is beautiful. The viaduct itself consists of 20 arches, and is one of the finest erections of that kind extant. The train arrived at the second stopping place, Hartford, at five minutes past eight o'clock; the distance performed by that time 31¾ miles. There is a handsome bridge at this station, and the cutting is about 33 feet deep. The stoppage here occupied three minutes. The road on either side of the Hartford Bridge is on the descent. At the end of the cutting, Vale Royal, one of the prettiest valleys in England, suddenly bursts on the eye. The railroad then proceeds through the rural districts of Cheshire, and to the passenger there is little to call forth attention until it reaches the level leading into Crewe, which is eleven miles in length. The first portion of this stage was performed rather slowly, owing to the stiffness of the rails, and the steam having been reduced by taking in water. The train reached Crewe at three minutes to nine o'clock. Crewe is 43½ miles distant from Liverpool; it is the third station on the line. The train left there at five minutes

past nine o'clock, about half an hour beyond the time fixed. There is a shed built for an extra engine, to assist in propelling the train up the Madeley inclined plane, but as yet no engine is assigned to that duty. The rise at the summit is 1 in 180. At half-past nine o'clock the train passed the station house. The down train was met at Whitmore Heath, fifty-four miles and a quarter from Liverpool. A few minutes afterwards, according to Birmingham time, it reached there at the half-hour exactly. It ought to have arrived at fifty-five minutes past eight o'clock, so that the Birmingham as well as the Liverpool train was about half an hour behind the proper time. The Birmingham train carried the London mail of the previous evening. The apparatus for supplying the engine with water was in an unfinished state, and considerable delay was thereby occasioned. It left Whitmore at twenty minutes to ten o'clock. We ought not to omit to mention the Madeley plane was ascended with great facility. The descent from Whitmore was performed with astonishing velocity. The one and a half mile from the fifty-eighth mile stone, or rather board, was done in two and a half minutes—so much for railway travelling. At the Penkridge station we met the mixed train, which left Birmingham at half-past eight o'clock. It had taken its departure from the station house at half-past ten, having done the twenty-four miles in two hours. The Wolverhampton station is about a mile distant from the town; an immense crowd was here collected to meet the train, which arrived there at five minutes to eleven o'clock. After taking in coke and water, the train again started. After passing through a short tunnel, we entered a deep cutting, the banks on both sides of which were quite covered with spectators. From Wolverhampton to Birmingham a general holiday appeared to be observed, and the scene was highly interesting both to the observed and observers. Tents were pitched in several fields, and parties given by the respective tenants in honour of the day. The weather was extremely beautiful, and the freedom from dust which exists on railways is another interesting feature connected with this branch of mechanics. The Newton-road station was passed at twenty minutes past eleven o'clock, and the train again entered on some deep cuttings, extending about half a mile in length. Between this and Birmingham we passed another train. The Liverpool train was at the moment proceeding with great rapidity—indeed that observation applies generally to the whole distance on the Birmingham side of Crewe. At half-past eleven o'clock the train arrived at its destination, all safe, and without an accident.

IRISH PATENTS GRANTED IN MAY, 1837.

Baron Henry de Bode, Major-General in the Russian Service, of Edgeware Road, Middlesex. For an improvement in Capstans. May 30.

NOTES AND NOTICES.

Exhibition of Fire Escapes, &c.—An immense concourse of people was collected on the wharf in front of Hungerford-Market on Wednesday evening, to witness an exhibition of fire-engines and fire-escapes. A compact and powerful engine belonging to St. Katharine's Docks having been put into thorough repair since the late fire, by the builder, Mr. Merryweather, engineer, of Long-Acre, was drawn up on the edge of the wharf, and by means of three lengths of suction-pipe, drew a supply of water from the bosom of father Thames, which it delivered about twelve feet above the flag-staff on the top of the Dolphin, a height of nearly one hundred feet from the ground, *and upwards of a hundred feet above the surface of the river, from whence the supply was drawn.* A set of Mr. Merryweather's improved fire-escape ladders having been raised against the Dolphin to a height of about forty-five feet, several descents were made to the great amusement of the lads who were thus lowered, and the satisfaction of the assembled spectators. Among those who took great interest in these performances, we observed the ingenious Captain Manby, Mr. Baddeley, and several other philantropic and scientific gentlemen."—*Morning Post.*

View from the Monument.—The New London Bridge, and its approaches, present a very imposing picture from the top of the Monument. King William-street, and the newly widened Princes-street, are particularly conspicuous; their spaciousness and elegance presenting a striking contrast to the mean and narrow appearance of most of the old streets in their vicinity. The Greenwich Railway is not so commanding a feature from the same spot as might be anticipated.

Horse-flesh at Discount.—The Grand Junction Railway, between Birmingham and Liverpool, being now completed, arrangements have been made by those concerned in the carrying trade for effecting the necessary alterations in the mode of conducting their business, Messrs. Pickford and Co. have announced the peremptory sale of forty horses, lately engaged in working their van between these two points, whose services were superseded the moment the indefatigable locomotives of the railway were brought into action.

Railways in Germany. — Notwithstanding the "pressure of the times" has extended to the Continent, the popularity of railway schemes is apparently anything but diminishing in Germany. The Prince Royal of Prussia has made himself conspicuous for his enthusiasm in their favour, and contributed not a little to bring them into vogue. Of course, the supply both of rail-bars and carriages comes principally from England. Austria is not behind hand; considerable curiosity has recently been excited at Vienna, by the appearance of a "model locomotive" which has been constructed, with all the latest improvements, by an eminent English engineer, in order to serve as a pattern for all other carriages to be used on railways.

New Method of Extracting Gold.—The St. Petersburgh letters are much occupied with a discovery relative to the working of the Russian gold mines, which, if truly stated, may come to have some influence on the circulation of the precious metals. A letter of the 26th ult. says : "There has been found out, it is said, in the Oural mountains a new mode of extracting gold from the earth, sand, or ore. The sand, or earth, has been put into a blast-furnace and melted, and the most extraordinary results obtained. By washing, the method hitherto pursued in Russia, if $1\frac{1}{2}$ zolotnicks of gold were produced from 100 poods of sand, &c., the expenses were about covered; 2 zolotnicks per 100 poods were worth working. Fine sand or earth rarely produced more than 3 zolotnicks, and 5 zolotnicks were quite uncommon. By the new process, on 100 poods of melted, they obtained 60 zolotnicks in some cases, in others 40 to 50 zolotnicks, and on melting 100 poods previously washed sand, they got 40 to 50 zolotnicks of gold. There is little doubt of the accuracy of these statements, but what the comparative expense of the two modes is, I cannot tell you, nor whether the Oural grows sufficient wood enough for fuel, and whether coal can be found there. 1lb Russian contains 96 solotnicks, 100 poods, are about 3,550 lbs. English weight."—*Times,* June 16.

Vicinage of Manufactories, and Railroads to Private Dwellings.—The immediate neighbourhood of a manufactory, to those having no interest in it, is generally considered a nuisance ; but if the branch of manufacture carried on, be not of itself, of an offensive or injurious kind, such as a gas work a soap work, a tannery, &c., and if it be properly conducted, and the moral conduct of its work-people properly enforced, we think the objections may be overcome. The exterior appearance of manufacturing buildings is now undergoing great changes in almost every part of the country; and instead of huge masses presenting a mean appearance, from the absence of architectural design, or deforming the landscape by their unsightly chimneys, they are becoming magnificent masses, in which the chimney, in the form of a lofty imposing column, is a feature seen at a great distance, on every side, and serves as a general ornament to the country. A railroad is a new feature in the suburbs of large towns ; and though a residence close along the line may not be agreeable to many persons, yet at a moderate distance it is quite the reverse, and indeed from situations looking down upon the line of road, we should think that it would form one of the finest artificial features, of the moving kind, that could be introduced into landscape, next to a canal or navigable river. We mention railroads, because we have been much struck with the carriages, passing along the line of the Manchester railway, as seen from the beautiful villas, particularly one erected from a design by Mr. Barry, situated on a high bank, which overlooks the valley through which the railway is conducted.—*Loudon's Suburban Gardener.*

Erratum.—In the note at the bottom of col. 1, page 121, for $8296 \times 18.5 \times 5 = 484400000$, read $5296 \times 18.5 \times 5 \times 1000 = 4.8840000$.

The Supplement to Vol. xxvi., containing Title, Contents, Index, &c., Medallic Portrait of his late Majesty, and Wyon's Chesselden Medal, engraved by Freebairn by Bates' patent machine, is published, price 6d. Also, Vol. xxvi., price 9s. 6d.

☞ *British and Foreign Patents taken out with economy and despatch; Specifications, Disclaimers, and Amendments, prepared or revised; Caveats entered; and generally every Branch of Patent Business promptly transacted.*

A complete list of Patents from the earliest period (15 Car. II. 1675,) to the present time may be examined. Fee 2s. 6d.; Clients, gratis.

LONDON: Printed and Published for the Proprietor, by W. A. Robertson, at the Mechanics' Magazine Office, No. 6, Peterborough-court, between 135 and 136, Fleet-street.—Sold by G. W. M. Reynolds, Proprietor of the French, English, and American Library, 55, Rue Neuve, Saint Augustin, Paris.

Mechanics' Magazine,

MUSEUM, REGISTER, JOURNAL, AND GAZETTE.

No. 727.　　　　　SATURDAY, JULY 15, 1837.　　　　　Price 3d.

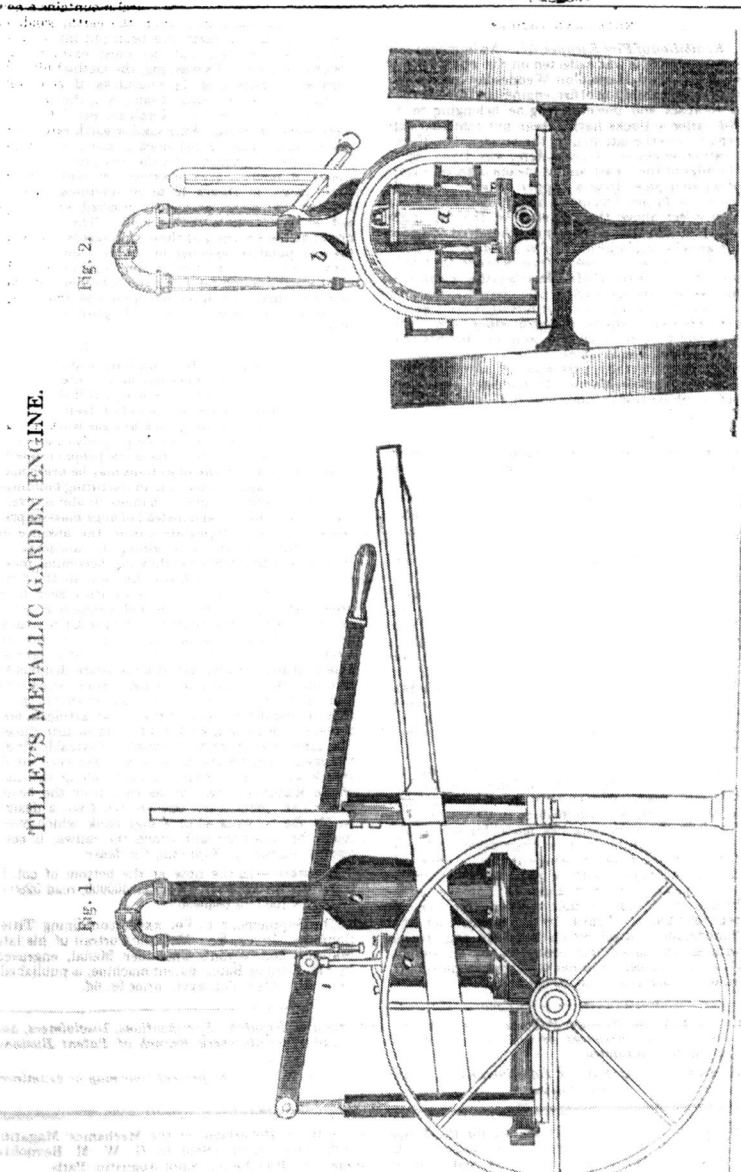

Fig. 2.

TILLEY'S METALLIC GARDEN ENGINE.

Fig. 1.

TILLEY'S METALLIC GARDEN ENGINE.

Sir,—During the temporary sojourn of a gentleman in London, some time since, from the scorching clime of Africa, he expressed a wish to purchase a good fire-engine : but the wood and leather in those of the ordinary construction were ill suited to his purpose, and, in fact, altogether unfit for a country, where heat and drought are aided in the work of destruction by the industrious ravages of the insect pests. Having been recommended to Mr. W. J. Tilley, engine-maker, Blackfriars-road, the gentleman called upon him and made known his wish, stating, that he wanted a fire-engine composed entirely of such materials " as the white ants could not eat." Mr. Tilley, having stated that he had no doubt he could furnish precisely the sort of thing that was required, immediately set to work and produced the " Metallic Fire-engine," which I had the pleasure of describing very fully in your 621st number (vol. xxiii, page 258). Since this one was made, the inhabitants of several hot climates have availed themselves of the certain protection afforded by these impregnable engines.   The East Indies, Italy, and other places have been furnished with " Metallic Fire-engines," in the construction of which, various little alterations and improvements have from time to time been introduced. A shallow trough, or pocket, has been added, lengthways of the engine, on either side, for holding the branch and suction-pipes ; a metal cistern has also been placed below the hind carriage, which affords the means of collecting a body of water from buckets, pails, &c., when the suction pipe is not employed.

The great advantage attending the employment of this peculiar form of engine has led to the application of the same mode of construction, in those of a smaller kind.   The accompanying drawings (see front page) represent a machine of this description, intended to be used as a garden, or extinguishing, engine, which, like the former ones, is composed entirely of metal, impervious alike to all the atmospheric vicissitudes, and the insinuating attacks of the insect tribes. In those countries where a shower is a luxury, and nature is greatly assisted by the powers of art, an engine of this kind is extremely useful for a variety of horticultural and other purposes, as well as being an efficient extinguishing engine in case of fire. This engine also comes within the means of numbers of persons, who have neither the money to purchase, nor occasion to employ the larger and more costly machine.

Fig. 1 is a side view of Tilley's metallic garden-engine, and Fig. 2 is an end view of the same as seen from behind ; a is the working barrel or cylinder ; b the air-vessel, standing upon a light frame-work of cast iron. The machine is mounted upon a pair of light iron wheels with broad rims, to prevent injury to the gravel walks of gardens, &c. The branch pipe is connected with the ascending pipe of the air-vessel by two brass elbows, screwed and swivelled, forming an universal joint, which supersedes the necessity for employing leather hose, and enables a person to direct the jet of water with the left hand, while the engine is wrought with the right.

Mr. Tilley has been particularly happy in designing these ingenious and eminently useful engines, which combine great simplicity of construction, with much convenience, and extreme durability.

I remain, Sir, yours respectfully,
WM. BADDELEY.

Wellington-street, Blackfriars Road,
June 28, 1837.

THE FIRST STEAM-BOAT PROJECTED
IN GREAT BRITAIN.

It is an interesting fact in the history of steam navigation, that the first attempt was directed to the sole purpose of towing ships, and well exemplifies the maxim that " Necessity is the mother of invention," for before that discovery extreme difficulty was often encountered to accomplish that necessary object, especially when the wind was unfavourable.

The first steam-boat projected in Great Britain was by Jonathan Hulls, who obtained a patent for his invention, dated the 21st day of December, 1736,* and in the following year he published a tract, containing a description of his machinery, the title of which is here presented to the reader at length :

* A description of Hulls' invention with an engraving is given in our 1st vol., page 97. Of this the writer of the present communication is evidently not aware ; he has furnished, however, some additional particulars not without interest.—ED. M. M.

" A Description and Draught of a new-invented Machine, for carrying Vessels or Ships out of, or into, any Harbour, Port, or River, against Wind and Tide, or in a calm. For which, His Majesty has granted Letters Patent, for the sole benefit of the Author, for the Space of Fourteen Years. By Jonathan Hulls. London : Printed for the Author, 1737. (Price sixpence.)" 8vo. p. 48.

The " draught" prefixed is a plate of a stout boat, with a chimney (as at present) smoking, a pair of wheels rigged out over each side of the stern, moved by means of ropes passing round their outer rims; and to the axis of these wheels are fixed six paddles to propel the boat. From the stern of the boat, a tow-line passes to the fore-mast of a two-decker, which the boat thus tows through the water.

The commencement of the little treatise is occupied by matter not immediately connected with the subject. He first treats of the Mechanical Powers, which he appers to have taken almost entirely from the " Mathematical Magic" of Wilkins, and he follows that author in one of his many absurdities, " that it is possible to make a Machine to lift up an immense Weight with a small string, or *even a hair.*" At page 14, he commences with fluids, and a number of theorems follow respecting the specific gravity of bodies, and the pressure of the air, together with their demonstrations, as also " Six Theorems extracted out of Archimedes's Tract, entituled De Incidentibus Aquæ, very necessary for the better Understanding of Several Experiments and conclusions herein contained," and he then describes his rude steam-boat. The work finishes with " Answers to some queries that have been made, concerning the possibility and usefulness of this Undertaking," which end thus, " The Scheme I now offer is Practicable, and if encouraged will be useful."

The humble manner in which Hulls writes contributes very much to favour his claim to the undisputed originality of the invention. Had he been such a boastful and self-conceited writer as the Marquis of Worcester, some doubt perhaps would still be entertained, but the style of his little treatise will, after an attentive perusal, persuade the impartial reader, that he is indebted to himself alone for the invention described in it.

Hulls' treatise is now very rarely met with, and a single copy has produced more than *three guineas*. The text has been reprinted at the end of Mr. Partington's Lectures, but the " draught" is omitted ; the imperfect manner, however, in which the reprint is executed, renders the original of as much value as before ; the copy in my possession is the only one with which I am at present ac-quainted.

J. O. H.

July 1, 1837.

FIRE ESCAPES.

Sir,—After the animadversions of your correspondents, Mr. H. Jenkins, and Mr. Baddeley, the first on the 17th of June, and the latter on the 1st of July, I feel called upon to trouble you again with a few observations.

The misrepresentations of Mr. Jenkins are what might be expected from one, that will not give himself the trouble to come at the truth, where it may so easily be obtained. Shortly after the loss of so many lives at the fire in Tottenham Court Road, in 1835, I attended two public meetings of the Association of that district formed for a *local* estab-lishment of escapes. The *room* in which they met to give judgment on the several machines submitted to their notice, I deemed *too small* to exhibit such as I had contrived, with any advantage ; and, information to that effect I couched in a *letter* which was sent to the *Treasurer, instead of the Secretary,* in consequence of which misdirection I presume, it was never laid before the Committee. Neither were my *machines* ever sent to them, which is evidence they were *not* rejected by that Association any more than by the *Humane Society,* as alleged by Mr. Jenkins. Having a desire to call the attention of that Association to some essential points regarding fire and escapes, I afterwards invited them by public placards to a more commodious room in Gower-street. There I gave a lecture on the subject, stating the propriety of forming a *fire brigade* as well as *escapes* to be distributed over the metropolis. I even advised them to adopt such escapes as might appear *more efficient* than my own. At the conclusion of the meeting, some gentlemen proposed certain resolutions. A second meeting took place at the same room ; a *committee* was formed, and ultimately, the *Humane Society* on the 22nd of March, 1836. A short time prior to its formation I was one of the committee, but through the advice of my friends, I *resigned* in order to prevent its being imputed to the Society, that they were favouring me more than any other mechanic; at the same time they pronounced that my escape was the *best.* The Society having advertised for escapes, the *model* of my *ladders* was the *last* inspected by their committee, and the *last* adopted, solely on account of the *expense* being more than the Society had then the means to defray, which occasioned other escapes of *minor* importance to take the lead. It was the efficiency of my ladders which induced the inhabitants of the Regent's Park district first to offer me their subscriptions, of which I received thirty pounds. The escape has since become the Society's by paying eighteen pounds for rent, &c., and not *fifty pounds* as set down by Mr. Jenkins; thus far he is answered.

Mr. Baddeley having become a member of the Humane Society must have faith in its utility, and as an *engineer*, he ought rather to advise the adoption of the most effectual means to save life in cases of fire, than throw a damper upon it. I am surprised, indeed, that he should count the life of a human being of so little importance as to signify that the sum of *thirty pounds* is too much to preserve it, thus making life a *second* consideration, and, the saving of property the *first*. Mr. Baddeley must recollect, that in, or about 1829, the generous and humane citizens paid Mr. Hudson eighty pounds for an escape, and does he suppose that the same feeling does not exist in the hearts of those residing out of the city ? From his account of the fire in Compton-street, one would be led to believe that the insurance companies ought to have every thing their own way; that their engines are to enter the crowd of spectators like *war-chariots;* and that a fire-escape is an intrusion. Mr. Baddeley ought to know *by instinct* that the escape was not sent from Robert-street for any other purpose than to exhibit its powers at a fire, and he cannot say that had the machine been stationed near to the fire, but that it might have been of infinite service at the commencement; for, his account of the courageous men who risked their lives, and the destruc-

tion of the escape, prove, that the object intended, to save life, may be effected by such men with the aid of the escape; in fact, we need nothing more to carry the objects of the Society into complete effect than contributions from the Humane.

Since Mr. Baddeley has not chosen to make himself fully acquainted with the peculiar advantages of my inventions, which has induced him to say what he cannot prove, I will set him right without a chance of contradiction. " The complexity of the escape," says Mr. Baddeley, " precludes the efficient working of it by persons not well practised in its use; and finally, the utter impossibility of applying it in many situations where a fire-escape may become needful. In all these points, Mr. Wivell's apparatus falls behind those of Mr. Ford and Mr. Merryweather." The contrary of all this was proved at the Society's first annual exhibition held at the Argyll Rooms on the 31st of March. There was no attempt made either by Mr. Ford or Mr. Merryweather to send their men up to the attic window, which was done by my machine; nor could their escapes be raised in an equally short space of time. As for Mr. Ford's escape, it was obliged to be in part put into a house passage opposite to the exhibition before it could be made to ascend the front of the building, a circumstance which was laughed at and ridiculed by the spectators. Mr. Baddeley seems not to be aware that my escape ladders can be varied at pleasure, so as to be placed *sideways*, as well as to front a house. The mode of turning them round by the lever end will permit of all the variety desirable in an escape, and I can vouch, that in case a house might fall into ruins while the *escape* should be in front, the purchase on the lever will prevent its falling; not so with any other of the patronized escapes. The *third wheel* belonging to my escape, as noticed by Mr. Baddeley, is an addition which can be dispensed with, where the escape has not to travel out of its district. When the wheel is removed, the escape can be made to go at a good speed, even if raised, and in that position it can be turned round corners and made to act in narrow streets or in courts. If this is not enough to satisfy Mr. Baddeley of his error, I will give him and the public an opportunity of judging whose machine is the best, in a fair trial of the machines whenever I may be called upon for the purpose.

I am, Sir, your obedient and humble servant,

A. WIVELL.

PRECIPITATION OF SATELLITES ON THE EARTH'S SURFACE.

Sir,—I, in common, I have no doubt, with many of your readers, looked at first upon the "Electrical Theory" as an ingenious fancy proceeding from the overflowing of a warm imagination. I have, however, lately had some conversation with several members of the Geological Society, and I find them strongly inclined to support that portion of the theory which supposes several satellites to have been, at remotely distant points of time in the history of our planet, deposited upon the earth's surface. I find also that M. de la Beche, V. P. G. L., strongly favours this view. According to Dr. Buckland, the total thickness of the entire series of the stratified rocks, taken in order, which at present covers the *original surface of the earth*, is not less than ten miles. It is difficult to conceive that this vast accumulation of solid matter should have been formed simply by the wearing away of mountain tops at one place, and upheaving of mountain masses at another point; but if we admit the deposition of a satellite, many of the difficulties with which geology is at present environed may be readily obviated. I have no intention, at least at the present time, to enter into the subject, but thinking that the author has been treated by some of your correspondents in a manner not the most courteous, I thought it right that they should know, that these views with respect to the satellites find a place in the highly scientific mind of M. De la Beche.

Yours, &c.

A GEOLOGIST.

N.B.—The "Electrical Theory" has been re-published at Calcutta.

HYDRAULIC WEIGHING MACHINES.

Sir,—In consequence of an answer from one of your correspondents, in No. 724 of your valuable publication, to a communication of mine respecting hydraulic weighing machines, inserted in No. 722 of the same work, under the signature of J. P. H., I am compelled once more to obtrude my observations upon your attention. I regret being obliged to do so, and trust that my subject will serve for my excuse.

For your correspondent's communication, I beg to return my best thanks, and to inform him that I should have noticed it before this, if I had not been waiting for information, which last night only I found I had no chance of obtaining for the present.

It is evident from the communication, that my claim to originality, in the application of the principle of the hydrostatic bellows, to the purposes of weighing, is good for nothing, inasmuch as your correspondent commenced selling machines, constructed on this principle, more than twelve years since, and, yet, I thought I had fair grounds for considering my claim a good one. I published my machine to the Society of Arts in 1835; I had in my possession various works on hydrostatics, published within a few years before my publication, in none of which was there any description of any thing like my machine, while this year, two works contained descriptions of similar machines. I, therefore, concluded, as no mention was made in works published before my publication, while in works published since, there was mention made, that my publication was the cause of the other publications; but it is now clear I was wrong.

Your correspondent says, "On referring to my books, I find I commenced selling them in January, 1825,—just ten years before 'J. P. H.' sent his to the Society of Arts." Now, while my good feelings make me place implicit reliance on his assertion, I would suggest to him, that his mode of proving his claim to originality, though the best in the eyes of a gentleman, is one which the world, in general, and a court of justice, in particular, would consider valueless; and, perhaps, rightly so; because, if it requires only an assertion to stamp a claim to originality, the claim he has set up, may be at once vitiated, by any person asserting that he made such machines twenty years before your correspondent commenced selling his. Your correspondent must, as a matter of course, have within his power other means of establishing his claim, than any he has yet shown; because, having made a new and curious article for sale since 1825, he must, between that time and the date of my publication, have advertised the machine; such a course, at least, would have been natural; because little profit could have been expected to be reaped from the sale of an article, of the existence of which very few persons could have any knowledge. I am sure your correspondent must be able to show he has done so much, and, that he should do it, I think absolutely necessary to the validity of his claim in the eyes of the world.

With respect to my observations upon your correspondent's machine, as described in the Engineers' and Mechanics' Encyclopædia, I think every one will allow that they were correct. I had no knowledge that the machine and the description were so different; but with the information I now possess, I beg to say, that, regarding simplicity of construction of paramount importance, your correspondent's machine is very much better than mine, as I made it; yet, it is still capable of great improvement.

In my communication, I said that cohesion and friction were the great points of deduction from the utility of hydraulic weighing machines. Your correspondent seems to have forgotten the cohesion, and to imagine that, in having got rid of friction, he has perfected his machine; whereas, he has only obviated the minor objection, leaving the major entirely untouched, as it will, and must, be under any possible arrangement of its parts.

Your correspondent has been pleased to hazard a correction of me, which I think I shall show to have been unnecessary; he says, " I must take the liberty of setting your correspondent right as to the principle of the machine. It has nothing to do with either the hydrostatic bellows or hydrostatic press, but merely the well known rule, that a floating body displaces exactly its weight of water; and in the weighing machine, as the water cannot escape, it runs up the sides; the pressure of the column of water thereby formed floating the cylinder." Without, for one moment, doubting your correspondent's explanation to be correct, I do mean to say, that the

explanation I gave, was also correct, and that it had more to do with the machine than your correspondent's. Mine brought the hydraulic weighing machine under a class, while his was so general, that there exists no machine, connected with liquids, to which it would not, perhaps, be applicable. I shall prove that the principle of the hydraulic weighing machine is, not only, that of the hydrostatic bellows, and hydrostatic press, but, that the effects of both the bellows and the press may, in a certain degree, be produced by the weighing machine. The hydrostatic bellows may be converted into a weighing machine, by substituting a glass-tube for the metallic-tube, and by affixing a graduated scale to the side of the glass-tube; or the metallic-tube may be used, by employing a floating graduated rod, instead of a fixed graduated scale. Such machines, it must be apparent, would be subject to objections, which, in my modification, I was desirous of obviating. I invented my machine from the hydrostatic bellows. I got rid of the resistance of the leather of the bellows by removing the leather itself; I kept the water of the bellows from running away by the casing of the machine; and I maintained the upper board of the bellows above the water, by thickening it, bringing it thereby into the form of a hollow floating box. The machine, as I constructed it, was nothing but the hydrostatic bellows, as it were, masked; and your correspondent's machine is similar. What is the result when a weight is put upon his machine? Your correspondent says, " as the water cannot escape, it runs up the sides, the pressure of the column of water, thereby formed, floating the cylinder." What takes place when a weight is put upon the board of a hydrostatic bellows? The water, as it cannot escape, runs up the tube; the pressure of the column of water, thereby formed, sustaining the board of the bellows in equilibrium. You will perceive that, in stating these results, I have in one instance used your correspondent's own words; while, in the other, the words are not very dissimilar. In the weighing machine, there are two columns of water to sustain the floating cylinder; while, in the bellows, there is but one to sustain the board in equilibrium. If it were wished to use the weighing machine as a bellows, it would only be necessary to place a weight upon the board, and pour water into the tube; when, we should immediately see the board, with the weight upon it, rise. If we wished to convert the weighing machine into a press, then it would be necessary to affix a frame to it, to keep the object to be pressed from moving upwards; when, if we placed the object upon the floating cylinder, and poured water into the tube, the object would be pressed against the frame, and the pressure would be increased as more water was poured in, until the water flowed over the exterior cylinder.

I think it will be admitted that I have now shown, that the principle of the hydraulic weighing machine has something to do with the hydrostatic bellows and hydrostatic press; that the weighing machine is the hydrostatic bellows masked; and that the principle of the weighing machine is that of the bellows and press, inasmuch, as the one may be made to perform, in some degree, in the manner I have described, the offices of the others.

I believe the hydrostatic bellows, the hydrostatic press, and the hydraulic, or hydrostatic, weighing machine, to be three machines of one class; the distinguishing principle of which class is, that, by which a pressure on a surface of small extent is equivalent to a pressure on a surface of large extent; this principle being the result of that well known property of liquids, by which they transmit pressure equally in all directions; the hydrostatic bellows, raising bodies; the hydrostatic press, compressing objects; and the hydraulic, or hydrostatic, weighing machine, estimating weight; the end of each of these machines being different, necessitating a different application of their one pervading principle.

More might be said, but more would be tedious. I, therefore, bring my observations to a close; in doing which, I beg to offer every apology for having trespassed so much upon your valuable space, and to subscribe myself,

Sir, your humble servant,

J. P. HOLEBROOK.

4th July, 1837.

168, Devonshire Place, Edgeware Road.

IRON NAVY.

Should England's bulwark fail—and Oak no
  longer grow,
Her iron plates may track the billows
  through.

Sir,—In times of prosperity and peace the advancement of science and enterprise generally keep pace with each other; the one has scarcely propounded her stores of intelligence, ere the other is ready at the call to carry forward with energy her schemes of beneficence and utility; and so leaving behind them the result of their united labours to the advantage of future generations.

The maritime connections of England form no mean portion of the sources of her prosperity; and, next to these, is the security afforded to maintain regularity and expedite her communications with different portions of the globe: and while, by the extent of her commerce on the one hand, her wealth is increased; so on the other, every improvement made to insure expedition and safety in the pursuit, is a benefit to the public weal, and a source of insurance to the timely return of her enterprise and activity.

Numerous have been the proposed improvements to afford safety, and insure expedition in our naval pursuits, and to preserve the lives of a valuable portion of our countrymen. Nothing seems so conspicuously to bear upon the subject as that of rendering vessels *sound*, and when propelled by steam, *safe*. With a view of combining these two important objects, it has been suggested, that iron will form an excellent substitute for wood, as one calculated to increase security, and to a very great extent afford benefit to the country's interest; the practical utility of the one, when compared with the other, and the peculiar nature of the material, under circumstances of emergency, seem to establish the opinion. For, suppose a vessel of oak, or other wood, to strike upon a rock, the result, as it frequently happens, is, that after collision, the vessel is so generally shaken, and her planks so loosened, that she immediately springs a leak, and if not stove in with the concussion, she requires all the art of the crew to save her and their own lives. In many cases, however, circumstances are not so propitious; the vessel is severely crushed at the part of contact, and immediately, begins to fill, and perhaps is never again heard of. Now, if an iron vessel, under like circumstances, strike a rock, the nature of the material of which she is constructed, yields to the shock, and in all probability it receives no further injury than a severe indentation at the place of contact; she may be lightened with success, and the crew with the remaining cargo saved from impending destruction.

In the event of fire, an iron vessel presents greater security, and the chances are greatly in favour, that the fire may be overcome before serious damage is sustained; there are no timbers, through which the destructive element can force its way, or afford draft for its support; its power therefore is more under the controul of the crew, and there is every probability of their being able under the severest circumstances to subdue its influence by their exertions.

In point of economy, it is allowed that an iron vessel may be built with a less outlay of capital, which would afford a strong plea in favour of their more general adoption for steam conveyance.

As respects oxidation, means may be adopted to prevent it, and I have no doubt, that when the subject is duly considered, improvements will be made in its application.

It was suggested in your Magazine by a correspondent (Mr. Aldersey), vol. xxii, page 477, that if compartments were formed in a vessel, it would render it more secure in case of accident; does not this deserve the attention of builders, where it can be done without interfering with a vessel's convenience for the reception of cargo?

I am, Sir, yours respectfully.

J. WOODHOUSE.

Kilburn, July 6, 1837.

MR. MURPHY'S WEATHER PREDICTIONS.

Sir, — By one of the "Notes and Notices" in your last number, I observe that the weather-predictor, Mr. Patrick Murphy, who proved himself so complete a quack at the beginning of the year (at the expense of the Meteorological Society, which disgraced itself by ushering his labours into the world) is still in the field, and has the unblushing impudence

to talk of the coincidence of his predictions with the fact. Dr. Birkbeck, it seems, has recommended Mr. Murphy to the patronage of government, and Lord Melbourne, I suppose, is expected some fine morning to put the great rival of Francis Moore on the pension list for a few odd hundreds per annum. It is to be hoped, however, that his Lordship, before he signs the order, will take the trouble to cast his eye over pages 287 and 415 of the *Mechanics' Magazine* vol. xxvi, from which he will be able to judge of the probable value of Mr. Patrick Murphy's services to the nation in the prophetic line. He will there find that Mr. M. having been unwary enough to publish his vaticinations *before* the time when they were to come true; the result was, that, while he predicted that the "tendency" of the month of January would be to "*drought*" the month was in reality one of the *wettest* known for years; that, on the 5th, when he told us to expect *frost*, we were in the third day of a very rapid *thaw*; and that every one of his prophecies was so flatly contradicted by the truth, that his only resource at last was to say, that his calculations would be found quite correct — *in America!*

And this is the person who talks so largely of his "discovery of principles for calculating changes of the weather,"—who is recommended to the Premier by the President of the London Mechanics' Institution—and whose calculations, according to the paragraph quoted by you from the *Times* "have been verified so as to place beyond doubt the correctness of the principles resorted to by him!"— Surely "the march of humbug can no farther go."—The only proper way of punishing so barefaced an impostor is in the hands of the press; no respectable periodical should throw away space in noticing his ridiculous attempts at attracting observation.

I am, Sir,

Very respectfully yours,

H.

4th July, 1837.

ON THE PROTECTION OF STEAM SHIPS FROM FIRE.

Sir,—From the extreme liability of steam-ships to accident by fire, it is matter of great surprise that no attention whatever is yet paid to their protection against the disastrous ravages of this element; so long ago as November 1827, I brought this matter under notice in your pages (vide vol. viii. p. 350) and suggested the employment of some extinguishing machinery, that might be connected with the steam-engine, in case of fire. Since that time, several valuable steamers have been either seriously injured or wholly destroyed, and a large number of human lives' have been sacrificed, both in this country and in America, for want of such a contrivance as I then suggested. Mr. Symington has renewed my suggestion in No. 725, p. 202, of your Magazine, and also alluded to the advantage that might be obtained by employing the power of the steam-engine to get rid of the water from a leaky boat. By making the suction-pipe of the force-pump or pumps communicate either with the water on the exterior, or in the interior of the vessel, at pleasure, by means of the common three-way suction-cock, several important advantages would result. Thus, for instance, upon a fire breaking out on board, a supply of water could in the first instance be drawn from without, but in the event of an inconveniently large body of water being thus thrown into the vessel before the fire was quite extinguished, by reversing the cock, the same water could be raised and again thrown upon the flames, and on their suppression be pumped overboard. In the event of springing a leak, the water could be got rid of in the same manner.

When we reflect that steam-boats, above all other vessels, are particularly liable to casualties, and at the same time have a power on board amply sufficient to avert almost every evil, it seems little less than criminal to withhold those few and simple equipments that would suffice to render them almost invulnerable. All our men of war, and most merchant vessels, have one or more fire-engines on board, and why not steam boats? Merryweather's compact and powerful yacht engine (a description of which appeared in your 645th Number*) has been found eminently useful upon several occasions of fire at sea: as this engine admits of being placed in a boat and taken alongside to windward of the

burning vessel, the crew are enabled to work it free from the annoyance of smoke, or apprehensions of personal danger. The portability of this engine likewise enables our gallant tars to land it, on the occurrence of a fire on the coast where they may happen to be stationed, and in this way they have frequently rendered most essential service to the inhabitants, and been the means of preserving lives and property to a considerable amount. My late much esteemed friend, the Hon. Wm. Pleace, had the greater portion of his valuable stores in Prince Edwards's Island, N. A., saved from total destruction by the gallant crew of H. M.'s frigate, the Ringdove, Capt. Palmer, who landed their engine on perceiving the outbreak of a fire in his premises, and afforded such prompt and efficient aid as was not to be obtained from any other source, at that time.

Valuable as are these machines, even when worked by manual labour, they can never be nearly so effective as those impelled by all-powerful, untiring steam; and I sincerely trust, that no steam-vessel will be hereafter sent to sea without some hydraulic machinery on board, capable of affording the protection so essentially necessary to this class of vessels.

The adoption of this simple and comparatively inexpensive plan, would convert every steam-boat, in case of need, into a powerful and useful *steam fire-engine*—an acquisition wherever it went.

I remain, Sir,

Yours respectfully,

WM. BADDELEY.

London, July 1, 1837.

WHEWELL'S HISTORY OF THE INDUCTIVE SCIENCES.*

This is a highly valuable work. The author, wisely considering that the compass of three octavo volumes is little enough for comprehending even the most succinct view of the multitudinous facts appertaining to the annals of scientific discovery, has avoided all speculative and discursive matter as much as possible, confining himself closely to narrative, and contenting himself with

* Vide Vol. xxiv. p. 226.

* History of the Inductive Sciences, from the Earliest to the Present Times. By the Rev. William Whewell, M. A., Fellow and Tutor of Trinity College, Cambridge, President of the Geological Society of London. In three vols. London, 1837. Parker: 8vo. pp. 473, 546, 586.

referring the reader, who may wish for a fuller discussion of certain subjects, to another work, which he informs us has already made some progress on its way to the press, devoted exclusively to the Philosophy of Inductive Science. The course pursued is a most judicious one, and probably the best that could be adopted, if not to please all parties, to offend none. It would be well if the theorist could always be kept perfectly distinct from the historian.

Mr. Whewell does not think it necessary to go back to any earlier period than that of the Greek school philosophy, and seems inclined to regard the father of historians, Herodotus, by virtue of his reasonings on the rising of the Nile, as the father also of inductive philosophers, although only, of course, in the same sense that "the child is father to the man." His first book is occupied solely by a general exposition of the scholastic philosophy, and the causes of its failure; the second embraces the history of the earliest stages of hydrostatics, optics, and harmonics; while the third is devoted to the most perfect of the sciences of antiquity,—astronomy, before, during, and subsequent to the memorable epoch of Hipparchus. In book fourth, the reader finds he has slept through the long and dreary night of barbarism, and is awakened to behold the dawn of science in the middle ages. It is, perhaps, in this part of his work that Mr. Whewell most departs from the strictly historical line he had marked out for himself, and indulges to the greatest extent in critical digression. Thus, we have separate chapters assigned to the consideration of the "Indistinctness of Ideas," the "Commentatorial Spirit," the "Mysticism," and the "Dogmatism of the Middle Ages;" and, finally, another on the "Progress of the Arts" in the same period, on which we shall beg leave to offer a few observations.

The tone of the chapter is altogether apologetical. As if feeling that the preceding ones contained too sweeping a denunciation of the science, or the want of science, of the era in question, Mr. Whewell proceeds to observe—

"The accusation of injustice to the state of science in the middle ages, if we were to terminate our survey of them with what has hitherto been said, might be urged from ob-

vious topics. How do we recognize, it might be asked, in a picture of mere confusion and mysticism of thought, of servility and dogmatism of character, the powers and acquirements to which we owe so many of the important inventions which we now enjoy? Parchment and paper, printing and engraving, improved glass and steel, gunpowder, clocks, telescopes, the mariner's compass, the reformed calendar, the decimal rotation, algebra, trigonometry, chemistry, counterpoint, which was equivalent to a new creation of music;—these are all possessions which we inherit from that which has been so disparagingly termed the stationary period. Above all, let us look at the monuments of architecture of this period,—the admiration and despair of modern architects, not only for their beauty, but for the skill disclosed in their construction. With all these evidences before us, how can we avoid allowing that the masters of the middle ages not only made some small progress in astronomy, which has, grudgingly as it would seem, been admitted in a former book; but also, that they were no small proficients in other sciences, in optics, in harmonics, in physics, and, above all, in mechanics?

"If, it may be added, we are allowed in the present day to refer to the perfection of our arts as evidence of the advanced state of our physical philosophy; if our steam-engines, our gas illumination, our buildings, our navigation, our manufactures, are cited as triumphs of science; shall not prior inventions, made under far heavier disadvantages,—shall not greater works, produced in an earlier state of knowledge, also be admitted as witnesses that the middle ages had their share, and not a small or doubtful one, of science?

"To these questions I answer, by distinguishing between art and science in that sense of general inductive systematic truth, which it bears in this work. To separate and compare, with precision, these two processes, belongs to the philosophy of induction, and the attempt must be reserved for another place; but the leading differences are sufficiently obvious. Art is practical, science is speculative; the former is seen in doing, the latter rests in the contemplation of what is known. The art of the builder appears in his edifice, though he may never have meditated on the abstract propositions, on which its stability and strength depend. The science of the mathematical mechanician consists, in his seeing that, under certain conditions, bodies must sustain each others' pressure, though he may never have applied his knowledge to a single case.

"Now, the remark which I have to make

is this : in all cases, the arts are prior to the related sciences. Art is the parent, not the progeny, of science ; the application of principles to practice forms part of the prelude, as well as of the sequel, of theoretical discovery. And thus the inventions of the middle ages, which have been above enumerated, though at the present day they may be portions of our sciences, are no evidence that the sciences then existed ; but only, that those powers of practical observation and practical skill were at work, which prepare the way for theoretical views and scientific discoveries.

· " It may be urged, that the great works of art do· virtually take for granted principles of science ; and that, therefore, it is unreasonable to deny science to great artists. It may be said, that the grand structures of Cologne, or Amiens, or Canterbury, could not have been erected without a profound knowledge of mechanical principles.

" To this we reply, that *such* knowledge is manifestly not of the nature of that which we call *science*. If the beautiful and skilful structure of the middle ages prove that mechanics then existed as a science, mechanics must have existed as a science also among the builders of the Cyclopean walls of Greece and Italy, or of our own Stonehenge ; for the masses, which are there piled on each other, could not be raised without considerable mechanical skill. But we may go much further. The actions of every man who raises and balances weights, or walks along a pole, take for granted the laws of equilibrium ; and even animals constantly avail themselves of such principles. Are these, then, acquainted with mechanics as a science ? Again, if actions which are performed by taking advantage of mechanical properties prove a knowledge of the science of mechanics, they must also be allowed to prove a knowledge of the science of geometry, when they proceed on geometrical properties. But the most familiar actions of men and animals do this. The Epicureans held, as Proclus informs us, that even asses knew that two sides of a triangle are greater than the third. They may be said to have a practical knowledge of this ; but they have not, therefore, a science of geometry. And in like manner among men, if we consider the matter strictly, a practical assumption of a principle does not imply a speculative knowledge of it."—Vol. i. p. 331.

Now, to most of this reasoning we demur, and to no part of it more strongly than that which asserts the barren and useless character of " science,"— most useless and most barren, indeed, if, as Mr. Whewell is of opinion, it

merely " rested in the contemplation of what was known," and added nothing to the existing stock of knowledge. A "mathematical mechanician"*may* "never have applied his knowledge to a single case," but it is quite fair to suppose, that, if he did so apply it, he would be able to suggest something new to the builder who proceeded by what is significantly called "the rule of thumb." This is what the whole question hinges upon. The defenders of the middle ages assert, that the monuments of art they have left behind could not have been produced without the aid of the lights which science gives. Mr. Whewell replies by propounding that science *never* lends any assistance to art, but contents itself with gazing on its productions ; and hereon issue is joined.

"Art is the parent, not the progeny, of science :" granted ; but, in its turn, science gives birth to art of a higher grade. So experiment must always precede theory ; but theory would be of mighty little importance if it came only after experiment had been exhausted. If Mr. Whewell were able to shew that the arts had always been *perfected* before the foundation of the related sciences, the fact would be conclusive in his favour ; but this, of course, he cannot do, simply because it is obviously and glaringly not the fact. It would, on the contrary, be easy to multiply instances, especially in recent times, of gigantic strides in the arts, the useful arts in particular, made by the immediate agency of science. As we shall soon see, Mr. Whewell himself alludes in this very chapter to some of them, and in so doing, necessarily overturns his own hypothesis. Nay, he does so in the very passage before us ; "the application of principles to practice," he observes, "forms part of the prelude, *as well as of the sequel*, of theoretical discovery." So, then, in spite of the purely contemplative character of science, "theoretical discovery" is to lead to practice, as well as to be derived from it,—a rather strange admission to occur so soon after the assertion that art is in all cases the precursor of science, and never its successor. Does it not pretty nearly amount to a giving-up of our author's side of the question ?

His farther arguments appear equally easy of demolition. We see no difficulty in allowing to the builders of Stonehenge and the Cyclopean walls the possession of a modicum of science, although of a much lower character than that of the architects of the middle ages. We also see no difficulty in denying the pretensions to science of the former, and at the same time admitting those of the latter. Stonehenge demanded for its erection considerable mechanical skill; but it is not said that this skill might not be of the nature of that which may be acquired by practice alone. On the other hand, it is expressly laid down, that "the grand structures of Cologne, or Amiens, or Canterbury, could not have been erected without a *profound knowledge* of mechanical *principles*." If so, why need we seek farther for proofs of the existence of science at the period of their erection? Mr. Whewell, it is true, goes on immediately to observe, that "*such* knowledge is manifestly not of the nature of that which we call *science*;" but it would require a keen eye to tell the difference. It is, perhaps, hardly possible to give a clearer definition of science, in a few words, than that it consists in a "profound knowledge of principles." Mr. Whewell is willing to concede the possession of such knowledge to the mediæval architects, from the inspection of their works: what, then, can be clearer than that those works are sufficient evidence to prove the existence of mechanical science in the times in which they were erected? If more be wanting, it is easy to adduce it from no more remote source than the pages of Mr. Whewell's own production. The following extract will show, by the admission with which it concludes, notwithstanding the cautious wording of the preceding portion, that our author himself bears testimony in opposition to his own view of the case:—

"No one who has attended to the architecture which prevailed in England, France, and Germany, from the twelfth to the fifteenth century, so far as to comprehend its beauty, harmony, consistency, and uniformity, even in the minutest parts and most obscure relations, can look upon it otherwise than as a remarkably connected and definite artificial system. Nor can we doubt that it was exercised by a class of artists who formed themselves by laborious study and practice, and by communication with each other. There must have been bodies of masters and of scholars, discipline, tradi-

tions, and precepts of art. How these associated artists diffused themselves over Europe, and whether history enables us to trace them in a distinct form, I shall not here discuss. But the existence of a course of instruction, and of a body of rules of practice, is proved beyond dispute by the great series of European cathedrals and churches, so nearly identical in their general arrangements, and in their particular details. The question then occurs, have these rules, and this system of instruction, anywhere been committed to writing? Can we, by such evidence, trace the progress of the *scientific idea*, of which *we see the working*, in these buildings?"—P. 347.

This is surely quite sufficient, so far as architecture is concerned. Mr. Whewell here admits all that his opponents are contending for,—that the architectural monuments of the middle ages prove, in the absence of any written evidence, very considerable pretensions to science on the part of their constructors. At one time, he seems disposed to deny that any such thing can be proved by any such means; but in this passage we find him distinctly speaking of the "scientific idea," of which "we see" the working in existing remains. It is possible, then, to infer the existence of science from other sources than direct historical record; it is reasonable to infer that a work requiring a profound knowledge of mechanical principles must have been guided by a "scientific idea," and that that "scientific idea" must have left some trace of its "working." This is quite enough, as far as architecture is concerned; and *ex uno disce omnes.*

But Mr. Whewell is of opinion, notwithstanding, that, if we allow the builder of Canterbury cathedral to have been a scientific character in his day, we cannot stop short of acknowledging the claims of every jackass on a common to the same distinction! Logic must certainly be at a low ebb at Cambridge, when a proposition so ridiculous as this can be put forward with even the semblance of gravity, by one of the professors of the university. Can he really perceive no difference in the quantity and quality of mind necessary to enable a donkey to find the nearest way to a bundle of hay, and that required for the design and execution of a beautiful and complicated structure, like one of our grand Gothic cathedrals? By the same rule, an animal of the same order would very appropriately fill a fellow's seat at college, or the presidential chair of the Geological Society. But this is all mere "midsummer madness," a specimen of absurd quibbling and fruitless trifling, which is sadly out of place where it stands. The actions neither of the ass nor the tumbler are supposed to be founded on a "scientific idea," or to result from a "profound knowledge of mechanical principles:" according to Mr. Whewell's own admission, the labours of the architect of the middle ages *are* so founded, and *do* so result; and herein is difference enough, and to spare, between the cases, —quite sufficient, at the very least, to make the pages devoted to the comparison fully as worthless as waste paper. By the same mode of reasoning (it might as well be christened at once the *asinine mode*) all the pretensions of modern, as well as ancient, science, may be disposed of in the most easy and comprehensive style. Is the proficiency of the age in chemistry spoken of; why, your jackass goes into the shade on a hot day, and so shews he is aware of the difference between heat and cold; is he therefore an adept in the science of chemistry? Again, we think we may be proud of our knowledge of hydrostatics. No such thing; every jackass takes advantage of its principles every time he drinks water from a pond; *ergo*, wherein does he differ from a Telford or a Rennie? The argument is wide enough in its sweep to take in the whole circle of the sciences.

Our author is as severe on the scientific pretensions of our own age, as far as they are connected with the arts, as on those of past times. He observes—

" As to that part of the objection which was stated by asking why, if the arts of our age prove its scientific eminence, the arts of the middle ages should not be received as proof of theirs; we must reply to it, by giving up some of the pretensions which are often put forwards on behalf of the science of our times. The perfection of the mechanical and other arts among us proves the advanced condition of our sciences, only in so far as those arts have been perfected by the application of some great scientific truth, with a clear insight into its nature. The greatest improvement of the steam-engine was due to the steady apprehension of an atmological doctrine by Watt; but what distinct theoretical principle is illustrated by the beautiful manufactures of porcelain,

or steel, or glass? A chemical view of these compounds, which would explain the conditions of success or failure in their manufacture, would be of great value in art, and it would also be a novelty in chemical theory; so little is the present condition of these processes a triumph of science shedding intellectual glory on our age. And the same might be said of many, or of most, of the processes of the arts as now practised."—Vol. i. p. 335.

Here we have our author divided against himself once more. Apparently forgetting how recently he had put forth the axiom, that "science is always preceded by art," he talks now of *arts* which have been perfected by the application of some great *scientific* truth; so that the possibility of science being in some cases the parent of art, is very clearly admitted. Nay, more, we are informed that "the greatest improvement of the steam-engine is due to the steady appreciation of an atmological doctrine by Watt," a substantial fact by way of a finishing stroke to our author's own art-before-science theory, which is, indeed, treated with little respect in the passage relating to the steel and glass manufactures. According to the view taken by Mr. Whewell in the earlier portion of the chapter, it is in vain to expect a chemical theory of the conditions of success or failure until *after* those conditions have been puzzled out by the blind and unguided efforts of art, in the way of experiment. We had thought it the peculiar glory of the inductive system, that it reasoned out theory from experiment, and then tested the results of theory by practice; thus making "art" the producer of science in the first instance, and afterwards its production. Mr. Whewell, as we have seen, holds that "science" is *always* the progeny of "art;" yet, in this one short extract, we find him not only bringing forward (in the steam-engine) a case in point of "science" being the producer of "art;" but talking of the advantages which a desiderated novelty in chemical *theory* would bring to the *practice* of some of our most extensive manufactures. Surely there is here no small degree of inconsistency! It must be allowed, that if the manufactures alluded to be in so deficient a condition, it is any thing but wise to thrust them forward in proof of the scientific attainments of our own time: but, according to Mr. Whewell's broad principle, it would be just the same if all its processes were perfect. Perfect or imperfect, science would have to bear no portion of either praise or blame, in virtue of its purely "contemplative" character. Mr. Whewell plays into the hands of his opponents, when he adduces the "present condition" of certain processes, as affording no "triumph" to the "science" of the age, for this is admitting what they contend for, i. e. that the state of science may be shewn by the state of the relative arts. The glass manufacture of the present day, it appears, is conducted in ignorance of the principles on which it depends; it would consequently be strange, indeed, to point to it as a proof of the progress of science in our own times; but the architecture of the middle ages betrays, in the monuments, which remain to us, a "profound knowledge of mechanical principles;" and it therefore seems quite reasonable to adduce those monuments in proof of the "intellectual glory" of the period which called them into existence. Wherever the arts have arrived towards perfection, it is at least presumptive proof that science has been there.

The long digression in which we have indulged leaves us only room for an enumeration of the contents of the remainder of the work. The fifth book is wholly occupied by the History of Formal Astronomy after the Stationary Period, rich in details of the discoveries of Copernicus and Kepler. This concludes the first volume. The second opens with the History of Mechanics, including the Mechanics of Fluids; Physical Astronomy follows, and the Secondary Mechanical Sciences, Acoustics, Optics, Thermotics, and Atmology, fill up the volume. Vol. iii. is of a more miscellaneous nature than the other two, chiefly because it has to do with more recent times, and with the divisions and subdivisions (sometimes not a little fanciful) of modern science. The "Mechanico-Chemical Sciences," Electricity, Magnetism, and Galvanism, lead the van, and the "analytical science"—Chemistry, comes next in order. Mineralogy, which Mr. Whewell designates, rather lengthily, the "Analytico-Classicatory Science," occupies one book (fifteenth), and "Systematic Botany and Zoology," another (sixteenth), under the head of "Classificatory Sciences." "Physiology and

Comparative Anatomy" figure as the "Organical Sciences," and the work winds up with a chapter on the "Palætiological Science,"—as Geology, with little mercy for the jaws of the pronouncers, is cognominated. It will be seen, that the matter of the book is much more branchy towards the end than at the beginning, and it is also (necessarily, perhaps) more diffuse and less compact; may it be added—less interesting? At any rate, the epochs into which it is divided, seem not quite of equal importance to those of earlier periods; the "epoch of Young and Fresnell," for instance, splendid as it may be, sinks a little in comparison with some of its predecessors, such as the epochs of Copernicus, of Galileo, or of NEWTON.

ANALYSIS OF SOLAR LIGHT.
(From the *Franklin Journal* for April).

Within a few days past, notices have been circulated in the public prints that Melloni had succeeded in depriving the sun's rays of all their heat, by transmitting them through certain media, consisting of water and coloured glasses; and also, that Mrs. Somerville, by means of a screen of pale green glass, had abstracted from them that property by which they darken the chloride of silver, and effect chemical changes.

Whilst these results have been obtained in Europe, experiments of a like character have been carried on in Virginia, the event of which is of far more interest to chemists, the effects being equally as certain, and the means being in the hands of every experimenter. Dr. Draper, professor of chemistry in Hampden Sidney College, found during the last year, that there are several solutions, which are transparent as respects the sun's light, yet opaque to his calorific ray; and others which are transparent both to his light and heat, but opaque to the chemical ray: for it does not follow, that a body transparent to light should be transparent to heat or the chemical rays. A solution of sulphate of copper and ammonia, and a decoction of tannin are both transparent to the light of the sun, yet they are nearly opaque to his heat. Nor is this condition of things at all regulated by colour; the first mentioned of those substances which is blue, the second which is brown, and the sulphocyanate of iron which is red, the chloride of chromium which is green, the muriate of cobalt which is pink, and the bichromate of potassa, which is orange, though they are all when in solution transparent to the rays of light, yet are either opaque or only translucent to the rays of heat. It has been found more recently, that solutions which are perfectly colourless and clear as water, exercise very different functions on the rays of heat, and though in an examination of upwards of two hundred and seventy such solutions, none have yet been found which are absolutely opaque to the rays of heat, there are some which approach that condition. Vegetable solutions, exercise a similar influence. Turnsole dissolved in water when the thickness is about a quarter of an inch, permits only about four rays of heat, out of every hundred which fall upon it, to pass through : this is a blue solution ; a decoction of Brazil wood which is red, a decoction of Logwood in alum which is purple, and tincture of turmeric which is yellow, have the same effect.

A solution of the chromate of potassa is nearly opaque to the chemical ray, but is transparent to the ray of light, and more than semitransparent to the ray of heat ; the bichromate of potassa seems to be absolutely opaque to the chemical ray, for a beam of light three inches in diameter, conveyed to a focus by a convex lens, after traversing such a solution one-fourth of an inch thick, did not blacken chloride of silver in an exposure of fifteen minutes. All the vegetable solutions above named are likewise nearly opaque ; but a solution of the sulphate of copper and ammonia, when in a mass thick enough to stop almost all the rays of light, is freely permeated by the chemical rays. It is curious that several *yellow* metallic solutions, as the chloride of gold, the chloride of platinum, the permuriate of iron, and the hydrosulphate of lime, act about as powerfully as the chromate of potassa, but this pecular tint is not always effectual in producing this result, for the yellow oil of turpentine, and the yellow ferrohydrocyanate of potassa, fail to prevent the blackening of the chloride.

These experiments therefore decide the question of the separate existence of calorific and chemical rays in solar light ; they also enable the philosophic chemist to insulate each ingredient, and operate upon it by itself, a matter of the utmost importance in the investigation of the properties of light.

ON THE CALCINATION OF ORES.

A most simple method for effecting this process is practised at the Iron works in Staffordshire, as well as at some of those in Scotland and Wales. It consists in spreading the ironstone intended for calcination over a bed of coal about a foot in thickness, adding occasionally a layer of small coal, until a heap is raised about eight or ten feet in height, and fourteen or fifteen in diameter ; the fire is then lighted, and the operation left to itself without any farther attention. The open fires vary, however, in their form. Another, and more economical mode is used

in South Wales, by which the refuse coal and coke are consumed in ovens or kilns, constructed for the purpose.

The form of the interior is, usually, a reversed cone or pyramid ; those which approach to an oval being also held in much esteem. The operation is easily conducted. The oven, or kiln, being first charged with coal and ironstone but not entirely filling it, when the fire begins to reach the upper part, small coal is thrown on alternately with the ores, until the kiln is filled. The lower part is then drawn out and left to cool, as in lime burning ; the kiln is recharged, and the process continued indefinitely.

In Wales it is generally contrived to erect the blast furnaces on the side of a hill, and the calcining ovens are built on a terrace surrounding it, to the height of the furnace mouth : the time for the operation is regulated so as to keep a supply only to the quantity required for smelting. At Newcastle-on-Tyne a similar method is practised, but the fuel consists of small coke.

At Bradford the ovens are rectangular, and about twenty-five feet in depth, fourteen long, and five wide, in the upper part ; towards the middle it takes the form of a truncated pyramid, whose base is about twenty inches diameter: small coke is used here also: at other works in the same vicinity, the ovens are of a similar shape to the furnaces, and about fifteen feet in height. These dimensions are, however, exceedingly variable, both in different counties, and some times in the same establishment.

At Pouldice, in Cornwall, the tin ores are roasted, to facilitate the subsequent separation by washing. The furnaces for this purpose have a fire place about one foot by four feet, on the same level as the part destined for the ores, and only separated from it by a course of bricks placed flat ; the furnace bed is about nine feet six inches by eight feet ; the height of the roof one foot ; its course nearly horizontal. In the front of the arch, near the door, is a vent, which after rising vertically, takes a course nearly horizontal, and discharges itself at the distance of a quarter of a mile into a large chimney, the upper part is formed of flat stones, which are easily removed for the purpose of clearing out the arsenic accumulated on its sides, which is sold for 10s. per ton: on the outside of the furnace is, also, a projecting or forge chimney, rising about fifteen feet. Similar precautions, favourable to the health of the workmen are in use in all the tin works throughout England, which have not yet been introduced into Germany. The charge of this furnace is six cwt., requiring 1½ bushels of charcoal to each roasting ; this is, however, variable, as well as the duration of the process, according to the nature of the mineral acted upon.

NOTES AND NOTICES.

Artesian Wells.—In the tertiary basin of Perpignan and the chalk of Tours, there are subterranean waters, which have an enormous upward pressure. The water of an Artesian well in Roussillon, rises from thirty to fifty feet *above* the surface. At Perpignan and Tours, M. Arago states, that the water rushes up with so much force, that a cannon ball placed in the pipe of an Artesian well is instantly ejected by the ascending stream. In Lincolnshire, where wells of this description have been long fully as common as in Artois (whence the name Artesian) they are very characteristically called *Blow Wells.*

Rival to the Hot Air Blast.—M. Teploff, of the Russian Mining Corps, states (Annales des Mines) that in the smelting furnaces of the Ural, where the quantity and velocity of the blast are properly regulated, 1.4 of pig iron is obtained by one of charcoal fuel, while in other furnaces they obtain but 4 and 6 by the same consumption of fuel. The velocity of the blast being increased, the heat within is increased without a corresponding consumption of fuel. In an experiment made by order of the government, it was found that one hundred cubic feet of air, under a pressure of two inches of mercury, produced the same effect as two hundred cubic feet, under a pressure of one inch, with this difference, that in the latter case, twice the fuel was consumed, which was required in the former case. In one furnace which is mentioned, 22,000lbs of iron were obtained in twenty-four hours, by 16,000lbs of charcoal. Previous to the due regulation of the draught, they consumed twice this amount of fuel for the same yield of iron. This economy is obtained by duly proportioning to each other the size of the blast pipe, and the pressure of the draught. The relation of these with each other varies with the furnace. Mr. Teploff, asserts that the results thus obtained exceed those with the hot air blast; but it does not appear that any comparisons have been made under his examination, and with the charcoal fuel.

Railway Dialogue.—The following (it is scarcely necessary to say) is from the newspaper press of brother Jonathan:—Two brothers recently from the old country, via Halifax, were lately walking up the Worcester Railroad, and their curiosity was somewhat excited by the iron tracks, but soon the cars hove in sight, and the following dialogue took place :—*Michael:* Och brother, d'ye see that quare crature a coming? *Patrick:* Troth and I do. What in the devil and his grand-mother's name, does it mane? *Michael:* Faith an' it is not me that is to tell ye, but an'ye don't stand out of the way, ye'll learn quite satisfactorily, I'm thinking. Don't ye min' how hard he brathes—he must have been running right tightly for a long space. [The car whizzed by.] *Patrick:* Och, Mike we're completely lost; for by my mother's milk, it is *Hell in harness*, and just the sort of coach I once dreamt the ould devil took the morning air in !

Free Trade.—From Bell's Comparative View of the external commerce of Bengal, for the year 1834-35, and 1835-36 (a Calcutta Annual) it appears, that since the abolition of the East India Company's monopoly, the quantity of native produce exported has gone on increasing till within the last year, it exceeded in value the total imports by 1,37,87,079 rupees.

Something new to Londoners.—A Calcutta paper (in the Calcutta and Saugor *railway* interest we

shrewdly suspect,) informs its readers, that " the south side of the Greenwich Railway *is planted with various forest trees, and forms a delightful walk for the citizens of London.*"

The Chemical Chair of the London University College, vacant through the lamented demise of Professor Turner, has been conferred on Mr. Graham, the Andersonian Professor of Chemistry at Glasgow. A better selection could scarcely have been made. Mr. Graham was first made favourably known to chemical philosophers by his discovery of the law of gaseous diffusion. He established by well devised experiments, the conformity of gases flowing through minute orifices, to the universal physical law that determines the issuing velocities of *non*-elastic fluids. During the last five years he has been diligently engaged in elaborate inquiries into the constitution of the salts, with special reference to the functions of their watery element, and has already published some results that are considered by good judges to affect materially the higher doctrines of chemical philosophy.

" *Mr. Herapath*" is the name of one of the disappointed candidates for the chair to which Professor Graham has been elected;—and we find from some letters we have received, that the gentleman in this predicament is generally supposed to be " Superintendent General John Herapath," of railway-evidence notoriety. The fact is not so. The Mr. Herapath, who was a candidate for the chair in question, is Mr. *William* Herapath, of Bristol, one of the best practical chemists of the day, and possessing as such very fair pretensions to the honour to which he aspired, a lover of truth and free enquiry, a gentleman, and (we should think) no *relation.*

Shalder's Fountain Pump.—Captain Greig, of the ship Caroline, in a letter dated 21st of March last, states, that in a late voyage the Fountain Pump "was the means of saving the ship and two hundred and thirty souls on board." The vessel was in so leaky a state, that "two seams in the bottom were partly left without caulking." The Captain adds, that the leather of the pump, " after serving two voyages between Quebec and London, does not appear to be the least worn."

The Railroad from Havanah to Bambano, on the south coast of the island of Cuba, is already in operation for four miles of its length, and it is calculated that before the close of this year five leagues of it will be completed. This is the first work of the kind in Cuba, but there are several others projected. The engines employed are from the manufactory of Messrs. Braithwaite and Co., of London.

Destructive Action of Copper on Ink.—The directors of the Bengal Bank lately refused payment of a number of bank notes, in consequence of their being without any signature. It appeared that they belonged to a Hindoo, who had kept them in a copper box. He asserted, that they originally possessed the signatures of the director, comptroller, cashier, &c., but that they had disappeared—he could not tell how. Mr. Prinsep, conjecturing that the ink had been acted on by the copper of the box in which the notes were kept, placed a paper written upon with English ink between two pieces of copper. After a short space of time, he found that the copper had decomposed the ink, and that the writing was completely effaced. He concluded that the statement of the Hindoo was correct, and recommended the bank not to refuse payment. The same destructive action is stated not to take place when China ink is employed.

☞ *British and Foreign Patents taken out with economy and despatch; Specifications, Disclaimers, and Amendments, prepared or revised; Caveats entered; and generally every Branch of Patent Business promptly transacted.*
A complete list of Patents from the earliest period (15 Car. II. 1675,) to the present time may be examined. Fee 2s. 6d.; Clients, gratis.

LONDON: Printed and Published for the Proprietor, by W. A. Robertson, at the Mechanics' Magazine Office, No. 6, Peterborough-court, between 135 and 136, Fleet-street.—Sold by G. W. M. Reynolds, Proprietor of the French, English, and American Library, 55, Rue Neuve, Saint Augustin, Paris.

Mechanics' Magazine,

MUSEUM, REGISTER, JOURNAL, AND GAZETTE.

| No. 728. | SATURDAY, JULY 22, 1837. | Price 3d. |

WOODHOUSE'S NEW ROTARY ENGINE.

Fig. 1.

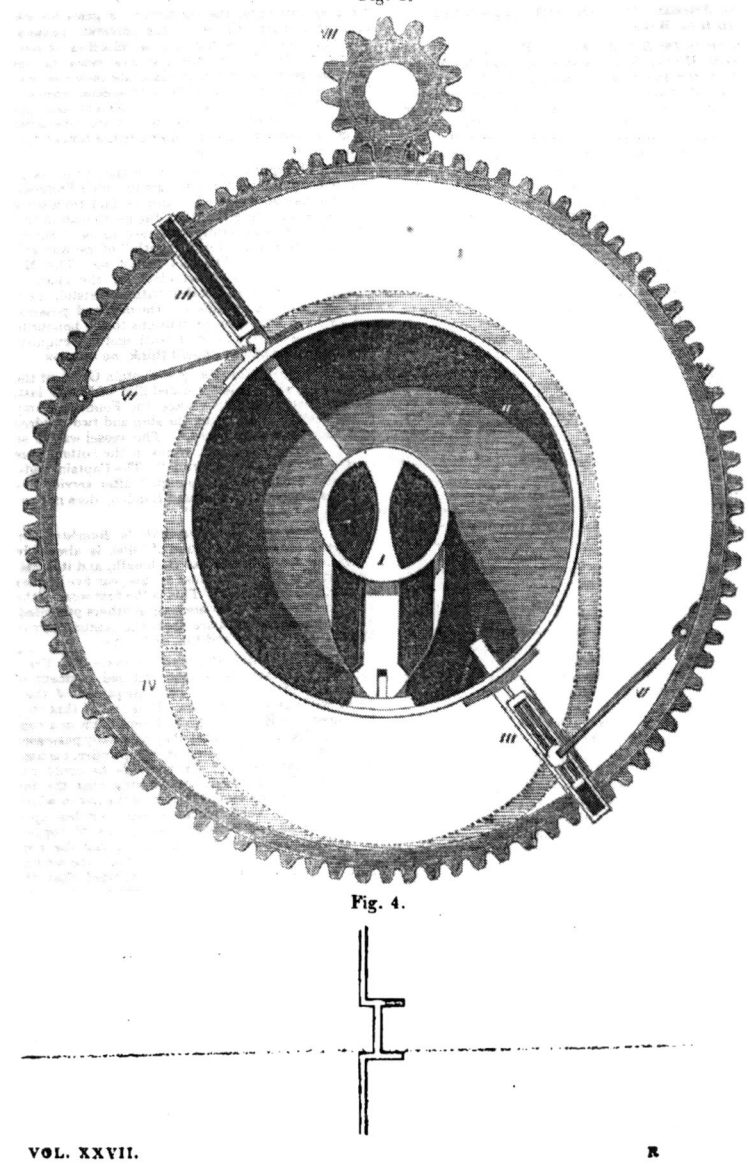

Fig. 4.

WOODHOUSE'S NEW ROTARY ENGINE.

Sir,—The numerous doubts which have been expressed by scientific men as to the practical advantage of giving a rotative action to steam power, are well calculated to damp inventive enterprize; yet such is sometimes the persevering incredulity of individuals, that notwithstanding all these doubts, the hope of success has not been subdued.

The advantages of reducing the bulk of the machinery in the case of locomotive engines, and affording a more ready application of power *without strain*, may in all likelihood, form sufficient inducements to perseverance; suffice it to say, that should the following be considered, as any advancement towards the attainment of the desired object, it is much at your service.

I am, Sir,

Yours respectively,

J. WOODHOUSE.

Kilburn, June 28, 1837.

Description.—The following are the probable advantages likely to be obtained by the use of a machine, such as is hereafter described :—1st, a direct rotary movement; 2nd, an equalization of power; 3rd, velocity more readily obtained; 4th, bulk of machinery much reduced; 5th, concussion avoided; 6th, facility of reversing the movement.

The Parts of the Machine are simply as follows.—In fig. 1., I is a central or fixed axis, through which the power is admitted and discharged; II., a cylinder; III., diaphragm plates, or slides; IV., an excentric guide; v., a cogged wheel, which, being affixed to, revolves with, the cylinder; VI., bearing cranks and rods; and VII., working axis. The last, viz., he working axis, it will readily appear, may be placed in any part, or two or more may be applied as found needful.

When power is applied through the axis I., the pressure forces itself against the abutment and other parts, but as the abutment is fixed, it affords a permanent resistance either way; the power then in its effort to escape, presses also against the diaphragm plate, which, as it laps within the cheeks of the cylinder, and is otherwise connected, causes the latter to revolve with the cogged wheel, the pinion, and the working axis. This rotary movement causes the reciprocating action of the diaphragms, whereby each alternately closes the chamber of the cylinder against the power, before the discharge of the other. Connected with a spare crank are two slides or rollers, which traverse the excentric guides; these, again, are connected with a rod and slide, that bed into grooves on each cheek of the cylinder; from this slide a rod is attached, passing through small packing boxes (fig. 2) into the diaphragm case, and attached to the diaphragm plate. The movement of the whole is thereby so connected, that it is impossible to throw it out of gear, however rapidly the machine is worked. The object of having the cases to the diaphragms is, that by their use, a large portion of friction is avoided, as they do not require packing, and slide up and down the cheeks of the cylinder free.

It may be objected that there will be a waste of power occasioned by the machine being continually in force, but the inquiry at once suggests itself—will not the velocity be thereby augmented, and if so, a grand purpose gained? The expansion of steam within a cylinder can only, after all, be a diminution of its power; *ergo*, a machine that does not require such accomodation to its defects, may claim consideration for utility, and even superiority, for many purposes. Waving the objection, however, this machine can also meet with like accomodation, if such were required, and the power be partially, or entirely shut off at each stroke. An equable motion is at all times desirable; to avoid concussion is a relief to the boiler and all parts of machinery,—in the case particularly of locomotive engines. Few have been long on board a steam packet, and not observed the trembling, occasioned by unequal force of the machinery—the immense strain also upon the axis, which the crank action occasions by the movement of the framework connected with it.

Fig. 1, illustrates the principle of the machine; the cheek of the cylinder being removed. The abutment is here seen, with the friction plate; similar ones are also placed at each end. A small quantity of packing may be placed at the bottom of the groove, but the plates, if well made, will not require it. The broad surface is kept against the surface of the cylinder, by the pressure of steam, as well as by its own gravity,—and its wear will improve its correct action. The diaphragms require no packing whatever;

Fig. 2.

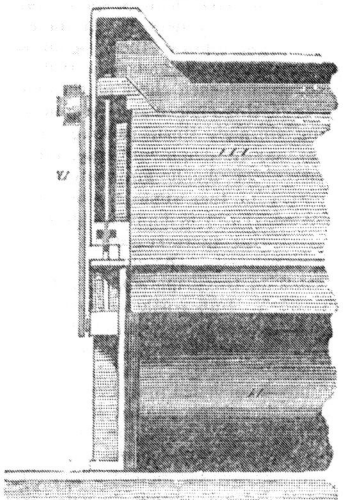

the groove in the cheek of the cylinder (fig. 4), if made true, will, when the plate or slide flaps upon it with pressure, prevent the escape of power, and the guide rollers will keep them well pressed upon the central axis; springs may be introduced if requisite, still further to regulate this pressure.

Fig. 2 is a section of the cylinder, &c. showing the roller and rods connected with the diaphragms, and the way they lap in the grooves of the cylinder.

Fig. 3, the eccentric guide, and method of constructing the two semicircular sections and the connecting pieces; by this means an eccentric of any dimensions may be made mathematically true.

Fig. 4, a section of the cylinder cheek, with the groove upon which the diaphragm rests when in action, and the outer groove in which the slide moves, that steadies the diaphragm rod.

As there may be many purposes to which this machine would be applicable, the frame work can be variously modified. For instance, should a locomotive

Fig. 3.

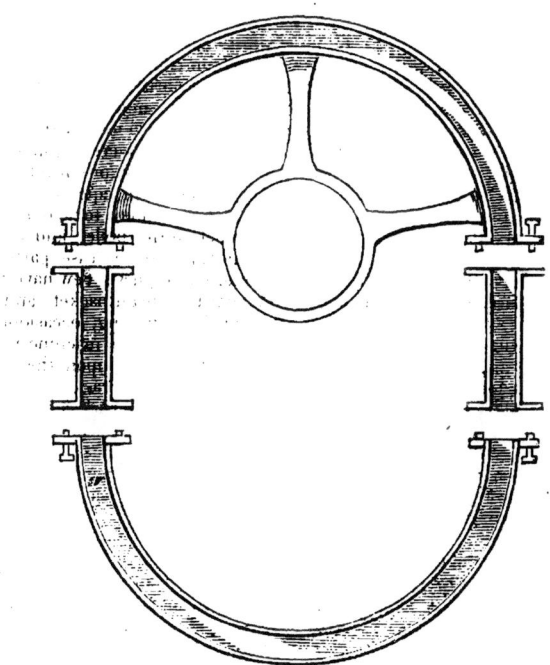

rail-road engine be fitted with one, the two axes may form those for the wheels, and be simultaneously acted upon without further means; in which case the machine will be central, in the carriage, and present no unsightly appearance.

As regards originality, the whole is to me new; but as the road has been traversed by numerous aspirants, there is little doubt but that many old features may be recognized. The principal claim will rest upon the excentric guide; and the method of connecting the rollers to the diaphragm plates—by means of which a reciprocating action is invariably maintained, and the possibility of derangement avoided.

In a model at the Adelaide Gallery, the diaphragms are not incased, the result is, an increase of friction; the area of the plates are each 6.18,—yet a power of 8lbs. to the inch would overcome the whole friction, and were they incased and the friction avoided, 3lbs. per inch power would overcome all that remained, and all power above that would be available. It will be observed that the model is not mathematically true, which operates very much against it, and increases friction.

The comparative lineal friction of a 10-horse engine, with that of a reciprocating of the same power, is for the former 142.81, and for the latter 146.72 inches, consequently, the proportion is in favour of this invention. I should rejoice in the opportunity of fair competition, and if a machine were well manufactured, I think there can be little doubt of its success.—J. W.

MR. UTTING'S ASTRONOMICAL TABLES.
—TO A SCOTCH DOMINIE.

Sir,—In your remarks on my letter (vol. xxvii, page 146) you seem much interested in Professor Struve's' observations on the planet Saturn and his ring, and on Jupiter and his satellites. You observe that different telescopes give different results. Very true, but you must be ignorant both of the nature of the instruments and their use, as well as of the doctrine of chances, to suppose for a moment, that two sets of observations would come out independently of each other, similar to those given by the Professor. Now we have eleven distinct observations out of the sixteen results,

each of which is given to the one thousandth part of a second; and if we allow that an observation may be correctly made to the one tenth part of a second (which is nearer than any instrument will give it correctly), there is in then a chance of one hundred to unity, that they do not come out the same in two observations; and the improbability, is all but infinite, when the eleven different observations are combined. The improbability that a constant difference should obtain between two sets of observations made with different instruments, is greater than that two sets of observations should come out precisely the same when both sets are made with the same instrument. I need not, however, make any farther remarks on this subject, as it amounts almost to an impossibility. It appears perfectly evident to me, that the difference between the results was intentional, and not produced by chance. The alteration of one letter, will, perhaps, render the title of these observations more consistent, i. e. for "deduced" read reduced. As it would be from a much greater number of observations, that the Professor found that the micrometer gave the diameters in the first instance, too large; and of course, the second set of observations, so called, would be reduced from the first, as "resulting from a much greater number of observations." But that the two sets of observations were independent of each other, I deny in toto.

You then proceed to test the length of my tropical year by metamorphosing my periods from days, hours, minutes, &c., into days and decimals! Now, if you will give me leave, I will substitute my own numbers as follows:—

days hrs. min. sec.   days hrs. min. sec.
27, 7, 43, 4.7129 × 29, 12, 44, 2.8547

days hrs. min. sec.
2, 5, 0, 58.1418

$$= 2360584''.7129 \times 2551442''.8547$$

190858''.1418

days hrs. min. sec.
$= 31556929''.8844 = 365$ 5 48 49.8844, which is less by .0011 of a second, than stated in my first table (vol. xxvi, page 378) owing to the periods of the moon containing only 27 and 29 days; whereas, that of the earth contains 365. Consequently, the decimals of a second in the moon's periods ought to be extended to five places, in order to being out the earth's period correctly to four places

of decimals: the earth's period being upwards of twelve times greater than those of the moon from which it is deduced; a nearer coincidence cannot therefore be expected. You, according to your system of computation make the difference .4426 parts of a second, instead of .0011 as above stated, your difference being 400 times greater than it is in reality.

You next proceed to test the periods of the earth and Venus, and make the *synodical* period* 583 days 22 hours 6 minutes 9.216 seconds. The period obtained from your own figures, comes out 9.204 seconds, a small mistake in your calculation of .012 of a second only. But this, however, is a greater error than you are likely to discover in my tables. In finding the *tropical* periods of the earth, you made use of the moon's *tropical* and *synodical* periods. On what authority did you take my *tropical* periods of the earth and Venus, and convert them into days and decimals, and then apply your own numbers for the difference of time, occasioned by the precession of the equinoctial points, in order to convert the *tropical* into *siderial* periods? Whereas, you had the *tropical* periods of the planets given in Table I. in days, hours, minutes, &c., and which you ought to have used instead of the siderial.† Was it not as easy to reduce the same to seconds, as to convert them into days and *decimals*, and then from *tropical* to *siderial* periods? Or did you adopt this plan in order to embarrass my calculations? Or to make the discrepancies more apparent? If so, you have missed your mark for this time. My

* Using the tropical periods from table 1, reduced to seconds, the synodic period of the earth and Venus comes out,—583 days 22' hours 7 minutes 52.5375 seconds, and the number of synodic revolutions in one conjunction of the sun, moon, planets, &c.,—156940.

† "A Scotch Dominie" has here fallen into an error by substituting the siderial for the tropical periods, as I never contended that if the sun, moon, planets, &c. were in conjunction, that they would again be in conjunction in the same point of the eliptic, or with the same fixed star. "The secular precession of the equinoctial points at the present time is 1 deg. 23 min. 30 sec. The above period contains ten revolutions of the precession, with a mean secular motion of 1 deg. 26 min. 5 sec. in a century; but I cannot at present state whether this comes within the limits of the secular variation. If so, the siderial periods of the planets will contain teh revolutions less, and the tropical periods of the satellites, ten revolutions more than are given in in the above tables." Vide vol. xxvi., page 379.—J. T

computations are open to investigation, but let it be done fairly, and I fear not the result, as my numbers are all given to the nearest unit in the last decimal place.

I am, Sir, yours, &c
J. UTTING

Lynn Regis, July 10, 1837.

A FEW WORDS TO NAUTILUS AND MR MACKINTOSH.

Sir,—I have a very short answer to give to your correspondent Nautilus, although he has thought proper in your last number to give a diagram in explanation of his geographical primer. I still adhere to my former statements. Indeed, far more has been already advanced upon that subject than was necessary; we cannot agree, and it is not absolutely necessary that we should.

I perceive a controversy is about to take place upon a far more important subject between Nautilus and O. N., relative to the possibility or impossibity of the astronomical question proposed by Nauticus. I have not yet found leasure to examine the solution which Nautilus has given for the question, in your last number; and, although I had, it would be unfair to both parties to give any opinion on the subject. O. N., however, I conceive is bound to make good the truth of his assertion. One parting advice I shall give Nautilus, which, I assure him, is kindly meant. And that is, for the future to endeavour as much as possible to keep his temper a little more under controul, than he has done in his last lucubrations: by losing his temper he gives his opponent perilous advantages over him.

In conclusion, I beg leave to add a few parting words to my late opponent, Mr. Mackintosh. I have examined his two propositions on the composition of forces, and I must in truth say, I read them with regret; a few more such propositions, would, I am assured, materially injure the high reputation which the *Mechanics' Magazine* has hitherto held in every branch connected with scientifical, philosophical, and mechanical subjects.

Yours, &c.
KINCLAVEN.

July 14, 1837.

NAUTILUS AND HIS IMPOSSIBLE ASTRONOMICAL QUESTION.

Sir,—In this day's Number of the *Mechanics' Magazine* your fastidious correspondent Nautilus (as Kinclaven has named him) has made a most ill-natured (and as I trust I shall be able to prove, an unwarrantable) attack upon me, because, I, forsooth, told him that a certain astronomical question proposed by your correspondent Nauticus (and which question, he, Nautilus, volunteered to give a solution of) involved an impossibility; notwithstanding this kindly meant advice, Nautilus undismayed by my assertion, has treated the scientific readers of the *Mechanics' Magazine* with what he himself calls (and which I suppose he believes to be) a true solution. He endeavours to make out that the stars γ draconis and polaris on the 1st of Feburary 1837, were both on the same azimuth circle at London at 8 hours 50 minutes 36 seconds Greenwich mean time. He has given us a formula for all questions of the same kind, but he has not thought proper to give us a demonstration of the formula. He says, " premising that the formula used is deduced from the commonest *problems* in spherical trigonometry."

Now if I must inform Nautilus that, suppose we should, for the sake of argument, grant that his formula is true; still we ought to ascertain before hand (if possible) whether the question we wish to solve by means of that formula is possible or not : formulas will not perperform miracles, or show us how to do that which common sense ought to have informed us is impossible. True, a *sound formula* will in most cases show us the absurdity of certain problems or theorms, where the thing to be done is founded upon either false or incongruous data ; and had Nautilus' formula been worth apples of gold (or even brass) it ought to have shown him upon its arithmetical application, that the problem he meant to solve was physically impossible. And now, Mr. Editor, with your leave I shall endeavour to demonstrate, that what I have asserted is true. Let P represent the north pole of the heavens, P' polaris, D γ draconis, Z the zenith of London, and draw the great circles P Z, P P', P D : and if possible, let Z P' D be an azimuth circle passing through Z,

and the two given stars P' and D. Then by the question we have given, P Z, P P',

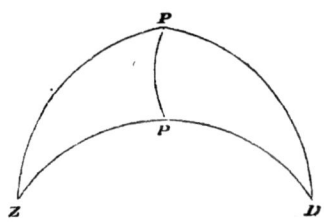

P D = 38° 30′, 1° 33′ 18″, and 38° 39′ 42″ respectively ; also the spherical angle D P P' = 106° 58′ 30″ = to the difference of right ascension between the two given stars. From which we deduce, from the " commonest principles of spherical trigonometry" the angle P P' D = 71° 12′ 4″, also P D P' = 2° 20′ 38″. And since the angle P' P D is greater than P P'D, hence P'D is greater than P D. Again, in the triangle Z P P' we find the P Z P = 2° 21′ 9″. Further, sin ½ (P P′ Z—P Z P′) 53° 13′ 23″ : sin ½ (P P′Z+P Z P′) 55° 34′ 32″ : : Tan ½ (P P′+P Z) 20° 1′ 39″ : Tan ½ Z P′. Now, as the first and second terms are of the same kind, and also the third and fourth, but the second term greater than the first; the fourth term will be greater than the third. That is, ½ Z P′ is greater than 20° 1′ 39″ or Z P′ is greater than 40° 3′ 18″ ; that is, Z P′ is greater than Z P. But it has also been shown, that P′D is greater than P D, much more then is Z D greater than Z P and P D ; that is, one side of a spherical triangle may be greater than the sum of the other two sides, which is absurd. Hence, the truth of Nautilus's grand formula (or his arithmetical application of it) falls to the ground.

In the above investigation, I have only considered the case when γ draconis is below the pole (I mean the pole of the equinoctial Nautilus) which is the only case Nautilus himself has taken into consideration : the same absurdity, however, might be shown would take place when γ draconis is above the pole.

Nautilus tries to rake up all he can against me. He quotes the following passage from my solution of the balloon question ;—" O. N. had occasion to refer to a table of meredional parts, which table has generally at the head of each column the initials ' M. P.' or ' Mer. P.' " &c. (page 212.)

This is miserable criticism, and is hardly deserving of a reply. But I must explain. The tables I made use of on the occasion, were those belonging to Professor Inman's Nautical Astronomy, and the table is headed *Meridional Parts*. The second solution of the balloon question is headed, " Solution on Mercator's Principles." Then follows what Nautilus states. " Lat. Vauxhall 51° 30′ 16″ (Mercator's Principles)" &c. Now what I really did write was (for I have a copy of the solution by me)" "Mer. pts." Your compositor, Mr. Editor, I suppose could not make out what was meant by the contraction_" Mer. pts", and seeing the article headed, " Solution on Mercator's Principles," committed the above *prodigious mistake*. If you should by chance have my letter still by you, you will find it is so as I have stated.*

Again, Nautilus snarls at me because I happened to give both the latitude and longitude of the place of observation in the question I proposed (see No. 719). The longitude of the place I proposed (Edinburgh) being small would make little difference in the solution; had the longitude, however, been great, for the solution I would have given, I certainly would have made it one of the elements. But in solutions, where it is allowed that two sides of a spherical triangle together, need not be greater than the third side, the longitude may be considered as perfectly unnecessary,—aye, and the latitude too.

In my first letter in the *Mechanics' Magazine* (No. 694), I fell into an error, which Kinclaven first noticed, and clearly demonstrated that I was wrong; I immediately saw my mistake, and lost no time in acknowledging it. Strange to say, Nautilus also fell into several mechanical blunders in his first letter in the *Mechanics' Magazine*. They were pointed out to him by an able writer, " S. W. S." of Leamington (No. 704), to which Nautilus never replied, and I believe I could assign two reasons why he did not. I shall always feel inclined to yield obedience to those whose mathematical attainments are superior to my own. So I shall willingly do to Nautilus when I

* We have referred to the M S., and find the fact to be as our correspondent suspects. The blunder was the compositor's.—ED. M. M.

find he is in that situation. But not till then.

I am, Mr. Editor,
Yours with respect,
O. N.

July 9, 1837.

THE LIGHT-POOL PIN MILLS.

In the Vale of Rodborough, on the road from Bath to Cheltenham, near Stroud, the traveller passes the Light-Pool Mills, where the patent solid head pin is manufactured on a large scale. The chief building is about 100 feet in length, and contains five floors, completely filled with machinery. A fine stream of water, equal in power to forty horses, acting on a large water-wheel, sets the whole in motion; the machines simultaneously performing the various functions with little noise or effort, while converting the rings of wire into pins, without the instrumentality of any manual assistance whatever.

The peculiar characteristic of the solid headed pin is, that the whole pin is formed of one piece of solid metal, the head not being separately spun and then put on in the ordinary manner, but compressed from the sold metal into a smooth round shape, thus rendering it firm and immoveable, and at the same time getting rid of the disagreeable consequences of its slipping and wounding the thumb, attendant upon the use of pins of the usual description. The metal employed is very hard, and thus the pins are exceedingly stiff and elastic, and a finely tapered point is preserved.

While one combination of machinery is drawing forward and straightening the wire, and cutting it off the requisite length, another apparatus in the same machine is forming and smoothing the point, a third compressing and shaping the head, and a fourth detaching and drawing out the pin in its finished state, which then falls into a receiver prepared for it. No less than forty-five pins per minute are made by each machine, and the whole manufactory produces the almost incredible number of three millions two hundred thousand pins, daily, or exceeding nineteen millions per week throughout the year.

An application was lately made to the Privy Council by Messrs. Tayler & Co., the proprietors of the patent for this manufacture (the invention of Mr. Lemuel Wright), for an extension of the term of the patent, and from the evidence adduced on the occasion, it appeared that enormous sums of money, and many years, have been expended in bringing the whole to its present high state of perfection. The Lords of the Council, who took great interest in the machine, had a model of it worked before them, in order that they might actually see pins produced by it. An extension of the patent for the term of five years was ultimately granted; but a poor reward, after all, for the genius and skill displayed in the invention, the capital adventured to bring it into use, and the prodigious saving of manual labour which it has accomplished.

VIATOR.

MR. DICKSON'S METALLIC NAVY— UNIVERSAL APPLICATION OF IRON.

Sir,—I have seen in your Number 727 letters from two correspondents, and also a letter in Number 725, on the construction of ships, and their safety from fire, the dangers of the seas, &c. It certainly is no detraction from the merits, or patriotic views, and benevolent intentions, of any gentleman, that not knowing what has been before done or suggested in any particular branch of science, he should publish his ideas upon the subject, although he afterwards find they have been anticipated by others. Instances of this kind are often recorded in your Magazine. I can assure you, Sir, that I have submitted a system of naval architecture to government, and also to some public companies, by which ships of war, and all other vessels, can be built of metal; and that they shall, on this plan, be cheaper, stronger (almost impregnable), far more durable, as well as safer, and lighter, than those built of oak, &c. in the common way. I have had the honour of an acknowledgment of this system from the First Lord of the Admiralty; but as you know, Sir, large bodies move slowly, and a change of system, like this, requires some time to be considered, and acted upon. With regard to the oxidation that will take place, it will not be so great an objection, as an entire iron ship would be, by affecting the compass. This evil I

have provided against; as well as the formation of compartments, by means of water-tight bulk-heads, so that if it were possible to force a hole through the sides, by striking against a rock, or otherwise, one compartment only would fill with water, and the ship would still keep a-float.

To your other correspondents, Mr. Symington and Mr. Baddeley, who suggest making the steam-engine on board to pump the water out of ships, as well as the water in which she floats, for extinguishing fires and other purposes, I beg to state that I did this twenty years ago; and no doubt several such apparatus are now to be found. I can also assure you, that I have an acknowledgment from government of being the first to propose *a steam-boat fire-extinguishing-engine*, which would throw more water (in one or more streams) than all the fire-engines about London together, and with a force sufficient to throw off any roof, and stop the progress of any fire, within its reach. The invention was also applicable to other purposes. I first proposed something of this kind to the Fire Brigade, when the Houses of Parliament were burnt down; and what has since taken place on this head is well known to the readers of your Magazine.

I cannot refer to your pages for an account of my first laying down a system of building an iron navy, because it was before the establishment of the *Mechanics' Magazine*. More than twenty five years ago I obtained a patent for making brewers' and distillers' utensils of iron (which the gas-works, &c. soon copied). At that time I made vessels as large as ships, as tuns, coolers, vats, and backs, which astonished those who saw them. This patent, the specification of which was published in the Repertory of Arts, opened such a field for the use of iron in architecture, &c., that many hundred thousand tons have been used through it. I was jestingly told that when I became Lord Mayor, the iron masters would build me an iron mansion house! I must conclude this epistle with an extract from the conclusion of my specification, which claimed the application of the invention to general purposes. After describing the manner of making the things for which the patent was granted, and their use in the construction of canals, locks, docks, inverted arches (which constitute ships), which I then and there said, "may justly be called building in iron—I, the said Jonathan Dickson, do hereby farther declare, that strong warehouses, manufactories, fortified places, stately mansions, elegant palaces, tombs, monuments, churches, and other places of divine worship, with their steeples or towers, to any extent, can of the aforesaid materials, and by the aforesaid principles, methods, and applications, hereinbefore described, delineated, ascertained, and made known, be permanently made, built, or erected, agreeably to any of the orders of architecture, in place of stones, bricks, and other terraqueous substances made use of the common way. In witness whereof," &c.

Yours respectfully,
JONATHAN DICKSON.

9, Charlotte-street, Blackfriar's Road,
17th July, 1837.

BALLOON-WAYS *versus* RAILWAYS.

Sir,—In all the schemes which have been hitherto proposed for the employment of balloons as conveyances from one specified place to another, it seems to have been assumed as necessary, that the motive force should be contained in the balloon itself. To construct an aërial vehicle thus capable of internal direction, is, indeed, an object worthy of ambition, and the glory of it, is, I have little doubt, reserved for some individual and some nation in the course of the next hundred years. But it strikes me that we have it already in our power, without any fresh invention, to turns balloons to infinitely more account than has been done hitherto.

In many parts of the new railroads, where there has been some objection to the use of locomotive engines, stationary ones have been resorted to, as every one knows, to draw the vehicles along. Why might not these vehicles be balloons? Why, instead of being dragged on the surface of the ground, along costly viaducts, or under disagreeable tunnels, might they not travel two or three hundred feet high? By balloons, I mean, of course, any thing raised in the air by means of a gas lighter than the air. They might be of all shapes and sizes to suit convenience.

The practicability of this plan does not seem to be doubtful. Its advantages are obvious Instead of having to purchase, as for a railway, the whole line of tract passed over, the company for a balloon-way would only have to procure those spots of ground on which they purposed to erect their stationary engines; and these need in no case be of peculiar value, since their being a hundred yards one way or the other would make little difference. Viaducts would, of course, never be necessary; cuttings on very few occasions indeed, if at all. The chief expense of balloons is in their inflation, which is renewed at every new ascent; but in these balloons, the gas once in, need never be let out, and one inflation would be enough.

These are the advantages to be derived by the proprietors of the balloon-way, which would, of course, be conveyed to the public in the shape of reduced fares. But the other advantages are manifold. All who have ever travelled by a balloon speak with rapture of the pleasure afforded them by the moving panorama of the country below; but a regret is frequently expressed that the car cannot be kept at a constant height of a few hundred feet, in order to enjoy the view to greater perfection. This very desideratum would be secured in the balloon-way. With regard to speed, it seems probable that a rapidity might be obtained which would leave the highest rate of railway carriages far behind. Friction might be reduced to a minimum.

I cannot conclude without expressing a hope that the first company which is formed for the purpose of constructing a balloon-way, will vote a handsome sum to the "ingenious proposer."

Yours respectfully,
P. P. C. R.

July 12th, 1837.

OLD AND NEW FIRE-EXTINGUISHING SYSTEMS.—MR. BADDELEY'S REPORTS.

Sir,—It is a pity that Mr. Baddeley did not think proper, in the first instance, to advance the true reason of his repugnance to enter the lists on the subject of fire-insurance. If he had done so, he would have spared himself the mortification of being compelled to acknowledge that his profession of anti-pathy to doing battle with a "·nameless knight" was but a mere feint to cover retreat, whose real motive was the fear of being unhorsed and overthrown. Had he pleaded at once want of "energy," and want of "leisure," occasioned by incessant occupation, no true knight, nameless or not, would have wished to take advantage of his weakness.   Nor would the confession have been so humi-liating as it now appears.   Mr. Baddeley vaunted, that if his assailant had but his vizor up, he would make mince-meat of him forthwith ; yet now he tells us his backwardness was occasioned by the want of "energy," generated by his "enduring the fatigues of business for fourteen hours per day," a reason quite as good for fighting shy of an open as of a masked antagonist.   Our friend has thus, by his want of candour, placed himself in a very conspicuous "false position," and there I leave him.

Mr. Baddeley commences his note by reciting his charges against me, of a "continual mis-statement of facts ;" but, to my surprise, concludes it without pretending to point out more than one solitary instance ; and if that be the strongest he can bring, what must the others be? The paragraph I quoted from a letter by "Wm. Baddeley," on the comparative efficiency of the old and new systems of fire-extinction, we are assured, does not relate to the new system at all. This is little better than a mere quibble. Any of your readers, by re-ferring back, as Mr. Baddeley rather in-considerately advises, to the mass of valuable information contained in his Annual Fire Reports, will at once per-ceive that, although the "London Fire-Engine Establishment" did not receive that name, or complete the whole of its arrangements, until the year 1832, the "new system of the fire-offices" uniting men and engines, and reducing their ag-gregate number, was in full operation the year before, and commented upon by Mr. Baddeley himself, in the extract given at p. 173. That extract remains, therefore, as germane to the matter as ever. Its every word bears directly on the question of "New System v. Old." "The co-operative system," observes Mr. Baddeley, "works exceedingly well for the insurance companies, but is not

equally advantageous for the public, *seeing that* the chance of prompt and effectual assistance, in case of accidents, *will always be in proportion to the number of men and engines that are distri-buted over the metropolis.*" Is it "arrant nonsense" to apply these remarks to a system, whose main feature is, that very "reduction in the number of men and engines," which Mr. Baddeley was of opinion must always operate against the interest of the public? (and if I recollect aright, this reduction has been carried to such an extent, that there are not now above half the number of fire-engine stations that were in existence under the old system).   Mr. Baddeley has evidently changed his opinion on this, as on many other branches of the subject ; then why not "make a clear breast" of it at once, as he seems half inclined· to do when he alludes to his having written the paragraph "five years and a half ago." This would be far bet-ter than affecting to deny the identity of the "new system" of 1832 with that of 1831, of which it is merely a revised and and improved edition, with a fresh *title-*page.

On every other point but this, Mr. Baddeley leaves me in undisputed pos-session of the field. Not one word has he to say in explanation of the awkward fact, deduced from his own Reports, that the number per annum of serious fires has increased, under the vigilant superintendence of the day-and-night Fire-Brigade, from *fifty-six* to *one hun-dred and thirty seven* (vide vol. xxvii. p. 36) ; not one syllable does he offer, to account for the hundred per cent. in-crease of fatal fires since the improved system has come into full operation ; nor does he touch, even for a moment, on that strange realization of the fondest anticipations of the friends of the new system,—the very remarkable increase in fires of first-rate importance and ex-tent ! Above all, he makes no attempt to reconcile his own assertion (vol. xxvii. ·p. 227), that "*every nerve has been strained* to render the Fire-Engine Es-tablishment *as efficient as possible*," with the position laid down by himself a week or two previous, that "the public will not, as P. R. states, 'be led to suspect,' but if they view the case aright, will positively *know*, 'that it is *not* the insurance companies' interest that property should be secured against calamity by fire' (AT THEIR EXPENSE) ' beyond a certain extent ;' that is, beyond the extent of their own liability"—(Vol. xxvi. p. 158.) The omission of these few points detracts a little from the completeness of the "reply."

In conclusion, allow me to hope that Mr. Baddeley will not for the future, as he seems too apt to do, consider any remarks applying only to his character of contributor to the *Mechanics' Magazine* in a personally-offensive point of view. In common with all the rest of your readers, I have too much respect for his highly useful labours to harbour the remotest intention of offence : but a suspicion (however groundless) to that effect seems the besetting sin of unanonymous correspondents, and is, perhaps, the greatest of the many disadvantages of the real-name-and-address system of magazine-writing. Mr. Baddeley, in his very mysterious concluding paragraphs, insinuates that "Aquarius" is not unknown to him ; yet every sentence he hazards on the subject serves to shew that he is completely in the dark, and none more so than that in which he covertly hints that any, even the slightest, "personal interest" in the matter is possessed by

Sir, your very obedient servant,

AQUARIUS.

14th July, 1837.

THE THAMES TUNNEL.

Report of the Committee of the House of Commons.

The select committee appointed to consider the papers laid before this house relating to the Thames Tunnel, and who were empowered to report the minutes of evidence taken before them to the house, have considered the matters to them referred, and agreed to the following report :—

" Your committee have taken evidence upon the subject of the engineering difficulties belonging to the undertaking, which they are of opinion will not be greater than are represented in Mr Walker's report. They have further considered the propable revenue to arise from the traffic through the Tunnel when completed, which, from the very nature of such evidence, must be in a great measure conjectural, they are not therefore prepared to give any decided opinion, whether the the revenue to arise from the proposed work will be sufficient to cover the Exchequer-bill

interest on the capital of 374,600*l.* proposed to be expended upon it.

" But looking to the importance of a work of this nature, for the first time now undertaken as a means of fixed communication, in situations where no other of an equally permanent nature may be available, and also that the sum of 180,000*l.* has been already expended upon the work by the proprietors, and the further sum of 72.000*l* by the public, they are of opinion, that it will be expedient to authorise the Treasury to continue the advances to the Thames Tunnel Company according to the act of Parliament.

" July, 1837."

[The best thing they could now do with this deplorable affair, would be to take the bricks out, and let the water in. The Committee recommend that £374,600 more should be advanced by the public to complete (?) this monument of miscalculation, blundering, and folly ; and yet they confess that they are not "prepared to give any *decided opinion* whether the revenue to arise from the proposed work, will be sufficient to cover the Exchequer Bill interest (3½ per cent. we believe) on the said £374,000 ; that is, in plain English, they recommend this immense sum to be taken out of the pockets of the people, without being certain that the security for its return is worth a single farthing ! Why, do they not know well—(known it is at least to all the world besides)—that the concern was never estimated by its projectors themselves, to yield more than 4 per cent. on a capital of £200,000 ? How then can it possibly pay 3½ per cent., or even 2 per cent. on £440,000, the amount to which the loan from the public is proposed to be augmented ? And if it will not yield 2 per cent., what else is the proposition of the Committee, but one for throwing a couple of hundred thousand pounds of the public money into the Thames ? We do not think there ever was a more scandulous job. Even if completed to-morrow, this great bore (in every sense) could effect no more for the traffic between the opposite banks of the Thames, than might be effected by a well-regulated steam ferry, for as many shillings as this will cost pounds.—ED. M. M.]

LANG'S ROPE-MAKING MACHINERY.

A pamphlet has been published at Greenock, containing an Exposition of the Principles of Mr. James Lang's invention for Spinning Hemp into Rope-yarns by machinery, and its effect on the strength and durability of Cordage. Of this Exposition the following extract will convey an outline :—

" It was only towards the end of the 18th century that the art of Rope-making engaged the attention of scientific men, and began to be conducted on scientific principles. Then it was discovered, that, by the mode of operation formerly in use, the yarns could not be brought to bear equally with each other; and, therefore, that a great loss of strength in the rope behoved to be the consequence. Great exertions were accordingly made by several intelligent individuals to remedy this defect, and between the years 1783 and 1807, no fewer than twenty-two patents were taken put for improvements in the art, and for machines of various descriptions,—these it is not to our purpose to describe. It may be sufficient to state, that the one invented by Captain Huddart of London, was greatly approved of, and obtained the highest celebrity. This plan was introduced into Greenock in 1802, by the late firm of Messrs. John Laird and Co., but was in some measure superseded a few years after by the method now in use, and which, by the application of the same principle, but of a more simple construction, was found to secure the same object, while, at the same time, it was better adapted for general purposes. For this improvement on Captain Huddart's plan we believe we are indebted to Mr. W. Chapman of Newcastle. The principle by which an increase of strength in the Cordage was effected (amounting to about 30 per cent.), is simply by so constructing the strand of the rope as that *every yarn is made to bear its own proportion of the strain.* That the application of such a principle shall be followed by such a result, must be apparent to every one, and *it is by carrying out this same principle to its full length*, as we shall afterwards show, that we have been enabled to effect an additional increase of strength, and, consequently, of durability to the rope.

" That a great improvement in ropemaking was effected by these gentlemen, there can be no question, but that perfection in the art might be attained, it was still necessary that the mode of preparing the yarns should also be improved. The usual process of hand-spinning was considered very defective, as evidently it did not impart to the yarns that degree of strength which it was thought the material was capable of affording. Endeavours were accordingly made to obviate this defect also. Three patents were even taken out for machines, but these were found not to answer expectation; those constructed by Mr. Chapman are still used by some houses in England, but as they are very defective, they have never been introduced into general practice. A moment's consideration must be sufficient to convince any person, the least conversant in rope-making, that, if the strength and durability of the rope depend on the proper arrangement and equal bearing with each other of the yarns in the strand, so its strength and durability must also depend on the just arrangement, regular twisting, and consequent equal bearing of the fibrous substances which are employed in the composition of the yarns. Indeed, after the improvement above alluded to, this was the only thing requisite to complete the scientific construction of cordage; and by the application of machinery, on a principle somewhat analogous to that which we have already referred to, this desideratum has also been supplied. Mr. Lang, who had for many years directed his attention to the subject, and was convinced of its practicability, upon taking the active management of our works, got a set of machines constructed under his own direction, which, on repeated trial, were found completely to accomplish the object. By this invention, the regular spinning of the yarns, which had hitherto been prepared in a tedious and clumsy manner by handlabour, is one object which has been effected; but this, although in itself important, is one of its least advantages. By the same plan, the hemp, to whatever purpose applied, being drawn over a succession of gills, or small hackles, is dressed in the highest degree; hence the fibrous substances of the hemp are regularly split and subdivided; they are also multiplied to such an extent as that their number in a Patent-spun yarn will be found more than double the quantity of those which compose a hand-spun yarn of equal grist; this, every one will admit, must increase its strength in no inconsiderable degree. Again, while the fibres are thus greatly multiplied, they are also completely elongated and laid straight, so as to admit of being regularly twisted, and each fibre being stretched its full length and laid parallel to the others, in the yarn, they are all made to bear at the same time, and equally, in the strain; thus every fibre of the hemp is called into action, and contributes its own proportion of strength to the fabric; this is certainly a most important feature in our Patent plan, and such a result could never be expected from the most careful and best conducted hand-spinning. But this is not all, by hand labour the hemp can only be spun from the middle, or *bight;* and therefore only one-half of the length of its fibre is extended in the yarn, consequently, some qualities of hemp have hitherto been considered inferior, because, on account of the shortness of their fibre, they would not admit of being doubled; thus, a material in other respects as good, while of lower price, has been rejected in the manufacture of cordage, not so much on its own account, but because, by the process of hand-spinning, only the one-half of its length could be employed. Now, Mr. Lang's plan has this additional advantage, that the hemp is spun by the end of the fibre, and thus, by having its whole length extended in the yarn, those qualities of hemp hitherto considered inferior, because shorter, may be applied with equal safety and advantage, and do in reality produce cordage as strong and as durable as the others. When we take into account the very depressed state of this branch of our manufacture, in consequence of the facilities enjoyed by our neighbours on the continent of underselling us in a foreign market, as also the present state of the shipping interest, it will, by every candid person, be acknowledged that an invention such as this, by which we are enabled to produce a superior article, and at a cheaper rate, ought, even in a political point of view, to be regarded as a public good; and is consequently entitled to public encouragement and support."

Professor Jameson, in his *Journal*, adds :— We have seen the rope-yarns, understand the machinery employed, have read carefully the exposition, and do not hesitate to say, that this new cordage has answered the expectation of those who have tried it, and that severely too, in many seas.

THE BRITISH POWER-LOOM, AND HINDOO HAND-WEAVING.

(From the *Madras Journal of Literature and Science*. Observations on the Flora of Courtallum, by Robert Wight, Esq., M.D.).

The Hindoo weaver, skilful, from long practice, in the use of his simple implements, and having no competitors, did not think it necessary to tax his ingenuity, for the invention of new and improved spinning and weaving machinery, but went on, as his progenitors had done, spinning and weaving, with a wheel and loom still of the simplest construction.

The process of fabrication, by such primitive methods, is so slow, that a man and his family, in constant employment, can do little more than support themselves by their labour. When, on the contrary, the raw material is exported at heavy cost to Britain, and manufactured there, with the aid of improved

machinery, it can be brought back and sold, after paying the expenses of a second voyage, from 20 to 30 per cent. under the produce of the same quality of the native loom. Owing to this difference, when the trade was thrown open, and free access was allowed to British manufactures, their cheapness soon drove the Indian ones out of their accustomed markets, and caused at first great distress to our manufacturing population. Now, however, the scales are re-adjusting themselves to our altered circumstances, and the advantages of the change are becoming evident. The exportation of piece goods, from the comparatively small quantity that could be produced for exportation, and the great expence of fabrication, never could return a proportional, if even a remunerating, profit to the country. The raw material, on the contrary, owing to the unlimited demand, the comparatively high price which it bears, and the small expence of preparing it for the market, not only remunerates, but returns such a profit, as to stimulate to a vastly increased production; when we add to this, that our growers can now clothe themselves with English cloth more cheaply than they formerly could with native, we can at once appreciate the advantages which India is in course of deriving from the English cotton manufactories; and how much her future prosperity must depend on the extension and improvement of her cotton cultivation. The fulfilling of these conditions is, in truth, indispensable to a continuance of that commercial prosperity, which is now beginning to dawn on us; since, unless we labour diligently to improve the quality, and diminish the exportation price of our cotton, great as the demand now assuredly is, we can scarcely expect that it will be able to hold its present place in the English market, when opposed by so many competitors, and, still more, by the long and expensive voyage required to bring it into that market.

PRACTICAL HINT TO MAGNETIC NEEDLE MAKERS.

(From the *American Railroad Journal*.)

Though the principle of the directive power of the needle is well known, we believe that the following case may not be of rare occurrence, and state it for the benefit of the makers and users of instruments.

A surveyor's compass had been ordered, which we procured and forwarded in complete order. It was returned, because when levelled by the bubbles, the needle was so much inclined as to touch the limb of the compass box.

When we received the instrument, no such

fault was found to exist, the needle was again found to be perfectiy free and horizontal when the compas was levelled.

This is easily explained. For every degree that we approach the North pole, the *dip* of the needle is increased by one degree nearly. The latitude of the place in question was more than two degrees to the north of this city. On examining the limb and ascertaining the space occupied by 2° 20', we were not surprised to find that this amount of devistion from horizontality, should cause the needle to touch.

The remedy was to place a counterpiece of brass or copper wire upon the needle, the adjustment being made here. On reaching the place of destination, the north pole will again be found to dip, and this is to be prevented by moving the counterpiece until the needle is exactly balanced.

These counterpoises in one shape or other were formerly quite common, but we have recently seen a vast number of instruments without any thing of the kind. Such a compass, though properly adjusted while in the shop, no sooner reaches a distance of sixty miles or more, to the North or South, than the respective pole will be found to have a tendency to dip by a very considerable and unpleasant amount.

We would recommend Instrument Makers to supply this counterpoise in all instances —for we are well convinced that they are often blamed for bad workmanship, when the very power that renders the needle useful is the true cause of the difficulty.

The dip not being constant in the same place, renders this adjustment still more necessary.

It need hardly be mentioned, that the construction of an extemporaneous counterpoise, can be accomplished by any one who uses an instrument.

HOW TO MAGNETIZE AND TEMPER STEEL AT THE SAME TIME.

M. Aime recommends the following method, which consists in tempering and magnetizing a bar of iron at the same time. To effect this, a bar of soft iron, curved in the form of a horse-shoe, is surrounded with a brass wire, covered with silk ; the two extremities of this wire are made to communicate with the poles of the voltaic pile ; a bar of steel, equal in length to the distance between the two extremities of the horse-shoe, is then ignited, and seized between a pair of pincers ; the two poles of the horse-shoe are then applied to the bar, and plunged into a bucket of water ; in the course of a minute or two after immersion, the bar is detached

from the horse-shoe, and a similar operation performed with similar bars extracted from the fire. In order to prevent the brass wire from softening, care must be taken in dipping the apparatus in water to envelope the two extremities of the helix in a rag covered with mastic. The ends of the conducting wire were soldered to the zinc and copper poles of the battery ; a single wire was employed. Aime, however, considers that it may be preferable to unite several into a bundle, or even to take a ribbon of copper covered with silk or varnish. The bar ought not to be detached too quickly from the horse-shoe ; it is necessary to wait until the interior of the steel has acquired a slight elevation of temperature, in order that the molecules may have time to arrange themselves, conveniently, for magnetizing and tempering. The duration of the immersion varies with the size of the bar, and the temperature which it possesses when taken from the fire.—*Journ. de Chim. Medic.*

REMARKABLE EFFECTS OF CONTINUOUS CURRENTS OF ELECTRICITY OF LOW INTENSITY.

The brilliant discoveries in electro-chemistry obtained by Sir Humphry Davy were effected, as our readers are aware, by the employment of voltaic currents of high intensity, elicited by means of large batteries. M. Becquerel afterwards drew attention to the chemical agency of feeble currents in reducing several refractory oxides to the metallic state; and Drs. E. Davy, Bucholtz, and Faraday, following in his footsteps effected decompositions of other substances by similar means. Mr. Bird, the Experimental Philosophy Lecturer at Guy's, has been recently prosecuting the same branch of inquiry with great success. From a communication made by him to the Royal Society, we find that he employed an apparatus analogous to that of Professor Daniell, for obtaining an equal and continuous current of low intensity from a single pair of plates: the metallic solution, in which a copperplate was immersed, being contained in a glass tube, closed at the bottom by a diaphragm of plaster of Paris, and itself plunged in a weak solution of brine contained in a larger vessel, in which a plate of zinc was immersed; and a communication being established between the two metallic plates by connecting wires. By the feeble, but continuous current thus elicited, sulphate of copper is found to be slowly decomposed, affording beautiful crystals of metallic copper. Iron, tin, zinc, bismuth, antimony, lead, and silver may, in like manner, be reduced, by a similar and slightly modified process ; in general appearing with metallic lustre, and in a crystalline form, and presenting a remarkable contrast in their appearance to the irregular, soft, and spongy masses obtained from the same solutions by means of large batteries. The crystals of copper rival in hardness and malleability the finest specimens of native copper, which they much resemble in appearance. The crystallization of bismuth, lead, and silver, by this process, is very beautiful ; that of bismuth being lamellar, of a lustre approaching to that of iron, but with the reddish tint peculiar to the former metal. Silver may thus be procured of the whiteness of snow, and usually in the form of needles. Some metals, such as nickel, which, when acted on by currents from large batteries, are deposited from their solutions as oxides only, are obtained by means of the apparatus used by Mr. Bird, in a brilliant metallic form. He farther found that he could in this way reduce even the more refractory metallic oxides, such as silica, which resist the action of powerful batteries, and which M. Becquerel could only obtain in alloy with iron. By a slight modification of the apparatus he was enabled to form amalgams both of potassium and of sodium with mercury, by the decomposition of solutions of chlorides of those bases ; and in like manner ammonium was easily reduced, when in contact with mercury, by the influence of a feeble voltaic current. In this last experiment it was found that an interruption to the continuance of the current, even for a few seconds, is sufficient to destroy the whole of the product which had been the result of the previous long-continued action ; the spongy ammoniacal amalgam being instantly decomposed, and the ammonia formed being dissolved in the surrounding fluid.

DESCRIPTION OF A PENDULUM ARTIFICIAL HORIZON, TO BE ATTACHED TO A SEXTANT OR QUADRANT FOR THE PURPOSE OF OBSERVING ALTITUDES BY DAY OR NIGHT AT SEA. BY LIEUT. BECHER, R.N.

A small pendulum carries an arm nearly at right angles to it, springing from the point of suspension, at which the whole rests on an agate point. At the end of this arm is a vane, perpendicular to the plane of the pendulum and arm, and having its upper edge cut horizontal, which forms the visible horizon. This apparatus is placed in a tube laid in the direction of the telescope, and attached to the sextant beyond the horizon glass ; the point of suspension rests on an arch within the tube, the rest of the pendulum hanging below, the vane being at the end nearest the horizon glass, its upper edge bisecting the space in the tube.

A disc is placed in the lower half of the tube, between the fixed horizon glass and the vane of the pendulum, and close to the latter without touching it ; in the upper edge of the disc in a small aperture or notch. A lens is placed in the end of the tube next the horizon glass, in order to shew distinctly the edges of the vane and this aperture ; at the other end is ground glass.

The sextant being held with its plane vertical, the reflected image is brought down to the horizontal edge of the vane, and the sextant is then oscillated in its own plane till the edge of the vane is seen exactly fair with the upper edge of the disc, or just covering the aperture. If the vane be above the aperture, this is discovered by the light appearing through two small holes in the disc. As the line of sight may not be exactly horizontal, its *error*, which is constant, is found by comparing the altitude obtained with that shewn by another instrument.

The pendulum moves in a small cistern, containing oil, to diminish its vibrations ; on turning up the face of the sextant to read off, the oils runs into another cistern. For observing at night, a small lamp is hung before the outer end of the tube.

On observing with the instrument in a steam vessel, the extreme error was 7′ 48″. The latitude, as found on board a small cutter in Sea reach by the altitudes of the moon and of *Jupiter*, agreed within 2′.

The error in observing is generally in excess.

NOTES AND NOTICES.

The Island of Juan Fernandez, on which Alexander Selkirk (Robinson Crusoe) was cast away, has been swallowed up by the recent earthquake which destroyed a great portion of Chili.—*West Indian*, 11th May.

Steam Ploughing, Harrowing, &c.—The Highland and Agricultural Society of Scotland has just offered a premium of £500 " for the first successful application of the power of steam to the cultivation of the soil, including the operations of ploughing and harrowing, and the other general purposes of the farm, for which animal power is now used." To this premium there is added the following note :— " The Society does not feel it to be necessary to express opinions as to the probability of a successful application of steam to tillage ; but it has felt it to be a duty imposed upon it by its constitution to bring the subject in a proper manner before the country." It is to be inferred from this, that the steam-ploughing experiments lately exhibited before this Society by Mr. Heathcoat, M. P., and spoken of in the newspapers as leaving nothing to be desired, are, after all, regarded by competent judges in the light of an entire failure. Such we learn, from other sources, to be pretty nearly the truth.

Organic Remains in the Sewalik Hills.—We ob serve in the Delhi Gazette that a magnificent collection of fossil bones was presented to the museum by Captain Cautley, of the Bengal artillery. These organic remains come from the range of hills formerly called Sewalik, which skirt the base of the Himalayah mountains from the Ganges to the Sutlege river, or from N. L. 30 to 31 deg. They abound in part of the range to the westward of the Jumna river, and belong to the genera mastodon, elephant, hippopotamus, rhinoceros, hog, anthracotherium, horse, ox, deer, antelope, canis, felis, garial, crocodile, emys, trionyx, besides fish and shells. Among the fossils, there were some considered to be new genera, and one which Capt. Cautley and Dr. Falconer have called sevatherium. The monkey of a large species has been found fossil in the Sewalik Hills.—*India Review,* June, 1837.

New Materials for Paper.—In the third volume of the Society for the Diffusion of Useful Knowledge's very interesting work on "Vegetable Substances," an account is given at some length of a series of ingenious experiments made by a persevering German on the manufacture of paper, by which he ascertained that there was hardly any vegetable whatever from which, in case of need, it might not be fabricated. We question, however, if even he, in the course of his very extensive researches, hit upon one singular substance from which it has recently been discovered by accident that this important article may be made. M. Larnandes, a printer at Moissac, a little more than three months ago, chanced to let fall on a table the juice of some love-apples, or tomatoes, as they are sometimes called. The table was very smooth, and when, three months after, M. Larnandes was going to clean it, he found to his surprise that the tomato-juice had, in drying, acquired the consistence of paper. He removed it with care, and found, that thin as it was, he could write on it with ease, and the ink did not spread. The discovery is likely to be of some utility in France, and most other foreign countries, though not in England. The post offices abroad very reasonably proportion their charges to the weight of the letter conveyed, and it is therefore of some consequence to write on the thinnest paper procurable.

French Patents.—In France, as in other countries, the number of patents granted has, for the last thirty years, gone on perpetually increasing. The present system commenced on the 1st of July, 1791, and the number from 1791 to 1793 was sixty-seven. The increasing fury of the Revolution, and the incessant wars of the infant empire, gave a check to the activity of inventors, and from the "year 1" of the Republic to "year 14th," and last, the number of patents was only 301. From 1806 to 1813, under the continued successes of Napoleon, some improvement was manifest; the number was 606. But it was under the Restoration that French industry was for the first time called into any thing like full developement; from 1814 to 1829, 3,383 patents were granted in France. The movement thus given has gone on increasing, and from the second revolution to 1836, the number has been 3,018, the last period of seven years thus nearly equalling the preceding one of fourteen. From the 1st July, 1791, to the 1st January, 1837, the whole number of patents is 7,375. Of these, 5,641 are of inventions, 1,734 of improvements and "importations," or, as we should phrase it, "communications from foreigners residing abroad."

New Method of Caulking Ships.—Mr. Yetts, of Yarmouth, has taken out a patent for a new method of caulking sea-boats, which renders them watertight, and prevents the oakum from being pressed out by the straining of the planks. Mr. Yetts effects this by introducing a narrow strip of caoutchouc (India-rubber) on each side of the threads of the oakum on the outer sheath of the vessel.—*Norwich Mercury.*

Prussic Acid.—A very simple antidote to the deadly effects of this poison consists in pouring cold water upon the head and spine of the person or animal affected by it. Dr. Copland first recommended the employment of this means of restoration in cases of poisoning by prussic acid, in the number of the London Medical Repository for June, 1825, twelve years since. He moreover advised having recourse to the same remedy in cases of poisoning by narcotics or substances exerting a suddenly depressing influence upon the nervous system. Some years after the recommendation of this treatment by Dr. Copland, the value of it was shown by Dr. Herbst and other physicians in Germany.

Boston Piggery.—About six miles from Boston, in West Cambridge, is the Boston Piggery. At least 700 hogs are here constantly kept in pork condition, *entirely* on the offal from the dwelling-houses in Boston, every one of which is visited in turn by the city carts. The offal increases, and the contractor calculates that it will be sufficient hereafter to fatten 1,000 hogs. He now receives four cart-loads a day, and pays the city 3,500 dollars a year, or about 2.75 dollars a load. He receives three dollars a day for what the hogs leave. The city treasury loses 1000 dollars a year by the operation, and it is said the man makes three times that sum. The pig pen is an enclosure of fifteen acres, with places of shelter from the storm. As the hogs attain their size, they are slaughtered on the spot,—the fat barrelled up, and the lean sold in the city. According to the rule in the country, the contractor should furnish each family in the city once a year with a spare-rib, for the food furnished the piggery.—*Springfield Journal.*

The London and Birmingham Railway Partial opening of the Line.—On Thursday last, the railway was opened for the conveyance of passengers and parcels between London and Box Moor (24½ miles), including the intermediate stations of Harrow and Watford. The distance is usually performed by the first class carriages in less than an hour. The fares average about two pence per mile.

The Supplement to Vol. xxvii., containing Title, Contents, Index, &c., Medallic Portrait of his late Majesty, and Wyon's Cheselden Medal, engraved by Freebairn by Bates' patent machine, is published, price 6d. Also, Vol. xxvii., price 9s. 6d.

☞ *British and Foreign Patents taken out with economy and despatch; Specifications, Disclaimers, and Amendments, prepared or revised; Caveats entered; and generally every Branch of Patent Business promptly transacted.*

A complete list of Patents from the earliest period (15 Car. II. 1675,) to the present time may be examined. Fee 2s. 6d.; Clients, gratis.

LONDON: Printed and Published for the Proprietor, by W. A. Robertson, at the Mechanics' Magazine Office, No. 6, Peterborough-court, between 135 and 136, Fleet-street.—Sold by G. W. M. Reynolds, Proprietor of the French, English, and American Library, 55, Rue Neuve, Saint Augustin, Paris.

𝕸𝖊𝖈𝖍𝖆𝖓𝖎𝖈𝖘' 𝕸𝖆𝖌𝖆𝖟𝖎𝖓𝖊,

MUSEUM, REGISTER, JOURNAL, AND GAZETTE.

No. 729.	SATURDAY, JULY 29, 1837.	Price 6d.

MR. COCKING'S PARACHUTE.

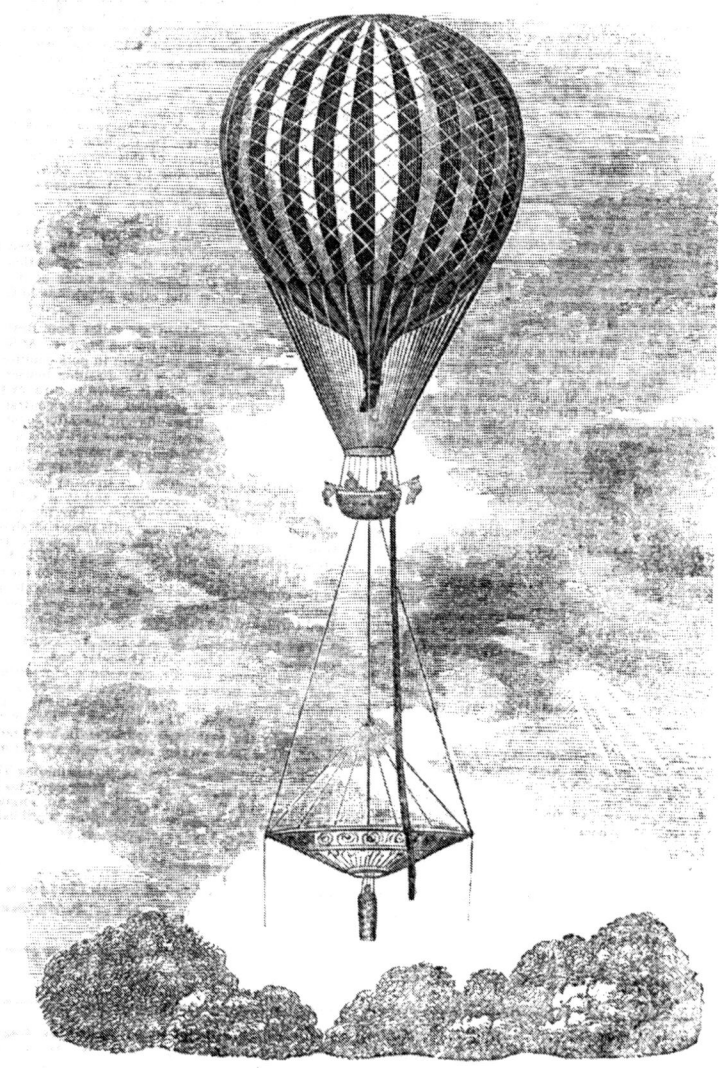

DESCRIPTION OF MR. COCKING'S PARACHUTE, AND NARRATIVE OF THE RECENT AND FATAL DESCENT.

Since the days of Garnerin, no one has had the courage—temerity we should have said—to venture a descent in a parachute, until the present melancholy instance. Whatever may be our opinion with respect to the ultimate success of aërial navigation, all will agree with us that no useful result could possibly have arisen even from the complete success of Mr. Cocking's attempt.

As considerable interest was excited in the public mind by so hazardous an enterprize, we employed an artist to make a sketch of the balloon and parachute at the time of its ascent, which our readers will find by referring to the description hereafter quoted from the *Times*, and the narrative of Mr. Green, he has executed with considerable fidelity.

The following description is doubtless either from the pen of the unfortunate experimenter himself, or under his dictation:—

Some account of the machine and apparatus which will be employed in the bold experiment to be made at Vauxhall Gardens on Monday next may, perhaps, be interesting to our readers.

The only parachute descent ever made in this country was that by Monsieur Garnerin, about thirty years since; and it was then remarked by many scientific men present, that the great oscillation which took place from the moment the machine expanded till it reached the earth, must have been attributable to some defect in the principle of its construction.

Mr. Cocking, a gentleman who has made the science of aërostation his study for many years, and who has also delivered public lectures on the subject, was present at Garnerin's descent, and has since devoted much time and labour to discover the errors in the parachute then employed. Like all inventors, he met with numerous failures and disappointments, but at length his efforts were crowned with success, at least as far as experiments could prove; and we believe the circumstance which first led him to adopt the form now about to be used, was the accidental dropping an umbrella from a balcony.

The umbrella fell the first few feet with the handle downwards, but after several oscillations its position was reversed, and having become inverted, it fell steadily to the ground.

Mr. Cocking from this occurrence felt convinced that the proper shape of such an instrument was exactly the opposite to that used by Garnerin, and that it should be a convex, instead of a concave surface, or a cone with its apex downwards.

Garnerin's parachute was merely made of a circular piece of canvass, with cords attached at short intervals around the outer edge, and all coming to one point below, to which the car was suspended, to which altogether weighed so little, that any common balloon was capable of ascending with it; but to keep the new instrument in its proper shape, numerous large hoops, wooden braces, and a variety of other apparatus, were necessary, which rendered the whole of so great a weight, that the persevering inventor, after all his labours, saw his models lie useless for years.

On learning the intention of the proprietors of Vauxhall to build a balloon of extraordinary dimensions, Mr. Cocking perceived an opportunity for introducing his parachute, and lost no time in communicating to them his plan. All difficulty was, however, not yet removed, for the very natural question arose as to what was to become of the balloon after the parachute should be detached from it, the custom having previously been to construct one of cheap materials merely to serve for the one ascent, and which was generally either lost or destroyed, having frequently been blown out to sea, for no aëronaut could be found who would undertake to ascend and suffer so great a weight to be instantaneously separated from the balloon. Mr. Green, however, stated his opinion that the object might be accomplished without accident to the aëronaut, and removed all difficulty by offering to make the ascent himself. All was soon arranged; a new parachute of extraordinary dimensions constructed, and Monday, July 24th, fixed for the experiment. Three hoops, the largest of which is 107 feet in circumference, connected by ten light spars of wood, form the frame-work of the machine. These are strengthened by a series of small lines stretching from the upper hoop to the lower, and the whole is covered by a fine cloth; the latter consists of twenty-two gores, 59 inches at their greatest diameters, and gradually diminishing to 11 inches, which, when sewed together, form a cone at an angle of 30°.

The car is of wicker, and its attachment to the lower hoop resembles that of the car of a balloon, which always retains its perpendicular whatever movement there may take place in the machine above. A strong rope will descend from the hoop underneath the car of the balloon, and, passing through an iron ring on the top of the main centre cord of the parachute, will ascend on the other side, and be made fast to the instrument commonly used by Mr. Green for liberating the balloon. From this a thin cord will hang down to the car of the parachute, and thus give Mr. Cocking the opportunity of making the separation at any moment he may deem favourable. The surface exposed to the action of the air is 124 square yards, and the weight of the apparatus 223 lbs. This, added to Mr. Cocking's weight, viz., 170 lbs., give the total of 393 lbs.; but it is calculated that the parachute is capable of descending with safety with a weight considerably greater, which is of course all in favour of the success of the experiment. The rate of the descent, as nearly as can be calculated, will be about 10 feet in a second, or six miles and a half an hour; but this will of course, in some measure depend on the state of the atmosphere.

From the *Morning Chronicle* of July 25th, we extract the following report of the circumstances attending the ascent:

"Vauxhall Gardens were crowded during the whole of yesterday afternoon by an immense assemblage of persons, drawn together to witness the hazardous and, we regret to add, fatal experiment of Mr. Cocking to descend from an altitude of upwards of a mile in a parachute of his own invention. The time fixed for the ascent of the aëronaut was five o'clock; but on our entering the Gardens at that hour, we found that the process of inflation of Mr. Green's Nassau balloon was not yet completed. This afforded us an opportunity of inspecting the parachute in which Mr. Cocking contemplated his awful descent, and we had some conversation with the unfortunate gentleman on the principle of his contrivance, and the altitude at which he proposed to sever his connection with the balloon of Mr. Green.

'Mr. Cocking, who was a gentlemanly man, short in stature, and somewhat stout, and apparently of the age of fifty-two or fifty-three, gave the most obliging answers to our queries, and explained that his parachute was constructed on a totally different plan from that of M. Garnerin. The latter he described as of the form of an umbrella, closed at the moment of descent, but expanded by the atmosphere as it approached the earth, and forming a sort of canopy over the aëronaut. His parachute, on the contrary, was in the form of an umbrella reversed, the cavity containing the air being turned uppermost, with the view, he said, of preventing the oscillation which proved so disastrous to M. Garnerin.

Mr. Cocking expressed by words the utmost confidence in the result of his experiment. When questioned as to the danger, he remarked that none existed for him, and that the greatest peril, if any, would attend the balloon of the Messrs. Green, when suddenly relieved from the weight of himself and the parachute (about five hundred weight).

Towards six o'clock, the Messrs. Green entered their balloon, which was allowed to ascend to an altitude of about forty feet, that the parachute might be brought directly under it, and securely fixed. It was seven o'clock before all the preparations were completed, at which time the whole apparatus was distinctly visible to every one in the Gardens. Considerable impatience had been manifested at the long delay which had taken place; but as the position of the parachute became more clearly defined, a general clapping of hands expressed the joy of the multitude. Another half hour passed away, during which time Mr. Cocking was engaged in earnest conversation with several of his friends. The band of the Surrey Yeomanry suddenly struck up the national anthem, which being considered the signal for the cords to be loosened, a loud huzza proceeded from the Gardens, and was re-echoed by the impatient mob outside. At this moment, a tube or pipe of linen was lowered by the Messrs. Green from the car of their balloon through the orifice in the parachute, and past the basket in which Mr. Cocking was to sit. This was for the conveyance of the ballast it is found necessary to discharge on the ascent of the balloon, and which, if it had been thrown out in the usual manner, would have lodged in the parachute. All the preparations having been completed, Mr. Cocking (having previously stripped off his coat as too cumbersome, and put on a light jacket) stepped into the car amid the acclamations of the company. Some of his friends offered him a glass of wine, which he drank, and having shaken them all cordially by the hand, little knowing that it would be the last time, the cords were loosened, and the balloon and its attendant parachute mounted into the heavens amid the renewed cheering of the crowd. The early part of the afternoon had been remarkably fine and clear, but about this time (half past seven) the sky had become somewhat overcast, and a breeze had sprung up. No apprehensions, however, were entertained, and the scene at that moment was as gay and cheerful as it is possible to imagine. Above was the majestic balloon, sailing rapidly aloft, its inmates waving their flags in triumph; below was the gaily dressed multitude, mixing their acclamations with the music of the band, and clapping their hands to the adventurous voyagers, little dreaming that the death-hour of the principal actor in the scene was rapidly approaching. The balloon had hardly attained an altitude of two hundred feet when the tube destined for the escape of the ballast from the car above, detached itself by some means or other from the basket of Mr. Cocking, and floated like a riband in the air.

We have since been favoured by an eye-witness with the following particulars of the fatal result :—Mr. R. Underwood, of Regent-street, followed on horseback in the direction taken by the balloon, to witness, if possible, the descent of the parachute, and from that gentleman we have learned the melancholy details which follow. Mr. Underwood was in the neighbourhood of Blackheath when he saw the cord which attached the parachute to the car severed. The parachute, thus left to itself, descended with the utmost rapidity, and swayed from side to side in the most fearful manner. Mr. Underwood anticipated the worst. In a few seconds, the dreadful oscillations still continuing, the basket which contained the unfortunate aëronaut broke away from the parachute, and Mr. Cocking was precipitated to the earth from a height of several hundred feet. Mr. Underwood immediately spurred his horse, and arrived in a field near Lee, where several labourers had picked up the parachute. They would not believe that a man had fallen with it, but on Mr. Underwood's explanations, and an offer of five guineas to whoever should find the body of Mr. Cocking, they commenced a diligent search. After traversing four fields they heard groans proceeding from a field called Burnt Ash, near Lee, and on going in that direction, they found the unfortunate Mr. Cocking literally dashed to pieces ! and just as they were loosening his cravat, he breathed his last in their arms.

We now take up Messrs. Green and Spencer's narrative (from the *Times* of July 26th), which is exceedingly interesting.

In consequence of the sad and fatal catastrophe which has befallen the late Mr. Cocking, I feel myself called upon to communicate to the public the whole of the particulars of my ascent with the Vauxhall Balloon, taking up with me Mr. Cocking in his parachute. The inflation commenced about 12 under the able direction of Mr. Hutchinson, the engineer of the London Gas Company, and was completed by five o'clock. Prior to the parachute being attached to the balloon I caused a trial to be made with the view of ascertaining whether the buoyancy of the latter was sufficient to carry up the former with safety. The result of this trial was, after some arrangements with respect to the ballast, of which I was compelled to give out about 650lb. in weight, had been effected satisfactorily. The abandonment of this large quantity of ballast I found to be absolutely requisite in order with safety to commence the ascent. The balloon was then allowed gently to rise a sufficient height to be conveyed over the parachute ; but in consequence of the great and unavoidable delay which was necessarily caused in affixing the two machines, the gas in the former became very considerably condensed, from a reduction of temperature. It, thereupon, became a matter of compulsion that I should get rid of 100lb. more of ballast, which I emptied out of the bags through a tube, constructed of canvass, and about fifty feet in length. The object in having this tube was, that any ballast I might deem it advisable to throw out during our voyage should take such a course as would entirely clear the broadest expanse of the parachute. The connexion between the balloon and the parachute was at length completed by the rope of the latter being made fast to the liberating iron by which Mr. Cocking was to free himself from the balloon.

It is but justice to myself I should here state, that I had on several occasions expressed my determination not to liberate the parachute from the balloon, upon the ground, setting aside any other consideration, that I might select a moment for severance when Mr. Cocking was not altogether prepared or ready for his descent, and therefore if any accident were to accrue to him, that I of course should be regarded as the responsible party, to whom blame would naturally attach.

Mr. F. Gye, every thing being in readiness, about 25 minutes to eight o'clock, gave the signal for the whole of the apparatus to be released from its trammels, and we instantly rose very steadily, taking an easterly course.

Mr. Cocking always desired that we should ascend to an elevation of 8,000 feet, about one mile and a quarter, at which height he proposed to detach himself from the balloon, and commence his descent. Finding, therefore, that our upward progress was very slow, I requested Mr. Spencer to discharge some more ballast, and he accordingly threw the contents of a bag weighing 20lb. through the tube already named. This proving of little avail, I directed a second and then a third bagful to be got rid of by the same means.

At this period we were floating over the Surrey Zoological-gardens, at an elevation of about 2,000 feet. It was at this moment that a portion of the lower end of the ballast-tube became detached, a circumstance which was caused by the occasional swinging to and fro of the parachute. This accident led to the inconvenience which I had foreseen some days before the ascent, and which led to the adoption of the tube, and of that of rendering it extremely difficult for us to discharge the ballast without its falling into the parachute.

Our inability to do this as we were then situated I communicated to Mr. Cocking, adding that under the circumstances it was impossible for us to rise any higher unless we were to attempt to throw the ballast in bags beyond the outer spread of his machine, a course of procedure which we considered to be attended with much danger to any person who might chance to be beneath, but that we would, if he wished it, make the experiment as soon as we had cleared the houses. Mr. Cocking replied " Very well, it is of no consequence ; if you think I have time to rise as high as I want, and to descend before dark." I remarked, " I think you have ; and you will then also have a more open country for the descent." We now continued to glide along guided by the pleasure of the wind at nearly the same elevation until we had cleared all buildings. During this time Mr. Spencer and myself were busily engaged in dividing our ballast into small parcels, so that we might be able to throw them over without injury to the parachute.

As soon as we found that we had arrived over the fields, and presuming that no danger could arise from the falling of the ballast, we quickly began to relieve ourselves of that essential commodity. In doing this our anxiety respecting any of it lodging in the parachute was much relieved by finding that that machine continually swung backwards and forwards, evidently occasioned by the operation of the currents through which we passed, so that we were enabled without any difficulty to cast away the bags without damage to the vehicle immediately below us. We continued to discharge ballast until we had lessened our quantity by 50lb., in addition to that already sent over. The balloon now began to rise, and soon entered a tier of clouds, when we lost sight of the earth. So great, however, was the resistance offered by the parachute to this denser atmosphere that we were again obliged, in order to attain the elevation Mr. Cocking pressed for (that gentleman considering that the greater the distance he had to fall, the greater would be the atmospheric pressure under the parachute, and therefore the easier descent) to rid ourselves of 400lb. more ballast, and even then, we only arrived at the height of 5,000 feet, which is a trifle less than a mile.

We were still 3,000 feet lower than Mr. Cocking's desired elevation.

" Whilst these operations were going on, Mr. Spencer and myself held a conversation with our appended neighbour and friend, which was entirely confined to the progress we were making upwards, Mr. Cocking manifesting much anxiety, and wishing to be informed how we were rising, requesting to to know when every additional elevation of 500 feet was accomplished.

As soon as we had attained the height of 5,000 feet I told him that it would be impossible for us to get up as high as he desired in sufficient time for him to descend by the light of day. Upon this Mr. Cocking said, " Then I shall very soon leave you ; but tell me whereabouts I am ?" Mr. Spencer, who had a few minutes before caught a glimpse of the earth, answered, " We appear to be on a level with Greenwich." I then asked him if he felt himself quite comfortable, and whether he found that the practical trial bore out the calculations he had made ? Mr. Cocking replied, " Yes ; I never felt more comfortable or more delighted in my life." Shortly afterwards Mr. Cocking said, " Well, now I think I shall leave you." I answered, " I wish you a very good night and safe descent, if you are determined to make it, and not to use the tackle." .

I should here observe, that with an anxiety to prevent any accident arising in the event of the violence of the wind rendering it impossible for a descent to be attempted, an apparatus had been constructed under the direction of Mr. F. Gye, to afford us the facility of assisting Mr. Cocking to haul himself up into the car of the balloon, and that this is the tackle to which I thus alluded.

Mr. Cocking to this question made no other reply than " Good night, Spencer ; good night, Green."

At this instant I desired Mr. Spencer to take fast hold of the ropes, and like myself to crouch down in the car. In consequence of being compelled to keep hold of the valve line, of course I had but one hand which was available for the purpose of safety. With that hand, fortunately, in the perilous situation into which we were speedily thrown, I was able to maintain my position.

Scarcely were these words uttered before we felt a slight jerk upon the liberating iron, but quickly discovered, from not having changed our elevation, that Mr. Cocking had failed in his attempt to free himself. Another but more powerful jerk ensued, and in an instant the balloon shot upwards with the velocity of a skyrocket.

The effect upon us at this moment is almost beyond description. The immense machine which suspended us between " heaven and earth," whilst it appeared to be forced upwards with terrific violence and rapidity through unknown and untravelled regions, amidst the howlings of a fearful hurricane, rolled about as though revelling in a freedom for which it had long struggled, but of which until that moment it had been kept in absolute ignorance. It at length, as if somewhat fatigued by its exertions, gradually assumed the motions of a snake working its way with astonishing speed towards a given object. During this frightful operation, the gas was rushing in torrents from the upper and lower valves, but more particularly from the latter, as the density of the atmosphere through which we were forcing our progress pressed so heavily on the valve at the top of the balloon as to admit of comparatively but a small escape by that aperture.

At this juncture, had it not been for the application to our mouths of two pipes leading into an air-bag with which we had furnished ourselves previous to starting, we must with within a minute have been suffocated, and so, but by different means, have shared the melancholy fate of our friend.

This bag was formed of silk, sufficiently capacious to contain 100 gallons of atmospheric air. Prior to our assent the bag was inflated, with the assistance of a pair of bellows, with 50 gallons of air, so allowing for any expansion which might be produced in the upper regions. Into one end of this bag were introduced two flexible tubes, and the moment we felt ourselves to be going up, in the manner just described, Mr. Spencer, as well as myself, placed either of them in our mouths. By this simple contrivance we preserved ourselves from instantaneous suffocation; a result which must have ensued from the apparently endless volume of gas with which the car was enveloped. The gas, notwithstanding all our precautions, from the violence of its operation on the human frame, almost immediately deprived us of sight, and we were both, as far as our visionary powers were concerned, in a state of total darkness for between four and five minutes.

As soon as we had partially regained the use of our eyes, and had somewhat recovered from the effects of the awful scene into which, from the circumstances, we had been plunged, our first attention was directed to the barometer. I soon discoved that my powers had not sufficiently returned to enable me to see the mercury, but Mr. Spencer found that it stood at 13-20, giving an elevation of 23,384 feet, or about four miles and a quarter.

I do not conceive, from the length of time I had been liberating the gas, that this was any thing like our greatest altitude for we were evidently effecting a rapid descent. This impression is corroborated by a rough calculation, which leads me to believe, knowing the customary rate at which the gas makes its escape, taken in consideration in conjunction with the length of time I had been pulling the valve-line, that we had lost at 30,000 feet of gas, or 180,000 gallons, a total of 5,000 feet more than my own balloon will contain.

It may be regarded as somewhat surprising that not a larger quantity had evaporated, especially when the size of the valves are considered, that at the top being nearly three feet in diameter, whilst the one at the neck of the balloon is upwards of two feet. The reason, however, is easily pointed out. The extreme rapidity with which we ascended, coupled with the consequent pressure of the atmosphere on the upper part of the machine, necessarily prevented much escape from the top valve. The same cause also forced an extraordinary emission from the opening at the neck, and I am decidedly of opinion, had it not fortuitously happened that the proprietors permitted this latter valve to be increased from 18 to 23 inches in diameter, that the balloon must have burst, and my companion as well as myself, been hurled headlong into eternity.

As I have stated, we were now rapidly on the descent, having got rid of all the unusual annoyances to which I have referred; and finding that we were proceeding downwards with the ordinary calmness and steadiness, although with much speed, we hastened to empty two tin vessels of water which we had taken up for the purpose, and to charge them with the atmospheric air through which we were then descending. Our desire was to effect this object at our greatest altitude, but from the circumstances which I have detailed we were unable to accomplish that end, and when the vessels were filled, the mercury in the thermometer had ascended to 17-50, or an elevation of 16,632 feet, about three miles.

When we had accomplished this matter, finding ourselves suffering severely from cold, we referred to the thermometer, which stood at 28, four degrees below the freezing point.

We were at this period apparently about two miles and a half above a dense mountain of clouds, which presented the appearance of impenetrable masses of dark marble, whilst all around us were shed the brilliant rays of the setting sun. We continued to descend with great rapidity, and as we approached the clouds that velocity considerably increased. At this time so large had been our loss of gas, that the balloon, instead of presenting to our sight its customary rotund and widely-expanded form, now merely looked like a comparatively small parachute, or half dome, without any aperture in its centre. We had parted with at least one-third of our gas, and were as far beneath the balloon itself as 50 or 60 feet.

Recollecting the late hour at which we quitted Vauxhall, I now began to be anxious about the time, and on applying to Mr. Spencer, ascertained that it wanted not more than a quarter to 9 o'clock. From this I was aware, notwithstanding in our then position we were blessed with a magnificent light, that on emerging below from the clouds darkness would have assumed her sable hue over the earth, and that we should have much difficulty, therefore, in ascertaining the nature and character of the country, supposing us to be over the land, on which we must effect our final descent. I, consequently, became extremely anxious to make our way through the clouds as quickly as possible, which having done we proceeded, until we had reached within some 300 feet of the ground, when we found it requisite, from our inability to ascertain the nature of the ground, the whole country beneath us offering the appearance of thick woods, to cast out every article of ballast and moveable matters, even to ropes and empty ballast-bags, in order to prevent us from coming in contact with what was supposed to be trees. After calling out for some time, and hanging out the grapnel, we heard voices in reply, and the parties speedily drew us to a safe place of landing, which proved to be close to the village of Offham, near Town Malling, seven miles west of Maidstone, and 28 from London.

The balloon was packed, and conveyed in a cart to Town Malling, where we were most hospitably treated and provided with beds by the Rev. Mr. Money, who, singular to relate, informed me that he is the son of Major Money, the aeronaut, who, on the 23d July, 1785, ascended from Norwich, and fell into the sea 20 miles off Lowestoff.

At half-past ten o'clock this morning we quitted Town Malling, and it was not until our arrival at Wrotham, at which place I inquired whether they had heard where Mr. Cocking had descended, that I became acquainted with the unexpected and melancholy result of his experiment.

I trust it is needless for me to say, how deeply the feelings of Mr. Spencer and myself were harrowed up by the said intelligence thus conveyed to us.

It is only due to the late Mr. Cocking I should add, that throughout the whole of our voyage, up to the moment when he released himself from the balloon, he displayed the greatest courage and fortitude, and the expression of his features, and the light and joyous, although earnest way, in which he made his inquiries and conversed with us, manifested his great satisfaction that at length a theory to which he had devoted the last 25 years of his life was about to be triumphantly put to the test.

We were up about one hour and twenty minutes.

Individually my opinion was, that having withstood the difficulties and severe pressure of the atmosphere in its ascent, Mr. Cocking's parachute would accomplish its descent with perfect safety."

Having disposed of the valuable statement of Mr. Green, (adds the *Times*,) we now proceed to a brief account of circumstances connected more immediately with the unfortunate victim.

When Mr. Cocking, who by profession we understand was an artist, and a man deeply practised in scientific matters, and about 60 years of age, made the proposal to the Messrs. Gye to come down in a parachute, he produced calculations, which he said, and we believe with truth, had received the sanction of several highly scientific gentlemen, (among others, Mr. Faraday has been mentioned,) demonstrating that such an experiment would be attended with success. A careful examination of these calculations corroborated the statement, and directions were given that every order Mr. Cocking gave with a view to the perfect construction of the machine should be instantly acted upon. Accordingly many hands, male as well as females, have been hard at work for some weeks. Various alterations, at the suggestions of Mr. F. Gye and other scientific friends, were made during the progress of manufacture, with a view to its increased strength, but Mr. Cocking's cry out was, ' Don't let me have it so heavy,' and even at almost the last moment he expressed himself as fearful lest the ropes were too cumbrous. Mr. F. Gye and the proprietors of the gardens were most anxious that the tin tube circle at the expansion of the parachute should have been constructed of materials similar to those of which the hoop to the grand balloon is composed, but Mr. Cocking was resolute in his objection, on the ground that it would be too heavy.

It is evident from the marks in the basket in which Mr. Cocking stood, that he must have remained in it until he reached the earth. This conviction is also borne out by the injuries apparent on the body of the deceased. The whole of the ribs appear to be broken or displaced ; in addition to the cut over the right eye, and the dislocation of the ancle, the whole of the skin around the neck is likewise exceedingly discoloured, as though the effect of a heavy

264

fall. When his friends went into the room in which the body was lying, it was with difficulty that the features could be recognized, although they did not display any distinct hurt except that above the eye.

We regret to say that the landlord of the inn at which the body lies was guilty of a violation of the ordinary forms of decency, by admitting the public to view the remains of the unfortunate gentleman, as well as the parachute, at 6d. a-head, and that when he was remonstrated with by Messrs. Gye, he defied them to prevent his doing as he pleased in his own house. One consequence of this course of conduct has been, that many parts of the parachute have been taken away by the curious, so that it will offer but very imperfect evidence to the jury. Ultimately an order was procured from a magistrate to restrain a continuance of this conduct.

ANOTHER DISCOVERER OF AERIAL NAVIGATION.

Sir,—That truly important and interesting subject, aeronautics, has lately and deservedly occupied a large share of your pages, and has made great advancement from the remarks of the numerous correspondents of your valuable and widely-circulated work. Among the most valuable suggestions on this subject are those proposed by Sir Geo. Cayley, to whom the science is greatly indebted, and to whom I have to return my grateful acknowledgments for the assistance I have derived, from the remarks contained in his paper on aerial navigation published in your 708th number, through which I have been led to the study and farther improvement of the science. Your last number contains a letter from P. P. C. R., who is justly of opinion that balloons employed as vehicles of conveyance "from one specified place to another," should have the motive force directed from the body of the balloon. I have recently matured a scheme in which I have secured this desideratum, together with the perfect command and facility of steerage in every direction. I have likewise provided for ascension and descension without the expenditure of gas or discharge of ballast. I have, in fact, the power of propelling my aero-vessel in any direction from one place to another, against the atmospheric current. After having secured to myself the advantages of the pecuniary benefits that may result from my improvements, the discovery will be made

public. Should P. P. C. R. or others of your interested correspondents be desirous of obtaining further information on the subject, I shall be willing to afford it as far as is consonant with my interest and safety. This science, if carried into active and effective operation, would be truly beneficial to mankind. The boon would be invaluable; man would then be in undisputed possession and dominion over earth, air and water. The merchant will be greatly benefited in the speedy and safe transmission of commercial correspondence. The statesman will avail himself of the means which it affords, in the facility of foreign communication, and dispatch of orders. The traveller and man of science will be assisted vastly in the exploration of unknown lands, whether in the regions of the scorching tropics or in the chilling ice-bound poles The barren and inhospitable desert, with its parching sands, its deceptive mirage, and its overwhelming simoom, will oppose in vain these hitherto alarming and sometimes fatal stops to the enterprising journeyer. The gloomy, savage, and intricate forest will offer no obstacle—mountain, flood, or morass will raise no barrier. The unbounded ocean may be traversed and divested of its terrors from rock or shoal, and the impenetrable and gigantic iceberg, in its adamantine chains, will resist no longer the persevering and triumphant march of man. The future traveller will be disburdened of those dangers and terrors, and privations of every shape to which those former searchers after knowledge were subjected. We have now arrived at the era in which aeronautics will take a most prominent and useful seat amongst the sciences.

PNEUMODOIPTOROS.

July 24th, 1837.

YORK CEMETERY CARRIAGE.

Sir,—I observed with much interest in your 722d number, Mr. Croft's design for combining a hearse and mourning-coach. My attention was drawn to the subject about six months ago, in consequence of the formation of a public cemetery in York, which being at a considerable distance from some parts of the city, suggested the idea of a carriage for the use of the poor.

The accompanying drawing is of a

carriage *drawn by one horse*, manufactured by Messrs. Morley, coach-makers, in this city, from a sketch which I laid before the committee of the cemetery.

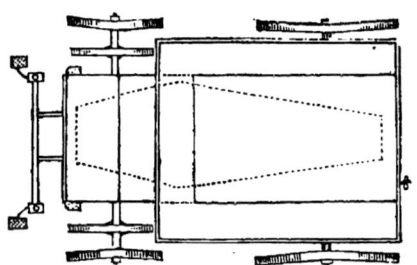

One of its members suggested that the body should be placed before the carriage instead of under it; and another design was made very similar to Mr. Croft's, (but much plainer.) The width, however, was thought too great for our narrow streets, and the original design was adopted, which if you think worthy of a place in your valuable Magazine, is much at your service.

The carriage cost £45; the Company propose charging the poor 3s. for the use of the carriage and horse, and 6s. to those in better circumstances, who choose to avail themselves of it. The carriage will contain six or eight persons, and there is room for the undertaker on the box.

I remain your obedient servant,

J. P. PRITCHETT,
Architect.

York, July 12th, 1837.

NAUTICUS'S ASTRONOMICAL QUESTION.

Sir,—I have to thank you for your kind insertion of my last, and also your correspondent Nautilus for his equally kind offer to gratify my request. My wish to trespass as little as possible on your valuable pages, alone prevented my inserting the formula I wished to have put into familiar rules; perhaps you will permit me to do so now. Dr. Tiarks, in his paper on determining the time by observations of two stars when in the same vertical, says, "The moment when the pole star and any other star during the period of its inferior revolution are in the same vertical, may be ascertained in the following manner:—Let l = co-latitude of the place of observation, d polar distance of the pole star p, D that of the other star S a, difference of right ascension of the same stars, t the angle Z P p, or the time elapsing from the upper passage of the pole star to its being on the same vertical with the other star S₁ P being the pole, and Z the zenith p the angle Z being the same in the two triangles, Z P p and Z P S, in which we have Z P = l, Z P p = t, P p = d, Z P S = t + a, and P S = D, we have these equations: $\tan Z = \dfrac{\sin t \cdot \tan d}{\sin l - \cos l \cdot \cos t \cdot \tan d}$ $= \dfrac{\sin (t + a) \tan D}{\sin l - \cos l \cdot \cos (t + a) \tan D}$ by which t may be determined." They give $\sin l$ (sin (t + a) tan D — sin t . tan d) = cos l . tan d . tan D sin a or $\dfrac{\sin t + a}{\tan d} - \dfrac{\sin t}{\tan D}$ $= \dfrac{\sin a}{\tan l}$.

I cannot but feel anxious for Nautilus's promised rules from the above formula, as I find the practical part of the problem extremely easy, not only with a transit, but with any instrument of similar construction.

On the evening of the 1st of July, in latitude 51° 40′, with a small theodolite, I found Capella passed vertically under Polaris, at 17 h. 17 min. 25 sec. siderial time; may I request Nautilus to take this as an example, and shew the error of my clock at the above time? I had not for some weeks verified it by a transit observation, but I believe it was not very wide of the truth. The polar distance of Capella on that day was 44° 10′ 26″, and of Polaris 1° 33′ 47″, their difference of right ascension 4° 3′ 35″. Nautilus will perceive that this method of procuring the time is very similar to the one he has pointed out, and that when I said I could make the observation in a few minutes, I of course meant that I had before roughly calculated the time, and adjusted the instrument. As soon as the lower star appears in the field of the telescope, I bring the centre wire accurately to bisect the pole star, and examine the axis by the level; as neither want much correction, I find I have plenty of time for this purpose before the passage of the lower star. Dr. Tiarks observes, that where extreme accuracy is required, the time elapsing between the two passages may be noted and allowed for, but for ordinary purposes this does not seem to be necessary.

I am sorry to notice, Mr. Editor, a snappish pettulance in some of your correspondents, which I am sure they would not indulge in, if they knew the effect it generally produces in the minds of your readers, an effect by no means favourable to them. Though no mathematician myself, I have had much intercourse with many, and I have always found those the most eminent and profound, who shewed the least arrogance or disposition to cavil at the real or supposed blunders of others. Surely, the kindness of Nautilus did not call for the rebuke obtruded by O. N., page 102, merely because I had not given some particular latitude and longitude in my question. The latitude certainly is a prominent part in the formula, but I only wished for a general rule, and an example for any latitude, and so, no doubt, Nautilus understood me.

I am, Sir,

Your very obedient servant,

NAUTICUS.

July 17th,

STEAM-BOILER EXPLOSIONS.

Sir,—From the numerous instances in which steam-boiler explosions have taken place, when the metal has to all appearance been good, it would appear that the question of such accidents does not rest more upon the weakness of the material, than the malformation of the boilers, as suited for purposes of safety. The statement given in your Magazine vol. xxi, p. 84, of the explosion of the boilers in the steam-boat New England, first inclined me to this opinion, which recent facts have tended to establish. The subject demands consideration, and the suggestions of Y Z, p. 213, will, it is to be hoped, elicit further remarks upon this important topic.

For Marine purposes, boilers are frequently made with a large portion of *flat* surface, presenting an extended area to the pressure of the steam and water, whereby the strength of the metal is placed at the greatest possible disadvantage. This was particularly the case with the boilers of the New England before alluded to, the ends of which were flat, and therefore ill suited to sustain any great pressure. The external support they may have received from the material in which they were bedded, though insufficient to resist the pressure upon it by the yielding plates, might have given an upward direction to the force at the time of explosion, by which the upper arch became inverted and folded over, producing the consequences that ensued.

In other boilers, and to give greater strength to the metal, the bottoms and sides are turned inwards, presenting a convex surface to the pressure of the steam and water; but experience has proved that this form is also defective. The great area exposed to the power is such, that the parts which have to sustain the aggregate, viz. the angles, are generally found to give way, or else the plates are crushed in the direction of their lengths, or line of the greatest pressure.

If I may be allowed to offer an opinion upon the subject, it is, that the form of all steam-boilers should be such, that the power within should act *entirely* in a line with the cohesive strength of the metal. I have seen calculations upon the subject, and found them to rest entirely upon this, though at the same time the form of the boiler was such, that the pressure within acted more upon the transverse than the cohesive power of resistance.

There is no form better suited than the spherical, but for convenience the cylindrical may be as advantageously applied. Our rail-road engineers have afforded us proofs of their superiority and perfect safety. The boiler lately patented by Mr. Symington, (p. 218,) demands attention in this respect, and though the circumstance of its safety is not there noticed, I cannot but think this is one of the greatest claims it has to superiority. I could wish to have seen the ends more convex; there is no reason why they should not be so. I have not the honor of knowing Mr. S., nor have I any further interest in the invention than what arises from its affording greater safety to the lives of all who embark with so powerful an agent as steam. The discerning will not fail to encourage so essential an improvement in the service of navigation.

I remain, Sir, yours respectfully,
JAMES WOODHOUSE.

Kilburn, July 8, 1837.

Sir,—It is now about one hundred and thirty-eight years since steam was introduced as a mechanical agent by Captain Savery; and yet, as appears from the frequent explosions of boilers which take place, and the conflicting opinions which are given as to the immediate cause of these melancholy events, the exact nature of this power is not properly understood, and more especially by those who are entrusted with its management. From the difficulty of conceiving that the power of mere steam is adequate to rend a strong new boiler, and to scatter the fragments in every direction to considerable distances, an opinion seems to be rapidly gaining ground that we are to ascribe these disastrous events to the formation and explosion of gases within the boiler. Now this opinion is either correct or otherwise. If the opinion that gases are formed within the boiler be correct, then the causes and manner of their formation ought to be investigated by competent persons without delay, that some means may be devised whereby we may be enabled to provide against the recurrence of these awful disasters. If, on the other hand, this opinion is founded in error, the sooner it is exploded the better; as by looking to many causes our attention is diverted from the real source of the evil, and thereby the danger increased instead of diminished.

Looking at the very elaborate experiments of the Franklin Institute, I must confess that I am somewhat sceptical with respect to this new doctrine. The experimental boiler of the Institute was in precisely that condition, which is supposed to be most favourable to the decomposition of water. Yet the experimenters were unable to effect the formation of hydrogen, and therefore, they came to the conclusion,—and that conclusion has gone forth to the world, that no gas is generated under the supposed circumstances. Now, although the experiments of the Franklin Institute are undoubtedly entitled to the highest respect, we must still bear in mind, that even with the utmost care and vigilance, aided by all the lights of modern science, there is still a possibility of error,—some trivial circumstance which escapes observation at the time, may vitiate an experiment, or even a series of experiments, and thus render them entirely valueless, as practical guides to the engineer. If it be a fact, that gases are formed within the boiler, and that we, reposing in confidence upon the conclusion of the Franklin Institute, neglect to seek out, and apply the requisite precautionary measures, we must expect at intervals a recurrence of these fatal explosions.

This is a subject of too much importance to be suffered to remain in its present obscure and embarrassed state. The The capital invested in steam-engine machinery, in England alone, amounts to many millions sterling, and from all appearances is likely to be extended indifinitely. The truth is, that steam power is too valuable to be given up, whatever disaster may ensue from its mismanagement; it therefore behoves us to exert all our means to obtain the complete mastery of this powerful agent. It appears to me, as the *Mechanics' Magazine* passes under the eyes of nearly all the engineers in the United Kingdom, as well as those of other countries, that through the medium of its pages a body of facts, deduced from actual practice, and not from experiment, might be collected, by which we should be enabled to arrive at satisfactory conclusions-

It may be proper here to remind the proprietors of steam vessels in particular, that their interests are deeply involved in the matter. It is expected, I understand, that a bill will be brought into Parliament to prohibit the further use of sheet-iron boiler, in steam vessels, in consequence, it is said, of iron decomposing the water, and generating hydrogen gas, thereby causing violent explosions. Nothing but copper boilers will be allowed, which, from their additional cost, unless they do in reality afford an adequate security, must be considered an unnecessary tax upon the proprietors of steam vessels.

I should be glad to see the subject canvassed in the pages of the *Mechanics' Magazine,* and would particularly recommend it to the notice of your able and intelligent correspondents.

Yours, &c.,
AN ENGINEER.

Limehouse, July, 1837.

ETTRICK'S THERMOMETER FOR CHEMICAL PURPOSES.

Sir,—In the year 1824 requiring a thermometer for ascertaining the heat of caustic liquids, the following was constructed at the time; being then unacquainted with the common one that folds back. As this is a decided improvement upon it, I shall be obliged by your inserting it in the *Mechanics' Magazine.*

Fig. 1, is an edge, and Fig. 2, a front view. A B the glass thermometer,

Fig. 1.   Fig. 2.

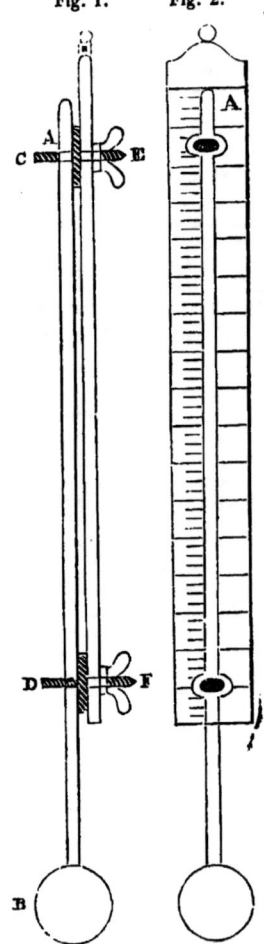

sliding through two pieces of brass C D having screws E F on the other side, for tightening the glass : a small piece of cloth should be applied under the glass at those places. The scale may be divided as is commonly done, *i. e.* beginning the divisions of the scale, when the thermometer is quite up : or, the scale may be marked, the divisions being commenced when quite down ; but, the better way would be, to divide it both ways.

Yours &c.

W. ETTRICK.

High Barns, Sunderland.

WOODHOUSE'S ROTARY ENGINE INVENTED BY BEALE.

Sir,—I hasten to inform you that Mr. Woodhouse has been anticipated by me in every particular of his rotary engine, and in a mechanical point of view, in a very superior manner. I long since constructed an engine on the same principle, of ten horse power weighing 2 cwt., which a boy could move, by the force of his lungs; and I myself have, with my breath propelled a model weighing 60 lbs. at the rate of 70 revolutions per minute; if I recollect rightly Mr. Maugham of the Gallery of Practical Science saw me do this considerably more than a year ago. I also beg to refer Mr. Woodhouse to my patent of the 25th February, 1835, and further to say, that I have sold a considerable number of such engines, and have likewise a number of orders for them in hand. Any gentleman wishing to see one of my patent engines at work, can do so any day at my factory at East Greenwich, between the hours of six in the morning and eight in the evening.*

I am, Sir,

Your obedient servant,

J. T. BEALE.

11 Church Lane Whitechapel.
22 July 1837.

CHEAP APPARATUS FOR ASCERTAINING THE SPECIFIC GRAVITY OF GASES.

Sir,—I have for some time past made use of a small apparatus for determining the specific gravity of gases, a description of which I thought might not be useless to some of your readers, who, like myself, cannot afford to purchase the expensive apparatus at present in use for that purpose.

It consists simply of a small *oiled silk bag*, and a very delicate balance furnished with a set of decimal grain weights. The bag holds about four ounces, and is rendered air-tight at the edges by means of a solution of India-rubber; it is fastened to a very small brass stopcock, which is contrived so as to hook on to one end of the beam of the balance instead of the scale-pan. To use this, I measure four ounces of dry hydrogen gas ; and having introduced it into the bag, I attach it to the end of the beam, and put a sufficient number of weights into the scale at the opposite end to counterbalance it. If I wish now to ascertain the specific gravity of any gas, say, carbonic acid, I introduce four ounces of it, previously dried, into the bag ; and having hung it on the end of the beam, I add to the weights already in the scale a sufficient quantity more to counterbalance it. The number of grains added, consequently being the specific gravity of the carbonic acid, when compared with that of hydrogen.

The advantages derived from using a square oiled silk bag for this purpose, in preference to a bladder or turkey's maw, are too numerous and evident to require pointing out.

By means of this little apparatus, I have been enabled to determine the specific gravities of several of the gases with great precision ; they differ, however, a little from those given in scientific works, for various reasons. Perhaps at some future time I may be able to collect together and send you a list of the different gases I have weighed, as compared with the weights hitherto given ; in the mean while, believe me,

Sir, yours truly,

J. F.

Near Sheffield, July 19th, 1837.

ADAMS'S "ENGLISH PLEASURE CARRIAGES."*

The word luxury is at no time much more than a comparative term. Many of the

---

* We shall be happy to publish a description of Mr. Beale's rotary engine, of which we have heard very favourable reports from parties who have seen it in operation. Perhaps Mr. B. will favour us with a copy, or a loan of his specification and drawings. —ED. M. M.

* English Pleasure Carriages ; their Origin, History, Varieties, Materials, Construction, Defects.

indulgences of one generation are the conveniences of the next, and the necessities of the third. They become so, because, though they are to the first generation real indulgences (that is, means of avoiding inconveniences already easily endured through habit), they are found to diminish suffering and increase enjoyment. The second generation grows up hoping and striving for, and partially enjoying the benefit of them; the third finds them absolute necessities, because having never been without them, their feelings, their plans, the whole train of their engagements, and the entire progress of their lives,—all suppose their existence and ready use. It is pleasant in this view to look along the history of "Pleasure Carriages," as given in this delightful book, and to remark the extraordinary contrast of the two ends of the tale; one, the rude and merely floating raft, and, perhaps, ruder sledge,—then luxuries and wonders; the other, the steamboat proudly defying the tide, and the locomotive distancing all animals in derision, become the daily sights and daily wants of the world. How many failing, yet not fruitless, efforts have been made in attaining this result;—how many murmurings against change have sometimes, and somewhile, hindered, to be at length overborne by the rush of improvement—how many fallacies in social theory have opposed themselves, and been exploded—how many wonderers at the ruinous luxury of the age, have quietly fallen in at the rear, to partake the good at first scorned—as much in pride as in virtue—it would take many and curious volumes to tell. Mr. Adams has told as much of it as his volume could in all reason be expected to give us, and more agreeably it will never be told again.

On his main subject, "English Pleasure Carriages," our author has hung notes and disquisitions on many related subjects; the following remarks are on one, which at all times frets more or less some members of the walking classes of the community:—

Improvements, and Capabilities; with an Analysis of the Construction of Common Roads and Railroads, and the Public Vehicles used on them; together with Descriptions of new Inventions; illustrated with numerous Designs; for the Use of Carriage Purchasers and Contractors. By William Bridges Adams. London: Charles Knight & Co. 1837; 8vo, pp. 315.

As this work may occasionally fall into the hands of readers who feel no direct interest in pleasure carriages, either as purchasers or constructors, some may perchance be inclined to question its utility, except as it relates to the mechanism of vehicular locomotion. They may perchance condemn pleasure carriages altogether, as luxuries unjustly engrossed by wealthy people. This would be as unjust as the sweeping condemnations so frequently passed on the public vehicles in the streets. Pleasure carriages are instruments of elegant human enjoyment; and to say that none ought to enjoy them because all cannot enjoy them, would be to possess a spirit akin to that of the " dog in the manger." If those who possess pleasure carriages were to enjoy them at the expense of those who do not possess them, the evil would be a monstrous one: but such is not the fact. Partial instances might be adduced; but they are only exceptions to the rule,—as, for example, the case of a swindler. But, after all, those who do not use pleasure carriages—as the mass of the community—though they do not benefit directly, still benefit indirectly by them. They are objects of beauty constantly exposed to public view, as much so as architectural creations—perhaps more so, being locomotive—and far more so, though in a humbler way, than paintings or statues. It is an undeniable fact, that the daily habit of beholding beautiful objects has an imperceptible effect in refining the national taste. Pleasing colours and pleasing forms tend to soften rugged natures; and whatever may be the disputes as to the evil or good resulting to a nation from the existence of a permanent leisure class, it is quite certain that if no part of the community be at leisure to study the arts of elegance, the public will be far less refined, far more devoid of taste, than if they have a standard—a type, as it were, to imitate, when any individual may acquire the means to imitate, without understanding the principles of that which he imitates."—pp. viii, ix;

How many of the aforesaid grumblers (a very small minority, we believe, of the classes to which they belong) will be convinced or reconciled by this reasoning we cannot guess; but it is clear to us that the same structure of society which permits the existence of " a permanent leisure class," makes the lowest classes better off than they would be without that structure. The system which would be at once most just, most permanent, and productive of most happiness, would be that which most effectually protected each member of the community from wrong, with the least interference with individual exertion. In this state of things, peculiarities of individual character would necessarily produce inequalities of condition—irregularities, however, by no means unjust, as far as society is concerned; for society in this sense of the term, does not produce them: indeed, without it, they would probably exist in a highly aggravated form. The man who now becomes wealthy by force of character, and founds a patrician family, would then by the same personal qualities, raise himself to the head of a troop of marauders, and leave a dynasty to be extirpated by the next successful aspirant; while those who are now his servants, or the poor of his parish, might then be the instruments, or the scarcely more pitiable victims of his ravages. As for abolishing the effects of individual character by artificial plans of society, few are wild enough to dream of it, after once thinking of it. Begging, then, a long step in the argument, it is lawful to ride in coaches—a conclusion at which we doubt not that many of our readers have arrived before this time, by many a route nearer than that we have taken. But the point being agreed, we go on.

Mr. Adams starts at the very beginning of his subject. His introduction leads through all the early contrivances for effecting change of place without weariness of limb. Riding on animals,—rafts,—canoes,—sledges, which he derives from rafts,—litters,—vehicles with rollers, suggested by the comparative ease with which fallen trees are moved,—wheels,—two-wheel carriages,—cars of various countries,—four-wheel carriages, contrived to turn, swinging braces, and springs,—till he fairly places us in an English carriage of the present day.

Following the early history of wheel carriages through the patriarchal and Egyptian periods, to the chariots of the Olympic circle, and of Rome, Mr. Adams comes to the rude conveyances of the Saxons and the middle ages. Among these curious particulars, we may notice that, at the Olympic games, "the renown attached to a winning chariot was as great as that now gained by a winning horse." We have noticed a singular fact, that among carriages built to the same plan, exactly of the same scantling, and by the same workmen, some are invariably preferred, on trial, by knowing drivers, as "running lighter" than the others. That this should have occurred, with the rude construction and workmanship, and equally coarse habits of comparison in mechanical affairs, existing in the Olympiads, does not surprise us; but that such a preference, so founded on undetected or unappreciated differences, should so frequently take place in the present state of the art of carriage building, is proof at least of the complexity of the problem, and of the need of its further investigation.

We may further notice, that though the Saxons evidently attempted to avoid the jolts of a quick motion on bad roads, by simply *suspending* the seat, no improvement of the principle was effected till almost our own times. So slowly does excellence grow! Astonished as we are, and justly, at the *total* progress made, we are often as much amazed, when we look into the history of the *parts* of a machine, at the tardiness of their perfection, and the almost total want of invention in those whose daily wants might seem imperiously to demand improvement. We stand, however, on too high ground to judge them fairly. Inventions are actually working for us and before our eyes, of which our forefathers neither hoped nor dreamed, besides which, evils which would now be intolerable to us, were to them, at worst, inconveniences which it were all very well to remove, but which yet might be very well endured.

The state of things in the middle ages is thus given:—

"The feudal times were obviously unfavourable to the use of carriages: the only seat considered befitting a knight was his saddle, —and the only place for a vassal, at the stirrup of his liege lord. The knights bestrode their coursers, and fair dames gracefully reined up their richly-caparisoned palfreys. In 1239, on the entrance of Frederic II. into Padua, ladies highly born, and sumptuously attired came forth to meet him on horses ornamented with trappings. But this state of things was to have its change, the more commodious though less picturesque wheel carriage came to make its innocent and bloodless *revolution*.

"Italy, France, Spain, and Germany take the lead of us in their records, and contend with each other for the honour of the first introduction of carriages. The earliest record we have found is upon Beckman's authority: he states, that when Charles of

Anjou entered Naples, (towards the end of the thirteenth century,) his queen rode in a *caretta*, the outside and inside of which was covered with sky-blue velvet, interspersed with golden lilies. That the example of the fair queen was speedily followed in France, though most probably at a humble distance, may be inferred from the fact of an ordinance of Philip the Fair being issued in 1294, (and which is still, according to Beckman, in preservation,) for suppressing luxury, and forbidding the citizens' wives the use of ' cars.' That these carettas were the same with the ' cars,' ' chares,' and latterly the ' charat,' in form, though differing in adornment, there is little doubt ; and although 'caretta,' and ' sky-blue velvet,' and 'golden lilies,' seem far more fitting to describe the car of Cinderalla, or of some radiant genius in a fairy pageant, there is little difficulty in believing that all the above-named vehicles had one universal family likeness, both in name and construction, to our common broad-wheeled cart ! In the ' Anciennes Chroniques de Flandres,' date 1347, a manuscript in beautiful preservation,—a work of art it may be called, from the brilliancy and delicacy of its finish,—is an illustration of the flight of Emergard, wife of Salvard, Lord of Rousillon. The carriage in which she is seated, is not only richly coloured, but the details of its construction are accurately supplied. The outer edges of the wheels are coloured grey, to represent a tire of iron, and the horses are attached to the carriage by a similar method to one now in use. The body of the cart or ' chariette' is of carved wood, and the hangings of purple and crimson, turned up in the centre. The Lady Emergard is seated inside, with an attendant behind, and her Fool in front. The machine is drawn by two horses, the charioteer sitting upon the left horse.

" That England was not far behind in the possession of the ' chare,' we have testimony, and that of an interresting kind, as it has thrown some light upon a part of the Lady Emergard's vehicle of stately clumsiness of which we had not till then discerned the use. In ' The Squyr, of Low Degree,' supposed to be before the time of Chaucer, (vide Ellis's Specimens of Early English Poetry,) the father of the Princess of Hungary thus makes promise :—

" To-morrow ye shall on hunting fare,
And ride my daughter in a *chare*.
It shall be covered with velvet red,
And cloths of fine gold all about your head ;
With damask white, and azure blue,
Well diapered with lilies new ;
Your pomelles shall be ended with gold,
Your chains enamelled many a fold.'"

" These pomelles* were doubtless the

handles to the rods affixed towards the roof of the ' chariette ;' and were for the purpose of holding by, when deep ruts or obstacles in the road caused an unusual jerk in the vehicle :—in the illumination they are gilded. This coincidence with the other of the ' lilies' in the ' caretta,' seems to identify the carriages as far as general construction is concerned.

" That the use of wheel carriages became common in England as they did in France, may be gained, amongst others, from Froissart, who, in speaking of the return of the English from Scotland in the reign of Edward III, tells of ' leurs charettes,' which were most likely of a similar form to those above mentioned ; though, as they were used for purposes of war, they were without any of the elegant appurtenances that were thought seemly for ladies of high degree."— Pp. 30, 31, 32.   *   *   *   *

" One of the most curious documents relative to this time, (the 15th century,) is to be found in Roubo's ' L'Art de Menuisier.' It has reference to the introduction of what would seem to us to be the first suspended carriage, although history ascribes this to a much later date. In speaking of a carriage brought from the King of Hungary as a present to the Queen of Bohemia, and which seemed to excite the wonder and admiration of the good Parisians, he describes it as ' *bralant* et moult riche.' What could *bralant* (quivering or trembling) mean, but that it swayed to and fro, from being suspended ? From this time covered carriages began to be used in France, though somewhat sparingly. They were forbidden for common use, even to women, as tending too much to the promotion of luxury ; and only those of the highest rank were permitted to use them. At all public ceremonies there is no mention made of state coaches, but of state horses and state mules. Even his holiness the Pope rode upon a grey horse ; though, to indemnify him for the exertion, his horse was led and his stirrup held by kings and emperors.

" As time went on, people became more philosophical ; and one evidence of this was, in preferring the ease that does no injury, to the self-denial that does no good ;—or rather, the ease that does good, to the self-denial that does injury. Covered carriages began to obtain more commonly, though at first their uses were confined to long journies or times of public ceremony. Hungary appears to have been the country out of which the coach was born ; though many

---

* Pomelle—probably a diminution of *pomme*, little apple—referring to the small round knob by

which the hand held on. Modern carriages still retain a similar appliance in the shape of inside lace-holders, even now that the improvements in springs and roads have rendered them useless except as ornaments.

nations contend for the honour of fathering the unwieldly child, which has in its turn been father to a numerous tribe of now rapidly-improving offspring. Denina contends for Spain ; Father Semedi, for Italy ; the ' Encyclopédie Française,' for France ; while we would put in a claim founded on the ' whirlicote,' which conveyed the mother of Richard II. from the terrors of Wat Tyler's mob. What these whirlicotes were, we have not been able to discover ; most probably the first rude attempt at the close carriage of a later period.* That the common people of this country had at this time their conveyances, may be inferred from the record of the bearing of King Richard's corpse,—' upon a chariette or sort of litter on wheels, such as is used by citizen's wives who were not able or not allowed to keep ordinary litters.' Anne, the wife of this king, granted an annual stipend during the life of Robert Westende, ' purvoiour de noz chariettes.''—pp. 33, 34.

The 16th century witnessed a large increase in the use of coaches by princes and grandees in Germany, and the 17th both in that country and in Spain. Edicts and reproaches, however, strove to repress their employment among the people. In France, however,—

" Even so late as Henri Quatre little advance had been made in emulation of the more luxurious Germans. It appears from a letter said to be still in preservation, that Henry the Great had but one carriage for himself and the queen : he says, ' I cannot come to you to-day, because my wife is using my coach.' This coach was probably the one in which he was afterwards assassinated. It is said, that immediately upon the murder, his friends about him let fall the curtains of the coach and drove to the palace. Carriages at this time used in France were made with a canopy supported by ornamental pilliars, and the whole surrounded by curtains of stuff or leather, which might be drawn up or let down at pleasure.''—p. 37.

We must not leave this curious chapter without noticing that about the year 1670 a machine was in common use as a public vehicle in Paris, as a substitute for a sedan chair, little if at all lighter than some of our modern cabs, (probably, however, carrying but one passenger,s and drawn by *one man !* " Ce qui," says Roubo, as quoted by Mr. Adams, "malgre l'usage, ne fait pas beau coup d'honneur à l'urbanite Francaise." Truly we

think so ! But they were suppressed for a time, lest they should *diminish* the demand for human brute-labour—not because they required it.

The second chapter is given to the history of English carriages. It commences with the coach built by Walter Rippon, in 1555 for the Earl of Rutland, and is continued by interesting particulars of construction, expense, the mistaken discontent of those who supposed that they should be injured by improvements,—to the close of the 15th century. In 1573, " my m^res coche. with all the furniture thereto belonging, except horses, cost £34. 14s., and the horses £21 .13s. 3d.''

" Vehicles of all descriptions now became general, and an outcry was speedily raised against them. In 1585, William Lilly, in one of his plays, complains of those who were accustomed to go to a battle-field ' on hard-trotting horses, now riding in easie coaches up and down to court ladies.' So high did the clamour run, that a parliamentary bill was in agitation to prevent the increase of coaches ; its alleged necessity being, that government would be at a loss to mount the army, owing to the increased use of horses amongst the common people.

" Meantime England was lending in turn to other countries what she herself had borrowed. Towards the end of the sixteenth century, John of Finland, on his return from England, among other articles of luxury took with him to Sweden the first coach that was seen in that country. Before that time, the nobles of Sweden when they travelled carried their wives behind them on horseback. The princesses travelled in like manner, and when it rained, enveloped themselves in a mantle of waxed cloth.

" In 1598 it was accounted a great marvel that the English ambassador to Scotland had a coach with him, as it was the custom for all public functionaries to add to their other toils of office that of making long journeys on horseback. James I. made his first progress from Edinburgh to London after this fashion. Stowe records his leaving Edinburgh on the 5th of April, and not reaching London till the 7th of May. We must cease to wonder at slow national progression, if all public business was conducted at a similar rate. Great part of the way where the country was favourable, the king hunted ; and on the day of his arrival, to avoid the extremity of dust, he rode from Theobaldes, through the meadows. At Stamford Hill he was met by the lord mayor, knights, and aldermen of London, in scarlet

---

* Querry—Whirling cot, or moving house.

robes, all on horseback, and ' multitude of people swarming in highways, in fields, on houses and trees, to behold the king, and with whom the name of the king was very strange, being full fifty years since their was a *king* in England.'

" There is a record by the same chronicler of the common use of carriages at this period. ' On the 8th of June following arrived at London, Monsieur de Rosny, great treasurer of France, accompanied with noblemen and gentlemen in great number. The same night they, *in thirty* coaches, rode to the French ambassador's leaguer, then lodged at the Barbican by Redcross Street.' Anderson places the period of the general employment of coaches in 1705, and, in his ' History of Commerce,' gives the following state of the number and increase of hackney-coaches in London and Westminster :—

In 1637 50
    1652 200
    1694, limited to 700
    1716 800

This does not quite agree with Old Parr's chronicler, who surely could not account fifty coaches in London a swarm sufficient to ruin the watermen or cause the gunpowder plot! What would he say now to the nine hundred omnibuses of modern growth, exclusive of the ancient-looking hackney coaches, and the endless varieties of the great mushroom family of cabs.

" It is a singular fact that in the earlier use of coaches in Scotland, that country was indebted to a native of Stralsund, in Pomerania, who, in the year 1610, offered to contract for a certain number of coaches and waggons, with horses to draw and servants to attend them. Accordingly, a royal patent was granted him, conferring an exclusive privilege, for fifteen years, of running between Edinburgh and Leith. In England, coaches were daily becoming more necessary to the good citizens; although, in many quarters, the prejudice ran high against their use. The most vehement outcries, as might be expected, were to be found amongst the watermen, whose ' rights' were most infringed upon. These, with their own poet Taylor at their head, now and then assisted by a stray pamphleteer or squib-writer, raised so formidable a complaint, that the matter was taken into parliamentary consideration, and there was some serious discussion as to the eligibility of checking the too frequent use of hired coaches ! The supposed necessity of such an injunction is almost to be wondered at when we consider that these vehicles were—without springs, and altogether clumsy and unsightly in their construction—vehicles in which people were, in the

words of Taylor, ' tost, tumbled, rumbled, and jumbled without mercy.' "—pp. 45, 46, 47.

It seems not to have been before the middle of the 17th century, that public coaches ran between distant parts of the kingdom. In 1673 they had met with the usual opposition to change : for it was gravely proposed "to suppress those within 50 or 60 miles of London," and to limit the longer ones to one set of horses for the whole length of road, or " to 30 miles per day in summer, and 25 in winter." What evils were not to be dreaded from the announcement that " that remarkable swift travelling coach, the Fly, leaves Birmingham on Mondays, and reaches London on the Thursdays following" ?

" Toward the end of the seventeenth century, improvements began to take place. In, Wood's Diary mention is made of a machine called the ' Flying coach,' which completed the journey between Oxford and London in thirteen hours ! The outcry lessened, and the imperfect vehicles and bad roads were left to passengers unmolested. What the latter were, may be imagined from the fact, that when Charles III. of Spain visited England, and Prince George of Denmark went out to meet him, both princes were so impeded by the badness of the roads, that their carriages were obliged to be borne on the shoulders of the peasantry, and they were six hours in performing the last nine miles of their journey!

" Abroad, little progress seems to have been made. In a curious collection at St. Petersburg, now in the possession of the Emperor Nicholas, and originally belonging to Peter the Great (recognised as Emperor in 1725), some specimens of antique carriages are still preserved. One is close, made of deal, stained black, mounted on four wheels, the windows of mica instead of glass, and the frames of common tin : the other is open, with a small machine behind of the shipwright emperor's invention—its purpose, to determine the number of miles traversed on a journey. In the same collection is the litter of Charles XII. used at the battle of Pultowa.

" During the eighteenth century, improvements were very gradually made in carriages, and but little progress in the rate of travelling. So late as 1760, a journey from Edinburgh to London occupied the time of eighteen days,—a part of the roads being only accessible by pack-horses. Within our own time, may be remembered the uncouth ' turns-out,' as a coachman would emphatically call them, both in private and public conveyances:—heavy coaches, laden with ill-packed luggage: miserable horses, bound in worse harness; all at the mercy of a red-faced, half-drunken, apoplectic coachman, with a wisp of straw for a hat-band, and buried under a weight of dirty drab capes and cotton neckcloths, looking as if he united the double capacity of driver and passenger, sufficient weight for the coach, being the passenger thereon."—pp. 54, 55.

Leaving now the history of carriages in the gross, we go on with our author to the detail of their parts and construction. Here, again, he begins certainly at the beginning, for his next chapter is a treatise on the mechanical powers; whether it was introduced under any great necessity, or to much advantage, does not seem quite clear. The subject might equally furnish a chapter on the history of the loom, the plough, the ship, or the steam-engine; and little of it seems to be connected by subsequent reasoning with the main object of the book. If, however, facility of expression, variety of illustration, and originality of thought have any redeeming power, the insertion of this chapter is amply excused. It is necessary, however, to remark, that besides adopting Mr. Farey's addition of the "funicular action" and the "hydrostatical action." To the common list of the mechanical powers, so called, he is desirous of adding two others, "the automatical action," which is merely a barrel-spring, and the "ponderatical action," which is a weight. He is led to this by having stated, and truly, that the lever, wedge, &c. "are not powers in themselves, but merely vehicles or instruments for the transmission of power." It seemed, therefore, to follow, that a weight or spring, as it gives back again only the power at first employed in winding it up, might be classed in the same list; the important distinction being overlooked, that the simple machines called mechanical powers, act only at the very instant they are acted on by what are called first movers, whereas the two "actions" he would add to the list, act in the absence of all other forces. If his classification be correct, he should add the "circumgyratory action," that of a fly-wheel, and with almost equal propriety the "expansive action," and the "electrical action." Throughout the whole chapter, mechanical powers, first

movers, and forces inherent in matter, are so mingled as to produce a striking view of the subject rather than a cautious and correct one.

The fourth chapter consists of a curious and useful enumeration of the materials employed in the construction of carriages, with valuable, and generally correct, observations on their origin and qualities. Ash timber of course occupies a prominent place: one observation requires remark. He says, "One of the qualities which render ash peculiarly valuable for carriages, is the absence of elasticity and consequent indisposition to alter its form by its own internal efforts." It is difficult to say what is the meaning given to the word "elasticity" in this and several other passages, especially as we know that ash yields further before it sets than almost any other timber of English or foreign growth, while the load it will bear ranks also very high in the comparison. The combined effect of these two qualities renders it more efficient in withstanding concussion than any other wood; and we suspect they both arise from greater equality of texture. This may in some round-about way agree with Mr. Adams's meaning of the phrase, "want of elasticity." We suspect that in this, as in some other cases, he has taken up some loose meaning of the word, different from that in which it is used by any of our mechanical writers. Our nomenclature of the properties of materials in relation to forces, is indeed by no means settled: nothing would tend more to the improvement of our arts and artizans than its amendment, and the common use of the amended terms in our workshops.

The fifth chapter describes shortly a carriage of each general class—the two-wheeled—the Phaeton—and the coach; and enumerates the parts of which the most elaborate of these vehicles is composed. The sixth contains some valuable remarks on wheels; it insists with great propriety on the necessity of making wheels elastic (in the sense of yielding considerably under concussion without breaking) to make them durable at travelling speeds. It is one of the consequences of the derivation of travelling vehicles from carriages of burden, that the present structure of wheel is used: its defects at speed are many and great; the remedy is not obvious, and we doubt whether any existing invention completely supplies it.

Axles come next to wheels. The contrivances which are most important, and in most general use, are well described and remarked on : the considerations necessary to the perfection of an axle are thus enumerated :—

" That there be sufficient bearing surface for the arm to rest on;

" That the box be of a convenient shape for insertion in the wheel ;

" That as large a body of oil as possible be kept in actual contact with the arm *by washing up as the wheel revolves;*

" That the column of oil may in no case be above the horizontal level of the leakage point while the wheel is at rest."—p. 115.

Now there are great doubts about this "*washing up;*" a Mr. Hynes, therefore, patented a contrivance some time since in which the working box was the internal cylinder of the two concentric ones of which the box was composed, the space between forming a capacious oil chamber, communicating with the surface of the arm by many holes through the internal cylinder. Whether this effectual mode of becoming independent of *washing up*, has been tried on any considerable scale, we do not know.

We come now to springs. The mention of " steel" gives occasion to a highly imaginative note, running rapidly and delightfully over the scenes in which it has figured as tool or weapon, from the days of Homer to those of Walter Scott. How much the world's condition has depended on this one substance! and how little do we really know of it yet! We suspect Mr. Adams has missed the true principle of the coach-spring; he says—

" In carpentry it is found that the longer the beam, the greater must be the thickness, and a given proportion between length and thickness is maintained throughout. The spring-makers recognise this principle in their longest plate, but do not keep it up throughout; for though the longest plate is thicker than the rest, all the others are mostly alike in thickness, though their length gradually diminishes."—p. 121.

Now this comparison of the plates of the coach-spring with the carpenter's beam does not hold: the longer beam must be thicker also, because of the greater leverage it gives to the load ;—in the spring the leverage is to every plate the same, namely, the length of the long-

est plate; the plates ought, therefore, to be of equal thickness. The beam of equal thickness, but of triangular horizontal section, is, if we may so term it, the primitive form of the coach-spring ; it becomes the practical form by being cut up longitudinally into strips of gradually diminishing length, which are laid, chiefly for convenience, under each other. A spring composed of plates of unequal thickness will require a greater weight of metal to render it capable of a given duty than one of equal plates. Iron work and lamps occupy the ninth chapter, and the tenth gives an interesting outline of the process of manufacture.

In accounting for the fact that most new carriages are of foreign origin, Mr. Adams says—

" Continental artists are very commonly enthusiastic lovers of their art; they try to improve it from liking for it, and when they fail, it is mostly from want of efficient workmen to further their designs. The demand with them is not sufficient to make every branch of their art a manufacture. In England, on the contrary, the manufacture of carriages is a work of many trades, and thus greater skill is produced in manipulation. But few carriage-builders care to introduce any thing new. If chance brings in a new fashion, competition is aroused, and does not subside till excellence, or something approaching thereunto, be attained. A foreign artist has mostly abundance of leisure time for his invention to work ; but if an English artist attempts to invent, his trade stops, and he will probably be designated for his pains by the contemptuous epithet of ' schemer,' even though his genius be that of a Watt"
—pp. 157, 158.

This is one among the thousands of proofs of the overwhelming influence of money-worship amongst us. Few men have stronger, or at least more enduring, motives than the respect paid them by their fellows ; and where as in England, this respect is regulated chiefly by the purse, "the enthusiastic lovers of their art" for its own sake will be few and far between. While we contend so earnestly for the superiority of English art, that we wonder any question was ever raised on the subject, we must also admit that to love art for its pecuniary results, and artists in proportion to their worldly success, is the way to counteract rather than improve the favouring influences to which we owe our pre-eminence.

There is scarcely a manufacture in

the kingdom of whom the following is not a correct picture:—

"Carriage builders have not been remarkable as a scientific body. They have been, strictly speaking, 'practical men;' and as the knowledge they have gained by experience has not been carefully hoarded in books, carriage construction has remained a sort of occult matter, without any specific theory attached to it. Each one, as he is fresh initiated, gains his knowledge as he best can from verbal instruction or from a new series of experiments, and thus a considerable portion of his time must elapse ere he can have verified his judgment. Enough of this knowledge exists in various brains, which might suffice for the construction of a sound theory; but it would be a difficult operation to gather it together, for many petty feeling would be at work. In the mean time all mention of theory, except in derision, is decried. By most experimentalists, the word *theory* is understood as synonymous with falsehood or absurdity,—as the very opposite of *practice*. It is clear that practice must be the ultimate verification of theory; but every true practice must have a true theory belonging to it. The *theory* of a subject is the *science* or philosophy of that subject: practice is the positive knowledge or proof of the soundness of the theory. But as theories are more plentiful than practices, and as many of them are not verified, there are, of course, many false ones. On this ground, unscientific experimentalists have acquired the habit of regarding all theory as false; which is about as reasonable as it would be to assert that because falsehood exists in the world, all truth must therefore be extinct. This peculiarity is not confined to carriage-building: engineering and architecture abound with it, and law and medicine are not wanting in it. The truth is, human knowledge is only got together by small portions at a time, in the school of experiment; and when that knowledge is considerable in any one branch, a true and verified theory may be constructed upon it. But when a great number of subjects have thus been analyzed and theorised, it is comparatively easy to construct theories by analogy, on new subjects, by sound principles. Newton's theory of the universe was just as true when he first developed it in thought, as after he had verified it by calculation."--pp. 159, 160.

In workshops at least, the true relation of theory and practice seems to be little understood. It is to be hoped, that the blunders of theorists and practicians will in time induce each, to be more sensible of the value of the other. Theory having extracted general rules from a multitude of observations on materials, substances, and what appear to be the ne-cessary relations of quantities, proposes by the aid of these rules to predict the results of any future set of circumstances; but then, as its first step necessarily is an enumeration of the circumstances of the proposed case, if it fails to enumerate them all, as it often does, it fails in its prediction also. Practice, on the contrary, proceeds by amassing numberless unconnected observations, as to cause and effect, and selecting from them for the same purpose of prediction such, if it happen to have them, as seem to fit the case proposed; but it fails, perhaps, oftener than it succeeds, from not seeing the differences between the assemblage of facts under which the rule was derived, from that to which it is to be applied. Theory and practice are then admirably calculated to remedy each other's defects; and before our mechanical arts will advance at the rate natural to them, the practician will gladly furnish his treasure of observations to be repaid by the invaluable generalisations of the theorist. We hope this day has already dawned.

We could easily supply illustrations of these remarks from this very subject of carriages, and the more readily, since the theory of the motion of a carriage on common roads at travelling speed, is perhaps a more complicated mechanical problem than any other. To shew the defect of theory, let us take this instance. Practicians assert that the narrower the tread of a carriage—that is, the shorter the axle-trees, the easier will be the draught; this the theorist denies, for it affects not either the weight, the friction, the velocity, the size of the wheels, or any other consideration which seems to him to enter into the question,—forgetting that his argument supposes the carriage to move in a straight line ;—that carriages rarely do so move,—that in passing into curves the velocities and momenta of the wheels are changed,—that this change requires force, and the more of it since the mean velocity of the wheels is greater than that of the body,—and that the amount of the change, and therefore of the force required, depends on the distance of the wheels from each other. Here, then, the practician has the start of the theorist, though theory, when put on the right scent, can well justify the conclusions of the practician. If it be needful to give a sample of the mistakes into which a very clever man may fall if he have not the aid of theory, it is sufficient to refer again to Mr. Adams's remarks on springs we have already quoted.

We wish we had an account like the following of the habits, qualifications, and earnings of the workmen in every other manufacture; nothing would so much contribute to a clear view of our social condition and our manufacturing capabilities. Our space and time will not allow us to pursue the reflections which this statement is calculated to suggest, especially when the situation of the workman engaged in more systematic manufactures is taken in contrast. We shall return to the subject next week.

"Body makers are very skilful joiners, using several kinds of wood, and working up many forms in which there is not a single plane surface. The essence of their art is to show perfect forms in the lines of their work without breaks or inequalities; and many of these lines are double convex or double concave. The principles of this work are essentially geometrical, and the more difficult forms of geometry are the most common. The workman must know how to draw well or he cannot work well; and to be enabled to do both he must possess correctness of eye and skill of hand. He has to make correct joints at every variety of angle, and has to resort to every mode of uniting his materials. The tenon and mortice, the scarf, the lap, the groove, the glue joint, the bolt, the screw, the nail, are all employed. The materials he uses are ash, elm, birch, mahogany, pine and deal; and he must also possess some skill as a metal-worker efficiently to fit the various plates of brass and iron which enter into the composition of his work. It is not absolutely necessary that he should possess taste, but fidelity in copying he cannot do without. And he must possess a capital in tools varying from thirty to forty pounds. As such men are not numerous they command high wages. They do not usually work by the day, like many other workmen, but by the piece. Two men working together have been known to earn in the space of a week £20; but it was by great exertion, working early and late, sixteen hours per day, and taking their meals on their work-benches. When in full work, very quick workmen will earn £5 per week; but as they seldom have full work the year through, they do not average more than four. Ordinary workmen do not earn more than £3, and on the average less than that.

"Carriage-makers are more akin to millwrights in the work they perform, though much less skill is required in geometrical knowledge. Their work is heavy, and requires great truth in all the framings; but the lines are on a larger scale than those of the body-maker, and therefore slight inaccuracies are not so perceptible. They have also few double convex or double concave lines and more plane surfaces. The materials they use are ash and elm, much of them in combination with iron work supplied by the smith. Neatness, but not extreme delicacy of work, is required in the carriage-maker: he requires fewer tools than the body-maker, and his earnings, while employed, are, by piece-work, from £3 to £2 per week, according as he may happen to be a good or indifferent workman.

"Carvers are the workmen who execute the ornamental wood work of carriages. Some of them are artists, furnishing designs as well as executing them, and of course are in such cases highly paid. Others are merely the executors of the designs of others. There are two classes of carving used in carriages: the simplest consists of the beads and mouldings on the framework of the body, and also on the carriage timbers; the other consists of leaf work and tracery, according to fancy, and is used to ornament blocks of various kinds, as well as the hind standards, and also on the timber ends. The designs for these purposes are similar to the scrolls and volutes used in architecture. The earnings of carvers are from thirty shillings up to four and five pounds per week, according to their skill; but, like many other workmen they are unemployed several months in the year.

"Coach smiths are the most skilful of all iron-workers. They have to work large and heavy bars of iron into forms containing several unequal curves, the thickness of the metal being also unequal. It is a work guided by the eye more than by measurement, and there are few straight lines to work from. The coach smith must be able to draw, or at least to criticise forms accurately, or he will not prove a skilful workman. He must possess considerable personal strength, and capacity to bear the heat to which he is exposed. He must be a good judge of the metal he uses, and so contrive his work that it may appear light, while capable of efficiently resisting the strain upon it; and it must moreover be truly wrought, being all intended to fix to wood work previously prepared. Men possessing so many different qualities are not numerous, and therefore are highly paid. Coach smiths are divided into three classes, fire-men, hammer-men, and vice-men. The fire-men are the class just described. The hammer-men aid them in their work, with the sledge hammer, when heavy blows are required to reduce the metal in size or form; they also blow the bellows and make up the fire, in short perform the office of labourers. And hence arises much injustice; if the hammer-man happen to be a skilful man, he frequently applies himself to work in the fire-man's absence. The fire-man, as soon as he discovers it grows jealous, quarrels with and discharges his hammer-man. Thus the hammer-men live in a position from which they are forbidden to emerge, even if they possess the necessary skill. The business of the vice-man is to file and smooth the work from the rough marks of the hammer, to fit joints, and finish screw bolts and nuts. Neatness and skill are required in his work, but not the precision of eye required in the fire-man. Fire-men mostly work by the piece, and earn from two to three and four pounds per week, according to the class of work : the hammer-men earn from twenty five to thirty shillings : the vice-men from thirty shillings to two pounds.

"Smiths have usually been esteemed a very drunken race ; but this estimate of them must be taken with a reservation. They were formerly much more so than at present like other mechanics ; but, like them, they are fast improving. Men who work hard in a heated atmosphere have a tendency to drink more than those who do not ; and with the imperfect arrangements which are so common in smiths' shops, it is not surprising that some of them should become confirmed drunkards. Contrivances will in time be resorted to, to enable the workmen to avoid the heat while working ; and probably tilt hammers will be so contrived that there will be no necessity to breed up hammer-men to a trade in which they can make no progress.

"Trimmers are to carriages, what upholsterers are to houses, in what regards the interior lining. They use similar materials, —as cloth, silk, morocco, canvass, webbing, curled hair, wool, flocks, &c. But, in addition to this, they have to use the more stubborn material of leather, in various ways, as for the coverings of folded carriage heads, in what is called ' open work.' Herein much judgment is required. The work of some trimmers is entirely confined to leather work, and their technical designation is ,' budget trimmers." They sew on the leathers to the iron frames, called dashing or splashing irons and wings, cover poles and shaft with leather in the wearing parts, cover the small cases called tool budgets, drag chains, safety chains, and ropes, and other similar work. In these employments, the men who cut out require much judgment, and also some taste, in order not to waste valuable materials, and also to make their work firm, and, at the same time, neat and agreeable to the eye. The earnings of trimmers who are skilful cutters, are from three to four guineas per week ; those who are merely workmen, earn from thirty shillings to fifty.

"Painters are an important branch of the

carriage trade, for on them the general good appearance of the carriage depends. The director or foreman must be an accurate judge of colours, as to their durability, and also as to the effect which varnish will have on them. He sometimes has to match a single pannel which has been damaged ; and it is a very nice operation to match a new colour to an old one, more especially when the colours are conspicuous. The mechanical skill required in painting is not very great ; that portion which consists in what is technically called " picking out," or painting fine lines of a distinct colour, on a ground work;—as black on yellow,—requires the greatest skill. The wages of a foreman are from two to four guineas per week. The ordinary workman can earn from twenty-five to thirty-five shillings, according to their skill ; and they are by no means too highly paid, considering the unhealthy nature of their employment, in heated apartments impregnated with mineral and other odours. Generally speaking, painters are more healthy of late years than they formerly were ; and this must be attributed to their increasing habits of greater personal cleanliness.

Brace-makers and harness-makers are generally ranked together, on account of the similarity of their work. The braces of a carriage serve to support the body on the springs, and also to confine its oscillations within certain limits. The braces are combinations of two or more straps of leather, increasing in number according to the strain they may be exposed to, and sewn together to form one substance. The cutter out requires considerable judgment as to the quality of his leather, and also to use economically parts of the hide which are fitted for different purposes, as they are not of a homogenous texture or substance ; he must also be able to calculate the requisite strength of material. The workmen who sew the material together require little more skill than shuttle throwers ; piercing the stitches with the awl is a mere matter of habit, which almost any person can acquire. The wages of a good cutter are from two to three guineas per week. The sewers earn from twenty-five to thirty shillings, according to their neatness of work. Their employment is unhealthy, as their work is always performed in a stooping posture, and working on black leather has a tendency to injure their eyesight.

" Sawyers do not require any great skill. Inferior carpenters and others frequently become sawyers. The work is rather laborious. Their earnings are thirty shillings per week. Very few carriage-builders now use pit-sawyers, as a single man at a bench with a small frame-saw is found far more efficient.

" Labourers are a class of people employed by coach-makers under one designation, but varying much in their skill and ability. The commonest class are those who wash carriages and move them from place to place. The next are those who are capable of polishing the metal work and leather, and keeping the paint in order.

" The next and most efficient class are those who possess a general knowledge of the mechanical construction of carriages, and are capable of hanging and unhanging them, separating their various parts, replacing damaged bolts or iron-work, nailing on the wearing leathers, painting the iron work, greasing, oiling, and adjusting the wheels. They must also be able to judge of the general condition of carriages, so as readily to detect defects which might render them unsafe in travelling. The weekly earnings of labourers are from twenty to thirty shillings, according to their skill.

" Axletree-makers are divided into forgers or fire-men, turners, and vicemen. The work of the forgers requires considerable skill and strength to unite large masses of iron at a welding heat, and to reduce them to accurate forms. Their work is akin to that of anchor-smiths. Axletree-turners must be very skilful, accurate workmen, to fix the patent oil axles truly ; for the common axles used with grease, inferior workmen will suffice. The vice-men also require much skill and practice in filing, to enable them to work true, which is absolutely necessary in axles. Were these men taught to work in wood first, as is the case with millwrights, skill would be more frequent among them than is the case at present. The forgers earn from two to three pounds a-week ; the turners, from two to three pounds ; the vice-men, from thirty shillings to two pounds, but the latter sum is not common.

" Spring makers require considerable skill, especially for the construction of circular or C springs with many plates. They work by the aid of a hammer-man like other smiths, and have a vice-man to finish their work. The modes of working being exceedingly imperfect, their work is empirical ; and thus some few by long practice acquire skill in tempering the steel, which others do not attain, simply for want of instruction. Spring makers earn from two to four, and occasionally six pounds per week ; the vice-men, and hammer-men, the same as in other cases.

" Wheelwrights must be skilful workmen, for their work is so severely tested, that if not true and sound, it must fail, and moreover the accuracy of it depends more on truth of eye, and skill of hand, than on any marks, guides, or rules. First rate wheel-wrights earn from two to three pounds per week ; but their work is very ladorious. Tire-smiths are a branch of the wheeling trade : an unskilful tire-smith does much damage in a short space of tine, and skilful ones are not abundant : their earnings are from three to five pounds per week, and occasionally more than that.

" Lamp-makers have no hard work to perform. Their work consists in cutting out thin metal and soldering it together. It requires neatness, but no considerable amount of skill or exactness. The effluvia of a lamp-maker's shop is unpleasant, but not positively unwholesome ; yet the sitting posture in which they perform their work is not favourable to health. Their earnings are from twenty-five to thirty shillings a-week.

Blind-makers, trunk-makers, and joiners are reciprocal trades. The amount of skill required by the workman is not very considerable. Their earnings are about thirty shillings a-week, and their work is very light. The joiners make wainscot cases, seat-boxes, &c.

" Turners are employed by carriage-builders to turn splintre-bars, splintres, drag-staves, raisers, and similar things. Their earnings are thirty shillings a-week.

" Lace-making formerly constituted an important branch of carriage-building, as skilled workmen were few, and they commanded very high prices for their labour. But the art of lace-making is no longer a sealed book ; the workmen have increased in number, and although a first-rate workman can earn three pounds per week, still he does not on the average work more than three or four months in the year, the total amount is very trifling. Formerly, lace-making was confined to London, but since the increase of carriages, it has become more of a manufacture, and is made wholesale at Manchester and other manufacturing towns. The London carriage lace-makers are, like most weavers, miserably poor and squalid, as is the case with all trades which are wearing out, or where the mode of operation is changing.

Curriers are the workmen who dress the leather which has been converted from the raw state by the tanner. Considerable skill is required in the operation of levelling the hides by a peculiar process, called shaving, and the work is laborious. When in work the men can earn from two to three pounds per week at piece-work ; but their numbers keep many of them constantly out of employment. Currying has generally been considered a profitable business for the masters; and the reason has been that considerable capital is required in it, combined with judgment in buying the material. Tanners do not give credit, and the currier has to lay in his stock of hides at particular seasons. Without great skill to judge of the quality of a very deceptive material, he may easily be ruined. It is a healthy trade for the workmen.

Japanners, in the leather trade, are those who purchase the glazed and enamelled water-proof leather used for carriages. Those who carry on this business are generally employed by the currier who finds the leather. Considerable knowledge of materials is required, as it is essentially a chemical art, and the material on which the japan is spread is very liable to injury. The workmen earn the same as other painters, and the employment is far from healthy, on account of the great heat necessary.

Ivory workers are divided into turners and carvers. The former earn from thirty to forty shillings per week, the latter considerably more, as they require more skill. The turners prepare rollers and buttons for glasses and blinds, the carvers cut out ornamental crests for seat cloths. Platers prepare the ornamental metal work, such as door handles, and the beading which covers joints, as well as buckles, and all the metal work used in harness. The earnings of the workmen are about thirty shillings per week.

Chasers emboss the crests, arms, &c., on the door-handles, heads and axletree caps, as well as other ornamental work.

The ordinary workman earn two guineas per week, but designers are paid much higher in proportion to their skill.

Embroiderers prepare crests and coats of arms to ornament the seat cloths. Their work being principally fancy, no fixed price is attached to it."

EXPERIMENTS ON THE ADHESION OF IRON SPIKES OF VARIOUS FORMS, WHEN DRIVEN INTO DIFFERENT SPECIES OF TIMBER. BY WALTER R. JOHNSON, PROFESSOR OF MECHANICS AND NATURAL PHILOSOPHY IN THE FRANKLIN INSTITUTE, PHILADELPHIA.

(From the *American Journal of Science and Arts.*)

In reference to railroad constructions, bridge-building, and several other useful applications in civil engineering as well as in naval architecture, the adhesion of spikes, bolts and nails of various forms becomes an object of much practical importance. In regard to railroads, this matter is worthy of more attention than might at first sight be supposed. Owing to the high price of iron, the flat rail is often unavoidably adopted in in preference to the edge rail; and whenever the speed of a train descending by gravity or impelled with great velocity by the moving power, is to be suddenly checked by the brake, the friction of the periphery of the wheel on the rail tends to drive the latter lengthwise, and thus to force all the spikes with which it is fastened into closer contact with the ends of the fibers which have been cut in driving them. If this partial or total dragging of the wheels along the rail take place sometimes in one direction and sometimes in the other, the spikes must be subjected to alternate impulses on the opposite sides. Indeed, whenever the motive power depends on friction for its efficacy, as in the case of the common locomotive engine, there is a constant succession of these two opposite dragging forces, the engine constantly tending by its driving wheels to urge the rail backwards, and the train by an equal but more extensively distributed action tending to urge forward all the rails over which it is at the same moment passing. So decided is this influence, that on a railroad where the transportation is all in one direction, and where the cars descend by gravity, I have seen rails entirely detached, or remaining loosely connected but by a single spike, while others clearly indicated by the inclined position of their upper faces or heads, that they were pressed into an oblique or leaning position the wooden sill.

This single case may serve to show the importance of attending to the character of the spikes used in similar constructions.

To determine some of the points relating to the forms of spikes, and the kind of timber into which they are driven, the following experiments were undertaken. They serve to show the relative economy of each form of spike, as well as its fitness for the purpose intended. The mode of executing the experiments was, to drive each spike to a certain distance above its cutting edge, into the edge of a piece of plank or scantling, and by means of a suitable apparatus, adapted to that purpose, to draw it out by a direct longitudinal strain. The machine employed for this purpose was the same as that which has been used for testing the strength of iron and copper, in experiments on the tenacity of materials employed in steam boilers. A strong band or strap of iron connected with the weighing beam of that machine, held the pieces of plank; and clamped pincers, with a suitable jaw, for taking hold of the head and projecting part of the spike, was attached to the opposite part of the machine, which being tightened by a strong screw held the spike firmly, while the application of weights upon the long arm of the lever drew the timber away, and released the spike. Care was taken to cause the strain to pass through the axis of the spike, and by a very gradual application of weights to avoid surpassing that force which was just sufficient for extraction.

The first experiment was upon one of Burden's patent square spikes, with a cutting edge, intended to be in all cases placed across the grain of the timber. This spike was .375 of an inch square, and was driven into a sound plank of seasoned New Jersey yellow pine, 3⅜ inches. The force required to extract it was 2052 lbs., and the exact weight of the part driven into the wood was 866 grains troy.

The second trial was upon a flanched, grooved and swelled spike, having the grooves between two projecting wings or flanches, on the same sides as the faces of the cutting edge. The other two sides were planes, continuing to the head. A cross section of this spike, taken 1¼ inches above its edge or point, had the form of fig. 1. At $\frac{8}{16}$ of an inch, that is, where the flanches project least from the edge, or where the swell between them comes nearest to forming a perfect square; the form is as shown in fig. 2; the dotted line in each figure, re-

Fig. 1.   Fig. 2.

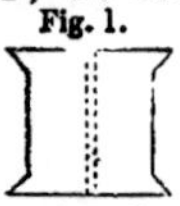

presenting the direction of the cutting edge. Towards the head of this spike, the flanching and grooving is suppressed, and the form becomes square. This experiment was made on the same piece of Jersey yellow pine as the first, and the weight required for extracting the spike was 1596 lbs. The weight of the part driven in was 708¼ grains. The cutting edge was irregular; the distance to which it was driven, was 3⅜ inches, as the first trial. To know the relative value of the two forms of spikes, we have but to divide the weight required for the extraction of each by the number of grains in the part which had been buried in the wood; thus, 2052 ÷ 866 = 2.37, and 1596 ÷

708.25 = 2.112. Hence, the plain spike had an advantage over the swelled and grooved one, in about the proportion 23 to 21. It should be mentioned, also, that the plain spike was drawn out by a very gradual addition of force, whereas the force of 1596 pounds drew the grooved spike immediately after its application. In the first trial, an attempt was made to detect any yielding or gradual retreat of the spike, before the final start, but none was observed.

The third and fourth experiments were made with the same spikes respectively as the first and second; but instead of yellow pine, the timber employed was thoroughly seasoned white oak.

The plain spike driven 3⅜ inches into that timber, required for its extraction a force of 3,910 lbs., and, as before, exhibited no signs of movement until the instant of starting, when it suddenly came out about one quarter of an inch, or as far as the range of motion and the elasticity of the machine would permit.

The flanched, swelled, and grooved spike, driven 3⅜ inches into another part of the same piece of plank, from which the plain one had been extracted, was drawn out with a force of 3,791 lbs. A slow motion to the extent of $\frac{1}{15}$ or $\frac{1}{10}$ of an inch was, in this trial, perceived to precede the starting of the spike, and was accompanied by a gradual protrusion of the fibres of the timber immediately around the iron. In these experiments, though the plain spike bore the greater absolute weights, yet when the weight of metal is considered, it is seen that the relative values of the two are 4.515 in the plain, and 5.354 in the grooved form. The various circumstances of the four preceding experiments are seen at a single view in the following table:—

TABLE I.

No. of Experiments.	Description of spike used.	Kind and condition of timber.	Breadth of spike.	Thickness of spike.	Depth to which it was driven.	Weight in grains for part driven in.	Force required to extract it in pounds avoirdupois.	Ratio of extracting force to weight of spike.	Date.
			Inch	Inch	Inch				
1	Burden's plain square spike....	Seasoned Jersey yellow pine	.375	.375	3.375	366	2052	2.368	Oct.27th, 1825
2	Flanched, grooved, and swelled .	Seasoned Jersey yellow pine	.375	.300	3.375	708	1696	2.254	....
3	Burden's plain..	Seasoned white oak.........	.375	.375	3.375	866	3910	4.515	....
4	Grooved & swelled............	Seasoned white oak	.375	.300	3.375	708	3791	5.354	....

REMARKS.

Experiment No. 1.—Force gradually applied, no motion previous to the starting.

Experiment No. 2.—Force applied at once.

Experiment No. 3.—Started suddenly.

Experiment No. 4.—Fibres protruded $\frac{1}{20}$ inch before spikes drew out.

Hence it appears, that in yellow pine the grooved and swelled form was about five per cent. less advantageous than the plain, while in the seasoned oak the former was 18½ per cent. superior to the latter. It is apparent that the advantage of seasoned oak over seasoned yellow pine for retaining spikes,

is, by a comparison of experiments 1 and 3, as 1 to 1.9; and, by a comparison of 2 and 4, it is as 1 to 2.37. In the preceding experiments, the spikes were driven into the timber, and immediately drawn out again. In the second series, the spikes were driven into their respective pieces of timber, and then soaked for a few days in water. The pieces into which the different spikes were driven, were as nearly alike as it was practicable to obtain them, being always cut from the same plank, avoiding knots, cracks, &c. The following table contains a view of the experiments after soaking the timber:—

TABLE II.

Timber soaked after the Spikes were driven.

No. of experiments.	Kind of spike used.	Kind and condition of timber.	Breadth of spike. Inch	Thickness of spike. Inch	Depth to which it was driven. Inch.	Weight in grains of the part inserted.	Force to extract the spike in pounds.	Ratio of the extracting force to the weight of spike.	Date.
1	{ Swelled and grooved ..... }	Chestnut unseasoned .	.375	.300	3.5	806.	1710.	2.121	{ Dec. 3, 1835.
2	"	Yellow pine seasoned.	.375	.300	3.5	806.	1668.	2.069	"
3	"	{ Hemlock partly seasoned ...... }	.375	.300	3.5	806.	1738.	2.156	"
4	"	White oak seasoned .	.375	.300	3.5	806.	3373.	4.184	"
5	"	{ Locust partly seasoned .... }	.375	.300	3.5	806.	4902.	6.081	"
6	{ Swelled and grooved, the swell filed away }	Chestnut unseasoned .	.390	.300	3.5	759.	1852.5	2.440	"
7	"	Seasoned yellow pine .	.390	.300	3.5	759.	1767.	2.328	"
8	"	{ Hemlock partly seasoned ...... }	.390	.300	3.5	759.	1296.8	1.576	"
9	{ Plain spike, filed lengthwise .... }	Chestnut unseasoned	.400	.394	3.625	933.5	1790.	1.810	"
10	"	{ Hemlock partly seasoned ...... }	.400	.394	3.5	933.5	1638.75	1.755	"
11	"	{ Locust partly seasoned .... }	.400	.394	3.5	933.5	3990.	4.167	"
12	"	"	.400	.394	3.5	933.5	4332.	4.640	"
13	{ Grooved and notched, or serrated .... }	White oak	.392	.315	3.675	759.	2622.	3.454	"
14	Burden's patent ..	"	.339	.329	3.625	639.	2152.	3.367	"

REMARKS.

Experiment No. 1.—In this and the four following, the thickness of the spike is that at the bottom of the grooves.

Experiment No. 4.—The oak used in this

experiment was firmer than that employed in the first series.

Experiment No. 5.—The timber had been slightly split by the driving of this spike.

Experiment No. 6.—The flanches remained after filing out the swelled part of the original form.

· *Experiment* No. 12.—Timber slightly split in driving the spike.

· The first five of the preceding experiments show that with a spike of given form and driven a certain distance into different timbers, the order of retentiveness, beginning with the highest, is as follows:—1, locust; 2, white oak; 3, hemlock; 4. unseasoned chestnut; 5, yellow pine. From the 6th, 7th, and 8th experiments, we see that chestnut is still above yellow pine, but that hemlock is inferior to both. By the 9th and 10th, it also appears that hemlock is still to be placed below chestnut. Comparing the 1st experiment in this table with the 6th, and the 2nd with the 7th, we perceive that the swell towards the point of the spike, was so far from being an advantage to it, that it in fact rendered the spikes less retentive than when that swelled part had been removed; so that, even could this form have been produced without any increase in the weight of the spike, it would still have been less advantageous than the simple groove without the swell; but when it is considered that the swell added 47 grs. (=806—759) to the weight, it is evident that the groove alone has a decided advantage over the other form. By the trials in unseasoned chestnut, (Nos. 1 and 6.) this advantage is 15 per cent. :

thus $\dfrac{2440-2121}{2121} = 15$; and by those on

yel. pine, (Nos. 2 and 7,) it is $\dfrac{2328-2069}{2069}$ =12.5 per cent. · In fact, after the ends of the fibres have once been thrust apart by the thick part of the swell, it is evident that when they come opposite to the cavity above the swell they must lose some portion of their power to press the spike and produce the retaining force of friction ; this force must then depend for its production on the action of those fibres of the wood which are opposite to the swelled portion, or between it and the point of the spikes.

In the next series of experiments, it was attempted to ascertain the relation between forms more diversified than had hitherto been employed.

As it is evident that the total retentiveness of the wood must depend, in a considerable degree, upon the number of fibres which are longitudinally compressed by the spike, it was inferred, that on the area of the two faces, which in driving the spike are placed against the ends of the fibres, must in a great measure depend the retention of the spike.

In this series, four kinds of wood and ten forms of spikes were employed.

A comparison of the results given in Table III. (on the opposite page) will show what order those forms would possess among themselves, in point of retentiveness, as well as the advantages of the respective species of timber into which they were severally driven.

This table furnishes three sets of comparisons for deducing the relative retaining powers of green chestnut, thoroughly seasoned oak, and equally seasoned locust. Thus the weight which in those three cases drew the square spike from the chestnut, was 1995; and that which extracted the broad flat one 2394; and that which drew the narrow flat one from the same timber was 2223. The sum of these is 6612. The sum of the three numbers for the same three spikes used with oak, was by experiments 5, 6, and 7, 13110; and the sum of the three locust, by experiments 13, 14, and 15, is 11280; these three numbers have to each other the relation of of 1, 2, and 2⅔ ; from which we infer that oak is almost precisely *twice*, and locust 2⅔ times as retentive as unseasoned chestnut. By comparing together the results of experiments 1 and 2, it will be seen that the weights required for extracting the two spikes respectively, are more nearly proportional to the breadth than to either the thicknesses, or the weights of the spikes. For the spike with a breadth of .405 inch and a thickness of .402, required 1995 lbs. for its removal, while that which had a breadth of .375 inch took 1873 lbs. Now .373 : 405 :: 1073 : 2033 for the calculated retentiveness, instead of 1995, as given by experiments ;—a difference of only + 38 lbs. between the observed and calculated results. Calculating the retention by the *weights* of the respective spikes, we should have 866 : 942 :: 1873 : 2987, or difference of 42 lbs., while using the thickness alone, we obtain .384 : 402 :: 1873 : 1960, a difference of an opposite kind of 35 lbs. from the observed result, the greater thickness yielding the less retentive power. This correspondence between the breadths and the extracting weights becomes still more apparent when we compare the third, and especially the fourth with the second experiment. Thus for the broad flat spike, (3d Ex.)—Compared with experiment 2, we obtain

By breadths, .373:.539 :: 1873:2701, instead of 2394, diff. 307
" weights, .866:.898 :: 1873:1942, " " " ⸻452
" thickness, .384:.298 :: 1873:1379, " " " ⸻1015

and for the thinner and lighter spike, (Ex. 4th.)—compared with the same,

By breadths, .373:.390 :: 1873:1958, instead of 2223, observed diff. ⸻265
" weights, .866:.566 :: 1873:1224, " " " ⸻999
" thickness, .384:.253 :: 1873:1234, " " " ⸻989

Nearly the same conclusions would result from a comparison of those trials, which were made on seasoned white oak and locust. Indeed, it appears that with a given breadth

TABLE III.

Spikes of various forms—Timber of different kinds.

No. of Experiments.	Kind of spike used.	Kind and condition of timber.	Breadth of spike. Inch	Thickness of spike. Inch	Area of two faces. Sq. in.	Depth to which driven. Inch	Weight of parts inserted. Grs.	Force to extract spike. Lbs.	Ratio of force to weight of spike.	Date.
1	Straight square.	Chestnut unseasoned.	.404	.402	2.83	3.5	942	1995	2.116	1835. Dec. 4.
2	Burdens patent.	"	.373	.384	2.64	3.5	866	1873	2.162	Dec. 8.
3	Broad flat.	"	.539	.288	3.77	3.5	898	2394	2.663	Dec. 4.
4	Narrow flat.	"	.390	.253	2.73	3.5	566	2223	3.927	Dec. 8.
5	Straight square.	White oak thoroughly seasoned.	.405	.402	2.83	3.5	942	3990	4.129	Dec. 7.
6	Broad flat.	"	.539	.288	3.77	3.5	898	5130	5.712	"
7	Narrow flat.	"	.390	.253	2.73	3.5	566	3990	7.049	"
8	Burden's patent.	"	.373	.384	2.64	3.5	866	3905	4.509	"
9	Cylindrical with cutting edge.	"	.485	Diam.		3.5	1211	3876	3.200	"
10	Grooved and swelled.	"	.375	.375	2.60	3.5	866	3727	4.624	"
11	Grooved but not swelled.	"	.375	.375	2.60	3.5	759	4247	5.662	"
12	Grooved, and bottom of grooves serrated.	"	.375	.375	2.60	3.5	500	2650	5.300	"
13	Square.	Locust seasoned 3 years.	.405	.402	2.83	3.5	942	5967	6.334	Dec. 8.
14	Broad flat.	"	.539	.285	3.77	3.5	898	7040	7.839	"
15	Narrow flat.	"	.390	.253	2.73	3.5	566	5273	9.316	"
16	Cylindrical, pointed with 15 grooves filed longitudinally from the point upward.	Ash seasoned.	.500	Diam.		3.5	929	2052	2.208	1836. Jan. 4.
17	"	"	.500	"		3.5	929	2309	2.507	"
18	Plain cylindrical, pointed scale not removed.	"	.500	"		3.5	1015	2451	2.411	"

REMARKS.

Experiment No. 10.—The measure in this and the two following cases as taken outside the flanches.

Experiment No. 12.—The weight of the part inserted is given by estimation in this experiment.

Experiment No 16.—In this and the two following experiments, the spikes were driven into the timbers in the direction of the length of the fibres.

on the face of the spike, a diminution of thickness is sometimes a positive advantage to the retentiveness of the timber; for in white oak, the spike which had a breadth of only .390, required as much force to extract it, as one of which the breadth was .405, though the thickness of the former was but .253, while that of the latter was .402; and on chestnut, thinner, narrower, and lighter spike, required absolutely more force to withdraw it than the other. This leads us to notice the different kinds of action of the respective spikes on timber of various kinds. In the softer and more spongy kinds of wood, the fibres instead of being forced backed longitudinally and condensed upon themselves, are, by driving a thick, and especially a rather obtusely pointed spike, folded in masses backward and downward so as to leave in certain parts the *faces* of the grains of the timber in contact with the surface of the metal.

That the view just presented is correct, seems also probable from what was observed in the case of the swelled spike. For while the grooved but unswelled one, driven into chestnut timber, (Table II. Ex. 6,) required 1852 lbs. to extract it, the grooved and swelled spike, (Ex. 1, same table,) took but 1710 lbs. And in Table III. Ex. 10, we find the swelled spike drawn from white oak by 3727 lbs. and the grooved but not swelled one, Ex. 12, requiring 4247. Hence it appears to be necessary, in order to obtain the greatest effect, that the fibres of the wood should press the face as nearly as possible in their longitudinal direction and with equal intensities throughout the whole length of the spike. Arranging the spikes according to the order of their ratios of retention to weight, as given by the experiments in Table III, from five to twelve inclusive, we have the following :—

1. Narrow flat spike, with a ratio of 7.049
2. Wide,   "   "   "   " 5.712
3. Grooved but not swelled, "   " 5.662
4. Grooved and notched, "   " 5.330
5. Grooved and swelled,   "   " 4.624
6. Burden's patent,   "   " 4.509
7. Square hammered,   "   " 4.129
8. Plain cylindrical,   "   " 3.200

Experiments 16, 17, and 18, of the same table were made by driving the spikes which were cylindrical with conical points into the timber endwise of the grain. This method of comparing two forms, the one grooved and the other plain, was adopted on account of the extreme liability of the timber to

split by driving spikes of these forms *across* the direction of the fibres. It was observed that on drawing these spikes, the holes were almost perfectly square. This resulted from the position of the rings of annual growth and the greater elasticity in some directions than in others. It is probable that if the filed grooves in experiments 16 and 17 had been covered with a scale of oxide, as was the case with the plain spike used in experiment 18, the former would have given a result somewhat higher.

When holes are drilled into stone blocks and afterwards plugged with timber to receive spikes in fastening on the chairs of edge rails, the method of experimenting just described finds an application, and it is probable that in such cases the grooved cylinder with a conical grooved point, may prove advantageous.

A few experiments were made to determine the effect of driving to different depths, on the total amount of retention. For this purpose two different spikes were selected, viz., the square hand-wrought spike, the section of which was .405 × .402, and the wide flat one of which the section was .539 × .288. They were respectively driven to a certain depth into unseasoned chestnut, and then subjected to a force just sufficient to start them. This force was noted, and the spike was immediately driven down one inch deeper than before, and the force again applied. All my experiments proved that when a spike is once started, the force required for its final extraction is much less than that which produced the first movement. This is readily accounted for on the principle that as the wedge shaped point was from half an inch to an inch in length ; and as this, on the starting back of the spike a very little distance, became mostly relieved from the pressure of the fibres, all that part of the retention which had been due to the wedge-shaped portion of the spike was at once destroyed. The following table will show, however, that

TABLE IV.—*Spikes driven to different depths.*

No. of Experiments.	Form of spike.	Kind and condition of timber.	Breadth of spike.	Thickness of spike.	Area of the two faces pressing the ends of the fibres. Sq. in.	Depth to which spike was driven. Inches.	Weight of the part inserted. Grs.	Force to extract the spike.	Ratio of force to weight of spike.	Date.
1	Squaare not filed.	{ Chestnut unseasoned.	.405	.402	.7695	1.9	483	1183	2.428	1835. Dec. 4.
2	" " "	"	'	"	1.1745	2.9	789	1995	2.528	"
3	" " "	"	"	"	1.5795	3.9	1095	2565	2.342	"
4	Broad flat.	"	.539	.288	.9702	1.8	442	1525	3.457	"
5	" "	"	"	"	1.5092	2.8	745	2594	3.482	"

the mere starting of the spike with parallel faces does not essentially diminish the retention, when again driven into the timber to a greater depth than before. But when a bar of iron is spiked upon wood, if the spike be driven down until the bar compresses the wood to a great degree, the recoil of the latter may become so great as to start back the spike a short distance after the last blow has been given. In this case a great diminution in the usual effect will be the consequence. This shows that a limit may exist to the force which we should apply in urging down spikes or bolts destined to fasten materials together.

By comparing experiments 1 and 4 together, it will be found that weight for weight the flat spike had when driven 1.8 inches, an advantage of 42.3 per cent over the square one ; and by a like comparison of experiments 2 and 5, it is evident the former had a superiority of 37.7 per cent. As the spike when driven in only 1.9 inches had a much less proportion of its parallel faces exposed to the reaction of the fibres and a greater proportion of the wedge-shaped point, it is reasonable to expect that the retention would not correspond precisely with the lengths inserted. It will be understood that when we speak of *cutting edges* and the wedge-shaped portion of spikes, whether square, flat, or cylindrical, the direction of cutting edges is always across the fibre or grain of the timber. It must be evident that the wedge-shaped part may be so acute, as to correspond nearly with two 'parallel faces, in which case, the tendency to retreat from the lateral pressures is small ; and the pressures themselves, increasing from the point upwards to where the spike is thickest, the total efficiency of a given length may be as great as that of an equal length of the parallel faces, and even greater, provided the thickness of the spike be so considerable as in driving it to produce much crushing and irregular folding of the fibres of the timber. If, on the other hand, the edge be very blunt, the tendency to recoil may be such as to diminish the adhesion, and in this case the effect of the wedge shape is negative In the other it may be positive.*

The *first, second* and *third* experiments indicate, in the tenth column of the preceding table, that beyond a certain limit the ratio of weight of metal to extracting force

* The following formula may represent the several experiments: $R = if + c$, in which R is the observed retention; $i =$ the length in inches of the part inserted; $f =$ the force of retention on one inch of the parallel faces, and $c =$ the differences between the retention of a parallel portion of the spike, and of an equal length of the converging faces near the point. The sign of ambiguity arises from the cause above explained.

begins to diminish, showing that it would be more economical to increase the number rather than the length of the spikes, for producing a given effect in fastening materials together. In this case, also, it will be perceived, that the adhesion has a much closer relation to the areas of the compressing faces of the spikes, than to their weights. For three of the experiments this ratio may be regarded as identical, and dividing, for each of the five experiments, the observed retention by the area of the two faces opposed to the ends of the fibres, we get a mean result, which proves that the absolute retaining power of unseasoned chestnut, on square, or flat spikes of from 1.8 to 3.9 inches in length, is about 813 lbs. for every square inch of those faces which condense longitudinally the fibres of the timber.

(*To be continued.*)

LIST OF ENGLISH PATENTS GRANTED BETWEEN THE 30TH JUNE AND 26TH JULY, 1837.

Henry Augustus Wells, late of New York, but now residing in Threadneedle-street, hat manufacturer, for certain improvements in the manufacture of hats. June 30; six months.

Freeman Roe, of Camberwell, Surrey, plumber, for an improvement in water-closets. July 7.

John James Waterstone, of Millbank-street, Westminster, surveyor, for improvements applicable to the intercepting and directing of currents and waves of water. July 10.

William Pringle Green, of Falmouth, Cornwall, Lieutenant, R.N., for improvements in capstans and machinery employed in raising, lowering, and moving ponderous bodies and matters. July 10.

William Chubb, of Portsea, Hants, manufacturer, for improvements in night commode pans. July 10.

Thomas North, of Mitre-street, New-cut, Surrey, card-paper and metal piercer, for an improvement in the manufacture of wire. July 19.

Whitmore Baker, of Dedham, Essex, veterinary surgeon, for an instrument or truss applicable to the tricking of horses' tails. July 19.

John Pearse, of Tavistock, Devon, ironmonger, for an improvement or improvements in the construction of wheels. July 19.

John Hartley Hitchin and Robert Oram, of Salford, Lancaster, engineers, for certain improvements in the construction and arrangement of cranes for lifting and removing goods, by which such machines are rendered more generally useful. July 19.

John Poad Drake, of Arundel-street, Strand, artist, for improvements in building ships, steam-vessels and boats, and also in the building of canal and river barges and lighters. July 19.

Sir James Caleb Anderson, of Buttevant Castle, Cork, Baronet, for certain improvements in locomotive engines, which are partly applicable to other purposes. July 19.

Henry Goschen, of Crosby-square, Bishopsgate-street, London, merchant, for improvements in preparing flax and hemp for spinning, being a communication from a foreigner residing abroad. July 19.

Joseph Henry Tuck, of the Rainbow coffee house, London, gent., for certain improvements in apparatus or machinery for making or manufacturing candies. July 25; six months.

John Melling, of Liverpool, Lancaster, engineer. for certain improvements in locomotive steam-engines, to be used upon railways; parts of which improvements are applicable to stationary steam-engines, and to machinery in general. July 26.

LIST OF SCOTCH PATENTS GRANTED BETWEEN THE 22ND JUNE AND 22ND JULY.

Alexander Macewan, grocer and tea-merchant, Glasgow, for a process for the improvement of teas as ordinarily imported. June 26.

James Leonard Clement Thomas, of Covent Garden, Middlesex, Esq., in consequence of a communication made to him by a certain foreigner residing abroad, for an improvement applicable to steam-engines and steam generators, having for its object the economy of fuel. July 7.

John Spurgin, of Guildford-street, Russell-square, Middlesex, M.D. for an improvement or improvements in the mode or means of propelling vessels through the water, and part of which means may be applied to other useful purposes. July 14.

George Nelson, of Leamington Priors, Warwick, gent., for a certain new or improved process or processes by the use of which the qualities of a certain gelatinous substance, or certain gelatinous substances called isinglass, may be improved. July 18.

Thomas Lutwyche, of Liverpool, manufacturing chemist, for certain improvements in the construction of apparatus used in the decomposition of common salt, and in the mode or method of working or using the same. July 20.

William Bell, of Edinburgh, Esq., for improvements in heating and evaporating fluids. July 21.

James Dredge, Walcot, Bath, brewer, for certain improvements in the construction of suspension chains for bridges, viaducts, aqueducts, and other purposes, and in the construction of such bridges, viaducts or aqueducts. July 22.

LIST OF IRISH PATENTS GRANTED IN JUNE, 1837.

Joseph Bunnett, of Newington Causeway, Southwark, window-blind maker, for improvements in window-shutters, which improvements may also be applied to other useful purposes. June 5.

William Cole, of Charing Cross, Middlesex, for certain improvements in carriages for railways or tram roads.

George Crane, of Yniscedwyn iron works, near Swansea, iron-master, for improvements in the manufacturing of iron. June 13.

Nicholas Troughton, of Broad-street, in the city of London, gent., for improvements in the process of obtaining copper from copper ores. June 14.

Bennett Woodcroft, late of Ardwick, Manchester, but now of Mumps, Oldham, for improvements in the method of printing certain colours on calico and other fabrics.

NOTES AND NOTICES.

" *General Herapath*."—Sir,—I perceive from one of your Notes and Notices, that you have quite misunderstood the purport of the note which I addressed to you. It was the *soi disant* " Superintendent-General John," to whom I alluded, but I did not mean to say that it was the Chair of *Chemistry* for which he was a disappointed candidate (though perhaps quite as fit for that as any other. What I wished to point out as worthy a note was the fact (an indisputable one) that the " Superintendent-General John" was a candidate for the *Natural Philosophy* Chair in the London University; and in spite of his claim to discoveries in natural philosophy, such as have baffled all other philosophers, whether ancient or modern, was sent *to the right-about*.—I am, Sir, your constant reader, W. N. IRBY, A.M.—15th July, 1837.

Science in the East.—We observe with great pleasure, from recent Calcutta journals and papers, that the new Governor-General, Lord Auckland, has commenced giving at the " Government House," a series of weekly parties, to which "gentlemen of scientific pursuits and attainments are invited, with the view of bringing forward interesting discoveries in general science." "At the Government House!" Who—fifty years ago—would have dreamt of so beneficent a sequel to a dominion established by the sword for the sake of pelf? The " India Review," a well-conducted and most useful monthly work, lately commenced at Calcutta under the direction of Frederick Corbyn, Esq., speaks of the event in the following modest but judicious terms:—" We know there are men in this country who will differ from us in regard to our expectations as to the great ulterior good to be derived from Lord Auckland's scientific parties. There are some who conceive that in India there is a deficiency of genius and talent. Granting the assertion to be just, by way of argument, yet we contend the encouragement thus given will inspire what D'Israeli calls ' *scientific industry*,' the art which seizes, as if it were, with the rapidity of inspiration, whatever it discovers in the works of others which may enrich its own stores; which knows by a quick apprehension what to examine and what to imbibe; and which receives an atom of intelligence from the minds of others on its own mind, as an accidental spark falling on a heap of nitre, is sufficient to raise a powerful blaze."

The " *Great Western*," a steam ship, of 400-horse power, built for the purpose of running between Bristol and New York, was launched at the former place on Wednesday, July 19, in presence of upwards of 20,000 persons. She is now on her way to London to have her engines put in.

The Supplement to Vol. xxvii., containing Title, Contents, Index, &c., Medallic Portrait of his late Majesty, and Wyon's Cheselden Medal, engraved by Freebairn by Bates' patent machine, is published, price 6d. Also, Vol. xxvii., price 9s. 6d.

☞ *British and Foreign Patents taken out with economy and despatch; Specifications, Disclaimers, and Amendments, prepared or revised; Caveats entered; and generally every Branch of Patent Business promptly transacted.*

A complete list of Patents from the earliest period (15 Car. II. 1675,) *to the present time may be examined. Fee 2s. 6d.; Clients, gratis.*

LONDON: Printed and Published for the Proprietor, by W. A. Robertson, at the Mechanics' Magazine Office, No. 6, Peterborough-court, between 135 and 136, Fleet-street.—Sold by G. W. M. Reynolds, Proprietor of the French, English, and American Library, 55, Rue Neuve, Saint Augustin, Paris.

𝕸echanics' 𝕸agazine,

MUSEUM, REGISTER, JOURNAL, AND GAZETTE.

| No. 730. | SATURDAY, AUGUST 5, 1837. | Price 3d. |

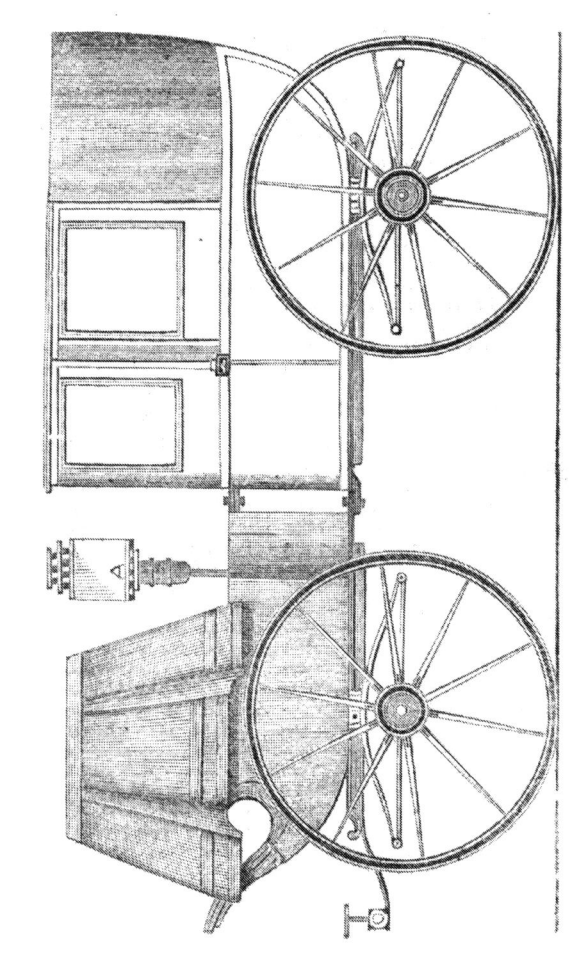

ADAMS'S EQUIROTAL TOWN CHARIOT.

ADAMS'S EQUIROTAL TOWN CHARIOT.

In our 23rd volume, p. 129, we gave a description of Mr. W. B. Adams's circular spring-wheel. We now extract from this gentleman's work on "English Pleasure Carriages," of which we commenced a critical notice in our last number, an account of another invention by him, to which that of the circular spring wheel appears to have given rise, and which promises to be of much more extensive utility; we allude to his *equirotal* carriage, so called from the wheels, both front and hind, being of the same size.

"Having been so far successful," he says, alluding to the circular-spring wheel, "in applying the wheels to a two wheeled carriage, a difficulty occurred as to their adoption to four wheeled vehicles. For hind wheels there could be no objection, as the size leaves abundant space for the springs; but in very small front wheels, the springs must necessarily be so much reduced in diameter, that they would cease to be springs and become rigid in the case of heavy carriages. For light carriages the objection would not be so great, as the metal might be very considerably reduced in thickness, in order to compensate for the reduced diameter of the springs; but still it would be disadvantageous. In this difficulty the author called to mind the fact, that wheels of unequal size to the same carriage were only a proof of defective construction; *equal sized wheels* being really the desirable point to aim at. After much reflection he constructed some models for the purpose of experiment, and ascertained that the lock or turn could be attained much more advantageously by placing the central pivot or perch bolt near the centre of the perch between the front and hind wheels, instead of placing it over the front axle, as is commonly the case. In the common mode the front wheels lock round on the perch bolt nearly at a right angle with the hind ones; and in turning, one of the hind wheels serves as a pivot, around which the front wheels describe a large circle. But when the perch bolt is placed at the centre of the total length, in the act of turning, both front and hind wheels lock together, and stand on lines forming the circumference of the circle in which the carriage is intended to turn, the two axles radiating towards a common centre. Thus, not only is the circle described by the common carriage larger than the improved one, but the resistance is greater,—in other words, the improved carriage will require less force to turn it. In the common carriage also, as the wheels must necessarily turn beneath the body, they must be kept small. In the improved carriage, with the perch bolt at a nearly equal distance between the wheels, the fore wheels have so large a radius that they do not touch the body in turning, and therefore may be made of the full size."

Mr. Adams then proceeds to describe various sorts of carriages constructed on this equirotal principle. We select for exemplification his town chariot, an engraving of which is given in our front page.

"At first sight the lines of this carriage do not appear so graceful to a superficial observer as those of the ordinary chariots, on account of the straightness of the bottom; but a closer examination will show, that with elliptic springs placed at the same horizontal level, no other line could be so advantageously adapted. The carriage is a whole composed of parts of equal sizes and proportions, and not filled in with heterogeneous ornaments for the purpose of covering defects. The central parts join together in lines which are portions of segmental curves; thus preventing a heavy appearance. The hind end curves upwards in the elliptic form; and the front, with a return curve, somewhat resembling the light figure head of a ship; thus denoting the line of progress. The lower line of the hammer-cloth is made to range with the central horizontal line of the body. The lamp, instead of being ungracefully attached to the fore part of the body, as is commonly the case, stands on a branching iron in the open space left for it between the body and the hammer cloth; thus becoming a prominent object like a classic pharos. The general harmonious appearance of the vehicle would, with unprejudiced observers, immediately obtain for it a preference over ordinary carriages, saying nothing of its mechanical advantages; but the eye, after being long accustomed to arbitrary forms, seldom remains unprejudiced, and it is difficult to divest ourselves of attachments that have grown on us by the force of habit. Thus, many persons are still found to prefer the barbarous grotesquerie which has caricatured the true Louis Quatorze taste, and to look with contempt, alike on the beauty of Greek simplicity and Gothic art.

"But leaving all questions of external appearance to be decided on their own merits, and taking the mechanical advantages for granted, the question of comfort remains to be considered. In this point of view, the carriage will be found to possess qualities not attainable in any of the ordinary vehicles. Though appearing larger than an ordinary chariot, it actually stands on a less space of ground, the axles being one foot nearer to each other than is commonly the case. But the whole of the length is usefully occupied. The body for the sitters, instead of being a cramped box, confining the limbs, as the ordinary chariots do, is in reality more nearly approaching the form of an apartment, being sufficient for two persons of the very largest size to recline at full length, without incommoding each other; while the bottom is straight like an ordinary floor. Britzschkas, it is true, also afford a facility for reclining at full length; but from want of space above for air, they are almost suffocating to the passenger; whereas, in this kind of chariot, ample space is afforded for air. On looking at the engraving, it will be seen that the ordinary appearance of the side door is preserved, though it is not in reality a door, but merely a window to draw up and down as usual. From the fore part of this apparent door the body is continued forward in a circular form, and thus the interior presents a large bow front, with a window on either hand, through which a perfect view is obtained on all sides. The floor of the body is in fact in the form of a horse-shoe. The doors open in the bow front on either side. This body is well capable of accommodating four or six people; and the locker in front will hold a very large quantity of luggage; while the coachman and footman go on the box. If required, a stand for the footman might easily be attached behind, by light iron stays or brackets. On a journey, imperials might be placed on the roof, and also on the fore locker; and supposing two persons only to occupy the interior, they might have a very convenient table before them. In addition to this, the author has contrived a very simple arrangement, by means of a large lamp below the bottom, to heat small water pipes carried round the interior, and thus maintain a comfortable warmth in the winter time. The ordinary mode of constructing carriages will scarcely permit this."

MACKINTOSH'S ELECTRICAL THEORY.
MR. THORNE'S REPLY TO A COUNTRY TEACHER.

Sir,—I read the last letter of your correspondent, the "Country Teacher," with satisfaction, for it made me see more plainly than ever, the manner in which he means to treat the propositions contained in the Electrical Theory; his style of answering these propositions may certainly mislead the unwary and unthinking, but I feel assured that it will be of no avail, when men duly qualified shall have to decide. The compliment which the "Country Teacher" has paid the Cambridge Professors, is certainly very flattering to them; but are we to judge, that because one is rather rash in giving opinions upon subjects which he has not duly considered, that he is consequently disabled from giving his opinion upon a subject with which he may be well acquainted? The attainments of Professor Faraday in electricity cannot be questioned. For my own part, I think he is one of the best fitted to form a judgment, and glad I am that this part of the theory has one, whose opinion is of so much weight, for its advocate. I am obliged to the "Country Teacher" for the information which he thinks he gives me, when he tells me that his authority is Newton; and that the principles of the equation "are as well known as that the three angles" &c.; but let me tell him, that although I might know, perhaps as well as himself, that the principles were generally known, still I might not be assured that these principles were correct, and therefore feel justified in rejecting them, as many eminent men have done before me—until I should be convinced of their correctness. I am not inclined to take the *ipse dixit* of any man, or set of men, but shall judge for myself, with their assistance. Similar dogmas to those of the school of Aristotle will not do for this age; for, although Newton, the master, may have said so, his authority cannot be taken on all occasions. The disciples of Newton, like those of Aristotle, venerate and worship their master, rather too much. If Newton had been perfect, the memory of Dolland and others would not have been immortalised. Newton certainly was a great man, and forwarded science in an especial manner, and as such, he will ever be respected.

The "Country Teacher" I find is rather inclined to concede the point, that the moon is not a solid body, and consequently, if it were deposited, the covering would not be so deep or thick as he stated; and also that the moon is the same in relative weight, whether hollow or solid. He says, that were it hollow, the depth of the covering would be diminished, but the weight would remain the same; and, as he calculates, each square foot would have to bear a pressure of 13.627 tons. Had not the "Country Teacher" penetration enough to perceive that such an admission is nearly all that was wanted to confirm my views with respect to the pressure and contortion of the strata? I asked (and the "Country Teacher" has given the answer, perhaps unwittingly), where the force requisite for this pressure was obtained? He answers, that every square foot would undergo by the deposition of a satellite, a pressure of 13.627 tons. This is a pressure quite sufficient to flatten the head of the *crocodilus priscus*, to which I alluded in my first letter.

I think I can perceive the meaning of the "Country Teacher's" observations on my remarks upon solidity and density; however, as yet I see no reason for relinquishing my opinions, nor shall I relinquish them, until some good reason presents itself. The opinions may be strange, but there are many strange things true. Did he ever remark the regular gradation of the density of the planets? If he has not, I can tell him, that it is even more regular than the number of moons: allowing the density of the sun to be $\frac{1}{4}$, within small fractions, Mercury is as 2, Venus $1\frac{1}{4}$, Earth 1, Mars .7, Jupiter .23, Saturn .02, Herschell not yet precisely calculated. Did the "Country Teacher" ever inquire into the cause of this regularly increasing density, for surely there must be some cause?

I did not mean at first to enter into a controversy upon Mr. Mackintosh's theory, of this kind; I intended not to advocate any particular point to the prejudice of another,—but to advocate it as a whole, whose principle feature is, the precipitation of the secondary on the primary bodies. In so doing, I have brought forward as proofs, geological phenomena, which appeared to me could have no other cause than these depositions. The "Country Teacher" will, I am sure, allow that what I have deduced from geology are facts. Although there may have been a great deal of "guess work" in the theories to explain the facts I have deduced, the facts were not guessed at, but observed. There are many geological phenomena which I own are yet not duly explained, but that they soon will be, appears a matter of certainty. The ground of argument I have taken in respect to the Electrical Theory,

gives but very little room for the exercise of mathematical talents; and I am afraid, that it is because geology depends so little upon the abstract sciences, it has conjured up the ire of those who would wish to appear before the world as profound mathematicians; and who desire it to be thought, that, with this knowledge alone can any problem be solved, whether relative to the state or motion of the heavenly bodies, to the construction of the globe, or even any thing which may be produced upon its surface. I shall answer the "Country Teacher" no further, unless he decidedly argues that there is no such thing as the acceleration of the moon, and that the phenomena I have mentioned, are mere fictions.

I remain, Sir,
Yours respectfully,
JOSHUA THORNE.

IMPROVEMENTS IN PUNCTUATION.

SIR,—It is certainly a remarkable thing, that while language itself is so proverbially subject to change, many of the little arts connected with its incorporation and preservation, are so particularly stationary. In nothing, I think, is this more striking than in the art of punctuation. For many years, nay, for many centuries, it has remained quite immoveable, and appears to have come altogether to a full stop. Judging from this circumstance, and from that of the same systems being so generally received by the different nations of Europe, one would be led to suppose that the art had arrived at the point of perfection; but will any one maintain that this is really the case? To me it appears full of imperfections. In thinking over the subject a few days ago, a few suggestions for improvement occurred to me, which, with your permission, Mr. Editor, I will proceed to point out.

The Spaniards have already introduced one improvement, which might, I think, be universally adopted with advantage. To every sentence which has a note of interrogation at the end, they affix an inverted note of interrogation at the beginning. This is indeed peculiarly necessary in their language, in which the words stand in the same order whether the purport of the sentence be interrogative or informative; so that, for instance, "*Muiró el Rey*," may mean either, "did the king die?" or "the king died." But the principle will apply in all languages—wherever it is needful to have one note of interrogation, it is quite as needful to have two. It is as necessary to show where a question begins as where it ends, perhaps still more so, in order that the reader may know in time to change his tone accordingly. In fact, though custom has reconciled us to the present usage, it is almost as bad as, if instead of two, we used only one bracket to mark a parenthesis. The same reasons that apply to the note of interrogation, will, of course, apply to that of exclamation.

A third "note" of an entirely new description, would, I think, be still more useful than either of the two already introduced. I have heard many passages murdered in reading, from the want of a mark of irony. Wherever this figure of speech is intended, it demands a total change of the voice—and it is for the very purpose of apprising the reader where changes of the voice are necessary, —where the author, if he were speaking instead of writing, would make use of them—that the whole system of punctuation has been instituted. The omission of a mark of irony, therefore, is a glaring defect, for which I hope some ingenious printer may, ere long, devise and introduce a remedy. He will have an opportunity of displaying his taste by selecting an elegant shape for the novel mark, which, of course, like the others, should be used both at the beginning and end of the passage it applies to.

My next alteration is the most important one I have to propose, for it would affect almost every sentence in every work. It is, however, merely an extension of the same principle which has already been recognised in the case of the parenthesis. Most sentences contain a number of parentheses, which are merely marked by the insertion of commas at every pause. I would propose, that in every case the *commencement* of these should be marked by an inverted comma thus, , while the *conclusion* should be pointed out by one in the ordinary shape. One instance will show what I mean. The following is taken from the article on copyrights in your 723rd Number, page 170. It is pointed thus:

" Yet, so it is, that while patentees are apparently left to struggle unpitied with all the ills that flesh is heir to, Mr. Serjeant Talfourd not only proposes, with apparently every chance of success, to confer on authors,—already in comparison so highly favoured,—a number of still additional favours, but maintains, that even then, they will be hardly treated."

I would propose to point thus :

" Yet so it is, that , while patentees are apparently left to struggle unpitied with all the ills that flesh is heir to, Mr. Serjeant Talfourd not only proposes , with apparently every chance of success, to confer on authors , already in comparison so highly favoured, a number of still additional favours, but maintains that , even then, they will be hardly treated."

Were this alteration introduced, it strikes me that the theory of punctuation would be rendered much more simple, and its practice much more easy. I, for one, am often puzzled under the present system to know where to place my commas. Your printers, will, I believe, be generally considered right in pointing the words, "but maintains, that even then," in the manner that they have done; that is, with a comma after " maintains" and none after " that ;" yet if a comma is intended to mark a pause, there surely ought to be none between " maintains" and " that," and there ought to be one between " that" and " even then," which latter two words, form in themselves a little parenthesis, and ought to be separated somehow. You will observe, that in my punctuation of the passage, the two little dashes which occur in the original are left out. They are in fact merely a defective way of supplying the same want which I propose to remedy in what appears to me a better. They serve the purpose of marking a slight parenthesis with the disadvantage of having the same mark at commencement and close; the very objection which applies to the comma as now used in similar cases.

It may perhaps be suggested that it would be better to employ two marks altogether new for this purpose instead of retaining one of the old ones. The remark may have some justice, but it is dangerous to propose too many innovations at once, and I have been afraid of affronting the prejudices of the eye.

I will only add, in conclusion, that the

hyphen might certainly be more liberally employed than it is now. In a former part of this letter the expression occurs "in thinking over the subject." The word over is here not an independent preposition, but an affix to the verb, and it would be better to write "thinking-over." Thus we should write without a hyphen, that a man "runs down" stairs, but with one, that one ship "runs-down"

another. In all the other Teutonic languages, also, such a compound as "coal and potatoe-dealer" would be written, "coal- and potatoe-dealer," with a hyphen after coal. But it is time to come to a period.

I remain yours,
Punctually,

NAUTICUS'S ASTRONOMICAL QUESTION.

Sir,—Your correspondents, Nautilus and O. N., have each of them said far more upon Nauticus's astronomical question than was really necessary. There have been faults on both sides. The only object I conceive that Nauticus had in view in proposing the question, was, to obtain an easy practical solution of it, and any one acquainted with spherical trigonometry might easily solve the question. Thus, in the spherical triangle P P′ D (see O. N.'s, diagram, page 244) we have given the two sides P D, P′ D and the included angle P′ P D, the angle P P′ D may be found, and in the triangle Z P P′, we have then given the two sides Z P, P P′ and the angle Z P′ P; hence the required angle Z P P′ can be found. All this is easy enough, although I must confess the calculation would be tiresome. The object therefore should be to determine the angle Z P P′ with the least possible cal-

culation. Nautilus has tried to do so in his solution (No. 726), but I must inform him that he has not discovered the shortest way in finding the required angle Z P P′. The following solution of Nauticus's question will convince him of this.

Call the polar distance of the lower and upper stars, a and b, A the difference of the their right ascension. L, the latitude of the place of observation. Then find x. So that,

1st, $\text{Tan } x = \text{Cosec } (a+b)$. $\text{Sin } (a-b)$. $\text{Cotan } \left(\dfrac{A}{2}\right)$

2nd, Find y. So that

$$\text{Cos } y = \text{Cos } \left(\dfrac{A}{2}-x\right) \text{ Tan } C.$$

$\text{Tan } L$. Then $y-\left(\dfrac{A}{2}-x\right) = $ hour angle

Z P P′ from which the time of observation is known.

Solution.

$(a+b)$	40°..13′..00″	Cosec ..	10,189983
$(a-b)$	37 .. 6 ..42	Sin ..	9,780514
$\dfrac{A}{2}$	53 ..29 ..15	Cotan ..	9.869407
x ..	34 ..40°..30	Tan ..	9.839974
$A-x$..	18 ..48 ..45	Cos ..	9,839957
$\dfrac{b}{2}$ ..	1 ..33 ..18	Tan ..	8,433714
L ..	51 ..30 ..00	Tan ..	10,099395
y ..	88 .. 8 ..56	Cos ..	8,509266

∴ 88.. 8.. 56—18—48.. 45=69°.. 20.. 11″=hour angle Z P P′. Differing from that of Nautilus by something less than 3½ seconds of time.

There are certain modifications in the above practical rule, which arise from this circumstance. The only auxiliary great circle that is required to be drawn is a perpendicular from P upon Z D. Now this perpendicular, according to the nature of the question, may fall between

D and P′, or between P′ and Z, or upon D Z produced (which last supposition would be the case in O. N.'s question). In my next communication I shall give a demonstration of the above, and point out the necessary modifications that can take place in the different varieties which may take place. Perhaps Nautilus will favour us with a demonstration of the above rule, or O. N. will try to do so; or if he will give us a demonstration of Nautilus's practical rule I shall forgive him for the mistakes he has formerly committed.

I am, Sir, yours, &c.

IVER M'IVER.

July 21, 1837.

VENTILATION.

Sir,—If any of your readers can help me out of a difficulty in which I am at present placed, I shall be much indebted to them, and the inquiry may perhaps lead to an improved method of ventilation. I have just put up a ventilator in an infant school of too limited dimensions, hoping thereby to relieve the excessive closeness and heat of the apartment. It is on the principle of Archimedes' screw; a helix of tin plate nearly 11 inches diameter, is wound round a small wooden cylinder, making four turns. This revolves within a cylinder of tin, let into, and fixed securely in, the wall. A pulley on the axis of the ventilator (3 inches diameter) is driven by a wheel 2 feet diameter; this is turned by one of the children who are delighted by an occasional permission to work it. The distance between the coils of the helix is about an inch and a half, and there is a space of about a quarter of an anch between their edges and the enclosing cylinder. Being made to revolve with ease about 500 times in a minute, I concluded that it must (as it were) screw the foul air out of the room; but scarcely any perceptible effect is produced.

I will take this opportunity of noticing that Mr. Woodhouse's rotary engine (described in your last Number) is not new. I have no doubt that he believed it to be so, but in the Register of Arts, vol. 1, New Series, he will find the exact counterpart of his invention in the shape of an engine patented in 1827, by Mr. Elijah Galloway; the only difference worth noticing, being that in Mr. G.'s engine, the piston and excentric guide revolve while the cylinder remains stationary.

The insertion of the above inquiry in your widely-circulated journal will much oblige,

Sir, your obedient servant,

J. R.

London, 26th July, 1837.

OLD AND NEW SYSTEMS OF FIRE EXTINCTION IN LONDON.

Sir,—I am well aware that it would not answer the purpose of "Aquarius" to be put right, and therefore I might spare myself any pains upon this head. At the same time I should be sorry for your readers generally to suppose that I had descended to a "mere quibble" respecting the Old and New systems of fire extinction in London, as charged upon me at page 250. The real fact, as can be proved beyond all question, is as I have already stated viz.; that the old system of firemen, &c., continued from the beginning of the eighteenth century up to the 31st December, 1832, after which day, a different system came into full and efficient operation. The partial reduction in the number of men and engines, made by some of the principal insurance conpanies in the course of 1829-30 (which Aquarius, in spite of truth and common sense, will insist upon calling a new system) was of the following nature: three of the largest fire-offices, that had been in the habit of running four engines each, for certain reasons agreed to drop one each, and only to run two engines to every fire between three offices, the firemen mutually cooperating and assisting one another, but each acting under their respective foremen. No change whatever took place in the system, which continued in every respect the same as it had been for a century previous, till January 1st. 1833 when the new system commenced, without any previous preparation, or intermediate transition, possessing no one feature in common with that which had so long preceeded it. The change of 1829-30 was a virtual reduction of the force, the new system of 1833 was a positive increase; the present fire-establishment continually paying more hands than were ever employed under the Old system.

"Aquarius" has more than once most unjustly intimated that Mr. Baddeley has evidently changed his opinion on this subject; allow me, Sir, to say that my opinions on this subject remain altogether unchanged; in proof of which I can appeal with confidence to all that I have either said or written in your pages and elsewhere: as also to many persons who have known my sentiments both longer and better than "Aquarius."

I have always held, and still hold, that

it is a disgrace to our legislature, that the protection from fire of the lives and property of the inhabitants of this metropolis* should be permitted to depend entirely upon the enterprise or caprice of a few trading companies; to whose gratuitous assistance the public are indebted far more deeply than they choose to acknowledge.

I remain, Sir,

Yours respectfully,

WM. BADDELEY.

London, July 25th, 1837.

P. S. I am sorry to find that some inconvenience has, in more than one instance, occurred from figs. 2 and 3 of Bunnett's patent revolving safety shutters, having been printed upside down, at page 177, through some inadvertence, and I take this opportunity of pointing out the mistake.

BUOYANT FLOAT PADDLE-WHEEL.

Sir,—Through your useful Magazine I beg leave to communicate a new kind of paddle-wheel. I think it not improbable that it will supersede all others, and that its powers will prove so great that boats and large vessels may be propelled with it by manual labor; and applied to steam-vessels, it will most materially lessen the power of steam required for other paddles, consequently save expense, and lessen the danger of a greater force of steam.

The principle of the plan is to bring into action the resistance of a buoyant body, for instance, a barrel, a hollow cylinder, or a globe, instead of the float of the common paddle-wheel; the pressure of the cylinders, being brought successively into action as the wheel revolves, at one time acting as an opposing power on the water to force the vessel forward, and then acting by their buoyancy in raising themselves, and aiding the working of the following cylinders. Assuming that the resistance of buoyant bodies will be greater than dead floats of the common paddle-wheel, and that the action of the buoyant body will relieve, or in a great degree get rid of, what is called the back water, the increase of power in the buoyant paddle-

wheel may be carried to any extent that you can construct cylinders, with safety.

The plan itself consists of a wheel with separate hollow buoyant barrels or cylinders, in place of the common paddle floats.

It is applicable to common paddle-wheels, and to any steam-vessel; but I advise it to be tried in a double boat by applying it between the two vessels. It may be placed so as to be taken out of the water when not working. In a small boat it may be worked by a crank handle on each side. The barrels or cylinders may be placed either horizontally or vertically. Five buoyant floats may be sufficient for a small wheel, but larger wheels will require more; and the velocity, with which common paddle-wheels work, will not be required, the force of the buoyant body being so much more efficacious than the dead float.

I give my plan through your meritorious work to the public, that they may have the advantage of it, without any patent right being taken out. Of the success of the plan there can be no doubt, for I have tried the effect of the buoyant float, upon a wheel with corks; a wheel with a string wound round it, and moved by the weight of a piece of lead, ran over the water, carrying the lead through the water with it; proving its motive quality and force, to be sufficient to bring with it the weight that moves it.

I am, Sir, yours, &c.

AN OLD CORRESPONDENT.

July 29th. 1837.

SIMPLE OXYHYDROGEN BLOW PIPE.

Sir,—As a constant reader of your valuable Magazine I beg to acknowledge the receipt of many useful hints; and shall be happy if in my turn, I can throw out something which may be useful to your numerous readers.

A friend of mine (C. Ingledew of Brighton) in using an oxy-hydrogen blow-pipe a short time since, adopted an arrangement which in my opinion, is exceedingly simple and compact: and, as it can be constructed at little expense I presume a sketch and description will not be altogether unserviceable to the scientific student.

I remain, Sir,

Yours &c.

SCIOLISTERUS.

Clapham, June 10th. 1837

---

* Even the small (though ancient) city of Chester has a regular " FIRE POLICE", for whom Mr. Tilley has just completed a splendid new fire-engine of the most approved kind.

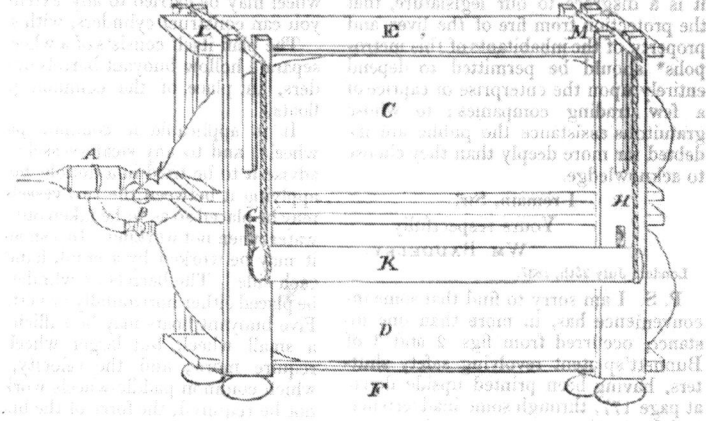

Description of the Engraving.

A represents Daniels' safety jet, (fitted with stopcocks to regulate the supply of either gas) firmly held by a screw in the projecting arm B. The gases are contained in the bladders C D, and the bladders are confined between the moveable boards E F; to the under side of F are attached the cords G H; these after passing over pulleys, shown in the side of the frame, pass under pulleys fixed to the ends of the weight K, and are attached to the projecting extremities of the cross pieces L M.

The action is so simple that I think it requires but little explanation. By the descent of the weights (of which only one can be seen in the diagram) the under board is drawn up, while at the same time the upper one is pulled down and thus both gases are simultaneously forced out.

In the diagram, two boards are represented in the centre of the frame; but I have just completed a blow-pipe in which I have placed only a single board with a small projecting piece, to which I have screwed the arm B; this perhaps will answer every purpose. A small hook might with advantage be placed in the centre of the weight K, to ease the pressure on the bladders occasionally, by hanging it on the centre board.

THE LATE FATAL PARACHUTE DESCENT.

(Further particulars, extracted from the evidence taken at the Inquest on the body of Mr. Cocking).

John Chamberlain, shepherd to Mr. Norman, of Burnt Ash Farm, in the parish of Lee, said that on Monday last, about a quarter past 9 o'clock, he saw the balloon and something hanging from it, which presently fell. At first it came down like thunder, that is with respect to the noise; it frightened all the sheep. It appeared to come down in a lump together, and he thought it turned over and came down on the slant. By the time it reached the ground he had got over the hedge, so that he could see it fall. The basket, or car, touched the ground first, and the other part of the parachute fell partly upon it. The machinery was broken to pieces, and covered a large space of ground. The deceased was in the basket up to his chest, with his head, of course, out; he was lying on his back, and the basket appeared to protect the body from any weight. He could not say whether the basket came down on the edge, or the bottom.

Mr. F. C. Finch, surgeon, of Greenwich, stated that his attention was directed to the balloon at a distance of half a mile. He saw the parachute detached and fall to the ground, where he thought he and his father arrived about two minutes after the descent. When he first saw the parachute it was descending very steadily, but it presently began to change its position, and assumed that of an oyster-shell diving through the water. It was coming down in a shelving manner, and made several gyrations, and then appeared to collapse, the circumference having given way. He should say that it turned over. He should think that the balloon, at the time of the detachment, was about a mile and a half high. The air appeared to afford more resistance to the car in which the deceased was than to the margin of the parachute itself. A very few seconds had elapsed from the time it was detached before it collapsed. It appeared on an exmination of the car that the deceased pitched on his feet. The injuries (which, in the opinion of witness, caused the death of the deceased) were received when he reached the ground. Indeed he did not see what was to kill him before. His moral life might have been gone but not his physical life. They knew of cases on a rail-road where there was an enormous speed without loss of life. The rail-road at Manchester, for instance. There it had been no uncommon thing for persons to travel at the rate of 60 miles an hour, without loss of life. Now, according to the statements, it was clear that the deceased descended only at the rate of 30, and therefore it must be perfectly apparent that the velocity of the journey could not have caused death.

By the Jury.—Was of opinion that the velocity that the deceased came down could not kill him. If he had been stopped in the same ratio as that with which he was descending he had no doubt of the deceased's coming down with safety.

Professor Airy, Astronomer Royal.— From the Observatory at Greenwich he saw the balloon shortly after its ascent from Vauxhall; the wind was then due west; but as the balloon rose he remarked that it appeared to come from the north. He took his eyes away from it for a short space of time, and when he again looked towards its direction he saw that the course was N. N. W. With regard to the parachute he was much surprised at its appearance, because he could not see the man who was said to have gone up in it. At this time he was using a common telescope. He presently heard a shout in the Park below him, and on looking up again he saw that the parachute had been cut away from the balloon; it very quickly changed its shape; it did not retain its original appearance more 3 or 4 seconds. He was quite confident that as far as it was possible to judge of time on such an occasion that was the extent, and he was fully borne out in his opinion by the ladies of his family, all of whom witnessed the sight. When they next came to look at the parachute it was in a collapsed state. The appearance it then presented was that of an umbrella about three parts closed, and

one portion of the canvass was flickering about with great violence. He watched the decent about half a minute, when he lost it behind the trees. He nevertheless exclaimed to his family that the person in it was certainly a dead man. He instantly put on his hat and walked over to Lee, where his expectation was realized. He was perfectly confident that the car could not have turned over, because had that been the case the party must inevitably have been thrown out. The car itself, too, would have got into some strange position. The parachute when he lost sight of it had come down about three-fourths of its space. It had gone down steadily, although it might have been sloping off from himself. It was difficult to estimate the best construction of such a machine, but in this of Mr. Cocking it had no power to set itself right, supposing it to be disturbed. If flattened by the air on one side, the regular forces acting upon it would make the danger the greater; the ring surrounding this was made of a tin tube hollow all the way round, he supposed for stiffness, but such tubes never should be trusted without stops which would enable them to resist tremor; if once flattened in the sides by a dent, they were highly dangerous. The tube was as bad a thing as could have been used; whalebone would have been much more desirable. He much preferred the principle of the old parachute to that used by Mr Cocking, as containing within itself the means of becoming right if meeting a trivial injury, whereas the present was the reverse.

Mr. Gye, one of the proprietors of Vauxhall, produced the following agreement, which was in Mr. Cocking's own handwriting :—

" Agreement made between Frederick Gye and Richard Hughes, esquires, of Vauxhall Gardens, on the one part, and Robert Cocking, gentleman, of No. 1, South-island-place, North Brixton, on the other. The said Robert Cocking undertakes to superintend and assist at the construction of a parachute of his own invention, on an entirely new principle, the expense of which parachute to be defrayed by the above Frederick Gye and Richard Hughes, and to be their exclusive property, subject to the following conditions; namely, the aforesaid Frederick Gye and Richard Hughes, bind themselves to the said Robert Cocking, on no account whatever to employ any other person or persons to make a descent or descents with the above-named parachute but the aforesaid Robert Cocking; and the said Robert Cocking binds himself to make his first ascent free of all demands or remuneration from Messrs. Gye and Hughes, except what may be occasioned by conveying back the para-

chute then and at all times to Vauxhall
Gardens ; and the above-named Frederick
Gye and Richard Hughes bind themselves to
pay to the said Robert Cocking, for the two
following descents after the first, the sum of
twenty guineas for each descent, and that
afterwards on all future descents with a
parachute, the said Messrs. Gye and Hughes
will pay to the said Robert Cocking the sum
of 30*l*. ; and the said Robert Cocking binds
himself to make descent with the parachute
as often as Messrs. Gye and Hughes shall
think proper (fair wind and weather always
considered) ; and the said Robert Cocking
binds himself not to construct a parachute,
or make descents for any other person or persons whatever but to the said Frederick Gye
and Richard Hughes ; and the above Robert
Cocking; further, to make descents in any
part of England, or on the continent, if required by Messrs. Gye and Hughes, for the
above-named sum of 30*l*.

    " (Signed)   ROBERT COCKING.
" July 21, 1837."

The Coroner here inquired the time that
the construction was commenced.

Mr. Gye could not exactly say the actual
time that the apparatus was commenced,
but Mr. Cocking was backward and forward with his plans, drawings, and calculations, about three weeks or a month.

The Coroner.—Who constructed the parachute ?

Mr. Gye.—It was made entirely under
superintendence of Mr. Cocking himself,
who did not wish that any one else should
interfere.

The Coroner.—Did you ever perceive that
Mr. Cocking had any misgivings as to the
success of his experiment ?

Mr. Gye.—I never saw a man so calm
and collected in my life as Mr. Cocking was
up to the last moment.

The Coroner.—Did you ever have any
conversation with the deceased as to the
chance of the experiment having a fatal termination ?

Mr. Gye.—I never anticipated a fatal result.

The Coroner.—Did any conversation take
place as to when the day should be fixed
whether Mr. Cocking should be obliged,
under all circumstances, to descend, or be
at liberty to change his mind ?

Mr. Gye.—None, for although this agreement was written two months ago, still it
was not signed till last Friday, and as late
as four o'clock on the day of the descent, I
had some communication with Mr. Cocking,
in the hearing not only of some of our workmen, but of two of that gentleman's particular friends, who have kindly attended here

to-day, in order, if you think it necessary,
to confirm my statement. (The coroner
and jury, however, appeared to feel so satisfied with the evidence of the witness as not
to think it necessary that either of these parties should be called). The conversation to
which I allude was couched, as near as I can
recollect, in the following words :—I said,
" Mr. Cocking, since you have been in these
gardens, you have probably acquired some
practical experience ; and if you now think
that your calculations are not likely to prove
correct, that you have not so much surface
as you think fit, that the machine is not of
sufficient strength, or that your nerves should
fail you, or that from any cause whatever
you would rather decline making the experiment, I beg of you to say so. Do not allow
any idea of disappointing the public, or of
any disgrace falling upon the Gardens, in
consequence of such a determination ; I will
willingly take the risk of that upon myself,
for they had better pull the Gardens to pieces
than that an accident should happen. If it
were to become necessary, we would return
the visiters the money they have paid."
Mr. Cocking replied, " My dear fellow, this
is very kind of you, but you know I have
shown my calculations to several scientific
friends, and I am fully satisfied of their accuracy." I then said, " There is one thing,
then, that I shall insist upon ;—if we succeed in removing the parachute from here
(it was then in one corner of the balloon-
ground) to the grass plot, and in getting it
safe out of the Gardens, and it stands the
pressure in ascending, I have not the slightest doubt but you will descend in perfect
safety ; but in case any thing should give
way during the ascent, or that at the last
moment you should feel disposed to abandon
the experiment from any nervous feeling, I
shall have a rope ladder put into Mr. Green's
car, up which you can climb and descend
safely with him in the balloon." Thinking
that his supposing himself to be the cause
of a public disappointment might induce him
to persist in making the descent against his
real wish, I laid out the following plan for
adoption, and arranged with Mr. Green accordingly. It was this :—Mr. Green was
to lower by a rope bags of ballast, equal to
the weight of Mr. Cocking, into the car of
the parachute, taking care, however, not to
separate the rope until Mr. Cocking had
ascended the rope ladder, but merely to
allow the ballast to hang so far down in the
car, that when the rope was cut, it should
fall to the bottom. This precaution was
necessary, as, if the weight of the ballast
had been on the car of the parachute before it had been relieved of Mr. Cocking's
weight, there would have been just double

the strain it was intended to encounter. Mr. Green approved of this plan, but made the very proper suggestion, which was adopted, that pullies and ropes should be substituted for the rope ladder; so that in case Mr. Cocking should be at all nervous, his reaching the car of the balloon should not depend solely on his own exertions, but that Mr. Green and Mr. Spencer should haul him up. As soon as Mr. Cocking was safe in the car, the parachute was to be liberated, and the public would be as much gratified as though Mr. Cocking had himself descended, with which it is possible they might never have become acquainted.

The Coroner.—Was this apparatus put into the car?

Mr. Gye.—I put it in myself.

The Coroner.—Was there not some apparatus attached to the parachute in order to guide it?

Mr. Gye.—Yes, there was, and that Mr. Cocking regarded as the most beautiful part of his invention. The witness here explained, that this effect was produced by the ropes which attached the car to the parachute passing through several blocks or pullies, which enabled Mr. Cocking to throw his whole weight on one side of the machine, and by altering the centre of gravity, make the instrument assume the form of an inclined plane. Mr. Gye then went on. Mr. Cocking made an experiment in my presence, which proved to me the capability of his machinery to produce the desired effect, for his model not only varied its course in the direction of the wind, but actually scaled down against it. [To illustrate the above, the witness produced two models of exquisite workmanship, made by the deceased, and which, as the witness observed, would go very far in producing a favourable opinion of his ability on the mind of any person, especially with regard to the subject of the present investigation].

The Coroner.—Pray, was not the upper ring of the parachute broken previous to the ascent?

Mr. Gye.—Bent, but not broken.

The Coroner.—How was this done?

Mr. Gye.—In order to move it from one part of the ground to the other, it was necessary to support it by men carrying short poles, and in consequence of the wind suddenly catching it, the whole weight of the parachute was thrown on one of these poles, the point of which had only two square inches of surface. These indentations were mended, and Mr. Cocking told Mr. Green that those were the strongest parts, and it has proved to be so, for the jury must have seen, on examining the remains of the tube, that it has not given way in any one of these

parts. The witness now produced two drawings by the deceased, and, at the wish of the coroner, explained the reasons given by Mr. Cocking for conceiving his own parachute to be superior to that of Garnerin. It was substantially this; that when the proper position of the old parachute was disturbed during its descent, and an oscillation commenced, the column of air underneath it became greater on the elevated side, therefore the constant effect was to increase that oscillation; but with the new parachute, the column of air became greater under the depressed side, and consequently had a tendency to raise it again into its proper position. Garnerin, whose weight was about that of the deceased, made his parachute, as I have been given to understand, 28 feet in diameter, Mr. Cockings was 34 feet, and which, if any gentleman present will be kind enough to make the calculation, will be found to give an immense increase of surface.

The Coroner.—Can you inform us whether there were any stops in the tin to prevent its collapsing?

Mr. Gye.—There were none. Mr. Cocking ordered every part of the material himself, and considered the tin tube strong enough without the stops; and I think the jury will be convinced that it was so by a test to which I will now submit a portion of it. The witness here produced a piece of tube three feet in length, on which were two joints in addition to the seam, and holding one extremity in his hand, requested a juror to take up the other. He then suspended a half hundred weight on its centre, without the least impression being made on the tube. A second was next suspended, but neither fracture nor indentation took place, and Mr. Gye stated his belief that it would well bear a third pressure of equal weight. The witness went on, at the request of the Coroner, to state that he had formed his opinion as to the cause of the accident, and having mentioned it to Mr. Green, found that he entertained the same. It was this,—that the deceased had, contrary to the caution given by himself, twisted the trigger line, by which he was to release the parachute, round his arm, and had thereby been pulled up out of the car as far as the ropes immediately above the lower hoop would allow his body to pass. The whole weight of the apparatus, as well as that of the deceased, instantly came upon this thin line, and it of course broke. The deceased then would naturally have descended much faster than the parachute, and as the car was directly underneath, must have fallen into it, and Mr. Gye was of opinion, that by his fall, which was about 11 feet, the ancle bone was broken. This fall produced a sudden jerk upon the parachute, and gave to the upper hoop a strain which it was never anticipated it would have to encounter. The deceased then being unable to bear his weight upon his legs, according to Mr. Gye's opinion, seems to have rested his chest upon the edge of the basket, and thereby caused the dreadful fractures on coming to the ground, noticed in the *post mortem* examination. The witness first conceived this idea of the accident from having been informed that a rope was found twisted round the wrist of the deceased ; but not succeeding in discovering the person who actually saw it, he, on Wednesday, at the suggestion of Mr. Green, in company with Mr. Spencer, and two friends of the deceased, examined the left wrist of the corpse, and found a deep indentation corresponding with the size of the trigger line around it. He thought the pressure on the parachute in ascending would be greater than that in descending, but was aware that on this, Professor Airy entertained a different opinion.

Mr. Monck Mason stated that he had taken an anxious, and, indeed, a painful interest, in the proceeding, from the certainty with which he had been long led to regard the result. In his opinion, whether the machine had broken in the descent or not, the main result would have been the same ; the insufficiency of the parachute to support the individual within the limits of velocity required by nature for the preservation of life was the real cause of the catastrophe. The rupture of the machine was merely an accident which had occurred during the consummation of his fate. So far from having been influenced in his opinions by the consideration of its strength; the conclusion to which he had arrived regarding the insufficiency of the means about to be employed was not only determined, but made known to the public before he had ever seen the parachute, or had any idea of the strength of the materials employed in its construction. He made known the result of his calculations some time previously; he informed Mr. Green of them ; on the night before the ascent, he communicated them to the public press*, in the hopes that

they might make a more powerful impression upon the parties concerned, as bearing with them the stamp of authority, which a public declaration of opinion always confers, and also in the hope that the public, being acquainted with the results, might be the more readily inclined to sanction the withdrawal of the attempt, if not absolutely to interfere to prevent it. Finding his remonstrances unavailing, on the following evening (the day of the ascent) he went to the Gardens, with the view of personally drawing the attention of the parties to the imminence of the case. He saw Mr. Cocking, and expostulated with him seriously upon his design. Mr. Cocking replied, that his friends had made experiments, and that he was fully satisfied of their correctness. He entreated him to observe, that the case was not one for experiment, but for calculations; the experimental part had long been determined. Mr. Cocking replied, as before, that he had no doubt

---

conclusion of the article "Aeronautics." Its principle seems to be an inversion of the preceding ones, in which the surface of least resistance is made to descend foremost. The chief object of this arrangement is said to be, the correction of the oscillating motion, which to a violent extent accompanies the descent, and the insurance of the speedy action of the machine after its detachment. The oscillations in question, however, do not appear to be in any way connected with the shape of the parachute. They are merely the consequence of a first irregularity impressed upon it, by the unequal extension of its parts in the act of opening. As a proof that the aberrations in question are entirely independent of the form of the parachute, or indeed of any other permanent condition of the descent, it may be observed, that the aberrations themselves are by no means permanently or invariably present, at times being much more strongly displayed than at others, occasionally wanting altogether, and almost always becoming fainter as the experiment draws to a close. The chief objection, however, the plan by which it is proposed to obviate them, is the great sacrifice which it occasions in the resisting powers of the parachute, to an extent indeed which gives us reason to entertain much apprehension concerning the issue of the experiment by which it is now to be illustrated. By a course of calculations, we learn, that the resistence exerted upon the base of a cone passing through the air (supposing it a plane) is to that upon its oblique presentation, in the proportion of unity to the sine of half the vertical angle. Supposing the apex of the cone in the present instance to be a right angle (from which we believe it is little removed) this proportion would stand in numbers—as one is to one divided by the square root of two ;—consequently, the loss of resistance occasioned by presenting such a cone point foremost, is equal to one-third of what it would have been, had the base been so disposed as to encounter the action of the air. Owing to this circumstance, the power of the projected parachute assuming its radius to be 17 feet, would only avail to retard the fall of the individual in the same degree as an ordinary parachute, whose radius was 14 feet. Now the descending velocity of such a parachute, charged with a weight of 484lbs., we ascertain from Dr. Hutton's theorem, would be exactly 20½ feet per second, and the force developed, the same as if the individual had fallen unprotectedly, from a height of 6 feet and a ⅓, very nearly twice as much as in these cases is generally considered to be the acmé of human bearing.

---

* The following is the substance of the letter alluded to by Mr. Mason ; it appeared in the *Morning Herald* of 24th July, the day of ascent :—" The plan which has been adopted as a novel one, has been long known to the scientific world, although, on account of certain inherent deficiencies, the practical cultivators of the art have declined adopting it. It was first promulgated in Paris about forty years ago, revived in England by Sir George Cayley, and published by him, with other notices on aerostation, in the 24th vol. of Nicholson's Journal. It was subsequently more fully developed and improved upon by Mr. Kerr, by whom it was, in several experiments, publicly illustrated, and is finally detailed in the Encyclopædia Londinensis, at the

us to his success. He again repeated his en-
treaties; that he would only for an instant
attend to what he had to say upon the subject. Mr. Cocking replied, that he had then
no time to spare, he must go and dress himself to ascend; but he would be happy to
meet him on the morrow and discuss the
point.

By a Juror.—He proceeded to remon-
strate with other persons, but was requested
to desist; among other persons, Dr. Faraday. He said that the friends of the deceased had satisfied themselves by previous
experiments; that it was now too late to
interfere, at the eleventh hour, and that all
would go right.

The Foreman of the Jury then read from
a written paper the following verdict.—"
We find that the deceased, Robert Cocking.
came to his death casually and by misfortune,
in consequence of serious injuries which he
received from a fall in a parachute of his own
invention and contrivance, which was appended to a balloon; and we further find that
the parachute, as moving towards his death
is deodand, and forfeit to our sovereign lady
the Queen."

———

Professor Faraday has subsequently
addressed a letter to the *Times*, explanatory of the part he took in this melancholy affair, which, in justice to that gentleman, we subjoin.

Sir,—Though very unwilling to appear in
the public journals or intrude on your kindness, I am induced, by what appears to me
an unnecessary reference to my name in the
late inquest, to ask of you the favour of publication for the present letter.

I knew Mr. Cocking long ago, was a fellow member with him at the City Philosophical Society, and heard him deliver the
lecture 23 years since, referred to by Mr. Gye
at the inquest; and the recollection of his
companionship, abilities, and kindness at
that time, adds greatly to my feelings of sor-
row for his melancholy death. I did not
know that he thought of putting his parachute to the proof by a descent, until I saw
his intention announced in the papers, and
did not see him, or the parachute, until the
day of the descent. He then asked me
at the Gardens my opinion of its safety,
and I said, that as to its capability of retarding his descent, it was purely a matter of calculation, into which I could not
go. He said that he had made both experiments and calculations, and was fully
assured the velocity of descent would not be
greater than that of a man falling from a
height of two feet. I then remarked upon
the weakness of the construction, especially

of the upper ring, and asked why he had not
given it a form better able to resist collap-
sion? Why it was not assisted by stretchers
or bracings, &c.? He gave me the same
answer generally that he had given to Mr.
Gye, that it was strong enough, and that he
objected to more weight above. I made
other objections, as for instance, to the
opening in the middle of the parachute, the
place of the centre of gravity, &c., but finding him perfectly satisfied with his preparations, and resolved to ascend (as is fully proved
by the evidence on the inquest), finding also
by the care of Mr. Gye, that every precaution was taken to enable him to abandon his
intention at any moment, I desisted from
making further remarks, which might tend
to disturb his presence of mind, though they
would not have prevented his ascent. I
however said not a word to him to advance his
going; but, being doubtful and anxious, had
expressed myself so to some on the ground,
and amongst others to Mr. Green, who
asking me whether I would rather be in his
or Mr. Cockings's situation, I said in his;
and this he told to Mr. Cocking in my
hearing. With these feelings on my mind,
I retired in part, and did not speak to Mr.
Cocking for the last hour and a half.

Hearing that Mr. Mason was disturbing
Mr. Cocking's attention, I did venture to
say to the former gentleman, that as Mr.
Cocking was resolved to ascend, I thought
it unwise. Mr. Mason told me that he had
made calculations, the result of which was,
that the descent would be a very rapid one.
I observed, that Mr. Cocking had also told
me he had made experiments and calculations, the results of which were, that the
descent would be slow. Mr. Mason's calculations and objections, as far as I know,
had no relation to the strength of the parachute, or to the actual cause of the failure
and sad result.

The opinion given by Mr. Green and Mr.
Gye (who appear to be the best judges under
the circumstances) regarding the failure of
the parachute, makes me glad that I said no
more to Mr. Cocking than I did. The retention of the rope attached to the balloon
at the moment of separation may have been
due to some disturbance of mind through
anxiety, thus bringing on the fatal termination; and I am very thankful that I, at
least, was not the cause of any such anxiety.

In conclusion, my sincere thanks are due
to the Coroner for his kindness and consideration. It is much to be desired, though
perhaps not to be expected, that others would
more frequently have the same thought.

I am, Sir, your obliged servant,
M. FARADAY.

Royal Institution, July 31.

EXPERIMENTS ON THE ADHESION OF IRON SPIKES OF VARIOUS FORMS, WHEN DRIVEN INTO DIFFERENT SPECIES OF TIMBER. BY W. R. JOHNSON, PROFESSOR OF MECHANICS AND NATURAL PHILOSOPHY IN THE FRANKLIN INSTITUTE.

(From the *American Journal of Science and Arts*.)
(Concluded from p. 287).

The accompanying figures represent the appearances of timber as developed by splitting the specimens, through the axis of the cavities, left by the spikes when withdrawn.

Fig. 1, is that presented by the locust timber, mentioned in Table II., experiment 11, in which the weight required to extract the spike was 3990 lbs. The upper part of the figure exhibits the rising up of the timber just as the spike starts. In every case this effect was found, on examining the timber, to have been of very limited extent.

1.   2. *Figures of Timber.* 3.   4.

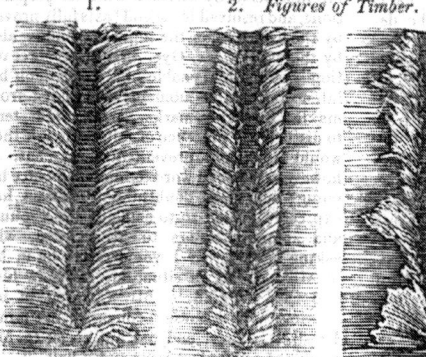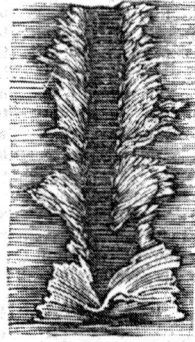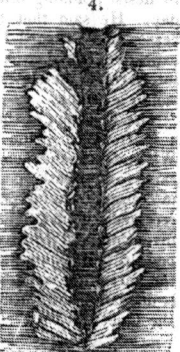

Fig. 2, represents the grain of chestnut timber as affected in experiment 3, Table III., with the broad flat spike, and other trials. At the point of inflection downward, the grain appears to be not only bent, but actually broken off.

Fig. 3, exhibits the appearance of a specimen of hemlock timber, used in experiment with the straight grooved spike, (Fig. 4, of spikes), in which the weight required to extract it was but 1296 lbs.—See Table II., Experiment 8th.

Fig. 4, conveys an idea of the manner in which a defective specimen of pitch pine was affected by a spike. The force required to draw this spike was so trifling, that it was not thought worth recording in the tables.

Figures of Spikes.

1.   2.   3.   4.   5.   6.   7.   8.

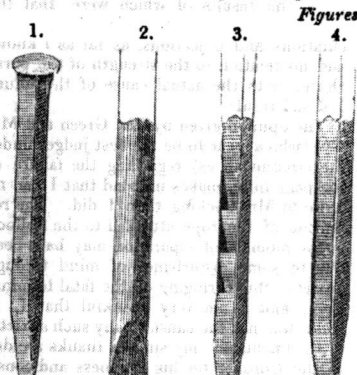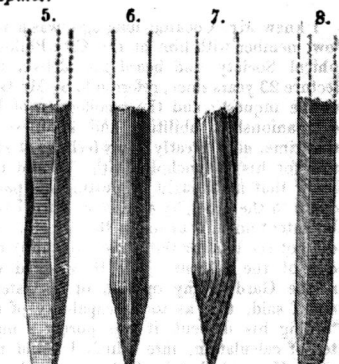

Fig. 1, is a square spike .405 of an inch wide on each face; referred to in Table III., Experiments 1, 5, and 13.

Fig. 2, is a cylindrical spike .485 inch in diameter, sharpened to a cutting edge.— See Table III., Experiment 9.

Fig. 3, is the grooved and notched spike, serrated in the bottoms of the grooves on the two faces, Table III., Experiment 12.

Fig. 4, is a spike with plain grooves on the faces, extending from the upper part of the bevel to the height of about 3½ inches.

Fig. 5, is a grooved and swelled spike, that is, having the groove deeper at the distance of two inches from the point, than it is at one inch from it. At the former, the depth of each groove is .066 inch.

Fig. 6, is a cylindrical spike .5 inch in diameter, tapering to a point.

Fig. 7, is a spike of the same diameter as the preceding, but having fifteen spiral grooves proceeding from the point upward.

Fig. 8, is a flat spike .390 inch in breadth, and .253 inch in thickness. See Table III., Experiments 4, 7, and 15.

Note.—The only series of experiments, analogous to those above detailed, which has fallen under the notice of the writer, was made in 1824 (see Gill's Technical Repository, vol. v. p. 248), by Mr. B. Bevan, on the adhesion of sprigs, brads, and nails, when driven into timber longitudinally and transversely. His operations were extended to several kinds of timber, viz., Norway deal, dry oak, elm, dry beech, and green sycamore. He employed some nails of a very minute size, of which 4560 were required to make a pound avoirdupois. One of these required 22 lbs. to extract it, when driven .4 of an inch into pine board. From this size he advanced by several gradations to the sixpenny wrought nail, of which 73 make a pound avoirdupois. Of the latter, he drove one to the depth of one inch successively into pine, elm, dry oak, dry beech, and green sycamore, and found the forces required for its extraction to be as follows :—

For Pine.. 187 lbs.   For Beech...... 667
    Elm,. 327   Sycamore... 312
    Oak.. 507

Mr. Bevan examined, to some extent, the difference between driving a nail by percussion with a hammer of known weight and range of fall, and forcing it into the wood by simple pressure. This curious inquiry did not, for obvious reasons, enter into the plan of the writer of this article. Mr. Bevan found, that to force a sixpenny nail into pine 1 inch, it took a pressure of 235 lbs. ; to extract it, 187 ; to force it in 1¼ inch, 400 ; to extract it, 327; to force it in 2 inches, 610 ; to extract it, 530.

NOTES AND NOTICES.

Legislative Procrastination.—The Chamber of Deputies, by coming to a vote to postpone all outstanding railway questions to next session, have put an extinguisher, for the present, on Mr. Cockerill's plan for a railroad from Paris to Brussels, and thus relieved for a time the anxieties of the inhabitants of St. Quintin, at the threatened deprivation to their city, of the advantages of improved communication. Railway matters seem to "hang fire" more in France, than in any other part of the Continent, generally further behind in the appliances and means of advanced civilisation : but parliamentary interference seems to be one of the chiefest causes of delay, *wherever* it is called into action.

Steam Explosion at Hull.—A member for the French Chamber of Deputies lately put the question, whether the French Ministers intended to institute any inquiry into the causes of the late explosion at Hull? To which Mr. Arago replied, that a committee of the Academy of Sciences was occupied in preparing a report on the causes of steam explosions in general, that at Hull included, which would be made public in due time. Both question and answer seem rather singular. If any scientific investigation into the causes of that explosion be necessary, it would seem rather to belong to the English than the French government to make one. Should any commission of inquiry on the subject be sent over the channel, we would suggest, that in the same humane spirit, our ministers should dispatch another to report on the late melancholy accident, by which twenty-four persons were destroyed at the Duke of Orlean's marriage at Paris.

Gamble, the engineer of the Union, has been acquitted on the charge of manslaughter.

Chinese Literature.—The study of Chinese appears to be making some progress on the Continent. The Emperor of Russia has appointed a Professor of that language at the University of Kasan, in the person of a Russian missionary long resident at Pekin; he has also purchased his Chinese library for three thousand rubles, and assigned him an annual salary of four thousand rubles, or about a hundred pounds sterling more than it is proposed to give the new Professor at the University of our own wealthy metropolis. The latter situation is, it is rumoured, to be offered to Mr. Kidd, now President of the Anglo-Chinese College at Malacca, one of the Chinese pupils of which has lately found employment under the Government of the Celestial empire, as a translator from the English. At Vienna, also, they are not inactive. Mr. Stephen Endlicher, an industrious and ingenious officer of the Imperial Library, has taken advantage of a recent visit of Baron Schilling de Constadt, the well-known linguist and traveller, whose gigantic stature and proportions found him such favour among the Tibetans, to draw up and publish a catalogue of the Chinese books and coins of the Imperial collection. The number of works, it appears, is 189; the library may perhaps be equal in this department to that of the British Museum, or even of the East India Company, but is certainly inferior to that of the Asiatic Society, or the London University; and all four of these are in our own capital, now pre-eminent for collections of Chinese literature. With regard to coins, there will probably be no reason for English readers to recur to the pages of Mr. Endlicher: a memoir on the subject, embodying information derived from Chinese authorities, by Mr. Samuel Birch, of the British Museum, was recently read before our own Numismatical Society,

☞ *British and Foreign Patents taken out with economy and despatch; Specifications, Disclaimers, and Amendments, prepared or revised; Caveats entered; and generally every Branch of Patent Business promptly transacted.*

A complete list of Patents from the earliest period (15 Car. II. 1675,) to the present time may be examined, Fee 2s. 6d.; Clients, gratis.

LONDON: Printed and Published for the Proprietor, by W. A. Robertson, at the Mechanics' Magazine Office, No. 6, Peterborough-court, between 135 and 136, Fleet-street.—Sold by G. W. M. Reynolds, Proprietor of the French, English, and American Library, 55, Rue Neuve, Saint Augustin, Paris.

Mechanics' Magazine,

MUSEUM, REGISTER, JOURNAL, AND GAZETTE.

No. 731.   SATURDAY, AUGUST 12, 1837.   Price 3*d*.

COLONEL MACERONI'S PARACHUTES.

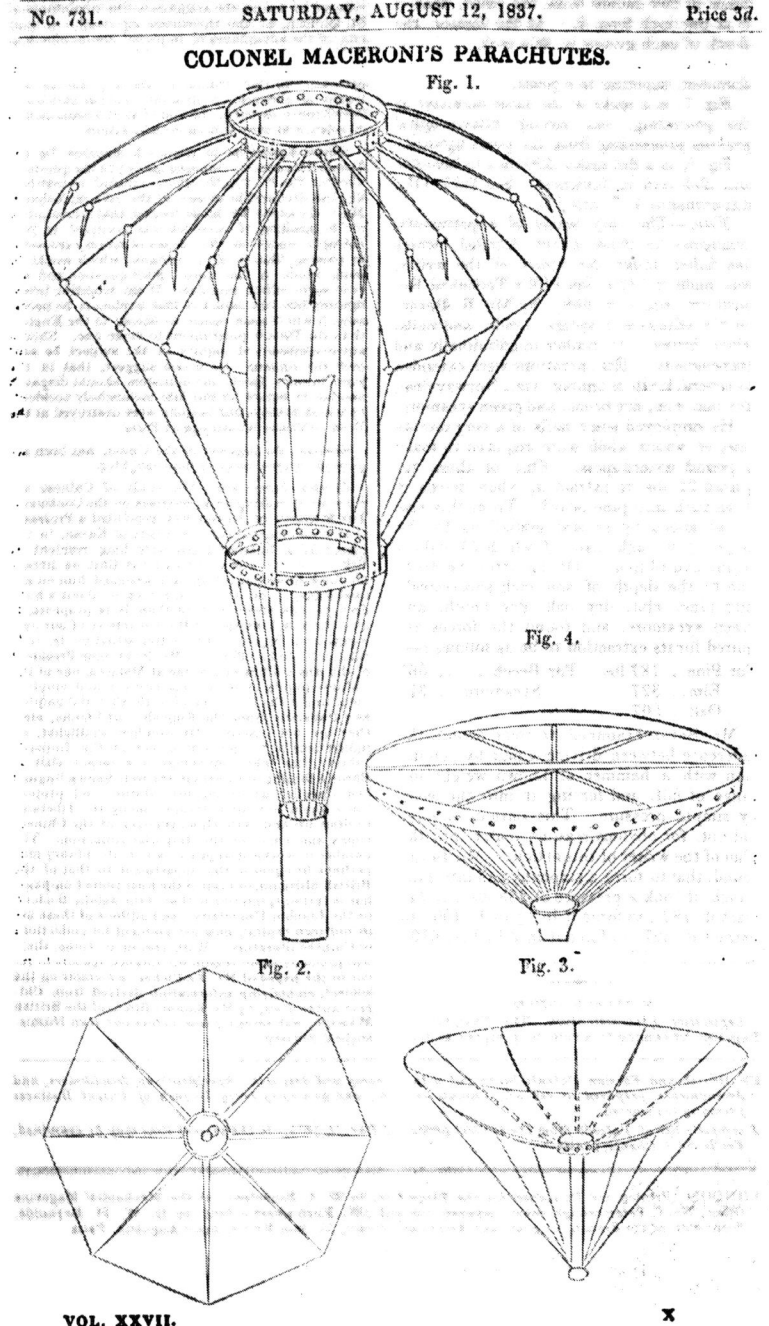

Fig. 1.

Fig. 4.

Fig. 2.

Fig. 3.

COLONEL MACERONI'S PARACHUTES.

Sir,—I read in the papers some days ago a confused, and, to me, unsatisfactory, description of a parachute, constructed by Mr. Cocking, on the principle of its presenting a convex surface downwards. The apparatus was of an extraordinary weight, more than that of a man! I have remarked, thirty years ago, that oysters, like a common tea-saucer, thrown into the water, will always fall bottom downwards, in consequence of the convex shape. But it is also necessary to know, that a flat surface, say, of three square feet, falling through the air, meets with double the resistance of a demi-spheroidal surface of equal diameter. The greatest resistance is from a concave descending surface, provided it can be kept from turning over, which it is naturally disposed to do. The proper, and perfectly efficacious, construction for a parachute, is similar to an umbrella; only, instead of the whalebones or canes being brought to a point and attached to a stick, they must be attached to a ring or hoop of wood, of a diameter equal to one-fifth or one quarter of the diameter of the parachute. Thus, there will be a large hole in the centre of the machine, through which the compressed and accumulated air will rush, and infallibly prevent its overturning, or even oscillating at all. I have tried this construction with heavy weights, and found it answer entirely.

To the central hoop must be attached four or more stout sticks of deal, of a length about equal to the diameter of the parachute; these brought down perpendicularly, are similarly fastened to another wooden hoop, equal in diameter to one-third or more of the parachute. Stays or braces of small cord are attached all round the circumference of parachute, and connected below to this inferior hoop, to which also is attached the basket to contain the aeronaut. Fig. 1 (see front page) is a sketch of this parachute. A second set of stays may be attached to the radial rods, by running rings, in a similar position to the metallic stays of an umbrella. Such is the proper construction of a parachute, in which (were I at liberty) I should feel no hesitation to descend from a balloon at any height. If this parachute be closed, it leaves an opening below, which will instantly inflate it upon falling.

For those who advocate a convex under surface to a parachute, the following are the two best ways of making such: Turn a flat round piece of deal, like a double Gloucester cheese. Bore eight or twelve holes in its periphery, into which properly insert by the butts as many East India bamboos, which taper to a thin point like a fishing-rod. Each bamboo being fifteen feet long, will form a circular frame of thirty-two feet diameter. A plan of this is shewn at fig. 2 (see front page). Over this stretch common calico. The whole will weigh only 20 lbs. The rope, to which is attached the basket of the aeronaut, being fixed in the middle of the wooden centre piece, the bamboos will bend gently upwards on the whole being pulled down through the air by a heavy body, and can never collapse. Fig. 3, shews this bamboo parachute descending. Another way would be, to form a hoop of beech 20 feet diameter; over this attach canvas, but loosely. The weght being applied to the middle of the slack canvas, will give the convex under surface desired, and slight stiff spars of deal placed across from one side of the hoop to the other, would prevent the possibility of a collapse, to which there is no disposition, as the pressure is equal all round. Fig. 4, shews this hoop parachute descending.

When I read the account of Mr. Cocking's parachute, I could not see the rationale of the thing, or how it was prevented from collapsing. A formation like a common umbrella, turned upside down, would have been far more sensible.

In 1804, a gentleman, whom I afterwards saw, leaped off the bridge of La Tenità, which connects two streets by passing over another street, 122 feet below. He fastened to his waist a common umbrella, only larger, like such as are used in gigs, and arrived safe to the paved ground, without injury. He took the precaution to affix stays all round, attached to the stick. This feat was witnessed by thousands, who still remember the fact.

Garnerin's parachute oscillated as described, only because the hole in its centre was not larger than the crown of a man's hat. After all, he was not hurt. For the double assurance of those who fear a too violent collision with the earth, helical springs at the bottom of the basket would serve as an auxiliary preventive to a shock.

There will be no shock with either of my parachutes, especially with the umbrella, fig. 1.

I have no veneration for ballooning, as I regard it as a perfectly futile attempt to navigate the air. Montgolfier balloons, as I have said, offer more chance of direction than those of gas. But bed is the best.

Yours, &c.

F. MACERONI.

MACKENZIE'S IMPROVED PARACHUTE.

Sir,—Public interest having been recently attracted to the subject of aerostation, and parachutes in particular, by Mr. Cocking's late unfortunate experiment, I take the liberty of troubling you with some suggestions relative to the subject, which you are at liberty to publish, should you so far think them worthy of attention, in your valuable miscellany.

I am, Sir, your obedient servant,

GEORGE MACKENZIE.
Architectural Draughtsman.

3, Claremont-row, Barnsbury-road, Islington,
August 2, 1837.

1st. Of whatever form a parachute might be made, would it not be advisable to place the aeronaut who is to descend by it, not quite in the lowest part of it, but, on the contrary, near the centre of gravity of the whole machine—the requisite stability being obtained by a weight, not of human, but of inanimate matter, suspended much below him, whose oscillations, should any occur, would not therefore much affect him, and which, by touching the ground before the basket in which he was placed, would soften much the jerk he would experience at the end of the descent, by lightening the parachute of much of the load which it had sustained, supposing it to be made of size proportional to the aggregate weight of ballast and aeronaut?

2nd. If the parachute be of a form adapted to continue, like a pendulum, any oscillations (which may arise, which appears to have been the case with M. Garnerin's), would not vertical sails or vanes, fastened about the lower weight, be useful in checking them?

3dly. In the construction of a parachute on the principle of Mr. Cocking's, or like an inverted cone, would not one or more annular tubes of flexible material, but inflated with air, like one kind of life-preservers against drowning, and three or four feet in diameter instead of three inches, be more efficacious in preventing the parachute from collapsing than the tin tube used in that unfortunate instance? In case of the union with this plan, of the one heretofore mentioned, of separating the aeronaut from the ballast which steadies the machine, the latter weight might be suspended by converging ropes from the outer annular tube, while the basket alone was hung to the middle; thus taking off much of the strain which would tend to produce collapse, as shewn in the accompanying

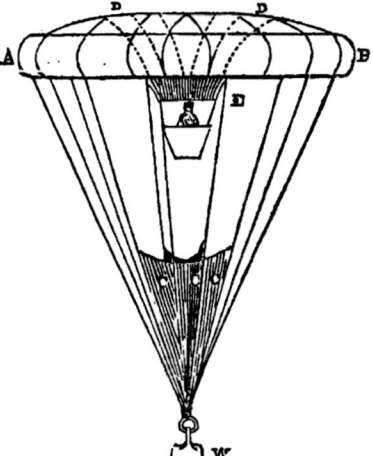

diagram, where the inflated annular tube A B has suspended to it the weight W, between the cords supporting which, are the four triangular sails c c, to check vibration in the weight, while the flexible part forming the area of the circle A B, curves over at D D to a conical shape at E, where it supports the basket.

4th. But perhaps the best parachute would be nothing else than a balloon, only inflated with common air, and with a funnel shaped piece at the bottom to catch the air to replace leakage or other accident, by means of a hole in the bottom (the neck), through which also the aeronaut might creep on approaching the ground, to escape the shock of the car coming in contact with it; there might even be a second car quite within the body of the balloon, and suspended from its inside by ropes radiating in all directions; thus the balloon itself would be a most efficacious spring to break the fall of the aeronaut. I am here supposing the above-named balloon to have been previously carried up by another, common one.

Before concluding, it may be well to explain, that the writer of this would not be understood to suggest or advocate the risking of any more human lives, in reducing to practice the foregoing, or any similar plans; at any rate, until their entire efficacy is proved by such experiments, as might be made at first with the inanimate machines alone, and their ballast, and afterwards with brute animals; of which, there should be tried not only those of smaller size and more active habits than the human, but also those of greater bulk and more clumsy form, to observe the effect of the descent upon them.   G. M.

PARACHUTE DESCENTS.

Sir,—The melancholy termination of Mr. Cocking's experiment has not been sufficient to deter the enterprising spirit of another individual, who, I have been informed, has since offered to renew the trial, and, it is to be hoped, upon more certain and cautious principles. Mr. Cocking's parachute was, as the distressing event proved, *greatly deficient in point of strength;* there should have been lines attached to the outer rim, supporting the car or basket; these would have afforded a bearing to counteract the pressure upon it, in its descent. Had this been done, in all probability it would have prevented the collapsing, and Mr. Cocking would have been preserved.

But I very much question if the principle of the inverted cone, after all, is correct; first, because it does not afford sufficient resistance, without requiring a more extended area, accompanied with the disadvantages either of increased weight or less proportionate strength. Next, because the difficulties of ascent are increased in exact proportion to the superior resistance which the hollow of the cone presents. By reversing its position, therefore, it is better suited to every purpose required—that opposed

to the ascent is less, and to the descent greater, presenting less risk both to the ascending and descending aeronauts. The rush of air would also converge to centre, and if the opening were left in the apex of the cone, to allow of its egress, oscillation might be avoided; an addition might also be made to serve as a helm, and direct the line of descent, which the aeronaut could command as he thought fit. But it is to be hoped, that before another individual risks his life upon so useless an enterprise, the experiment will be tried by attaching a weight of any required density, to the parachute, and upon the result of this, the attempt could be proved safe or otherwise; the experiment would of itself afford sufficient interest, and be certainly more creditable to the public, than if another individual were to place himself in such peril previous to using every possible precaution for his safety.

I am, Sir, yours respectfully,
JAMES WOODHOUSE.

Kilburn, July 21, 1837.

SIR HUMPHRY DAVY'S PRESIDENCY OF THE ROYAL SOCIETY.

Sir,—Mr. Herapath having published ten letters more of the private correspondence which he falsely alleges caused "the expulsion" of Sir Humphry Davy from the presidency of the Royal Society, I shall, with your leave, take up, and proceed with, my analytical exposition of this correspondence, from the point where I left it in my letter in your journal for May last.

The reader will recollect, that the term *expulsion,* was latterly softened down by Mr. Herapath into "*forced retirement,*" and that again into "*resignation,*" which led me to remark, that it was manifest from this, he was desirous of wriggling out of the charge of expulsion altogether. One would have thought that here were variations enough for one tune; but Mr. Herapath, as if intent upon shewing the infinitude of his suppleness, or wrigglesomeness, has favoured us with yet one change more. The charge is now, that the correspondence ended in the *expulsion, forced retirement, resignation,* or—"*exit*" of Sir Humphry Davy from the chair. Rather than go on *backing out* at this rate, he had better make a clear breast of it at once, and honestly and contritely confess that the charge amounts to just nothing at all.

Mr. Herapath, having given up pedagogueizing at Bristol for something in the same line at Cranford, wrote both to Mr. Davies Gilbert and Sir Humphry Davy (Letters X. and XI., 11th January, 1821), apprising them of his change of residence, and pressing for a decision on his "paper," which he hints, would, if favourable, be of some consequence to him "*in his business !*" Mr. Davies Gilbert (good natured man!) replies (Letter XIII., 14th January, 1821), that he hopes sincerely his "academy will answer his every expectation," but that being no longer President of the Royal Society, he can say nothing about "the paper" which he had put into the hands of Sir Humphry Davy on the day of his election. Sir Humphry Davy replies (Letter XII., 13th January), that he had read the paper, that is to say, "those parts of it *which are intelligible*," but is by no means "impressed with a conviction of their truth."

"The pressure of your gravific fluid, for instance, taking away *weight*, must depend on the *motion* of its particles; and yet you counteract this pressure by *heat*, which you consider as *motion*"!!!

Sir Humphry concludes by politely inviting the author of this rare theory to favour him with a call at his house in Grosvenor-square "any Wednesday evening after nine o'clock," when he would "always find some of our most distinguished men of science with him."

Herapath says, that he accepted the invitation, and "attended Sir Humphry Davy's evening meeting," 17th January, 1821.

"We had a long chat together in the rooms, in which he spoke very kindly and encouragingly, and hoped, alluding to my paper, that I would not be discouraged by the opinions of one or two, laying an emphasis of contempt on the word 'opinions,' adding, 'there are two or three in the council who are determined it shall not pass.' He introduced me to Dr. Young, who, on my asking him, said he had not seen or heard of the paper, yet in a few minutes after, discussing the mode of making some experiments, he observed, 'but you, in your paper, say * * *.'"

I will not assert that every word of this statement is false, but I will say that I do not believe a single word of it, —which is a fact. Sir Humphry Davy had already communicated to Mr. Herapath, in writing, his own deliberate opinion, that his theory had no truth in it, and justified that opinion by a specimen, which shewed that it was deserving only of contempt; and yet he would have the world believe, that when he afterwards, and for the first time, met Sir Humphry Davy, the president forsook all the distinguished and *really* scientific men around him to chat familiarly and long,—most "kindly and encouragingly," with this country pedagogue—this Cranford *academician*, and strove hard to throw all the blame of the rejection of his paper on others of the Council. The thing is incredible—nobody will or can believe it. Sir Humphry had too much tact—leaving out of the question truth, honour, consistency, every thing else—to be guilty of such baseness. And Young, the polished and high-minded young—he, too, must, on the credit of this indiscriminate libeller, stand convicted of uttering a gross and wilful falsehood ! Faugh !

Mr. Herapath afterwards sends Sir Humphry Davy (Letter XVI., 5th Feb., 1821) some "experiments on temperature," which, he says, present "a striking agreement with the theorem" given in "the paper," about which he had been so long pestering the Society.

"That these experiments, if they are allowed to be correct, are a decisive proof of my theory of the constitution of the gases, and, therefore, of my theories of collision and heat, no one, I think, can deny ; and if they are not allowed to be correct, it will remain to be shewn wherein I have erred, and *what kind of miracle it must have been to produce so imposing an agreement.*"

Sir Humphry Davy, who was no stranger to the "kind of miracles" by which such "agreements" are sometimes produced (as to which the reader may peruse with profit an amusing chapter in Mr. Babbage's book on the Decline of Science), replies (Letter XII., Feb. 28, 1821), "You speak of mixing mercury in vessels of hammered tin, a metal which is rapidly dissolved by mercury!!!" Sir Humphry adds, "I have likewise submitted it (the account of the experiments) to a very able philosopher, who has added a note at the end, which alone would shew that in its present state it could not with propriety be communicated to the Royal Society." The "very able philosopher" alluded to appears to have been Dr. Roget, and the note (as now given by Mr. H.) is as follows:—

"If (as Mr. Herapath maintains) the temperature of melting ice be to that of boiling water in the subduplicate ratio of 8 to 11, that is, as $\sqrt{8}$ to $\sqrt{11}$, or 1:1.1726: Then the difference of the temperature between is to the total temperature of ice reckoned from the real zero ::1.1726—1 (or, 0.1726):1::180° :1043°, and not 480°, as Mr. H. makes it, from having calculated according to the *simple*, and not the *subduplicate*, ratio.—P. M. R."

Sir Humphry begs, under these circumstances, to be informed " in what manner he may *immediately* return the two papers."

Mr. Herapath states, that before receiving this letter, he " had seen Sir Humphry Davy again, but found him very unlike the kind, affable man" he was at his first visit, January 17th.

" He affected the great man—talked dictatorily (*sic in orig.*)—was going to upset me at once by some experiments of De Luc; but though I saw the book *under* his fingers, *he* would not take it *down*, probably well knowing *he* would have confirmed me, as I then told *him* the experiments *he* alluded to would."

Nice grammatical English this; but let that pass. When it is considered that Sir Humphry Davy had by this time satisfied himself that neither "the paper," nor " the experiments" furnished in corroboration of it, were fit for presentation to the Royal Society, and more especially, what his notions must have been as to the kind of miracles by which the " striking agreement," or, as Mr. H., with more propriety, perhaps, calls it, " *imposing* agreement," between the theory of the paper and the results of the experiments was accomplished, the want of cordiality evinced by Sir Humphry at this second interview can hardly be wondered at. What community of feeling could there possibly be between two experimentalists of such opposite character ?

After such decisive evidence of the real opinion which Sir Humphry entertained of Mr. Herapath and his "experiments," the reader will scarcely be prepared for the next curious particular which comes in my way. The account of the "experiments" was sent to Sir Humphry Davy on February 5, and the letter pronouncing them unfit for presentation to the Royal Society, is dated February 28th ; and yet we are expected to believe, that during this short interval of twenty-three days, Sir Humphry Davy expressed himself as follows:—

"Mr. Gilbert informed me that Davy spoke *in very high terms* of the experiments"!!!

Not even on the respectable authority of Mr. Gilbert nimself would I credit such a statement, and still less am I disposed to do so when all the proof we have of it is the assertion of Mr. John Herapath that Mr. Gilbert said so and so *sixteen years ago ;* the said John Herapath being the same person who has before represented Mr. Gilbert himself to be a great story-teller (see my letter of May last), and the no less estimable Dr. Young to be a still greater.

Here, for the present, my task of dissection ends (would *the subject* did not smell so rank!); but having arrived at that stage of this little history where the cause of quarrel between the parties was complete, and war (to *expulsion*, if not to the knife) was about to commence, I may as well mention, before concluding, that Mr. Herapath now tells us that after all he was "not ambitious to appear in the Philosophical Transactions!" The grapes were sour.

I am, Sir, your obedient servant,
PHILO-DAVY.

Camden Hill, August 2, 1837.

SIR SAMUEL MORLAND'S SPEAKING-TRUMPET.

Sir,—The invention of the speaking-trumpet has been demanded for many ; but without inquiring into the validity of their various claims, it is certain that we are indebted to Sir Samuel Morland for the instrument in its present state.

In 1672, Sir Samuel published a description of the speaking-trumpet, in a small tract entitled, " A Description of the Tuba Stentorophonica, an Instrument of excellent use, as well by Sea as by Land," (fol., 8 leaves). From this very rare treatise, the following particulars are taken, which are interesting, inasmuch as they shew the gradual experiments that he made, before the instrument attained a comparative degree of perfection :—

The first trumpet that he constructed, "although," says Sir Samuel, "the invention had been long before digested in my thoughts," was made in glass in the year 1670, being about 2 feet 8 inches in length, the diameter of the greater end 11 inches, and that of the other end 2½ inches. "With this," he says, "I was heard speaking at a considerable distance by several persons, and found that it did very considerably multiply the voice."

The next tube that Morland made was of brass, 4½ feet feet in length, the diameter of the greater end being 12 inches, and that of the less 2 inches; and in order that no part of the breath might be lost, he caused the mouth-piece to be constructed like a pair of bellows, so that by opening and shutting, it might precisely correspond to the movement of the mouth. With this instrument, trials were made in St. James's Park, where King Charles, Prince Rupert, and Lord Angier heard him speaking very distinctly at the distance of half a mile.

Much encouraged by these trials, and his Majesty's approbation, Sir Samuel constructed three more of these instruments, of copper, in the form of common trumpets. The first measured 16 feet 8 inches in length, the diameter of the greater end 19 inches, and of the little end 2 inches; the second, 21 feet in length, the diameter of the great end 2 feet, and that of the other end 2¼ inches; the third was 5½ feet long, the diameter of its great end 21 inches, and of its little end 10½ inches. With these trumpets; he was heard speaking at the distance of nearly a mile and a half.

Sir Samuel afterwards enters into a philosophic disquisition on the nature of sound, and the best form of the speaking trumpet; but he does not come to a conclusion on the last point, which is still dubious. It is now generally agreed that the efficiency of the instrument does not depend so much on its form as its length.

Morland concludes his pamphlet with "an account of the manifold uses" of this instrument, which are excusably magnified; the reader who is curious in such matters, can peruse it at the British Museum, but space will not permit me to give an example.

J. O. H.

A.]½, August 7, 1837.

ON THE SYMMETRIZING POWER OF THE EYE. BY THE REV. J. MACIVAR, A. M.

Let the surface of a glass mirror be sprinkled over with some powder, as, for instance, with flower from a dredging-box. This done, on looking perpendicularly down upon the reflecting surface, at the distance of distinct vision from it (unless the eye be too long-sighted,) the powder will appear, not irregularly scattered, as it really is, but symmetrically distributed in two systems of beautiful radiations, having the pupils of the eyes for their centres.

The phænomenon is sufficiently remarkable to strike even those who are not otherwise curious in such matters. It may be observed, however, that as every eye cannot catch it at once, it is better to commence by using one eye only, as this gives only one system of radiations, which, being more simple, is more easily observed. If this phænomenon has not been already attended to (and I do not recollect to have seen it noticed anywhere,) it is, I think, well worthy of investigation. Some facts are, indeed, immediately obvious respecting it. Thus, as to the region in which the physical part of the phænomenon takes place, it plainly appears that it is not either the humours or retina, as is generally supposed in reference to other phænomena of the same order, but a more deeply seated part of the apparatus of vision. For if it were any of these anterior parts, or even the retina itself, the centre of the radiant system would certainly change its place when the eye was made to wander over the mirror. In point of fact, however, that centre does not change place except when the whole head is moved, in which case it does so proportionally.

I ascribe the phænomena to a peculiar mode of action in the nervous part of the apparatus of vision, proper to it as an elastic tissue, in virtue of which it tends, like the tissues and media experimented on by Chladni, Savar, Faraday, and others, and doubtless all elastic tissues and media, to distribute all motions impressed upon it in symmetrical systems; a view of the matter having very interesting bearings upon the principles of tastes,—during the investigation of which it was, that this experiment first occurred to me,—and one calculated to explain several seemingly unaccountable phænomena as to the distribution of sensibility in the retina.
—L. & E. Phil. Mag.

We have caused the following autographs to be engraved from the Royal warrants for two patents, which have recently passed through our office. The signature of our late Sovereign is one of his latest, executed when the hand of Death was strong upon him (the warrant is dated June 12th,—he died June 20th), and shews, combined with the feebleness of age, a degree of pains-taking strikingly characteristic of that anxiety for the dispatch of public business, for which his Majesty was, to the last, so laudably distinguished. The autograph of our Queen, (whom Heaven long preserve!) evinces, for one so young, singular firmness and decision. We trust that in matters of business (matters political we meddle not with) her Majesty will take the late King for her model, rather than the royal voluptuary that preceded him. In the time of George IV., warrants for patents were frequently delayed for several months, for want of the royal signature, and not seldom warrants were signed out of their regular order, so as literally to make the last first, and the first last. But during the late reign, we never knew, nor heard of, a patent being delayed on this account a single day, far less of any inventor losing his precedence through the official neglect or laziness of the sovereign.

PRODUCTION OF POWER FROM THE DECOMPOSITION OF WATER.

Sir,—The means of setting "the Thames on fire" have long been known, but the advantage of so doing has not yet been proved. After superseding coal in lighting our houses and streets, perhaps the next application of galvanic action to useful purposes will be the separation of metals from their ores; and judging from the experiments of Becquerel, Fox, and Crosse on these substances, even this generation may probably witness their success. On observing your correspondent Mr. Fry's idea of using water for fuel (burning water, in fact), I recalled to mind, and extended a speculation which may cause the mining steam-engine, and its tremendous powers, to be spoken of in 1937 as matters of history, viz., that all the water at the bottom of mines should be decomposed by a galvanic apparatus, to save the expense of pumping it to the surface : the mine to be lighted with the hydrogen, and the men supplied with good air from the oxygen; and, further, if these gases were evolved under considerable pressure, such pressure might be used under pistons to raise the ore, &c., leaving the gases at atmospheric pressure, for air and light; and the surplus, if combined to produce heat, would smelt the ores cheaper, perhaps, than by the direct application of galvanic agency.

There seem, however, to be limits to the production of power from given quantities. The cost, also, of a given power is a primary object,—as for instance, that of muscular action; — and coach masters in supplying the demand for quick travelling, exceeding the limits of humanity, are well acquainted with the cost of animal power: the facts stated in their petition against the Manchester and Liverpool railway, proved the necessity of locomotive steam-engines, even for moderate velocities.

The cost of the conversion of water into steam, and the limits of its power, are now tolerably well known, though at its first introduction, indefinite notions of its unlimited capabilities, appear to have been entertained—similar to those which are now afloat in the world, respecting galvanic agency, arising from a consideration of its enormous power, without reference to the space through which that power can be exerted. Though the in-tensity of the galvanic force seems as yet unascertained, yet its space of action is known to be but small: in fact the gross moving power requires to be better understood;—perhaps it will be best ascertained either by the failure, or success of its application to machinery.

In the pendulum scheme of galvanic motion, the return action of the ball brings it close to the moving power, which thus exerts a fresh impulse, apparently just sufficient to produce motion. The manufacturer will ask—What available power is left? In consequence of the small space of the action, possibly the rapid generation, by galvanic agency, of gases under pressure, is a more feasible idea; the power obtained might then be simply represented in pounds one foot high, or in proportion to the volume in cubic feet of the gas produced × by its pressure in pounds per square foot; and its cost, by the intensity of the galvanic action, in the destruction of zinc, or other producing agents. Perhaps the water might be recomposed by the same agency, and then a vacuum could be obtained under the piston, and we might have high and low pressure engines,— one cylinder being made proportional to the oxygen, the other to the hydrogen.

It is seldom recollected by persons engaged in untried means of producing power, that the thing wanted can be reduced to pounds one foot high ; if not as regards the power itself, yet the effect produced can always be managed to be so measured. The purchasers of machines generally regard them as mercantile commodities, and look to the cost of the work done, including the first price and daily expence ; consequently, extravagant schemes are, and will be tried, which, from a more distinct perception of the cause of failure, may lead in other hands to beneficial results.

I am, Sir,
Yours &c.
N. S.

P. S. The question raised by another correspondent relative to the formation of mountain ranges by fallen satellites, in preference to internal action, is best referred to existing facts.   In one case the surrounding strata ought to be depressed and dip under the mountains ; in the other the upheaving strata should, partially at least, overlay the mountain sides.   N. S.

ADAMS'S ENGLISH PLEASURE CAR-RIAGES.

(Continued from page 181.)

Our readers will have been struck with the great difference between the earnings of some classes of workmen employed in building carriages, and those engaged in many of our staple manufactures. The three or four pounds per week of the body makers contrast strangely with the 10, 12 or 14 shillings per week of the weaver or stocking-maker. We cannot at present enter on so extensive a subject, and we advert to it merely for the purpose of inciting enquiry and eliciting discussion. In the mean time we commend to our readers the following extracts as suggesting some important views :—

" Notwithstanding the apparently high wages earned by the greater part of the workmen employed by carriage builders, but few of them, and those only among the most skilful, enjoy constant work. High wages have produced the common effect of increasing the numbers of the workmen beyond what are necessary for the demand. The consequence has been, that inferior workmen have been found willing, occasionally, to work at a lower rate of wages, for small masters, who work on speculation, and get carriages up cheaply with inferior materials, for the chance of ready-money sale. In order as much as possible to counteract this, and prevent the low rate of wages from becoming general, many of the workmen have joined together in a Trades Union, binding themselves not to work for low prices. The consequence is, that there are two classes of men,—those who belong to the Union, and those who do not : but this makes no actual alteration in their relative condition as to their earnings. The most skilful men belong to the Union rather for the sake of quietude and remaining unmolested, than from any value they attach to it, because they know that with or with or without the Union their skill can always command constant employment at the highest rate of wages. The other Unionists share amongst them just as much employment as there may happen to exist ; and they would do just as much without the Union, inasmuch as it neither increases nor diminishes the total amount. If they be good workmen, they get employment ; and if they be bad ones, the Unions cannot procure it for them. And those, who do not belong to the Union, are in the same precise condition : those who employ them select the most skilful, and leave the others without work,

unless under the pressure of necessity. The only advantage the Unions can appear to hold out, is the prevention of interlopers from working at the trade, without serving a regular apprenticeship to it : but as these interlopers can work in other shops, not belonging to the Unions, they are not in reality kept out, but do the Unionists great mischief by working at a lower rate of wages. It has been supposed by many, that great mischief may result to the public from the general customs of Trades Unions ; but the supposition is unfounded. On the contrary, experience and discussion will most probably convince the Unionists that combination cannot raise their rate of wages ; and the elements of dissolution are moreover constantly at work amongst them. They are not an equal body, but one composed of classes taking rank one after another. In the carriage manufacture it is peculiarly so. The body-makers are first on the list ; then follow the carriage makers ; then the trimmers ; then the smiths ; then the springmakers ; then the wheel-wrights, painters, platers, brace-makers, and so on. The body-makers are the wealthiest of all, and compose amongst themselves a species of aristocracy, to which the other workmen look up with feelings, half of respect, and half of jealousy. They feel their importance, and treat the others with various consideration, according to their station. Carriage makers are entitled to a species of condescending familiarity ; trimmers are considered too good to be despised ; a foreman of painters they may treat with respect, but working painters can at most be favoured with a nod. A smith is considered quite unendurable,—a regular drunken, beer-drinking ' Ironsides ;' and a plater is contemptuously denominated ' bead-sticker.' A wheelwright is held to be a kind of rough wood-chopper ; and a brace-maker, a mere vulgar ' snob.' The other classes partake of the same feelings of caste in their various proportions. A body-maker is considered a ' good catch' as a husband for the daughter of an ordinary mechanic ; and the carriage maker excites much anxious feeling on the part of mothers, who consider marrying to a carriage maker as important a matter as vulgar-minded mothers in the classes just above them consider ' marrying to a carriage.'

" All these things of course create much jealousy and bickering. The progress of democracy is not likely to be advanced by the agency of Trades' Unions formed of such ingredients."

The preceding extract shows clearly the non-effect of combination in *maintaining* the price of labour ; but we may further remark, that if the efforts of the workmen employed in the fabrication of instruments of pleasure, of any kind, could succeed in *advancing* their price, it is clear that the use of them must be contracted by the advance; and still more so, than in proportion to it : and those classes which would be excluded from the use of them by the advance, would expend as much of their spare income as might be thus rendered idle, in other means of enjoyment. Many workmen would thus be deprived of their customary employment, for the purpose of raising the wages of a small number, who still continued to retain it. A competition must then ensue between the employed and the unemployed classes, the result of which would be the return of prices to their old level, or even below it, and the return also, after a time, of the old demand for labour. Every scheme for interfering with the free disposal of property or labour, by the individual rightfully possessing, it becomes in practice wholly abortive, except for evil; though in some cases it requires considerable care and research to show the particular way in which the result works itself out.

The world presents to view on every side, and has done so in every age, a strong tendency in society to split itself into sections, of which some assume to be of higher rank than others. The mythic dawn of the ages when Egypt reared, by the labour of servile myriads, her massive and extending temples, witnessed the operation of the same principle which now breaks up a shop of coach makers into jealous castes. Whether this tendency is to be deemed a good, to be regulated and improved, or an evil, to be opposed and exterminated, is a grave question. At present, however, it seems to be an effectual security against the success of any wide-spread confederacy to endanger the general fabric of society.

The 13th chapter is given to a subject which no writer on " English Pleasure Carriages" can now dismiss in silence,—steam locomotion and railways. We pass over the clever and often (not always) correct remarks, with which it commences to give the following striking and novel view of the probable effects of rail roads on the demand for pleasure carriages.

" But even in the present condition of steam-coaches, enough has been done to excite the prejudices of many carriage builders, who fear lest their should be encroached on. They fear it may be possible for steam to supersede horses in pleasure carriages. To analyse this we must first define what is meant by pleasure carriages. All carriages which carry human beings may be called pleasure carriages, inasmuch as they are constructed to avoid the pain of walking; but the best definition of a pleasure carriage is, one not used for the purpose of business, or mere conveyance between near or distant places,—but for the purpose of pleasant exercise in the open air, or to facilitate the intercourse of social life, not as a matter of necessity, but of enjoyment. For pleasure carriages as thus defined, it is not likely that steam will be considered available. The reasons are sundry. In the first place, steam is a mere labourer —a drudge who performs his work without speech or sign, with dogged perseverance but without emotion. By dint of the garb in which he is clad, the machine which serves him for a body, he sometimes puts on the appearance of a live thing, shaking his polished metal clothing like an armed knight: but this is only when he is stationary. His travelling garb is rough and rude, his breadth is sulphureous, his voice is hissing, his joints creak, the anointing of his limbs gives forth an unpleasing gaseous odour, he carries with him a kitchen and a fuel chamber, and his whole appearance is black and unsightly. He may be personified when speaking *of* him; but no one pats his neck or speaks *to* him in a voice of encouragement. It is not so with a horse or horses. They are beautiful and intelligent animals, powerful, yet docile ; creatures that respond to kindness, and shrink from cruelty and injustice. The driver and owner can love them or feel proud of them; they step with grace, and can vary their form and movements in a thousand ways. They are creatures of individual impulses; and although injudicious treatment occasionally reduces them to blindness by artificial means, —though injudicious custom chooses to govern them by the sense of feeling rather than by the inflection of the voice modulated to their ear, still their is felt towards them a species of companionship. The man who rides a horse, feels a pleasure when the creature responds willingly to his purposes ; and when he responds unwillingly, he feels a pride in the exercise of his power to compel him to obedience. Even when a horse is vicious, there is a pleasurable excitement in riding him. The rider's nerves are strung, his senses are quickened ; eye, hand, and ear are alike on the alert; the blood rushes through his veins, and every faculty is aroused There is a feeling of proud consciousness that his individual skill and dexterity can render his life as secure in peril as other men's are under ordinary circumstances. Many men there are who prefer a horse to a certain extent dangerous.

> ' Oh ! the blood more stirs
> To rouse a lion than to start a hare.'

" Most men like a horse with vivacity, and few choose one which is merely adapted to work,—at least for riding. And thus it is with driving to a certain extent,—that is to say, for pleasure purposes. The carriage is built to harmonise with the horses, and the horses are selected to set off the carriage well. The carriage and horses form a combination ; and if they possess not harmonising points, they are unsightly. A cart-horse in an elegant carriage is as much an anomaly as a blood-horse in a heavy cart.

" But there are persons who merely need a carriage for the purpose of moving in the open air without personal trouble, and to whom a machine would be preferable if it afforded them the same facilities, together with a diminution of the inconveniences. In its present state, steam is not capable of supplying this purpose. The boiler and appurtenances are necessarily of great weight ; and the smaller they are made, the more proportionately heavy do they become as regards the work they are capable of performing. Fire, even of coke or charcoal—steam—the empyreumatic odour arising from heated oil, together with hissing noises, are nuisances of great amount. A steam gig or chariot would undoubtedly be a great acquisition for night work, saving horses and servants alike from illness and annoyance. It is a painful sensation to be at the opera and be conscious that the horses and servants are suffering pain, and perhaps imbibing the seeds of disease, exposed to rain, snow, or frost ; but as these are only casualities, they will be endured, rather than the certain annoyance from steam in its present state will be submitted to. For short trips by sea, steam is endured, because it is certain in its time, and against its inconveniences are to be set the fearful inflictions of protracted periods of sea sickness in sailing vessels ; but if it were a question of a permanent dwelling on the sea, most persons would prefer a sailing vessel to a steamer."

" The constructors of pleasure carriages have not only nothing to fear from the encroachments of steam, but, on the contrary, they may regard it in the light of an ally. Since the invention of steam-boats, the facility of exporting carriages to Ireland and the Continent, without the necessity of expensive packing, and without the uncertainty of arrival, has led to a greatly increased demand. In spite of the unwise exclusion contemplated by the custom-house laws of France, English carriages are now commonly seen in Paris and other parts, and they are universally preferred. On an infinitely greater scale will carriage-keeping be promoted by the introduction of rail-roads. Time was, that travelling coaches were something like baggage waggons, and travelled as slowly. People wanted to travel faster, and their baggage was sent by the waggon, as heavily-laden vehicles would not bear rapid motion. But the vehicles were improved, the baggage was lightened, and goods and passengers again travelled together. But the vehicles were wanted for other purposes than mere travelling ; they were needed as pleasure carriages in towns. Invention was set to work, and the same vehicle was made to show like a town coach one day, and like a travelling coach the next. But such vehicles were necessarily imperfect. The springs which are adapted to carry a light weight easily are not adapted to carry a heavy weight, and vice versâ: and a carriage must necessarily lose much of its beauty when used for travelling. These disadvantages have prevented many persons from keeping carriages, and have obliged some few to keep two carriages. But another motive has perhaps been still more forcible. In travelling with a carriage rapidly, it is necessary to go with post-horses ; or to travel by very easy stages, with a single pair. Few persons like to travel slowly, and fewer still, to leave their horses behind them and be deprived of their use ; and as the habits of those who keep carriages are mostly migratory at particular periods of the year, they would rather cease to keep horses and carriages than be confined to one spot. The desirable thing is to have one pleasure carriage perfect in all its parts, and to be able to convey it, servants, horses, baggage and all, at a rapid pace, from one point to another, without injury to carriage or horses ; to have the perfect use of it at any required spot, with as much facility as though the owner had not left his home.

" Steam locomotion on rail-roads will accomplish all this. The driver or the owner may drive the vehicle, with the family, servants, baggage and all appurtenances, on to a platform securely railed round, and steam will do its office in conveying them to their destination, without concussion, and without damage to the vehicle. When this shall come to pass, pleasure carriages will increase in number manifold."

The author demonstrates (no difficult task) that in most cases where steam locomotion on common roads would answer, it would pay still better to lay down a railroad ; and in the following extract .

from a subsequent chapter, he disposes of the objection to railways on the score of their enormous expense, in a manner equally striking and just :—

" The experiments on railroads have been condensed into the space of a few years, and we look at the cost of them in a mass ; but we say nothing of the cost of the experiments spread over a long number of years, by dint of which our common roads have attained their present state of perfection. The same reasons which hold good for applying iron to the bearing surfaces of our wheels, will be found ultimately to hold good with regard to the bearing surfaces of our roads, whether our draught power be steam or animals.*

A chapter on taste; one describing the different kinds of carriage now in use; and another on the preservation of carriages, complete the book so far as relates to vehicles of known construction.

The remainder of the book (about one fifth of its entire bulk) is occupied with descriptions of the author's patented inventions. Indeed it seems to be a peculiarity attaching to books on this subject, that their author's own novelties should originate them. The principal of these inventions, is a contrivance for turning carriages in less room than ordinary, though the fore-wheels are as large as the hind ones. This is effected in carriages of all kinds having four wheels, the omnibus and waggon included, by making the body in two parts, and uniting between the wheels by joints—one at the floor, and the other as much above or below, it as conveniently may be. The principle is ingeniously and tastefully applied to almost every description of pleasure carriage. We gave a view of the " Equirotal Town Chariot," in our last number with the author's account of it. Of the merit of this invention it is perhaps premature to speak with confidence. The advantages of close turning, and large wheels are not doubtful, but it is not to be expected that they will be attained on the first trial without some drawback. To turn closely requires more power than when the change of direction is not so suddenly made ; but

this is of little importance at the instant it is needful to turn so closely. Nimrod's assertion quoted in a note at page 285—" That if the body of a coach could be made to lock with the carriage, she would go round a corner in full speed without danger"—is scarcely correct, since a body as flexible as a rope, but as high from the ground, and as narrow on the base as a coach, must necessarily be in danger of upseting on turning at high speed very suddenly, from its centrifugal tendency alone. It is not, therefore, in the close turning in which this contrivance would be useful, that high speed and great power would be wanted. Mr. Adams's attempt to introduce high fore wheels, contrasts very advantageously with the preposterous arrangement of some lately-built omnibuses, where the greater part of the load is laid on the small fore wheels. The body will require much skill in the construction of its framework, as well as great strength and good workmanship in the joints to render it capable of enduring the incessant longitudinal vibration of travelling speeds on pavements and other rough roads. To Mr. A.'s perseverance and fertility of invention, however much may safely be left.

The remaining inventions are,—his spring wheel (described in our 23rd vol., p. 129)—a coach spring exactly like an archer's bow—the back being attached to the body and the string to the axle ;—and a deep cranked axle built of wood and iron. Remarks and suggestions on the construction of railroads and adaptations of the above-named inventions to railroad purposes, conclude the book. They are all distinguished for originality and boldness of design—and well deserve the serious attention of every one who is engaged in the construction of wheel carriages of whatever kind.

If Mr. A. sees objects too rapidly, and too few of them at once to form opinions likely to bear the test of future and broader inquiries,—he has on the other hand gathered from all times and regions innumerable topics of embellishment, and germs of improvement. No constructor of carriages can safely be without the book, and few who use them will choose to be so. There is no such book in the language. Felton's, besides being out of date altogether, is workshoplike. Fuller's highly useful work is strictly confined to its professed subject.

* One important item in swelling the costs of railroads, is, the increased value of the land purchased for them, saying nothing of the jobbing. The common roads have been made by small portions at a time, and improved gradually. To make a new line of common road now, for a great distance, would be found a sufficiently costly undertaking.

If the critical mechanic find few chapters in Mr. Adams's book without disputable points, he will be pleased with the novelty and variety of illustration, the vigour of thought and the suggestiveness everywhere displayed. Mr. A. has elevated his theme above its native technicality, by clever disquisitions on almost every connected subject, and rendered it an object as attractive to a cultivated taste, as it is important to the physical comforts, and material interests of life.

Before we conclude, we ought perhaps to observe, that Mr. Adams's numerous quotations are uniformly given without any reference to book, page, or date,—a fault which recoils on himself with double vengeance, since it deprives his work of the value as an authority, it would otherwise have undoubtedly acquired.

TELEGRAPHIC COMMUNICATION BETWIXT EDINBURGH AND LONDON.

(From the *Scotsman*).

It has been found by experiments made with a view to ascertaining the velocity of electricity, that it is transmitted instantaneously, by means of a common iron wire, a distance of eight miles; and electricians of the first eminence have declared their opinion that, judging from all scientific experience, the electric or galvanic influence would be almost instantaneously transmitted from one end to the other of a metallic conductor, such as ordinary copper wire of moderate thickness, of some hundred miles in length.

If this scientific theory is correct, it follows that a wire, secured by a coating of non-conductors, and protected from external influence or injury, and laid under the turnpike-road between Edinburgh and London, could be the means of distinctly indicating to a person stationed in London, that such wire had been electrified or galvanized in Edinburgh—the transmission of the electric or galvanic influence being clearly discernible by various well known means.

How, then, is this scientific fact to be applied to purposes of practical and general utility? Simply by laying as many wires separated from each other as will correspond to the letters of the alphabet, and preconcerting between the persons stationed at two extremities of the line of communication, that each individual wire is to represent a particular letter; because, if the person stationed in Edinburgh can, by applying the electric influence to any one wire, instantaneously apprise another person stationed in London that a particular letter of the alphabet is thereby indicated, words and sentences *ad infinitum*, may be communicated, and the idea of a perfect telegraph would be realized.

Without experience, it is impossible to say with what rapidity this electro-magnetic telegraph could be worked; but, in all probability, intelligence could be conveyed by such a medium as quickly as it is possible to write, or at least to print; an apparatus could be constructed somewhat resembling the keys of an organ, by which the letters of the telegraph could be touched with the most perfect ease and regularity.

It has been mentioned, that the transmission of the electricity or galvanism could be discernible by various means well known. If any indication, however slight, is made, that is enough, all that is wanted being that it should be perceivable by the person placed to watch the telegraph.

It has been assumed, that the electric current is capable of transmission by means of a single impulse from Edinburgh to London. But it is not indispensable that so great a distance should be accomplished at once. Intermediate stations for supplying the telegraph with new galvanic influence could be resorted to, and its perfect efficiency still preserved.

The best mode of troughing or protecting the metallic conductors, and separating them both from each other, and from the surrounding substances by which the electric or galvanic influence might be diverted, would, of course, require considerable scientific and mechanical skill; but the object appears perfectly attainable. Insulating or non-conducting substances, as gumlac, sulphur, resin, baked wood, &c., are cheap; and the insulation might be accomplished in many ways. For example, by laying the wires, after coating them with some non-conducting substances, in layers betwixt thin slips of baked wood, similarly coated, the whole properly fastened together and coated externally. These slips might be perhaps ten yards long, and at the joinings precautions for the expansion and contraction of the wire by the change of temperature, might be adopted. The whole might be enclosed in a strong oblong trough of wood, coated within and pitched without, and buried two or three feet under the turnpike road.

The expense of making the telegraph proposed is, of course, an important element in the consideration of its practicability and utility.

The chief material necessary, viz., copper wire, is by no means expensive. It is sold at 1*s*. 6*d*. per pound, of sixty yards in length. The cost of a wire from Edinburgh to London, say 400 miles, would thus be about 900*l.*; but say for solderings, &c., 100*l.* additional, or that each copper wire, laid from Edinburgh to London, would cost 1,000*l.* sterling, and that the total expense for the wires necessary to indicate separately each letter of the alphabet, would be 25,000*l.* The purchase of so large a quantity would, of course, be made at a considerably less price; but probably one or two additional wires might be needed, and the circuit of the electrical influence must be provided for by one or more return wires.

The coating, separating, and troughing of the wires can be accomplished by low-priced materials, and the total expense of the whole work (except the price of the wires), allowing a large sum for incidental expenditure, has been roughly estimated at 75,000*l.*, making a maximum expenditure of, say, 100,000*l.* for the completion of the telegraph. For a proportional additional sum it might be extended to Glasgow.

As to the working of the telegraph, it is apprehended, that even if the speed of writing were not attained, there could at least be no difficulty in indicating one letter per second. At this rate, a communication which would contain sixty-five words would occupy about five minutes. This is supposing the vowels to be all indicated. But abbreviation in this, and many other respects, would no doubt be contrived; and the number of words in the communication supposed, are greater than necessary for an ordinary banking or commercial letter, or for friendly inquiries and responses. Supposing, however, that each communication was to occupy five minutes, and to be charged five shillings each, if the telegraph was worked twelve hours a-day (that is, six hours from each end), it would produce a revenue of 36*l.* daily, or 10,800*l.* per annum, supposing there were 300 working days in the year. If, however, the plan is practicable, the public intelligence that would, no doubt, be transmitted by the telegraph would be sufficient to keep it in operation night and day.'

Arrangements are being made for having the necessary experiments tried on a metallic conductor of fifty or a hundred miles in length, and if the same instantaneous and perfect indication of the passage of the electric or galvanic fluid is found to take place, as in the case of the recent experiments at the University, the triumph of the scheme would be complete.

NOTES AND NOTICES.

Cook-omotion.—Sir Samuel Morland, who lived at Vauxhall House in 1675, had a 'coach with a moveable kitchen, with clock work machinery; in which he could make soup, broil steaks, or roast a joint of meat. When he travelled he was his own cook. Sir Samuel was as eccentric in his tastes, at home as abroad; the side table in his dining-room, was supplied with a large fountain, and the glasses stood under little streams of water.

Immense Tuns.—The Heidelburg great tun appears to have been a vain boast; there is at Beaufoy's vinegar works, at Lambeth, a vessel full of sweet wine, containing 59,109 gallons; and another full of vinegar, containing 56,799 gallons; the lesser of which exceeds the Heidelburg tun by forty barrels.

Singularly Shaped Hail Stones.—On the 14th of May, M. Elie de Beaumont being at Clamart, in the direction of Plessis Piquet, witnessed a remarkable hail storm, which proceeded from a cloud of small extent, and low in height above the surface of the earth. The stones were singular in form, being all *angular* and *pyramidal*; the opposite face to the pyramid was *curved*, and appeared to be the segment of a concentric sphere. All were composed of very distinct fibres directed spherically, and at the same time presenting marks of concentric zones; they were white and semi-opaque; they appeared to have been spheres of ice, as large as a pistol or musket ball, and formed by progressive movement, but all broken before they reached the earth.—*Gazette de France.*

A society for the encouragement of the study of electricity has been formed in London.

New Plan for Propagating Apple Trees.—A new plan for increasing plantations of apple trees has lately been carried into extensive practice by the horticulturists of Bohemia. *Neither seed nor grafting is required.* The process is to take shoots from the choicest sorts, insert them in a potatoe, and plunge both into the ground, leaving but an inch or two of the shoot above the surface. The potatoe nourishes the shoot, while it pushes out roots, and the shoot gradually grows up and becomes a beautiful tree, bearing the best fruit.—*Suabian Mercury.*

Watering Vegetables.—A solution of soda has been applied with great success. The difference between vegetables so treated, and those watered in the usual way is very conspicuous. Vegetable marrow in common mould has been found to surpass plants grown in a bed of dung. The proportion used is one pound to fourteen gallons of water.—*Enniskillen Chronicle.*

Uses of the Sun Flower.—The value of this plant, which is easily cultivated, and ornamental to the garden, is scarcely known in most parts of the kingdom. The seed forms a most excellent and convenient food for poultry, and all that is necessary is to cut off the heads of the plant when ripe, tie them in bunches, and hang them up in a dry situation, to used as wanted. They not only fatten every kind of poultry, but greatly increase the quantity of eggs they lay. When cultivated to a considerable extent, they are also capital food for sheep and pigs, and for pheasants and partridges. The leaves when dried form a good powder for cattle; the dry stalks burn well, and form an abundance of alkali; and in bloom the flower is most attractive to bees.

Light evolved from Insects.—A singular phenomenon was witnessed on Tuesday evening, in the city of Canterbury. The residents within and near the precincts of the Old Castle, at the southern entrance of the city, were alarmed in the night by a stream of red light, apparently issuing from the old ruins, as if a fire was raging below. On repairing to the spot it was discovered that the light emanated from an innumerable swarm of small insects, which had collected on the walls and about the old ruins. The moon was not visible, and, with the exception of the spot on which they had located, all was darkness. With the morning sun the little creatures disappeared. About thirty years ago a similar phenomenon was witnessed on these walls.—*Kentish Gazette.*

New Food for Silk Worms.—An experiment, possessing much interest and importance to the rearers of silk worms, has just been made at Epinal, by which it appears that the leaves of the scorzenera, a plant well known in the culinary art, have been used with much success for feeding those valuable insects.—*Sussex Agricultural Express.*

Science in the Legislature.—The new parliamen will, to all appearance, have a smaller number of scientific members (always few enough) than the last, which, in its turn, had fewer than that which preceded it. Sir George Cayley will have no seat in the first parliament of Queen Victoria, while Mr. Babbage is farther off the object of ambition than ever. Mr. Ewart, the magnanimous trumpeter of foreign art, and would be patron of foreign artists at the expense of English, has lost his election for Liverpool. Mr. Morrison, also, who was a sort of representative of the artistic-manufacturing interest, has disappeared from the house, and, as far as is known, has left no successor. The principal scientific men who remain there are Mr. Heathcoat, the member for Tiverton, well known for his inventions in lace machinery, and the (said-to-be-unsuccessful) steam-plough: Mr. Handley, the member for Lincolnshire, whose exertions to introduce steam-machinery in agriculture have been great and long-continued; and Mr. Jephson, the member for Mallow; who holds a high reputation in the mechanical world. We believe Mr. Rotch, the barrister, better known to fame as the inventor of the patent screw-fid, has not secured a seat on the present occasion, or, of course, he would have to be added to the scanty list.

Steam Communication with India.—There is now some tangible ground for the belief, or rather the hope, that this great object will very shortly be accomplished. Those two slow moving bodies, Government and the East India Company, have at length progressed so far, in accordance with the recommendation of the House of Commons' Committee (which ought to have taken effect years ago) that the steamers necessary to complete the line are at length ordered to be fitted for their stations, and are expected to commence plying almost immediately. It is to be hoped there will now be no more slips "betwen the cup and the lip," but it has been more than suspected that the East India Company took up the scheme only for the purpose of more conveniently overlaying it. We think, however, public opinion is now so strong upon the subject, that this is now beyond their power, and that the long-desired communication is at last in a fair way of being established.

Schmidbauer's Power-Carriage. — In a paragraph in the German papers we find some information of Schmidbauer's "Power-Carriage," which we learn with amazement from the same authority has been attracting universal attention for several years past. This famous carriage is, it appears, set in motion by the action of an hydraulic press, and was to display its powers by going up hill with as much ease as over level ground. Two mechanicians of the name of Mannhardt and Drossbach, have recently examined its construction and given the result to the public. They pronounce the principle to be worthless, its application clumsy, the construction of the vehicle disgraceful, its performances contemptible, and the whole concern a humbug. The "Hamburg Correspondent" adds, that "it is understood that from thirty to forty thousand florins (three or four thousand pounds) have been expended by Englishmen on the construction of this carriage, a fact," it remarks, "by no means incredible, since Messieurs, the British, often sacrifice the highest sums to the oddest ideas." We are afraid that to this charge we can hardly plead "not guilty."

First Railroad from Paris.—The railroad from Paris to St. Germain, the first constructed in the neighbourhood of that capital, was intended to be opened, if possible, on the occasion of the annual festivals, in honour of the three days of July. It was, however, only found practicable to make an experimental trip on the 30th of that month, some of the rails having then only been laid down the preceding night, and the public opening has been deferred to the 15th of August. A railroad to Versailles is, it appears, in contemplation, and is considered more likely to pay than any other in the neighbourhood of Paris, especially since, by the alteration of Louis Phillip's new museum, which outdoes all former outdoings in that line, the daily number of passengers has been increased from fourteen or fifteen hundred to fourteen or fifteen thousand; and though, of course, not likely to continue at that extreme height, will in all probability, considerably exceed for the future what it formerly has been, even in its palmiest times. The *Constitutionnel* indulges in a view of congratulation at the completion of the St. Germain railroad, which seems a little too lofty, when it is considered how far their despised neighbours of Belgium, have been allowed to outstrip the now dilatory French, in this important branch of commercial enterprise. The same journal refers with great satisfaction to the prospect now it appears entertained of dispensing with the use of English iron in the construction of the railways; but although the writer is very indignant at the notion of being "tributary," to England for iron, he appears to entertain no sort of objection to being "tributary" to England for the invention, or rather of taking it without paying tribute at all. Let the French invent a method of guiding balloons, and we hope the English will exhibit a range of ideas a little superior to the meanness and malice of borrowing the discovery, and at the same time prohibiting the importation of French silks for the manufacture of the article.

Steam Vessels in Sweden.—The progress of Sweden in steam-navigation may be considered as very creditable to that country, when we reflect that in spite of great natural resources, it is at present the poorest in Europe. The number of steam vessels now in activity amounts to twenty-six, of which four belong to the government, and twenty-two to private individuals. The horse-power of the four government steamers is stated at 275, and that of the private ones at only 899;—the average, therefore, for one of the former is 68 horses, and for one of the latter 40, or one-tenth of the power of the large steamer just launched at Bristol, to run between that port and New York, three of a similar size to which would exceed in power the whole Swedish twenty-six. Four other steam-vessels are now, however, in course of building for the Swedish government, and it is intended to go on gradually adding more and more to the navy.

To Dilute Ink.—One of the best substances for diluting ink that has become too thick for use is a strong decoction of coffee, which appears in no respect to promote the decomposition of the ink, while it improves its colour, and gives it an additional lustre. This useful discovery was made by Dr. Bostock, the chairman of the committee of chemistry, and is communicated in a valuable article "On the improvements in black writing ink," inserted in the 47th vol. of the *Transactions of the Society of Arts, &c.*

Erratum—in a few impressions of our present number, p. 310, col. 1, line 14, for "reiterated," read "reckoned."

☞ *British and Foreign Patents taken out with economy and despatch; Specifications, Disclaimers, and Amendments, prepared or revised; Caveats entered; and generally every Branch of Patent Business promptly transacted.*

A complete list of Patents from the earliest period (15 Car. II. 1675,) to the present time may be examined, Fee 2s. 6d.; Clients, gratis.

LONDON: Printed and Published for the Proprietor, by W. A. Robertson, at the Mechanics' Magazine Office, No. 6, Peterborough-court, between 135 and 136, Fleet-street.—Sold by G. W. M. Reynolds, Proprietor of the French, English, and American Library, 55, Rue Neuve, Saint Augustin, Paris.

𝕸𝖊𝖈𝖍𝖆𝖓𝖎𝖈𝖘' 𝕸𝖆𝖌𝖆𝖟𝖎𝖓𝖊,

MUSEUM, REGISTER, JOURNAL, AND GAZETTE.

| No. 732. | SATURDAY, AUGUST 19, 1837. | Price 3d. |

DR. HARE'S NEW AIR-PUMP AND CONDENSER.

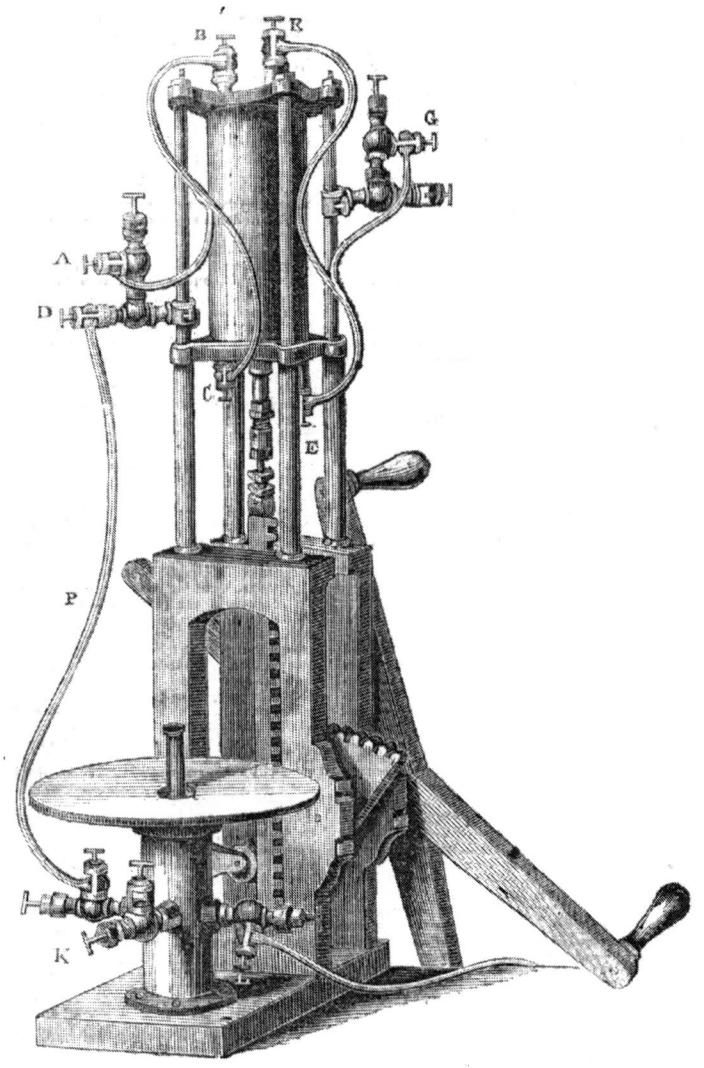

DESCRIPTION OF AN AIR-PUMP OF A NEW CONSTRUCTION, WHICH ACTS EITHER AS AN AIR-PUMP, OR A CONDENSER, OR AS BOTH ; ENABLING THE OPERATOR TO EXHAUST, TO CONDENSE, TO TRANFER A GAS FROM ONE CAVITY TO ANOTHER, OR TO PASS IT THROUGH A LIQUID. BY R. HARE, M.D., &c.

This pump has one iron chamber,* one piston and four valves. When in operation, it is always simultaneously exhausting and condensing ; and, of course, accomplishes as much, in a given time, as two chambers of the usual construction, of the same calibre and stroke. A suction valve is placed at each end of a steel rod, which slides through the packing of the piston,† so as to be airtight, and to be pressed in opposite directions alternately. It is of such a length, that while it forces one valve, towards which the piston moves, against its seat, closing a corresponding aperture, it withdraws the other valve from its seat, and, consequently, opens the aperture with which this valve corresponds. Hence, with every reversal of the motion, the aperture previously opened, will be shut, while that previously shut will be opened. Between the apertures thus alternately opened and shut, and the valve cock A, a communication is made by means of a forked leaden pipe, communicating with the valve cock at A, and with the apertures at B and C. The valve cock, by means of a gallows screw D, communicates, when desirable, with any receiver by another flexible leaden pipe P.

Two other analogous and corresponding apertures E, R, which communicate in like manner with a valve cock G, are furnished with two valves opening outwards. These, when not subjected to any pressure from within the chamber, are kept in their places by spiral springs. They act as valves of efflux, and, like the valves in other condensers, are opened by the pressure of the air condensed by the piston as it approaches them, and are shut by springs when the piston moves in the opposite direction. It is well known, however, that this mode of opening valves, if unassisted, always allows a small portion of condensed air to remain in that portion of the chamber and of the passage leading to the valve, which the piston cannot be made to occupy entirely. This disadvantage is diminished in the case of the valves which I am describing. A stem proceeding from each valve enters the chamber so far, as that the piston cannot finish the stroke without coming in contact with the stem, and moving the valve sufficiently to allow the air to escape, without suffering any resistance from the valve and its spring.

The means by which the apertures of the suction valves communicate with a valve cock A, and may be made to communicate with the receiver through the pipe P, have been explained. By like means the communication, existing between the apertures of the valves of efflux and a valve cock G, may be extended from this valve cock to any receiver. In fact, it is only necessary to vary the situation or number of the pipes, by which communications with the chamber are effected, in order to cause the apparatus to perform the part of an air pump, a condenser, or both. When employed to transfer air, it would be more correctly designated as a forcing air-pump, than as a condenser.

The disk of brass in front of the pump, serves as an air-pump plate, when connected with the pump by means of the pipe P, as represented in the drawing. (See front page.) It is supported on a hollow brass cylinder, furnished with valve cocks as at K L, in order to allow various experiments to be performed by means of the tube, in the axis, surmounted by a cup of copper. The tube being open at the lower end, the cup is accessible to an incandescent iron. This contrivance facilitates the exposure of substances to heat, either in vacuo, or in any gas. When boric acid and potassium are thus heated, boron is evolved. By means of a similar arrangement, heating chloride of calcium with potassium, I obtained a potassuret of calcium, which decomposed water and yielded a solution which was rendered milky by carbonic acid.

When a glass globe of fifteen gallons is exhausted over this plate, and filled with oxygen gas, phosphorus having been previously placed in the copper cup, on heating the phosphorus, a combustion ensues of trascendent splendour.

For this and other experiments, the hollow cylinder, which supports the air pump plate, may be screwed into a hole in a table and placed at any convenient distance from the air pump. With this view, there is a conical screw cut upon the lower end of the cylinder,

The mechanism by which the piston is moved, is too obvious to need description. There is, however, a peculiarity in the construction of the piston rod, which is of great utility. The rod is hollow, having been sufficiently reduced in diameter from a piece of gun barrel by the wire-drawing process.

---

* The diameter of the chamber in the instrument represented in the figure is three inches ; the length is ten and a half inches, allowing a stroke of about eight inches, taking off the thickness of the piston. In order to render this instrument unsusceptible of injury from mercury, it was constructed altogether of iron or cast steel.

† This contrivance was suggested to me by an excellent pump with glass chambers, obtained many years ago from Pixii. In that pump a steel rod is made to open and shut one valve : in mine the same rod opens and shuts two valves.

The bore of this *hollow* rod is occupied by a solid rod, which extends from the metallic disk, at the farther end of the piston, to the rack. To the other disk, the hollow rod is fastened. The leather packing between the disks, being turned in the lathe so as to fit the calibre of the chamber accurately, is made more or less tight by the action of a screw just above the rack. Hence the pressure may be regulated without taking the pump apart, which is always troublesome, and at some periods impracticable within the time at command.

With respect to the efficacy of this pump, satisfactory proof was given some time since, at the Franklin Institute, when it raised the mercury very near to the height of that in the Torricellian tube.

Having been in possession for many years of an elegant air pump with glass chambers furnished by Pixii, we have been induced to give the preference to the new instrument, in all cases where a perfect exhaustion has been desirable.

Of the three valve cocks, one usually communicates with a gage; since, instead of an instrument of that nature permanently associated with the pump, and which is subjected to exhaustion by means of a lateral communication with the perforation leading to the cavity of the receiver, I employ a moveable barometer gage, which is made to communicate with the receiver directly. The operator is thus enabled to observe the quantity of gas in the receiver, after the communication with the air pump is arrested by closing the valve cock through which it was established.—*Trans. Amer. Phil. Soc.*

HUTCHISON'S, AND BACON AND KILBY'S GAS BURNERS.

Sir,—In my former communication, I meant no more than to protest against the merit of an invention being conferred on Mr. Hutchison, which I believed, and still believe, to be justly due to others. Clovis would have been secure from any further notice from me, had he confined himself within reasonable bounds; but the misrepresentations of his last letter, imperatively demand, if unintentional, correction, and if wilful, exposure.

Clovis favours us with two diagrams which he introduces with a perverted quotation. "Here are the counterfeit representations of two burners. A. Hutchinson's.—B. Kilby and Bacon's." B, is in very truth a "counterfeit representation" of Bacon and Kilby's burner. It is neither it,—nor in the least like it. There is no such thing as a "broad and

circular ring brazed in the upper surface" of Kilby and Bacon's burner; the one he comments on is not Kilby and Bacon's, and therefore, any reply to his objections is unnecessary.

No such explanation, however, can qualify the assertion, made by Clovis, that Mr. Rutter's eulogy in your 603rd number, does not apply to the burner patented by Kilby and Bacon, but that it is confined to "an adjunct to a burner, called a gallery cone." Now Mr. Rutter fixes his praise as plainly as words can do it on "a burner," not a gallery cone,—stating the improvement to consist in the apertures by which air is admitted to the flame, being contracted as regards both the interior and exterior of the burner; and he expressly particularises the burner as patented by Messrs. Dixon, Walsall, knowing it only as an article in the market by the name of the manufacturer stamped upon it; and he adds, that "he knows nothing whatever of the manufacturers themselves." Clovis can hardly be ignorant that the burner of Messrs. Dixon, which was the subject of Mr. Rutter's remarks, is identical with the burner patented by Kilby and Bacon, for he says, "the burner of 1829, was before him as he wrote," and if it was, it must have been stamped with the words, "E. and W. Dixon, Walsall."

Clovis again says, that the merits of this burner "are yet to be discovered—hitherto they have remained in profound and undisturbed obscurity." Here again he is in error. In Liverpool, Sheffield, Leeds, Birmingham, Manchester, and a great many other towns, it has almost altogether superseded the sale of the old Argand. If not so much so in London, the fact is easily accounted for by the circumstance, that the burners are in the great majority of cases supplied by fitters on contract, to whom the cheapest burner is therefore obviously the best. Nevertheless, they have had a considerable sale in London, whilst the sale of Hutchison's, I believe, is confined entirely to the company of which he is, or was, the engineer. But the manner, in which Mr. Rutter speaks of becoming acquainted with this burner, is sufficient to show that it has not "been buried in profound obscurity."

As to the "experimental observations" with which Clovis has favoured us, tending chiefly to show that by excluding air from flame, you deprive it at the same time of oxygen, I feel no disposition to disturb so profound a truth. But I deny that his speculative inference from that fact, of the inferiority of Kilby and Bacon's burner, is borne out either by experiment or observation. And to prove what I say, I would again adduce the testimony of Mr. Rutter (grounded on numerous detailed experiments) who dwells not only on the economy, but also on the peculiarly *steady light* of the burner in question. Or if any of your readers should prefer the evidence of their own senses, they may satisfy themselves of the faultlessness of the burner in this respect by a single *" experimental observation"* of the way in which the splendid shop of Everington on Ludgate Hill is lighted.

Clovis then considerately informs us, that " the principle of an invention cannot be protected by a patent," and that, " principle cannot be monopolised." For his luminous exposition of this occult doctrine, your intelligent readers must feel duly grateful. I much question, however, whether the invention of Messrs. Kilby and Bacon will serve to illustrate his proposition, as he would charitably lead us to infer, and I would invite him to peruse their specification before he again draws his *partial* diagrams and fallacious conclusions.

This point however, as well as Mr. Hutchison's pretensions to originality, will be speedily determined by an authoritative tribunal, whose judgment I am content to await. Meanwhile, I cannot share in the amiable pleasure which Clovis anticipates from " the decision of the court, establishing an instance of that absurd enthusiasm which leads inexperienced persons to expend and waste money upon crude, useless, and imaginary inventions." I am not able to join him. To my mind, such instances, when they happen are rather to be lamented. The race we know is not always to the swift, nor the battle to the strong, and the failure of honest exertions, from whatever cause, ought surely to awaken sympathy and regret, rather than exultation. Where indeed a man seeks to appropriate to himself the labours of another, to which he has not the least right, his disappointment may afford more legitimate satisfaction.

I am, Sir, your obedient servant,
JUSTUS.

METALLIC VALVES FOR FIRE-ENGINES.

Sir,—Under the article "Fire-engine," in the " Engineers' and Mechanics' Cyclopædia," by L. Hebert, in speaking of Newsham, it is observed, "that the description of his fire-engine will be read with much interest when it is considered so perfect was his machine, that at the expiration of above a century, we still find it nearly as he left it."

A considerable number of engines, some vibratory, others rotary, have been introduced; but all these have been found wanting in efficiency and durability, as compared with that of Newsham. When it is considered that fire-engines generally meet with the most unaccountable neglect, it will be seen that permanency of working condition is a most important feature in machines of this description.

The only alteration of Newsham's engine that has made any way in public estimation is the re-arrangement of parts introduced with a view to increased efficiency and durability by Mr. Charles Simpkin, who, in the year 1792, patented an improvement in fire-engines, " which consisted principally in the employment of separate chambers for containing the valves, instead of placing them within the cylinders and air-vessels, as was done previously. Mr. Simpkin (afterwards of the firm of Hadley, Simpkin, and Lott), Long Acre, London, materially altered the internal arrangement of the working parts, and constructed an engine much more compact and convenient than any of its predecessors. As a travelling engine, it was infinitely superior to any previously built ; the only method of conveying Newsham's engine about, was by placing it in a cart or waggon made purposely for it, and many of our metropolitan readers will recollect that the London Assurance, Royal Exchange, and Phœnix, Fire Offices, continued to run Newsham's engines in this manner to the end of the year 1832, when these and other offices combined in forming a general fire-engine establishment, which adopted Simpkin's form of engine."*

Another improvement, which accompanied those already noticed, was the introduction of perpendicular metallic, in lieu of horizontal leather, valves.

* The Engineers' and Mechanics' Cyclopædia, vol. i. p. 509.

As this particular form of valve has not yet appeared in print, and is not nearly so well known as it deserves, although at this time employed in all parts of the world, I send herewith a sketch of a metallic valve from a fifth size fire-engine, constructed by Mr. Merryweather, successor to Messrs. Hadley,

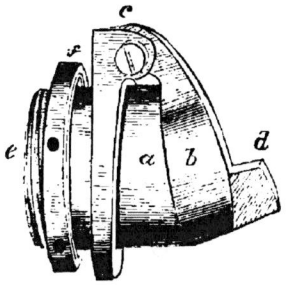

Simpkin, and Co. : *a* is the valve-seat; *b*, the valve hinged on to a shoulder at *c* by two screw pins; *d* is a projecting piece of metal, which, striking against the cover of the valve-chamber, limits the opening of the valve to any approved extent. These valves are very beautifully executed, the valve being so accurately fitted to its seat by grinding, as to close the opening in an air-tight manner. The mode of fixing the valve in its place is as follows :—Perpendicular partitions are cast in the sole of the engine, which forms the valve-chambers, with a circular opening of a proper size to receive the neck of the valve *e*, upon the end of which a strong screw is cut. The valve being put in its proper situation, with a stout leather washer between the partition in the sole and the shoulder or flanch *c*, the ring-nut *f* is screwed up tight on the opposite side of the partition, making a good sound joint.

From the circumstance of the valve hanging almost perpendicularly, a very small force is sufficient to open it; but in proportion to the extent of its opening, is its tendency to shut quickly increased. From the peculiarity of position, and the small quantity of surface presented by the valve-seat, there is no place for the lodgment of foreign matters that would otherwise injure the action of the valves and obstruct the working of the engine. The manner in which the valve is hinged to the shoulder, also causes it to open clear away from the seat, leaving a free passage for the water, and any impurities with which it may be charged.

These valves have now in almost every instance superseded those of leather, the perishable character of which have led to frequent and serious failures in the time of need; "there's nothing like leather" —for boots and shoes, perhaps, but in hydraulic machinery this commodity can be most advantageously dispensed with.

I remain, Sir,
Yours respectfully,
WM. BADDELEY.

Wellington-street, Blackfriars Road,
August 5th, 1837.

REMARKS BY MR. ADAMS, ON THE REVIEW OF HIS " ENGLISH PLEASURE CARRIAGES."

Sir,—While recognizing with pleasure the approbation bestowed on my volume by your periodical work, I wish to avail myself of a portion of your columns as an arena open to all appellants, in order to reply to some objections of the reviewer. First, as to elasticity. " One of the qualities which render ash peculiarly valuable for carriages, is the absence of elasticity, and consequent indisposition to alter its form by its own internal efforts." I agree with the reviewer, that the meaning of this sentence is obscure. The meaning I wished to convey is, that ash timber is little liable to warp, and is moreover very plastic. Even this must be qualified, for some ash is brittle, while other kinds, especially that which is white in colour and wide grained, is exceedingly tough, and may be made to take any required shape. It is difficult to define, in common language, what elasticity is. All bodies possess elasticity, varying from the extreme of brittleness to the extreme of toughness—from a block of marble to a piece of sponge. Yew and lancewood are the most elastic woods when the elasticity of a spring is required, and, like all elastic woods, are subject to fracture, as is the case with tempered steel. Fir also is an elastic wood, but it is very brittle, probably owing to its porous texture, which permits the fibres to crush on compression. It is the plasticity of ash, as opposed to elasticity, which constitutes its fitness to resist fracture on concussion, and renders it little liable to warp, in comparison with other woods of equal density and irregular grain.

The mode of constructing wheels which I consider the best to ensure the elasticity requisite to prevent the mischievous effects of concussion when travelling at speed, will be easily understood by the accompanying sketches. Fig. 1 re-

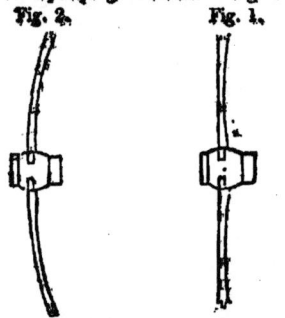

Fig. 2.   Fig. 1.

presents a nave shewn laterally with two opposite spokes framed into it. These spokes are lightened out on their front sides, leaving their ends of full size. Fig. 2 shews the spokes forcibly bent over to the front by the action of the shrinking tire.

The greatest strain on a wheel is at the nave, and the greatest concussion at the periphery, consequently those are the points of wear. If, therefore, the spokes be of equal strength throughout, they must shake loose in their framings. But if they be reduced at their mid-length, they will possess an elastic action available to elude concussion, and relieve the framings from the strain.

The reviewer says, speaking of Mr. Hynes' patent axle-box, "whether this effectual mode of becoming independent of *washing up* has been tried on any considerable scale, we do not know." There must be an error here. If the circular magazine be filled with oil, it will remain full so long as the wheel be not in motion, but the moment the motion begins, the oil will be pumped away and discharged at the shoulder collar; and this process will go on till the surface level of the oil be at the level of the under surface of the axle arm, when the wasteful expenditure will cease, and the remainder of the oil will be economically used.

Speaking of carriage springs, the reviewer says, "in the spring, the leverage is to every plate the same, namely, the length of the longest plate; the plates, therefore, ought to be of equal thickness * * *. A spring composed of plates of unequal thickness will require a greater weight of metal to render it capable of a given duty than one of equal plates." If, by the word "duty," the reviewer means *power of resistance,* he is right, and in this sense, a spring composed of a single plate equal to the total of the laminæ will perform still more duty. But the real duty of a spring is to yield—not to resist, and in the act of yielding, a luminated spring, composed of several plates, sliding on one another, varies the leverage of the different parts. A reference to the subjoined figure will clearly shew this. A shews a straight

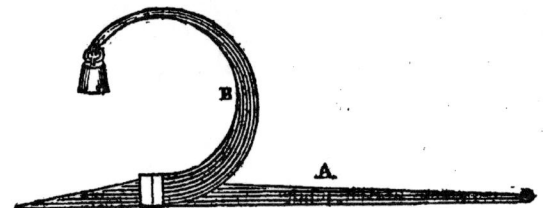

figure composed of several plates; B shews the same spring bent into a circular form, a form which all straight springs, when in action, approach to, more or less. The inner plates of B being curves of less diameter than the outer ones, have a greater power of resistance, i. e. the strain on their fibres is greater, and the only mode of making

the strain equal to the outer plates, is to reduce the thickness in the same proportion as the diameter. Therefore, though the theory of the reviewer is sound, it does not hit the case, because the enumeration of the circumstances is deficient, resistance being substituted for yielding.

With regard to the fact that two carriages built precisely alike, as far as external evidence goes, will not run equally light, there are several circumstances that may explain it. If it be an under-spring carriage, a variation in the play of the springs may arise either from varying friction in the plates, or from the centres of motion at the spring ends being untrue, and either of these causes will materially affect the draught. There may also be an inaccuracy almost imperceptible in the adjustment of the axles, so that the two hinder wheels be not at a right angle with the line of draught. The motion of a carriage somewhat resembles that of a vessel on the water. It is not in a straight line, but in a series of curves to right and left alternately. It is therefore most important that both the vessel and the carriage should be of flexible structure, in order to diminish friction. The French privateers, during the war, were occasionally constructed with wedges in their beams, so that, when chased, the obstruction of the wedges would afford greater flexibility and speed. The fastest rowing boats we know of are the Deal gigs and the Thames wherries, and flexibility is in them even a more prominent quality than lightness. The facility of draught in my equirotal carriages is not owing merely to the increase of size in the front wheels, but also to their flexibility arising from their vertebral construction and the perfect action of the bow-springs, which yield in all directions to every inequality. The front portion of the carriage also acts as a lever to the hind part, so that whenever the front wheels are turned to a curve, the hind ones are turned to follow the same curve. This same quality prevents the necessity of a drag chain and shoe, for in going down hill, supposing the front wheels to follow a straight line, if the hinder axle be drawn to an angle of greater or less inclination, by any simple purchase, any amount of friction may be given to the hinder wheels. The importance of flexibility as an aider of draught cannot be better illustrated than by a reference to the almost bye-gone days of hackney-coaches. It is well known that those useful vehicles were remarkable not merely for the play of their springs, but also of all their screw bolts and joints without exception. Their movement, therefore, was exceedingly easy, if not graceful, and the power of the lean horses was suffi-

cient to keep them going. This gave rise to an occasional practical jest when the coachman stayed too long at the public-house. Some wag would screw up all the loose bolts during his absence, and when he returned to ply the whip, the result was either a break down, or a total stoppage, which no horse "steam" could overcome. It was probably after some such prank as this that the author of the Pickwick papers describes the horses "as about to assassinate the coachman."

It is generally assumed that the motion of carriages on our modern railroads is in a straight line, where curves do not intervene. But such is not the fact. No rails are really straight lines. They are a series of small sinuosities, and the carriages which run on them having fixed axles are—supposing those axles to be perfectly parallel—only calculated to run in straight lines. But if those axles be not perfectly parallel, then the carriages are only adapted to run on curves corresponding to the angle at which the axles are set. The result is, a large amount of concussion, friction, and destructive wear. The wheels follow the draught on the straight line or the curve, to whichever their adjustment disposes them, and are met by a sinuous projection, which throws them off just as the course of a river is turned by a rocky point; they again follow their course until they meet another obstacle, and the same results are renewed. The only remedy for this is, to construct the carriages so that the action of the draught may regulate the adjustment of the axles, and this once done, a curved line of road would be found as available as a straight line, wherever it may be desirable to avoid expensive obstacles. But, with your permission, I will enter more at large on this subject at a future opportunity, and meanwhile remain

Yours obediently,

WILLIAM B. ADAMS.

121, Long Acre, August 8, 1837.

WHISHAW'S ANALYSIS OF RAILWAYS.

The somewhat old-fashioned amplitude of Mr. Whishaw's title-page, which we have copied below,* will serve to give a

* Analysis of Railways; consisting of a Series of Reports on the Twelve Hundred Miles of projected Railways in England and Wales now before Parlia-

tolerably correct idea of the nature of his very laborious work. And yet, notwithstanding all its particularity, the reader can hardly help feeling disappointed, on penetrating into the body of the book, to find it so excessively temporary in its character. In a pamphlet, the stamp of permanency is not looked for, but it is a different matter when a portly octavo *volume* is in the question. It is grating to the feelings to find that an entity so outwardly respectable is destined, from the nature of its matter, to become in a great degree superannuated within three weeks after its first appearance, and, after flourishing for a few short months, to be cast aside with as little unconcern or impropriety as "yesterday's paper." Yet so it is. Mr. Whishaw confines his attention solely to the projects *now* (or rather *then*, for the title-page is already out of date) before Parliament. The few railways completed come not within his ken ; the many begun, or for which Acts have been obtained, lie beyond his range of vision, and it rather unfortunately happens, that these two classes include by far the most interesting parts of what might, from the general title, most naturally be supposed to form the staple of an "analysis of railways." But Mr. Whishaw will have nothing to do with substantiality ; he deals only, ponderous as his production may appear, in details of the gossamer dreams of projectors, and elaborate plans, elevations, and sections, of castles in the air. It is therefore no wonder that his volume should be bulky, or, at the same time, that its utility should be less apparent than its bulk.

Proceeding in alphabetical order, Mr. Whishaw first gives a minute account of the direction of each proposed line, with reference to mansions, parks, houses, and other remarkable objects, by measurement in chains. All this, of course, may be supposed to be vastly interesting to the parties concerned, but it is undoubtedly "caviare to the general." If

ment, together with those which have been abandoned for the present Session; to which are added, a Table of Distances from the proposed London Termini to eight well-known Places in the Metropolis ; a Table exhibiting the Length, Cost, Tunnelling, Curves, &c. of each of the Railways for which Bills are now in progress through Parliament ; with a Glossary, and other useful Information. By Francis Whishaw, Esq., Civil Engineer, M. Inst. C. E. London ; 1837. Weale. 8vo.; pp. 312.

the same process were gone through with actually existing railways, the result would be a very dry collection of names and distances ; but it is still worse when the same thing is gravely done with respect to all the lines projected, many of which will never be executed at all, while many more will be so materially diverted from their present intended course, that the measurements now given will be useless. A precise account of all the bearings of the course of one Brighton railway, *in esse*, might pass muster, but in Mr. Whishaw's elaborate work, we have similar details of four or five Brighton lines *in posse*; and, to puzzle matters still more, it is almost certain that not one of these lines will be that finally adopted ; in which case, of course, our author's information on the subject will at once become mere waste paper.

After the detailed account, Mr. Whishaw invariably gives the particulars of the curves under three-quarters-of-a-mile radius, of the gradients, length of planes, and so forth, and of the tunnels and viaducts, winding up with the contents of the excavations and other earthworks required, the number of crossings of roads, canals, and navigable rivers, and a few general "remarks." To all this mass of matter, the last head, perhaps, excepted, the same objection applies ; and even, in a great degree, to that, as Mr. Whishaw declines to present his readers with his own opinions on the comparative merits of the various lines, or to do more than point out now and then some of their most obvious peculiarities. We could have wished that he had given himself more latitude as a critic, since, as he tells us in his preface, one of the main objects of the work is to enable the public to separate the schemes of real utility and practicability from the very numerous ones of an opposite character. Mr. Whishaw puts the materials for judging in the hands of the public, that is, if the public had been bred under a civil engineer : he should have gone farther, and have shewn how the materials were to be used, after providing them to hand. Mr. Whishaw shrinks from the task, on account of its apparent invidiousness ; but those who would enlighten the world on the subject of projected railways must not content themselves with such a milk-and-water excuse as this. The critical remarks might, and should, have been the most valuable parts of the volume; as it is, they make a feature of the least conceivable importance. The compilation of the work, from the original parliamentary documents, must have been an extremely laborious undertaking, but at the same time, requiring nothing more for its execution than persevering industry; an "analysis" of the working merits, the *real* probable cost (not that laid down in the engineer's estimate), and the *real* probable profit or loss of each line, would have demanded talents of a far higher order; but it would also have been of an incomparably higher value.

The concluding pages of the volume contain a good deal of miscellaneous information on railway affairs, in a form less tabular, and therefore more attractive, than that of the main body of the book. Such, for instance, as the following general view of the extent, expense, &c. of the projected lines of last session:

"The number of proposed railways, including diversions, extensions, and branches, in England and Wales, for which plans have been lodged in the Private Bill Office in the present session, is seventy-five, of which only forty-eight are under the consideration of Parliament; these amount in length to twelve hundred and thirty-three miles, and are estimated at the sum of thirteen millions three hundred and fifty-two thousand seven hundred and twenty-six pounds,* or fifteen thousand six hundred and ninety-five pounds per mile. The whole length of tunnelling is twenty-five miles; and the number of bridges, exclusive of viaducts and culverts, two thousand eight hundred and twenty-five, or nearly two and a third per mile. The weight of iron required for the rails is one hundred and ninety-three thousand five hundred tons; and of stone for the blocks, two millions six hundred and seventy thousand tons. The area of land required to be taken is upwards' of fifteen thousand acres; and of felt for the chairs, one hundred and thirty acres. These railways, if carried into execution, would employ at least five thousand men, and fifteen hundred horses, for three years.† The principal competing lines are the five Brighton, the two Birkenhead and Chester, and the South Union, and Manchester, Cheshire, and Staffordshire Railways.

* This sum is exclusive of the proposed Brighton lines, one of the southern lines from Manchester, one of the Birkenhead and Chester lines, the Great Western, Southampton, North Midland, and Eastern Counties, diversions; and also, the line from Gillingham to Exeter.

† For the earthwork alone.

"The proposed railways, in England and Wales, abandoned in the present session, are twenty-seven in number, amounting in length to seven hundred and ninety-four miles; the length of tunnelling is about eight and three quarter miles; and the number of bridges, one thousand five hundred and ninety-five, or about two per mile."—P. 263.

The concluding glossary is no unessential portion of the work. In good truth, so many new words have been coined within this year or two by railway speculators, that such an addition to the dictionary began to be imperiously required by "the public in general," that they might know what they were speaking about when the "crack" topic of the day came under consideration. Mr. Whishaw does not content himself with doling forth such small lumps of information as that "terminus" in the railway-tongue stands for "end" in English, but finds room to go into matters a little more at length. Thus, under the head of "locomotive engines," he favours us with the following interesting pieces of information :--

"Locomotive engines, of very imperfect construction, were in use in use for a long time previously to their introduction on public railways. The Stockton and Darlington Railway is the first on which this masterpiece of human skill was introduced as a substitute for horse-power. Many of the engines still used on this line are very ponderous and heavy, but still they are powerful. The Lord Brougham may be quoted as an example; it is an engine 16 feet in length, supported on six heavy wheels, each three being connected together with cranks; these wheels are each 4 feet in diameter; the whole weight is about 12 tons. The two cylinders are placed in front of the chimney, and are each 14 inches in diameter, the piston of each working vertically, and communicating with the cranks beneath attached to the wheels.

"On the Manchester and Liverpool Railway, the proportion of the number of engines in daily use, is almost one to every three miles, and about as many more under repair; among those at present in use, may be mentioned, the Collier, the Mercury, the Rapid, the Hercules, the Ajax, the Speedwell, and the Thunderer.

"On the Dublin and Kingstown Railway, where the passenger-traffic is very considerable, the trains starting from either end of the line almost twenty times a day, the number of engines is nine; they are severally called the Manchester, the Britannia, the Vauxhall, the Kingstown, the Dublin, the Comet, the Vittoria, and the Stanley. Three of these were built by Messrs. Sharp & Roberts, of Manchester, and have 11-inch cylinders and 16-inch stroke; and the remainder by Mr. Forrester, of the Vauxhall Foundry; the weight of these engines is from about 9 to 10 tons; many of them are of elegant design.

"On the Leicester and Swannington Railway, where the tonnage of coal alone, from Mr. Stephenson's and other collieries, is about 500 tons a-day, the number of engines is seven. The Atlas and Vulcan, each with six wheels, are two of the most powerful engines at present in use on any line of railway, having cylinders of 16 inches diameter, and 20-inch stroke; they are built for heavy loads and slow speeds. The Hercules, Goliah, and Samson, have each 14-inch cylinders and 18-inch stroke; and, lastly, the Comet and Liverpool, 16-inch cylinders, and 14-inch stroke.

"The valuable work on locomotive engines, by the Chevalier de Pambour, contains the best possible information with regard to the construction of the locomotive engine."—P. 279.

DEMONSTRATION OF NAUTILUS'S ASTRONOMICAL FORMULA.

Sir,—Iver M'Iver tells me in this day's number of the *Mechanics' Magazine*, that he will forgive me for my past mistakes, provided I can give a demonstration of the truths of Nautilus's astronomical formula, for determining the time when two given stars will be in the same azimuth circle. With this request I willingly comply, and the more readily so, as Nautilus informs us that the truth of his rules are founded upon some of the simplest *problems* (theorems or propositions would have been a better term) in spherical trigonometry.

In the first place, I beg leave to make some corrections in Nautilus's notation (press errors I believe them to be). For x^1, x^2, x^3, read x_1, x_2, x_3.

Demonstration.

Let Z represent the zenith of the observer, P the pole, D and R the positions of the lower and upper stars. Draw the great circles D O, P N perpendicular to R P, Z D and using the same notation with Nautilus, we have,

By spherics, cos. A : 1 :: tan. P O : tan. P D ∴ tan. P O = tan. x_1 = tan. cos. A; hence O R = $P^1 \pm x_1$ (according as the perpendicular D O falls above or below the point P). Again, sin. O R :

sin. O P : 1 tan. D P R : tan. P R N; hence tan. P R N = $\dfrac{\text{sin. } x_1 \text{. tan. A}}{\text{sin. } \left(P^1 \pm x\right)}$

Also cos. R P : cot. R P N : : tan. R P N ∴ cot. R P N = tan. R P N. Cos. P^1 = $\dfrac{\text{sin. } x_1 \text{ . tan. A . cos. } P^1}{\text{sin. } \left(P^1 \pm x_1\right)}$ = cot. x^2 = sin. x^1

tan. A . cos. P^1 . cosec. $\left(P \pm x_1\right)$. Lastly, cos. Z P N : cos. R P N : tan. R P^1 : tan. Z P; hence cos. Z P N = $\dfrac{\text{cos. R P N . tan.}}{\text{tan. Z P}}$

P R = cos. x_2. tan. P^3. tan. L = cos. x^3 ∴ $x^3 \pm x^4$ = hour angle Z P R.   Q. E. D.

Demonstration of Iver M'Iver's method.

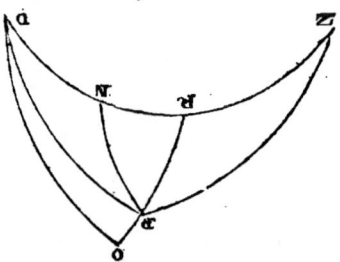

1st. Let the perpendicular (see the above diagram) P N fall between R and D, then cos. N P R : cos. D P N : : tan. P D : tan. P R; hence, by composition and division, cos. N P R + cos. D P N : cos. N P R — cos. D P N : : tan. P D + tan. P R : tan. P D — tan. P R. That is from two well known trigonometrical theorems. Cot. A : tan. $\frac{1}{2}$ (D P N — N P R) : : sin. (P D + D R) : sin. (P D — D R). Therefore, tan. $\frac{1}{2}$ (D P N — N P R) = tan.

$\left(\dfrac{A}{2} - N P R\right) = \dfrac{\text{cot. A . sin. } (d-b)}{\text{sin. } (a+b)}$ =

cosec. $(a+b)$. sin. $(a-b)$. cot. A = tan. x. Therefore the angle N P R = $\dfrac{A}{2}$ — x. Again, cos. Z P N : cos. N P R, tan. $P R$: tan. Z P ∴ cos. Z P N = $\dfrac{\text{cos. Z P R}}{\text{tan. Z P}}$.

tan. P R = cos. $\left(\dfrac{A}{2} - x\right)$ tan. b . sin. L = cos. y: hence $y - \left(\dfrac{A}{2} - x\right)$ = hour angle Z P R, the same as is stated by Iver M'Iver.

When the perpendicular P N falls between Z and R, by pursuing a similar process we find,   tan. $\left(\dfrac{A+RPN}{2}\right)$ = cosec. $(a+b)$. sin. $(a-b)$. cot. A. In this case the < N P R = $\left(\dfrac{x-A}{2}\right)$ and the hour angle Z P R = Z P N + N R P = y + $\left(\dfrac{x-A}{2}\right)$. Lastly, when the perpendicular falls upon D Z produced, we still find the angle N P R = $\left(\dfrac{x-A}{2}\right)$ But in this case the angle N P R being greater than Z P N, we have the hour angle Z P R = N P R — Z P N = $\left(\dfrac{x-A}{2}\right)$ —y : these are the modifications (I presume) which Iver M'Iver alludes to in his letter in the *Mechanics' Magazine* of this day. I am afraid Nautilus will find some difficulty in extracting any thing useful from Dr. Tiarks astronomical equations (see No. 729); for any practical purpose they are not worth one farthing.

I am, Mr. Editor, yours, &c.

O. N.

August 5, 1837.

OBSERVATIONS ON THE DUTY PERFORMED BY THE CORNWALL STEAM ENGINES. BY JACOB PERKINS, CIVIL ENGINEER.

(From the *Franklin Journal* for May).

The true cause of the great difference of duty performed by the Cornwall and the best Boulton and Watt engines, has been a matter of serious inquiry for the last fifteen or twenty years. But within the last two or three years, the difference has been so astonishing as to induce many engineers to suppose that some part at least was owing to trickery.

If we do not admit the fact of the superiority of the Cornish engines, the cause will not soon be found. I must say, that after much thought, investigation, and experiment, I believe that the Cornwall engines do at least three times the duty that the best low pressure, condensing, double stroke engines do; and I have no doubt that I see the reason of it.

Having, in the first place, visited the Cornwall mining establishments to judge for myself, I very soon came to the conclusion, that the advantage which the Cornish single stroke engine has over the reciprocating double stroke engine is much more owing to the difference in the construction of the engines, than in that of their boilers. Very few engineers know the great value of using high steam expansively, and many of those who admit it, do not know how to apply it properly.

The repeated experiments which I have made have satisfied me that the single stroke engine is far better calculated for taking advantage of the valuable property which the expansion of high steam possesses than the double stroke. In the first place, there should be no steam lost between the steam-pipe and the piston, which cannot be avoided in a double stroke engine. In the second place, at the end of the stroke the steam should be allowed to escape without any reaction, and this cannot take place, when the induction and eduction pipes are used at each end of the cylinder, as is the case with the double stroke engine.

If the induction pipe is large enough to allow the steam to escape freely so as to prevent loss by reaction, then the eduction-pipe would be much too large for the induction pipe, and much high steam would be lost, without having the benefit of expansion. In fact, it is impossible to get the steam on and off soon enough in the double stroke engine. The loss from this cause is much greater than is generally believed. It is supposed by some that there is a loss by having the steam on one side of the piston only; it is, however, quite the reverse. It is very well known that the larger the piston the greater is the saving, particularly in the piston itself. To make the single stroke engine consume the same steam as a double stroke engine, the cylinder must be double the area.

If it should be said that much time and power is lost by not having the steam on the piston on the return stroke, it may be said in answer, that if only fifteen strokes are made in a minute, there would be but two seconds between the working strokes; and that the fly, when the fly is used, must be very light indeed to show any variation of speed. When worked in the Cornish fashion without the fly, no power can be lost between the strokes.

I do not mean to say, that all the gain is to be attributed to the single stroke engine ; there is undoubtedly much power saved by dispensing with the fly wheel, where the work to be done is pumping water. This is proved by the fact, that a single stroke, balance bob, low pressure, pumping engine will raise 33,000,000 lbs. ; while the double stroke low pressure engine with a fly-wheel will raise but 22,000,000 lbs. The fly is a power which will not, like steam, wait to accommodate itself to the stubborn visinertia of the water, neither will it accommodate itself to the going off of the steam, consequently much power must be lost. When one watches the beautiful accommodating action of the Cornish pumping engine, he will readily see, that there must be great loss in using the ponderous fly. When the steam is first let on to the piston, the pressure, although 40 lbs. to the square inch, it seems too little for its work, and appears to labour hard to get the water in motion, but at the end of the stroke, although the steam has expanded down to 10lbs. to the inch, the work seems quite light. Here the expansive property of high steam is beautifully exemplified. To begin the lift 40 lb. to the inch seems not enough, but when the stroke is ended, 10 lbs. seems more than is wanted. How is it with the condensing double stroke engine? Is not the power the same at the end of the stroke as at the beginning?

I cannot believe that the enormous quantity of 125,000,000 of water was raised one foot high with 84lb. of coal without the assistance of a little air, which certainly can be used without being readily detected. To show how I learnt this singular fact, I must be allowed to relate a curious trick which was attempted to be passed off on me in America about forty years since. Two honest farmers, one day called on me to see if I would join them in a patent of great importance; they stated that the discovery would prove that the law was erroneous which stated that water would rise only about 32 feet in a vacuum. I told them it was contrary to what I had learnt and declined having anything to do with it; they, however would not be put off. They said that they had brought with them an exhausting pump, which had raised water 100 feet by rapid exhaustion, and that they would pay all the expenses of fitting it up, and that I could then see who was wrong. One of them averred that he was a ruined man if he had been deceived. I was so satisfied that he had been imposed upon that I readily agreed to test his pump. I had a leaden pipe attached to the double barreled exhausting pump, and the situation I had fixed upon happened to be 44 feet from the water to the pump. When the pump was put in action, it, to my great surprise, delivered the water at the pump spout. I then set myself to work to discover the cause, which was not ascertained until the third day; I observed that the water appeared full of air bubbles, it then struck me that air was allowed to mix with the water in minute portions, by which means the column of water became expanded; I then placed my ear close to the pipe and soon discovered a singing noise, and by clasping the tube with my

hand the noise stopped and the water ceased to flow. Here was the trick; by examining the tube I found that it had been perforated with a small pin-hole unknown to me, which admitted just air enough to expand the column. I then charged the men with the imposition; one denied it, but the other looked pale, and acknowledged he had done it by the direction of the inventor, who said it must be kept a secret, otherwise the invention would be infringed upon. They were now made to understand that they were duped, and were soon on their return home, minus 3000 dollars.

Having seen that a column of water might be expanded by admitting air under the lower clack, I was induced to inquire, while in Cornwall, of an engineer, if he had ever known air to have been admitted under the clack; after expressing his surprise at my question he admitted that it was common, but that it was not acknowledged, since every one wished to have it appear that they had done as much duty as possible.

Since the quantity of water pumped was known by the number of strokes per day, and as the contents of each stroke was known by its length, and by the diameter of the plunger, if the air which the water contained was not allowed for, more work appeared to have been performed than had actually been done.

My friend stated that it had been found advantageous to allow air to be admitted in small portions, for it made the pump work more lively in consequence of the spring it gave to the column of water and caused less strain to the machinery, but that he never knew the air allowed for. Although this circumstance of admitting air to mix with water serves to lessen the amount raised, yet this cannot, I think, be more than 15 or 20 per cent., and I fully believe, 90,000,000lbs. have been raised one foot high by a bushel of coal.

ON THE MANUFACTURE OF WHIM-ROPES FROM IRON WIRE.

(Being the Substance of a Communication from Mr. Albert, of Clasthal Royal Britannic Hanoverian Mining Councilor, to Dr. Karsten, Royal Prussian Privy and Mining Councillor, and Member of the Royal Academy of Sciences in Berlin, Editor of the " Archives of Mineralogy, Mining, Metallurgy," &c.)

(From the " *Archiv fur Mineralogie, Geognosie, Bergbau und Huttenkunde,*" conducted by Dr. C. J. B. Karsten. Berlin, 1835.)

The great annual expense of providing ropes for the shafts in the mining district of the Upper Harz, and the circumstance of the hemp being only procurable by importation from abroad, led me during several years to make a series of experiments for the sole application of iron to this purpose. These experiments terminated in new methods of manufacturing whim-ropes, and of obviating their weight, by the adoption of endless chain; but yet my object was not accomplished. However, it occurred to me subsequently, at the commencement of last year (1834,) that iron wire might be plaited or twisted together so as to form a whim-rope; and the results of my experiments were so completely satisfactory, that arrangements are now making in these mines for the general adoption of ropes of this description. The manufacture of them from iron wire is, in fact, a very simple, and not an expensive, operation; and yet there are a great many apparently insignificant circumstances which materially delay the work, and occasion impediments, which can only be obviated by obtaining an accurate knowledge of them. I have, therefore, resolved to describe the process and its peculiarities, and hope thus to render some service to practical science.

In the first place, the iron wire employed is of the sort numbered 12, in the Royal Foundry of the Harz, of the diameter 0,144 inches; and ten feet of the wire weigh 13,91 Loth, Cologne weight, or seven and one-fifth ounces avoirdupois.

This wire is drawn by a machine, in lengths of 60 to 130 feet; and to facilitate the work on the straight-rope course, and to avoid weakening the wire by violent bending, in order to bring it into a straight direction, it is so arranged, that after the last heat, the drawing is performed with a single wire on a cylinder of twelve feet in diameter. The price of this wire is at present 9 dollars, 10 groschen current, for 110 lbs. Cologne, or about £1. 7s. per cwt.

For the preparation of the wire, the following implements are requisite:—

1. A large smith's vice, about 70 lbs. in weight, attached to a frame of the usual height.

2. A small hand vice, about 6 lbs. weight.

3. Iron winches (fig. 1) made of one

Fig. 1.

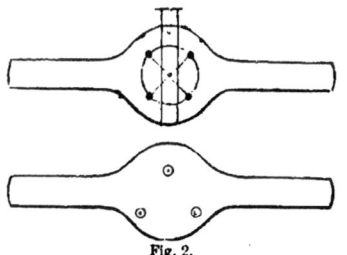

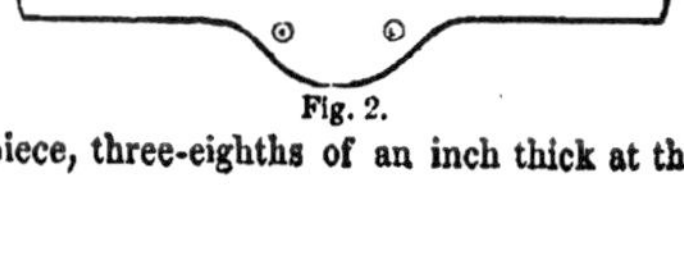

Fig. 2.

piece, three-eighths of an inch thick at the

middle, with a round handle at each end, altogether fifteen inches long. The centre forms a flat surface, containing five holes of about three-tenths of an inch diameter. The four outmost holes lie in a circle at one and a quarter inch distant from each other. At the centre of the circle is a similar hole, connected with the other holes by grooves of about one-fifth of an inch in width. This communication may be suspended by means of pegs, introduced through small openings on the narrow side of the winch, pushed before the holes, and fastened by their elasticity, or if required, by grooves made to fit. The holes must have no sharp edges. If dispatch is required, three such winches will be necesssary.

4. An iron winch (fig. 2) of the same construction as the former, with this difference, that it contains only three holes of half-inch wide, without connexion with each other.

5. About eighty boards, of six inches square, half an inch thick, with four round holes of one-quarter inch wide, two inches apart in the square (fig. 3.)

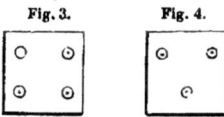

Fig. 3.   Fig. 4.

6. About ninety similar boards of hard wood, with three round holes of half-inch wide, at equal distances from each other (fig. 4.)

7. A cast-iron trough one-quarter of an inch thick, three feet long, ten inches wide, eight inches deep, and about 60 lbs. in weight, or a similar one of plate iron.

8. Some files for sharpening the ends of the wires, knippers to take off the ends, and pliers to lay on a thin band of wire at particular parts of the chain.

Method of Manufacturing the Rope.—The work requires a covered walk at least 130 ft. long. The wires are laid in a straight line one beside the other, and the ends sharpened with the file before they are applied to the holes. Four wires are fastened to the large vice at the end of the walk, previously to which thirty or forty four-holed boards, and behind them the four-holed winch (No. 3) have been pushed along them, the boards being arranged at the distance of three or four feet from each other, to prevent one wire from touching the other. Along the whole length of the walk, workmen stand at six to ten feet apart, holding the wire up, when trussels or props are not provided, and turning it with a uniform and constant motion. With the length above supposed, about ten persons would be required; although a machine is now being made for the purpose; which will, however, only be advisable when a large number of ropes are to be prepared. At the end of the walk, opposite the vice, a trusty workman is placed, to keep the ends of the wire constantly separate while they are being turned. At the vice two men are stationed; and one turns the iron winch (No. 3) in such a manner, that at every complete revolution of the winch he advances six inches forward. At first this distance may be regulated by measurement, but in a short time practice gives the necessary correctness.

The second workman at the vice follows the turner with the small hand-winch (No. 2), secures in it the twisted rope at every two feet, and holds the winch steady, so that the turner can advance further.

As the turner proceeds, the boards (No. 5) are pushed towards the other end, and the workmen as they reach it successively, are for the time no longer required; as often as the winch is turned once round, so often all the four wires must be turned throughout the whole length of the rope; but during this turning no twisting takes place, but only a motion upwards and downwards, as well as from left to right.

When the turner has proceeded with his work to the end of the walk, and a cord of four wires is thus completed to the above length, this cord is for the present laid on the ground. The workmen who have been spared, as above described, have meanwhile provided the wires intended for the second cord, with the dividing boards (No. 5,) and after them with the second winch (No. 3.) The four wires are then inserted in the vice, the turner recommences his work as before; and after that a third cord of four wires is formed by the same process.

It will be requisite to make one of these three cords considerably longer than the others, and the last is preferable for that purpose, as the turning winch (No. 3,) and the boards (No. 5) can then be put on at once, so that turning is not meanwhile delayed. When the three cords of the length of the walk are completed, they are then turned together to form the main rope, the ends of each cord being now put through the ninety boards (No. 6,) which are pierced with three holes, the second turning winch with three holes, (No. 4) is put on, and the ends of all the three ropes are at once attached to the main vice (No. 1.) The workmen are again distributed along the walk, and the turning proceeds as at first; yet, with this important difference, that as soon as two feet of the rope are turned, the main vice is opened, and the whole of the workmen move two feet forward in that direction, and the finished rope, as it becomes longer,

is rolled behind or beside the vice in the form of a coil or ring, at least nine feet in diameter.

Fig. 5.   Fig. 6.

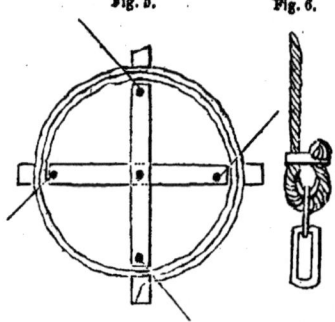

For this operation a cross is placed on the ground, so as to be easily turned round, formed of two strong pieces of deal (fig. 5) resting on a pivot in the centre. After thus completing a rope of three cords and twelve wires, it is lengthened by repeating the same process, when the single wires are to be joined to those of the next rope.

After many trials, I have found it best to unite them by means of friction, in the following manner:—on working to the end of one wire, a new one is inserted into the same holes of the boards, (No. 5) along with it, so that at the ends of the wires which are nearly worked off, two wires always lie together for the length of forty inches. When the turner arrives with the winch (No. 3,) at the commencement of a fresh wire, he thrusts it into the centre hole by the sharpened point, and almost into the middle of the four turned strands of the rope in progress, where it is fastened by binding it round a few times with thin wire, mainly for the purpose of ascertaining at any time where the end of a wire is to be found, since it is desirable to bring it, if possible, to the inner part of the main rope, when the latter is to be turned. The rope is then turned twenty inches farther, in such a way that the fresh wire remains firmly seized in the middle of the former. The corresponding peg of the two in the winch (No. 3) is now drawn out, the wire which is nearly worked off is pushed out of its hole in the circle of the winch, and inserted into the centre hole of the same winch; and in its place the forward end of the fresh wire is removed from the centre hole, and inserted into the vacant hole in the circle, when the peg is again pushed forwards.

On continuing the turning, the remaining twenty inches of the old wire likewise occupy the centre of the rope, and are again bound round at the ends with thin wire. The firmness of this binding consists in the circumstance that every wire in the main rope or chain is not exposed at the exterior surface for more than from six to nine inches; as it then enters the interior, where the tension retains it firmly in its position, even although a single wire at the surface should occasionally be worn away or otherwise rendered useless. The marking of the places where the ends are fastened by the thin wire, enables the workman to distribute these fastenings in an equal manner through the rope, which indeed often takes place of itself from the regular length of the wires, and is often effected by the breaking of the single wires. There should not be more than two ends of different ropes at the same point.

By the method described, a rope of any length may be made, adapted to the depth of any particular shaft. If the covered walk be 130 to 140 feet long, thirteen workmen will be wanted, who may be kept fully employed; of these, five or six must be men on whose care reliance may be placed; the others may be invalids or boys. On an average, these thirteen persons in one hour can finish fifty feet of rope, at least.

The rope when completed must be covered with an adhesive composition, which on cooling still remains *flexible*, in order to defend it against the damp of the mines. For this purpose there may be used the refuse of artificial grease or oily composition; and in default of these, a mixture may be employed, consisting of one-third of oil, and two thirds of colophonrium or rosin. The iron trough (No. 7) is filled with this composition, and a coal fire maintained under it till it becomes heated to the temperature of boiling water; the rope is then drawn slowly through it, so that it may become sufficiently heated in the fluid, and all the interstices become filled with the grease, and consequently devoid of air. In an hour and a half 700 feet may be thus greased by eight workmen. When many ropes are to be made, a machine may be employed for this purpose, which, however, would produce no saving, if the work be on a small scale. To 700 feet of rope, there will be required forty to fifty pounds of the composition.

To join the rope to the chain on which the bucket hangs, I have found the following to be the simplest method:—The end of the rope is heated gently, to the length of eight inches, and then bent round an iron clamp, in the form of the half of a chain link, hollowed from beneath (fig. 6.) A wrought-iron ring, of one inch in breadth, previously drawn along from the opposite extremity of the rope, is then driven down to the clamp,

and the ends of the wires are separately turned through the ring, and fastened or beaten down over it, after which the whole is fastened with wire or strong cord round it; or if greater security be desired, it is enclosed in molten lead. A chain-link is suspended in the grooved clamp before closing the chain, or it may be done afterwards if a snap-link be employed, which may be opened and shut.

As long as this process presents no manifest disadvantages, it will not be requisite to adopt any superior or more difficult methods. The heated part of the rope should not extend upwards above the ring. After various trials the weight of a rope of 700 feet, without the composition, was found to be only three cwt. one quarter, or from three to four pounds every seven feet. The expense, on a close calculation, for manufacturing a rope of 3920 feet, including every outlay, to the time of fixing it to the whim, is 220 dollars, namely, 171 dollars for the wire, and 49 dollars for wages, or about 31*l.* 10*s.* for the whole, reckoning seven dollars to the pound. Each single wire will bear a tension equal to ten cwt., and the whole twelve, consequently, 120 cwt. The weight of metal used at once is about ten cwt.

It is indispensible that the rope should be coiled within the limits of its elasticity; and, therefore, it is not advisable to have the coils of less diameter than nine feet. The cage of the whims of the shafts in the Harz are in general twelve feet in diameter. The small weight of these ropes, with wheels of twenty-eight to thirty feet diameter, freely admits of the use of buckets from nine to ten feet in height, when, in case of iron chains being employed, only four feet would be allowable with an equal power of the water-wheel. The larger diameter allows, with a slow motion of the wheel, a greater velocity, with advantage to the machine. If every bucket be made of the breadth of three or four feet, the ropes will not wrap or entangle over each other, even at the depth of 1400 feet or more, by which the injury arising from friction is avoided. The working of these ropes, in reference to the supply of water to the wheel, has proved highly satisfactory, although varying, according to circumstances. At one shaft a saving of one-fourth to one-fifth of the water was the result, as compared with hempen ropes, the work being equal. At another the saving was one-third to two-fifths. In regard to durability and economy, a positive result cannot be given, since none of the wire ropes which have hitherto been in use are yet worn out. At the Caroline shaft, which, on an average, required 3010 feet of fresh hempen rope annually (the total quantity in use being 3640 feet,) at a charge of 860 dollars, about 123l. sterling; there have now been wire ropes employed thirty-four weeks, which are still perfectly fit for use. So much, however, has already been saved as would suffice to make new ropes. At the present period (April, 1835,) ropes of this description are used in four of the principal shafts of the Upper Harz. In a few weeks they will be employed in two shafts more, and they will be gradually adopted, in a manner compatible with a due regard to the interest of those manufacturers who have heretofore supplied the hempen ropes and iron chains. The adoption of the wire rope is a matter of essential importance for the mines of the Upper Harz, where more than 84,000 feet of rope, (partly hemp and partly iron) are in constant work, and where every year upwards of 38,500 feet of new rope are required.—*Mining Journal.*

LIST OF IRISH PATENTS GRANTED IN JULY, 1837.

William Gossage, of Stoke Prior, Worcester, for an improved apparatus for decomposing common salt, and for condensing and making use of the gasious product of such decomposition, also containing improvements in the mode of conducting these processes. July 14.

Alexander M'Ewan, grocer and tea merchant, Glasgow, for a process for the improvement of teas as ordinarily imported. July 14.

Peter Spence, of Henry-street, Commercial Road, Middlesex, chemist, for improvements in the manufacture of Prussian blue, prussiate of potash, and plaster of Paris. July 17.

Charles Brandt, of Upper Belgrave-place, Middlesex, merchant, for an improvement in the mode of evaporating and cooling fluids. July 17.

George Goodlet, for an improved method of boiling, drying, or evaporating, concentrating and treating, also applicable to distilling spirits from grain, wash, or other articles, and rectifying. July 21.

John Spurgin, of Guildford-street, Russell-square, Middlesex, M. D., for an improvement in the mode or means of propelling vessels through water, and part of which means may be applied to other useful purposes. July 28.

NOTES AND NOTICES.

Medal Striking.—We have much pleasure in announcing to the friends of the fine arts that Mr. Pistrucci, chief medallist in the Royal Mint, has discovered a method by which he can stamp a matrix or a punch from a die which has never been touched by an engraver, and shall yet make a medal identically the same with the original model in wax, an operation by which the beauty and perfection of the master's design are at once transferred to any metal, whether gold, silver, or copper, by striking it according to the usual process. It will at once be seen that this is a very different operation from that by which cast medals are manufactured. It is as simple as it is ingenious, and Mr. Pistrucci having no intention of taking out a patent for the dis-

covery, and being anxious to give to the public the full benefit of it, in the different processes of manufacturing plate, jewellery, and all kinds of ornamental work in metal, announces that the whole of the process consists of the following method :—The model being made in any substance, wax, clay, wood, or other fit material, a mould of it is taken in plaster, from which mould, when dried and oiled to harden it, an impression is taken in sand, or other similar substance which may be preferred, and from this again a cast is obtained in iron as thin as possible, that the work may come up sharply, and the iron attain the hardness almost of a steel-die hardened. This cast-iron impression is then flattened mathematically true on the back, and fixed in a steel die, the hollow of which is turned to the exact size of the cast iron, and it is set within the rim or border, hammered as close as possible, so as to form a collar. The metal upon which the impression is to be struck (to form either the medal itself or a steel matrix, if desired) is to be fashioned into the shape of a cone in the ordinary way, perfectly flat at the base, heated red-hot, and placed at the bottom dish of the press. When the die, fitted as above, having been previously placed at the top dish, and the workmen quite ready to give the blows instantly, three or four, as may be required, a perfect impression of the cast-iron will be attained without the least injury to it. Of course it will be necessary, previous to the die being used, for the artist to polish the surface. Mr. Pistrucci's first experiment was successfully performed upon a punch of hard copper, with his model of the medal of Sir Gilbert Blane, being nearly three inches in diameter; and he has no doubt that it will equally succeed on a steel punch, perhaps, too, without its being necessary to heat it. When the process above described shall have been brought to the perfection of which it is capable, there can be no doubt that in the execution of works of this description it will not only be the saving of the labour of months or years in the engraving of dies, and, consequently, of great expense, but the work to be executed will in all points be, in an instant, an exact fac-simile of the original conception of the artist, instead of representing, as at present, merely the handiwork of the engraver, copied from such original. It will also dispense with the use of the very expensive machinery, such as the *tour à portrait*, introduced into the mint by Mr. Pistrucci several years ago, which, however apparently correct in its productions, can never give a perfectly true semblance of the original, even to the limited extent to which it is applicable. And we may possibly be led by it to discover the mode by which the artists of antiquity succeeded in producing these beautiful coins, in which the softness and boldness of the fleshy parts have never yet been equalled by any modern engraver in steel.—*Times.*

Magnetic Observations.—Baron Alexander von Humboldt, in an advertisement inserted in the *Prussian State Gazette,* of the 4th instant, announces that Professor Parrot, of Dorpat, has undertaken a scientific journey to the North Cape, and has expressed a wish that corresponding magnetic observations should be made by scientific men in different parts of Europe on the 21st. 24th, 28th. or 31st of the present month of August with a view to advance the theory of the magnetism of the earth. The traveller wishes the observations to be taken at intervals of five minutes from noon on any one of the above days, till noon on the following day, by mean Gottengen time.

☞ *British and Foreign Patents taken out with economy and despatch; Specifications, Disclaimers, and Amendments, prepared or revised; Caveats entered; and generally every Branch of Patent Business promptly transacted.*

A complete list of Patents from the earliest period (15 Car. II. 1675,) to the present time may be examined, Fee 2s. 6d.; Clients, gratis.

LONDON: Printed and Published for the Proprietor, by W. A. Robertson, at the Mechanics' Magazine Office, No. 6, Peterborough-court, between 135 and 136, Fleet-street.—Sold by G. W. M. Reynolds, Proprietor of the French, English, and American Library, 55, Rue Neuve, Saint Augustin, Paris.

Mechanics' Magazine,

MUSEUM, REGISTER, JOURNAL, AND GAZETTE.

No. 733. SATURDAY, AUGUST 26, 1837. Price 3d.

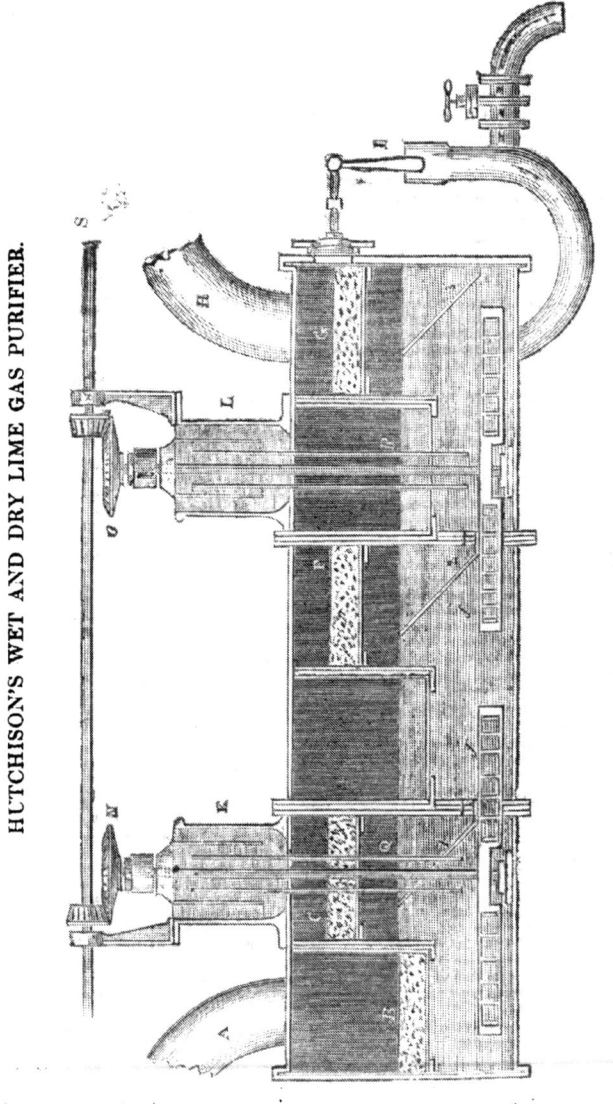

HUTCHISON'S WET AND DRY LIME GAS PURIFIER.

HUTCHISON'S WET AND DRY LIME GAS PURIFIER.

The excessive impurity of the coal gas manufactured previous to the year 1805 (when lime was first used in the purifying process) occasioned considerable perplexity to all the parties who were engaged in its production.

In giving the following description of Mr. Hutchison's purifier, it will not, perhaps, be considered out of place, to relate the circumstance which led to the accidental discovery of that affinity which exists between lime and the sulphuretted hydrogen, with which coal is combined. The occurrence took place while Mr. J. Hutchison was exhibiting some of his early experiments, before the gentlemen who originated the first metropolitan gas company.

The apparatus which he used upon those occasions consisted of a retort placed in a vertical position over a furnace, the lower part of the retort being surrounded by a groove, as shewn in the sketch at *a*. This groove, after the

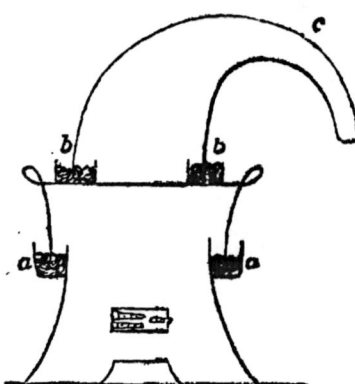

charging of the retort, was usually filled with clay or sand, and either of those substances sealed the gas, and prevented its escape : *b b* is another joint at the junction of the conducting pipe, and the upper part of the retort.

A few minutes previous to the commencement of one of the experiments alluded to, it was observed by an attendant that there was neither clay nor sand in readiness; and as a number of persons interested in the result of the exhibition were present, it was necessary to provide a substitution for the sand. This substitute consisted of a portion of slacked lime, which was being used at the time, in repairing the premises where Mr. Hutchison and Winsor were performing the experiments. (This was in Green-street, Grosvenor-square).

During the process, it was remarked by several of the gentlemen present, that there was a total absence of that noxious effluvia which, during former exhibitions, rendered the gas so offensive; and Mr. Hutchison being the only person in the room acquainted with the circumstance that lime was used, instead of sand, in forming the joint, it occurred to him that this happy effect was produced by the action of the lime upon the impure substances exhaled from the decomposed coals; and having satisfied himself of this truly important fact, he adopted various methods of applying lime, in order to render the gas fit for practical purposes. He first mixed dry lime with the coal before being placed in the retort; but this injuring the quality of the coke, the method was abandoned. The lime was then placed in thin layers upon perforated iron plates, which being laid upon the surface of the coals in the retort, absorbed the noxious gases as they became disengaged. This arrangement was also given up, and ultimately the lime was applied in separate vessels.

It was this accidental discovery which, more than any other part of their interesting experiments, induced seven of the gentlemen who were present to lay the foundation of a gas company, by immediately subscribing a fund of 700 guineas, with which sum active operations were commenced; and shortly after this nucleus of the Chartered Company, lighted the public lamps in Pall Mall.

The enterprise was greatly encouraged by the Prince of Wales, who evinced considerable interest in its success. The Duke of Athole, also, and Ludovic Grant, were the chief promotors of the scheme; indeed, the latter gentleman was appointed chairman of the infant gas company.

That the illuminating qualities of the gas produced might be displayed to the best advantage. The Prince ordered his conservatory in the rear of his mansion at Pall Mall to be lighted, and the gas-fittings were constructed for the purpose by Hutchison. Immediately after this exhibition, six elegant lamps were placed upon the noble portico or colonade which occupied the principal front of Carlton House, and lighted by the early specimens of coal gas.

The original projectors of the company were indefatigable in their exertions, to season public opinion in favour of this new light.

The various products which resulted from the distillation of coal, such as the tar, ammonia, and coke, were exhibited to the royal family by the Duke of Athole, and a portion of the salts manufactured from this material was presented to the Queen.

Thus, under the fostering patronage of royalty, and the direct influence of court, aided by the spirited efforts of the public, a system of beautiful artificial illumination was established, which has since become of the greatest consequence to the country.

Until within the last four years the machinery employed in the process of purification has been so defective, that in most instances the gas was permitted to escape into the gasometer, without having been sufficiently exposed to the perfect and uninterrupted action of the cream of lime with which the purifier was charged.

The sketch (see front page) represents a longitudinal section of the purifier for which Mr. H. secured a patent right in 1833. All that have been constructed upon this principle are still in operation, and in no respect, since the first introduction, have they failed to produce the important effects which now renders coal gas innoxious.

The judicious arrangements and relative adaptation of its parts, necessarily subject every particle of the gas to the influence of the lime.

The gas immediately after passing through the condenser, and entering the purifier, becomes separated by means of the partition by which the machine is divided, so that the sulphuretted hydrogen which forms one of its constituent parts, instantly combines with the lime-water, and this process being repeated in each of the purifiers, the gas passes in a perfect state to the exit main.

The perforated plates and oblique shelves shown in the drawing in conjunction with the two agitators, offer the necessary obstructions to what would

otherwise be the too rapid progress of the gas through the purifier.

Another advantage which this invention possesses over any other now in use, is that of its combining a wet and dry lime apparatus; this peculiarity in its construction, renders it very serviceable to gas works.

Mr. Green, the aeronaut, has on several occasions complimented the London Company on the purity of the gas, which by means of the apparatus has been supplied for his balloons.

The splendid balloon, which in the month of November last, conveyed this enterprising gentleman and his companions to Germany was inflated by gas which was passed through this purifier under the immediate inspection of Mr. Hutchison himself. Mr. Green, who I believe may be considered an excellent authority upon this subject, has declared, that the gas cleansed by this purifier is the best in quality that has ever been used for the purpose aerostation.

Description.—The pipe A, is that through which the gas is conveyed from the condenser into the purifier. The first obstacle which obstructs its direct passage, is the perforated plate B; the gas is here separated, and its volume minutely subdivided, so that the cream of lime, which is continually preserved in uniform action by the fans *f* and *f* is made to exert its attractive influence in, abstracting the sulphuretted hydrogen.

The parts indicated by the letters C F and G are upon the same principle as B, and serve to multiply the necessary obstruction to the gas escaping, before it has beeen sufficiently washed.

The oblique shelves 1, 2 and 3, are also for the same purpose.

K L are two hydraulic seal caps, which prevent the escape of gas from the perpendicular tubes, in which the spindles Q and R revolve; S is a horizontal shaft upon which are placed two vertical cog wheels, which by means of manual or steam power give a rotary motion to the bevelled cog wheels N and O, and to these are attached the spindle of the agitators *f f*.

The plate G is covered with a layer of dry lime which receives the gas, after it is passed through the liquid in the bottom of the tank, therefore, whatever impurities may have escaped from the

z 2

cream of lime, are completely extracted by the last stage of the process.

I is the feed pipe through which the purifier is supplied with the lime-water.

B. W.

from England to Rome in one night, by means of a flying horse!

Yours obediently,

J. O. H.

August 20, 1827.

INVENTION OF BALLOONS.

Sir,—Aerostation having of late occupied so much of the public attention, I thought that the following notices of a few supposed early approaches to the invention of the balloon, might not be unacceptable to your readers.

In a work by Silvester, translated from a poem by Du Bartas, published at London in 1592, the following curious lines occur:—

" Againste one ships that skips from stars to
    grounde,
From wave to wave (like *windy balloones*
    bounde)."

Whether these " windy balloones " were of a similar nature to the modern machines of the same name, is, I think, a matter of doubt: a notice of the above lines was first made in the Gentleman's Magazine for the month of May, 1834.

From the following very singular passage from Bishop Wilkin's " World in the Moon," it is evident that the author had in view the heated air balloon:—
" Suppose a cup, or wooden vessel, upon the outward borders of this elementary air, the cavity of it being filled with fire, or rather, ætherial air, it must necessarily remain swimming there, and of itself can no more fall, than any empty ship can sink."

Roger Bacon not only asserts the possibility of flying, but affirms that he himself knew how to make a machine with which a man might be able to convey himself through the air like a bird; but Dr. Hutton has proved, that if it consisted of the same method which he describes, the machine would be crushed inwards by the pressure of the external atmosphere.

Father Lana, as late as 1670, in a work entitled the " Prodoma," has revived the project of Bacon as his own invention.

The tales of Deadalus and others concerning the art of flying, can only be regarded as empty fables; *ab uno disce omnes.* According to Richard of Bardney, Bishop Grostest made a journey

THE VELOCIPEDE.

Sir,—I should feel much obliged if yourself or one of your talented correspondents would explain, why the numerous and ingenious attempts made to effect locomotion by the velocipede, have hitherto proved abortive: what is the rationale of a velocipede? does it diminish friction, or has it hitherto only transferred it in a disadvantageous manner, and what is the desideratum? Can a man employ his muscular power to effect a greater velocity than walking or running, by mechanical interventions, without a proportionate exhaustion; or has nature placed a limit that no ingenuity can pass? There is a wide difference between the actions of walking and that of rolling; is not the latter a positive mechanical advantage? in point of fact, is the velocipede a toy or a machine? There seems some analogy between skating and velocipeding, and I know from experience that I can attain a velocity of eight or ten miles an hour by the former, with the same exertion that I could obtain four or five by walking or running: what is the rationale of this? If the efficiency or non-efficiency of the machine were calculated and proved, it would, doubtless, save the waste of much ingenuity and labour.

I have read your notices of Mr. Adams's work on "Pleasure Carriages," with much pleasure, but, in reference to his invention or plan for keeping the wheels equal, by enabling the vehicle to lock without the usual bearing on the front wheels, I cannot help doubting whether a great disadvantage would not arise, to the direct progression of the carriage. In the ordinary construction, the connection of the motion of the four wheels is well maintained, the weight bearing equally on them all; but, if the connection between the wheels were broken, as it would be by Mr. Adams's central joint, the weight upon either pair of wheels, *being divided*, would, I conceive, create a tendency to a vacillating motion in the direct progress of the carriage; the wheels being constantly liable to be thrown out the same line.

Your obedient servant,

A CONSTANT READER.

August, 14, 1837.

STEAM NAVIGATION TO AMERICA.

Sir,—An article on " Steam Navigation" appeared in a recent number of the Edinburgh Review (No. 131), in which the writer endeavours to prove that Dr. Lardner is correct in the conclusion to which he came in his paper on that subject laid before the British Association, Sept. 1836,—viz., that a profitable and permanent connexion could not be effected between New York and England in one trip.

As the subject is one of general interest, and of great importance to the commercial interests of this country in particular, great care should be taken not to discourage the spirit of enterprise,which has prompted three different parties to make the attempt to establish steam communication with the United States, nor to afford an excuse for the East Indian Government to fall back into its former inertness upon the subject of a steam communication with India, now that it has been just roused into action, by the determined and persevering importunity of its subjects there. It is essential to a fair trial of any project, that the best means be employed to accomplish the end designed. If a vessel whose speed is only five miles per hour be employed to perform a certain passage in a given time, when one whose speed is ten miles an hour can be had, it is evident that the experiment is not a fair one. So in reasoning upon the practicability of any scheme, like that of steam navigation to the United States, if a number of vessels be selected whose size, speed and performance, are notoriously less than those of many other vessels which are actually in existence, it is evident that however correctly the size, speed, and performance of the selected vessels may be given, it does not prove that the scheme is impracticable with vessels of larger size, greater speed, and better performance.

The writer of the article " Steam Navigation" in the Edinburgh Review has given us a very full and elaborate table of the consumption of coals, average speed, &c. of eleven steam vessels, from which he most logically and correctly proves, that with such vessels, a steam communication with New York is impracticable. Had his researches been somewhat more extended, it is very possible that he might have have found, at least eleven other steam vessels, whose average speed would have shown that instead of twenty-four or twenty-five days, it would be possible to perform the same distance in fourteen or fifteen days.

The Reviewer states that Mr. Field considers that great improvements have been made in marine engines since 1834. The performance of many of the new steam vessels fully bear out Mr. Field in the opinion which he is said to have given. Yet, by a strange perversity, he adopts as data the performance of steam ships, most, if not all of them, built before that time, and concludes, that a steam communication with New York is impracticable !

The Admiralty steamers are the data upon which his calculations are made; yet he has not informed us whether they slackened their speed during the night, as I believe is the practice in her Majesty's service.

The writer contends, that any inferences from coast and channel trips are fallacious; but he has not shown us why they are so. It is well known, that on the coast and in the channel, the short cross sea which is so frequent, retards the progress of steam vessels much more than a long rolling sea, and therefore a priori, this affords a good test by which to try the performance of a steam vessel.

The use of salt water for raising steam is admitted to be a great obstacle to the performance of long voyages, but it is also admitted, that fresh water may be substituted with good effect; the recent improvements in condensation, warrant us to expect that it may be done with success.

But the great difficulty is, the quantity of coals required, which the Reviewer says, will prove an insuperable obstacle to long voyages. In this particular it seems highly probable that he will be found to be in error, for upon his own showing, the larger vessels require a smaller power in proportion to their tonnage than the smaller ones. And of the vessels which he has selected as the data upon which he makes his calculations, there are only three which are now deemed large vessels,—viz., the Medea Steam Frigate, of 807 tons ; the Dee, of 639 tons; and the Private Steamer A, of 660 tons. The two first are constructed for war, and are therefore not to be expected to have sufficient capacity for carrying a large supply of fuel; and the Private Steamer A, is not sufficiently described, for the public to form any judgment as to the quanty of fuel she will carry.

The Reviewer states that a steamer of 1,200 tons, with 300 horse power, will only stow 500 tons of coals. In this statement it is evident that he has taken the nominal tonnage as the actual weight she is capable of carrying ; whereas, it is usually found that a vessel will carry about 50 per cent. more than her nominal tonnage ; thus, a vessel nominally of 1,200 tons is capable of carrying with safety 1,800 tons. If then the power be equal to 300 horses, the weight of the machinery and water will be, say 400 tons. The consumption of coals per day with boilers of the best construction, will be 72,000 lbs. per day, and for fourteen days will be 450 tons, leaving 950 tons for spare coals, merchandise and stores.

Another important feature which has been overlooked, is the fact, that large vessels are propelled at a much greater rate with the same proportion of power to tonnage than smaller ones. Hence, if the Dundee and Perth, which are about 650 tons, are propelled at the rate of 9.99 miles, nearly ten miles per hour, a vessel of 1,200 tons may be reasonably expected (having the same proportion of tonnage to power) to be propelled at a greater *velocity*, but if, contrary to all experience, she should not go faster, then she would perform the distance between New York and England in fourteen days; and if the currents and winds should be favourable, in much less time, as it is found that with a strong wind in such a direction, that a steamer can set her sails, her speed will be accelerated about a mile, or mile and a half per hour.

Let us take the large steam ship now building in London for the British and American Steam Navigation Company, and try what her capabilities are for performing the intended voyage. Her nominal tonnage is 1,795 tons ; she is to be propelled by two engines of 220 horse power each, which will require 47 tons 2 cwt. 3 qrs. 12 lbs. of coal per day of twenty-

four hours ; if her speed is only nine and a half miles per hour, she will perform the passage in fourteen and a half days, and consume during that period 683 tons 11 cwt. 1 qr. 20 lbs. of coals.

Take the estimated weight of her machinery, boilers and water at 600 tons, and (allowing 50 per cent. on the consumption of coals as a reserve) the weight of fuel at 1,025 tons, we have 1,625 tons for machinery and coals. Now the calculated displacement between the light and load water line amounts to about 2400 tons, thus leaving about 800 tons to be occupied in stores, merchandise and passengers. From a drawing which I constructed, in order to be submitted to the directors, I found by calculation, that with her machinery, coals and merchandise, she would draw only 16 feet of water, if built after my design ; and, although built from another design, I do not think that her draft of water will be greatly different, probably rather more than less, when fully equipped.

Some of your readers may be impatient at this mode of meeting the question, and wish for some facts upon which they too may reason and come to a conclusion for themselves.

In 1825, the Enterprise, a vessel of about 400 tons, effected her passage from England to Calcutta in 113 days, 64 of which she was propelled by steam, and 49 by sails alone.

In the present year, the Atalanta steam ship, of about 650 tons, effected her passage from England to Calcutta in 91 days, 23 of which she was in port, and under weigh 68 days only.

Here then is a striking instance of the improved state of marine steam engines, and of the advantage which a large vessel has over a small one in making her passage. The average speed of the Enterprise, taking the distance at 15,000 miles, is 132¾ miles per day, or about 5½ miles per hour ; whilst that of the Atalanta is 220⅞ miles per day, or 9¼th miles per hour for the whole distance.

The average speed of her Majesty's steam vessels on the Mediterranean station was, some time since, officially stated to be 7¼th miles per hour, which is 1⅕th miles more than the average given in the Edinburgh Review ; taking the highest number as correct, it is much below the rate of most merchant steamers, under much more unfavourable circumstances. For instance, those between Scotland and London come to an average speed of upwards of nine miles per hour; those between Glasgow and Liverpool, perform that passage in, from seventeen to twenty-four hours; and from the books of one company, I found on inspection, that the average time occupied in the passage, both winter and summer, was nineteen hours; and it was thought that some new boats, which were then nearly ready would make the average still less, now the distance by sea being considerably more than 200 miles, the average speed of the steam vessels employed in that trade, must considerably exceed ten miles per hour. The voyages now regularly performed by the merchant steamers to the Peninsula and into the Mediterranean, warrant us to expect that a steam communication will be effected with New York in one trip.

It would be unjust not to refer to the Columbus, a steam ship, fitting upon Mr. Howard's principle for the purpose of attempting the passage to New York. She is capable, I am informed, of carrying a sufficient quantity of coals to supply the engine for upwards of forty days, and will use *fresh water* only for raising steam.

Excuse my trespassing so long on your time, and believe me,

Yours truly,

GEORGE BAYLEY.

LATE EXPLOSION OF THE "UNION" STEAMER.

Sir,—Having formerly had a good deal to do with the early establishment of steam navigation on the Thames, I naturally take an interest in every thing relating to the subject, which I meet with in your pages. A good deal of discussion, I observe, has arisen in consequence, of the explosion of the "Union" Steamer at Hull, some attributing the disaster to an insufficiency of water in the boiler, and the generation of hydrogen gas; while others contend that it was occasioned by the undue accumulation of steam. But in assuming the first to be the cause, I would ask, is it possible that gas *can* be generated in a boiler under the circumstances in which that of the "Union" was placed just previous to the accident? And if so, (I speak not as a chymist), how does the necessary admixture of the gas with

atmospheric air take place, which air, it must be understood, has to enter from *without*, *against* highly elastic vapour *within* the boiler? Supposing, however, these two preliminary difficulties satisfactorily disposed of, how, in the next place, I would ask, is ignition to take place within the boiler? I should certainly be disposed to deny that power to the overheated state of the plates; because I have seen numerous instances, and could, I dare say, point out some at the present time where the feeding apparatus having become suddenly out of order, the water in the boiler has fallen below the flues, and the consequence has invariably been, *not an explosion from the generation of gas, or any other cause*, but simply the bending of the weak, because hot plates, which compose the top part of the flue, by the pressure of the internal steam, generally, however, confined to that part immediately over the fire. Besides, I should be inclined to think, that an explosion from the ignition, or even the generation of gas, could not occur without being attended with some very unusual and remarkable appearances, such as the safety-valve being in full operation, without and discernible cause (hydrogen gas being invisible), and the appearance of a flash at the time of the explosion, none of which, I think, have yet been observed. Indeed there appears (to me at least) so many objections to, and difficulties attendant on the assumption of explosions of steam boilers being occasioned by gas, that any further observations on this view of the subject seem to be superfluous, I shall therefore, in the few remarks which I have now to make, confine myself to that opinion which assigns the cause to the undue accumulation of steam. It unfortunately happens generally, (the scientific would say *fortunately*) that on these occasions no person of observation, and scientific attainment is present, hence, all the information which is afterwards attainable, in addition to what the wreck supplies, is just so much as the interested proprietor, the culpable engineer, or uninformed passengers are able or willing to furnish. From this cause arises much of the mystery and obscurity in which all such unfortunate occurrences are more or less involved, and the absence of full and correct information prevents the real cause from being understood.

Were it possible to be otherwise, I have no hesitation in saying, that in most cases, the cause of explosion might easily be explained, and satisfactorily accounted accounted for. There are, it is true, in the steam engine, matters "not dreamt of in our philosophy," and circumstances often arise in its operations which would require a Watt to explain; but such occurrences are "few and far between," and rarely takes place except in old delapidated engines, and therefore do not apply to the majority of those used in steam navigation. In the case of the "Union," the explosion seems, as far as can be gathered from the evidence, to have taken place under anything but extraordinary circumstances. The *facts* (with the *opinions* we will not now meddle) appear to be, that the water in the boiler, as indicated by the guage taps was high enough, that the boiler was of sufficient strength, and in good repair, and that the safety-valve was in proper order, and had been observed to be in proper action just before the accident; so that all things considered, the explosion would appear to have taken place very gratuitously. I have, however, little doubt of there being much more than has hitherto met the eye or ear, which for reasons before alluded to, is with difficulty now attainable, but without which, it would be impossible to discover the real cause, or to arrive at any thing like correct conclusions. Previous to adding my opinion of the cause to those already offered, I may observe, that as an indication of the height of the water in marine boilers, nothing can be more fallacious than gauge-taps, as *commonly* used, the more especially as they invariably indicate the water to be much higher than it really is; when, however, instead of being simply inserted in the front of the boiler, as they usually are, they are attached to a *pipe*, the upper end of which is in communication with the steam at the *top*, the lower one with the water from the *bottom* of the boiler, must at once become the most correct, certain, and durable indicators I have yet seen. The plan, which did not originate with me, was first tried in 1825, and was afterwards introduced into every vessel which subsequently came under my management, and I have no doubt continues in use to the present time. The state of repair in

which the boiler was at the time of the accident, appears to have been in every respect satisfactory; indeed, from knowing by experience that boilers have been in constant work, when corroded to such a degree, as to be reduced in places to the thickness of a shilling, I should be disposed to consider the explosion entirely uninfluenced by the strength, or state of repair in which that of the "Union" was at the time of the accident; it may not, however, be amiss to observe, that marine boilers, from the peculiar shape which their confined situation renders necessary, are never so strong as those where such restrictions are not imposed; and it often happens, that in small vessels, they are still further weakened by being made in one part, instead of two or three separate divisions, as is the case in the larger vessels. I am not contending that either the one or the other of these defects, would separately, or combined, under ordinary circumstances, cause an explosion; but whenever an accident of this nature happens, I have no doubt, that in combination with other causes, they are of extreme importance, especially that of the shape, which, from being flat, is by the internal pressure of the steam, changed to a round form, and the parts of the boiler thereby loosened, and the iron fractured. From the absence of all information respecting the dimensions of the boiler, and power of the engines of the "Union," there is nothing, or next to nothing, to reason upon; but the few facts which may be collected from the evidence, may perhaps enable us to imagine a case which will have some degree of analogy, to what actually took place. If then, for example, we assume the boiler to have been of the usual form and strength, and for the sake of the argument 15 feet square, its top or roof would present an area of 225 superficial feet, and at the ordinary working pressure of marine condensing engines, would be exposed to a strain equivalent to about fifty tons. Under the most favourable circumstances as to form, materials, and workmanship, such a boiler, composed of 5-16th plate, should require a force of 1,800 tons to effect a permanent change in its structure, which, of course, is the commencement of fracture; but in boilers, as in machinery, "partial strength is universal weakness," or in other words, its ultimate strength would only be equal to its weakest part, whatever strength their might be elsewhere. Hence, if we take into consideration the weakness arising from the causes before alluded to, which are more or less present, if not perceived, in the very best constructions, we may safely venture to consider the ultimate strength at one-half, or even less than one-half of 1,800 tons. Here then we only require a pressure of 50 or 60lbs. to the square inch to blow the top of such a boiler completely away. That a pressure equal to, or very much exceeding this, is perfectly attainable in the boiler of a condensing engine, may easily be conceived, by supposing a fortuitous combination of circumstances to arise, and which in point of fact, I believe did exist at the time of the explosion on board the "Union;" that is to say, the vessel lying to, the engines standing, the fires burning fiercely, no water going into the boiler, and either from the *smallness* of, or *some other defect* in the *one* safety-valve, only a *part* of the rapidly accumulating steam escaping from the boiler. Imagining this state of things to continue but for a *short* time, it cannot excite much surprise that a violent explosion should be the consequence, nor can their be a doubt that the same thing would again occur, under the circumstances before mentioned. The common sense view of the subject here offered, is the result of a good deal of experience, and some observation; if it is a correct solution of the difficulty (and to myself it appears clearly so), there needs but little discussion respecting the remedy, which, in conjunction with sober, careful and intelligent engineers, must consist of TWO *well-constructed, and sufficiently large,* LOCK-UP *safety-valves.*

A variety of observations, respecting the periodical inspection of steam vessels, and the education of engineers, suggest themselves, but having extended my remarks already to an inconvenient length, I will for the present conclude, renewing the subject, if there should appear to be occasion, at some future opportunity, and accompany my remarks with some sketches of the guage-taps before alluded to, and the best form of safety-valves, &c.

I am, Sir,

Yours very respectfully,

JOHN LEONARD.

Railway Office, Crauford,
Äugust 15, 1837.

MR. WIVELL'S FIRE-ESCAPE; HUMANE SOCIETY FOR PREVENTING LOSS OF LIFE BY FIRE.

Sir,—At page 227 of your 727th number, Mr. Wivell has put forth a few observations in reply to the animadversions of Mr. Jenkins and myself; nothing that Mr. Wivell has brought forward, however, goes in the slightest degree to affect the statements of which he complains; with some few and unimportant variations in detail, his remarks are, upon the whole, confirmatory of the statements advanced.

With reference to myself, Mr. Wivell argues, "that having become a member of the Humane Society, I *must* have faith in its utility!" I need only just say, that *wishing* and *hoping* for, is one thing,—but being convinced of its utility, is another, and a widely different thing; Mr. Wivell will please to mark the difference.

Mr. Wivell also expresses some surprise that I "should count the life of a human being of so little importance as to signify that the sum of *thirty pounds* is too much to preserve it." If these were my sentiments, he might well be surprised; but such they are not. I most undoubtedly object to spend *thirty pounds* upon any ONE fire-escape, while I know, that machines of equal, or even greater efficiency, can be provided for one-sixth of that sum.

By adopting fire-escapes at about five pounds each, six may be stationed in a district where only one of the more expensive kind could be provided. The probability of saving life increases nearly as the square of the number of escapes, so that in any given district the chances of saving life would be *thirty-six* times greater with the cheap, than with the dear escapes.

Mr. Wivell says, "Mr. Baddeley *must* recollect, that in or about 1829, the generous and humane citizens paid Mr. Hudson eighty pounds for an escape!" Now, Mr. Editor, it is very hard upon me, that in order to oblige Mr. Wivell, I *must* recollect what really never took place. If Mr. Wivell will consult the information afforded in your well stored volumes of the period to which he refers, he will find the fact to be, that Mr. Hudson was the founder and gratuitous secretary to the first society for preventing loss of life by fire, and in that capacity, expended something very much like the sum mentioned, upon a clumsy machine, which, like some of a more recent date, was never worth what it cost for house-rent.

The funds thus wasted, emanated not from citizens alone, but from humane persons in various parts of London and its suburbs. Mr. Wivell's boast of his escape having been "patronized" and "adopted" by the Society, looks rather awkward when he tells us it was only received as a gift, with a goodly list of subscribers as an accompaniment! while the apparatus of others has been adopted and patronized by purchase.

According to my notions of these matters, Mr. Wivell's escape will be dear to the Society at the cost of its rent, to say nothing of the thirty pounds subscription money; in ten years (should the Society last so long) it will have cost them a sum equal to the providing and maintaining in efficient working order, thirty other fire-escapes, which number would afford all needful protection, to at least six such districts as that in which this one machine is now stationed.

When I observe the gratifying list of subscribers now belonging to the Society, I cannot help thinking that under proper management, half London might, ere this, have been provided with fire-escapes; one or more persons in each district might, I apprehend, be found willing to take charge of them and superintend their practical application in time of need.* Rewards might have been bestowed upon all who could be shewn to have exerted themselves in the preservation of life; this having been done, the Society would have proceeded with considerable eclat, and with a greatly augmented list of subscribers, from whom the needful supplies would have been forthcoming, for extending the benevolent object of the Society.

I remain, Sir,
Yours respectfully,
WM. BADDELEY.
London, August 4th, 1837.

ACCIDENTS IN COAL PITS.

Sir,—Your ready insertion of my previous letters, induces me to proceed with their subject, by placing another in your

* The Society have one of Mr. Ford's fire-escapes stationed in the Strand, but it was not forthcoming at the late melancholy and fatal fire in Holywell-street.

hands. I have already asserted, that in the present system of coal-mining every thing is considered of more value than human life; and, that it is solely a money question, I may add, one of no great amount, whether explosive accidents shall continue to be very common, or become very rare occurrences. To these assertions I challenge contradiction. Let coroner's inquests, in such cases, return verdicts of "*culpable* homicide" against mine-owners and mine-managers, where on their parts there appears to have been *culpable* neglect; violent deaths in coal mines will then, I am satisfied, no longer be almost of daily record. Making these observations, on due consideration, I hope and trust, that they will not be passed over heedlessly, by the influential and humane.

I shall now, agreeably to my former promise, refer to the Report of the late Parliamentary Committee "On accidents in mines," in the hope of rendering it something better, than "a dead letter," which, as to the attainment of its proper object, it has hitherto been, and I am sorry to add, if left to the coal proprietors, is likely ever to be.

Having, however, Sir, a strong desire not to encroach, in this instance, too far on your valuable space, and above all, not to write more than would perhaps be read by those whose attention I wish to engage, I shall confine my present remarks chiefly to an outline of the subject, in the hope that its filling up, will receive the aid of some of your highly-talented correspondents. The Report in question, commences stating, that the committee had called before them in the course of their inquiry "witnesses connected with all the great Mining Districts in the Kingdom." That they had also examined plans, diagrams, and a great variety of safety lamps. That they had also obtained ample proofs of the calamities which had occurred in coal mines from sudden explosions of fire-damp, foul air, and sulphur, which terms are severally, locally applied to carburetted hydrogen gas so copiously evolved in many of these mines. Few collieries, it is added, are entirely free from fire-damp, but in many, the quantity is so large, that in spite of the skill and unremitting attention, which they assume is exercised, the risk is constantly great. They then state, that according to the list drawn out for them, which they properly consider "defective and vastly short of the full number," the fatal accidents for the last twenty-five years amount to 2070. They further observe, that taking a period of eleven years previous to the introduction of Sir H. Davy's Safety Lamp, and eighteen years since, in the counties of Durham and Northumberland, where it has been more used than in any of the other mining districts, fewer persons were destroyed in the former, than in the latter period. This evidence against the assumed safety of the Davy Lamp, strong as it is, is nevertheless softened down by the excuse, that many mines of a more dangerous nature, have been worked since this lamp was introduced. Or in order words, that it has sometimes to meet, when ventilation is overpowered or neglected, that which it was alleged by Sir H. Davy, it would effectually resist, and which, it appears, it will not—an explosive atmosphere. For what else has it ever been valued? The Committee, after this lame and impotent excuse, on a point that has an important bearing on the whole inquiry, observed, that in addition to explosive gases, mines are sometimes infested with gases destructive to life, though not explosive: that inundations have been frequently destructive, (on one occasion, it appears nearly 100 persons were drowned in a mine) and that then, there remains *a long list of casualties,* some of which they *conceive are wholly beyond human controul.* They then point out that the only means of preservation, as applied to the former, may be divided under three heads, viz., *Ventilation, Safety Lamps,* and *Maps* or *Plans* of the under ground workings.

Having proceeded thus far with these observations of the Committee, it will be necessary to notice particularly the matters they consider within human management. The first is ventilation. It will be seen, by a perusal of the evidence obtained from the persons practically, and therefore best acquainted with its nature, that ventilation is always uncertain in its effect, even when under the best possible management, which it now evidently is not, being, by the admission of all, left, in many of its most material points to the care of children of a tender age. The Committee say, and on such a matter their precise words cannot be dispensed with. "On ventilation, and the daily unceasing strict discharge of the duty by every person (towards it) engaged about the mines, from the scientific professional viewer, the wasteman, the overman, the deputy, the lamp keeper, the pitman, down to the trapper, often a boy, young and thoughtless, who manages the air doors (most important matters,) depend the safety of *hundreds of men and boys* from *minute to minute;*—one act of omission of assigned duty, one solitary moment of neglect, may cause the instant destruction of life and property to an indefinite extent." This is indeed a frightful picture of the present state of hundreds of coal mines, and of thousands of human beings, and it is no less frightful than true, and no less true than uncalled for, except by ignorance, obstinacy, and avarice on the part of coal owners and their worse managers. Both are equally implicated in this charge. In the first place, it may be asked,—why is life to be periled by the employment of children in such important duties? and in the next, why should unsafe lights be used in any coal mine, whether called Davy Lamps or Candles, when safe ones can, as shown by the Committee, be obtained? For, mark, Sir, no interruption of the ventilation of a coal mine by any sudden rush of carburetted hydrogen, the gas referred to in this case by the Committee, whether from the bursting of blowers, falling of the incumbent strata, or the wilful or accidental neglect of *one or of all the persons employed in the mine,* could produce any fatal result, unless the gas were ignited, which could not happen were a really protected light used. I again say, let coroners look to this matter, and let the members of the legislature do so, and that speedily. To stop a wanton, and therefore unnecessary sacrifice of life, when within their power, is a duty both owe to society.

The next part to notice, is what the Committee say on the Davy Lamp. It is important in many respects. They assert with great truth, that the principles of its construction (so much then for Sir H. Davy's claim to its invention) were practically known to the witnesses, Dr. Clanny, and Stephenson, the present eminent engineer, before he (Davy) brought his powerful mind to bear upon the subject, and they add, strangely enough (as will apper from what closely follows) produced an instrument *(a lamp)* which will hand his name down to the latest ages. What can they mean?—if the following paragraph is intended to have any meaning. They say, " the attention of your Committee has been drawn by different witnesses to contingencies in mining, under which the Lamp of Sir H. Davy ceases to afford adequate protection." One of these contingencies, be it known, is its being exposed, which the lamp must necessarily be, in some of its commonest uses, to a current of air, which may be or not explosive. The Committee continue, " Of the possible existence and nature of those contingencies, your Committee have ascertained that the inventor (Sir H. Davy) was well aware, and they regret *that the cautions he gave to some of his immediate friends were not made more public ?*" That this secret was confided to very few persons, and long remorselessly sepulchered in their bosoms, need not be here insisted upon, when it will be found by a reference to the published evidence, that the persons to whose management some of the most extensive and most dangerous mines in the kingdom were at that time given, were left totally ignorant to this astounding fact. They heard it, as Mr. Stephenson stated, he did, " for *the first time* in *that* (the Committee) *room.*" Sir H. Davy unfortunately is dead, and can make no atonement for the past. But some of the depositaries of this sad and fatal secret are alive and rich. They have therefore still time before the grave also closes over them to make some reparation, not to those who now crowd the church yards of Durham and Northumberland with their scorched and mutilated bodies, for the dead cannot be recalled to life, but to their wretched widows and helpless orphans, hundreds of whom are at the present moment in want and misery, because it was considered *indelicate,* and not to the pecuniary interest of the mine owner, to tell the truth of Sir H. Davy's Lamp. *Nor has it yet been fully told where it ought most to be known.* Here I must for the present stop. To extend my letter any further, would be to fall into the error I have promised to avoid. I shall, however, Sir, with your permission, take the first opportunity of continuing the subject. In the meantime I hope that what I have stated will awaken the many who are now slumbering, to a sense of duty.

I remain, Sir, yours, &c.

CARBON.

MR. DE LA BECHE, AND THE SATELLITE DEPOSIT THEORISTS.

Sir,—In a work by Mr. De la Beche, published in London in 1834, entitled, " Researches in Theoretical Geology," the preface commences with these words: " Although the theory of central heat, and the former igneous fluidity of our planet, have been much dwelt on in the following pages, the author trusts that he will not be considered so attached to these views, as not to be ready to reject them, and embrace others, which may afford a better explanation of observed facts, should such be brought forward." Apparently, a sort of apology for strong views derived from the doctrine of central heat, and a promise to avow any change of opinion on increased knowledge. In 1835, " How to Observe," by Mr. De la Beche, was published by Knight, in London ; it contains no directions "How to observe" satellite deposits. It is, however, impossible to prove that no half understood conversation, or joke, has not given rise to the second-hand assertion, as would seem, of his belief in a doctrine relative to satellites so much at variance with those published in his work on theoretical geology.

The propriety of bringing forward an assertion, the truth of which is more than doubtful, is most questionable.

Geological observers are unanimous in their opinions, that mountain masses elevate the surrounding strata ; and the satellite deposit theorists are bound to shew, either by their own observations, or from those of others, that the usual conclusions are erroneous ; that instead of being elevated, the strata run under such mountain masses, otherwise the satellite deposit must remain an astronomical dream ; and even if this proof ever should be afforded, no difficulty in re-respect to the time requisite for the formation of mechanical rocks containing organic remains, as in the Alps, would be obviated, since it would be merely removed to another sphere, where the formation of 10,000 feet of mechanical deposits would require as long a period as in our own planets.

I am, Sir,

Yours, respectfully,

N. S.

August 11, 1837.

HYDRAULIC PENDULUM.

Sir,—I beg to contribute to the amusement of the numerous readers of the *Mechanics' Magazine*, by sending you a sectional drawing of an "hydraulic pendulum," intended to raise water by the alternate action of inclined planes. The

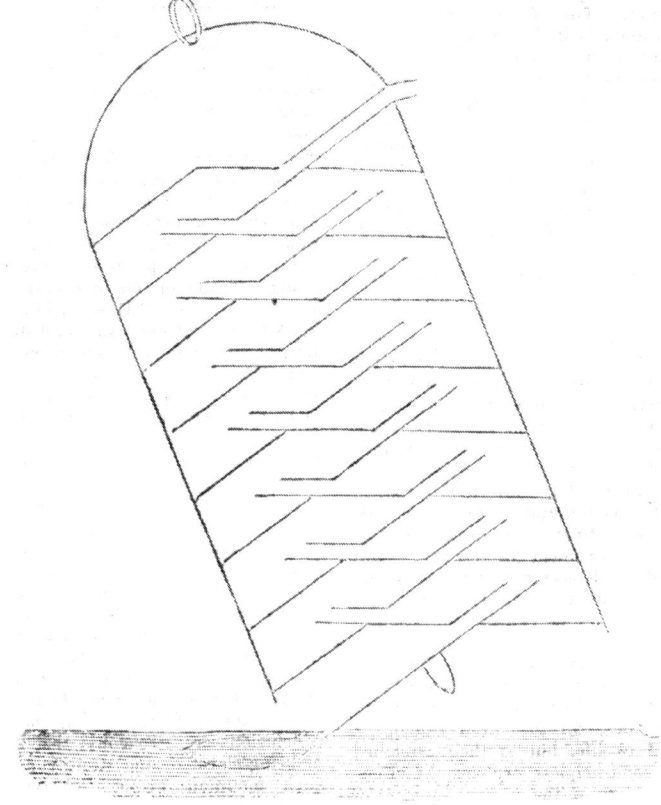

drawing presents a lateral view of the model, with one side removed so as to shew the internal arrangement. The apparatus is suspended from the upper part, so as to allow of a motion similar to that of a pendulum; and it will be evident on a little inspection, that on the first movement to the right (in the position represented), the spoon attached to the lowest box or division will dip into the water beneath, a portion of which will be taken up on the returning oscillation, and conveyed by the inclined plane forming the bottom of the box, to the corresponding lowest division on the other side. The return of the water being prevented by short delivering pipes projecting into each box, the machine will gradually fill by a continuation of the motion, till the discharge commences to take place from the highest pipe, at every alternate oscillation. Your practical readers will have already foreseen the defect in this contrivance, which is, that all the boxes on one side only being full, at the same time, the weight of the water therein contained destroys the regularity of motion: on which account I have been in the habit of considering it ever since its invention, about four years ago, as incapable of being applied to any useful purpose. It has, however, lately occurred to me, that a rotary motion might be given to the apparatus by making it turn on centres at the top and bottom, in which case the inclined planes would act as before, and the inequality of motion might be counteracted by a fly-wheel, and its position, at an angle of 70°, as shewn in the drawing, would probably give it a decided advantage over the well-knewn screw of Archimedes. I beg to apologize for taking up so much space in your most useful publication, and am, Sir,

Your very obedient servant,
RICH. JA. IREMONGER.

London, August 10, 1837.

MR. BUCKINGHAM'S VOYAGE ROUND THE WORLD AGAIN.

It will probably be within the recollection of most of our readers, that Mr. Buckingham, the Eastern traveller, some years ago, projected a voyage round the world, for the somewhat undefined purpose of "sowing the seeds of civilization;" and that the amount raised by subscription not being sufficient to carry the scheme into effect, the whole affair ended in nothing more than "sowing the seeds" of an annuity of 35l. for the lives of Mr. and Mrs. Buckingham. After a repose of some years, occupied in sitting in Parliament for Sheffield, lecturing in favour of temperance, &c. &c., Mr. Buckingham has set about raising the ghost of his old fantasy. He is about to leave England, in the first instance, for the United States, in which he proposes to take an extensive lecturing tour; after which he will set out (at his own expense?) on a trading voyage to all the least known parts of the globe, maintaining himself by the profits of commerce, and partly, perhaps, by the copyright of his travels, a volume of which he intends to get out regularly every three months, at whatever part of the world he may be, and send home, and to America, for sale. There could be no objection to all this, if all were fair and above-board; but it is not at all unreasonable to suspect that the whole plan is only the prelude to a desperate assault on the pockets of Brother Jonathan. At all events, Mr. Buckingham is determined to leave no stone unturned, in the subscription line, in England. For somewhere about the tenth time, books have been opened at various bankers, previous to his leave-taking, for the receipt of donations from the admirers of this *persecuted* individual, the (avowed) object of which is, not to raise a crop of civilization, but—to secure an annuity of 100l. to Mr. Buckingham, and 80l. to his wife, an object which bids fair to be attained; making another rub for the most ill-used man on the face of the earth!

ANOTHER RUPTURE IN THE THAMES TUNNEL.

Yesterday afternoon the Thames Tunnel became quite filled with water which flowed from an aperture from above. It would appear from the report supplied to us on the subject, that generally there existed some necessity for keeping the pumps at work, for we understand, that a little before twelve o'clock at noon the water was found to increase considerably; but in the course of the afternoon the quantity had somewhat diminished, although it slowly gained upon the pumps, and as the tide rose it was found impossible to keep pace with the increased influx of water, when Mr. Page, the acting engineer, considered it necessary to send for Mr. Brunel, who was in town attending a meeting of the directors.

At five o'clock, finding it was quite useless to proceed in the attempt to check the steady increase of the water, which had risen ten feet, the attention of the engineers and workmen was turned to securing all parts of the shield, which operation was carefully and deliberately performed. The curiosity of the men, who were anxious to watch the gradual rise of the water, rendered it very difficult for the engineer to withdraw them, even when it became expedient to do so. At half-past five o'clock the Tunnel was filled, every one having previously retired, and it is gratifying to add, that no accident has occurred to any individual. Soundings were immediately taken by the engineer, and the displacement of ground having been ascertained to be of limited extent, steps were taken forthwith to stop the aperture from above, as upon former occasions, in order to resume the pumping as soon as possible.—*Times, 24th August,* 1837.

WARMING BUILDINGS.

The first requisite is a complete combustion of the fuel; and the second, a complete delivery of the heat evolved in the place intended to be warmed. Nothing could be more wasteful of fuel than common open fire-places; only one part in fifty radiates into the room, the great body of heat going up with the draft of the chimney. If a kettle of water be placed before the fire, it will not boil in less than twenty-four hours: placed over the fire, it boils in half an hour. If a man stand in front of the fire, he gets only half warmed; the half next the fire is warmed, while the half away from it is chilled; but, if he were to place himself in the line of the draft over the fire, he would be burnt to a cinder all around. The ancient Romans understood these things better than the moderns; they carried their flues horizontally under the pavement of the chamber to be heated. A stove on the same principle was erected at the County Fire Office ten years ago, which has answered perfectly; and Mr. Beaumont has erected similar stoves at the elephant-house in the Regent's Park, at Sudbury Grove, at St. James's Church, and other places, with similar success. These simple contrivances produce a saving of eleven-twelfths of the fuel consumed to obtain the same warmth by hot-air and hot-water stoves, and with perfect freedom from dirt, dust, smoke, and impurity of every kind. He was sure they only required to be more known to be adopted in all the churches and chapels throughout England.—*Architectural Mag.*

LOWNDS'S EVER-POINTED PENCIL AND PEN-CASE.

The exterior tube of this case is open at its two ends only, not having any longitudinal slit to admit a slide for protruding the point, this being effected in a different manner, to be presently described. This exterior tube as represented at fig. 1, has a plain surface, but it may be ornamented in any way which may be preferred. Figs. 2 and 3 show the interior tube which fits into fig. 1, within which fig. 2 is made to slide. The upper part of fig. 2, contains the pen-slide and holder, and also the reservoir for spare pencil points; the latter consists of a tube concentric with the tube *a*, and its place is represented by the dotted lines; it reaches down to *b*, where it is soldered to a diaphragm, or partition, reaching across that part of the tube, and extends up to the upper end of *a*, and is there enclosed by a small screw cap; its length is sufficient to enable it to contain two lengths of pencil points. The pen holder is situated in the space between those two tubes, and this is slid out by means of the small screw button *c*, working in the slot *d*, the tube *a* being reduced, or flattened, to allow the head or button *c*, sufficient space without obstruct-

ing the passage into the exterior tube. When the pen is retracted there is sufficient space between the reservoir and the tube *a*, to carry two extra steel pens with perfect convenience. Fig. 4 is the screw cap, or head of the pencil case; *e* is a tube, having a screw cut on the outside of it, the female screw into which it works being cut in the inside of the upper end of *a*, the exterior of which tube passes within the cap, whilst the tube *e* admits the point of the pen; by this arrangement the whole length, nearly of the cap is saved in the length of the pencil case.

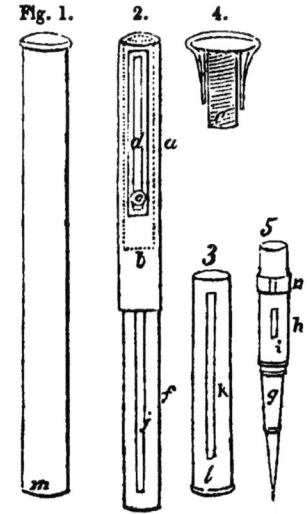

Fig. 1. 2. 4.

The lower end of the interior tube, fig. 2, is that which receives the pencil point and its appurtenances, to be now described. Fig. 5, which contains the lead, is, at the lower part *g*, made, in all respects, like those in general use; its upper, or cylindrical portion, *h*, is to occupy the part *f*, of the tube fig. 2; *i* is a projecting check piece, or feather, which when fig. 5 is in its place, occupies the slot *j*, and also the slot *k* in fig. 3, this latter tube fitting on to *f*, fig. 2, the two slots *j* and *k*, being made to coincide, and the feather *i* rising high enough to pass through both of them. When the respective parts 2, 3, and 5, are put together, the whole is to be passed into the exterior tube fig. 1, the lower end *l* of fig. 3, is then attached to the lower end *m* of fig. 1, by soft soldering them together, and on screwing the head fig. 4, into its place, the instrument is complete.

Operation of the Instrument.—When the pencil point is within the case, the feather *i* occupies the upper ends of the slots *j* and *k*;

and to cause the point to protrude, the tube fig. 2 is drawn up by means of the head fig. 4; this tube sliding in the exterior tube, and also in fig 3; the drawing up of the interior tube brings the lower part of the slot *j* into contact with the feather *i*, which consequently checks it; on pushing the head down, the pencil point is protruded, and ready for use; and when no longer wanted it may be readily pushed back by the finger. To cause the cylindrical part *h*, of fig. 5 to slide freely and evenly within its tube *f*, it is surrounded at *n* by a divided spring ferule, which is in part received within a groove turned in *h* for that purpose. When the pen is to be used the tube is to be drawn out, the head unscrewed, and the pen protruded; by means of the button as before described; the head may be screwed into the opposite end, a female screw being cut within *l* for that purpose.

NOTES AND NOTICES.

New Bee Hive.—An inhabitant of Connecticut, Mr. Judd, has invented a contrivance, by means of which bees are made to build their cells, and deposit their honey, in the chamber of a dwelling-house, in neat little drawers, from which it may be taken fresh by the owner, without killing the insects. The hive has the appearance of, and is, in part, a mahogony bureau, or sideboard, with drawers above, and a closet below with glass doors. The case, or bureau, is designed to be placed in a chamber of the house, or any other suitable building, and connected with the open air, or outside of the house, by a tube passing through the wall. The bees work and deposit their honey in drawers. When these, or any or them, are full, or it is desired to obtain honey, one or more of them may be taken out, the bees allowed to escape into the other part of the hive, and the honey taken away. The glass doors allowing the working of the bees to be observed; and, it is added, that the spaciousness, cleanliness, and the even temperature of the habitations provided for them in this manner, render them the more industrious.

Arsenic in Candles.—At a late meeting of the Medico-Botanic Society, Mr. Everitt made some remarks respecting the tests for arsenic, and afterwards demonstrated its presence in the composition candles. Having fully proved the existence of the poison in the candle, in the proportion of at least two grains in each (and he stated his belief that four grains were a more correct statement,) he then proceeded to assign a reason for its use. Candles which are made of tallow are of too low a melting point to admit of the use of a curved wick. Stearine or spermaceti, either of which has a much higher melting point, is, therefore, employed in making the composition candles, and to prevent its running into grain or crystalizing, a certain quantity of wax was added, which, it was found, would fully answer the purpose. It was afterwards discovered that a small quantity of arsenic would effect the same object, and it being considerably cheaper, it was adopted into use. The professor further stated that, when he had made the discovery, and it had become bruited abroad, his opinions were confirmed by two or three manufacturers who acknowledged using the poison. He left it to the members of the profession to determine whether arsenic thus volatilised, and coming in contact with the lungs, would prove deleterious. Judging from the effects of other gases, he thought it would be injurious.—*Lancet.*

Electric Telegraphs.—The idea of electric telegraphs appears to have spread with electric rapidity. The invention has almost simultaneously made its appearance at four different places, at such a distance from each other, that it must apparently have been invented four times over, as it would otherwise almost require the electric telegraph itself to have conveyed it quick enough. At Frankfort, on the Maine, at Paris, at Edinburgh, and at Munich, the discovery is being prosecuted with interest and ardour; and the Germans already claim to have invented a method which will only require one-tenth of the expense of the Scotch one, but have not yet made public what it is. What if, after all, the quadruple invention should turn out good for nothing, The idea of a musical telegraph has also been brought forward at Vienna, where they appear to be unconscious that a series of lectures on that subject, in which a plan for one was developed, was delivered about a couple of years ago at Paris and London, before Louis Philip and Queen Adelaide, by an ingenious Frenchman, M. Sudre.

Guttenberg's Monument.—The 14th, 15th, and 16th of August were celebrated by a succession of feasts and festivals on the inauguration of the monument of Guttenberg, the inventor of printing, at Mayence. Time has at length brought his due honours to Guttenberg, and "the curious," it appears, are not behindhand with their old associate, as they poured in such hosts into Mayence, that the hosts of the town were incapable of receiving them. A crowd is, perhaps, in its proper place at a festival in honour of the press.

New Method of Engraving discovered by Mr. John Burnet. We do not mean that any of the effects which he is enabled to produce by this new process are finer than could have been produced heretofore, but simply that the price at which he can offer copies to the public is so small as to bring works of the highest class of art within the reach of all but the very humblest classes. What, for instance, will the reader say to a series of engravings from the Cartoons of Raffaelle, the paper of each to be of the finest quality, and of the size of 34 inches by 24, and the size of the prints only varying according to the shape of the original, each to be sold for *four shillings* instead of four guineas! The thing is scarcely credible to those who know that probably fifty per cent. is the allowed profit to the trade, that fifty per cent. of the remainder is the expense of the paper and the printing of each single engraving, and that not more than one shilling therefore can remain to remunerate the artist! We have only seen one of the proposed series—Paul preaching at Athens; the style of which is broad, bold, and admirable, superior, in our opinion, for all artistic purposes, to the over-wrought works of Holloway. Copies of this work, framed in the cheapest possible manner, like an almanac, if the economists so desire it, ought to be hung up in every school-room and every Mechanics' Institute in the kingdom. Here is a means of education offered which costs nothing either of money or time; and it would make itself felt now or hereafter, not only its moral and humanising influences, but in the arts and manufactures of the country. We earnestly hope that this subject will be considered worthy of attention by all whose voices are potential for good or ill in the conduct and management of such institutions.—*Athenæum.*

W. E.'s proposed communications on electricity and mechanics will be acceptable.

☞ *British and Foreign Patents taken out with economy and despatch; Specifications, Disclaimers, and Amendments, prepared or revised; Caveats entered; and generally every Branch of Patent Business promptly transacted.*
A complete list of Patents from the earliest period (15 Car. II. 1675,) to the present time may be examined, Fee 2s. 6d.; Clients, gratis.

LONDON: Printed and Published for the Proprietor, by W. A. Robertson, at the Mechanics' Magazine Office, No. 6, Peterborough-court, between 135 and 136, Fleet-street.—Sold by G. W. M. Reynolds, Proprietor of the French, English, and American Library, 55, Rue Neuve, Saint Augustin Paris.

Mechanics' Magazine,

MUSEUM, REGISTER, JOURNAL, AND GAZETTE.

No. 734. SATURDAY, SEPTEMBER 2, 1837. Price 3d.

RAUB'S SAFETY APPARATUS FOR STEAM BOILERS.

Fig. 1.

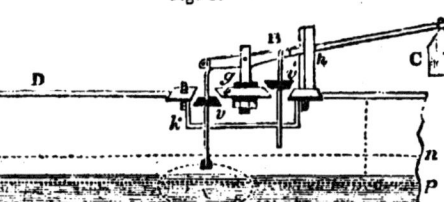

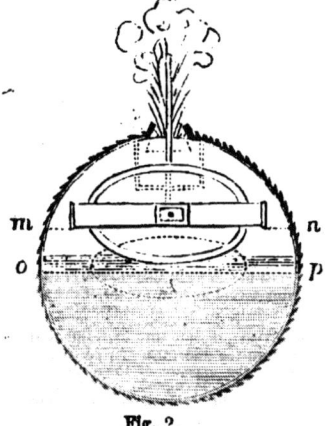

Fig. 2.

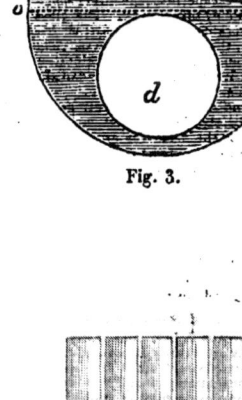

Fig. 3.

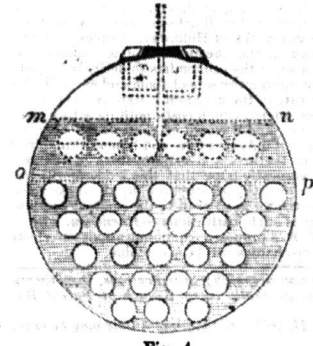

Fig. 4.

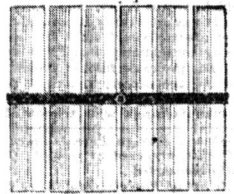

Fig. 5.

A A

MR. SAMUEL RAUB'S SAFETY APPARATUS FOR STEAM BOILERS.

(Communicated to the *Franklin Journal* by Professor W. R. Johnson).

This ingenious, but simple and efficient plan for indicating the deficiency of water in a steam boiler, is presented in the accompanying sketch, fig. 1 (see front page). D is a vertical section through the length of a cylindrical steam boiler, without an interior flue; *m n* is the ordinary water line, and *o p* is the fire line of the same boiler. On the top of the cylinder is rivetted a plate of brass *e*, serving for valve scats, and through the centre of this plate passes the upright iron pillar *g*, with a fork at top to receive and support on an axis, the lever B. On opposite sides of the axis, and at equal distances from it, are attached to the lever the rods of the two equal valves *v* and *v'*, the former of which opens inwards, and the latter outwards, so that any pressure of steam within the boiler which tends to open the one, tends by an equal force to close the other; but any force which is applied to either arm of the lever, tends to affect both valves in the same manner. *h* is a simple guide rod, in the slit of which the lever plays, and *k* a guide for the valve rods on the inside of the boiler. A is a solid, or hollow, metallic body, having, from its form when hollow, a specific gravity rather greater than that of water, and is kept, generally, quite immersed in the liquid; but when from any cause left uncovered by the water, it tends to descend by a force which is measured by the weight of such a bulk of water as there may be of the solid laid bare. Thus, if there be one cubic foot of the solid above the level of the water, the force it will exert to open the valves will be about sixty-two pounds. This equality between the bulk of the body uncovered and the weight of water which measures its gravitating power, is the consequence of being counterpoised by the weight C, which, under ordinary circumstances, is just sufficient to keep the valves at their seats, when A is completely immersed. It is evident that as the valves are similar, and of opposite tendencies when urged by the steam, and as they are attached at equal distances, on opposite sides of the fulcrum of the lever B, they are, under all circumstances of pressure in the boiler, equally prone to obey any external force; and as the relation between the specific gravity of water and that of an immersed incompressible solid is not changed by the circumstance of both being under a pressure of steam, no impediment is felt to the action of the valves when the steam is up, more than when the boiler is filled with cold water and common air.

It is true, the relation of the specific gravity of the solid, and of the steam in which it is immersed when not covered with water, is changed with the pressure of steam; because, unless surcharged with heat, the latter has its *density* increased in proportion to the pressure, but the relation between the density of water at all known temperatures, and of steam at any working pressure, is such as to preclude the supposition that the buoyant power of the latter can ever become sufficiently important to modify the action of the immersed body. Thus, since water is 815 times heavier than common air, the latter will buoy up a body immersed in it, 1-815th part as much as the former fluid. Hence, any solid immersed, and floating indifferently in water in vacuo, at 60°, and then raised above its surface, would there weigh one eight hundredth part more than if raised into a medium of the density of common air; but if raised into a medium having a density of *common steam*, that is, vapour which counterpoises the pressure of the atmosphere, it would weigh only one 1696th part less than when raised out of water into a vacuum. If the steam into which it might be raised were at a pressure of two atmospheres, the weight lost by a change from a vacuum to steam of that tension, would be nearly 1-848th of the whole weight; and if of ten atmospheres, 1-169th of the same amount; and as the last mentioned pressure is probably above the mean working pressure of high pressure boilers, it is evident that the greatest difference between the effect of the immersed body when tried in atmospheric air, and in high pressure steam respectively, would be only about one half of 1-170, or one 340th of the weight of water which is equal to its bulk. This, in the case of a float having a bulk of one cubic foot, would be less than one-fifth of a pound. Hence, if an apparatus of this kind be properly adjusted at common temperature, and while the steam chamber is yet filled with atmospheric air, it would not be sensibly diminished in efficacy by a pressure of steam of twenty atmospheres, or twice as great as the highest working pressures now deemed useful in the steam engine. With regard to the form of the immersed body, the inventor has not restricted himself, but practice will doubtless indicate the propriety of making its vertical dimension small, so that when the water once comes down to its upper surface, its whole bulk may become as speedily as possible uncovered, and effective towards opening the valves. This condition must, however, be made consistent with the free escape of steam, generated below the immersed body, to the steam chamber above; hence a division of the body into several distinct portions, united by inflexible bars, may sometimes be found expedient.

Fig. 2, represents the form and action of the apparatus in a common cylindrical boiler. The depth of the body A is about the same as the distance between the lowest safe water line and the highest fire line outside of the boiler; it might be as much less than this, as it should be found convenient to make it, and its upper surface should, when suspended in the water, be coincident with that of the water at the moment it has come down to the level just indicated. In this figure the apparatus is represented as in action, the same as in fig. 1.

In fig. 3, is seen a vertical section of the apparatus, such as may be used in cylindrical boilers, with interior flues. Two distinct portions of the immersed body, A A, are united by an inflexible rod, curved upwards to conform, when required, to the exterior of the flue d. This arrangement facilitates the escape of steam generated by the top part of the flue. The marks for water lines and fire lines are the same as in figs. 1 and 2.

Fig. 4, represents a tubular boiler, with the immersed body formed of a series of pieces of tube, closed at both ends, and connected together by rods into a kind of grate-formed assemblage, as more distinctly seen in fig. 5. The tubes used in this apparatus may be of the same diameter as those constituting the boiler, or of any less size, affording ample freedom for the escape of steam through their interstices, in its passage from the boiler tubes below, to the steam chamber above.

In figs. 2, 3, and 4, the interior valve only is exhibited; the rest of the apparatus being entirely the same, whatever is the form of the immersed body, or of the boiler in which it is used.

REWARDS TO ENGINE-KEEPERS.

"Statuta pro publico commodo late interpretantur."[1]

Sir,—It is sincerely to be wished that all persons charged with the application of beneficial statutes, especially when vested with discretionary power, would carry out the original intentions of the framers of such statutes, with judgment and liberality.

Among other instances that might be quoted, in which the reverse of this is the case, I may mention the arbitrary manner in which rewards are given to firemen, under the provisions of the well known Building Act (14° Georgii 3d cap. 78.)

In the greater number of parishes, it has hitherto been the practice, to pay the full rewards* for engines brought to any house on fire, and half the rewards, according to the nature of the case, for fires in chimneys; which adjudication has usually been considered satisfactory by the engine-keepers.

In some few parishes, however, especially of late, a short-sighted policy has obtained, calculated to prove exceedingly mischievous in its effects, and to entirely destroy the wholesome stimulus intended to be produced, by the framers of the act in question. Thus, for instance, it not unfrequently happens, that the magistrate making the award, guided by a spirit of wisdom extremely paradoxical, almost invariably gives the full reward to the engine-keepers for their attendance, in case the building in which the fire originated, and perhaps one or two others adjoining are burned to the ground; but, should the firemen by prompt attendance and extraordinary efforts, confine the flames to the floor or apartment in which they originated, it becomes a trifling matter, and the rewards are limited to one half, or perhaps a third of the sum named in the act!

Again, should the firemen on arriving at a fire, attempt, and successfully accomplish its suppression by the aid of buckets only, they are deemed unworthy of reward; but should they at once set their engine to work, and render *the damage done by water* three times as great as that occasioned by the fire itself, they will have little or no trouble in obtaining the full reward. One remarkable instance of this kind came under my own observation a short time since; a fire broke out in the premises of an engineer, and the firemen being sent for, were promptly in attendance; on examining the nature and contents of the premises in the parts adjacent to the fire, they found the consequence of throwing in a large body of water would be the destruction of a large stock of costly patterns; the firemen accordingly set to work with buckets of water, cutting away and extinguishing the fire piecemeal, and in about an hour

---

* The rewards are, thirty shillings for the first engine; twenty shillings for the second; and ten shillings for the third; with ten shillings to the turncock, whose water first arrives at a fire. The latter functionary frequently finds himself cut off with half a crown, after quitting his bed at dead of night to lend his needful aid'

A A 2

had removed all apprehension of further danger. The owners of the premises in question, expressed themselves highly gratified with the skill and care displayed in the conduct of the firemen. The sapient *authorities*, however, upon whom devolved the rewarding of the men, resisted their claims, because they had not set their engines to work ! The employment of the engines would have involved infinitely less labour, and less risk to the firemen, than the course they adopted ; but the amount of property destroyed would have been incomparably greater.

It is well known that parish engine-keepers receive a very paltry remuneration for their services, and the rewards alone make the office desirable. If, therefore, these rewards are cut down, below the amount of expenses unavoidably incurred in getting out and working an engine, the engineer is compelled to withhold his attendance, which is at present actually the case in several metropolitan parishes. Or, if the engineer should attend with his engine, he has no inducement to incur the additional expense of working it, even if necessary. I have frequently known parish engineers, to be money out of pocket by their attendance at a fire, besides the risk incurred, and the labour of clearing up and oiling the engine, hose, &c. afterwards. This ought not to be; the object contemplated in offering the reward, was to hold out *inducement* for prompt attendance and efficient services at fires.

Modern legislation on this subject is calculated to produce the most alarming results, by tending in the first place to discourage the attendance of engines altogether; in the second place, to offer a high premium for an increased extent of damage either by fire or water, or by both !

Some alteration of the statute regulating the rewards to firemen has been mentioned at different times, but the subject is a very difficult one to legislate upon, and one in which great latitude must necessarily be given, for a discretionary application of its enactments; in this matter—

" Whate'er is best administered, is best."

The churchwardens, magistrates, and others, who have the adjudication of these cases, would do well carefully to investigate each claim as it is brought before them, and decide fairly upon its real merits, with that degree of liberality' which the interests of society so eminently require. The saving a few pounds annually to a parish collectively, by wringing them from a class of men by no means overpaid, may very likely be the means of taking thousands from the pockets, and prove the ultimate ruin, of some respectable and industrious parishioner.

I remain, Sir,
Yours respectfully,
W. BADDELEY.

London, August 22, 1837.

SUB-MARINE NAVIGATION.

Sir,—Sailing under the water has been a favorite scheme for many centuries. When we reflect on the advantages of such a contrivance, the marvel at this ceases. The following lines contain an account of some of the attempts made two hundred years since towards its accomplishment.

Among the manuscripts of Dr. Birch in the British Museum, is a tract bearing the signature of the celebrated inventor of logarithms, entitled, " Secret Inventions, profitable and necessary in these days, for the defence of this Island, and withstanding of Strangers, enemies to God's truth and religion." This small treatise thus concludes:—"These inventions, *besides devices of sailing under the water*, and divers other devices and stratagems for harassing of the enemies, by the grace of God and work of expert craftsmen, I hope to perform. John Napier, of Merchiston, Anno Dom. 1596, June 2."

It merely appears from this document, that the invention of a sub-marine vessel was premeditated by Napier, but we possess no proof that he ever attempted its construction. The exploit, was, however, performed in Napier's life-time by Cornelius Dreble, a celebrated Dutch chemist.

This mechanist is reported to have constructed a vessel for king James I, which he rowed under the water in the Thames. It carried twelve rowers, besides several passengers, the air breathed by whom was made again respirable by means of "a certain liquor."

The preceding narration must be taken with some limitation. That Dreble did make an experiment of a similar nature is beyond the possibility of a doubt, from the many notices we have of it by contemporary writers; but that he succeeded so far as to propel the boat in a given direction, and provided for the consumption of pure air by the above method, is almost beyond the limits of credibility, when we consider the period in which the experiment was performed. Bishop Wilkins, in 1648, thus makes mention of it:—"That such a contrivance is feasible and may be effected, is beyond all question, because it hath been already experimented here in England by Cornelius Dreble, but how to improve it into public use and advantage, so as to be serviceable for remote voyages, the carrying of any considerable number of men with provisions and commodities would be of such excellent use as may deserve some further enquiry." This evidently implies that Dreble had not attained any practical proficiency in his instrument.

As customary with the Bishop, exaggerations occur throughout his chapter on Dreble's vessel. The following extract, which is intended to point out one of the uses to which such a machine might in course of time be applied, will amuse the reader:—"All kinds of arts and manufactures may be exercised in this vessel. The observations made by it, may be both written, and (if need were) printed here likewise. Several colonies may thus inhabit, having their children born and bred up without the knowledge of land, who could not chuse but be amazed with strange conceits upon the discovery of this upper world!"

The two preceding extracts from Wilkins are taken from his Mathematical Magic, book 2, chap. 5, p. 179, and 190.

J. O. H.

August 28, 1837.

MR. UTTING'S ASTRONOMICAL TABLES.

Sir,—In testing the accuracy of Mr. Utting's length of a mean tropical year, from the formula $\frac{PS}{S-P}$ (see No. 722) I calculated the length of the mean solar year to be 365^d 5^h 48^m 49^s + a fraction somewhat less than half a second. Mr. Utting, however, from the same formula has calculated the length of the tropical year, and has found it to be no less than near half a second more than I had calculated it to be; the difference being so

small, rather than go over the calculation again, I shall concede this point to him. Still, however, according to his own hair splitting calculation, there is an error of of .0011 of a second, and this would produce a mistake of 4^m 35^s. 9944 on the grand conjunction feat. Mr. Utting alludes to this error, and tells us, that if he had calculated the decimal of the seconds of the moon's periodical period to five places (!) instead of four, all would have been right. That is, Mr. U., by his (yet unexplained) method could determine the length of the mean periodical revolution of the moon, true to the hundred thousandth part of a second, and the length of the mean tropical year, to the ten thousandth part of a second—Prodigious accuracy! But what is the real fact of the case? Why, that astronomers at this minute are not agreed in the length of a mean tropical year to a single second, instead of the ten thousand part of one. By taking the mean between several of the best authenticated of their periods, I find the result produces 365^d 5^h 48^m 49^s 3—. And with regard to the mean synodic period of the moon, it is known, perhaps, to greater accuracy than any other of the heavenly bodies; for, from observations made on eclipses of the sun and moon, from a period 720 years B.C. down to the present time, it is found that a mean synodic period of the moon is 29.530588 days, or 29^d 12^h 44^m 2^s. 8. If, therefore, instead of Mr. U.'s manufactured synodic period, we substitute 29.530588, then 91640740+ 29.530588 = 3103248.062+ and 29.53+ × 062 = 18 hours 17 minutes; that is, the moon would arrive 18 hours 17 minutes too early at the grand conjunction post. Perhaps your learned correspondent Joshua Thorne could suggest to Mr. Utting some method by which the moon might be made to stand still until all the other planets came up to the said line of conjunction.

Mr. Utting would fain wriggle himself out of the blunders he has fallen into in respect of his method of determining the synodic periods of any of the planets. His manner of computing their synodical periods is evidently derived from the theorem $S = \frac{T'T'}{T-T'}$ and if this theorem is right, there is no doubt, from the way in which he has contrived to manufacture the tropical periods given in his first Table, that $\dfrac{91640740}{S} = \dfrac{G}{S} +$ will always be a whole number, or very nearly so. It is true, he has not given us the above theorem (or any theorem), but I can easily demonstrate without any arithmetical calculation, that his rule is the same as that which is deducible from the theorem $S = \dfrac{T\,T'}{T - T'}$. Assume $91640740 = G$. Let N be the number of tropical revolutions the earth makes in the time G; n, the number Venus (or any other of the planets) makes in the same period. Then by Mr. Utting's 1st Table, $\dfrac{G}{N}$ and $\dfrac{G}{n}$ are both whole numbers (or very nearly so). Then, according to Mr. U.'s principles $S = \dfrac{G}{n - N}$; and, consequently. the number of synodic periods will be $G + \left(\dfrac{G}{n - N}\right) = n - N =$ to a whole number. Now Let T = tropical period of the earth, T' that of Venus (or any other planet). Then, $\dfrac{G}{T} = N$ and $\dfrac{G}{T'} = n$; therefore, $\dfrac{G}{T'} - \dfrac{G}{T} = n - N$; hence, $G = \dfrac{(n - N)\,T\,T'}{T - T'}$ ∴ $\dfrac{G}{n - N} = \dfrac{T\,T'}{T - T'}$; but according to Mr. U.'s principles $\dfrac{G}{n - N} = S$; hence, $S = \dfrac{T\,T'}{T - T'}$. But this I positively deny, and again assert, that (see No. 726); $S = \dfrac{P\,P'}{P - P'}$; and further, I assert that in no case in the solar system is $\dfrac{T\,T'}{T - T'} = \dfrac{P\,P'}{P - P'}$; and these facts, Mr. Editor, are as well known to every one who has attentively studied the motion of the planets, as that 6 times 7 is equal to 42, is known to every tyro in arithmetic.*

Mr. Utting will, I trust, now see the reason why I was obliged to metamorphose his tropical periods into sideral revolutions; had he given the sideral periods, it would have saved me a good deal of trouble. There are several other

* A very good and full demonstration of these facts, are given in the treatise on Astronomy, published under the superintendence of the Society for the Defusion of Useful Knowledge.

inaccuracies Mr. U. has fallen into which I might here notice, but as I am on the eve of a jaunt to Rob Roys country, I must defer doing so until I return.

I am, Mr. Editor,
　　　　Yours, &c.
　　　　　A Scotch Dominie.
Forfarshire, Augsut, 18, 1837.

QUESTION BY A TOWN TEACHER.

Given $\left\{\begin{array}{l} x\,y = a\ x + n\,y \\ y^2 - x^2 = n^2 \end{array}\right\}$ to find x and y by quadratics.

QUESTION BY A CAMBRIDGE STUDENT.

At what distance from the sun must a superior planet be placed, so that its periodic revolution may be n mean solar days, and determine the limits of possibility.

WOODHOUSE'S ROTARY ENGINE.

Sir,—The plan of the rotary engine I sent you was one of my own invention solely, notwithstanding the resemblance it may have to any other invented previous to its existence; my object has always been to avoid any thing like imitation.

Having arranged my plan, and executed drawings I left them with a patent agent, who politely gave me his opinion, that if I could incase the diaphragms, so as to avoid the friction of the surrounding packing plates, it would greatly improve the arrangement. This was about the latter end of June, 1836. This gentleman, at the time informed me that an engine had been patented, somewhat resembling it, but could not at the time mention the name of the patentee: this induced me to peruse several works, when I discovered Mr. Galloways, as the only one at all similar. Your correspondent, J. R., whose observation I have this moment read, states it as an " exact counterpart" of that invention, (p. 295); but upon comparison there is a manifest difference. First, the one requires two valves, acting alternately for the admission of steam, which the other does not ; these valves also require the further addition of tappets, &c., which to the other would be needless; the diaphragms also in the one act as stationary abutments to the power, which in the other are the moving levers; in the one, the access of power is constant; whereas, in the other it requires to be shut off at every stroke.

or half revolution. It cannot, therefore, with justice be said, that the revolving of the central axis and excentric guide, are the "*only difference.*" Would that all who have invested property in securing a patent, were as free from infringement upon patent right, as these two engines present. As to the resemblance my engine may have to Mr. Beale's " superior," I shall decline further remarks, until we are favoured with a description of it; from what I have seen of that engine, it is *only* suited as a stationary one, and not at all calculated to any other purpose, where a jerk, or other casualty might throw the diaphragms out of play, and lose power without limit; as to velocity it is quite out of the question, unless by auxiliary machinery; besides, if I am not mistaken, Mr. B.'s engine is incapable of a reverse movement, which for locomotive purposes is indispensible; as it respects the central admission of steam, it is quite clear that " Hero" has a prior claim to its application, even before the use of the cylinder was applied.

The circumstance of the engine being called " New" is the only doubt I have

respecting it, for after all, it can only come in with the rest as an *attempt at improvement* to obtain a rotary action. " Nothing new under the sun."

A word before I conclude on *steam boiler explosions*. The observations of Mr. Leonard upon this subject, seem to establish the advantage of using cylindrical boilers exclusively for all purposes; added to which, the advantage of having capacious lock-up safety-valves, would, in all human probability, exclude the possibility of accident from the sudden expansion of steam, owing to an insufficient supply of water on the one hand, or a check to the emission of steam from the boiler when the engine is stopped, and insufficiently capacious outlet to the accumulated power of steam, on the other,

Trusting that I have not trespassed needlessly upon your valuable pages, or the attention of your readers with this subject.

I remain, Sir,

Yours respectively,

JAMES WOODHOUSE.

Kilburn, August 26, 1837.

MR. ADAMS'S EQUIROTAL CARRIAGES.

Sir,—In your number of August 26th, a correspondent in noticing the construction of my carriages, appears to entertain the notion that the horses can have no control whatever upon the guidance of the hind wheels, which he imagines are left at liberty to deviate from the track of the front ones with every obstruction or inequality of the road. This is a fallacy, which I understand many persons have taken up, and which I now propose to refute. The fact is, that with

my carriages the hind wheels must of necessity follow in the tracks of the front ones, owing to the position of the central working joints; and the defect thus improperly attributed to them, is in reality a defect peculiar to the existing class of carriages on four wheels. A reference to the accompanying sketches must convince all who are capable of reasoning on the subject.

Fig. 1 is the plan of a four-wheeled carriage of the ordinary construction,

Fig. 1.

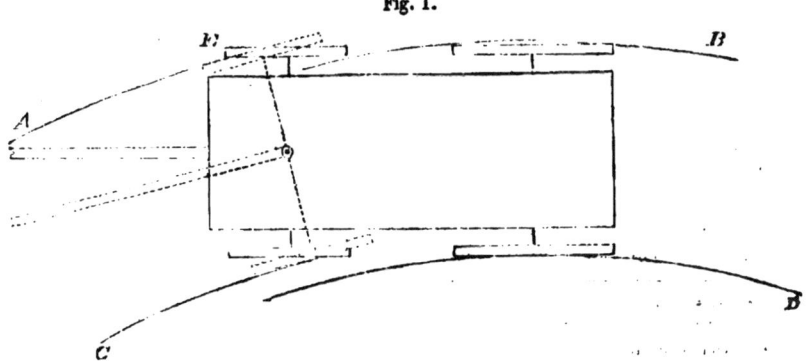

locked, at about the average angle used in turning or going round the corners of ordinary streets, as is shewn by the dotted lines. The vanishing point of the angle formed by the lines of the two axles, will be found at the distance of 27 feet from the front wheel E, conse-quently the four separate circular tracks, A, B, C, D, on which the four wheels run, will be comprised within a circle of not less than fifty-four feet in diameter.

Fig. 2, is the plan of an equirotal car-riage of my improved construction, the dotted lines shewing the angle of turn-

Fig. 2.

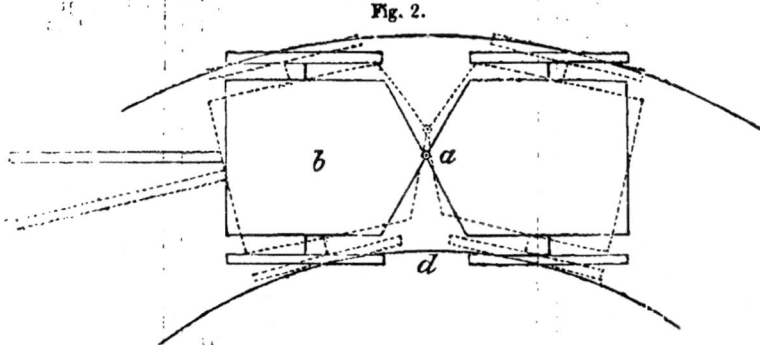

ing exactly the same as fig. 1. But the turning centre being carried back to *a*, instead of being in the ordinary position, *b*, the front portion of the carriage, to which the horses are attached, acts as a lever on the hind wheels, so that they also lock, and consequently the vanish-ing point of the angle formed by the two axles will be found at the distance of 15 feet from the track *c*. Thus, the two circular tracks, *c*, *d*, on which the four wheels run, will be comprised with-in a circle of 30 feet in diameter, instead of 54, as is the case with the carriage fig. 1.

Carriages must either run on straight lines or in curves. Practically, they scarcely ever run in straight lines; their line of progress is a series of curves alternating to the right and left. With the ordinary carriage, the horses have no guiding power on the hind wheels, be-cause their centre of motion is round the perch-bolt, which has no leverage on them; and, as the draught acts on them from a distant centre, they have a con-stant tendency to run in a straight line, as a string holds a kite. Therefore, when the front wheels turn at an angle,

the hinder ones must travel some dis-tance, with considerable friction, before they can adapt themselves to the changed direction; and this friction must be very great, when unsteady horses or crowded streets cause the direction to be very frequently changed. We may under-stand this better by imagining a waggon drawn by a single cord without shafts or pole to steer it.

The equirotal carriage cannot have the fore wheels turned at an angle, without the hinder ones being turned to a corre-sponding angle, and, therefore, the hinder part is under perfect control, which the hinder part of the ordinary carriage is not. Supposing, therefore, that an equi-rotal carriage were descending a hill, keeping a straight line—if the hinder wheels were set at an angle by means of blocks and pullies on the axles, the speed of the carriage might be checked at plea-sure by the driver, without the necessity of using a drag, and the amount of check regulated by the greater or less declivity.

I remain, Sir,
Yours obediently,
WILLIAM B. ADAMS.

121, Long Acre, Aug. 26, 1837.

TO OBTAIN A ROTARY MOTION AT ANY DISTANCE, BY THE ACTION OF TWO DOUBLE CRANKS.

Sir,—A model of the machine, of which I send you a description, was constructed last year, and forwarded in September to the Adelaide Rooms, Low-ther Arcade, where I presume it is now lying. Yours, truly,

W. ERRICK.

Sunderland, 17 July.

Description.—A B (fig. 1), a shaft, having two cranks, E and F, standing at right

angles or ninety degrees to each other.
C D, another similar cranked shaft,

Fig. 1.

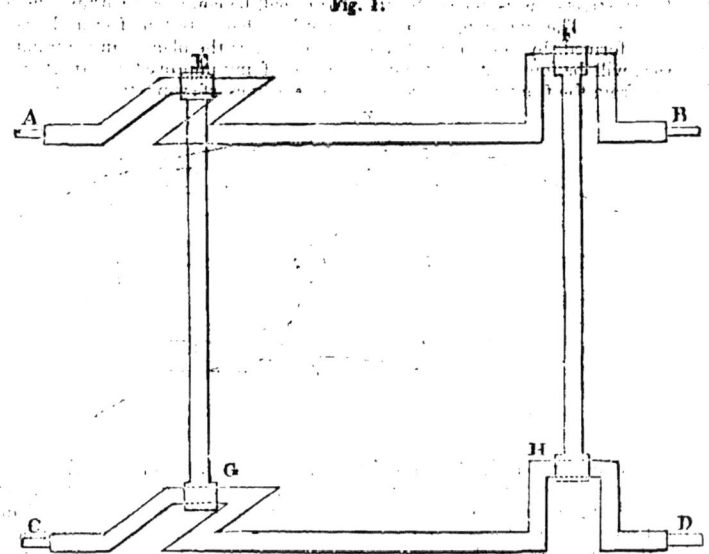

having the similar cranks G and H,
standing directly opposite to those on
A and B. These cranks are connected
by the rods E G and F H. It will
readily be seen, that by this construction the least motion in one shaft will
cause a corresponding one in the other,
by reason of the secondary crank putting

the other past the centre. Lest there
should be any doubt respecting the perfect action of them, the following diagram (fig. 2) will fully explain it, and at
the same time prove that equal arcs are
passed over in equal times by the corresponding cranks :—

Fig. 2.

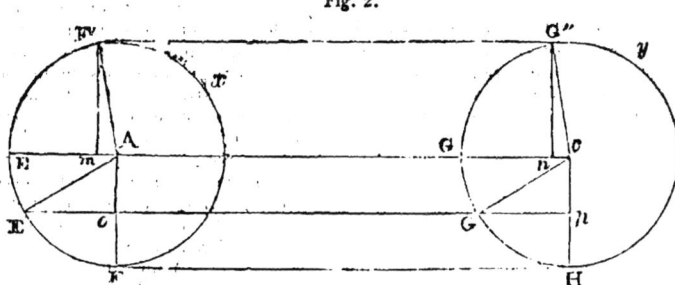

Let E A and F A represent the arms
of the cranks E and F in fig. 1; and G C
and C H, those of G and H : circles being
drawn from the centres of motion A and
C. Suppose the points G E to be connected by a line, and F H also by another, which lines shall represent the
radius rods E G, F H respectively. Now,

as the cranks E A, F A, and G C,
H C are equal and fixed, and stand at
the same angle to each other, whatever
motion the arm C H may acquire, the
other, G C, will also receive. The same
may be proved of the arms E A, F A;
consequently, if the points H or F be
moved through any number of degrees,

the points G and E will be moved through an equal number. Now, as the circles E F x and G H y are equal, and the line E A G C in the line of the centres; if we take a line equal to C A, and apply it at G, it will extend to E. For the same reason, a similar line applied at H, or right angles to the line A C from the centres of the circles, will reach to F, the point at right angles to the line A C from the centre A, Therefore, the lines E G and F H are equal, being equal to the distance A C. If we now suppose the arms C H and A F to have moved to C G′ and A E′, and the arms C G and A E to C G″ and A E″; then, as the arc H G′ is supposed to be equal to the arc F E′, the angle p C G′ is equal to the angle o A E′; and as the lines C G′ and and A E′ are equal, as also the angles C p G′, A o E′ being right ones; the distance p G is equal to the distance o E′; therefore, G′ o plus o E′ are equal to G′ o plus G′ p, equal to C A, equal to H F. Also, because the arc G G″ is

equal to the arc E E″, the angle G o G″ is equal to the angle E A E″, and the angle c n G″, A m E″ right ones (the lines n G″, m E being perpendicular to the line E A G C), the angle C G″ n is equal to the angle A E″ m, and the line c n equal to the line A m. Therefore, C n plus n A equal to m A plus, A n equal to A C, equal to F H; consequently, the connecting rods must be of equal lengths for all points of the circumference of the circles, and the pairs of cranks at right angles to each other; Q E D. This form of the double crank is of much more use than it might at first sight be imagined, for by it we may greatly improve and simplify several valuable machines, to a few of which I will now advert. It is admirably adapted for locomotive carriage wheels, to which I believe it has been applied, and is still used, for keeping one of the cranks of the centre, for the purpose of starting; and this is the only use to which the principle has been applied. I may, there-

Fig. 3.

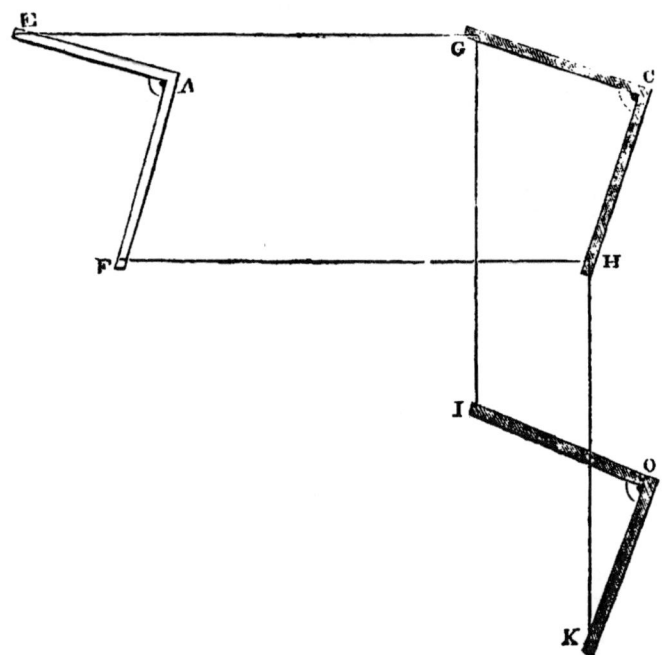

fore, say it has not been used to give motion, which is the object of this paper

to suggest, but, to retard one already acquired. In the paper-mill, it might be applied in the place of the endless strap that drives the cylinders carrying the copper web. In very large foot boring or turning lathes, where slow motion is required, it could be applied with advantage, by making one of the cranked shafts the mandril, and the other the treddle-shaft, when the fly might be dispensed with. It might likewise be used for lathes turned by steam, which would dispense with the long straps. In orreries and other machinery, where large intermediate cogged wheels are applied for conveying the power to a distance, the principle could be applied with great advantage. But the most singular application of it is in being able to convey the rotary motive power at a right or any other angle to the original motive force, as shewn in the diagram on the preceding page.

Where E A F, G C H of fig. 3, represent the similar double cranks of fig. 2, and E G, F H, their radius rods. The crank I O K, with its radius rods G I, H K is for obtaining the rotary motion at a right angle to the original motion. By additional cranks, the motion might be conveyed in a circle.

W. E.

LONDON AND BIRMINGHAM RAILWAY.—
EIGHTH HALF-YEARLY REPORT.

Birmingham, 18th August, 1837.

The directors on the present occasion of submitting their half-yearly report, have the satisfaction to announce, that the expectation they held out in their last Report of a partial opening of the line in the course of the present summer, to the extent of twenty-one miles out of London, has now been fully realized. Early in the month of July, the engineer having reported that the works of the twenty-four and a half miles, between the Company's station, at Euston-square, in London, and Boxmoor, were in a fit state for use, the directors decided that this portion of the railway should be opened to the public, on the 20th of that month. The trains commenced running accordingly on that day, and although the traffic has hitherto been merely derived from excursions of pleasure and curiosity, and from the journeys of the comparatively few individuals who reside in the immediate vicinity of the line, and although the departures of the trains (in consequence of the progress of the works connected with the entire completion, and finishing off, of this portion of the railway), are at present confined to three from each end, the number of passengers has already

exceeded anticipation, and proved fully equal to the means for their conveyance.

On the 16th instant, being 28 days from the first opening, 39,855 persons had been conveyed by the railway, being an average of 1,423 per day, for which the daily receipts average 153l.; during the last week the daily average of numbers has advanced to 1,807, and of receipts, to 189l.

The directors are assured by the engineer that the works which at present interfere with mid-day trains will be entirely completed, and that the whole of this part of the railway will be in excellent travelling order in the course of a month, by which time the stationary engine for the incline of the extension line will be in readiness for work, and an ample supply of locomotive engines at their command. Full effect will then be given to provisional arrangements, which have been already entered into with the principal coach proprietors, for bringing the passengers by their respective coaches upon the railway, as fast as it is in readiness to receive them, which arrangements, and others calculated to bring an immediate and active traffic upon the railway, all the parties concerned appear most anxious to carry on with spirit, whenever the directors feel satisfied that they are in a situation to perform punctually and efficiently what the company will then have to undertake.

The directors cannot but notice the great advantage arising from the gradual opening of successive portions of the railway; opportunity being thus afforded for organizing the arrangements required in the carrying department, and for progressively adapting them with the benefit derived from experience on a small scale, to more extended operations, whilst the road is becoming gradually and safely consolidated, and an important revenue is afforded by a limited number of passengers' trains.

The advance made towards the entire completion of all the works of the London and Birmingham railway, and the near approach of the time at which the whole line will be opened to the public, appear to the Directors to require, on their part, a communication to the proprietors of the most exact information which it is now in their power to obtain, as to the ultimate cost of the whole undertaking, the periods at which each portion of it may be reasonably expected to be opened for business, and the probable traffic. They have, in consequence, required from the engineer carefully revised estimates of the cost of all the works in his department which are still unexecuted, and such a statement of the probable cost of those remaining works, of their entire sufficiency for the purposes of the traffic of all descriptions to be anticipated on opening the whole line, and of the exact periods at which, in all probability, each successive portion cannot now fail to be executed and completed, as he may be willing should go forth to the proprietors with the full sanction of his name and professional character.

The details will be annexed to the Report, and the directors cannot but remark with pleasure upon the assurance they have from Mr. Stephenson, at this advanced period of the works, that not only will a few weeks see the railway at the London end, opened from Boxmoor to Tring (a further advance of seven miles), but that in the course of December next it will extend in perfect working order for business, sixteen miles farther, to Denbigh Hall, at the crossing of the Holyhead road, and at the Birmingham end as far as Rugby, making the whole length of railway which will be entirely completed, and which the directors therefore hope to have opened to the public *on the first of January next*, 27 miles. They have thus reasonable ground to hope that at this early period the entire line of railway communication between London, Birmingham, and the principal places in Lancashire, will be open to the public, with the exception only of *an interval of thirty-five miles* of excellent turnpike road between Rugby and Denbigh Hall. The engineer states that the proprietors may calculate with perfect confidence on the entire completion of the whole line, and of the works connected with it, in the course of the autumn of 1838.

The proprietors will see by the annexed revised estimates that the expectation of the entire completion of the railway and stations in efficient working order from end to end, and of the ample carrying establishment now contracted for, within the capital of 4,500,000*l.*, is confirmed and strengthened by the further means of calculation afforded by the nearer approach of all the works to their termination. As far as relates to the

cost of stations, engines, carriages, waggons, and, indeed, every item of future expenditure, excepting the unexecuted works in the engineering department, there is scarcely any opening for error or question, and the directors think that the confident manner in which Mr. Stephenson has expressed his conviction of the sufficiency in all respects of his present revised estimates (confirmed by the circumstance that works in the hands of the Company have been let, and executed by sub-contractors considerably below the engineer's estimate) affords every security and assurance of accuracy that can be obtained on this subject. It should also be mentioned, that no credit whatsoever is taken for a considerable extent of unoccupied land in possession of the Company for re-sale, as opportunities offer, and that the engineer's estimate for the carrying department includes a much larger extent of stock than will be required in the first instance, if at all. The directors, therefore, do not hesitate to express their confident expectation that the proprietors may calculate upon having the railway completed, and in full operation, within the present capital of 4,500,000*l.*, sanctioned by Parliament; and that if there should eventually prove to be any further excess in the engineering department, or if the extent of the future traffic should render expedient any extension of the works at present contemplated, the additional capital cannot be required until a large revenue has rendered it easy of attainment, and placed the proprietors in a situation to judge of the propriety of such farther outlay.

As the undertaking approached completion, the probable amount of traffic to be expected became a point of great interest. In order to obtain as near an approximation to the truth as the circumstances of the case admit, a sub-committee was appointed to examine into the subject. The result of their investigations may be stated as follows:

	Per Week·
That the gross receipt from passengers *now* travelling by coaches on the roads parallel immediately contiguous to the line of railway, without assuming any increase, amounts at railway prices to	£6,789
That the gross receipts from persons now posting on the same roads amount to.	729
That the gross receipts from parcels now carried by coaches on the same roads amount to	1,571
That the gross receipts from goods *now* conveyed by waggons and canals on the lines between London and Birmingham, not including iron, timber, cattle, minerals, or other goods, which pay low tonnage, amount to.............	8,120
That the total gross receipts from the foregoing sources, assuming no increase, amount per week to	£17,209
That the total annual receipts amount to....................................	£894,868

The data from which these results are obtained will be found in the Report to the

Board by the sub-committee appointed to investigate the subject; copies of which document may be had by the proprietors, on application to the secretaries.

The directors congratulate the proprietors upon the completion and opening for traffic of the Grand Junction Railway between the Liverpool and Manchester line and Vauxhall near Birmingham, and upon the commencement of the works of the Midland Counties and North Midland Railways, connecting the London and Birmingham line with Yorkshire and the Midland Counties; all which lines form tributary streams, the full value of which to the main trunk can scarcely be over estimated. The Birmingham and Gloucester, and the Derby and Birmingham Railway Companies, also appear to contemplate the use of the entrance into Birmingham and the stations of the London and Birmingham Railway. The directors have the pleasure of communicating the entire success of the opposition announced in their last Report to the attempts to establish injurious rival lines, uncalled for by any public necessity. The judicious regulations now adopted by Parliament relative to all new

lines of railway, afford ample grounds of security against the recurrence of projects of a similar description.

The directors have to announce, that the Act authorizing the Company to raise an additional million, and for other purposes, received the royal assent on the 30th June, and that in pursuance of the resolution of the special general meeting f the same date, an additional capital of 625,000l. has been created, under the powers of the Act, in 25,000 shares of 25l. each, which have been offered to the proprietors of 100l. shares, in the proportion of a 25l. share for each 100l. share. It is proposed that the new shares of 25l. each, which form an integral part of the capital stock of the Company, shall be entitled to the same rate of dividend as the original shares of 100l. each, without distinction as to the time of the payments of the calls which shall have been made respectively when a dividend is declared.

By the statements of accounts now to be laid before the proprietors, it will appear that—

The receipts to the 30th of June, were £3,181,069 15 8

The disbursements 3,102,272 8 5

And the balance of cash in the Company's hands at that date........ 78,797 7 3

The proprietors in referring to the account of capital, will observe, that there remains of the 4,500,000l. a sum of 1,329,282l. 17s.

3d. applicable to the further expenditure of the Company, which, in the annexed estimate is stated at 1,313,698l.

R. Creed,   ⎫ Secretaries of
C. R. Moorson, ⎭ the Board.

Engineer's Estimate of the Periods at which different Portions of the Line will be completed.

	Miles.	
From London to Boxmoor	24½	Open.
" Boxmoor to Tring	7½	" October, 1837.
	32	
" Tring to Denbigh Hall (at the crossing of the Holyhead Road)	16 ⎫	" January, 1838.
" Birmingham to Rugby	29 ⎭	
	77	
" Denbigh Hall to Blisworth	13	" May, 1838.
	90	
" Blisworth to Rugby	22½	" Autumn of 1838.

Total 112½ Miles.

OPENING OF THE RAILWAY FROM PARIS TO ST. GERMAIN.

We extract the following amusing account of this event, from the letter of the *Times* correspondent. . . . .

――――――

St. Germain, Aug. 26.

Paris has put on her seven-leagued boots, and reached St. Germain in a stride! The

chateau of Louis le Grand, and the fine terrace sweeping through the forest until it is lost in distance, have kindly consented to approach the metropolis for the gratification of the numerous *quidnuncs* who inhabit it; and St. Germain, with all its interesting scenery, although, if we are to credit the map, it is twelve good English miles from Paris, is now more accessible than the windmills of Montmartre. This *triomphe merveilleuse*, as the Parisians delight to call it, is the work of that grand miracle-monger of the nineteenth century—steam ; a trip on the railway is now the "*plaisir inconnu*," the "*emotion sans égal;*" and if there be throughout the length and breadth of Paris a single café or coterie, or in the faubourgs a "Merchand de Vin," *alais* "dramshop," where the praises of railroads in general, and of the railway to St. Germain in particular, has not formed the inexhaustible topic of conversation for the last four and twenty hours, I will suffer myself to be impaled alive like a frog in a gourmand's clutches, and fricasseed without mercy.   *   *   *

The train started at twelve to the instant, and then was the clatter of voices raised ten fold. "*Il part—ce coursier de feu, et de fumée!* He snorts! he snorts! His prodigious tail of vapour floats in the firmament! *La voila!*" Even when the engine had attained its extreme velocity, the rattling of tongues was continued, one person shouting into a second's ear, and a third shrieking at the extreme pitch of his voice, "*Cheval magnifique!* Noble and intrepid horse, which nothing can stop! He devours the way before him—he snorts! *vraiment*, he snorts! He is clothed with thunder, like the horse of Job! *Corbleu!* what a delicious motion—*n'est-ce pas?—Oui—c'est le plus grand plaisir du monde!*" Away clattered engines and voices to the same tune, to the end of the journey. If you wish for a genuine specimen of an enthusiast, you have only to clap a Parisian for the first time in his life in a flying "locomotive." In the carriage in which I fixed myself were some half-dozen piquantly-dressed soubrettes and grisettes, distinguishable by the extreme neatness of their *fichus de dentelles a la paysanne*, and their mignonnes lace caps. Of these no fewer than three affected dizziness, faintness, &c., and finished *par s'etre évanouies* on the bosoms of the gallants by whom they were accompanied. Altogether it was a most precious living comedy, worthy of a place in Paul de Kock's "*Tourlourou sur les mœurs Parisiennes.*" Until I reached Paris, I laboured, in common with most people, under the absurd misconception, that the true "land of Cockaigne" is London. For genuine Cockneys you must come to France.

An hour's walk in the forest of St. Germain, after my arrival, was positively delightful in the extreme. In no direction could you turn without meeting elegantly-dressed Parisian ladies (and all other dressing is out of the question) moving along as gracefully as swans in the Cydnus, to which

their white muslin dresses, which are very much the rage here, in no small degree assimilated them. What charming bonnets adorned with waving feathers, or with those ambitions, but not less elegant, wreaths of flowers, which are only made to perfection here, and exhibit the very acme of taste! And then the eye is so pleasingly relieved by the graceful contrast presented by an unbonnetted girl, wearing one of those exquisite little caps ; or by the outlandish helmet-shaped casquette which some rustic belle delights to select for her coiffure. The Bois de Boulogne never presented a more animated scene.

For statistics, it will be sufficient to state, that the *materiel* is composed of 105 vehicles, capable of containing 4,070 persons, and of transporting the entire population of Paris to St. Germain in the course of one fine Sunday. The railway 4½ leagues in length, passes through a beautiful country, traversing no fewer than eighteen bridges, three of which are across the Seine. The vehicles are all intended for the transport of passengers, and will be occupied principally on Sundays. There is a tunnel Batignolles, which is divided into two galleries, being about 400 metres, or a quarter of an English mile long. The construction is very solid, the rails being fifteen times heavier than those upon the Liverpool and Manchester road.

MR. COAD'S PLAN FOR CONSUMING SMOKE.

Mr. Richard Coad, of this town, has taken out a patent (sealed July 10, 1835) for an invention of his for getting rid of the nuisances from steam-boats and factories, by making the chimneys consume their own smoke. To borrow a passage from a contemporary to explain this, "The smoke is a certain quantity of the inflammable matter of the coals, which is lost by evaporation, instead of being burnt." Now, Mr. Coad's method consists in supplying this smoke with the quantity of heat that is necessary for its perfect combustion ; and this is effected in a very simple and ingenious manner. An apparatus, consisting of a series of small tubes, or chambers, so constructed as to expose a large surface to the action of the heat, is placed in the lower part of the chimney beyond the boiler ; one end of the series communicates, by an open orifice, with the external air, while the other opens into a slit in the bridge of the surface. This is the whole contrivance, and it acts thus : —The superfluous heat in the chimney raises the temperature of the iron tubes to a high degree, and the draught in the chimney causes a current of air in the fire through every aperture, and consequently, through the heated tubes; a current of hot air is thus thrown into the flame at every point where the smoke begins to be formed; and the effect is, that the deposition is prevented, and the flame and heat of the fire are both much increased, and not a particle of the smoke escapes from the top of the stack. It will be seen from the foregoing statement, that the means by which Mr. Coad accomplishes this object are as simple as they have hitherto been found effective; and the saving in fuel, from the peculiar operation of the invention, we are assured by several persons of experience, will be immense. The principal merit of Mr. Coad's patent consists in bringing back the caloric, which in almost every instance is entirely lost to the manufacturer. We trust, for the sake of the health of the town, that no feeling of dislike to new inventions will prevent the use of this apparatus from becoming universal.—*Liverpool Telegraph*, Dec. 14, 1836.

LIST OF ENGLISH PATENTS GRANTED BETWEEN THE 29th JULY AND THE 24th AUGUST, 1837.

William Palmer, of Sutton-street, Clerkenwell, manufacturer, for improvements in printing paper hangings. July 29; six months.

James Matley, of Paris, and of Manchester, gent., for a machine, called a tiering machine, upon a new principle, for supplying colours to, and be used by block printers in the printing of cotton, linen, and woollen cloths, silks, paper, and other substances, and articles to which block printing is, or may be applied without the aid or assistance of a person to tier upon. August 2; two months.

Archibald Richard Francis Rosser, of New Boswell-court, Middlesex, Esq., for improvements in preparing manure, and in the cultivation of land, being a communication from a foreigner residing abroad. August 2; six months.

Alexander Macewan, grocer and tea merchant, Glasgow, for a process for the improvement of teas as ordinarily imported. August 5; six months.

Richard Thomas Beck, of Little Stoneham, Suffolk, gent., for new or improved apparatus or machinery for obtaining power and motion, to be used as a mechanical agent generally, which he intended to denominate Rotæ Vivæ, being a communication from a foreigner residing abroad. August 9; six months.

William Gossage, of Stoke Prior, Worcester, manufacturing chemist, for certain improvements in the processes or operations connected with the manufacture of alkali from common salt, and with the use of the products obtained therefrom. August 17; six months.

William Gillman, of Bethnal Green, engineer, for an improvement or improvements in steam boilers, and in engines to be actuated by steam or other power. August 17; six months.

Henry Shuttleworth, of Market Harborough, Leicester, gent., and Daniel Foot Taylor, of the Priory, Gloucester, pin manufacturer; for certain combinations of, and improvements in machinery for making pins; in pursuance of the report of the Judicial Committee of her Majesty's Privy Council, being an extension for the term of five years from the 15th of May, 1838, the expiration of the former

letters patent, granted for the term of 14 years to Lemuel Wellman Wright.

John George Hartley, of No. 11. Beaumont Row, Mile End Road, Esq., for an improved application of levers for the purpose of multiplying power. August 22; six months.

Thomas Du Boulay, of Sandgate, Kent, Esq., and John Joseph Charles Sheridan, of Lewisham, in the same county, Esq., for improvements in drying and screening malt. August 24; six months.

James Crellin, of Liverpool, and James Holt, of the same place, plumbers, for certain improvements in water closets. August 24; six months.

Robert Brown, of Water Side, Maidstone, Kent, engineer, and iron founder, for certain improvements in the construction of cockles, stoves, or apparatus for drying, or stoving hops, malt, grain, or seeds. August 24; six months.

William Hearn, of Southampton-street, Pentonville, Middlesex, engineer, and William Davies, of Upper North Place, Grays Inn Road, Middlesex, plumber, for a certain improvement, or certain improvements in the construction of boilers for the generation of steam, and heating water or other fluids. August 24; six months.

William Southwell, of No. 5, Winchester Row, New Road, Middlesex, pianoforte maker, for a certain improvement in pianofortes. August 24; six months.

LIST OF SCOTCH PATENTS GRANTED BETWEEN THE 22d JULY AND THE 24th AUGUST, 1837.

Godfrey Woone, of Berkeley-street, Middlesex, gent., for an improved method of forming plates with raised surfaces thereon, for printing impressions on different substances. Sealed 24th July, 1837.

Robert Griffiths, of Smethwick, near Birmingham machine maker, for improvements in the manufacture of burrs, or nutts, for screws and nails, or spikes and bolts. August 9.

William Henry Goschen, of Crosby Square, Bishopsgate-street, London, merchant, in consequence of a communication made to him by a certain foreigner residing abroad, for improvements in preparing flax and hemp for spinning. August 9.

John Paul Newmann, of Great Tower-street, London, prussiate of potash maker, by his invention, and partly from a communication from a foreigner residing abroad, for improvements in the manufacture of prussiate of potash, and prussiate of soda. August 9.

Andrew Smith, of Balper, Derby, millwright and engineer, for a certain improvement, or improvements in printing machinery. August 17.

NOTES AND NOTICES.

Railway Returns.—The receipts of the Grand Junction Railway from Birmingham to Manchester and Liverpool, up to the 20th August last, being only forty-seven days from the time when it opened, amounted to no less a sum than £35,534! The first weeks receipts were £3,224. 15s. 7d.; the last £6,394. 1s. 8d., showing an increase in one short month of nearly double. The whole of this large revenue has been derived from passengers, and light parcels alone—the necessary arrangements for carrying goods, not being as yet completed. The returns from the posting of the London Birmingham Railway, which has been opened, namely, that from Euston Square to Boxmoor, are equally encouraging. On the 16th of August, being twenty-eight days from the first opening, 39,855 persons had been conveyed, being an average of 1,428 per day, for which the day receipts averaged £153. During the week subsequent to the 16th August, the daily average of numbers had advanced to 1,807; and of receipts to £168.

Turf for Steam Boat Fuel.—It is an interesting fact, that turf is now used as fuel on board the steamers plying between Limerick, Clare, and Kilrush. The Garryowen has made the passage between Kilrush and Limerick, fired with turf, in three hours and twenty minutes.—*Irish Paper.*

Some months ago we were informed that our neighbour, Mr. George Crane, of the Yniscedwin Ironworks, had directed his attention to the application of stone coal to the smelting of iron ore. From our knowledge of the indefatigable industry and perseverance with which this gentleman follows up every pursuit in which he may be engaged, we entertained a confident, and, as the result proves, a well-grounded hope that his efforts will prove successful. For many weeks past we have been anxiously expecting a confirmation of the very favourable reports which had reached us of the successful progress of Mr. Crane's experiments. Undaunted by the failures which had attended similar attempts, Mr. Crane in the autumn of last year secured a patent right, and by a method hitherto untried (viz., the application of hot blast to his fuel) he most fully succeeded; and the peculiar adaptation of anthracite coal to the reduction of iron ore is now fully demonstrated. We were aware of the peculiar properties of anthracite coal, and that the veins with which this district abounds affords from 87 to 93 per cent. of carbon; it did not, therefore, occasion us surprise when we learned that Mr. Crane anticipated that by the successful introduction of this fuel a description of iron would be produced very nearly resembling in its quality that formerly obtained by the use of vegetable charcoal. In this also his anticipations have been fully realized, and we cordially congratulate him on the result. That most important manufacture, the iron trade, has been hitherto of necessity confined to such parts of this country where bituminous coal prevails; and a large portion of the mineral district, where anthracite coal abounds, has been excluded from its advantages. Our local knowledge enables us to state that iron stone in great abundance is found to alternate with this peculiar fuel, and the eventual effect of this most important discovery must therefore be to induce the erection of iron works over a large extent of country from which this manufacture has hitherto been wholly excluded.—*Cambrian.*

Accidents in Coal Pits—Errata.—Sir, you will oblige me by correcting an error of the press in my last letter. It being one of figures, is material. Instead of the Parliamentary Committee saying, as there printed, "taking eleven years previous to, and eighteen years since, the introduction of the Davy Lamp, *deaths,* from explosions in the coal pits of Durham and Northumberland, have been more in the latter than the former period; it should have been, the same length of time *before and after—eighteen years.* While on this part of the subject, it may be well to point out to your readers, that, judging from the present case, little reliance ought to be placed on what are called the official returns of coroners. In this instance, an order was sent, bearing rather an unusual authority—no less than that of the Secretary of State for the Home Depart-

ment, requiring a return of the number of persons destroyed by explosions in the coal pits of Durham and Northumberland, during a given, and no very distant period, on whom coroners inquests had been held. *According to law, inquests ought to have been held on all.* Now, what was the return thus called for? Why, seventy-six for Northumberland, none for Durham!! The Committee, however, found, from the account on which they made their report, and which account, as far as it went, was confirmed by several of the *mining witnesses,* that the proper number of deaths, during the period referred to, in these counties alone, instead of only seventy-six, was 1025!! Of these, they state, 538 had happened since the introduction of the Davy Lamp. This account, great and surprising as it is, the Committee say, they have reason to consider "*vastly short of the proper number.*"

Your obedient servant, CARBON.

August 30, 1836.

Progress of Civilization.—A coffee-house has been established in "Warren-Square" at Houaruru, the capital of the Sandwich Islands, by a Mr. John Butler, who has succeeded in obtaining the patronage of all the "rank and fashion" of the city, especially by the unrivalled excellence of his *spruce-beer.* His tables are doubtless well supplied with the current periodical literature, as the Sandwich Islands themselves support a newspaper, and, we believe, a magazine into the bargain; while, no further off than at Van Diemen's Land, the natives, (who, it will be remembered, were hunted, a year or two since, to an island out of the way of the settlers), contribute their share in the shape of an aboriginal gazette."

Letting off the Steam.—There is nothing pleases us more in these dull times than the rhetorical affluence of the *Express.* The messages of the Lottery Mayor are prosy compared with the figurative articles of that paper. Witness the following grand burst of metaphorical eloquence, in a paragraph describing the greatness of the American people:—
"Steam is the quill our poets indite with. The earth is our big book. Railroads are the tracts we make upon it. Niagara is its title-page. Two oceans are its binding. The Mississippi is but a stitch in it. We are a steam people, and steam was designed for us—proof, the birth-place of Fulton—and such originals the jog-trot old world can never understand. True, the 'Hero of New Orleans' generated a little too much steam upon the currency, which burst the national boiler; but as soon as we can find out the killed and wounded, we shall light up the fires, and whiz off again."—This is a specimen of writing on the high pressure principle.—*Plain Dealer.*

Improvement in the Steam Engine.—Professor Nollett, employed in the museum of the state, has just completed a most important invention—viz., a steam engine exempt from all danger of explosion, not expensive, occupying but little space, and the moving power of which, at the same temperature as the ordinary machines, has a power six times as great, reducing by one-fifth the consumption of fuel, which is an immense advantage, not only in respect to economy, but to the smaller space which may be required for the stock of coals.—*Brussels Paper.*

LONDON: Printed and Published for the Proprietor, by W. A. Robertson, at the Mechanics' Magazine Office, No. 6, Peterborough-court, between 135 and 136, Fleet-street.—Sold by G. W. M. Reynolds, Proprietor of the French, English, and American Library, 55, Rue Neuve, Saint Augustin, Paris.

Mechanics' Magazine,

MUSEUM, REGISTER, JOURNAL, AND GAZETTE.

| No. 635. | SATURDAY, SEPTEMBER 9, 1837. | Price 3d. |

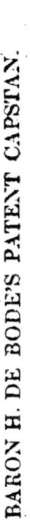

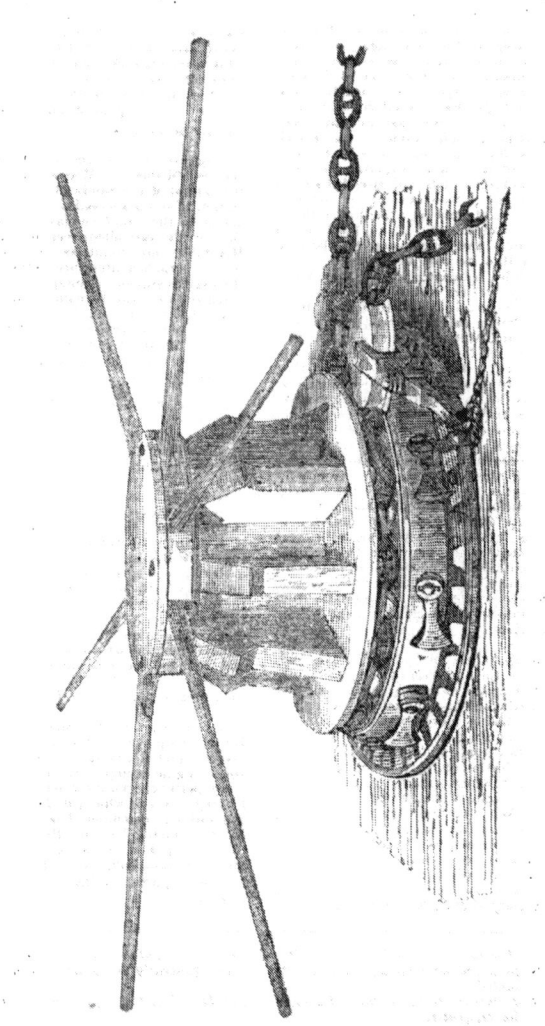

BARON H. DE BODE'S PATENT CAPSTAN.

BN. H. DE BODE'S PATENT CAPSTAN.

The object of this improvement upon ships' capstans is to obtain a simple, economical, and effectual preventive against the well-known effects of surging, which attends the use of the old capstan.

The patent capstan may be worked with or without a messenger, and consists of the application to the capstan, in present use, of a cast-iron concave ring, with alternating stops, fixed to the base of the capstan, and directly over the pall head round which the cable, chain, or messenger, makes but one turn.

The effect of the stops in holding the cable or messenger fast is ensured and increased by a compressing wheel, regulated by a lever; by which combination surging is effectually prevented, and the anchor heaved without risk or inconvenience.

Any sized chain or cable may be used with the patent capstan.

It occupies no more space when fitted than the ordinary capstan, and the apparatus can be applied in a few hours to any capstan already fixed, and in use, without disturbing it in any way.

Fewer hands are required to work the patent capstan, as the men are not obliged to "hold on" when at work.

The strain is directed to that point of the spindle which offers the greatest strength and resistance, whereby the old capstan may be made to perform a considerable increase of duty.

In heeling vessels, when repairs are required in ports unprovided with dry docks, as well as in hauling ships up the patent slips, this capstan offers complete security from surging.

The patent capstan may be seen at work at the offices of Messrs. John and Edmund Walker, 105, Upper Thames-street.

CAOUTCHOUC ROOFS.

Sir,—As yours is a repository for many crude (as well as perfected) inventions, which may afterwards be the groundwork for others of the greatest value and importance to the public, I beg to request you will lay before your readers the following suggestion for a new application of caoutchouc or India-rubber.

I have long thought, that if the tops of houses could be flat, and have reservoirs of water upon them, that water might be made available as a supply for domestic purposes to every room in the house, and also that screw hose might be fitted thereto for the purpose of extinguishing any fire in the room where it originates on its first discovery. Hitherto, lead has appeared the most suitable material for roofs, but weight, price, and contraction by the heat of the sun have been great objections. May not India-rubber be advantageously substituted? If prepared in large sheets one-eighth or three-sixteenths of an inch in thickness, they might be laid on, and afterwards the joinings made perfectly secure by the solution of caoutchouc; and in case of damage from any cause, it might easily be repaired by the same means. Some of your more scientific readers can give the necessary strength of wall and timber for bearing the various depths of water which might be required. I apprehend that in large buildings, such as the new Houses of Parliament, it would not only be advantageous as a preventive of fire, but also more economical.

Yours,
A CONSTANT READER—Z.

MR. DICKSON AND THE CORNISH ENGINEERS.—OBSERVATIONS ON THE CONTROVERSY BETWEEN THOSE PARTIES, BY A PRACTICAL ENGINEER.

Sir,—In your No. 732 are some observations by Mr. Perkins on the performance of the Cornish steam-engines as stated by different parties concerned therein. For several years past, those performances have been doubted by some, and questioned by others, until at last, Mr. Dickson, in your No. 669, unhesitatingly charged the Cornish engineers with calculating most erroneously the performances of their steam-engines. In No. 675, is the Cornish engineers' defence, and in No. 680, is Mr. Dickson's reply; after which, Mr. Enys writes a second letter, in No. 688, and Mr. Dickson replies to this last, in No. 692.

The public, and particularly those interested in this kind of property, have derived great satisfaction at seeing errors of so much consequence so clearly exposed by Mr. Dickson, virtually admitted too, as they have been, by Mr. Enys, who took upon himself to be the champion of the Cornish engineers. Mr. Dickson, after showing their calculations to be erroneous, calls upon them for (what he, or any other person had a right to demand) a practical proof that they could raise their millions of *pounds weight of water* to any convenient height, say one hundred feet, yards, or fathoms; as to the hackneyed phrase of one foot high, it will not do in practice. Mr. Dickson has clearly pointed out the mode of ascertaining the quantity (or weight) of water to be raised, and has allowed ample time for them to clear themselves from suspicion. In the meanwhile, that the public may really know what can be done with a bushel of coals, (although Mr. Enys has said, that "they regard with the utmost apathy, the opinions, or assertions, of engineers of other parts of the kingdom), Mr. Perkins has, it appears, made a tour through Cornwall, and observed the operation of some of those stupendous engines, whose like are not to be found elsewhere.

The result of Mr. Perkins' observations is twenty-five per cent. in favour of Mr. Dickson's charge and protest against the Cornish engineers. He says, "I cannot believe that the enormous quantity of 25,000,000 of pounds weight of water was raised one foot high with 84 lbs. of coal (one bushel), without the assistance of a little *air*, which certainly can be used without being readily detected." He then gives an instance how he learned to detect the error. Mr. Dickson, who is a practical man, seems to have known all about it. In his letter in No. 669, he says, "it is well known how difficult it is to make a pump to deliver a quantity of water at a great hight, to agree with the calculation or the measurement of that part of the pump *supposed* to be filled and emptied every stroke, any admixture of *air*, &c. will produce a variation from the calculation." And he emphatically adds, "perhaps some *imperfection in the pump-work* has led some of the reporters to make an alteration in their figures. In another part Mr. Perkins says, that "while in Cornwall he inquired of an engineer, if he ever had known *air* to be admitted under the clack. After expressing his surprise at my question, he answered that *it was common*, but that it

was not acknowledged, since every one wished to make it appear that he had done as much duty as possible, and farther, that he never knew the air to be allowed for!!" Shame upon those corruptors of science, professors and practisers of the useful arts, who aspire to eminence by depreciating the eminence of others, and rendering the best of sciences subservient to deception! I hope it is not yet reduced to this, that those who are the most dexterous in this way are considered (even in Cornwall) to be the best practical engineers. What a dilemma some of them might possibly now be in with their employers, were they to cause the tests of truth and justice to be applied to the fulfilment of their engagements!

After all this, I hope the Cornish engineers will bestir themselves, and get those blemishes removed by the practical proof suggested by Mr. Dickson, before some other "engineer from other parts of the kingdom" shall make a tour through Cornwall, and cut off perhaps another 25 per cent. from their performances. The amount will then be nearer what Mr. Woolf brought it to, and which Mr. Dickson has stated were likely to be obtained from the powers of steam employed in due subordination to the laws of hydraulics. I am, &c.

P. E.

M. DE LA BECHE AND THE SATELLITE DEPOSIT THEORY.

Sir,—In your last number, 733, there is a communication signed N. S., the object, or purport of which it is somewhat difficult to perceive; unless it be to call in question an assertion made by me in a former number, that M. De la Beche, had in conversation advanced an opinion in some respects favourable to the views advanced in the Electrical Theory with respect to the presumed deposition of satellites. Whether that conversation was "half understood," or the opinions advanced only in "joke," M. De la Beche alone can tell. But the fact of the conversation having occurred as stated, is not to be overthrown by the half-and-half sort of denial of N. S.; and if N. S. knows anything of the matter, he is perfectly aware of this;—as to the "propriety of bringing forward the assertion" that such conversation had taken place, that is quite another affair. For my own part, I hold that such "bringing forward" is most proper, seeing that it was not a *private* conversation, having been held in a place, and amongst men where all opinions upon matters of science are supposed to be common property. For, after all, an opinion is but an opinion, and standing high as Mr. De la Beche confessedly does in that department of science to which he belongs, it is not to be supposed that his scientific reputation is likely to be compromised by his having avowed, whether inadvertently or otherwise, a leaning to a theory, which, if not true, is certainly bold and original; more especially when it is considered, that he himself, in his work on theoretical geology has promulgated views of a speculative character, quite as much at variance with the commonly received notions upon this subject. Although I would not take upon myself to say that the speculations of M. De la Beche "must remain an astronomical dream," I can see as much "propriety in bringing forward such an assertion" in reference to the speculations of M. De la Beche, as to those of Mr. Mackintosh. Not that I intend by this to condemn either the one or the other; indeed it appears to me, that the speculations of those gentlemen run much closer together upon many points than N. S. seems to be aware of.

I do not know that I am called upon to say more at present. Had N. S., by going into the subject at length, attempted to show that the views of the "satellite deposit theorist" are erroneous, he would have conferred a benefit upon science, and an obligation upon

Your obedient servant,
A GEOLOGIST.

August 28, 1837.

MR. WIVELL'S FIRE ESCAPES.

Sir,—I beg to return you my best thanks for the publication of the correspondence between Mr. Baddeley and myself, touching the *first* adaptation of *wheels* to fire escape *elevators* and *ladders*. Mr. Baddeley's *references* have been examined minutely, but without discovering the mention of wheels being applied to any such machines, antecedent to my design, which appeared in 1829. Mr. Hudson's plan is a *roller*, and not wheels, the inefficiency of which

must be well known to Mr. Baddeley, and others who have had their *run* upon wheels through thick and thin up to the present time.

At page 345 of your last number, Mr. Baddeley's remarks on my former communications are somewhat flippant. Nevertheless, as I court inquiry, rather than shun it, I embrace the earliest opportunity of replying to them "I object," says Mr. Baddeley, "to spend thirty pounds upon one escape, while I know, that escapes of equal, or even greater efficiency (than Mr. Wivell's) can be provided, for one-sixth of that sum." Now I have already called upon Mr. Baddeley for his proof of his statement by a public exhibition of all the Society's escapes; but this call Mr. Baddeley has thought wise not to notice,—thinking, probably, to quash all further proceedings by words of empty sound. Had not public opinion been with me, I should not have presumed to claim the superiority of invention over the *five pound bubbles of the earth*,—for such they appear to be in every sense of the word, from whomsoever blown. When Mr. Baddeley speaks of "*efficiency*," I understand him, to refer rather to *cheapness* than utility, for escapes that cannot be made to take persons from the garret-windows, and from the roofs of houses, are unworthy of the title *efficient*, the more especially when they cannot accomplish the great desideratum of affording relief to persons above cornices, such as are often to be found under attic windows. If Mr. Baddeley is not possessed of sufficient comprehension to estimate the full worth of a machine that can effect as much, I beg him to bear in mind, that the Humane Society for the protection of life from fire, have lately come to the conclusion that my invention is the only *efficient escape*. I shall therefore conclude this subject with a little advice to Mr. Baddeley, in return for *his* to older heads than his own, not to prejudice the merits or demerits of an invention, without first making himself acquainted with its full power.

I am, Sir,
Your most obedient, &c.
A. WIVELL.

August 27, 1837.

THE NINTH BRIDGEWATER TREATISE.

Mr. Babbage, will, we fear, add nothing to his reputation by the publication of his new work,* the more especially that its appearance is quite uncalled for. The Eight Treatises, for whose production the last of the Egertons left by his will a thousand pounds a piece, have been duly written, printed, and published, exciting in their progress a greater degree of attention than can usually be expected to fall to the share of any " performances" so regularly made to order; all this having been effected, it might reasonably be supposed that " these" would be " an end." Mr. Babbage, however, has thought fit, without the prospect of a thousand pounds before his eyes, to enter the arena as an amateur, although urged neither " by hunger nor request of friends." Mr. Babbage's situation in life places him, we believe, far out of the reach of the former stimulus, and as to the latter, if he had any advisers of his present venture, they are assuredly not of the number of his *friends*.

The production is called in the title-page " A Fragment," but in truth it can hardly pretend to a more honourable name than that of a fragment of fragments,--almost every chapter being composed of mere scraps of composition, without any attempt to unite them into one whole : some chapters have no end ; many more have no beginning ; and one at least may be fairly said to have neither beginning, middle, nor end.† A more hasty, ill-concocted affair has seldom issued from the press, at least in the garb of a grave scientific treatise. The petty arts of the printer even have been called into action, to give that *appearance* of solidity and respectability to the volume which its literary importance failed in imparting. Its pages are printed as widely as possible ; while, in order to swell out its sides to a thickness in some degree commensurate with that of its eight more regular predecessors, the

paper used is of a most extraordinarily substantial character : and yet, with all these appliances and means, the object is but imperfectly obtained, it having been found impossible to dress up an octavo of two hundred and forty pages into the " counterfeit presentment" of a portly tome of some three or four times the quantity of matter : and, after all, out of these two hundred and forty, there are not above one hundred and sixty of original text, the rest being composed of notes, of which, by far the major part are not composed by Mr. Babbage, and have before appeared in print. So much for minor faults.

The professed object of the work is to rescue the character of the cultivators of the exact sciences from a slur cast upon them by the Rev. William Whewell (the historian of the Inductive Sciences) in the Treatise which he produced as part of the series to which Mr. Babbage desires us to consider his " Fragment" as a supplement. Mr. B. undertakes to refute the notion that the studies of the mathematician are inimical to his progress in theology, and at the same time to give the general reader higher and sublimer views than he has ever heretofore possessed of the highest and most sublime of sciences. And how does he propose to effect all this ? Where does he take his stand to accomplish this grand and noble object ? Whence is he to gain the point of view from which he is to see into the depths so immeasurably farther than Paley or any of his predecessors ? The truth might be guessed at in vain for centuries. In a word, Mr. Babbage's coign of vantage, is neither more nor less than—Mr. Babbage's own calculating-machine!

It is perhaps hardly necessary to do more than state the plain fact, that the main object of this Ninth Bridgewater Treatise is professedly, to *raise our conceptions of the power and wisdom of the Creator, by comparing the mechanism of the Universe with that of Mr. Babbage's calculating-engine !* The bare announcement that such is the staple of the book supersedes the necessity of comment. The sooner it is consigned to oblivion, the better for the author's reputation in every respect ; it is, in all points of view, to be deeply regretted that the author's own judgment, or that of his friends (if

* The Ninth Bridgewater Treatise. A Fragment. By Charles Babbage, Esq. London, 1837. Murray, 8vo., p. 240.

† Chapter 14th, which is *verbatim et literatim* as follows : " Thoughts on the Origin of Evil. I had intended to have put into writing the substance of an interesting discussion I once had with a distinguished philosopher, now no more ; but other demands on my time have prevented the completion of this intention.

————————————————," p. 156.

any were consulted) had not kept it from being hurried through the press, and before the public.

We can, however, without impropriety, copy from the appendix, a note on the present state of matters with regard to the machine itself: although it were to be wished that the information afforded had been of a much more explicit character. The language used is so vague and indeterminate, that most readers will still be unable to decide whether the inventor or the government is most in fault.

" The nature of the arguments advanced in this volume having obliged me to refer more frequently than I should have chosen, to the calculating engine, it becomes necessary to give the reader some brief account of its progress and present state.

" About the year 1821, I undertook to superintend, for the Government, the construction of an engine for calculating and printing mathematical and astronomical tables. Early in the year 1833, a small portion of the machine was put together, and it performed its work with all the precision which had been anticipated. At that period, circumstances which I could not control caused what I then considered a temporary suspension of its progress; and the Government, on whose decision the continuance or discontinuance of the work depended, have not yet communicated to me their wishes on the question. The first illustration I have employed is derived from the calculations made with this engine.

" About October, 1834, I commenced the design of another and far more powerful engine. Many of the contrivances necessary for its performance have since been discussed and drawn according to various principles; and all of them have been invented in more than one form. I consider them, even in their present state, as susceptible of practical execution; but time, thought, and expense, will probably improve them. As the remaining illustrations are all drawn from the powers of this new engine, it may be right to state, that it will calculate the numerical value of any algebraical function; that, at any period previously fixed upon, or contingent on certain events, it will cease to tabulate that algebraic function, and commence the calculation of a different one, and that these changes may be repeated to any extent.

" The former engine could employ about 120 figures in its calculations; the present is intended to compute with about 4000.

" Here I should willingly have left the subject; but the public having erroneously imagined, that the sums of money paid to the workmen for the construction of the engine were the remuneration of my own services for inventing and directing its progress; and a Committee of the House of Commons having incidentally led the public to believe that a sum of money was voted to me for that purpose, I think it right to give to that report the most direct and unqualified contradiction."—p. 170.

THE ELECTRICAL THEORY OF THE UNIVERSE.

Sir,—Kinclaven in no very measured terms (No. 715) has told the author of the Electrical Theory of the Universe, that he is profoundly skilled in the science of equivocation; this grave charge Mr. Mackintosh never thought proper to clear himself of. I observe that another able writer, N. S., has brought a similar charge (No. 733) against one of Mr. M.'s supporters, who styles himself a geologist: and I am sorry to say, Mr. Editor, that I have more than once had a complaint of a like nature to bring against Mr. Joshua Thorne, who really appears to me to be a more finished adept in the fudge disseminating system, than either Mr. M. or the geologist.

In vol. xxvii, page 84, Mr. Thorne says: " However some of your readers may laugh at the idea of a resisting medium, and the consequent approach of the planets to the sun, as well as the satellites to their primaries, I know I am supported by most astronomers, and the greater number of scientific men (Mr. Mackintosh for one), who are capable of judging; and being thus supported, it does not become me, in a paper like the present, to reiterate opinions so well known, and so generally received."

The above quotation reads very well; it has only one fault, and that is rather a grievous one—namely, that it does not contain one word of truth. I challenge Mr. Thorne to produce a single writer on physical astronomy, and that for a period of 52 years back, who ever promulgated such false principles. It was in the same fashion that the satellites of John Herapath wished to back their primary, but their gross misrepresentations soon brought themselves and their master into merited contempt, and this is fully recorded in the *Mechanics' Magazine*. Think of this, Mr. Thorne.

It was Dr. Halley, as stated by Kinclaven (No. 690), who first discovered (about a century ago) that the mean motion of the moon was accelerated; and how to account for this perplexing anomaly of the lunar motions completely resisted the united efforts of all the cultivators of physical astronomy from the time of Halley up to 1785, in which year, that prince of mathematicians and astronomers, La Place, found out the cause of this anomaly; he has demonstrated in the most incontrovertible manner that this acceleration (or secular equation of the moon) is periodical, and confined to small limits. In the interval of time between Halley and La Place, various attempts were made to account for this acceleration. In chapter 6, page 93, vol. 1, of Ferguson's Astronomy, he, in a very fanciful manner attempts to prove that the world is not eternal, and that it neither could have existed from eternity, nor would exist to eternity; and this, I presume, is the only authority that Mr. Thorne, or Mr. Mackintosh could produce for their strange whims. Sir David Brewster, in his edition of Ferguson's Astronomy, gives the following note to the said chapter :—

"The acceleration of the moon's motion, to which Mr. Ferguson here alludes, amounts to about $11'' 8'''$ in a century. It was generally ascribed to some resistance opposed to the motion of the moon; but M. De La Place, has lately discovered, that it arises from a diminution in the eccentricity of the earth's orbit. This, as well as other irregularities in the solar system, generated by the mutual action of the planets, *are all periodical*. They are confined within narrow limits, and are *balanced* by irregularities of an equal and opposite kind. *There is no possibility, therefore, of that general union of the planets in the centre of the system which our author apprehends.* By the most simple law, the diminution of gravity as the square of the distance increases, the planets are not only retained in their orbits when whirling round a central sun, but an *eternal stability is insured to the solar system.* The little derangements which affect the motion of the heavenly bodies are apparent only to the eye of the astronomer; and even these after reaching a certain limit, gradually diminish, till the system, regaining its balance, returns to that state of harmony and order which preceded the commencement of these secular irregularities. Even amidst the changes and irregularities of the system, the general harmony is always apparent; and those partial and temporary derangements, which, to vulgar minds, may seem to indicate a progressive decay, serve only to *evince the stability and permanence of the whole.* In the contemplation of such a scene every *unperverted mind* must be struck with that astonishing wisdom which framed the various parts of the universe; and *bound them together by one simple law,"* &c.

And that simple law is nothing else but universal attraction. It is now universally admitted by all the astronomers of the present age, that there no longer remains any phenomenon in the system which is not deducible from the Newtonian theory of gravitation.

In number 724, page 183, Mr. Thorne remarks : "I will again put to your correspondent, the 'Country Teacher,' the fallacy of his equation (!). If he will turn to page 360, No. 681, he will find an extract from Dr. Wilkinson, who says, that the mass of the earth is to the mass of the moon as 49.22 is to 1. But, the 'Country Teacher' says, it is as 71 to 1; so here are two mathematicians who have come to quite a different conclusion on the same point; and I will not take upon me to decide which is right."

Mr. Thorne has for once acted wisely, not giving any opinion who was right or wrong, for as sure as he tried it, as sure would he have blundered. But I must inform Mr. Thorne, that I never made such an assertion as that the mass of the earth is to the mass of the moon, as 71 to 1. What I really did assert, No. 711, page 494, was, "by the best authority the quantitity of matter in the earth, is to that in the moon as 71 to 1." This is another of Mr. Thorne's misrepresentations. But it will be of no service to him, for every one knows, and more particularly those, who pretend to have a knowledge in physical astronomy, ought to know, that mass and density are two very different things ; thus a cubic foot of gold, and a cubic foot of silver have equal masses, but their density, or weight, if brought to the test, would be found to be very different. Now it is well known, that the mean density of the earth, is to that of the moon, as 99 is to 68, and taking Dr. Wilkinson's mass of the earth to be 49.2 times that of the moon, then we have

$$\frac{49.2 \times 99}{68} = 71\frac{66}{85} \text{ that is ; the mean den-}$$

sity of the earth would be $71\frac{66}{85}$ times that of the moon, which differs very little from what I stated it to be.

Kinclaven recommended Ursa Major to take a spell at the Tutors' Guide; I think Mr. Thorne ought to do so too. Still, Mr. Editor, I have not entered upon that part of the subject which I promised to do at the end of my letter, No. 724, but as this letter has already extended to a sufficient length, I must postpone doing so at present.

I am, Mr. Editor, yours, &c.

A COUNTRY TEACHER.

HUTCHISON'S, AND BACON AND CO.'S BURNER.

The burner of Kilby and Bacon (it would appear) is now "disowned" by Justus. The injurious effects produced on artificial light by the errors in its construction (of which an exposition was given in a former number of the *Mechanics' Magazine*) have no doubt induced this gentleman to form so wise a determination.

To refute the unfounded charge of wilful misrepresentation so strenuously urged against me, it is necessary that I should state—that the diagram B. in No. 725, is a fair transcript of Kilby and Bacon's burner, procured expressly from their London agent. Having been invited by Justus to procure the specification, I had the satisfaction within the last hour of doing so. The diagram B, and the figures represented in the specification are certainly not the same. They disagree (not in principle) but, in arrangement. On the next column is a faithful copy of the burner as depicted in the enrolled document. Your impartial readers will readily perceive the amount of difference between the two drawings. "The broad circular ring" which Justus denies the existence of, is, in this drawing, placed *one-eighth* of an inch below the upper surface of the cylinder. It will be difficult to conjecture the degree of credit which Justus can possibly derive from the discovery of this *unimportant* dif-

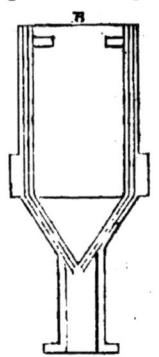

ference, as the absurdity of the principle which guided the original inventor, is evidently more apparent in this instance than in the case which I have already illustrated. The merit of inserting a "broad circular ring" in an argand tube being the "improvement" contended for by Justus, I cannot imagine by what process of reasoning, or peculiarity of vision he has been led to infer that Hutchison's conical burner is entitled to be called a "colourable evasion" of Kilby and Bacon's. Hutchison's lengthened experimental knowledge in all that relates to gas machinery, would be more than a guarrantee against compromising this knowledge by interposing between the atmosphere and the fluid of a burner "a circular ring."

This is the sole peculiarity in Kilby's patent, and Hutchison's is not incumbered with any such contrivance. As has been already repeatedly stated, his improvement consists in uniting *the transverse of sections two cones.*

It is evident, that Justus himself, notwithstanding the hot-headed zeal which he displays in this affair, is either incapable of describing the advantages of his pet burner, or what is more probable, the invention will not yield him the opportunity. To him, the subject is no doubt a most ungrateful one, otherwise it is natural to infer that his last epistle would have been accompanied with *a correct diagram* of the patent. Instead, however, of performing this necessary office, Justus leaves the execution of that onerous duty to the antagonist whom he has selected.

We are assured that Kilby's improvement has been extensively patronized in

Liverpool, Manchester, "*and a great many other towns.*" This may be as Justus reports, and if in reality it is so, I contend that it is not therefore necessary to be inferred that its excellence has recommended it.

I have not the means of ascertaining what progress has been made in the improvement of gas machinery in the " great many towns" spoken of by Justus. But it is generally known, that in those towns *he has* named, the method of generating gas, and indeed their whole system of apparatus is exceedingly objectionable. The minor offence, therefore, of adopting an ill-constructed burner may surely be pardoned.

Justus must have been unusually deficient in tangible grounds for argument, when he resorts to so weak a subterfuge, as to attribute the very limited sale of his burner in London to its being more expensive than those that are usually supplied by gas fitters. If this can be admitted as a plea in favour of his client's improvement, it may with far greater propriety be applied to Hutchison's. For, without doubt, the double-coned burner must be more difficult to execute, both in the cutting and finishing processes, than the *simple* contrivance of Kilby and Co., where the only mechanical ingenuity required is to insert " a broad circular ring" in an argand tube.

If this writer is in the smallest degree acquainted with the cost of gas fittings, he must be convinced, that all the argand burners in the metropolis might be spoiled by the introduction of "*the flat ring*" at the rate of one penny each.

Justus unfairly avails himself of that panegyric which Mr. Rutter inadvertently wrote in favour of Kilby's burner, and with most discreditable zeal endeavours to impress upon the public mind the belief that the invention of his friend's is the identical one praised by Mr. R. We are informed that Mr. Rutter " fixes his praise as plainly as words can do it on a burner, not a gallery cone." Without intending any disrespect to Mr. R., I trust that gentleman will pardon me, if I presume to suppose, that he (like many other clever men), may occasionally be led into error through the contrivance of designing persons. Mr. Rutter's knowledge, I have reason to believe, is of a more solid

nature than to induce him to eulogize a " thing" so utterly destitute of merit as this burner. The gallery cone, the name of which, very probably was not at the time known to that gentleman, is the invention that has been praised, and the burner of Kilby and Co. *with this cone attached to it*, must have been exhibited to Mr. Rutter, in order to obtain his recommendation.

I submit the case as it now stands (divested of all ambiguity) to the impartial judgment of the parties interested in this controversy.

If Mr. H. was guilty of the baseness which has been imputed to him, he would not deserve that reputation which his abilities as an inventor have obtained for him; neither would his services be *continued* as engineer to the London Gas Company.

It would be equally absurd and unbecoming in a gentleman who is employed in remodeling so many gas establishments, to appropriate the title of being the inventor of (to say the least), one of the worst burners that has yet been contrived.

I am, Sir,

With sincere respect

Your obedient servant,

CLOVIS.

August 21, 1837.

___

NOTE ON O. N.'S DEMONSTATION.

Sir,—I must confess I did not expect that O. N. would have given such demonstrations as he has done (No. 732), for the two methods of determining the polar angle Z P R, when the two stars R and D are in the same azimuth circle; more ingenious demonstrations, in my opinion could not have been given. Well, according to promise, I freely forgive O. N. for the mistakes he made in his first letter in the *Mechanics' Magazine*, although I must say, I can hardly conceive how so good a geometer could have fallen into them. Still, however, in candour, I must inform O. N. that his two demonstrations, ingenious as they are, have evidently been composed in a hurry. Thus, in the first it is stated, " tan x, = tan. cos. A ;" this should have been tan. x, = tan. P D cos. A. Again, in the second method it is said, " sin. (P D + D R) : sin (P D—

D R)," this should have been, sin. (P D +P R) : sin. (P D—P R). These two mistakes (if they are not press errors), are not errors in judgment as the preceding steps of the demonstrations fully show; they are errors arising from writing in too much haste—from a fear, perhaps, that some one might have made them out before him.

Well, Mr. O. N., now that you have done so well, will you be so good as give a solution of your own question, and inform us why the perpendicular P N must fall upon D Z produced? Determine also, if you please, the greatest latitude of the place of observation, when the question just ranges within the limits of possibility.

I am, Mr. Editor,
Yours, &c.
IVER M'IVER.
September 1, 1837.

THE INFANT SCHOOL VENTILATOR
(page 295).

Sir,—Allow me to ask the Infant School Master, who figures in No. 730, if he considers, that the revolution of an Archimedes screw, when altogether immersed in a fluid, would produce a circulation of that fluid through it? He seems altogether to forget that it is gravity, and not velocity, which causes water to rise in the machine so named. If he must have an infant tread-wheel, let him erect a vane-wheel, similar to that within the new-invented, —100 year-old— fire-blowers. Had he made his enquiry *before* he went to the expense of erecting his "helix," it would have been as well.

I am, Sir, your obedient servant,
NAUTILUS.

REMARKS UPON THE USE OF PNEUMATIC ENGINES, AS APPLIED TO MINES, AND ON THEIR APPLICATION TO OTHER PURPOSES. BY JACOB PERKINS, C. E.

(From the *Franklin Journal* for June).

The Pneumatic engine which is the subject of these remarks, although it has been more or less used for a long time, has, from some cause, had its properties overlooked and neglected in a remarkable degree. This instrument certainly cannot be used as a prime mover, yet for distributing power it can be employed to great advantage. Some years since Mr. Hague obtained a patent for the application of it to the working of coal mines, &c., and the result has astonished all the engineers who have made themselves acquainted with the facts relating to it, which, to believe, they say, must have been seen. In one of these mines where the engines are performing the work, usually performed by horses, the most distant pneumatic engine is seven miles from the mouth of the shaft, where the prime mover, the steam engine, is at work; and the most distant pneumatic engine can be set at work as quickly, and as powerfully, as any one of those which are intermediate, although some of them are but a short distance from the steam engine. The most extraordinary part of the operation is that of the air being exhausted simultaneously from each end of the main pipe, although seven miles distant from the air-pumps. The complete ventilation of the mine is a very important result. The air which is used to work the pneumatic engine is the foul air of the mine, which is delivered at the surface of the exhausting pumps. But the most curious, and apparently paradoxical, feature of this engine is yet to be explained.

Having recently witnessed some of Mr. Hague's pneumatic experiments, I was powerfully struck with the amount of work the pneumatic engine performed, and which led me to study its operation. I had been acquainted with the fact, that the sudden compression of air, by which its atoms are brought nearer together, caused a great increase of resistance by the repellant power of the heat thus generated, so that it required a pressure of much more than two atmospheres to force the air into one half its original bulk, and that after the air had been allowed time to part with this extra heat, it would then occupy but one-half of its original space. I then asked myself, if so much power be lost by compressing the air and liberating the heat which it contained, why would not the expansion of the air take away resistance until the air had time to recover the heat and become of the same temperature before as it expanded. Now, if there is a gain by the sudden exhaustion of heat, by the expanding of the air, thereby diminishing the resistance on the eduction side of the piston, we see a natural cause for what is said to take place as to the gain of power in the pneumatic, over the steam engine, which puts the pneumatic engine in motion. It is confidently stated, that the pneumatic engines, at work in the mines, do much more duty than the steam-engines working at their mouths.

To take advantage of this hitherto unobserved law, the pneumatic engine must be modified in such a manner as to allow the free access of the atmosphere, so that it may work on the induction side of the piston by its whole weight. In the present pneumatic engines, the induction pipe is much too small, which causes the air to be more or less wire-drawn, so that the whole weight of the atmosphere cannot act with its full effect. This is the improvement which has grown out of having discovered this law, which has hitherto been unnoticed, and for which a patent is in progress. It is intended also to patent the application of the pneumatic engine to other useful purposes. For instance, it is proposed that an immense air-vessel be laid under the surface of the earth, and that this magazine of power be laid as near to where the pneumatic engines are to be worked as may be most convenient. The air-vessel may be exhausted by water power, by wind, or by steam. If steam is used as the prime mover, the proper place for the steam-engine would be at the coal mines, where the coals would cost comparatively nothing, since the transportation, as well as the duties, would be saved, and the culm, which, with a properly constructed furnace, would answer well to raise the steam, and of which vast quantities are lost, may be had for taking away. It matters not at what distance the prime mover should happen to be from the main air-vessel, if the power should be used in great manufacturing towns, as the exhausting pipe would constitute a part of the air-vessel. This principle applied to rail-roads, would be of the utmost consequence on account of the immense saving of wear and tear. All the present projected rail-roads, and even as many more, may be worked by small stationary engines. These stationary pneumatic engines may be placed at convenient distances to set endless chains and ropes in motion at pleasure, according to circumstances. When these engines stop, there is no power lost, as there is in the present locomotive and stationary steam engines, by the waste steam blowing off; these, also, are always ready for action.

In some situations, there are immense water-falls running to waste, the power of which might be used also at any distance to exhaust the air-vessel. There is at this moment a project on foot in Virginia, for working by water power a rail-road three hundred miles in length; it so happens, that a series of water-falls runs nearly parallel to the proposed rail-road, and a survey has been made by engineers; and although the cutting of a great number of canals from the different falls, to move the carriages by a series of water-wheels, at a great expense, has been recommended, a very favourable opinion has been entertained of the proposition. This new project will, however, very shortly be laid before those concerned.

There are situations, such as waste lands, heaths, &c., where a forest of self-acting wind-mills might be placed to exhaust the air from extensive magazines, by which means an immense deposit of power may be accumulated, and used as occasion requires for working the pneumatic engines, rendering this uncertain and unsteady power available for many purposes. These wind-mills may be so constructed as always to face the wind, and so as to require no attention day or night; should the air-pumps vary ever so much as to their speed, no injury would result.

Facts shew, that in adding heat to atmospheric air, its power rapidly increases; if so, must it not be admitted, that by extracting heat the power is rapidly diminished? What is the limit? May we not suppose, that if all the heat were taken from the air, the atoms of air would settle into a liquid, and a vacuum take place? The atoms of air being separated by heat, and by heat only, it follows that in the absence of heat a perfect contact of the atoms of the air must result, and perhaps a solid be formed. Steam deprived of a given portion of its heat liquifies, and if, of another given portion, it becomes solid, with an unknown quantity of heat still remaining, for philosophers have not been able to determine the natural zero. The operation of heat on water and on air is widely different. To obtain the pressure of an atmosphere by expanding air, it has only to expand to double its bulk; but to obtain the pressure of an atmosphere by the expansion of water, it must increase its bulk nearly 1800 times; it takes but about double as much heat to expand water 1800 times, as it does to expand air twice. If adding heat to air increases its power so rapidly, why should not the subtraction of heat diminish its power in proportion? Now, if advantage be taken of the extraction of heat by the sudden expansion of air, which necessarily takes place on the eduction side of the piston of the pneumatic engine before it has time to regain the heat lost by expansion, by allowing the weight of the atmosphere to act with its full effect, it must be admitted more or less power is gained.

The amount of steam, or fuel, lost in working locomotive, as well as stationary, engines, cannot be less than 50 per cent. The loss that takes place by coals burning to waste, whilst the engines are standing still, is not the only loss, for the motion of the locomotive shakes out and scatters its lighted fuel all along the road. There is much more heat lost from radiation, and from the motion of locomotive steam-engines, than from stationary ones. The great importance of being able to dispense with the ponderous locomotive steam-engine, from its being the principal cause of the destruction of rail-roads, in consequence of their great weights as well as the consequent friction on the rails, is perfectly apparent.

This system of applying pneumatic power is particularly applicable to uneven countries, for at an inclined plane the power may be so regulated that the speed need not be diminished for want of power.

The power of the falls of Niagara, which is now running to waste, might, should this system be found capable of adoption, be made available, and all that section of country, surrounding this mighty agent, might be supplied with a very cheap and convenient power for all manufacturing purposes, as well as for rail-road travelling.

BENNET'S STEAM ENGINE.*

(From the *Journal of the American Institute*).

A model of an engine, constructed upon the principles of those which are to be employed in propelling Capt. Cobb's steamer between this and Liverpool, has been at the Repository of the Institute for several weeks past. A throng of visitors have constantly surrounded it. Between the hours of eleven and one, Mr. Bennet has attended, and explained its operations. It has undergone the scrutiny of great numbers of scientific professors, ingenious and experienced mechanics and engineers, citizens and strangers.

Mr. Bennet, by request, has gindly given all the explanations requisite to a perfect understanding of its operations, and answered the ten thousand questions that have been propounded, with a clearness, simplicity, and patience, that is highly creditable. He has invited objections, that he might have an opportunity to meet them, and if found to be serious, that seasonable remedies might be provided. The examinations have resulted in a general conviction that the world is about to realise a new improvement, not inferior to that of Watt and Bolton—an improvement that will effect a new era in ocean navigation, and bring all parts of the world in approximation to each other. A voyage to Liverpool, it is believed, may, by the power of this engine, be accomplished in ten days, with one-tenth of the fuel heretofore required.

We have requested Mr. Bennet to give a minute description, accompanied with a drawing, which, we hope, will enable the readers of the Journal who have not visited the Repository, to comprehend what to us was incomprehensible, till we examined the

model, and heard the explanation, how the fire and the water could be brought and continued in actual contact with each other, and, rapidly generating the steam, still kept in control, and its potency safely directed to propel the car or the ship.

The following is the description which Capt. Bennet has been so obliging as to prepare for us :—

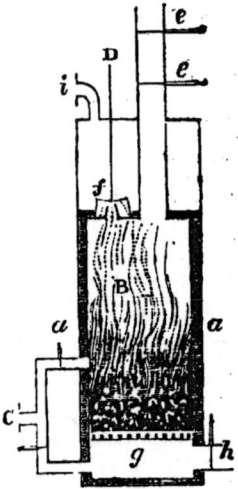

The engine for the Liverpool packet, is a double horizontal high pressure engine, 35 inch cylinder, 6 feet stroke, with two blowing cylinders, of half the capacity, worked by the piston-rod of the steam cylinder passing through the lower or extreme head, and into the blowing cylinders; consequently, both will be of the same motion. Pipes C, with the necessary valves attached to the blowing cylinders, convey the air to the steam generator, whose outer case, *a a*, is 4 feet diameter, and 12 feet high, and the inner case, or furnace B, is 3½ feet diameter, and 9 feet high. Smoke and feed-pipe D, is constructed with two slides, *e e*, which closes the pipe perfectly tight when thrust into it; their uses will hereafter be explained; *f* is a cup-valve in the steam chamber, placed over a short pipe or nozzle on the upper head of the furnace, and fitted to its seat perfectly tight, with a rod extending through the upper head of the outer case; *g* is the ash-pit below the grate; *h* an opening into the ash-pit, with a slide to close it tight, when necessary.

In order to put the engine in operation, and successfully use all the advantages of this generator over any other, it will be necessary to set open the feed and smoke-pipe D, and the pipe h, as now represented; introduce fuel down the feed-pipe, in sufficient quantity, and to ignite it. Previously fill the space between the outer and inner case with water up to the dotted line, half way up the cap-valve f, which will completely immerse the furnace; and when steam is generated of sufficient elasticity to start the engine, say 75 lbs. per square inch, close the pipes D and h, with their respective slides; then start the engine in the usual way, by opening a communication with steam-pipe i; then the blowing cylinders will force their charges of air through the pipe C into furnace B, partly taking its course through the mass of fuel on the grates, a sufficient quantity being introduced above the fuel to burn the smoke, which can be regulated by slides in the branch pipes, terminating the air-pipe C. You will discover that there is no escape for the air thus forced into the furnace until its elasticity is, by the continued blast from the blowing cylinders, a little superior to the steam in the steam-chamber, when the cap-valve f will rise from its seat, and the air, flame, and gases arising from combustion, will be forced to pass under the edges of the said valve out into the water; and in this process, all the heat generated will be imparted to the water, without the possibility of escaping otherwise.

" By the repeated experiments I have heretofore made, I find that one foot of air blown into the furnace to promote combustion, by the expansion it undergoes, and by the addition of the gases and steam, is augmented in bulk at least five times its original size, or, to speak briefly, there is five times as much compound steam, as air, forced into the furnace; consequently, it will take one-fifth part of the power of the steam to operate the bellows, plus the friction, or this is nearly the power; but I forbear at present, nor is it necessary, to speak at large on that subject in this paper.

" By a careful examination it will be seen that the pressure of steam will wholly depend upon the proportion of the size of the blowing cylinder to the steam cylinder. In my engine now building, the blowing cylinders each contain 20 cubic feet; the steam cylinders, each 40 feet; but the steam being cut off when the piston has made but one half its entire stroke,—which reduces its size, as a measure to deal out the steam, to exactly the size of the blowing cylinder—the measure of the air forced in by the blowing cylinders being augmented, by passing through the generator, to five times its bulk, has to be forced into a space in the steam cylinder of just its original bulk; it will, therefore, exert a force equal to five atmo-

spheres, which will be 60 lbs. to the square inch above the atmospheric pressure.

" This force, per inch, will not be exerted during the whole length of the stroke of the piston, but only half way, or to where the steam is cut off; and at the end, its elastic force is reduced to about 20 lbs., which will make the average pressure 50 lbs. per square inch, and the piston contains 962 square inches, which multiplied by 50, will produce 48,100 lbs., the whole average force the piston moves with. It is calculated to have the engine make thirty-five double strokes per minute; hence, the piston will move 420 feet per same time, which multiplied by 48,100, produces 20,202,000 lbs.; the weight that the piston would lift 1 foot high per minute, divided by 33,000, being what a horse power is estimated at, gives 612 horse power for each steam cylinder. But the power abstracted to operate the blowing cylinders, and overcome the friction, I allow nearly equal to the power of one of the cylinders; therefore, I estimate the power of the engine at 612 horse power.

" The amount of fuel consumed, will depend upon the amount of air forced into the furnace by the blowing cylinders; and my two blowing cylinders, at every revolution, would force in 80 feet, if there were no leak either in piston or valves, and no space between said piston and valves for the air to compress in, and not be wholly forced out; therefore, probably not more than 75 feet will be expelled each revolution of the engine; and as it takes all the oxygen contained in 175 feet of atmospheric air to burn one pound of carbon, and 525 feet to burn one pound of hydrogen, I am of opinion, that to allow 225 feet to be necessary to burn one pound of fuel, will not be allowing too much; and, as before stated, 75 feet will be forced into the furnace at each revolution, it will therefore take three revolutions to burn one pound; and as a cord of yellow pine weighs about 2100 lbs., it will take 6,300 revolutions to burn one cord, which, divided by 35, the motion of the engine per minute, will give three hours for each cord, which, compared with the engine of the steamer Erie, on the Hudson, of little less or nearly the same power (600 horse power), will consume forty cords in ten hours, or twelve cords in the same time my engine will one cord."[*]

---

* The intelligent reader will not fail to perceive that this last miracle of art of our friend Jonathan, is nothing more than a new, but by no means improved edition of the blast-engine of Messrs. Braithwaite and Ericsson, which proved in its application to steam-vessels a failure, for the same reason that his will assuredly fail also,—the rapid clogging up with clinkers, and wasting of the fire-bars, through the intensity of the heat, to which they are subjected.—ED. M. M.

MR. ROBERT STEPHENSON'S REPORT, ON CAPTAIN ALDERSON'S REPORT TO THE DIRECTORS OF THE WESTERN LINE OF RAILWAY FROM LONDON TO BRIGHTON.

Gentlemen,—I have received Mr. Till's (secretary to Stephenson's line) letter of the 27th July last, requesting me to furnish you with such observations as appear to me to be called for by Captain Alderson's Report, and also to report to you my opinion generally of the line selected by him, in order that such opinion may be laid before the subscribers to the Western line, that they may individually consider the propriety of availing themselves of the option of taking shares in the Direct Line, under the terms of the Act which has passed.

Many of the points raised by Captain Alderson in his Report are of so much interest to the profession of which I am a member, and involve consequences of so much importance to the public as subscribers to railroad undertakings, that I shall feel it my duty to reply to them in a more detailed manner than is, perhaps, absolutely necessary upon the present occasion.

It may be sufficient for the present purpose to observe, that Captain Alderson asserts, that the Western Line is the best in an engineering point of view, but recommends the adoption of the Direct Line, for the following reasons:—that it acommodates Lewes and Newhaven ; that it secures to Brighton exclusive advantages which it at present possesses, and of which it ought not to be deprived ; and that the termini are preferable, especially that in London ; the Greenwich Railway being, in his opinion, well calculated for a main trunk line southward, and that Company having, as he was informed, the means of adapting it to the increased traffic which would in consequence fall into it.

Upon each of these points I will offer some brief observations ; and, first with respect to Lewes and Newhaven. Captain Alderson has not pledged himself to the accuracy of the estimates ; on the contrary, he states that he believes those for the Direct Line to be insufficient ; but he has nevertheless adopted them as the basis of a tabular calculation, from which it appears that the estimated cost of the Western Line and of the Direct Line to Brighton, are within a fraction the same, and that there is an increased cost in the Direct Line of upwards of 200,000l. for the branches to Lewes and Newhaven. As those branches run from Brighton, and not from any intermediate point, it is obvious that the Direct Line affords no greater facilities for them than the Western Line does either in point of expense or otherwise ; I have never advised

their adoption, though I was well aware that *Parliamentary interest would be gained by doing so*, because I have been satisfied that they never would pay the expense of their own maintenance, and would therefore prove a ruinous drawback from the fair profits of the concern.

Looking also to what I have considered to be the interest of the subscribers, I freely admit that I have not taken the same view that Captain Alderson has of the claims of the people of Brighton : I have been anxious to consult their convenience in the selection of the terminus as far as was consistent with the adoption of a line of cheap and easy construction, and the prospect of an extensive traffic ; but, acting as I have for shareholders, whose money is to be embarked in the undertaking, I could not recommend the sacrifice of their interests to the maintenance of a supposed monopoly ; and I am, besides, convinced that no such monopoly can be maintained ; for when railroad communications are opened to Southampton, Dover, and other places on the coast and elsewhere, it will be found that a cheap line and low tolls will be the only real securities, and that the accommodation or exclusion of Shoreham or Worthing are to the people of Brighton themselves matters of very secondary importance.

With respect to the Greenwich Railway, and its capabilities for adoption as a main trunk out of London, little need be said ; the character of that line, and its want of a depôt, so essential to the existence of any line of railroad, are matters of public notoriety ; and the probability of the Company having the means to add an additional width to the road to accommodate any increased traffic, the necessity of which is stated by Captain Alderson, can be estimated by yourselves. There are, however, other difficulties of an engineering nature in this line, which have always influenced me, but which do not seem to have occurred to Captain Alderson ; and the same apply to the Croydon line, in connexion with it, in which there is the inclined plane of one in one hundred for two miles and five-eighths, not even adverted to by him. Had Captain Alderson sufficiently considered these points, had he adhered to his former principle* (which he stated to be a near approximation to accuracy) that 20 feet rise may be regarded as equivalent to one mile in distance, instead of being only equivalent to a fifth of a mile, which last principle he now, for the first time, adopts in his Report on the Brighton lines; and thereby gives an

* Vide Captain Alderson's Report on the Manchester and Cheshire and South Union Railways.

undue advantage of near five miles in distance to the Direct Line ; and, had he considered the interests of the subscribers, as well as those of the inhabitants of Brighton, I have no doubt that he would have come to a different conclusion ; but the Legislature having now passed a Bill for the Direct Line, in consequence of his Report, I now proceed to the second point which you require of me, namely, my opinion of the line selected by Captain Alderson.

In doing this, I find some difficulty ; because, though Captain Alderson has pointed out several objections to the plan of the Direct Line, and has suggested various modes of correcting some of them, I have nothing before me to shew which of these modes, or to what extent it is proposed that they should be adopted.* Captain Alderson states, that the cost of the Direct Line from Croydon to Brighton is likely very much to exceed the Parliamentary estimates ; and, however it may be altered or modified, I entirely concur in this opinion ; and without going into any detailed statement of the engineering difficulties, I find myself called upon to state generally, that having now had to struggle practically with works of more than ordinary magnitude and difficulty on other lines of railway, and having had ample opportunities of carefully weighing those circumstances which justify the adoption of such works, I am satisfied that the views which have hitherto guided me in laying out the Brighton Line will be found ultimately correct; more especially, when it is remembered, that the average works of excavating, embanking, and tunnelling, per mile on the Direct Line exceed, by nearly 50 per cent., those of any other railway in existence, or, I believe, seriously contemplated ; and, in taking this simple view of the case, it must be borne in mind that the difficulties and dangers attendant on works of this kind arise more frequently from their unusual magnitude than from the other minor features. An important question, however, for consideration is, of what is the Brighton Line to consist ; is it to be a line from the Croydon Railway, or from Earlswood Common to Brighton. Looking to the clause in the Act, which gives to the South-Eastern Company the option of taking, after completion, the twelve miles of the road, upon which alone a double traffic can be contemplated, and for the construction of which the Brighton Company are, I

observe, to find the capital (I mean the twelve miles from Croydon to Earlswood Common), I consider that the Brighton Line will, very probably, be confined to twenty-nine miles, viz., from Earlswood Common to Brighton ; in that case three companies, and in the other case two companies, will possess a power of a very dangerous character over the interests of what will remain of the Direct Line ; and if circumstances should compel them to exercise this power by the infliction of their maximum tolls, the Brighton Company might be left without the means of making any return to the shareholders ; so that, in point of fact, the interests of the Brighton Company are absolutely dependent upon the very doubtful prospects of the other lines.

Another subject of the greatest importance is the traffic; and with reference to this question I must look at the relative merits of the Direct and of the Western Lines. On the direct Line there is not one town or place of any importance which is likely to bring traffic into it : the only towns near which it passes being Cuckfield and Crawley, it can derive no material advantage from any branches connected with it ; for on the one side the eastern traffic will necessarily be absorbed by the South-Eastern Railway; and, on the other side, if branches should be made to connect the line with any of the western districts, such branches will be rather for the benefit of the Greenwich, Croydon, and South-Eastern Companies, than of the Brighton Company, on whose road such traffic would pass for a very short distance ; and if the South-Eastern Company should avail themselves of their power to purchase the Merstham portion, they might not run upon any part of it. Upon the Western Line, on the contrary, there are the following places :—Ewell ; Epsom, with its crowded races ; Leatherhead ; Dorking, placed in a neighbourhood of almost unrivelled attraction ; Horsham, the site of an important corn-market ; Henfield, Beeding, Steyning, and Shoreham. In addition to these towns actually upon the line, there are Arundal, Worthing, Chichester, Bognor, and Portsmouth, the traffic to which places must use the Western Line for at least twenty-eight miles ; and there is the intercourse between Brighton and Windsor, and Oxford through Horsham, which also must use the Western Line for twenty miles. Taking all these circumstances into account, I am convinced that a Western Line would have a very large intermediate and ulterior traffic, of which the Direct Line will be destitute.

I shall conclude by stating, that in giving my consideration to a Brighton railway, it has always appeared to me that it was es-

* In consequence of this Report, a tunnel of 1,320 yards has been adopted at Merstham. The length of the tunnel at Balcombe has been increased from 470 yards to 850 yards; and the tunnel at Clayton Hill has been increased from 850 yards to 1,700 yards; but I have nothing before me to show whether any or what alterations are to be made in the slopes.

sential in justice to the shareholders, that the line should be so designed as to embrace as much collateral and ulterior traffic as possible; and that as Brighton, in common with other watering-places, owes its present importance mainly to fashion, every security ought to be taken that the line should be as much as possible removed from the risk of caprice. For this purpose I have uniformly recommended the Western Line; and when I consider the local and lateral advantages which it will possess, and the importance of the districts that it will accommodate, I cannot but think that it will at no very distant time be executed; and whenever it is, I am of opinion that the cheapness of its construction, together with its local advantages, will enable it to carry the Brighton traffic on terms which would be ruinous to the Direct Line.

For these reasons, gentlemen, I adhere to the opinion which I gave long since, and at a period when I might fairly be considered to be unembarrassed by prejudice: I have now carefully reconsidered that opinion, and I am more than ever convinced that the Western is the only line which with safety to the subscribers, can be adopted.

I am, Gentlemen,
Yours very faithfully,
ROBERT STEPHENSON.

Great George-street, Wesminster.
August 15, 1837

NOTES AND NOTICES.

Instantaneous artificial Congelation.—In freezing water by the vaporization of Hydric, commonly called Sulphuric, Ether, there is much labour in pumping, and the etherial vapour condensing in the pump, disqualifies it for nice experiments until cleansed. Dr. Hare finds that the interposition of sulphuric acid lessens the requisite labour, and protects the pump. By means of a globe or bottle with two tubulure, and a glass funnel with a cock, the acid being in the globe, the water in a retort, and the ether in a funnel, while the two former are exhausted, on allowing the ether to descend upon the water, the congelation of this liquid is instantaneous.

Process for Ink devoid of Free Acid.—Writing ink is usually constituted of the tanno-gallate of iron and a portion of sulphuric acid which had existed in the copperas, or sulphate of iron employed as one of its ingredients, the tanno-gallate being suspended and the acid dissolved in the water. This free acid is injurious to iron pens. Dr. Hare has observed that when an infusion of galls is kept over finery cinder till saturated, it forms a beautiful ink, in which of course there is no free acid. This ink is rather more prone to precipitate than that made with sulphate of iron, and this propensity is not counteracted by the addition of gum arabic. But,

on the other hand, it has the advantage of being easily suspended again by agitation, not forming any concrete matter insusceptible, like common ink grounds, of that distribution in water, which is necessary to good ink. The tanno-gallate of iron when obtained from a filtered infusion of galls and finery cinder, as above described, on being evaporated to the consistency of thick molasses, gum arabic in due proportion having been previously added, forms a pigment which might, it is conceived, supersede India ink. When completely dried it glistens like jet.

Antiseptics.—It is because salt is the most agreeable preservative of meat that it is used for this purpose, and by no means because it is the most effectual. According to the experiments of Sir John Pringle, it is the most feeble of all the substances tried by him. Saltpetre he found to possess no less than four times the preservative power of salt: on this account, and on account of the property which saltpetre possesses of giving a pleasing redness to beef, it is always an ingredient in the brine with which meat is preserved. Some suppose, however, that it has also the effect of hardening the fibre. Some other experiments of Sir John Pringle are more curious than useful; they add nothing to our means of preserving flesh, on account of the disagreeable taste of the substances employed. Thus sulphate of potash had twice the preservative power of common salt; sal-ammoniac three times; carbonate of ammonia, or of potash, four times; borax twelve times; succinic acid twenty times; and alum no less than thirty times. Perhaps some practical hints may be derived from the last-mentioned fact. Of all the antiseptics tried, he found camomile-flowers to be most powerful in its effects; and, on account of their bitter taste, we may add the least useful. He estimates the preservative power to be 120 times greater than that of salt. Nay, he found that meat in which the putrefactive process had taken place, was restored by camomile, and that it remained sound for a year after. Camphor seemed to have 300 times the power of salt.—*Donovan's Domestic Economy.*

Railroads in Prussia.—A letter from Berlin, of the 30th ult., has the following passage:—Amidst the present commercial crisis which paralysis every branch of business, and inspires general mistrust, railroads are still the subject of vast speculation. The shares of companies founded here are rising, and those in railroads which have not yet received the sanction of government, the Frankfort and Halle, for instance, are at premium of from 8 to 10 per cent. The Breslau shares have risen 1½ per cent.—*Berlin Gazette.*

Mr. Weather Prediction Murphy.—Again! In a letter to the *Times* of Thursday last, Mr. Murphy predicts that the autumnal equinox will "set in upon the 13th inst., and continue during the two following days," and, "that from the absence of these storms last spring, they are the more likely to be violent." Mr. M. says, nothing, however, of the *whereabouts.* Does he mean, as in a former instance, to include the whole globe in his calculations?

Nautilus.—With pleasure. He will be so good as direct his bookseller to make the necessary application.

Erratum.—In the Cambridge Student's astronomical question, p. 366, for "periodic revolution," read "synodic revolution."

☞ *British and Foreign Patents taken out with economy and despatch; Specifications, Disclaimers, and Amendments, prepared or revised; Caveats entered; and generally every Branch of Patent Business promptly transacted.*
A complete list of Patents from the earliest period (15 Car. II. 1675,) to the present time may be examined, Fee 2s. 6d.; Clients, gratis.

LONDON: Printed and Published for the Proprietor, by W. A. Robertson, at the Mechanics' Magazine Office, No. 6, Peterborough-court, between 135 and 136, Fleet-street.—Sold by G. W. M. Reynolds, Proprietor of the French, English, and American Library, 55, Rue Neuve, Saint Augustin Paris.

Mechanics' Magazine,

MUSEUM, REGISTER, JOURNAL, AND GAZETTE

| No. 736. | SATURDAY, SEPTEMBER 16, 1837. | Price 3d. |

URI EMMON'S PATENT IMPROVED SINGLE RAIL, RAIL-ROAD.

Fig. 1.

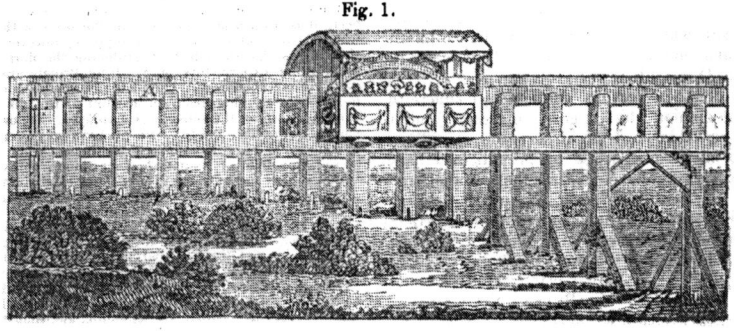

Fig. 2.

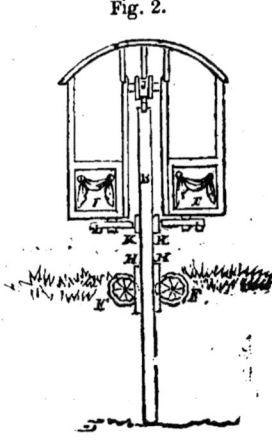

URI EMMON'S PATENT IMPROVED
SINGLE RAIL, RAIL-ROAD.

(From the Patentee's Specification in the *Franklin Journal* for June).

The general construction of the single rail which I use is the same with that for which letters patent were obtained by a certain Henry R. Palmer, in England, in the year 1821. This single rail is elevated upon posts set in the ground, the rail being secured on the tops of the posts, and covered with an iron plate on its upper side. The strength of the rail must be such as to sustain the load which is to bear upon it, and this will be governed by the distance of the posts apart which support it.

The accompanying perspective drawing fig. 1, represents the rail, supported upon posts, and covered by the iron rail plate. The posts may sometimes be mortised into a ground sill, but as ground is generally uneven, and as this mode of constructing railroads is intended to obviate the necessity, in the greater number of cases, of excavating and embanking, by giving the posts the proper length to reach the level of the rail, a horizontal ground sill can rarely be used; and it is desirable to be able to fix these posts firmly at their lower ends, by means which shall be adapted to uneven ground, be efficient without being costly, and be well calculated to keep the posts in a vertical position, and allow of their adjustment when necessary. To effect this I take trunks of trees, from which I hew off a portion of one side, so that they will lie along against the posts, as shown in the transverse view, fig. 2, at F. These logs may be buried partially, or wholly, in the ground, and they must be bound together by bolts, or cross ties, in any convenient way. Between the vertical posts and the above named logs I insert wedges H, H, by the driving of which the posts may be, at any time, firmly fixed in a vertical position, and regulated as may be desired. When the vertical posts are of considerable length, lateral braces must be used, and these may rise from cross sills which rest upon the trees or logs, and which may serve at the same time as cross ties to those logs.

Where it has been proposed to use a single rail, such as I have described, it has also been intended to construct a car, or carriage consisting of two parts to be suspended from the rail, one part

on each side thereof with wheels between them, near their tops to bear upon the rail, in a manner analogous to that shown in the transverse view, where I I are the two parts of the car, or carriage, and J one of the running wheels. The main improvement which I have made in this part, consists in the employment of guide rails K K, which run along on each side of the posts, to which they are firmly fixed. These may ordinarily be placed about three feet below the top of the rail, and opposite to them; upon each section of the car, or carriage, I place friction rollers, or wheels L L; which generally run free of the guide rails, but come into contact therewith, when, from any cause, the carriage leans more towards the rail on one side than on the other. Other modes of fixing guide rails and friction rollers may be devised, which will be substantially the same in operation as that above described; as, for example, there may be an edged rail running along, under one section of the car, or carriage, supported by arms from the vertical posts, and two friction rollers attached to the under side of the section of the car, or carriage, may bear, one on each side of such edge rail or plank. Such a plan, however, would not, in my opinion, be equally good with that first described, and I give it therefore, merely as an exemplification of one variation of my plan. The turn-outs which I intended to use resemble those described by the beforenamed Palmer, and I do not, therefore, claim anything new in this part of the structure. But what I do claim as of my invention, is the manner herein described of fixing and regulating the vertical posts by means of logs placed in the ground along their lower ends, with wedges to be driven in between the logs and the posts. I also claim the employment of guide rails and friction wheels in a single rail rail-road placed in the manner, and for the purpose described, whether the same be effected precisely in the way herein set forth, or in any other analogous thereto, and producing a like result.

MR. COAD'S PLAN FOR CONSUMING
SMOKE.

Sir,—Having perused a paper in your Magazine of the 2nd inst., on "Mr.

Coad's plan for consuming smoke," and knowing your love of truth and accuracy, I am sure that any remarks will find a ready insertion in your pages which may elucidate matters of so great importance as the consumption of smoke from steam engine and other furnaces, and thereby effecting a considerable saving of fuel, and getting rid of a great public nuisance.

I have some knowledge of Mr. Coad's plan, and wish to show how widely the statements in the paper alluded to, differ from those made in the specification of that gentleman's patent. It is stated, that " a current of hot air is thus thrown into the flame *at every point* where the smoke begins to be formed." Now, this is perfectly at variance with the specification, in which he states that he effects his object, " by means of currents of fresh atmospheric air; and introducing the same below the boiler *at or near the bridge* of the furnace for the purpose of consuming the smoke." Again, he says, " my invention consists in abstracting the waste heat or caloric, from the vapours escaping up the flues or chimney by means of currents of fresh atmospheric air, made to pass through pipes or chambers placed in, or in connexion with such flues or chambers, and directing the said fresh atmospheric air so heated, and obtained, on to the uninflamed smoke or gases arising from the combustion of the fuel *at or near the situation of the bridge of the furnace,* for the purpose of promoting a more perfect combustion of the smoke and inflamable vapours *at that point of its egress."*

Further, in describing the apparatus, he says, " the lower extremities of the said pipes lead into a larger tube H H, which forms a *passage to the bridge* N, and there terminates in a long slot or opening, or a series of small openings *at, or near the top of the bridge,"* and at the conclusion of the specification, he states that the heated air " is discharged *at the bridge of the furnace* for the purpose of inflaming the smoke as " herein before mentioned." Now I beg to say, that from the foregoing extracts from Mr. Coad's specification, it is quite clear that the statement in the paper in question in your last Magazine, that by Mr. Coad's invention, " a current of hot air is thus thrown into the flame at every point where the smoke begins to be formed," is incorrect, for his plan is to throw *it in at the bridge of the furnace,* and of course, after the flame has been formed and is passing away from the fire into the chimney.

I beg also to call your attention to the description of his apparatus in the article referred to, which runs thus: —" An apparatus consisting of a series of small tubes, or chambers, so constructed as to expose a large surface to the action of the heat, is placed in the lower part of the chimney beyond the boiler, one end of the series communicates by an open orifice with the external air, while the other opens into a slot in the bridge of the furnace." Now, the inspection of the specification will show that all Mr. Coad's variations of apparatus are the very reverse of what is here described, and consist of tortuous, or up and down system of pipes through which air can only be thrust by a forcing or blowing apparatus, to which he indeed resorts, and which he describes.

Now let any practical scientific man examine Mr. Coad's specification, and reflect on all these tortuous systems of pipes, which, in his drawings he points out, and on the sending in of the air at the bridge of the furnace, and of course beyond the fire where the smoke is generated, and I am sure they will see that the whole is a theoretical scheme which never has been, nor ever can, by any of the arrangements of apparatus which he has described, be reduced to practice; and further, it is obvious from the statement that "a current of hot air *is thrown into the flame at every point where the smoke begins to be formed,"* that Mr. Coad is become aware that air ought to be so thrown into the flame at the moment the inflammable gases are generated, to produce the combustion of the smoke, and not to be thrown into a mixture of smoke with carbonic acid, and other inflammable gases which is always to be found at the bridges of furnaces.

Your obedient servant,
PLAYFAIR.

September 9, 1837.

AUTHORITIES FOR A RESISTING ETHE-RIAL MEDIUM; REPLY OF MR. THORNE TO THE " COUNTRY TEACHER."

Sir,—The "Country Teacher" accuses me of being a good disseminator of fudge, and devotes a long paragraph of your valuable Magazine to an *accusation* of this kind *by way of argument*. He then gives a quotation of one of my former letters, which he says reads very well, but there is one very grievous fault, which is, that it does not contain one word of truth ; and challenges me to produce one single writer for the last fifty-two years back who has promulgated such false (as he calls them) principles.

If the " Country Teacher" will turn to the Treatise of Astronomy by Sir J. Herschell, which forms one of the series of Dr. Lardner's Cabinet Cyclopædia, he will find at page 309, his (Sir J. H.'s) opinions on this subject; he says, when speaking of Encke's comet, that, " on comparing the intervals between the successive perihelion passages of this comet (Encke's), after allowing in the most careful manner for all the disturbances due to the actions of the planets, a very singular fact has come to light, viz.: *that the periods are constantly diminishing ;* or in other words, that the mean distance from the sun, or the major axis of the ellipse is dwindling by slow, but regular degrees ; this is evidently the effect which would be produced by a resistance experienced by the comet from a very rare etherial medium pervading the regions in which it moves ; for such resistance, by diminishing its actual velocity, would diminish also its centrifugal force, and thus give the sun more power over it to draw it nearer. Accordingly, (no other mode of accounting for the phenomena in question appearing,) this is the solution proposed by Encke, *and generally received.* It will, therefore, *probably fall ultimately into the sun,* should it not first be dissipated altogether,—a thing no way improbable when the lightness of its materials is considered, and which seems authorised by the observed fact, of its having been less and less conspicuous at each reappearance." And, again, a note on the following page says, " should calculation establish the fact of a resistance experienced also by this (Biela's) comet the subject of periodical comets will assume an extraordinary degree of interest. It cannot be doubted that many more will be discovered, and by their resistance, questions will come to be decided, such as the following :—What is the law of density of the resisting medium which surrounds the sun? Is it in rest or in motion? If the latter, in

what direction does it move? Circularly round the sun or traversing space? If circularly, in what plane? It is obvious that a circular or vorticose motion of the ether would accelerate some comets, and retard others, according as their revolution was relative to such motion, direct or retrograde. Supposing the neighbourhood of the sun to be filled with a material fluid, it is not conceivable that the circulation of the planets in it for ages, should not have impressed upon it some degree of rotation in their own direction. And this may preserve them from the effects of accumulated resistance." And in the next page, 311, Sir John again says, when speaking with respect to the change of dimensions of the comet of Encke, as it approaches to, or recedes from the sun :—" M. Valz, who, among others, noticed this fact, has accounted for it by supposing a real compression or condensation of volume, *owing to the pressure of etherial medium* growing more dense in the sun's neighbourhood." May I also be allowed to reiterate the words of M. De la Beche in his Researches in Theoritical Geology when he says that recent astronomical researches have rendered it extremely probable that the planets move through a resisting medium. Assuming this to be true, it follows that all such bodies, with their attendant *satellites must eventually fall into the sun ;* and consequently, there is no real stability in the solar system, it being one of constant, though quiet and long-continued change.

Now Sir, after these full and fair extracts, I would ask your readers, whether the words I made use of were not correct, that the theory of a resisting medium is generally received? The extracts show that it was proposed by Encke, received by Sir John Herschell, made use of in argument by M. De la Beche, and as Sir John Herschell says, generally received.

Yours respectfully,
JOSHUA THORNE.
London, September 9, 1837.

MR. UTTING'S ASTRONOMICAL TABLES.
TO A SCOTCH DOMINIE.

Sir,—When I sent my remarks on your paper (vol. xxvii, p. 224), I had not then seen your last letter, (vol. xxvii, p. 214), as I take the *Mechanics' Maga-*

zine in monthly parts. I do not, however, consider it necessary to enter into a confutation of all your solutions, as your principles of calculation are the same in your last letter as in the one which precedes it, and which I have proved to be erroneous.

At page 460, vol. xxvi, you say, " but I will ask Mr. Utting from what authority has he deduced the periodic times of the planets given in his first table ; for I find that none of them agree with the best modern discoveries; the periodic time of the earth is very nearly true, but of the others, some are minutes wrong, some hours, some days, yea, even months wrong."

Now, I have before stated, that the greatest difference, which is in the periodic time of the planet Uranus, is little more than five hours (instead of months!) as computed from the periodic times given by Sir John Herschell in his Treatise on Astronomy, the accuracy of which you acknowledge, thus :—" I have never seen Sir John Herschell's Astronomy, but I have no doubt that the mean siderial periods of the planets are all, as far as is known, correctly given;" (vol. xxvii, p. 214); whence it follows, by your own admission, that the periods which you gave (vol. xxvi, p. 461) were erroneous; for that they cannot both be correct is very evident. So much for your knowledge of the best modern discoveries!

You then proceed, " but I will inform Mr. Utting, that had I been disposed to calculate the grand period of conjunction of all the planets, I never would have put myself to the trouble of converting the mean time of the siderial revolutions into mean tropical periods; I should have at once converted the mean siderial revolutions into mean synodical periods," &c.

But let me ask you, how would you have obtained the siderial periods of the planets in the first instance? You here betray your ignorance of the subject you attempt to elucidate. The periodic times of the planets are obtained from observations of their transits relative to the fixed stars, made during a considerable period of time; from which their motions in longitude are obtained, and thence their secular motions, siderial, tropical, anomalistical, and synodic

periods : any one of which is found with nearly as much ease as another, the secular motions of the earth's perihelion and equinoxial points being given.

You next attempt to convict me by the application of your well-known astronomical theorems ; but as I have before proved, that the error originates in your reductions and transformations, it is quite unnecessary for me to enter into your arithmetical operations. Or otherwise how could you expect that, after reducing the moon's periods from hours, minutes, &c. to decimals of a day, you could obtain the earth's period therefrom correctly, it being twelve times greater than those of the moon from which you had to obtain it ! (vol. xxvii, p. 147). My periods are given to four decimal places of a second. You have given yours to seven decimal places of a day only.

My numbers are reduced to a denomination 86400 times lower than yours; consequently, your decimals ought to have extended to nine or ten places instead of seven. For example, take the moon's period = 29 days 12 hours 44 minutes 2.8547 seconds, which, reduced to days and seconds will be as follows :—

Viz: 29 days 45842 sec. 8547 decimals.

By your own reduction (vol. xxvii, page 147) : 29 days 5305886 decimals.

Thus, you see that you are two decimal places deficient. Now if two numbers are given, with their difference, to find a fourth, you must at least have three more, or ten decimal places, if you expect your results to agree with mine; which almost any school-boy could have told you.

Again, page 216, you say, " In short, Mr. Utting has confounded tropical periods with periodical revolutions," &c.

Now, Sir, I beg to state that Mr. Utting has done no such thing. My periods are designated by their proper appellations, and are in reality such as I have described them.

You are pleased to call them (*i. e.* the siderial periods) *periodical periods,* which is an improper designation. Are not tropical, anomalistical, and synodic periods, *periodical* periods also?

I trust, Sir, I have now fully confuted your attempts to prove the inaccuracy of my tables. Your objections have had a tendency to establish their correctness, rather than the contrary. In conclusion, I recommend you to make yourself more perfect in the principles of arithmetic, before you again assume the office of *critic ;* as all that you have hitherto advanced in opposition to my period of conjunction, has been a tissue of misrepresentation, and erroneous calculations.

I am, Sir, yours, &c.

J. UTTING.

Lynn Regis, September 6, 1837.

P.S.—What I advanced in opposition to the two results of *Professor Struve,* being independent of each other I still maintain, but I beg to observe, that I do not, nor ever did, assert him to be an impostor. I know not where the misrepresentation originated. You may be the author of the notice in the journal referred to, for what I know to the contrary, as you seem to have a fellow feeling for its author.

Since writing the above, I have been doubtful whether your erroneous calculations were wilful or made through ignorance. I, however, pledge myself to confute *every calculation* you have made, which differs from my results, if required, provided you affix your name to your next letter.

THE GIRAFFES.

Sir,—In the following remarks, I do not wish to disturb Mr. Kyan's patent, or ruffle his placidity, I only venture to doubt the questionable propriety of adopting his process for the *wood* used in the construction of the enclosures of the animals in the Regent's Park Zoological Gardens, especially that of *the Giraffes.* These beautiful and delicate creatures are *incessantly licking the paling ;* and though the quantity of *corrosive sublimate* may be insufficient to prove promptly *fatal,* yet I fear, it must seriously affect their health. Their constitutions are very different from those of " Solyman the sublimate eater."

I applied the tip of my tongue to the wood, and feel fully satisfied of having detected its presence by the taste.

I asked a question or two from the surly Cerberus who was stationed to watch them, and who growled forth any thing but a direct answer; indeed, he was too intent on reading a newspaper to attend either to the giraffes or to me.

I have not yet seen the giraffes in the " Surrey Zoological Gardens," but I was considerably impressed with the difference in their physiognomy, in comparing the *present* appearance of those in the Regent's Park, with what I had witnessed at the period of their introduction into the Gardens. Their former sprightliness, and the cheerful lustre of their now *tearful* eye, are gone. I had a few days before seen the beautiful specimens of the giraffe in the *Jardin de Plantes* at Paris, which is my opinion yields an additional proof.

I again repeat, I *fear* they are *not healthy.* I would now simply put the question for the consideration of those more immediately interested, how far it is fairly attributable to the *corrosive sublimate,* in which the timber has been steeped by Kyan's patent process ?

I remain, Sir,

Your very humble servant,

J. MURRAY.

London, September 7, 1837.

STEAM NAVIGATION TO INDIA AND AMERICA.

Sir,—In common with the rest of the readers of the *Mechanics' Magazine,* I have read with much interest the remarks of your valuable correspondent, Mr. Bayley, on the subject of steam navigation to America, and am glad to find, that the opinion of a gentleman, whose authority, as a practical man ranks so high, is decidedly on the side of the practicability of the project. I believe he will carry such an immense majority with him, that even Dr. Lardner, the almost solitary *croaker* at the plan, would, now that he sees how closely the time approaches for a most vigorous attempt, or rather attempts, to carry it into execution, would be glad to draw in his horns a little, and to have the world forget that he once denounced a voyage by steam to the United States as being about as feasible as a voyage to the moon! He *has,* in fact, shown his consciousness of having gone too far in that too hasty declaration, by endeavouring to explain away the main force of the expression; but he still thinks it fitting and proper to do all that in him lies to throw a wet blanket on the scheme, and, by every means within his reach, to thwart the hopes of its projectors, or at any rate, to frighten its less steadfast supporters. Luckily, none of the parties concerned seem to think it worth their while to take any notice of the worthy doctor's well-meant labours. With them, words are but wind! and they seem determined, either to show the fallacy of his objections by making the voyage while he is occupied in proving its utter impossibility, or to have the warrant of experience, as well as the dictum of a one-sided theorist, against them, ere they give up their well-grounded hopes of success. The refutation of the doctor might, perhaps, safely be left to time; but it is not by any means desirable that, because it is evident his croakings will not do so much mischief as they might have done, they should therefore be allowed to go forth to the public unchallenged, and do what small harm they may. Mr. Bayley, therefore, has done "yeoman service to the cause," by showing up the hollowness of the foundation on which Dr. Lardner rests his argument against the plan, as he has so completely done in the *Mechanics' Magazine*, No. 733.

I say, Dr. Lardner's argument, because it is as notorious as the sun at noon-day, that the writer of the article on steam navigation in the Edinburgh Review, whose positions Mr. Bayley so satisfactorily demolishes, is neither more nor less than the learned doctor himself: so that the coincidence in opinion between the two is a matter but little to be wondered at. By the way, I think the only writer who has yet stood forward in support of the doctor's views on the subject, happens to be this same critic of modern Athens: *i. e.* the ideas of Dr. Lardner, the lecturer, have been most warmly seconded, and enforced by that very impartial personage, Dr. Lardner, the reviewer! There is some advantage, at any rate, in being not "two single gentlemen rolled into one," but one learned doctor split into two. If nothing else, it insures a very striking similarity of opinion between the originator of the argument and its supporter!

Dr. L. has appeared in yet another character, on behalf of his rash, but darling assertion; that of author of a pamphlet on Steam Communication with India, in the course of which he dwells at some length on the impossibility of

steaming more than a certain distance in a certain time, and without stopping to take in coals. Unluckily, the very week in which this pamphlet appeared, the intelligence arrived that one of the East India Company's steamers, by the Cape of Good Hope had gone *still further and still faster* than the extremest limit fixed by the infallible doctor in his study,—and that, too, without his leave and license, first had and obtained! If folks go on in this way, it is ten to one but the voyage direct to New York may be fairly steamed off by about the time the doctor has his next article on its folly ready for the press. The paper of Mr. Bayley, will, at least, prevent the readers of the *Mechanics' Magazine* from feeling the least surprise if this shocking event should actually take place.

It is to be regretted that Dr. Lardner should persevere in his course with such obstinacy. He seems to think it a point of honour to maintain the entire correctness of his first adverse opinion, "come what come may"—albeit, such a spring of action is sadly unphilosophical. Another motive also appears to carry weight; the doctor, for some reason or other, is a thick-and-thin advocate of a grand central Irish railway, and is for demolishing everything that in the least degree "stands in its light." Actuated by this motive, he desperately endeavours to persuade the good people of England, that it will be far better for them to land (themselves and goods) at Valentia Island, the western extremity of *his native country*,—travel per railway again to the eastern coast,—embark there once more, —disembark on the eastern shores of Wales, and mount a railroad again for their final destination,—than to be steamed off to that destination at once, without the trouble and expense of disembarking, loading, unloading, re-embarking, re-disembarking, re-loading at all! This *trait* in itself speaks volumes as to the dependence to be placed on the doctor's *reasonings*, when his *feelings*, of nationality even, stand in his way.

I may as well observe, that the pamphlet I have alluded to is well calculated, notwithstanding this incidental blemish, to further the cause of steam communication with India by the Red Sea, although it contains scarcely anything in its favour that has not already been repeatedly urged on the attention of Government and the East India Company, two slow-moving bodies, that, it is now pretty certain, are *at last* about to stir in that long-agitated matter to some purpose.

I remain, Sir,

Very respectfully yours,

H.

London September 6, 1837.,

HOW TO EFFACE "INDELIBLE MARKING INKS."

Sir,—A friend of mine, Mr. J. Francis, of Brighton, on the 25th of last March, whilst experimenting on nitrate of silver, discovered a very ready and simple means of removing the stain of this salt, and consequently of *all indelible marking inks*, of which this salt constitutes the base. All that is necessary to be done to remove the mark or stain of these inks from any article, is to immerse it in a little of the liq. amon. fortiss. of the chemists' shops. In about ten minutes the colour will be much faded, and in a few minutes more, it will totally have disappeared.

Marking inks have acquired their fame, by no method having hitherto been applied to remove oxide of silver, without injuring the fabric of the article: this oxide is produced by decomposition of the nitrate of silver, (after writing with the marking ink) either by application of heat, or by exposing it to the sun's rays. Liquid ammonia dissolves this oxide without leaving the slightest trace of its previous existence.

Yours, &c.

I. T.

Near Sheffield, June 17, 1837.

Query.—Would not the exhibition of liq. amon. gradually remove the dark colour produced on the skin of persons, by the internal administration of nitrate of silver?—

IMPROVEMENTS IN THE ROYAL OBSERVATORY, GREENWICH.

Since the appointment of Professor Airy, as astronomer royal, various important improvements in this establishment have been effected, or put in a course of accomplishment.

In the first place, a large portion of the Royal Park has been enclosed, and annexed to the Observatory, for the purpose of magnetic observations; and there is every prospect, that such observations will be commenced in the course of the ensuing summer.

The library, as Professor Airy found it, contained the germs of a most valuable astronomical and mathematical collection; but almost every set of works continued in series was imperfect; and much was wanting in the modern works of continental astronomy. At the Professor's application, sums exceeding 200*l*. were placed at his disposal, by the Lords Commissioners of the Admiralty, for the completion of the library. Much has already been done; and before long, it is expected that the library will be made, without any great expense, a most valuable and practically useful collection. Mr. Airy attaches great importance to this part of the institution, for the following reason :—The natural tendency, in an office so much pressed with routine-work, and with official business having no very close relation to science, is, to be degraded into a mere bureau of clerks; and it is difficult even for the director to resist the contagion. The only antidote is, to place in the power of all, the means of acquaintance with the literature and the foreign systems of astronomy: to make the principal persons at least familiar with the speculations of ancient, and the theories of modern, times. It is only thus that the character of astronomer can be made to predominate over that of mere observer or mere calculator.

The only changes which have been made in the instruments of the Observatory are the following :—The attachment of the telescope on Troughton's circle has been altered, the connexion being now effected by clamps similar to those used on Jones's circle and on the Cambridge circle, instead of the grasp of the spokes by which the telescope had been held in the same position for several years. The acting part of the zenith tube has been completely remodelled. Micrometers have been placed in the microscopes for viewing the top and bottom of the plumbline: the original telescope-micrometer has been discarded, and a new one mounted, requiring only a small range of screw, and liable to none of the flexures to which the old one was exposed.

Mr. Airy having understood that Mr. Maclear, astronomer at the Cape of Good

Hope, had with great care ascertained the precise locality of the Abbé de la Caille's observatory, and had taken measures for connecting, by triangulation, that spot with the new observatory, he ventured to suggest to the Lords Comsioners of the Admiralty the propriety of enabling Mr. Maclear to verify the astronomical part of the measure of the arc of meridian if he should think fit; and he pointed out Bradley's sector as an instrument which, with a change in its mounting, would be well adapted to this purpose. Their Lordships were pleased to direct that the necessary change should be made; and that instrument is now in the hands of Mr. Simms for repair and alteration.

A valuable telescope of 6¾ inches aperture has been presented to the Royal Observatory by the Rev. R. Sheepshanks; and, with the approbation of the Board of Admiralty, Professor Airy has taken measures for mounting it equatoreally in the South Dome; a situation greatly preferable to those of the existing equatoreals. The artist employed in constructing the mounting is Mr. Thomas Grubb, of Dublin.

The observations of 1836, with the exception of some small matters relating to the equatoreal observations and the solar eclipse, are entirely reduced and ready for press. Of the results, the following are the most interesting. The circles exhibit precisely the same kind of discordance between determinations by direct vision and determinations by reflection, which was formerly noticed by Mr. Pond, afterwards by Professor Airy, and more lately by Mr. Henderson and Mr. Maclear; and its quantity is nearly the same. Correcting for this, and using Bessel's refractions, the Professor finds (from more than 1300 observations) that Mr. Pond's latitude requires to be diminished by nearly one second. The accurate agreement of the results from stars in different zones seems to shew that Bessel's tables represent the Greenwich observations well. The discordance of the obliquities deduced from the two solstices is a very small fraction of a second. The right ascensions of the Nautical Almanac require to be diminished generally about 0ˢ·13. The result of the reduced observations of α Lyræ is not yet wholly investigated, but they appear to shew no signs of sensible parallax.

Complaint, we find, is made of a want of hands to reduce the astronomical observations made in a satisfactory manner; or, to speak more properly, of much of the time of the present assistants being wasted upon business not strictly within their line of duty, namely, the daily comparison and official work relating to the government chronometers. Either, the establishment should be increased, or the charge of the chronometers transferred to some other department.

MR. PISTRUCCI'S METHOD OF MEDAL-STRIKING, NOT NEW.

Sir,—I wish to offer a few remarks on an article which has gone the round of the papers, claiming for Mr. Pistrucci the merit of inventing a method of impressing dies with a cast punch from an original model, and thereby saving the time of the artist, and expense to the public.

In the first place, the method was known and practised by my grandfather, as far as it was practicable, fifty years since; and not only by him, but by his brother artists of the time. It was carried to its utmost extent in the coining of the old penny, at Matthew Bolton's mint, Soho, near Birmingham, in 1797, and has been continually used by medalists in general from that period. How Pistrucci could have strained his modesty so far as to claim the plan he details, in the face of British artists, as an original invention, I am at a loss to account for. He says, a cast is obtained in cast iron as perfect as possible; but is quite silent as to the means of procuring this perfect cast (in fact, as perfect as the hubs taken from the original dies, as used in the mint, which hubs are as perfect as the coin, and are transferred to the money dies, so as to give little or no trouble to the engraver); he should tell the public how they are founded; why does he not do so? Why, because he knows it to be utterly impossible to cast any metal hard enough for the purpose in sand or loam, or any other composition.

But, admitting for a moment the practicability of the process, will he persist to tell the real professors of the art, that a heated die will only want polishing on the surface? He knows, if he has yet learned what every apprentice should know the first year of his time, that a heated die will scale, and that this scale must be removed by acid, which leaves the pure steel in a very imperfect state; so much so, that an expert engraver would rather do a die in the usual way twice over: and again, with regard to his expecting to put these cast iron hubs into soft steel cold, I tell him his hopes are vain. It is really too bad for this foreign cameo-sculptor to pilfer from native workmen a little knowledge, and then attempt to deceive the public by claiming it as his own.

Being a subscriber to your Magazine from its first number, and never having troubled you with a line before, I beg your insertion of the foregoing.

Yours, &c.
JOHN BADDELEY.

63, Compton-street, Clerkenwell.

AUXILIARY RULES FOR WORKING NAUTICUS'S ASTRONOMICAL QUESTION.

Sir,—In order to render the formula, and example, furnished by me at page 212 more complete, I beg to add the two following short rules, by the aid of which the ambiguity of the combination, sin. $(x + P')$, forming the arc x^2, and that of $(x^2 + x^3)$, forming the hour angle, may be avoided.

For the first $\left\{ \begin{array}{c} + \\ - \end{array} \right\}$ when A. $\left\{ \begin{array}{c} > \\ < \end{array} \right\}$ 90° (*vice versâ* when the polar dis. exceeds 90°).

For the second $\left\{ \begin{array}{c} - \\ + \end{array} \right.$ when A $\left\{ \begin{array}{c} > \\ < \end{array} \right\}$ 90°, and the azimuth is north.

$-$ .... when the azimuth is south.

I hope the method will now be intelligible, without there being a necessity for occupying your space by putting the rule into words; and I trust that Nauticus will find no difficulty in working the question last proposed by himself at page 266. He will find that the siderial time of observation was $17^h 17^m 21^s$, shewing an error in his clock of $+ 4^s$.

The method to be deduced from the equations quoted by Nauticus from Dr. Tiarks, is scarcely worth the trouble of solving. As Nauticus, however, seems to wish very much to have it done, I am happy in obliging him.

Let | l = co. lat. | D = polar dis. of lower star | d = that of the upper | A, or a = diff. in R.A. | x = the hour angle.

$$\frac{\text{Sin. } (x + a)}{\text{tan. } d.} - \frac{\text{sin. } x}{\text{tan D}} = \frac{\text{sin. } a}{\text{tan. } l}$$

And let (tan. d. tan. l.) = m. (tan D. tan. l.) = n. (tan. d. tan. l. sin. a.) = p.

$$\therefore m. \text{ sin. } (x + a) - n. \text{ sin. } x. = p.$$

by expansion—m. (sin. x. cos. a. + cos. x. sin. a.)—n. sin. x. = p.

$$\therefore (m. \cos. a - n) \sin. x. + m. \cos. a. \cos. x. = p.$$

$$\therefore \text{Sin. } n. + \frac{m. \text{ sin. } a. \cos. x.}{m. \cos. a - n.} = \frac{p.}{m. \cos. a - n.}$$

$$\text{Let } \frac{m. \text{ sin. } a.}{m. \cos. a - n.} = \text{tan. } \theta.$$

$$\therefore \text{Sin. } x + \text{tan. } \theta, \cos. x. = \frac{p.}{m. \cos. a - n.}$$

$$\text{or, } \sin, x. \cos. \theta + \cos. x. \sin. \theta = \frac{p.}{m. \cos. a - n.}$$

$$\therefore \text{Sin. } (x. + \theta) = \frac{p.}{m. \cos. a - n.}$$

Whence the formula is derived as follows :—

$$\text{Sin. } (x. + \theta) = \frac{p.}{m. \cos. a - n.} \quad \Big| \quad \text{Tan. } \theta = \frac{m. \text{ sin. } a.}{m. \cos. a - n.}$$

In words, it gives the following rule, m., n., and p. retaining the same values :—

To log. sin A, add log. *m*, and find the nat. number of the sum; from which subtract the nat. number of log. *n*; find the log. of the remainder, and call its arithmetical compt. *s*.

To log. cosine A, add log. *m* and *s*; the sum is log. tan of arc *θ*.
To log. cosine *θ*, add log. *p* and *s*; the sum is log. sine of arc *(θ+x)*.
From which *θ* being subtracted, *x* is found.

Example.

<table>
<tr><td></td><td></td><td></td><td>R. A.</td><td>Polar Disc.</td><td></td></tr>
<tr><td></td><td></td><td></td><td>h. m. s.</td><td></td><td></td></tr>
<tr><td>1 July, 1837.—Stars Polaris ...</td><td>1</td><td>1</td><td>4——</td><td>1.33.47</td><td>} Lat. 51.40, long. 38.20.</td></tr>
<tr><td>Capella ...</td><td>5</td><td>4</td><td>39——</td><td>44.10.27</td><td>}</td></tr>
</table>

A..60 . 53 . 45	Sin.. 9.941381		
D..44 . 10 . 27	Tan.. 9.987478	Tan D.. 9.987478	Tan *l*.. 9.898009
d.. 1 . 33 . 47	Tan.. 8.435960	Tan *l*:.. 9.898009	Tan *d*.. 8.435960

Log. *p*... 8.364819	log. *m*... 9.885487	log. *n*.. 8.333969

Log. *m*.. 9.885487	9.885487
Sin. A.... 9.941381	Cosin.. 9.686993

Log. *s*. ... 0.453349	9.572480	Nat. numb... 373663

	Tan. .. ⌈ 0.280017	8.333969	Nat. numb... 021576
θ... 62 . 19 . 15 ...... { ══════	Log. ⌈ 9.546651	352087
Cos. ... ⌊ 9.667003		
	0.453349	*s*. .. ⌊ 0.453349	Arith. comp.

Log. *p*. .. 8.364819

θ+x.178 . 14 . 55 Sine..... 8.485171

x.115 . 55 . 40................ =7ʰ 43ᵐ42.7ˢ

R. A. polaris 1 . 1 . 4

————————17ʰ 17ᵐ 21.3ˢ sidereal time.

Nauticus can now please himself. He will, however, I fancy, agree with me, that the method proposed at page 212 is simpler, if not more concise, than this; there are, to be sure, many repetitions in this method, which only require copying down, and it therefore appears longer than it really is; but the necessity of converting logs. into natural numbers, and conversely, adds greatly to the trouble and risk of error. Indeed, if it were not for this consideration, there is another method, which would be shorter than either of the others, viz.—

D = 44 . 10 . 47	Cosec .. 0.058619		
d = 1 . 33 . 47	Cotan.. 0.012522		
A = 60 . 53 . 45	tan .. 8.435959	Nat. cotan.. 556690	Log.tan. 8.435960

8.507101	Nat. numb.. 032144	Cotan *l*.. 0.101990

θ 18 . 49 . 35	Nat. tan.... 524546	Cosin *θ*.. 9.947221

(Δ—*θ*) 88 . 14 . 55	Cosine.. 8.485171

x or Δ 115 . 55 . 40 = 7 . 42 . 42.7

R. A. P. 1 . 1 . 4

17 . 17 . 21.3 sidereal time of observation.

I have neither time nor space now to write out a rule for this last method; but, if demanded, I shall introduce it into some future communication.

It may now be expected that I should say something about the assertion so confidently made by " O. N." of the impossibility of such questions as the present; but that writer has laid himself so hopelessly prostrate by his unhappy exhibition at page 246, that it would be merciless to be otherwise than brief in replying to him. His whole "*investigation*," as he calls it, diagram and all, involves such inconceivable absurdity, that with any other signature than " O. N.," I should have pronounced it to be a hoax : he thinks that he has satisfactorily proved that the zenith distance of a star can be *greater* than its polar distance, and the co-latitude, taken together; which never was, will, or could be the case under any circumstances whatever; and moreover, these three are portions of great circles which must always intersect, and consequently form a triangle ; save and except the instant when the star is on the meridian. But this is not all, for having taken the trouble to wade through " O. N.'s" demonstration, in order to discover the particular obfuscation under which he labours, I find that he has, as usual, been manufacturing a rule for himself, or rather, an analogy that Napier never dreamed of. At page 246, col. 2d, line 16th, he has substituted the sign $+$ for $-$; and this happens to make *all* the difference, nor can it have been a blunder of the compositor's making ; for, on it is based the whole structure of the " investigation."

Now, after this, do not the remarks, with which he prefaces his letter, appear too ridiculous? Wherein he talks of having in vain "*warned*" Nautilus of the impossibility of the question, &c., and how Nautilus was " *undismayed*" thereat? And is it not too bad, that because one may sometimes loath the augean labour, of sifting through similar rubbish, one must, months afterwards, be taunted with one's forbearance, as if what was unworthy of an answer must therefore necessarily be unanswerable? And then the compliments these worthies pay each other! Not long since, a correspondent of yours discovered that " O. N." was an " able mathematician," and now,

" O. N." " sends round the joke," by dubbing " S. W. S." an " able writer !"

To Kinclaven, as he has withdrawn from the field, I shall say nothing ; the accusation of want of temper in an opponent is almost invariably made by those who get the worst of an argument. I have never had, in these discussions, even an excuse to lose mine ; on the contrary, I have been thoroughly amused throughout.

I remain, Mr. Editor, yours, &c.
NAUTILUS.

PNEUMATIC BAROMETER.

Sir,—In perusing the 699th Number of the *Mechanics' Magazine*, I was much struck with your correspondent, Mr. Ollivier's, ingenious suggestion of " A Pneumatic Watch Mainspring." Would not, however, such a motive force require a corresponding regulating power to compensate for the changes in atmospheric pressure produced by meteorological variations, or different altitudes? But if no such regulating force were applied, would not the "*rate*" of Mr. Ollivier's proposed clock be a delicate and accurate measure of the mean atmospheric pressure during any period of days, weeks, or months? And might not the principle be still farther applied in the construction of an instrument more portable and less liable to derangement than the common mountain barometer? I scarcely know whether this be an original suggestion, or whether it deserves a place in your pages.

Your constant subscriber,
C. H.

DAVENPORT'S ELECTRO-MAGNETIC
ENGINE.

(From the American Correspondence of the *Morning Herald*).

I did not write by the packet of the 16th, because I had made an appointment, for the next day, to go and see the electro-magnetic machines of Mr. Davenport, and which I considered well worthy to be the subject of a letter, provided there were any grounds for the vast expectations founded upon them, not only by the inventor and his friends, but by every person who had examined them, and heard the explanations of Mr. Davenport. Having seen them, I am free to confess that I cannot discover any good reason why the power may not be obtained and employed in sufficient abundance for any machinery—why it should not supersede steam, to which it is infinitely preferable on the score of expense, and safety, and simplicity. I do not very clearly understand the principle (something about changing the poles from positive to negative, or from north to south), and *vice versâ*, in rapid succession ; but this is of little consequence, as I shall be able to send you, probably by the next packet, a pamphlet containing a full exposition, with illustrative engravings. Mr. Cook, who is associated with Mr. Davenport in the patent, is now engaged in preparing this pamphlet, and he has promised me the first copy that is printed. They have patented their invention in France and England.

Before I saw the machines, I had two doubts as to the more extended application of the power. One, whether the enlargement of the apparatus would be attended by any very great increase of the power ; the other was founded upon what I supposed to be a necessity in the construction of the machine. I had understood that the revolving wheel was formed of iron bars, upon which the coated wire was wrapped, or wound, in order to form the communication with the galvanic batteries, or cylinders of alternate zinc and copper ; and that this wheel revolved within the periphery of a fixed circle, also magnetized, and having on its inner surface certain points at which the points or poles of attraction and repulsion were established. Somehow or other, I had formed the idea, that the space between the outer surface of the revolving wheel, and the inner surface of the fixed circle, was of necessity exceedingly minute, so that in fact they did all but touch ; and I conceived that it would be impossible to construct large machinery with such nicety of adjustment as to effect and retain this close proximity, without the danger of coming into actual contact. But I find that the space between is ample to allow of any reasonable play ; even in the small machines, with the comparatively trifling degree of power employed, it is full a quarter of an inch ; and with the increase of power, it may doubtless be enlarged.

The last machine constructed by Mr. Davenport occupies a surface of about 18 inches square, that is, 18 inches on each side, and consists merely of a platform, having upon it an iron circular frame, with an arch extending from side to side above it, a spindle in the centre playing in this arch at top and in a socket below, and on this spindle an incomplete wheel, formed of two cross pieces of iron, with segments of a

circle at the four extremities. It is, in fact, a wheel, with four breaks in its periphery. Some hundreds of feet of isolated, or coated, copper wire are wound around the cross pieces, and also round the fixed circular frame ; the connection with the galvanic batteries, which are three small cylinders, each consisting of six concentric tubes of zinc and copper, the outer one scarcely larger than a quart pot, is, as usual, by small rods of copper. The revolving wheel is six·inches in diameter, and weighs about six pounds. Attached to the upright spindle is a small cog wheel, which may be made to work in other wheels, with axles, for the purpose of shewing how great a weight can be raised from the ground.

With the three batteries acting on it, the revolution of the wheel was 1,000 times in a minute ; and these 1,000 revolutions raised a weight of 200 lbs. one foot. The first machine made by Mr. Davenport, which is much smaller and has but one battery, raised but 24 lbs. He is confident that with a number of batteries, or one very large one —say as big as a barrel, there would be power enough to drive the largest machinery, while the cost of construction would be reduced to a fifth, or perhaps a tenth, and that of attendance, fuel, &c., now forming so heavy an item in the expenses of steam-power, would be almost done away with. Half a barrel of blue vitriol, and a hogshead or two of water, would send a ship from New York to Liverpool ; and no accident could possibly happen, beyond the breaking of some part of the machinery, which is so simple, that any damage could be repaired in half a day. Surely it is a great and vastly important discovery, and the wildest imagination can hardly grasp the wonders in achieving which it may, and doubtless will, become the instrument.

TEMPORARY CAISSOON FOR STOPPING OUT WATER WHILE REPAIRING SEA-COCKS OF STEAM-VESSELS.

(From the *Nautical Magazine.*)

The following description of a temporary caissoon, applied to H. M. steam-vessel Dee, for the purpose of excluding the water whilst one of the sea-cocks was ground in afresh, by Com. W. Ramsay, R. M., displays that ingenuity under difficulty, for which our seamen are celebrated :—

In describing a caisson that was used by H. M. steam-vessel Dee, under my command at Port Royal, in the month of August, 1835, the simplicity of the details are such, that it may perhaps be thought by some hardly worthy the attention of the readers of the Nautical ; but as all who may have to encounter a similar difficulty may not know how easily it can be overcome, is a sufficient reason for giving them. It is necessary first to state, for the information of those who are not much acquainted with the fittings of steam-vessels, that there are several sea-cocks, which, when turned, admit the water through the bottom of the vessel for various well-known purposes. The most common plan is to have a pipe, which communicates with the sea. About a foot from the outside of the vessel is the cock, upon which another pipe is fixed, which conveys the water to its destination. Now these cocks, by constant use, are liable to leak; when this occurs, the water flows in a stream into the vessel, and the only remedy to be applied is to remove the cock, and what is technically called, grind it in afresh, and then replace it. This is, of course, effected without danger when the vessel is in dock, but it is evident, that if attempted when she is afloat, without some method of preventing the water rushing in, if the pipe inside cannot be stopped, which would be very doubtful, the vessel would fill with water.

This being premised, it may be now stated that the sea-cock on the larboard side of H. M. steam-vessel Dee was found to be leaking very much. It was considered that taking off the cock, and trusting to being able to stop the pipe from inside would be dangerous, besides the difficulty, perhaps impossibility, of putting the cock on again when reground, with such a rush of water as it is evident would take place. As there are no locks at Port Royal, the only plan was to stop the aperture (by which the water enters the vessel) outside, until the necessary repairs were completed.

The vessel was first given as great a heel as possible to starboard, by which the hole to be stopped was brought within four feet of the water's edge; next, having procured several feet of two inch fir plank, a box was made which had three sides, and a bottom, of the following dimensions: the back was five feet deep by four broad, the sides three feet broad, the bottom of course extending from the back to the ends of the sides. The way in which it was rendered watertight was this: two folds of very thick fearnought boiled in a mixture of tallow and tar, was placed between each joining of the planks, and the whole was kept together by the means of iron bolts, which were driven quite through.

Now, it was necessary to obtain the exact curve of the vessel's bottom, that the sides of the caissoon might be cut to answer to it. This was effected by means of a long stripe of lead, which was forced during a calm against the vessel's bottom. The curve being thus obtained, the sides and bottom of the caissoon were cut to their proper shapes; small grooves were cut in their edges, and four folds of fearnought, prepared as above, were nailed on. The nails were driven along the grooves, so that when the caisson came to be pressed against the vessel's bottom, there might be nothing to prevent a good fit. Two large cleats were then nailed upon the vessel's side, on the exact spot that the top of the caissoon would be, so that once forced down into its place, it could not rise again. As near the surface of the water as possible, two strong screw eye-bolts were fixed to the vessel's side, through which lashings were rove, and a tackle got all ready.

The caissoon was now put over, forced down under the cleats mentioned above, the lashings encompassed it, which were hauled tight by the tackle, by which means the caissoon was forced against the vessel. A small pump that had been prepared before, was then placed in it, by the aid of which, and bailing, all the water was got out of the caissoon in about ten minutes, after which one man occasionally bailing kept it quite dry. Having this to work in, the aperture was soon secured, the cock taken off and ground afresh. When that was finished and put in again, the caissoon, which had been allowed to fill with water was pumped out, the lead and plank had been nailed on to keep the water out, of the ship was taken off, and the whole business was finished without the slightest stop, impediment, or difficulty, in about forty-eight hours.

STEERING FROM THE BOW, THE BEST REMEDY FOR STEAM-BOAT ACCIDENTS.

Sir,—The late serious steam-boat accident on the river Thames, I mean the encounter of the Monarch and the Apollo, appears to claim the attention of persons who have had opportunities of considering such things and of suggesting practical remedies.

In the United States of America every steam-boat has the steersman placed so far forward in the vessel that he can readily distinguish, even at night, any vessel which is meeting him, or any boat or other obstacle which lies in his course. The utility of this method of steering any vessel moving so fast as a steam-boat in a crowded river, even in day-time, need scarcely be insisted upon. But when the darkness of night is superadded, its advantages become still more obvious, and the plan ought certainly be adopted in every boat navigating the river.

In practice nothing can be more simple than the American mode of steering. The tiller is generally shipped abaft the rudder, in order to leave the quarter-deck quite free for the passengers. The tiller-ropes are then led, through blocks, on the quarter, and along small trunks, to the foremost part of the vessel, where they are again rove through blocks, and made to pass round the barrel of an ordinary steering-wheel, which being raised on a platform, to the height of 10 or 12 feet above the deck, and not far from the bows of the ship, the helmsman can distinctly see ob'ects before him, and by the proper movements of the wheel really avoid them.

It has been objected to this adaptation of the steering process that the weight and friction of the ropes would be so great that the proper degree of celerity of movement could not be commanded. But I have myself often, and with the greatest ease, steered boats as large as any of ours on the Mississippi and elsewhere, and I know that in other respects there exists no technical difficulties in the way of its universal adoption.

It is well known to professionel men that only one person can steer a ship properly in an intricate navigation; and even those who are not bred to the sea will understand that when a vessel going at the rate of many miles an hour is threading her way amongst shoals and boats, and numberless vessels, some meeting her, some crossing her, and some going in the same direction, there ought to be the most immediate communication between the sense of sight which is to distinguish these objects, the practised intellect which is to decide what is proper to be done, and the hand by which the regulating impulse is to be given to the guiding power. In other and plainer words, the helmsman ought to see what he is about, and not to act by the command of another.

In America the pilot himself is always at the wheel, and being raised up in the manner I have described, in the bow of the vessel, he can distinguish every obstacle, and know at once how best to steer clear of it. With us the matter is very different. The helmsman is fixed in the worst position possible, at the very sternmost part of the vessel, where he can see nothing—1st, owing to the want of elevation; 2d, to the intervention of the masts and the chimney; 3d, to that of the crowds of passengers and their carriages and luggage; and, 4th, to his being at the whole length of the ship further from the object to be avoided. To remedy this inconvenience what is done by us? The pilot stations himself on the top of one paddle-box, the captain on the other —both bad positions for seeing directly ahead. Only one of them ought to call out to the steersman what to do; but, as the responsibility is shared by both, each of them does in practice interfere, as I have often indeed heard contradictory orders

given by them respectively, while the bewildered helmsman knew not which way to turn the wheel. All this is bad enough in day-time, but I need not say how the confusion is worse confounded when it is dark, and when it is blowing and raining, and when several men have to be stationed along the deck to pass the word, as it is called, from the pilot to the helmsman, especially when the noise and bustle amongst the passengers hunting for their carpet-bags, increase the difficulty. My wonder accordingly has much more often been excited how these vessels get on at all, than that occasional accidents should occur.

I must add, that when the remedy is so simple, so cheap, and when it has been so extensively tried and found effective, it is altogether inexcusable in those who have the power to regulate such things that this plan has not been universally adopted in our river boats. I have taken the liberty repeatedly to endeavour by letters, by personal remonstrance, and by publications in the scientific journals of the day, to rouse the steam companies and captains to the importance of this point, but hitherto in vain. I venture now to hope that you will take it up, and assist me with your powerful pen in obliging those who have so many lives, and so much valuable property under their charge, to adopt at least one very obvious means of adding to the safety of their boats. It is indeed ridiculous to think, that while every method which ingenuity or skill can devise for adding to the speed, beauty, or comfort of these vessels, is at once eagerly adopted, a mode of securing their safety which ample experience has shown to be most efficacious should be treated with neglect.

The only objection 1 have ever heard urged against this plan of steering is, that when the vessel left the river and entered a rough sea, the steersman would be needlessly exposed in the bow, and that, in point of practice, he would be better if placed abaft, in the usual situation, than so far forward. In answer to this, it need only be said that nothing could be easier than to have another wheel and tiller ropes, fitted in the ordinary way, but the tiller not shipped till required, at which time the tiller used for the wheel in the bows might be unshipped or the ends of the tiller ropes cast off. In short, I think you will take my word for it that, technically considered, nothing can be more simple than this device, which, by placing the whole power of guiding the steam-vessel in the hands of the pilot (or of a man who stands by his side), will not only essentially add to her safety, and that of all the other boats on the river, but enable her speed to be greatly accelerated without incurring nearly so much risk as at present.

I shall only further remark, that I cannot help thinking that when lives are lost, or property destroyed on these occasions, a very serious responsibility falls on those who, having the means in their hands, stop short in the outfit of their vessels, in applying those methods of security which they, or those who have attended to the subject, know to be highly conducive to that object.

I remain your obedient humble servant,

BASIL HALL, Captain R. N.

Dunglass, Sept. 9.—*Times.*

[A striking illustration of the evil consequences of the existing state of things, will be found in the evidence given by the mate of the Monarch, who was at the wheel on the night of its collision with the Apollo, at a late inquest on the body of one of the sufferers. He says, " his business was *not* to keep a look out, but to attend to the orders of the captain and pilot * *. It was his duty to obey the orders he received, and not to ask the reason of them."—ED. M. M.]

NOTES AND NOTICES.

Bridge or Tunnel from Dover to Calais.—Mr. W. Coppett, an English engineer, is now on his road to Paris to lay before the French government a project for constructing a passage to cross dryshod from Calais to Dover. He at Havre explained his plan to the public. Mr. Coppett asks of France only one milliard, and as much from England. With this trifling sum, he will make cones like those employed at Cherbourg between fifty and sixty years ago. If the government does not approve of this system, he has in his pocket three or four others. For instance, he will make a tunnel under the sea from Dover to Calais, introducing from one end to the other cast-iron pipes 18 feet in diameter. This last mode of communication, according to Mr. Coppett, would cost only one milliard, to be paid in equal portions by both countries.—*Daily Paper.*

Filtering Machines and Infernal Machines.—A Frenchman, of the name of Alleume, has lately got into a pretty scrape by the ignorance of the Belgian police upon scientific matters. It appears that he invented a machine for filtering and clarifying water, which he took with him from Paris to Brussels for the purpose of procuring a patent. The police, however, mistaking his filtering, for an infernal machine, he was arrested and thrown into prison, as a conspirator either against the French or Belgian king. After a confinement of two months, he was acquitted, but interdicted from France, and ordered on board a vessel for England, where he arrived without money or friends. The Lord Mayor, to whom his case was made known, a few days ago, recommended him to represent his case to King Leopold, now in England.

Pulverized Cork Beds.—Will it be believed, that a mattress made of this material, weighing only 25 lbs., cannot be sunk by the weight of seven men? And that one or two persons might float on it in the midst of the ocean with as great security from drowning as if on board ship? Yet such is the fact, as demonstrated by experiment. The beds, cushions, &c. made of this material are more elastic, soft, and comfortable than those of the best hair, and never become matted.—*New Era.*

The Circular Cut.—Most persons remember their surprise, when children, at the great length of thong supplied from a small piece of leather by the spiral, or, as it is technically called, " the circular cut." The wonder was worked up into a fable, for Dido was said to have obtained the ground on which Carthage stood, by bargaining for as much as a bull's hide would enclose, and then cutting the hide into thongs, so as to take in a space far larger than the seller expected. This story has gone the round of the world. A friend of ours was informed in Persia, that the English obtained possession of Calcutta by the very same stratagem; the Chinese tell the story of one of their emperors; and the North American Indians believe that this was one of the countless artifices by which the white men deceived their brethren.—*Athenæum.*

Galvanic Telegraph.—The mode of making instantaneous communications by galvanic power has been put to the most decided test on the London and Birmingham Railway, under the direction of Professor Whetstone and Mr. Stephenson, the engineer. Four copper wires, acted upon at each end of the line at pleasure, by the agency of very simple galvanic communicators, have been laid down on the line of the railroad to the extent of 25 miles. They are enclosed in a strong covering of hemp, and each terminus is attached to a diagram, on which the twenty-four letters of the alphabet are engraved, in relative positions, with which the wires communicate, by the aid of moveable keys, and indicate the terms of the communication. The gentlemen to whom we have referred, we believe, are fully satisfied that communications to almost any extent may thus be made instantaneously by the agency of galvanism.—*True Sun.*

Gigantic Road Scraper.—A machine has just been introduced for scraping macadamised roads, and is now in use in Hyde Park, where it appears to do its work much more effectually, and in much less time, than the large hoe hitherto used for this purpose. The main objections to it are its weight, and that it appears to be only applicable to roads in good order, having a perfectly even surface.—*Morning Herald.*

Steam Navigation of the Jumna—India.—The Agra Ukhbar of February states, that a measure had been determined on by the supreme government, which was calculated to give impulse to the already fast advancing prosperity of Agra, and the permanent steam navigation of the Jumna. With a view to that object, three iron steam-boats, of the utmost possible buoyancy, had been ordered from Maudeslay and Co., and would probably within a year be plying on the Jumna. It is added, that this, with the presence of two boards now at Allahabad, and the influx of small capitalists, will give to Agra an European population, and activity unsurpassed by those of any city in the Mofussil. Other measures for the improvement of local trade had been submitted to the local government, such as the erection of wharfs, marking the channel of the Jumna, &c.

☞ British and Foreign Patents taken out with economy and despatch; Specifications, Disclaimers, and Amendments, prepared or revised; Caveats entered; and generally every Branch of Patent Business promptly transacted.

A complete list of Patents from the earliest period (15 Car. II. 1675,) to the present time may be examined. Fee 2s. 6d.; Clients, gratis.

LONDON: Printed and Published for the Proprietor, by W. A. Robertson, at the Mechanics' Magazine Office, No. 6, Peterborough-court, between 135 and 136, Fleet-street.—Sold by A. & W. Galignani, Rue Vivienne, Paris.

Mechanics' Magazine,

MUSEUM, REGISTER, JOURNAL, AND GAZETTE

No. 737.]   SATURDAY, SEPTEMBER 23, 1837.   [Price 3*d*.

ETTRICK'S IMPROVED MARINER'S STEERING COMPASS.

Fig. 1.

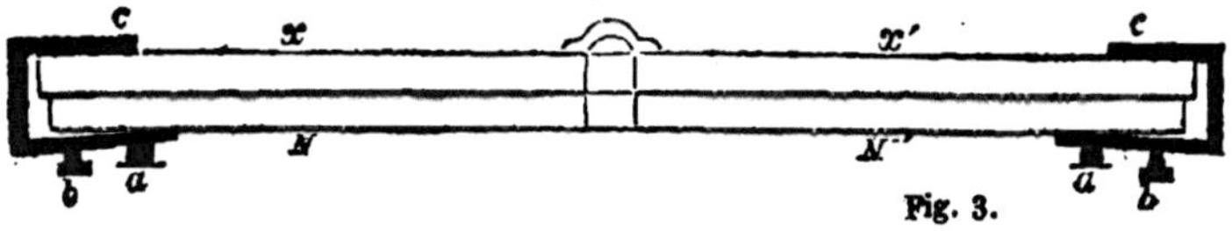

Fig. 2.

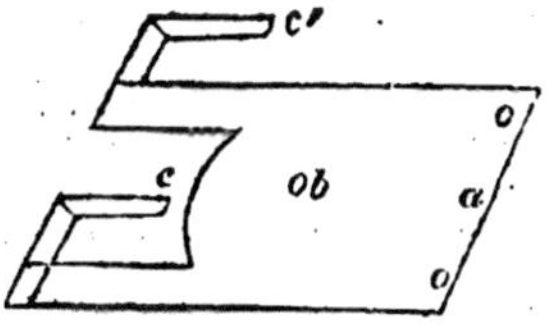

Fig. 3.

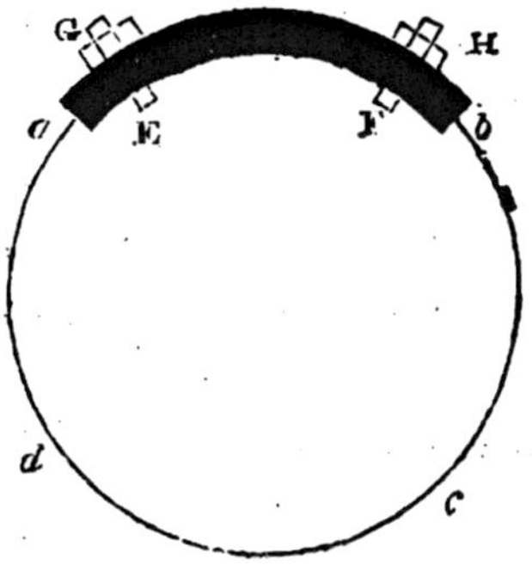

Fig. 4.

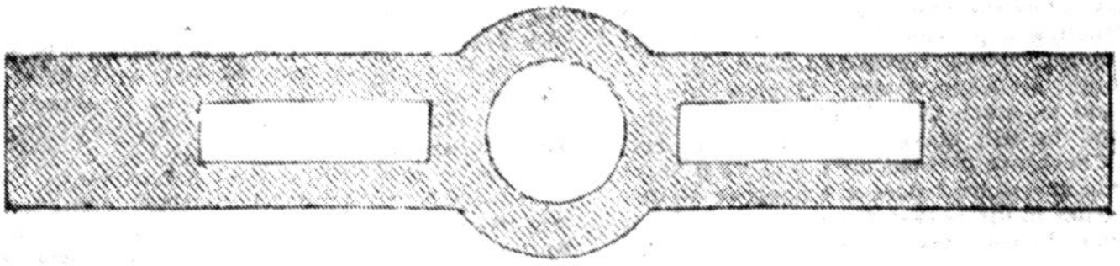

Fig. 5.

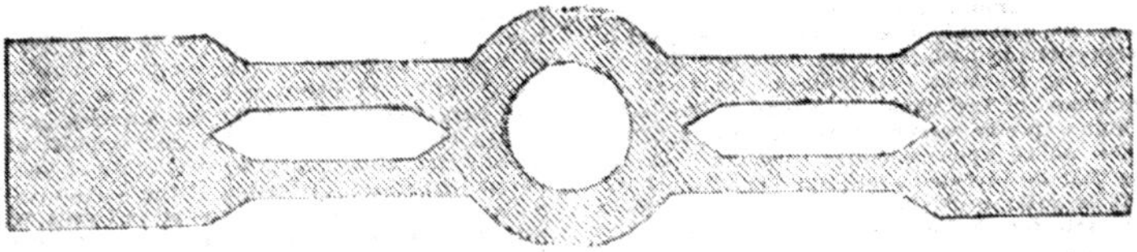

Fig. 6.

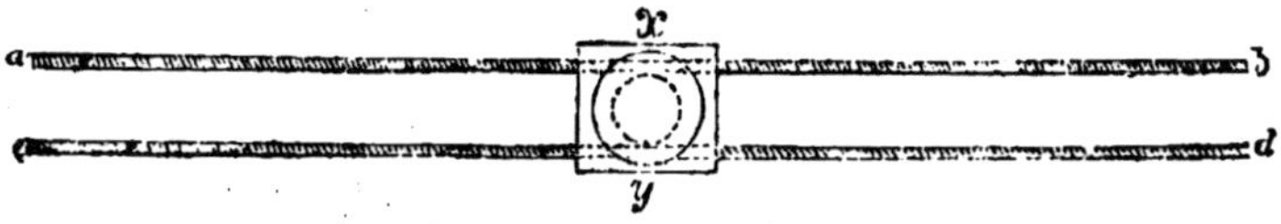

Fig. 7.

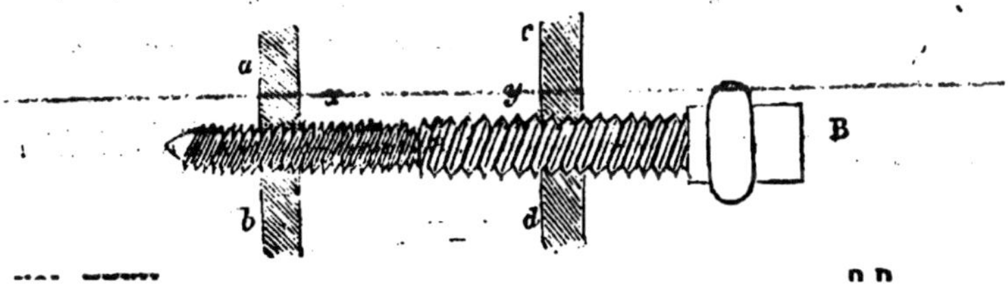

ETTRICK'S IMPROVED MARINER'S STEERING COMPASS.

Sir,—It always appeared surprising to me that the needle of the mariner's steering compass should be placed upon the card according to the cardinal points, whereby an error of many degrees, nay, some points, would be caused in the course of a vessel, if an allowance were not made for the magnetical variation by the commander, in laying down his course, or by the helmsman in steering; the latter of which must be liable to serious errors, not only because the person at the helm in merchantmen is generally an extremely ignorant man, but also because the points do not fall in with the degrees. It was a long time before I could satisfy myself that it was the universal practice with nautical men to have their cards placed as here stated; but upon inquiry, I find it general, not only in merchant vessels, but also in her Majesty's Navy; nor am I aware that it has been proposed to place them otherwise: probably the reason may be, that the variation is not stationary, and that it is not only altering annually, but is also different at different parts of the world, which would cause continual alterations of the card in respect to the needle; and according to the present method of fixing, it would be impossible. I propose, therefore, either to cut two circular grooves the length of the extreme variations of the compass in the card near to the division upon the outer edge and concentric with it, and fasten the card upon the needle by two brass screws, so as to allow of a free adjustment, or else by two light brass clamps with screws as shown in fig. 1,which method I prefer to the former one, because the card is not weakened by any holes.

It may be remarked, that the card is very securely fastened upon the needle by screwing down the agate cap tight, and that the only use of the lead clenches as at present used, or the brass clamps which are proposed to be used in lieu thereof, are merely for keeping down the outer edge or divisions close upon the needle, which would otherwise rise up and cause great errors in reading off the degrees or points upon the card. This end is thoroughly accomplished by the clamps a a′ fig. 1, which are fastened to the needle N N′ by the two screws or clenches as shown at a in fig. 2. To draw the points C C′ of the clamps upon the card x x′ in fig. 1, there are two screws b b′, which may be turned by hand, and are inserted into the under side of the clamps, and press against the needle N N′. It can scarcely be objected to these clamps, that their weight will preclude their general introduction, when it is stated, that with the clamps, their tightening screws need not weigh more than one-twentieth part of the weight of the needle with its card and cap. It may now be stated, that it is not proposed to correct the whole variation of the compass by this addition of two clamps, but merely the annual one, and that the local variation would be much better done by moving the line of direction upon the compass-box, called the "Lubber's Point" by mariners; which would answer the same purpose as moving the needle. This can be effected in a very simple manner, by merely applying a piece of sheet brass on the inside of the brass compass-box, and putting another piece on the outside of it; the two being secured together by two sliding screws,which work freely in long slits or grooves made in the side of the box (fig. 3) parallel to the upper edge of it. The inner, or first-mentioned piece of sheet brass, has "Lubber's Point" drawn upon it, and the outer piece of sheet brass, a line or Nonius engraved upon it, which, by applying close to a graduated segment of a circle of forty or fifty degrees, admits of great accuracy in the adjustment of "Lubber's Point." In the steering compass card now described, there is no tangent screw for accurately adjusting the Nonius, though therewould be very little difficulty in adding one, which would be a considerable improvement; because the Nonius would be retained by it in the place where it was set, without any tightening of the nuts.* As stated before, I propose to place the needle upon the card according to the variation at some particular place of note, as Greenwich Observatory, and that as soon as the mariner finds any deviation from that variation, by his azimuth compass, then to correct it by the "Lubber's Point." As an additional weight has been laid upon the needle by this alteration, I thought that it might be possible to lighten it, and still retain the same quantity of directive power. It appeared to me, that as the magnetism does

---

* Since this paper was written, a tangent screw has been added.

not circulate from pole to pole as formerly supposed, but is merely stationary at, or near, the ends or poles, that there could be no objection to the removal of part of the metal near the middle parts, only leaving sufficient near the poles, as three-fourths of an inch, or one inch as shown in fig. 4. It must be remarked, that this form is highly objectionable, if the magnetic fluid is distributed in the needle, as supposed by some. The greatest objection that I conceive can be made to a removal of part of the metal, is the liability of the magnets having a multiplicity of poles; but, by trial I do not find it to be so, and therefore it ought not to militate against the introduction of such form.

The metal might be removed from the middle parts of the needle, or from the outer edge, though probably it would be the best to take off equal quantities from both, as in fig. 5.

Whilst I am speaking of the forms of compass needles, it may not be amiss to mention one with wires or rods, which would answer extremely well for the steering compass; a b, and c d (fig. 6.), two steel wires passed through the brass cap x y, which is circular, as the present form, except the lower part of it, which is square, through which the steel rods are passed, and secured by screws, soft soder or otherwise. By this form, the rods are not pierced or damaged to form the centre of suspension.

As it is desirable to do away with all possible sources of error to the mariner, I would suggest that an error might be committed by the helmsman in respect of the cardinal points, in reading off the the course, and that this liability of error might be avoided by colouring the points upon the card after the following manner. Because the cardinal points have a more conspicuous appearance than the intermediate ones, north-west and north-east, south-west and south-east, I propose to mark the latter in preference to the former, and I consider that yellow, brown, red and green, would answer as well as any of the colours, because they can be distinguished from each other by candle light. In conceding this, I beg to say, that as it is proposed to put the needle upon the card so as to adjust it for the variation, it will be necessary, not only to have the card accurately balanced, after the needle is fixed or clenched upon it, but also to balance the

needle after being magnetised before the card is applied; for if that is not strictly attended to, the card will dip in different positions of the needle with respect to the cardinal points of the card. It is also to be remarked, that the same thing must be attended to in the case of the compass-box, with respect to the two plates of brass for adjusting "Lubber's Point." It might easily be corrected by applying a piece of brass on the light side of the box, which might be made adjustable, to or from the axes of the box by screws; but a more simple method would be to make the adjustment at once by the screw proposed to be applied for moving the plates of "Lubber's Point", as in fig. 7, where a b represents a stud in the sliding plate of "Lubber's Point," and c d a stud in the compass-box, and x y, the screw with a heavy handle B. The screw is double, and has a right and left-handed thread.

W. ETTRICK.

STEAM VOYAGE UP THE NIGER.

There is an old Spanish saying, "Time and I against any two," which was a prodigious favourite with Sir Walter Scott. Old Chronos is undoubtedly a most potent auxiliary, but there are another "two," which, when united, are capable of effecting no small wonders with very little assistance from "him of the scythe and hour-glass:"—to wit, British enterprise and the power of steam. One of the latest proofs of this position is afforded by the work which has just appeared, devoted to a narrative of the last expedition into the interior of Africa;[*] an expedition undertaken by a company of private merchants, the moment that the true course of the mysterious Niger became known to the world by the perseverance and good fortune of Richard Lander, and carried into effect by means of vessels propelled by steam, and one of them composed entirely of iron. Time works many marvels, doubtless, but he was an unimportant agent in this affair, since two or three years only passed by, from the discovery of the mouth of the Niger, ere our adventurers, aided by the mighty

[*] Narrative of an Expedition into the interior of Africa, by the river Niger, in the steam vessels Quorra and Alburkah, in 1832, 1833, and 1834. By Macgregor Laird, and R. A. K. Oldfield, surviving officers of the Expedition. In two volumes, London, 1837. Bentley, 8vo, pp. 467, 455..

genie, steam, whose aid they invoked, had penetrated into the bowels of a land which had never before, since the world began, witnessed the presence of a white man,—had subjugated to commerce the mighty stream whose waters had never borne on their bosom a single messenger of civilisation; and (to descend from the heroics) had bartered away Manchester calicoes and Sheffield cutlery for elephants' teeth and palm oil, in kingdoms, the knowledge of whose existence was but a thing of yesterday!

The expedition, which was fitted out from Liverpool, in 1832, in all its chief objects proved a total failure. One grand cause of this was, that excessive mortality, among the Europeans, which threatens to prove an insuperable barrier to the progress of *(white)* civilisation in Africa. The crews of the two steamers, the Quorra and the Alburkah, consisted, at the starting of the expedition, of forty individuals, all men in the very prime of life and strength: when it returned, three years only afterwards, the only survivors were *four* out of the *forty!* Lander himself, after escaping the pestilence, to which he had some reason to think he had become seasoned, fell beneath the blow of the assassin: of the rest, some were poisoned, but the great majority were laid low by the horrible fever of the coast, which, as if to warn them from the inhospitable shores of " the white man's grave," attacked them with the utmost fury on their very first arrival. Notwithstanding the ravages of death, however, the survivors persisted in the expedition, and succeeded in navigating the Niger as far up as the city of Rabbah, situated in a populous country in the very interior of the continent. Although successful in thus demonstrating that the great and untried difficulties of the nautical part of the task were not insurmountable, the expedition was nevertheless quite a failure in a mercantile point of view; it was expected that it would lead the way in opening a new and extensive market for the manufactures of Great Britain, and that in the process, the originators of the plan would inevitably amass a large fortune. The reverse, it appears, has proved the case; we are led to believe that the result of the experiment has been a heavy pecuniary loss, and that, whatever may be the ultimate prospects of British commerce on the banks of the Niger, the present expedition, has been to all concerned a disastrous one in every respect. The name of Africa is but too often the prelude to tales of misery and misfortune!

The " Narrative" of the voyage is composed of the separate journals of the only two officers of the expedition who reached their native country alive. Mr. Macgregor Laird, who was one of the original promoters of the enterprise, and had a pecuniary interest in its success, became, partly through the vacancies caused by death, one of the most active conductors of its fortunes: Mr. Oldfield was at first the junior, and very soon the only surgeon, and was likewise compelled by circumstances to take a very active part in the general details of the expedition. Mr. Oldfield's journal is by far the longer of the two, and embraces, perhaps, the greater number of points of interest. There is a striking family likeness, however, in all books of travels in Africa, and the journals of these gentlemen will not prove an exception. So far as they are occupied with the mere names of the barbarous villages lining the banks of the Niger, they can hardly be expected to prove of any considerable interest to the reader, or to convey any very valuable information. This kind of matter, forms unfortunately a large proportion of the whole : while the ever recurring accounts of the progress of disease and death among the whites, and of the horrid barbarities and wretched superstitions of the natives, combine to cast an aspect of the deepest gloom over a considerable section of the work. Nevertheless, all this shade is not entirely unrelieved by light ; we catch a glimpse now and then of some of the manners and customs of the country, which are not quite so revolting to the feelings as their treacherous poisonings, or their more open human sacrifices. It is pleasing to get a glance at the domestic life even of " the untutored African," and not always unprofitable to pay some attention to the "arts and manufactures" practised among the rudest and most unpolished of mankind. Unluckily, most travellers are not much in the way, and still less in the habit, of gratifying this kind of curiosity, and it is found much easier to swell out a volume with long details of the endless and pointless court ceremonies, or ridiculous mummeries of some black potentate or priest, than to paint the peculiarities of a country, its people and productions, with the precision, the fidelity, the *truth* of old DAM-PIER. We are afraid Mr. Oldfield is hardly an exception to the rule : the mass of his matter is of the regular staple, and so similar to that of many of his predecessors, that the reader might easily fall into the belief that he had before him a volume of Clapperton or Lander. His information on *interior* subjects is extremely scanty, and what there is, is not of the best quality. The talent for observation is probably one not very easily acquired, nor is it every one who sets out with the predetermination to see everything worth seeing, and note everything worth noting that will effect his object. Mr. Oldfield appears not to be of the number of the gifted few. The following specimen, will, we think, be sufficient to bear out our opinion: the reflection we have taken the liberty to mark with italics is certainly remarkable for its profundity. Such as it is, this extract embodies a considerable cantle of the information afforded by Mr. O. on the state of the useful arts in the interior of Africa. The scene is at Egga, a town of some importance; after a notice of a visit to the market-place, he goes on to observe—

" From the market I went to several yards and dye houses. In most of the dye-yards there were nine large pots, four feet by three, with larger ones stuck in the ground. The principle articles employed to obtain the dye were trona, and the bark of a tree resembling the *cortis cinchor*, and indigo in its natural state. The indigo appeared of a superior quality ; and *no doubt, if these people possessed better means,* they might *bring the art of dyeing to much greater perfection.* The sides of several of the vessels were perforated with holes to allow the liquor to run off ; and in the yard were tobes, cloths, and leather, undergoing the process of dyeing. The glazed appearance on the tobes, which have a coppery colour, is produced by rollers of wood pressed on them. On one side of the yard spinning and weaving were going forward, the spinning walk being thirty yards long. The process of weaving is similar to what I have before observed in Africa : it is conducted by one man, who has an instrument something like our shuttle, which he runs through the threads perpendicularly, instead of horizontally, as is the case with our weavers. The widths are not more than three or four inches. Their cotton is exceedingly fine, but I believe there is little of it cultivated. * * * * At a short distance from the Mallam's, I heard some smiths at work, and took an opportunity as I passed of inspecting the forge. There were two fires, with a wall about four feet high. The fires were placed on the inner side of the wall, while a boy was working two goats' skins sewed together, one end terminating in a point. This rude substitute for bellows was inserted in an aperture in the wall which led to the fire, and was worked by a little boy, who appeared to understand his office very well. There were two smiths at work making axes, iron braces, and nails for canoes ! Their hammers were large pieces of iron, while stones supplied the place of anvils, and charcoal was used for the fire. I also visited a manufactory where upwards of twelve persons were employed in making wooden spoons."—vol. ii, page 112.

Mr. Laird, like his colleague, pays little attention to matters not immediately connected with the object of the expedition, but it may not be irrelevant to quote a passage or two from his department, relating to a subject which has heretofore been noticed in our pages,— the " free negro colony of Liberia," an establishment set on foot by the Americans with a view of perpetuating the system of slavery in their land of perfect freedom, by " draining off " the superabundant " free coloured population," and so preserving their *property* from the contamination of contact with men of their own hue in a state of liberty (if a state of unceasing contumely and persecution can so be called). It may be recollected, that the Americans carried their philanthropy to such a height, that a year or two ago they actually sent a sort of missionary to England to solicit subscriptions in aid of their righteous cause, and among the many false representations by which the honourable gentleman, entrusted with the mission, endeavoured to get his fingers into the pockets of John Bull, was one to the effect that Liberia was in the most flourishing possible condition, and had already done wonders in civilising the barbarous natives in its neighbourhood. According to his statements, if they had but money enough, the Liberians would soon civilise Africa from one end to the other! Let us see what an unprejudiced observer has to say as to the system pursued in peopling the colony, and the much-vaunted efforts of its inhabitants for the regeneration of their *native* country,—as the American slave-owner delights to call it, albeit, all the Liberian

colonists are his own fellow countrymen—

" It may be said that free negroes are not
forced to go to Liberia, and, perhaps actual
force may not have been, and may not be,
resorted to ;—but what is the case ? First,
their lives are rendered miserable by a continued series of petty oppressions, and then,
Liberia is held out to them as a sort of paradise of plenty and freedom, where no white
man is to be allowed to tyrannise or op-
press. An intelligent mulatto said to me
on my questioning him off the subject, ' it
was not exactly kidnapping, but we were
inveigled away under false pretences.'

" As to civilising Africa by means of
Liberia, it is well known, that from the time
the colony was first established it was constantly at war with the natives, until their
partial extermination left the strangers in
peaceable possession. It is true, they assert
that they bought the ground with the right
of extension ; but this only adds hypocrisy
to cruelty.

" As to the commercial situation of the
colony, the Americans have certainly not
shown their usual acuteness in the choice of
natural advantages : instead of fixing their
head quarters at the mouth of some considerable river, they have taken possession
of the most unhealthy and sterile part of
the coast, with no inlet into the interior ;
the consequence of which is, that they are
dependent on the uncivilized negroes on the
Grain coast for their supplies of food. It appears questionable whether Liberia will ever
raise food sufficient for a very moderate population, and it certainly never can export
any quantity of tropical produce. During
the time we remained in the river St. Paul,
our vessels were crowded by respectable
intelligent mulattoes, all of whom, with the
exception of the coloured editor of the
Liberia Gazette, and one or two others in
the pay of the society by whom they are
sent from America, complained bitterly of
the deceit that had been practised towards
them, and of the privations under which
they were then suffering. It was often a
source of regret to me that I had not ac-
ceded to their wishes, and taken some of
them on board our vessels, as they were
fine intelligent men, who would have been
invaluable to us in the interior."—vol. i,
page 41.

Such is the Liberia, which, in the
speeches of the itinerant ambassador of
slavery and intolerance, burst on the delighted gaze as a perfect picture of Paradise on earth. What with John Bull's
better knowledge of the motives of the
humane originators of the " American
Colonization Society," and the reports
on the actual state of affairs, of eye-wit-
nesses like Mr. Laird, we are sadly afraid
that England will never have the honour
of another visit from Mr. Elliott Cresson.
The amount of his collections would not
pay for the voyage over !

STEAM NAVIGATION TO AMERICA AND INDIA.

Sir,—Since my communication which
you inserted in No. 733, upon the subject of steam navigation to India, I have
been informed that the " Atalanta" sailed
again from Bombay on special service,
with 300 troops on board, on the next
day but one after her arrival at that port ;
thus proving the excellence of her machinery, and the possibility of conti-
nuously working a steam engine for a
considerable period without injury. It
places the reasonings of Dr. Lardner on
this point in a very questionable shape,
and affords us humble mechanics something like a reasonable hope that the
passage to New York may be accomplished in one trip, although Dr. Lardner has pronounced it to be next to impossible.

The steam ship called the " Great
Western" has arrived in the river Thames
for the purpose of receiving her engines.
She was built at Bristol by Mr. Pattison,
and measures about 1320 tons, old
tonnage ; when first launched she drew
eight feet eight inches water abaft, and
seven feet eight inches water forward ;
with 600 tons of coals on board, she
draws eleven feet three inches water in
the river Thames, or about eleven feet at
sea, which shows that the displacement
of the first two feet four inches above
the light water line, is equal to 600 tons,
and as she may be safely put down to fifteen feet water, the next four feet will
displace, at least, 1200 tons more, making
her total displacement 1800 tons at the
least, which may be thus distributed : 500
tons for machinery, 800 tons for fuel,
and the remaining 500 tons for additional
stores, merchandise and passengers. She
has now the greater part of her stores
on board, as cables, anchors, sails, &c.
which of course leaves nearly the whole
500 tons for merchandise and passengers.

She is fitting up in a very commodious manner for the convenience of
passengers. The saloon will be very
lofty and airy, and the state rooms (sleep-
ing cabins) are large and convenient.
The paddle or main beams are formed

of four pieces of timber, each twelve or thirteen inches square, confined together at the ends, and separated to the distance of six or seven inches in the middle of their length on the same principle as the bow beams of Mr. Smart.

Her size, when seen by herself, does not appear so great as it really is, and it is only when on board, or seen alongside other vessels, whose size is known, that her magnitude is appreciated. She is nearly as long as the large steam vessel "Victoria," now building in the river Thames, but is not so wide, nor so deep as that ship.

The East Indian Government have purchased another steam ship, the "Waterford," to send out to India. It is said that she is to be called the "Semiramis." It is matter of regret, that a vessel expressly built for the conveyance of merchandise should have been purchased for this purpose;—it is not giving the trial of steam communication with India a fair chance. For, although well adapted for the purpose for which she was built, she is evidently not suitable for a steam frigate or a packet. One would have thought, that with the practical experience which the East India Company must possess, as to the rapid destruction of timber from the effects of climate, &c. in their Indian Possessions, they would have selected a vessel built with the most durable materials to send out, and not one in which red pine is so largely used as in the "Waterford."

Advices have been received from the "Berenice" (the last steamer dispatched by the Hon. East India Company) from which it appears that her progress has been more rapid than that of the "Atalanta" during the same part of the voyage.

I am, Sir, yours, &c.
GEORGE BAYLEY.
London, September 11, 1837.

HINTS FOR NEW MANUFACTURES—
LAY FIGURES, STEEL VIOLIN BOWS,
LOCOMOTIVE ENGINE CHIMNEYS,
AND SPARK-ARRESTERS.

Sir,—As you considered my communication on the hydraulic pendulum not unworthy of insertion in your valuable pages, perhaps the present suggestions may be interesting to some of your readers. I would suggest to those whom it may concern two articles of foreign production, the manufacture of which, has not, I believe, as yet, been attempted in England.

First, in point of importance, both in regard to the talented set of artists, whom the subject interests as consumers, and in regard to cost, which point is the most interesting to the manufacturers, I would mention the lay figures or mannequins which, for the information of many of your readers who may not be aware of their use, it were as well to describe. The said lay-figures are imitations of the human form, generally of the natural size, having their frame work made of wood, finished at the joints with such mechanical contrivances as allow of the limbs being made to imitate the articulation of the human frame, and of being placed in any position the painter may wish, whereon to arrange such drapery or dresses as the country, era, or subject of his painting may render necessary. The figures are fitted up, if I may be allowed so to express myself, by rolls of cloth representing the muscles and flesh, and covered with silk. The price, including duty and carriage from Paris is, as I understand, from thirty to thirty-five pounds.

2dly, I would mention the violin and violincello bows made of steel, also of French production, which are much in use among many eminent musicians.

Surely England is pre-eminent in all manufactures in steel, and need not fear competition in this branch of industry, if some of her talented manufacturers thought it worth their while to apply their energies to the subject. The price of steel bows in England is from 1l. 10s. to 2l. 10s.

Lastly, in reference to a subject of paramount importance, viz., the prevention of sparks issuing from locomotives: would not the adoption of a spiral chimney favour the conversion of the rotary motion, thus given to the smoke and steam, into a vertical motion to be continued to a short distance from the highest point of the chimney by a horizontal pipe, after which, the lower half of such pipe might be cut away for a certain length, and a tray, containing wet sponges or water might be suspended beneath, wherein the ignited particles of fuel would fall by their natural gravity?

The spiral chimney would also allow of the height being reduced, so that the usual gauze hood might be without inconvenience considerably enlarged, in which case the sum of the apertures, even of a finer gauze than is at present employed would present an equally free,

or even freer exit to the smoke and steam, according to the dimensions of the hood employed,

Your must obedient servent,
R. J. IREMONGER.

APPENDIX TO A PAPER ON THE CONJUNCTION OF THE SUN, MOON, PLANETS, ETC. BY J. UTTING, C. E.

(Vide *Mechanics' Magazine*, vol. xxvi, p. 378.)

Sir,—Having entered into an investigation of the motion of the equinoxial points, I find, that according to La Place (Systeme du Monde, 4th edit., 1813, page 300), the solar, or tropical year is shorter at the present time by 13 sec. French, or 11.232 sec. English, than it was in the time of Hipparchus; or about 1950 years from the publication of La Place's Systeme du Monde. But the accelerating and retarding motions in the planetary system are not uniform; neither indeed can this be the case, or they could never change from a retarding to an accelerating motion; and it is very probable that for four or five centuries on either side of the maximum or minimum point, no difference would be discovered in the

length of the solar year by the best observations.

Now, half a period of the precession is about 12545 years, and the time since Hipparchus, about 1950 years; hence

$$\frac{12545 \times 11.232 \text{ sec.}}{1950 \text{ years}} = 72.26^*,$$

the mean diminution or acceleration of the solar year. Consequently, in 12545 years, or half a revolution of the equinoxial points, the year would be shorter or longer alternately by about 72¼ sec., which would cause an increase or decrease in the secular precession of the equinoxes, of 4′ 56″. 8, according with the present diminution of the tropical year.

The mean sec. prec. stated in vol. xxvi, p. 372...... 1° 26′ 5″
The sec. prec. at the present time................ 1 23 30

Difference at the present time below the mean...... 0   2 35

Now, supposing that the diminution of the solar year has nearly approached its limit, the double of the above difference, or 2′ 35″ × 2 = 5′ 10″, which will be the total variation; differing from the above result (4′ 56″. 8) by about 13 sec. only! It is very probable, however, that the solar year is not at the present time arrived at its minimum: neither are we certain that the mean diminution of the solar year, as above stated, is equal to the mean diminution for its whole period. Thus, I have, I presume, sufficiently established the probability that ten revolutions of the equinoxial points are performed in 250904 solar, or 250894 siderial years.

The reason why I did not hit upon this before, was in consequence of my taking the diminution of the solar year from Mr. Bailey's Tables = 4.21 sec., which gave the sec. prec. for half the period of the equinoxes = 1′ 51″ only: whereas, the difference between my mean prec. above stated, and the precession at the present time, was 2′ 35″, which doubled, gives 5′ 10″; being nearly three

times greater than that given by the diminution of the solar year, according to Mr. Bailey's statement. It is also given wrong in Mr. Pond's translation of La Place's Systeme du Monde. La Place, in former editions of this work, stated it at 12 sec.; in Mr. Pond's translation it is 3″. 8. It appears that Mr. Bailey, as well as Mr. Pond, has taken them as seconds of a degree, instead of seconds of time, and La Place's numbers, were both, in consequence, reduced incorrectly. According to the French division of time, 10 hours make a day, 100 minutes one hour, and 100 seconds one minute. The siderial year is expressed thus: in days and decimals = 365.256384. In seconds thus: 36525638.″4†, or 365 days 2 hours 56 minutes 38.4 seconds, so that in the French notation, no reduction is necessary to convert days and decimals into hours, minutes, &c.; as this is effected by merely pointing off one place for the hours, and two places each for the mi-

* According to La Place, this diminution may amount to 120 sec.; or 103.68 sec., English.
† Vide Systeme du Monde, 4th edit., page 216.

nutes and seconds. It is to be regretted, that this system is not universally adopted, both as to time and angular measurements : thus, the diameter of a circle being unity, its circumference is 3.1415926535, &c., or would be equal to 314° 15' 92". 6535. &c. But the sacrifice of the very valuable instruments, and astronomical and mathematical tables now in use, will, in all probability prevent its being adopted. This division of the circle, was, if I recollect right, proposed by the late Dr. Hutton.

Periods of the moon's longitude, perihelia, and node ; the satellites of Jupiter, Saturn, and Uranus ; the sun's longitude, and perihelia, the obliquity of the ecliptic, and last, not least, the precession of the equinoxial points, as stated in my paper (vol. xxvi, p. 378), all agree remarkably well, with modern observations. Now, presuming that the secular variations are positive or negative at the present time ; this does not at all militate against the probability of the conjunction taking place ; as they may assume an opposite character before the period is half terminated.

There is no deviation in my Tables from the most correct statements of the elements of the planetary system at the present time ; but what may be compensated by the secular inequalities of the planetary motions.

I am, Sir, yours, &c.
                    J. UTTING.
Lynn Regis, September 8, 1837.

VENTILATION BY SPIRAL SCREWS.—
WOODHOUSE'S ROTARY ENGINE.

Sir,—Permit the " Infant Schoolmaster " to say a word to Nautilus. I am informed that Capt. Ericsson has patented a propeller for steam-boats, the acting part of which is very similar in shape to that of my ventilator, and that a speed of six or seven miles per hour has been therewith obtained. If this be true, Nautilus's objection of course falls to the ground. The propeller, I should say, is wholly immersed in water, as the ventilator is in air. Why should not such a screw have the same effect upon the fluid in which it is immersed, as an ordinary one has upon its nut ? The true impediment to success in the case of air, I take to be, that at the necessary velocity, the friction of the air against the thread of the screw is too great to permit the entrance of so subtle a fluid ; while

density of water allows sufficient hold to be taken of it (so to speak) to produce a visible effect, Some air does undoubtedly find its way through, and on diminishing the number of threads, I found the effect to be a little increased, which confirms my opinion.

With regard to Mr. Woodhouse's engine, my expression " exact counterpart" was perhaps too strong, as it is certainly more simple in its parts, and probably more uniform in its action, than Galloway's ; but I was forcibly struck by the main feature of the eccentric guide and radial valves being common to both, and which I did not remember to have seen in any other engine. As to the central introduction of steam, there is no other way of introducing it if the cylinder revolves; indeed, Mr. Woodhouse disclaims the invention of this method.

Your obedient servant,
                    J. R.
London, 16th September, 1837.

SOLUTION OF A TOWN TEACHER'S ALGEBRAIC QUESTION, No. 737. BY H. R. B., MANSION - HOUSE, HAMMERSMITH.

Given $\begin{cases} x\,y - a\,x + n\,y \\ y^2 - x^2 = n^2 \end{cases}$ To find x and y.

From the first equation we have $x = \dfrac{n\,y}{y-a}$; hence, by substitution $y^2 - \dfrac{n^2\,y^2}{(y-a)^2} = n^2$. Clearing of fractions, and transposing $y^4 - 2\,a\,y^3 + a^2\,y^2 - 2\,n^2\,y^2 + 2\,a\,n^2\,y = a^2\,n^2$; adding n^4 to both sides : $y^4 - 2\,a\,y^3 + a^2\,y^2 - 2\,n^2\,y^2 + 2\,a\,n^2\,y + y^4 = n^2\,(a^2 + n^2)$. Extracting the root $y^2 - a\,y - n^2 = n\,\sqrt{a^2 + n^2}$; therefore $y^2 - a\,y = n\,(\sqrt{a^2 + n^2} + n)$. Complete the square $y^2 - a\,y + \dfrac{a^2}{4} = n\,(\sqrt{a^2 + n^2}$

$+ n) + \dfrac{a^2}{4}$ Extract the root :—

$$y - \frac{a}{2} = \sqrt{\,n\,(\sqrt{a^2 + n^2} + n) + \frac{a^2}{4}}$$

$$y = \frac{a}{2} + \sqrt{\,n\,(\sqrt{a^2 + n^2} + n) + \frac{a^2}{4}}$$

Or assuming $\sqrt{a^2 + n^2} = d$,

$$y = \frac{a}{2} + \sqrt{\,n\,(d + n) + \frac{a^2}{4}}$$

By a similar process we find :—

$$x = \frac{n + d}{2} + \sqrt{\left(\frac{n + d}{2}\right)^2 - n^2}$$

                    H. R. B.
September 5, 1837.

DURABILITY OF VARIOUS KINDS OF WOOD.

(From the *Nautical Magazine*).

The following are the particulars of experiments made on several kinds of wood, 1⅛ inch square, and 2 feet long, placed vertically in the ground, and about 1 foot 6 inches exposed to the atmosphere, on the 1st of January, 1831; examined at two different times, viz., the 8th May, 1833, and and the 24th February, 1836:—

Species of Wood.	Remarks, 8th May, 1833.	Remarks, 24th February, 1836.
English Oak	Much decayed and diminished in weight.	Very much decayed, especially those of open grain.
Italian Oak	Good, but decay had commenced on surface.	Do. do. rather less than the English.
Adriatic Oak	Very much decayed.	Very much decayed, excepting one piece, very good.
Leaf or Live Oak	Very good.	Three much decayed, the rest tolerable.
Canada White Oak	Very much decayed.	Very bad and rotten.
Memel do.	Ditto.	Ditto.
Dantzic do.	Ditto.	Exceedingly bad.
Mahogany hard	Good.	Tolerably good.
Do. soft	Much decayed.	Very bad, totally decayed.
Libanus Cedar	Good.	Tolerably good.
Pencil Cedar	Very good.	All very good, as put in the ground.
African, No. 1	Very good.	A little decayed, and inclined to doat; better than English oak.
African, No. 2	Very good.	Worse than No. 1.
Teak, heavy	Very good.	Rather soft, but good.
Teak, light	Good.	Soft ¼, but good.
Teak, part of Hasting's mizen-mast	Good.	Soft ¼, the rest indifferent.
Fir, Dantzic	Much decayed.	Very much decayed, rotten all through.
Fir, Riga	Much decayed.	As bad as the Dantzic.
Fir, Memel	Much decayed.	Very bad, rotten.
Fir, Red Pine	Much decayed.	Very rotten, much like the Dantzic and Riga.
Fir, Yellow Pine	Very much decayed.	Very rotten.
Do. Virginia Pine	Decayed.	Very rotten.
Do. Pitch Pine, heavy	Decayed ⅛ of an inch, the rest good.	Decayed ⅛ of an inch, the rest tolerably good.
Do. do. light	Very rotten.	Very rotten.
Polish Larch	Decayed ¼ in the surface, and lost in weight.	Decayed ¼, the rest a little decayed.
Scotch do. Treenails	Surface ¼ in. decayed and brittle.	Surface ⅛ in. decayed, the rest brittle.
English Elm	Very rotten.	All rotten.
Canada rock do.	Ditto.	Rotten.
American ash	Ditto.	Ditto.
Locust Treenails	Good and retained their weight.	⅛ in. rotten, the rest as sound as when put in the ground.
Scotch Larch do.	Surface ¼ decayed, and very brittle.	¼ in. rotten, the rest brittle.
Stinkwood dark col.	Surface not decayed, but very brittle.	This piece was misplaced.
Cowdie	Surface ¼ decayed, and very brittle.	Rotten.
Stinkwood light col.	Surface ⅛ decayed, and brittle.	Rotten.
Poonah.	Surface a little decayed, and become light.	Surface ⅛ decayed, the rest good, better than African.

Note.—Riga preferable to all the Fir, and Dantzic next.

GREENHOUSES AND CONSERVATORIES.

(From Loudon's *Suburban Gardener*, No. III.).

The custom of rearing plants in pots, and keeping them in the windows of dwelling-houses, is of great antiquity; though it is only in modern times, and chiefly since the days of Louis XIV, that a house for plants has become a conspicuous feature in the elevation of a mansion. The most ancient description of plant-house is what is called an orangery; in which, formerly, orange trees, planted in large boxes or tubs, were kept during the winter, and set out of doors during the summer, season. Such houses almost always fronted the south; the back wall was of masonry, the roof covered with slates, tiles, or lead, and the front contained a range of large glass windows. Beneath the floor there was sometimes a flue for heating; and at other times this purpose was effected by means of German stoves. As the object of the orangery was merely to keep the trees from the frost, and they were not expected to grow while in the house, this description of building suited them perfectly; and it might still be very properly added to a mansion, provided no other plants were placed in it than orange trees, and a few other evergreen trees or shrubs, and succulent plants; such as myrtles, olives, cactuses, agaves, aloes, &c. Such houses, however, are totally unfit for plants which grow or flower in the winter season; such as camellias, heaths, acacias, and all those Cape and Australian trees and shrubs which, by their flowers and newly produced foliage, constitute the great charm of British conservatories during the winter months. To render an orangery fit for keeping such plants, it is necessary that the roof should be entirely of glazed frames, to admit perpendicular light, without which no plant in a growing state can thrive; and when this is the case according to the common usage of gardeners, the building is no longer called an orangery, but a conservatory, a word which appears to have been first applied to plant-houses by Evelyn, in his Calendarium. A further alteration or improvement in such houses consists in forming beds of earth in the floor, and planting the trees and shrubs in them, instead of keeping them in tubs and boxes. This, indeed, is the description of the modern conservatory, which is almost the only kind of plant-house now attached to first-rate mansions. The term green-house is now generally confined by gardeners to houses having glass roofs, which are kept at the same temperature as the orangery or conservatory, but where the plants are grown in pots, which are usually small, and elevated upon stages, so as to bring them at

once near the light and near the eye of the spectator. The characteristic of a conservatory is, that it grows a few plants to a large size, and so as to produce scenery of a magnificent exotic aspect; while that of a green-house is, that it produces a great many different kinds of plants, of small size, which may be considered as merely living botanical specimens of exotics. The green-house is, consequently, much better adapted for the smallest description of suburban residences than the conservatory; and a modification of the green-house, which may be called a plant cabinet, or cabinet green-house, in which a few choice plants are kept, and always taken away and renewed as they begin to fade, is, perhaps, still more appropriate. What are called plant-stoves, tropical plant-houses, or hot-houses, in the proper sense of the word, are unfit for being attached to dwelling-houses, from the great heat and moisture required to render their atmosphere fit for the plants of hot climates.

The enjoyments afforded by a green-house, however small, to the female part of the family are very considerable; and, where there are children, these enjoyments may be mingled with useful instruction, by teaching them in it the names and nature of plants, and their culture and management at seasons, or during weather when it cannot be done out of doors. A green-house also affords exercise, in shifting, potting, tying up, pruning, &c., in cold and wet weather, and at periods of the year when nothing can be done in the open garden. At the same time that we recommend a green-house, it is proper to state that, where the mistress of the house has not a taste for plants, and and is not in the habit of working among them herself; and where this taste does not exist in any part of the family, and no gardener is kept, a green-house is in danger of becoming a nuisance, rather than an ornamental appendage. In such a case, where it is determined to produce the effect of a green-house, for the sake of fashion, or the reputation of being fond of plants, or some similar motive, the best mode is to engage with the nearest nurseryman or florist to keep the green-house furnished with plants, at so much per annum or per month. By this means, it will always look well; but, as none of the beauty which it presents will be the result of the care and attention of any part of the family, of course the enjoyment derived from it cannot be anything like so great as where the contrary is the case. * *

In whatever manner a green-house, or plant-house of any description, is attached to a house, means ought always to be provided for warming, ventilating, and watering the plant-house, altogether independently of the dwelling-house; for few things are more disagreeable and unwholesome to human beings, as well as injurious to furniture, and the walls of the room, than the close damp effluvia of the earth, water, and plants of a conservatory. For this reason, the plants grown in conservatories immediately attached to drawingrooms should be such as are natives of very dry climates (for example, the Cape of Good Hope, Australia, &c.), and, consequently, require very little water; and the gardener should contrive to give his his waterings either late in the evenings, or very early in the mornings, when there is no chance of the conservatory being in use by the family. Previously to the hour when it is expected the family will walk in the conservatory, it ought to be thoroughly ventilated, so as to carry off the damp; and the surface of the ground ought never to be kept very moist, in order to produce as little evaporation from it is as possible.

In large houses, few objects connected with them produce a more splendid effect, or contribute more to luxurious enjoyment during winter, than a large well kept conservatory. It should be of considerable length and breadth; at least twice the length of the drawingroom, and broad rather than narrow; with a glazed roof, and with both sides glazed, if the length is in the direction of south and north; but with a wall on the north side, if it is in the direction of east and west. It should be separated from the drawingroom by glass doors or windows, opening down to the floors; the piers between these ought to be as slender as is consistent with strength, and the style of architecture of the house; while the glass should be in very large plates, and, if possible, one plate only to each window or door, so as to give the idea of the drawingroom and conservatory forming but one room. A drawingroom, in the form of a pentagon or an octagon, projecting from the body of the dwelling-house, might be enclosed, on every side but that on which it is entered from the house, by a conservatory; and this, if 100 feet deep, and from 30 feet to 40 feet in height, with a broad walk radiating from the window in the centre of each of the outer sides of the drawingroom, would render the allusion to a summer-house in an Eastern garden complete. Some of the paths might be covered with gravel, and others with turf, the gravel being kept perfectly smooth and firm by frequent rolling, so that no part of it might stick to the shoes, and be carried into the drawingroom. It order that the gravel paths may be kept perfectly dry, the flues and hot-water pipes by which the house is heated should be carried under them; and, to contribute to the same end, when the plants are watered with the syringe, the walks should be covered with canvass. While this attention to dryness would contribute to the enjoyment derived from the conservatory in the winter season, a certain kind of attention to moisture might be made to contribute equally to enjoyment during the spring and summer months. What we propose is to be effected by producing artificial rain, in the manner invented, successfully carried into execution, and practised for the last ten years, by Messrs. Loddiges, in their magnificent palm-house at Hackney. The mode by which artificial rain is produced is both simple and unexpensive, requiring merely that lead pipes should be conducted horizontally close under the glass roof, pierced with small holes, and supplied from a cistern at a higher level. The holes may be pierced in the pipe with a common sewing-needle; and the distance of the pipes from one another may be from 8 feet to 12 feet, according to the height of the roof above the heads of the plants. The water can be turned on and off such pipes at pleasure, by stop-cocks properly placed.* * In warm summer evenings, when the weather is dry and sultry without, to sit in a drawingroom, and see and hear a shower falling in the conservatory, cannot fail to impart a sensation of refreshing coolness, as delightful to the spectator as it is invigorating to the foliage and roots of the plants. In the case of all conservatories which are immediately connected with the drawingroom, a superior gardener ought to be kept, with abundance of assistance; otherwise the plants cannot be maintained in that high degree of order and keeping which is essential to the effect of this appendage, and without which, as we have already observed, it becomes a nuisance, great in proportion to its pretensions.

For this reason, where a first-rate gardener, and abundance of hands, are not kept, we would recommend the conservatory to be separated from the drawingroom by a lobby; in which there should be openings, so arranged as to secure a constant ventilation: or it may be connected with the house by means of a corridor, or other covered way; in which case, however, it is seldom completely seen from the drawingroom; and, consequently, a great luxury of the conservatory, that of looking down its main walk from the drawingroom window, and feeling as if we were sitting in a bower in an Eastern garden, is lost.

The slope of the roof ought never to be less than 45°; and, in order that this slope may not be carried so high as to be too conspicuous over the parapets, the roof of every wide house ought to be in several spans, with wide gutters between. This is beautifully exemplified in the magnificent conservatories at the Grange, of which a section will be found in the first volume of the Gardener's Magazine; and also in that at Woollaton Hall, near Nottingham; and in several other conservatories put up in different places by Messrs. Clark and Jones, of Lionel Street, Birmingham; and Messrs. Cottam and Hallen, of Winsley Street, London.

PERPETUAL MOTION.

Two classes of persons are inveigled into this hopeless quest: the first is the projector,—generally a man who can handle tools, and who is gifted with some small power of invention,—a faculty,—as Mr. Babbage justly. observes, by no means rare, and of little use unless coupled with some knowledge of what others have done before him. Of the inventions already made,—of the experiments which have been tried and have failed,—our projector is usually profoundly ignorant. What are called the laws of mechanics, namely, general truths which were established by the observations of scientific men in times past, and which are now admitted by all who take the trouble to investigate them, he has either never heard of, or chooses to set at nought without inquiry. The other class is that which finds capital. The projector, having perhaps exhausted his own funds, takes his scheme to some person who has a little money to spare, and dazzles him with the prospects of sudden and splendid wealth; little by little he is drawn into expenses which neither of them perhaps had anticipated. Failure after failure ensues, but still all is to be right at last. The fear of ridicule,—the necessity for retrieving, the one his capital, the other his credit,—these motives carry them on till the ruin of both puts a termination to their folly.

Unhappily, however, the stage is quickly occupied by other adventurers, profiting nothing by the fate of their precursors; and yet one would think that a very slight consideration of the subject would be sufficient to shew the absurdity of the undertaking. What is the object aimed at? Is it to make a machine which, being once set in motion, shall go on without stopping until it is worn out? Every person engaged in the pursuit of the perpetual motion would perhaps accept this as a true statement of the object in view. Yet nothing is more easy than to make such a machine. There are from ten to twenty of them at work at this moment on the Rhine, opposite Mayence. These are water-mills in boats, which are moored in a certain part of the river; and,

as the Rhine is never dry, these mills, which are simple in their construction, would go on for years,—go on, indeed, until they were worn out. But if this instance were mentioned, the projector would perceive that the statement of his object was imperfect. It must run thus:—a machine which, being set in motion, shall go on till worn out without any power being employed to keep it in motion.

Probably few persons who embark in such a project sit down beforehand to consider thoroughly what it is they are about to undertake, otherwise it could hardly require much knowledge of mechanics to see the impossibility of constructing such a machine. Take as many shafts, wheels, pulleys, and springs as you please; if you throw them in a heap in the corner of your room, you do not expect them to move; it is only when put together that the wildest enthusiast expects them to be endowed with the power of self-movement; nor then unless the machine is set going. I never heard of a projector who expected his engine to set off the moment the last nail was driven, or instantly on the last stroke of the file. And why not? A machine that would continue to go of itself would begin of itself. No machine can be made which has not some friction, which, however slight, would in a short time exhaust any power that could have been employed merely for the purpose of setting it in motion. But a machine, to be of any use, must not only keep moving itself, but *furnish power;* or, in other words, it must not only keep in motion, but it must have power to expend in some labour, as grinding corn, rolling metals, urging forward a vessel or a carriage; so that, by an arrangement of parts which of themselves have no moving power, the projector expects to make a machine, self-moving, and with the power of performing some useful task!

"Father, I have invented a perpetual motion!" said a little fellow of eight years old. "It is thus: I would make a great wheel, and fix it up like a water-wheel; at the top I would hang a great weight, and at the bottom I would hang a number of little weights; then the great weight would turn the wheel half round and sink to the bottom, because it is so heavy, and when the little weights reached the top, they would sink down because they are so many, and thus the wheel would turn round for ever." The child's fallacy is a type of all the blunders which are made on this subject. Follow a projector in his description, and if it be not perfectly unintelligible, which it often is, it always proves that he expects to find certain of his movements alternately strong and weak, not according to the laws of nature, but according to the wants of his mechanism.

If man could produce a machine which would generate the power by which it is worked, he would become a creator. All he he has hitherto done,—all, I may safely predict, he ever will do,—is to mould existing power so as to make it perform his bidding. He can make the waterfall in the brook spin his cotton, or print his book by means of machinery; but a mill to pump water enough to keep itself at work he cannot make. Absurd as it may seem, the experiment has been tried; but, in truth, no scheme is too absurd for adoption by the seekers after perpetual motion. A machine, then, is a mere conductor of power into a useful channel. The wind grinds the corn, —the sails, the shafts, and the stones are only the means by which the power of the wind can be turned to that particulor purpose; so it is the heat thrown out by the burning coal which performs all the multifarious operations of the steam-engine, the machinery being only the connecting links between the cause and the effect.—*Penny Magazine.*

GRAND JUNCTION RAILWAY BETWEEN BIRMINGHAM, AND MANCHESTER, AND LIVERPOOL.

An annual general meeting of the proprietors of this undertaking was held at Liverpool on Thursday, the 7th instant.

The Report of the Directors, after congratulating the proprietary on the opening of the line for that most important branch of its traffic, the conveyance of passengers, thus proceeds :—

" The time is gone by for expatiating on the general utility of railways ; on the speed, safety, economy, and comfort which they afford, and on the mighty changes they are destined to effect in all the arrangements of society ; but it has fallen to the lot of this company to be the first to exhibit to the country the practical working of a railway nearly a hundred miles in length, and forming the main route through the heart of the kingdom to Scotland and Ireland, and to the populous manufacturing and commercial districts of the north. The opening of a railway of this character and extent may be said to be an event of national importance ; and the results will be looked to with intense interest by the public at large, and especially by those who have embarked their property in enterprises of a similar kind. The experience of the first two months has been as satisfactory as the most sanguine could desire ; most of the direct public conveyances have been superseded, and many of the collateral ones have been diverted upon the railway ; private travelling on the line of country traversed by the railway has been annihilated ; whilst, at the same time, the posting upon all the routes pointing towards it has been stimulated in an extraordinary degree. Liverpool and Manchester have been brought within a night's post of London—an advantage in which not only places bordering upon the railway have participated, but others lying considerably wide of and beyond it ; the extent of which accommodation will be best appreciated by the fact, that no fewer than about 740 mail bags are taken up and set down every day of the several stations on the railway. Much credit, indeed, is due to the Post-office authorities for the prompt and efficient manner in which they have adapted their system to the new order of things ; and, though the Directors are of opinion that the remuneration is by no means adequate, either with reference to the service performed or the great benefit derived by the public, they have felt it to be their duty to afford every facility, and to consider the profit to the company in this case as a matter of secondary importance."

The gross receipts from the opening on the 4th July to the 2nd September have been as follow :—

		£.	s.	d.
For the week ending July 8th		3,224	15	7
,, ,, 15th		4,910	19	11
,, ,, 22nd		5,452	10	7
,, ,, 29th		4,673	12	10
,, August 5th		4,887	4	0
,, ,, 12th		5,873	19	1
,, ,, 19th		6,394	1	8
,, ,, 26th		5,649	5	8
,, Sept. 2nd		5,395	16	9
		£46,462	6	1

Of which receipts, the following is an analysis :—

		Passengers.		Receipts.		
		1st Class.	2d Class.	£.	s.	d.
1.	Liverpool to Birmingham..........	5,708	2,840	7,893	9	6
2.	Birmingham to Liverpool..........	6,542½	3,576	9,198	19	6
3.	Stations on the Line to Liverpool ...	4,870	3,300	3,536	1	9
4.	Liverpool to stations on the Line ...	4,441	3,320	3,190	10	0
5.	Stations on the Line to Birmingham..	5,067	4,297½	2,191	0	6
6.	Birmingham to Stations on the Line..	5,748½	5,263	2,476	6	0
7.	Manchester to Birmingham*........	2,588	978½	3,425	19	0
8.	Birmingham to Manchester*........	2,567	1,241	3,535	15	6
9.	Stations south of Crewe to Manchester*	800½	674	895	15	6
10.	Manchester to Stations south of Crewe*	640½	651½	825	14	6
11.	Stations north of Crewe (inclusive) to Manchester	1,656½	1,440	721	13	6
12.	Manchester to Stations north of Crewe (inclusive)	1,637½	1,919½	803	7	6
13.	From one Station to another	6,621	15,840½	3,247	19	0
		48,888	45,341½	41,942	11	9
	Parcels................................			2,396	1	4
	Gentlemen's carriages....................			1,483	6	0
	Horses................................			520	7	0
	Expresses..............................			120	0	0
	Total			£46,462	6	1

The Directors admit that the receipts may have been swelled by novelty and a favourable season of the year ; but they very fairly desire it to be remembered on the other hand, that they have derived no aid from the carriage of merchandize and live stock ; that three coaches, besides, are still running from Liverpool, and five from Manchester, to Birmingham, or to London, which cannot long survive the competition of the railway. The traffic of the line will not, they think, be fully developed until the opening of the London and Birmingham railway, " when the increased facilities of intercourse with the metropolis will give an impulse and a motive for travelling to which it is not easy to prescribe limits."

The gradients of the railway are stated to have, in no instance, been found an impediment. The engines can surmount the Madeley summit with a train of more than 200 passengers and their luggage (a load far exceeding the average), without any material diminution of speed ; nor is there any difficulty experienced in the same engine performing a trip to Birmingham and back again in the day.

The Directors propose to effect a more convenient and direct communication between the London and Birmingham and Grand Junction at Birmingham. The destination, they say, of a large majority of persons travelling upon the railway is to parts beyond Birmingham ; and to these, the annoyance and loss of time in the change

of coaches and transferring of luggage will be a constant source of complaint. To such as are unacquainted with the localities, it may be necessary to state that the two railways, though coming from opposite points, enter Birmingham almost parallel to each other ; the consequence of which is, that the coaches, having arrived by the one line, must be turned singly upon a turn-plate, and remarshalled in a train, before they can depart on the other. It is to avoid this detention that the Directors propose to carry an embankment from the present temporary station at Vauxhall to join the London and Birmingham about a mile from their own station. The length of this branch will be about three-quarters of a mile, and the cost of making it is estimated at 20,000l. to 25,000l. The object is not so much the saving of distance as of time. It would reduce the stoppage at Birmingham to a few minutes, and would enable the train to proceed uninterruptedly for 200 miles, with merely a change of engine at Vauxhall, where a fresh one would be in readiness to start, whether the train was before or after its time.

Annexed to the Report was a statement of accounts, from which it appeared that the capital expended upon the works, including the purchase of the Warrington and Newton Railway, and of engines, coaches, and waggons up to the 30th June, is 1,469,811l. 4s. 5d. There still remains 10l. uncalled, of which 5l. per share will be required in the present year ; and the rest in the first half of the next, for the completion of the road, the stations, and the purchase of additional stock.

* The traffic between these four points only and Manchester would be affected by the lines from Manchester to Stafford and Manchester to Crewe.

NOTES AND NOTICES.

Paper Casts of Sculpture.—My servants made me casts in paper of the sculpture on the walls of these two rooms, that is, of all the sculpture in the three large plates which I now publish. This method of obtaining fac-similes of sculpture in basso-relievo is very successful, and so easy, that I had no difficulty in teaching it to my Arabs. I found stiff, unsized, common white paper to be best adapted for the purpose. It should be well damped, and, when applied to sculpture still retaining its colour, not to injure the latter, care should be taken that the side of the paper placed on the figures be dry—that it be not the side which has been sponged. The paper, when applied to the sculpture, should be evenly patted with a napkin folded rather stiffly; and, if any part of the figures or hieroglyphics be in intaglio or elaborately worked, it is better to press the paper over that part with the fingers. Five minutes is quite sufficient to make a cast of this description. When taken off the wall it should be laid on the ground or sand to dry. I possess many hundred casts, which my Arabs made for me at Thebes and in the Oasis. Indeed, I very rarely made any drawings of sculpture without having a cast of the same; and as the latter are now quite fresh as on the day they were taken, the engraver having not only my drawing but also these indubitable fac-similes, is enabled to make my plates exactly like, and quite equal to the original.—*Hoskins's Visit to the Oasis.*

Steam Boats in Switzerland.—According to the accounts from Switzerland, several of the Cantonal Governments have determined to build steam-boats to run on their inland lakes. This plan will produce great advantages, by opening a more ready communication between Zurich, the Grisons, and Italy. When the boats intended to navigate the Lake of Geneva commence running, travellers may go from Geneva to Berne in one day.—*Gazette de France.*

Queen Anne's Farthings.—Much misconception prevails amongst the vulgar as to the scarcity and value of Queen Anne's farthings. There are six farthings of this queen, one of which was circulated as currency, and if in fine condition, is worth from seven shillings to a guinea. The other five are what are called pattern pieces,—that is, coins struck for approval, but never issued for circulation; and their value varies, according to their condition and scarcity, from one to five pounds, though No. 4, which is scarce, and the existing specimens of which are not in good preservation, might, if very fine, bring 10*l.*, or even more. But there are also very many brass farthings of this queen, altogether worthless; yet, when ignorant people get hold of one of these, they often fancy their fortune is made, and tramp up to London even from Ireland, to the no small annoyance of dealers and the officers of the British Museum, as well as to their own dismay when they find they cannot turn their brass into gold.—*Spectator.*

Preservation of Vessels from Fire.—A plan for extinguishing fire on board vessels having gone the round of the newspapers a few days since, I beg leave to call the attention of your readers to the second volume of your valuable Magazine, p. 394, where they will there see a similar suggestion by a

season, and proposed for their approbation twelve years ago, which, if it had been adopted, would have saved many lives and thousands of pounds. I merely point out this to shew the value of your plan, wherein are many useful hints expressed by ingenious minds, who, having the will, have not the means, of bringing them forward for the benefit of mankind. I am, &c., A. M. G. London, Sept. 18, 1837.

A New Light.—A chemist having found, after many experiments, that a void produced by electricity in a glass vessel became luminous, has, at last, succeeded in forming a long bottle, of 3 inches by 30, from which having exhausted the air, and otherwise acted upon it by a galvanic battery, a light is now emitted, being hung up in his apartment, equally clear, but not so oppressive to the eyes, as that of the sun.—*French Paper.*

Lime.—Lime is said to be an excellent remedy for burns or scalds: equal proportions of lime, water, and any kind of oil, made into a thin paste, and immediately applied and repeatedly moistened, will speedily remove the effect of a burn; and if applied later, even when the blister has risen, the remedy never fails. This paste has been known to stop effusions of blood, when almost every thing else has failed. Dry lime thrown into a flesh wound is always healing.

Effect of Climate and Cultivation on Vegetables.—The myrtle tree, which, with us, is a small shrub, grows in Van Diemen's Land to the height of 290 feet, and has a trunk from 30 to 40 feet in circumference. The wood resembles cedar.—The Chinese have an art by which they are able to produce miniature pines, bearing a perfect resemblance to the gigantic specimens of America, and only five or six inches high.

The Queen's New Dessert Service.—There has lately been exhibiting, at the Griffin warehouse, (late Weeks's Museum,) Piccadilly, an elaborate specimen of skill and excellence in one of the foremost of British manufactures. It is a splendid dessert service of porcelain, made for her Majesty, by Messrs. Brameld, of the Rockingham Works, near Rotherham, Yorkshire, of British materials. The designs, which are original, are by Mr. Brameld; and the pictorial embellishments have been executed by the artists of the Rockingham Works. It has taken five years to complete this extraordinary labour of British art, the charge for which is upwards of 3000 guineas. The service consists of 200 pieces, viz., 56 elevated vases, baskets, &c., and 12 dozen plates. The service, by its lightness and elegance, will relieve the massive gold plateau, candelabra, &c., which are used at the royal state dinners.

Literary Patents.—Pope took out a patent for the translation of the Odyssey, and at the time I commenced business, it was not uncommon for booksellers to take out patents for new books.—*Tegg's Remarks on Copyright.*

The Notice of the Pulverized Cork Beds, given p. 408, was extracted from an American paper. We are not aware of any article of the kind being manufactured in this country.

The British Association.—We shall devote an extra sheet next week to giving an abstract of the proceedings of the Liverpool meeting.

☞ *British and Foreign Patents taken out with economy and despatch; Specifications, Disclaimers, and Amendments, prepared or revised; Caveats entered; and generally every Branch of Patent Business promptly transacted.*

A complete list of Patents from the earliest period (15 Car. II. 1675,) to the present time may be examined. Fee 2s. 6d.; Clients, gratis.

LONDON: Printed and Published for the Proprietor, by W. A. Robertson, at the Mechanic Office, No. 6, Peterborough-court, between 135 and 136, Fleet-street.—Sold by A. & W. Galignani, Vivienne, Paris.

Mechanics' Magazine,

MUSEUM, REGISTER, JOURNAL, AND GAZETTE.

No. 738.]　　　　SATURDAY, SEPTEMBER 30, 1837.　　　　[Price 6d.

PARIS AND ST. GERMAIN RAILWAY.

PARIS AND ST. GERMAIN RAILWAY.

The last "movement" of the Parisians has been by steam. The present *point d' appui* of the excitement of the capital of *La Belle France*, is the result of its first attempt to annihilate distance by the aid of mechanics. [Of the opening of the railway from Paris to St. Germain, we extracted an amusing account from the letter of the *Times'* Parisian correspondent, in our 734th number; and we now present our readers with an engraving of the works at the Paris terminus, copied from a lithograph lately published there; and also with a map of the line.

We shall go more into detail in our notice of this railway than we are in the habit of doing, in the first place, because it forms one of the first practical results, in this branch of art, of the usual superabundance of French theorising; and secondly, that the principal features of the line may be pointed out to such of our countrymen as may be visiting the French capital, who will of course not fail to take a trip by steam to St. Germain. The account which follows is made up partly from personal observation, and partly from the Parisian periodicals and papers of the day.

On entering the station at the Paris terminus and paying for your place, you are immediately struck with the prominent manner in which the national taste for gaudy display, is introduced into an undertaking where everything is of great weight and giant strength. Having obtained your *billet*, on which is marked the number of the place you are to occupy, you are, on producing it to a *gendarme*, ushered by him into a magnificent saloon, which in the evening is lighted with fine chandeliers. This saloon is in the form of a lunette, with a railing in the centre, to divide the high price from the low-price passengers; each point of the lunette, is the exit from this saloon to the stairs, (see engraving on front page) which lead to each side of the railway; the walls of this waiting saloon are divided into compartments, beautifully painted and decorated in the Louis quatorze style; as also with medallion portraits of celebrated engineers and men of science. The four principal compartments contain very spiritedly painted figures, emblematic of Science, Industry, Commerce, and Agriculture. In smaller compartments are tablets on which are inscribed the names of Newcomen, Savery, Watt, Washbrough, Trevethick, &c., Papin occupying a place in the centre tablet, in consequence, perhaps, of some new discoveries of Baron Dupin, proving him to be the inventor of railways and locomotive carriages! Elegant and soft cushioned seats, covered with scarlet damask, are provided for the waiting passenger, who is enjoined in the announcements to be at the rendezvous a quarter of an hour before the appointed time of starting—more than half the time occupied in journeying the 11½ miles. The windows of this saloon overlook the railway. The building, the interior of which we have just described, is over the commencement of the first tunnel, which is at a little distance from the extreme end of the railway, the line after emerging from it, continuing for a short distance, and terminating in a similar building; and the part between these two erections forms a kind of head, analagous to the basin of a canal, where passengers enter the carriages, and the waggons are loaded. The path by the side of the train is here elevated so as to be over the wheels, and level with the floors of the carriages; thus a passenger has merely to walk into the vehicle, any accident from falling being rendered impossible. The same plan is adopted on the Birmingham line, but on the Greenwich, the height to which a passenger has to mount is extremely inconvenient, The reader will perceive that the view of the railway on our front page is taken from the building at the extreme end, and looking on to the building across the neck, if we may so speak, of the line. The former being the *entrée*, and the latter the *sortée*, and having similar flights of steps, as is partially seen in the engraving.

The general design of these buildings, and the grand flights of steps, from a point of view taking in the whole, is of a very bold and striking character; and the effect of this design, from being executed in stone, in fact almost cut out of a bed of stone, comes with much force upon an eye accustomed to the dullness of the brick and mortar structures of this country. The facility with which stone can be procured, being often dug from the quarry, hewn into blocks, and used, nearly all upon the same spot, gives the

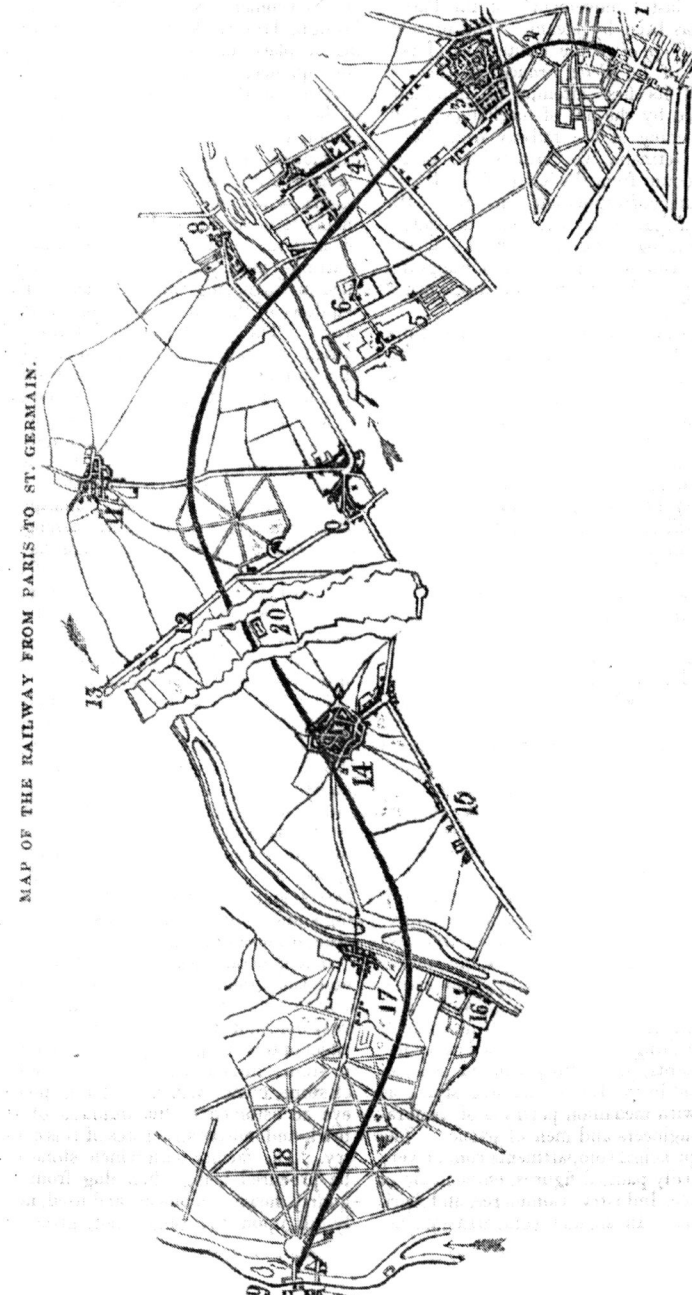

MAP OF THE RAILWAY FROM PARIS TO ST. GERMAIN.

1. The intended extension of the Railway to the Madelaine. 2. The present Paris terminus in the Place de l'Europe, at the end of the Rue Tivoli. 3. The Village of the Batignolles, under which the Railway passes in a tunnel. 4. Clichy la Garenne. 5. Village of Villiers. 6. Courcelles. 7. The river Seine. 8. Asnières. 9. Courbevoie. 10. Park and Chateau of La Garenne. 11. Colombes. 12. Bridge of Besons. 13. The Seine. 14. Nanterre. 15. Rueil. 16. Croissy. 17. Chatou. 18. Forest of Vesinet. 19. Le Pecq, upon the left of the Seine, and facing the terminus of the Railway.

Parisians a great advantage over us, in the power of making a display of taste in the execution of their public works.

The law authorising the formation of a company for the construction of the railway from Paris to St. Germain, was passed on the 9th of July 1835. It commences, at present, in the Place de l'Europe, on the north of Paris, but it is intended to continue it, by the Rue Tronchet, nearly to the Madelaine, in the very heart of Paris; the termination is at the port of Le Pecq, at St. Germain. The length of the line is 18,430 metres, or 11.160 miles, English. At Paris, it it 40.55 metres above the level of the sea (about 127 feet English) and at Le Pecq, 31.497 metres (about 101 feet), the difference in height between the extremities being 8.071 metres (about 26 feet). The railway passes under the Place de l'Europe in a tunnel of 264 metres, or 844½ ft.; then through a cutting, walled in on each side until it enters another tunnel of 403 metres, or 1292 feet in length, which leads as far as the Rue de la Paix in the village of the Batignolles; it then passes under the exterior Boulevart and the Rue des Dames and Rue de la Paix, and various other streets, by means of bridges. Immediately past that which carries the Rue Cardinet over the railway, are large warehouses occupying an area of 250 m. by 100 m. (800 feet by 320) for receiving goods and merchandise brought to Paris by the railway. The line now proceeds on an embankment until it crosses the Seine a little way past Asnieres by a bridge of five arches of 30 metres each, (about 96 feet); it then continues in a direct line from its first curve before the Batignolles for about 4500 metres (three miles), when between Colombes and Asnieres, there is a curve of 2000 metres (about 1¼ miles) radius. In another direct line it then proceeds as far as the two bridges over the Seine a little way past Rueil, where the railway takes another curve of a similar radius to the last. These bridges cross two arms into which the Seine is here divided, embracing the Isle du Chiard; one bridge is of three arches of 28 metres (89½ feet) each, In another direct line it then traverses the Forest of Vesinet and terminates at Le Pecq, in a large depôt for passengers, and for warehousing merchandise brought up by the rivers Seine and Oise to proceed to Paris by the railway; or

which has been brought from Paris to be taken on by these rivers.

The whole length of railway is divided into three straight lines, and three curves. Each curve is on a level, and each straight line is an inclined plane of 1 mil. in each metre (or 1 in a thousand). It was calculated by the engineers that the same power required by the locomotive to ascend this incline, would be required to turn each curve, in going from St. Germain to Paris; and that the power necessary to turn the curve in going from Paris to St. Germain would be obtained from the impetus acquired by the train in descendtng the inclines; so that thus the locomotives would always be kept at an uniform power of traction. On approaching Paris the terminal curve diminishes to from 900 to 800 metres (960 to 852 yards), this being rendered necessary by the locality, and it also serves to deaden the speed of the train as it approaches the end of its course.

By the railroad, the distance between Paris and St, Germain is only a third of the length which it is by the river Seine; the navigation between these two points is, besides being so circuitous, extremely difficult, and at times impossible. This remark, however, merely applies to the carriage of heavy goods, as no passenger ever thought of travelling to St. Germain by water. Even by the steam packets which were established about a year ago between Paris and Rouen, from the circuitousness of the route, and the difficulty of navigation, it was found necessary to convey passengers by diligences to a point about 15 or 16 miles down the river, where they then embarked in the steam vessel.

The "matériel" possessed by the administration of the railway, consists of a motive force of 12 locomotives of different powers; equal in all to 360 horses. The means of transport consist of—

		Persons.
5 Close carriages, having accommodation for	}	150
2 Open carriages		80
8 Diligences		240
20 Waggons "furnished"		800
70 Waggons "unfurnished"		2800

Altogether there are vehicles for 4070 persons. There are four double lines of rails from Paris to the Batignolles; three from thence to near Asnieres, and two from thence to St. Germain. As yet, however, only one track is completed, for a considerable distance.

The rails on this line are of great solidity, being twice the weight of those on the Liverpool and Manchester, the former being about 60 lbs. per lineal yard, and the latter only about 30 lbs.

The breadth between the rails is 1½ metres, (about 5 feet); between the lines 1.80 m. (about 6 feet) and on each side 1.45 m. (about 4½ feet). The tunnel of the Batignolles is divided into two galleries, in each of which are two tracks of rails; one gallery was commenced on the 7th June, 1836, and finished, 9th March, 1837; the other is not yet completed. The breadth of each gallery is 7.40 m. (about 23 feet), the height 6m., (about 20 feet.

The number of persons going between Paris and St. Germain before the establishment of the railway, by public and private carriages, was estimated at 400,000 a year, or about 1100 per day; it was anticipated that this number would be increased in a tenfold degree; nor do we think the expectation likely to be disappointed: during the day the railway trains are always full, and on fine evenings and Sundays the crush to obtain places, is as suffocating as at the gallery door of a London theatre during the Christmas holidays.

The railway from Paris to St. Germain presents a summary of all the works that any undertaking of a similar nature, is usually called upon to execute. Two tunnels, the one with four double lines of rails under two parallel arches or galleries; the other with also four lines under a single arch. Three grand bridges over the Seine, of which one is of three arches of 150 metres, (480 feet); fifteen bridges for roads and streets, the names of which it is needless for us to mention, to pass over the railway; cuttings to the depth of 17 metres (60 feet), embankments to the height of from 10 to 20 metres (32 to 64 feet), and a stone quarry traversed.

The landscape, on the route of the line, is not of any particular interest. On crossing the Seine at Asnieres, are seen the magnificent Arc de Triomphe d' Etoile and the church of St. Dennis. The succeeding country is of a varying character. The forest of St. Germain, near which it terminates is the most extensive in the neighbourhood of Paris, containing 5,550 French acres. Its vicinity to the railroad

is already attracting there a new stream of population. The *Maisons Laffitte*, and its vast park of 1500 acres is now, says a Parisian journalist, being transformed into a *delicieuse colonie*, where are building under the direction of a young architect, M. Duval, "les constructions les plus variées, les plus agréables, les plus capricieuses, qu'il soit possible de voir". This *delicieuse colonie* is, thanks to the railroad, within forty minutes journey of Paris; and for 8000 francs, or £320, one may become the proprietor of an acre of land, well covered with wood, a pretty house and garden, and near the banks of the Seine.

The railway trains leave Paris at intervals, ten times a day; as also the same number of times from St. Germain. The departures are so arranged, that no more than one train shall be journeying on the railway at once; the time occupied in performing the trip, being from 25 to 30 minutes: indeed this arrangement is at present necessary, as for a great part of the length, the line is only a single track. The fares are from 1 to 2½ francs.

The utility of the railway-system as applied to France cannot be questioned. In the neighbourhood of the capital its effects will be most beneficial. The supplying of the markets of Paris, says a writer in the *Revue Britannique*, with articles of daily consumption, especially milk and vegetables, has been becoming more and more difficult from the increasing population; the great demand impoverishing the lands in the neighbourhood; the kine are being constantly drained to the last drop, and the gardens permanent dung-hills. The swiftness of transport on a railway, he adds, being 6 or 7 times that of carriages on common roads, the produce of places six or seven times further distant from Paris than are at present available, would thus be brought into the market. And if lines were to radiate in all directions from the capital, with connecting branches, from 36 to 49 times the present extent of country would be laid under contribution for the supply of Paris.

On the other hand we have heard it objected, that the system of centralization, which gives Paris such a hold upon the whole country, would be increased by railroads; we think, however, that the effect would be the contrary, and that the general adoption of the railway system

from the capital to the provinces, and
from one province to another; would tend
to equalize rather than centralize, influence and wealth, as well politically as
commercially.

SPEED OF AMERICAN STEAMERS.

Sir,—At the meeting recently held at
Liverpool by the British Association for
the advancement of Science, I perceive that doubts were thrown on the
statements of Professor Henry of New
York, relative to the speed attained by
steam boats navigating the Hudson
River.

Professor Henry said " he had himself often gone the distance of 150 miles
in nine hours; and he had stated that
the current was very trifling. Indeed
what current there was, was reversed by
the oceanic tide ascending the river." To
which Dr. Lardner replied,—" from his
own experience he utterly disbelieved,
that the extent of fifteen miles an hour
could be attained *except by boats of a
very peculiar description.*"

Professor Henry only stated, what is
so well known to those who have been
on the Hudson, that the only wonder is,
that the remark excited observation.
How did Dr. L. ascertain that the Americans had not boats of a *very peculiar
description?* Surely he ought to have
ascertained the fact before he volunteered
so uncourteous a contradiction. So far
back as April 1833, I sailed the distance
in eleven and a half hours, and that was
not then considered a quick passage.
Perhaps it may be unknown to many of
your readers, as well as the Doctor, that
the boats navigating the Hudson are
built chiefly of pine and cedar, as light
as possible, and only for sailing in smooth
water; indeed so disproportioned are the
timbers to the weight of the engine when
in motion, that the decks are kept in
continual vibration. The dimensions of
one of their small sized boats, the "Cham-
plain," was given me by the engineer
while on board in 1833 :—

Length of boat	180	feet
Breadth ditto..............	28	"
Ditto paddles.............	14½	"
Diameter of ditto	22	"

Boilers on deck, four, for the purpose of
distributing the weight.

Engines, two, 80-horse each.
Cylinder, forty-two inches.
Stroke, ten feet.

Strokes per minute, twenty-three.
Consumption of pine wood per trip, thirty
chords, at four dollars per chord.

The De Witt Clinton is 238 feet long,
independent of her false bow, which may
be seven feet more; has one engine of
180-horse power, with a sixty-five inch
cylinder, and ten feet stroke; the beam
works on an erection of wood, raised
from fifteen to twenty feet above the
deck.

When we consider that the chief part
of our river boats are short, and strongly
timbered for the sea, with their engine
and boiler in the hold, a supply of heavy
coal for fuel, we need not be surprised
that they are unable to attain the speed
of boats built on the American principle.
If Dr. Lardner never travelled in the
United States, "his own experience"
cannot apply to their boats; and consequently, proves nothing. He disbelieves
the Professor's statement, because at
variance with his own experience—How
modest! It is to be hoped that foreigners will neither judge of the modesty or
courtesy of our scientific countrymen, by
this rash exhibition of ill nature and in-
decorum; had the Doctor suppressed
his impatience a little longer, he might
have learnt that the secret of their speed
lay in their sharp bows, and light draft
of water, in presenting a diminished
surface to the action of the opposing
forces, or resisting medium. Perhaps
inquiries are beneath the Doctor's notice.
Has he been so long accustomed to teach,
that he has forgotten to learn? But we
suppose Dionysius must still be absolute
at Syracuse.

I have the honour to be,
Your most obedient servant,
JOHN GALLOWAY.

87, Piccadilly, Manchester, September 18, 1837.

RYAN V. COMMON SALT.

Sir,—I am not one of those who
have indulged in fearful apprehension of
the consequences likely to arise from the
general use of kyanised timber, on the
health of her Majesty's lieges by sea or
by land; neither can I agree with Mr.
Murray, who, in Number 736, page
398, inclines to attribute the present
sickly appearance of the giraffes in the
Zoological Gardens, Regent's Park, to
the circumstance of their continual licking of the kyanised palings. Those per-

sons who have studied the economy of these curious animals, well know the difficulty experienced in naturalizing them in our extremely variable climate; and to the effects of climate alone, may their present state very fairly be ascribed.

The following extract from Dr. Granville's description of the salt mines at Saltzburg, in his recent work on the Spas of Germany, is somewhat curious, and well worthy of something more than " passing notice."

" As it was discovered that, where the wood was most exposed to the action of the salt earth, it became harder and harder, and was scarcely ever after liable to decay, all those piles which, when fixed, are not necessarily in contact with the salt parts of the mountain, are previously soaked in brine. Now here is a hint for a rival company to Kyan's monopoly, which I am convinced offers no greater security against the decay of wood than strong brine would. It will be found on trial, that the *bichloride of sodium* in this respect is as efficacious as the *bichloride of mercury* employed by Kyan."

Dr. Granville appears to have a good deal of reason on his side, and should the fact prove to be as he asserts, which I think very probable, the preservation of our timber will become a cheap and easy process; free from all the objections (just or unjust) that have been made from time to time against Mr. Kyan's patent process.

I remain, yours respectfully,

WM. BADDELEY.

London, September 18, 1837.

EXPERIMENTS IN ELECTRO-MAGNETISM.

Sir,—I have completed an electro-magnet, which is made from a half inch rod, and is three inches in length. I calculated it would support about ten or twelve pounds; but to my great surprise it sustained thirty-five pounds, with a battery only 2½ inches high, and 2½ diameter. Encouraged by this experiment, I commenced a trial of the helix, which I believe has the property of suspending a needle in its centre; I wound three layers of copper-wire, about one-sixtieth inch diam., and covered with cotton, on a glass tube, one inch diam., brought the three wires together, and soldered them to a piece of large copper-wire at each end of the helix. I then amalgamated the ends of the large copper-wires, and made the connexion by dipping them into the cups of a battery six inches high, and four in diameter ; but there was not the slightest effect produced on the needle, though the acid was very strong. I tried it next with a tube half inch diam. ; then there was a little effect obtained. Lastly, I tried it with a tube quarter inch diam. and four layers of wire, and it then drew the needle a little way in, but would not, as I expected, suspend it, although I tried it with fine soft iron wire, fine magnetised needles, very strong solutions of different acids, and was particular about the amalgamations. If any of your numerous correspondents can give me any information respecting the cause of my failure, and give a few practical hints, through the medium of the *Mechanics' Magazine*, it would greatly oblige,

Your constant reader,

S. C.

Weymouth, September 16, 1837.

APPEARANCE OF A LUNAR RAINBOW.

Sir,—It has been observed that Lunar Rainbows are very rare, and have been seen only when the moon was at the full, Whether they can be seen only at the full, I am not prepared to say, but the one which I am about to describe certainly did happen at that period.

It was on Thursday evening the 14th inst., at a quarter past eight o'clock, and six hours forty-seven minutes after full moon, that I was walking out in a field adjoining the house in which I reside, when on looking at the sky in a north-western direction, I was struck with the appearance of something which seemed like a rainbow. Never having seen one by night myself, and knowing it to be of very rare occurence, I hastened to call the rest of the family out to witness this extraordinary phenomenon.

The weather in the course of the day had been very rainy, but had cleared up a short time previous to the appearance of the bow. The wind was moderate, blowing from the west. The moon was shining as brilliantly as I ever remember to have seen her ; not a cloud was near; and over-against her in the north-west

partments on each side, leav-
space at each corner, equal to
. The men are placed as usual
tions of AB, CD and should
nt colours. Two sets of men
isite. The partners or allies
, sit side by side, as AB, CD.
will be able to communicate
ons to each other. Suppos-
e the antagonists of AB, C
must both be check-mated
r the other be conquered; if
the players be check-mated,
main powerless and inactive,
her be moved nor taken; but
lly be able to relieve him, he
iately return to the charge,
ole of his men come into
fore.
s are the same as in common
fore the parties are in fact ex-
ross-fire combined with the
his antagonist before him.
e be calculated to make the
about them, this is the one;
it excites is said to be beyond
and which is much increased
liberty of communication
parties interested. The de-
gram exhibits at once the
board, and the situation of

DOUBLE CRANK ROTARY
MOTION.

bserve in your publication
r 2nd., a letter from a cor-
(Mr. Ettrick) with a de-
a machine, by which a
n may be obtained, in any
m the original motive power;
of which he states to have
cted last year, and placed in
Rooms. My object in now
ou, is merely to say, that I
milar arrangment of double
year 1835, indeed, it forms
ture of a machine, I at that
nced the construction of, but
not yet had time to mature.
wever, at the same time con-
as not aware of its utility or
I perused your correspon-
iption, otherwise, I should
ed my claim to the invention
his time.
I am, Sir,
Yours respectfully,
AMATEUR MECHANIC.
nsbury, 15th September, 1837.

GOWLAND'S ARTIFICIAL HORIZON.

Sir,—At the late meeting of the British Association, in Liverpool, Mr. William Ettrick gave a description of several artificial horizons; among others, of
one invented and constructed by himself.
This instrument consisted of a black
glass plane, with a pendulous rod attached to the under surface, and was
supported by centres playing in gimbals.
The rod had a weight affixed to its lower
end, for the purpose of maintaining the
horizontal position of the plane.

Under these circumstances I deem it
right to state, that in the early part of
the year 1835, Mr. Gowland, chrono-
meter maker, of Leathersellers Buildings, London-wall (the ingenious inven-
ter of the triple-pointed steel pens, &c.),
showed me an artificial horizon which
he had introduced, consisting of a flat
plate of opaque black glass, which floated
upon the surface of mercury contained
within a circular box, somewhat resembling a large tobacco-box. The glass
was of a very beautiful jet black colour,
and was levelled with extreme care, the
positive efficiency of the instrument
mainly depending upon the accurate
parallelism of the two faces. Suspended
by centres, moving in gimbals, with a
weightier rod screwed to the bottom of
the box, this horizon, would be adapted
to use on ship-board. For the purpose of
land-service, however, the plumb-rod is
unnecessary, the instrument being complete in its original simple and compact
form. The portability of Mr. Gowland's
artificial horizon, with the circumstance
of its requiring no verification or adjustment previous to using, sufficiently accounts for the high value that has been
attached to his instrument, and justifies
the preference it has attained over some
other inventions of a similar nature.

Extraordinary care must of necessity
be used in affixing the pendulous rod to
Mr. Ettrick's glass plane, so as to obtain
a true horizon, and I apprehend it must
be liable to derangement in use. In Mr.
Gowland's apparatus no such nicety is required; self-adjustment always takes place.

The tremulous motion of the mercury,
which is so decidedly objectionable to its
use for a reflecting surface, is nullified by
the superincumbent plane of glass, while
the true horizon is always obtained without trouble, and with great certainty.

WM. BADDELEY.
Wellington-street, Blackfriars-road,
September 26th 1837.

DISCOVERY OF KREOSOTE; ITS USE IN PRESERVING ANIMAL SUBSTANCES, ETC.

For several years past, the dry distillation of organic substances has engaged the attention and exercised the interest of European chemists. This process consists in subjecting them, when deprived of moisture, to a high temperature. By this means the elementary principles of the body are acted on; they enter into new combinations, so that the products are the result of its destruction or decomposition by heat.

In 1830, M. Reichenbach, a chemist of Blansko, while engaged in the investigation of this curious interesting subject, discovered kreosote and five other substances, all of more or less value in medicine and the arts. and all produces of the destructive distillation of vegetable matter. Kreosote, however is by far the most important of all these products, both on account of its chemical proprities and its numerous practical applications. It was first discovered by Reichenbach in impure pyroligneous acid. and afterwards in all the tars.

It is an oily transparent fluid, and when pure perfectly colorless; its odor is very similar to that imparted to meat by wood smoke, varying, however, accordingly to the species of tar used in its manufacture. It is readily combustible in the atmosphere and burns with much smoke.

Kreosote has been successfully applied to the preservation of fresh meats, and hence may hence may become an important article in domestic economy. The meats intended to be preserved should be immersed in a solution of one part of kreosote in a hundred of water. Here they should remain from twelve to forty-eight hours, according to their size, when they are to be dried, either in the sun or before the fire, and afterwards set aside for six or eight days, at the end of which period they will be found to have acquired the consistence, appearance, smell and taste of the finest smoked meat.

Kreosote is probably the most efficient substance yet discovered for the preservation of dead bodies of whatever kind.—Birds poisoned with it, resist putrefaction for a great length of time, and the bodies of animals may be mumified, so as to keep them sound for an indefinite period by immersing them in a solution of kreosote in water, or by injecting a mixture containing kreosote into the blood vessels.

And, indeed, from recent investigations, it has been ascertained, beyond a doubt, that the tarry and resinous substances from which kreosote is cheifly manufactured, were the very articles used by the ancient Egyptians in the process of embalming, and by means

of which their mummies have been handed to after ages—mementos of the science and skill of that gifted people, as imperishable and as wonderful as the pyramids themselves.

It is stated in the Asiatic Journal for February, 1836, that Lieut. Col. M. C. Bognol presented to the Royal Asiatic Society a human hand and a piece of beef, preserved by means of a preparation of vegetable tar found on the borders of the Red Sea, in the vicinity of Mocha. The Bedouin Arabs with whom he conversed on this subject, were of the opinion that this vegetable tar, called in their language Katran, was the article chiefly depended on by the ancient Egyptians in the process of embalming. They also believed that large quantities of camphor, myrrh, aloes, and frankincense were used; but these are evidently not essential, as the tar alone penetrates and discolours the bone. The only use now made of this tar, is as a plaster or ointment for the sore backs of horses and camels, rot in sheep, and lastly, in the preparation of the heads of criminals sent from the distant provinces to the seat of government. The tar is obtained from the branches of a small tree or shrub, which is found in most parts of Syria or Arabia Felix.

The process by which kreosote is procured is complex and difficult; that of Reichenbach has been simplified and improved by other chemists. The following is the mode recommended in the Annales de Chimie et de Physique of July, 1835, by M. Koene. The tar derived from pit coal is distilled in a retort provided with a long tube, having a large mouth. Under this is placed a receiver. The oil which comes over first swims on water; and it is necessary to remove from time to time the products of the distillation, till an oil is obtained which sinks in water. When this is found to be the case, the product is collected. The heavy oil obtained during the distillation condenses not only in the receiver, but also in the tube of the retort, where it unites with the naphthaline, forming a buttery substance. By applying a gentle heat, the mass will drop into the receiver. The product is now allowed to remain in a cool place for some hours, after which it is pressed. The expressed naphthaline still contains oil, which is separated by heating it with its own weight of acetic acid till it melts. After allowing it to cool, the crystallized naphtha is pressed; and the acid adhering to the kreosote is saturated with sub-carbonate of potash. The kreosote is now to be shaken for a quarter of an hour with phosphoric acid, the proportions being half an ounce of the acid to twenty ounces of the oil. The mixture ought then to be agitated with its volume of water, and afterwards distilled with a graduated heat, care being taken to separate the oil which floats on its surface. The rectified oil is now to be dissolved in its own volume of a hot solution of caustic potash, of the specific gravity 1.120. When it has been allowed to cool for half an hour, the oil upon the surface is again removed, and the heavy oil again treated with the caustic potash, only a fourth part, however, of the solution being this time employed.

On uniting the solutions of potash, a slight excess of diluted phosphoric acid is added, and the free kreosote which floats on the surface is separated. It is again rectified; and the first product, which is chiefly water, being rejected, the kreosote comes over quite pure.

Kreosote has now been a sufficient length of time before the public to enable us to ascertain pretty certainly and accurately its real value as a remedial agent.

Reichenbach, among his first experiments, applied the kreosote to slight scalds, in which he found it eminently beneficial. In the treatment of burns, it has been employed in France, having, it is said, a remarkable tendency to cause the sores to cicatrize from the circumference to the centre, thus preventing those irregular contractions, which often produce permanent disfigurement.

There is scarcely any disease, in which, according to the concurrent opinion of numerous physicians, kreosote has proved more beneficial than in the toothache. It has been employed on the continent for this purpose, ever since its discovery; and for the last two years, it has been prescribed very extensively in Edinburgh, and Dr. Cormick says, with great success. But unless there be a cavity in the tooth through which the kreosote may be applied to the nerve, as a general rule, no advantage will derived from it. Where the pain is merely rheumatic, a solution of kreosote and water is highly useful, relieving more speedily, certainly, and for a longer time, than any other remedy.

Various explanations of the operation of kreosote in these cases have been offered, but none seem satisfactory.

1. It has been supposed that the remedy produced its effect by destroying the nerve; to this it has been objected, that if the nerve were destroyed, the pain would never return, whereas, in most cases, the pain returns after a considerable lapse of time. But the de-

struction of the nerve, it may be rejoined, may be partial only, sufficient to paralyze its sensibility for a while, but not sufficient to prevent a return of this sensibility.

2. The kreosote may unite chemically with the albumen of the fluids, which are always exuding from a carious tooth, and thus form a crust to protect the nerve from the action of the atmosphere.

3. It may, perhaps, afford relief by stimulating the loaded vessels of the nerve, causing them to contract and expel the blood with which they are surcharged.

The best method of introducing the kreosote is by means of a camel's hair pencil. After this has been done, the cavity should be filled with cotton saturated with pure kreosote, care being taken, if possible, to prevent any adhering drops from touching and irritating the adjacent soft parts. If this should happen, however, the pain is but momentary, and is not attended with any serious consequences.

Dr. Elliottson has published several interesting cases of cutaneous diseases, in which the kreosote has effected a cure after various other means had been tried in vain. It has also been recommended in chilblains. Dr. Halm, of Stuttgart, says, that whether they are ulcerated or not, he accomplishes a cure in the course of a few days with a solution of kreosote in water. Several caution should be borne in mind, in the application of kreosote to ulcers. It is of great importance in regulating the solution, to remember that water dissolves only one-eightieth part of its weight of kreosote. If a small excess of kreosote be present, it will float on the surface in the form of minute globules ; and, of course, when the lint or brush is dipped in the solution, these globules will adhere, and thus a much stronger preparation than was intended will be used.

Of all the beneficial effects of kreosote, however, there is probably none more important than its power of allaying the irritability of the stomach, and of controlling the most obstinate cases of nausea and vomiting. Its power, in affections of this character (says Doctor Cormack) exceeds all other all other known remedies; and Doctor Elliottson says, that he never knew it fail to arrest vomiting, proceeding from functional derangement merely. Doctor Elliottson also prescribed it with great advantage in a case of vomiting from arsenic ; and severally times successfully for sea-sickness.—*American Journal of the Medical Science.*

PROCEEDINGS OF THE LIVERPOOL MEETING (BEING THE SEVENTH) OF THE BRITISH ASSOCIATION FOR THE ADVANCEMENT OF SCIENCE.

*President—*EARL OF BURLINGTON.

September 11—16, 1887.

(Select notices, extracted and abridged from the Reports in the Athenæum of the 16th and 23d of September.)

SECTION A.—MATHEMATICAL AND PHYSICAL SCIENCE—FIRST SITTING.

*President—*Sir D. BREWSTER.

Read, " Suggestions as to the probable causes of the Aerial Currents in the Temperate Zones," by Mr. W. R. Birt.

Read, a communication from Col. Gold, late of the Royal Artillery, " On the possibility of effecting Telegraphic or Signal Communications during Foggy Weather, and by Night, in all seasons." The author calculates that the transit by his means would be thirty times quicker than by the mail, even when conveyed by the rail-road, at the rate of twenty miles per hour.

Read, a communication, forwarded to the Association by N. L. Beamish, Esq., " On an improved mode of constructing Magnets," by Mr. Cunningham, of Cork. The author stated, that he had tried steel of various qualities, but could not succeed in making magnets sufficiently powerful. While thus engaged, he met with a communication from Mr. Knight, jun., to the Society for the Encouragement of Arts, describing a new mode of construction, and recommending common blister steel, of an open grain and highly carbonized, as the best material for the purpose; and since much hammering is highly injurious, he advised that the steel should be procured of the size exactly suited to the required magnets, which would obviate the necessity of forging, except at the centre of the rod, to give it the horse-shoe form. The author stated, that it would be an obvious improvement upon this method, to give iron the required form previous to its conversion into steel, as this would render any further disturbance unnecessary. It occurred to him, while reflecting upon the very large quantity of carbon in cast iron, that it ought to be admirably adapted to this purpose, and, in order to test the correctness of his opinion, he got three small castings made of the horse-shoe form, each weighing seven ounces; on touching these with a small compound magnet in the usual manner, he was very agreeably surprised to find them absorb and retain the magnetic influence in a degree superior to any steel ones he had ever previously constructed; he stated, that he had no doubt that they would be further improved if heated red-hot, and very slowly cooled, which would make the metal softer, and the grain more uniform; and they might afterwards be hardened at the poles to produce the maximum effect. He considered this result of much importance, as it will enable us to construct compound magnets for magneto-electrical machines with great facility, and at a very trifling expense, as any number could be cast from one timber pattern.

Mr. Christie stated his regret that the gentleman, whose communication had been just read, had not entered into numerical details, stating as well the power of the steel magnets which he had previously made, as the actual and comparative power of the cast-iron magnets, which he seemed so much to prefer. It must be obvious, that without this information, no scientific person could at all confide in the vague statement, that magnets made in one particular way were " superior" to those made in another way, for both might be badly made, and the difference might not be of much practical importance. He strongly doubted the value of cast-iron as a material for the construction of magnets.—Mr. Holden said, that he preferred steel tempered blue, or to spring temper, and was, on the whole, inclined to agree with the last speaker, in doubting the value of the material proposed. He knew that cast-iron was capable of receiving strongly the magnetic influence, and bars of cast-iron, as long as they retained their upright position, were found to possess polarity in a very high degree; but he doubted whether, if they were removed from their upright position, they would long retain their polarity to any considerable extent.—Mr. Peacock fully agreed with Mr. Christie.—Mr. Christie stated, that, at the very last meeting of the Association, in Bristol, the Rev. Mr. Scoresby had made a communication respecting the construction of magnets, and the material he preferred was evenly-tempered steel, of the blue temper, such as watch springs, or ladies' busks. He had also strongly reprobated the leaving any part of a magnet soft, and hardening the rest.—Mr. Snow Harris observed, that, from many trials, and much experience, he was convinced that hardened steel wire, just as it is to be had in the shops, without any further working it, or putting it into the fire, or altering its temper, was the best material for constructing small needles, intended to retain their magnetism permanently; and this latter consideration was of the utmost consequence when constructing needles for philosophic research—as, for instance, upon the magnetic intensity at various places, since the slightest alteration of power, in that case, would most materially and injuriously affect the result.—Prof. Henry had tried cast-iron, and had found that it did not retain its magnetic power so effectually as common steel.

Mr. Lubbock then gave an account of the Discussion of Observations of the Tides, obtained by means of the grant of money placed at his disposal at the last meeting of the Association. He trusted that when members saw the results published in full, as they would shortly be in the Philosophical Transactions, they would not deem their importance disproportionate to the great labour and expense which had been bestowed upon them. He also wished to inform the Section that he had lately received, through the kindness of M. Arago, the printed Brest Tide Observations from January 1807 to the end of December 1835, and the use that they should be put to remained to be determined. He was disposed to believe that little more could now be obtained from the best observations than had already been, from the comparison of the London and Liverpool observations; it would, however, be desirable to determine the semi-menstrual inequality in the height at Brest, which might be done from the observations of a single year, and it would be also desirable, no doubt, to compare the observations of identical tides of London and Brest which might now be done; but on the whole, the labour and expense of a full discussion of them would be so great that he much doubted whether the advantages that would result would compensate for them.

The Rev. W. Whewell explained to the Section the results of the observations made within the last year, by the aid of his Anemometer. He had exhibited the instrument in an unfinished state at the Dublin meeting, and in a more matured state of its existence at Bristol; it had since received some valuable improvements, which were suggested by the practical working of the machine. It might suffice at present to say, that in it a small set of wind-mill vanes, something like the ventilators placed in out windows, were presented to the wind by a common vane, let the direction of the wind blow how it might: the aërial current as it passed set these vanes into rapid motion, and a train of wheels and pinions reduced the motion, which was thence communicated to a pencil traversing vertically, and pressing against an upright cylinder, which formed the support of the instrument. Ten thousand revolutions of the fly only caused the pencil to descend the one-twentieth of an inch. The surface of the cylinder was japanned white, and the pencil as the vane wavered,

kept tracing a thick irregular line, like the shadings on the coast of a map; the middle of a line was readily ascertained, and it gave the mean direction of the wind actually exhibited before the eye by a diagram, while the length of the line was proportionate to the velocity of the wind, and the length of time during which it blew in each direction; which therefore gave what he called the integral effects of the wind, or the total amount of the aërial current which had passed the place of observation in the direction of each point of the compass, during the interval which had elapsed since the time of last recording the instrument. This, it was well known, was a subject of much importance in meteorological speculations, but has not been hitherto accomplished. Anemometers on this principle had been also erected by Professor Forbes and Mr. Rankin, at Edinburgh, and by Mr. Snow Harris and Mr. Southwood at Plymouth; but he was not at present prepared to state the results of these observations, though they had little doubt they would be interesting and useful.

Mr. Osler, of Birmingham, read an account of a new Registering Anemometer and Rain Guage, now in use at the Philosophical Institution at Birmingham, illustrated by diagrams, giving a condensed view of the observations recorded during the first eight months in the year 1837.

He observed that the results obtained by this instrument are essentially different from those produced by the Anemometer exhibited by Professor Whewell. In this instrument the direction of the wind is obtained by means of the vane attached to the rod, or rather tube that carries it, and consequently causes the latter to move with itself. At the lower extremity of this tube is a small pinion working in a rack, which slides backwards and forwards as the wind moves the vane, and to this rack a pencil is attached, which marks the direction of the wind on a paper ruled with the cardinal points, and so adjusted as to progress at the rate of one inch per hour by means of a clock. The force is at the same time ascertained by a plate one foot square, placed at right angles to the vane, supported by two light bars running on friction rollers, and communicating with a spiral spring in such a way that the plate cannot be effected by the wind's pressure, without constantly acting on this spring, and communicating the quantum of its action by a light wire, passing down the centre of the tube to another pencil, below which it thus registers its degree of force. The rain is registered at the same time by its weight acting on a balance, which moves in proportion to the quantity falling, and has also a pencil attached to it, recording the result. The receiver is so arranged as to discharge every quarter of an inch that falls, when the pencil again stands at zero.

Mr. Whewell spoke highly of the construction of this anemometer; he had no doubt but that a very slight modification of the mode of registering its indications would cause it to answer every purpose which he had lately described as desirable. In its present form, however, it was the force of the aërial current, which is indicated, not the integral effect. He also highly commended the rain-guage, and the method of showing in one diagram to the eye so many important meteorological phenomena. Professor Lloyd stated, there was a very simple method of causing the anemometer of Mr. Osler to give the integral effect of the wind, and that was to cut out the paper covered by the tracings of the pencil indicating the force of the wind, and to weigh it; for it was easy to perceive, that since the ordinates of the curved spaces covered by those tracings were proportional to the force, and, therefore, the velocity of the wind, and the abscissæ to the time, the areas represented the integrals, or the total amount of the aërial current.— Mr. Ettrick asked. whether some other method of supporting the cylinder which moved backward and forward as the force of the wind varied, rather than friction rollers, would not be desirable—such, for instance, as bridle rods, or other means known to practical mechanics, and he was sure, well known to Mr. Osler. Mr. Osler replied, that many methods of supporting this part of the apparatus had been tried and laid side, as not answering; among the rest, bridle rods.

Professor Powell then communicated the progress of his inquiry into the subject of Dispersion of Light, since the last meeting of the Association. The results would, he said, appear in the next volume of the Transactions of the Royal Society.

SECTION B.—CHEMISTRY AND MINERALOGY.
—FIRST SITTING.
President—MR. FARADAY.

The first paper brought before the Section was one by Mr. G. Crane, of Yniscedwyn, "On the Use of Anthracite Coal, by the Combination of heated Air to the Purposes of smelting Iron Ore." The reduction of the quantity of fuel expended, to less than a third of that before required of the bituminous kinds for the production of one ton of pig iron—the increase of from forty to fifty per cent. upon the former make by this process,—and the increased strength of the metal when compared with that before obtained by him, from the native ores of the South Welch Basin, with the use of the coke of the bituminous veins and cold blast, were the leading points of the paper. Mr. Crane

dwelt on the abundance of this variety of fuel, of which there are large deposits in Wales, Scotland, Ireland, Sardinia, France, Transylvania, and particularly America.

The Secretary read a paper, by Mr. Golding Bird, "On the Crystallization of Metals by Galvanic Influence." To M. Becquerel we are mainly indebted for the knowledge of the power of a single galvanic circle in producing powerful voltaic decompositions, whilst to our own countrymen, Dr. Faraday, we owe that most important piece of information, that poles, or *attracting surfaces*, are by no means requisite to the crystallization of a metal'; and that all that is necessary for the reduction of a metal from the salt or oxide is the mere passage of a voltaic current. That this current may be of the weakest intensity has been shewn by Dr. Bird in an essay lately read before the Royal Society of London. The apparatus contrived by Mr. Bird was very simple, consisting of an external cylinder of glass, capable of holding about half a pint of fluid, filled with a solution of common salt (chloride of sodium); into the contents of this cylinder was plunged a second and smaller cylinder, furnished at its lower extremity with a plug of sulphate of lime: this second glass cylinder was filled with a solution of sulphate of copper; into the latter a plate of copper, furnished with a conducting wire, was immersed, whilst into the solution of salt a plate of zinc, also furnished with its conducting wire, was plunged. Under these circumstances, a current of electricity is developed, the plate of zinc becoming positive, and the plate of copper negative, although the *intensity* of the current could be scarcely supposed sufficient to the production of chemical action. Mr. Bird has, however, shewn, that when the connecting wires of the two plates of this elementary battery were immersed in a saline solution of a compound salt, the most important physical and chemical changes were produced; and that if, instead of immersing these wires in fluids, they are twisted together, so as to insure metallic connexion, it will be found that the electric current developed will produce most interesting and unexpected effects, on the metallic solution present in the smaller; for, although it might be anticipated that the copper would be reduced, yet we should expect that this reduction would be most obvious at the surface of the negative electrode; which, however, Mr. Bird has shewn not to be the case; for, on examining the plug of sulphate of lime (plaster of Paris), closing the smaller cylinder, and separating the solution of sulphate of copper from the brine, it was found that beautiful and hard crystals of metallic copper were deposited in it, not in a confused manner, but in veins precisely resembling those met with in mines, of which, however, it is scarcely necessary to observe, they presented but a miniature resemblance. From this, it appeared, that the *mere passage of an electric current*, independent of the presence of the poles, was sufficient to effect metallic reductions, supporting, in a satisfactory manner, the experiments of Dr. Faraday on this subject. The metallic crystals thus obtained were very hard and brilliant, resembling, in a striking manner, those produced in the vast theatre of nature; indeed, some specimens exhibited by Mr. Bird, obtained by the aid of his miniature apparatus, precisely, and, indeed, so closely, resembled the most perfect forms of native and ruby copper ore, that they would probably defy the most expert mineralogist to discover their true origin. These effects were, moreover, by no means confined to salts of copper; for, when solutions of antimony, lead, tin, zinc, bismuth, silver, or other metals, were placed in the inner vessels, instead of a solution of copper, the metals were, in every case, reduced, partly on the plate of copper which served for the negative electrode, but chiefly in crystals imbedded in the mass of plaster of Paris closing the inner cylinder.

To one circumstance, Mr. Bird particularly called the attention of the meeting, viz. the danger of considering the chemical changes produced in the bowels of the earth as in the first place depending upon metallic veins themselves; for, although it was evident that by the action of heat upon them, thermo-electric currents may be, and no doubt are, developed, yet we must regard the first physical cause which induced the deposition and formation of these very veins; and this cause, it is evident, can be none other than, in the first instance, chemical action.

SECTION C.—GEOLOGY AND GEOGRAPHY.— FIRST SITTING.
President—Rev. Professor SEDGWICK.

The first communication was from Mr. Whewell, "On the Changes of Level of Land and Water," which have taken place, or may be likely to do so. He mentioned that this was one of the questions proposed by the Association, and for which a grant of money had been voted; namely, to ascertain with great accuracy the differences of level of a number of points in two straight lines, at right angles to each other, and terminating on the sea coast. Although a portion only of the task prescribed had been performed, he could vouch for the accuracy of the survey which had been made in a line from Bridgewater to Axemouth. The gentleman who effected this survey was Mr.

Bunt, of Bristol, and the line is the same as that chosen formerly for a ship canal, between Bristol and the south coast of Devon.

The next communication brought forward, originated also from a question proposed by the Association at a former meeting, and submitted to a committee. This committee undertook to make experiments, for the purpose of determining the quantity of silt in sea water at different depths; but of their number the only gentleman who had performed an extensive series of experiments, was Captain Denham, of Liverpool, who now made a report to the Section, of which the following is a brief outline.

He stated that the proportion of insoluble matter contained in the Mersey, amounts to twenty-nine cubic inches in the flood, and thirty-three inches in the ebb, in each cubic yard of water; evincing a preponderance of one in eight in the matter of the ebb, or 48.065 cubic yards of silt, &c. which is detained by the banks outside the Rock Narrows each tide, with the exception of what the succeeding ebb disturbs, at the exhausted stage of the former ebb. Thus, the ebb of to-day ranges over sixty-four square miles, and the next ebb over forty-four square miles, reducing by one-third the first day's layer; that being the relative proportion of silt held in solution, and deposited over the outer area, at the northern margin of which the cross-set of the Irish Channel ebbs, limits the deposit by sweeping into broad water what may extend so far. Now the excess of silt, on the 730 refluxes of tide that occur in a year, amounts to 35,087,450 cubic yards, capable of spreading a layer, if equally disseminated, of twenty-one inches thick over the first tide area; one-third however is disturbed, and carried over to the second tide area; or there is an uniform increase of the banks, and decrease of water in the channels of the estuary of the Mersey, amounting to seven inches per annum. This deposition of matter is however very unequal, some parts of the coast and of the banks receiving great accumulation, while others are often taken away. At the quarantine ground, the bed of the river shoaled up twenty-two feet in eight years, and then eleven feet in two years, over a space of half a mile long by one-quarter a mile wide; and yet this was swept away in eighteen months. Captain Denham had been examining the port of Liverpool, for fourteen years; and he infers from his observations, that a time will arrive when no access to this port could exist, unless man sets bounds, by his ingenuity, to the operation of tidal action. He made a number of local observations, which showed the diligence he had exercised in both planning and executing whatever he conceived might benefit this most important port; and he finished by an explanation of his principle of a constant sea level, which he had ascertained to be at three hours before, or three hours after high water, and by exhibiting the instrument which he had employed in drawing up water from different depths.

Mr. De La Beche pointed out the great importance of these experiments, both to the scientific and the practical man, in affording information concerning operations and works on the banks of estuaries and rivers. He conceived that the utmost caution should be used in making embankments, as in most instances they had proved detrimental to the navigation—Mr. Yates spoke also of the enormous quantity of silt determined by Captain Denham, as being of vast importance in illustrating the opinions of Mr. Lyell, on the changes produced on the earth's surface, by causes still in operation. He alluded to a communication made some time ago by Mr. Horner on a similar point, namely the quality of earthy matter contained in the waters of the Rhine.—Lord Northampton gave Captain Denham's experiments as an example of the importance of the British Association, and of its peripatetic character. The important port of Liverpool has been ever in great danger of having its navigation seriously injured by the accumulation of silt at the mouth of the Mersey. In consequence of a question proposed by the Association, the true nature of the case had been discovered, and remedies pointed out.

SECTION D.—ZOOLOGY AND BOTANY.—
FIRST SITTING.
President—W. SHARPE MACLEAY, F.L.S.

Mr. Gray offered some remarks on the supposed production of insects, by the experiments of Mr. Crosse, and referred to two experiments made by Mr. Children in a manner perfectly identical with those of the former. The solution of silica was obtained from Mr. Garden, in Oxford-street, and in one experiment it was sealed up, whilst in the other it was exposed to the air; but in neither case was there any appearance of insects. The insects had been very indefinitely described by Mr. Crosse, some having six, and others eight legs. It was no proof that they could not have been produced from the water used in the experiment, because it was boiled, as that would not be sufficient to destroy the eggs of the insects deposited therein.—Rev. Mr. Hope remarked one peculiarity, that no one had given the insects a specific name, and that they merely appeared to belong to the commonest species of Acari.—The Chairman mentioned

the circumstance, that the seeds and germs of animals and vegetables are earlier and more quickly developed in a current of electricity, and that in all probability, these favourable circumstances operated upon the eggs of the insects produced in question. It was well known that seeds would retain their vitality for an indefinite period of time, and there was no reason why any limit should be put to the vitality of the eggs of animals.

The Rev. Mr. Hope read a letter from Sir Thomas Phillips "On a Method of destroying Insects which affect Books and Manuscripts, particularly the *Anobia*." For the purpose of preserving books, he had used paste, in which corrosive sublimate was mixed, which would for some time resist their attacks. He had effected the destruction of *Anobium striatum* in his library, by placing in different parts of it pieces of beech plank, smeered over in summer with pure fresh paste. It was soon discovered which pieces of the wood were infected, by the saw-dust, and these were removed and burnt. So injurious is this species, that he considered that one impregnated female would be sufficient to destroy a whole library. He had also observed two other enemies—a small brown beetle; and one much larger, introduced from Darmstadt or Frankfort-on-the-Maine, which was not very abundant, although very destructive. This latter was about six times the size of the former, of a black colour, with white spots or stripes, belonging to the modern family *Curculionidæ*, and being most partial to the books bound in oak boards.

Mr. Curtis suggested the employment of spirits of turpentine, as the effect of corrosive sublimate, and other poisonous substances, only lasted a short time, and soon stained the leather.—The Chairman remarked on the destructive effects produced by Dermestes in his library in Cuba. It was probable that the insects which attacked the paper were different from those which attacked the paste, the former being Acari, and the latter small coleopterous insects. He had found no method of preservation so effectual as to give the books a free current of air, and, for this purpose, he was always accustomed to leave his book-case open, the books being placed about two inches from the wall, so as to allow a free circulation.—Mr. Hope remarked, that the infusion of quassia had been esteemed a preventive; and Mr. Gray stated, that, in Geneva, the water used in the manufacture of paper was that in which quassia had been infused.

Mr. Golding Bird referred to the observations of Mr. Gray, with respect to the production of insects, as stated by Mr. Crosse in his experiments, which he had repeated on a large scale, but without any result, although he had continued them for some weeks, varying them in every possible form. He also explained that such could not have been produced from the silica, as this was precipitated from the mixture of the alkaline solution of silica and muriatic acid, the fluid passing through the filter being nothing but very dilute muriatic acid.

SECTION E.—ANATOMY AND MEDICINE.

*President--*WILLIAM CLARKE, M. D.

The second report of the Sub-Committee, appointed by the Association to investigate the Motions and Sounds of the Heart, was read by Dr. Charles Williams.

Before describing their last investigations, the Committee stated that they had found frequent opportunities of confirming the conclusions of their former researches on the natural sounds of the heart ; and these conclusions not having been shaken by any subsequent experiment, or well-founded objection, the Committee consider them established ; viz., that the first sound of the heart is *essentially* caused by the sudden and forcible tightening of the muscular fibres of the ventricles when they contract ; and that the second sound essentially depends on the reaction of the arterial columns of blood on the semilunar valves of the arterial orifices, at the moment of the ventricular diastole. Certain other circumstances were stated, as being capable of adding to, or modifying these sounds.

The chief subjects of their present inquiry were, the unnatural, or morbid sounds, sometimes heard in the heart and arteries ; and in investigating the causes of these sounds, which Laennec compared to blowing, filing, sawing, purring and cooing, or musical sounds; they sought to determine, 1st, What is the essential physical cause of these sounds ; and, 2nd, In what manner disease can develope this physical cause—A correct answer to these inquiries would determine the value of these sounds as signs of disease.

The Committee found that they could produce precisely the same sounds in every variety, by impelling, in various modes and degrees, a current of water through India-rubber tubes ; and by numerous experiments, they ascertained the relations which the character of these sounds bore to the nature of the impediment, and to the force of the current. They obtained similar results on experimenting on the arteries of living animals, and discovered, that in the human subject the same sounds may be produced by simple pressure, not only in

VOL. XXVII.

the arteries, but in the veins also. They found that ,the sounds heard in the neck, described by some eminent French writers under the names *bruit de diable*, and *bruit de mouche*, as signs of a particular morbid condition, which requires the use of certain remedies, may be produced at will, by the pressure of the stethoscope on the jugular veins of the healthiest persons, and is therefore not necessarily a sign of disease, but has probably been accidentally caused by the same pressure in many cases in which it has been considered as a morbid sign.

The Committee conclude, in answer to the first inquiry, that a certain resistance to a moving current is the essential physical cause of all the various sounds in question, and that this resistance is generally given by some pressure on, or impediment in, the tube through which the current moves ; but that sometimes the resistance is caused by a change in the direction of the current, by which it is made to impinge on the walls of the vessel which contains it.

The second inquiry the Committee think can be fully answered only by extensive clinical and pathological observations, with due regard to the previous investigations ; but they have planned some experiments that promise to elucidate certain obscure points of the pathology and diagnosis of diseases of the heart and arteries, the knowledge of which would be of direct practical advantage. These points the Committee propose to investigate, if the Association think fit to re-appoint them to this office.

SECTION F.—STATISTICS.—FIRST SITTING.

President—Lord SANDON, M. P.

Colonel Sykes read a summary of a paper " On the British Collectorate of the Deccan." In the Deccan artisans of various kinds do the work of the farmers in their respective branches, and are paid by allotments of land, and a per centage on the produce; thus, the barber shaves for his land, the tailor makes clothes for his land, &c.—which land is cultivated by them to produce food. The revenue derived by the government was 82 per cent, in the aggregate from land, and altogether averaged 8s. per annum for each individual. The native manufacture of silk and cotton has been almost suppressed by the machinery of England. There are few other manufacturing products of any value, and these are not produced in the Company's territories, with one or two slight exceptions. The transit duties on the conveyance of goods are exceedingly onerous, and form a great impediment to commerce.

At the conclusion of the paper, a vote of

F F

thanks was passed to Col. Sykes. In the course of a discussion which took place at a later period in the day, several questions were put to Col. Sykes, in reply to some of which he stated, that the wages of a head carpenter, as compared with the price of grain, were from 25s. to 30s. a-month; a common carpenter, 31s. to 35s.; a smith, the same; field labourers, 14s. a-month for a man! from 7s. to 14s. for a woman, and 6s. for a boy, finding themselves in everything, and working from sunrise to sunset. He was afraid that the loss of the two principal manufactures was not made up or compensated by any increase of raw produce for exportation. The cultivation of various articles might be greatly increased to the advantage both of the natives and of the people of this country : for example, several kinds of oils, and many species of fibrous plants, suitable for cordage. The breadth of land under cultivation has not been increased of late years. The instruments were so rude and simple, that were not the returns naturally so great, and the cost of production so trifling, the people could not live. The condition of the labouring classes is little better than that of the people in many parts of Ireland. The system of transit duties was under the serious consideration of government. Until within the last twenty years, there had been constant intestine wars, which were now put an end to under the influence of the British government.

Mr. G. R. Porter, read "A Brief Memoir of the growth, progress, and extent of Trade between the United Kingdom, and the United States of America." He began by observing, that in these days of watchfulness and severe scrutiny into every branch of public expenditure, it would hardly be credited that there is not a trace to be found in the Journals of the House of Commons of any account of the produce of the taxes having been called for by Parliament during the whole course of the American war,—a fact attested by the late Mr. George Rose, who having been for many years a Cabinet Minister, knew well the importance of such returns.

The British Colonies (Mr. Porter continued) which now form part of the United States of America, were, with the exception of Georgia, all founded in the seventeenth century. The date of the first settlement of each individual colony was as follows :—

Virginia	1607	Maryland	1633
New York	1614	Connecticut	1635
Massachusetts	1620	Rhode Island	1636
New Hampshire	1623	North Carolina	1650
New Jersey	1624	South Carolina	1670
Delaware	1627	Pennsylvania	1682
Maine	1630	Georgia	1733

It was not until more than a century had elapsed from the period referred to in the foregoing extract, and when they had secured their independence, that any part of the raw material employed in the cotton manufacture was received from the British plantations in America. A few bags of cotton, arrived in 1785 and 1786, were apparently of foreign growth, and had been transmitted to America from the Spanish main. Cotton was raised in gardens in the United States before 1786 ; but that was the first year in which it was cultivated by planters as a crop; and 1787 was the earliest year in which any of the growth of the country was exported.

Before the separation of the British provinces from the mother country, the statements which were given concerning their trade exhibited that of each province separately. Attention was then directed to a table which contained the official value of imports and exports from and to each province, for the years 1701, 1710, 1720, 1730, 1740, 1750, and 1760, and thereafter for each individual year to 1783, when the independence of the United states was fully recognized. For a long period up to that event the operation of the navigation laws had given to this country a monopoly of the trade with its colonies ; and Mr. Porter considered it worthy of remark, that so long as the American provinces continued thus connected with England, the increase of the commercial intercourse bore a very inadequate proportion to their increasing population. In 1749 the number of inhabitants in the provinces was stated to be 1,046,000, and the official value of exports and imports was 2,117,845l. Assuming that that the population between 1749 and 1774 increased steadily at the rate afterwards exhibited by the census of 1790, the number of inhabitants in 1774 must have been 2,803,625. If the trade had increased in an equal ratio, the imports and exports in 1774 would have amounted to 5,676,523l. ; whereas the actual amount was only 3,964,288l., showing a deficiency of 30 per cent.

Another table exhibited the official value of our imports and exports from and to the United States collectively in each year from 1784 to 1835. The earliest census for the United States was taken in 1790, when the population was found to be, 3,929,328. The official value of our trade with the United States in that year was 4,622,851l. In 1800 the population was found to have increased to 5,309,758. At the same rate of increase the trade in that year should have been 6,246,925l.; but as it actually amounted to 9,243,432l., the increase was greater than that of the population by 48 per cent. In 1810 the population was 7,239,903, and the trade 10,427,722*l.* If the proportion of 1790 had been preserved, the amount would have been 8,517,739*l.* The excess, after allowing for the increased population, was therefore 22 per cent.; but if the comparison is made with 1800, it appears that the increased trade is not quite 13 per cent., while the population was augmented at the rate of 36 per cent.; there is therefore a virtual deficiency of 23 per cent., which Mr. Porter considered ought to be ascribed to the operation of the Orders in Council issued in retaliation of the Milan and Berlin decrees of Napoleon. Pursuing the comparison to 1820, we find that the population was then 9,638,166, showing an increase over 1810 of 33¼ per cent.; on the other hand, there is a falling off in the official value of the trade between the two countries at the rate of 27 per cent. This circumstance Mr. Porter attributed to causes of a temporary nature, capable of easy explanation. On the renewal of the intercourse between England and America, after the peace in 1815, our merchants and manufacturers, stimulated doubly by the deficiency of British goods in the American market, and their superabundance and consequent low price at home, made such large shipments of manufactures to the United States, that a glut was there produced, and as this occurred simultaneously with a considerable derangement of the currency in the commercial cities of America, English goods were sacrificed at ruinous prices. In the meantime, the commercial distress which had visited our own country was passing away, and an effective demand for our products had arisen from other quarters, as appeared from the fact, that although the real value of British goods exported to the United States, which, on the average of the five preceding years, was near 9,000,000*l.*, fell in 1820 to 3,875,286*l.*; the general exports from the United Kingdom to foreign countries were greater in 1820 than they had been in the preceding year.

In 1830, the date of the last census, the population of the United States was 12,856,165, and the official value of the trade with this country 16,292,639*l.* The increase, as compared with 1790, was 227 per cent. on the population, and 252 per cent. on the amount of trade. If the comparison is made with the remaining decennary periods, it will be found that the increase in 1830 was as follows:—

	Increase per Cent.	
	Population.	Trade.
Compared with 1800	142	76
— 1810	77½	56
— 1820	53¼	115

The increase of population in the United States, between 1820 and 1830, was at the rate of 3¼ per cent. per annum. If we assume that the increase has since gone forward at the rate of 3 per cent. in each year, the number of American citizens in 1835 must have been 14,784,589. The official value of their trade with this country in that year was 25,671,602*l.* A comparison of this amount with the value of the trade in the years of the different enumerations exhibits the following results:—

	Increase per Cent.	
	Population.	Trade.
Compared with 1790	276	455
— 1800	178	177
— 1810	104	146
— 1820	53	239
— 1830	15	57

But Mr. Porter considered that it was not simply with reference to the numerical increase of the citizens of the United States that we should consider this question of the increase of our trade. During the forty-seven years that have elapsed since the first census was taken, in 1790, at least 11,000,000 of the inhabitants have been added to their number, being equal to an increase of 276 per cent. But during that time we are fully warranted in believing that the wealth of the country has been augmented in a much greater proportion; and it may be fairly presumed that, but for the untoward interference of wars, and of that which is scarcely less inimical to national prosperity than war —commercial jealousy, the dealings between the two countries must have become far more considerable than they are. During the period in question, America has added materially to her means of consuming foreign products by the extent to which she has carried the cultivation of exportable products. In 1791, the whole export of cotton from the United States was under 200,000 lbs; and it was shown by accompanying tables that the average annual importation of American cotton into this country during the last ten years, has exceeded 225,000,000 lbs, the value of which cannot have been less than 7,500,000*l.* per annum. In 1836 our importation was 289,615,692 lbs., which, at the average price of the year, probably produced more than 10,000,000*l.* sterling.

The intercourse between this country and the United States is important, not only to our merchants and manufacturers, but also to our ship-owners, and that in a continually augmenting degree. The tonnage of vessels which entered the ports of the United States from foreign countries, in each year from 1821 to 1836, distinguishing American and British from other shipping, was as follows:—

Years ending 30th Sept.	American.	British.	Other Foreign Vessels.	Total.	Centesimal proportion of British to American Tonnage.
1821	765,098	55,188	26,338	846,624	7.21
1822	787,961	70,669	29,872	888,502	89.7
1823	775,271	89,553	29,915	894,739	11.55
1824	850,033	67,351	35,016	952,400	7.99
1825	880,754	63,036	26,891	973,681	7.15
1826	942,206	69,295	36,359	1,047,860	7.35
1827	918,361	99,114	38,475	1,055,950	10.79
1828	868,381	104,167	46,056	1,018,604	11.99
1829	872,949	86,377	44,366	1,003,692	9.89
1830	967,227	87,231	44,669	1,099,127	9.02
1831	922,952	215,887	66,061	1,204,900	23.39
1832	949,622	288,841	104,197	1,342,660	30.41
1833	1,111,441	383,487	113,218	1,608,146	34.50
1834	1,074,670	453,495	114,557	1,642,722	42.19
1835	1,352,653	529,922	111,388	1,993,963	39.18
1836	1,255,384	547,606	132,607	1,935,597	43.62

The most important part of our trade with America consists in our exports of manufactured goods. The following table exhibits the declared value of those exports in each year from 1805 to 1836, with the exception of 1812 and 1813, the records for which two years we destroyed at the burning of the Custom House in London.*

Declared Value of British and Irish Produce and Manufactures Exported from the United Kingdom to the United States of America, in each year, from 1805 to 1811, and from 1814 to 1836.

Years.	Amount.	Years.	Amount.	Years.	Amount.
	£.		£.		£.
1805	11,011,409	1817	6,930,359	1827	7,018,272
1806	12,389,488	1818	9,451,009	1828	5,810,315
1807	11,846,513	1819	4,929,815	1829	4,823,415
1808	5,241,739	1820	3,875,286	1830	6,132,346
1809	7,258,500	1821	6,214,875	1831	9,053,583
1810	10,920,752	1822	6,865,262	1832	5,468,272
1811	1,841,253	1823	5,464,874	1833	7,579,699
1814	8,129	1824	6,090,394	1834	6,844,989
1815	13,255,374	1825	7,018,934	1835	10,568,455
1816	9,556,577	1826	4,659,018	1836	12,425,607

One thing which cannot fail to strike any one on inspecting this table is the large amount of our exports in the three earliest and two latest years of the series, when compared with those occurring in the intermediate years. The extent of the shipments of 1815 Mr. Porter considered as the result of the renewal of commercial intercourse after the war. The years 1805, 1806, and 1807, 1835, and 1836, followed long periods of friendly intercourse. The serious falling off that occurred in 1808 and 1809, Mr. Porter, as already stated, attributed to the effect of our celebrated Orders in Council, issued in retaliation for Napoleon's Milan and Berlin Decrees. Nearly one-third of our foreign export trade in 1805, 1806, and 1807, was carried on with the United States.

The high degree of importance to each country of the trade which it carries on with the other was evident from the Tables appended to the Memoir. The proportions which that trade bears to the entire foreign trade of each country are as follows:

* This omission is less to be regretted, because of the unfortunate state of hostility into which the two countries were plunged during those years.

Centesimal Proportion which the Trade between the United Kingdom and the United States of America bore to the whole Foreign Trade of each country respectively, in each year, from 1821 to 1835.

Years.	Centesimal Proportion which the Trade with England bore to the whole Foreign Trade of the United States.	Centesimal Proportion which the Trade with the United States bore to the whole Foreign Export Trade of England.
1821	35.95	16.95
1822	39.16	18.57
1823	32.70	15.41
1824	31.75	15.86
1825	37.67	18.31
1826	29.60	14.77
1827	35.03	18.87
1828	34.75	15.78
1829	33.75	13.45
1830	33.13	16.02
1831	41.78	24.36
1832	35.99	15.00
1833	35.41	19.86
1834	39.61	16.43
1835	41.76	22.31

The proportion which our export trade with the United States bore to our whole export trade was, in—

1805	..	..	..	28.91
1806	..	..	..	30.31
1807	..	..	..	31.80
1836	..	..	..	23.28

Mr. Porter stated that in the foregoing observations all remarks upon the state of convulsion into which this most important branch of our foreign trade has lately been thrown had been avoided, partly because its occurrence is too recent to allow of a sufficiently calm estimate being made of the cause or causes which led to the catastrophe, but chiefly because it would be difficult, if not impossible, to enter upon that subject without departing from that line of strict statistical research which it is desirable to preserve in the proceedings of this Section of the British Association, In conclusion, he remarked that the shipments of British produce and manufactures, in the year 1836, amounted, according to the value declared by the shippers, to 53,368,571*l.*, of which sum America took 12,425,605*l.*, or 23.28 per cent. The total shipments in 1835 amounted to 47,372,270*l.*, of which America took 10,568,455*l.*, or 22.31 per cent., the difference between the two years being, on the total shipments, 5,996,301*l.*, and on the shipments to America, 1,857,150*l.* Without admitting or denying that these figures give evidence of over-trading, he called attention to the circumstances of the two people—namely, that the means of obtaining the comforts of life are enjoyed by a larger proportion of them than is the case with any other people; that the habits and predilections of the citizens of the United States lead them to give a preference to British goods; that ours is the cheapest market in which they can procure many articles necessary to them; and that we are, out of all proportion, their best customers for the raw produce of their soil; and he asked whether, if the trade of the two countries were put upon a proper footing, and conducted upon enlightened principles, that amount of traffic could be considered excessive which gives annually to every citizen of the United States articles of British growth and manufacture to the value of sixteen shillings and ninepence three farthings!

A report " On the State of Education in the Borough of Bolton in 1837," was read by Mr. Ashworth.—The Return made to Government in 1833 on the state of education has been found very defective. In Bolton there have been no means of testing its correctness. But, if accurate, there has been a very remarkable increase in the number of scholars, being 25 per cent. more of day scholars and 40 per cent. more of Sunday scholars.

There are now 21 Sunday schools with 9,867 scholars, or 19¾ per cent, of the population, of whom about 2000 may be estimated as being in attendance both at daily schools and Sunday schools, leaving the number of 7,867 or 15¾ per cent. of the population receiving instruction at Sunday schools only.

There are 66 day and evening schools containing 3,227 scholars, or 6⅖ per cent.

Total number of scholars 11,094, or about 22½ per cent. of the present population, estimated at about 50,000.

Children equal in number to 20 per cent.

2,014 scholars in 4 schools connected with the Church Establishment.
1,085 scholars in 1 Roman Catholic School.
6,768 scholars in 16 schools belonging to various classes of dissenters.

In Bolton there are 5 charity schools with 692 scholars, including the 2 infant schools. There is also a grammar school, whose scholars have been entered at 120, being the number reported to government, the master having declined to give our agent any in-

of the population are not in attendance at any school whatever.

In the Sunday schools were found—

formation on the subject. The income was stated to the committee to be 450l.

Of superior schools for the children of persons in good circumstances there appear to be 17 with 721 scholars.

Of common boys' schools there are 15 with 851 scholars.
Of common girls' schools . . . 5 — 209 —
Of Dame schools . . . . . . 23 — 634 —

—944 being boys and 750 girls, all the boys' schools containing some girls, and *vice versa.*

Extracts from the reporter's notes will show that even this limited education is of a very inferior quality :—

" I find that in many of the schools there are, in many cases, from 20 to 100 scholars, crammed into a dirty room or cellar, without air or ventilation, the effluvia from whose breath and clothes is exceedingly offensive, and must be very injurious to the children's health. In most, too, ordinary household occupations have been carried on by the old women along with the teaching of the scholars. In some instances the neighbours were sitting over the fire in the school, smoking their pipes to chat and gossip.

" A good deal of the bad morals, bad manners, and absurd prejudices, which we find amongst our population, are perpetuated by the example of the teachers and their associates. It was sometimes difficult to get questions answered. To the inquiry as to the method in teaching arithmetic, several of them replied, ' *Why th' graidley owd-fashioned road.*'

" One of the masters, whose head was bound up with a dirty rag, and whose house, in a back street, seemed never to have been cleaned, told me, in answer to the question whether he was educated for the employment, that he was so educated, adding, ' *My feyther larnt eight parts of speech be-sides English, and Parson Fonds toud him tin he could teych him, no feer.*' Upon my remarking that I supposed he would also have been liberally educated, he said, ' *Oh, yes, I larnt accidents and grammar.*' His occupation he said had been that of a navi-gator, or, as he explained the term, ' he had worked at making lodges and reservoirs.' Necessity, not fitness, seems in almost every instance to have been the cause of the teach-er's adopting this employment, as is evident

by a perusal of the answers which they have given on being asked what inducement led them to undertake the profession of a schoolmaster. ' Old age, and to get a liv-ing.'—' My husband left me with four small children, and I undertook it to get a living.' —' My husband could not keep me, so I took this because I could get nothing else.'—One man gave as his reason that he had lost his left arm, and a woman that she had lamed her foot. Another old woman said she kept a Dame-school because ' she *geet* poor, and was a widow.' "

An abstract of the Report made by the Regents of the University of the State of New York, on Education," was then read by Dr. W. C. Taylor.

SECTION G.—MECHANICAL SCIENCE.—
FIRST SITTING.

President—Rev. T. Robinson, D. D. F. R. S.

Dr. Lardner read a paper by Mr. Reming-ton, " On the Railway Balance Lock."

This balance lock is designed to raise or lower a train of carriages by a horizontal motion. The trains are proposed to be elevated on a stage of wood or iron raised or lowered by wheels and axles upon train plates or rails laid in a series of inclined planes ; the construction of which was ex-plained by a diagram. The stages are pro-posed to balance each other as far as their own weight will suffice, and the power re-quired is to be supplied by a stationary steam-engine. The author believed that this system would be found superior both in cheapness and despatch to any system of inclined planes ; he described it as an at-tempt to convert a railway into a series of level planes broken by steps. Its general principle was to lift the trains from a lower to a higher level, by a single line of rails placed on a platform which was to be raised perpendicularly between the walls of the lock. At the sides of the platform are wheels or rollers, which are intended to play in diagonal grooves in the walls, the platform being connected by wrought iron rods with a superior bar; there is a similar platform on the other side of the engine; and the trains are raised by a series of levels.

Mr. Williams' paper on the Treffos Pump was next read. Great difficulties arise in the case of the common pump, wherever there is a long column of water between it and the well. It is proposed by this pump to keep up a continuous motion in the column, however long, thus permitting the pump to be placed in the most convenient position; it was said to save the power by which a long column of water is set in motion afresh at each stroke of the pump, and to save expense in the dimensions of the supply pipe by keeping up the continuity of the action, a purpose hitherto attained imperfectly by the use of two or more cylinders acting in succession, which Mr. Williams thought complicated and inapplicable to the purposes of the common house pump. Mr. Williams places an air-tight vessel or chamber, which he calls a "treffos," adjacent to and of somewhat larger dimensions than the cylinder of a common forcing-pump, the bottom of each being connected by a suction pipe. The treffos is to be quite filled in the first instance with water through an aperture in the top, and to be completely closed when the pump is set in motion. As the piston ascends, the water below rises in the cylinder and falls in the treffos, until the water is on a level in each, there being no atmospheric pressure in either.

Mr. Evans thought the proposed plan rather disadvantageous than otherwise. He and Mr. Adams considered that it was only an enlargement of the common pump, and subject to the same defects, the friction being greatly increased, moreover, by the use of a pipe of so small dimensions as that proposed, three-fourth of an inch. The difference of friction was very perceptible between pipes of $1\frac{1}{4}$ inch and $1\frac{1}{2}$ inch diameter; it must, therefore, be very greatly increased, indeed, in a pipe of three-fourths of an inch; while the employment of the second valve was also objectionable. If three valves were to be employed, the same effect might be obtained without the large chamber. Mr. Knight inquired whether the pump could be removed to a distance from the well, a case in which the common air vessel could not be used. The Secretary explained that such was Mr. Williams's assertion, the advantage consisting also in equalizing the current, and in the certainty of obtaining a cylinder full at each stroke. The object was to render the piston independent of the supply

pipe, but dependent on the larger vessel. It was answered, that for the certainty asserted to be given, the action of the piston must still be depended upon.

The Section then proceeded to the consideration of Mr. Henwood's paper "On the expansive Action of Steam in the Cornish Mine Engines." Mr. Henwood exhibited tables and diagrams illustrative of the various elements which influence the expansion of steam in the cylinders of some of the large pumping engines in these mines. The diagrams pointed to differences in the early part of the stroke depending on the quantities and pressures of the steam in the boilers, on the dimensions of the valves, and on the load of the engines; in the middle of the working stroke of all of them, parabolic curves described the pressure of the steam at successive instants, and at the end of the return stroke another parabola indicated the saving obtained by expansive working. In three engines at Huel Towan, East Crinnis, and Binner Downs, the relative duties performed by one bushel of coal were respectively 86, 73, and 73 millions of pounds lifted one foot high, and 1085, 870, and 1006 *tons* lifted the same space, for *one farthing of expense*.

A long and desultory discussion followed. Mr. Henwood stated it as his belief, that in instances where results considerably differing from those given by him had been obtained, as where the *duty* had been reported to be 120 millions instead of 80; some deception had been resorted to, probably by the workmen, in support of the qualities of their favourite engines, such as putting in a very large quantity of coals before the engine commenced, and then removing it prior to its being inspected. In his own experiments, he had never known the duty to be more than 91 millions, the lowest being 70 millions. In answer to a question put by the President, as to how he determined the quantity of water raised in determining the duty, Mr. H. stated the loss of water to be about one-tenth. His experiments, in answer to a question put by Mr. Ilam, he stated to be of from twenty to thirty hours. Doctor Lardner said, the question before the Section was of great importance in a general point of view, being, in fact, this:— "What amount of mechanical virtue resides in a quantity of coals of given quality?" Mr. Taylor had last year informed them that 125 millions of pounds were raised a foot high by the combustion of a bushel of coals, though it had previously been much doubted whether 110 millions could be so raised. Mr. Ilam, replied that in no instance, at least from a long experiment, had the duty much exceeded 90 millions. Mr. Galloway had, from an experiment of twelve hours, obtained a duty of 125 millions, where it had formerly been estimated at 80 millions, but he was probably deceived in the way described above. In another instance, 90 or 91 millions were found to be the correct duty where 127 millions had been reported to be so. In answer to a question from Mr. Guest, Mr. Henwood stated that the engines did best duty at a velocity of from 5 to 7 strokes a minute, the length of the stroke being ten feet: he now confined his observations to pumping engines, without reference to winding or stamping engines, Some single engines working expansively did better duty than double engines working not expansively, the duty of the former being 30 or 40 millions of pounds, that of the latter not more than from 10 to 20 millions. The variation of the strokes was not more than two or three inches in ten feet. At the end of the stroke a bell is touched by the engine, and is not left untouched more than once in a thousand times. Mr. Evans had made an experiment on this subject by suspending a piece of jack-chain corresponding to the length of the stroke, and had found that in the best engines there was an intermission sometimes every fifth or sixth time, sometimes every eighth, or ninth; the variation being sometimes scarcely perceptible, sometimes half an inch, sometimes 5-8ths of an inch. Mr. Henwood mentioned that the engine *must* reach within three or four inches. Dr. Lardner inquired whether the indicator was used to estimate the vacuum as well as the steam. Mr. Henwood said they applied it to steam only, as being what was to them most important.—Mr. Webster knew an instance where a rotary engine altered did rather more duty than a single pumping engine. The discussion ended by Dr. Lardner's declaring his intention to propose a recommendation that measures be taken to determine the duty of double engines expansive and not expansive, acting as used in manufactures; as also the pressure of the steam, the quantity of the water and the size of the valves.

The attention of the Section was next occupied by Mr. Russell, of Edinburgh, " On the Mechanism of Waves in reference to Steam Navigation." Mr. Russell had, at previous meetings of the British Association, given an account of his investigations on the resistance of fluids to the motion of vessels, and ascertained the law of interference of the wave in modifying the nature and amount of that resistance. Since the last meeting of the Associations he had extended his observations to a variety of subjects of practical importance, and amongst others to the improvement of the navigation of such rivers as the Thames and the Clyde, in which steam navigation was extensively employed. In these rivers it was found that steam navigation was conducted under very great disadvantages when compared with the open sea. Mr. Russell had discovered that in shallow water one great impediment to high velocities was the generation of, which he termed, the great wave of translation of the displaced fluid,—not undulation of fluid, but translation of one part of the fluid, reaching to the whole depth with equal velocity. When the vessel is propelled, the water heaped on its side generates this great anterior wave of translation, which increases as the velocity increases; the section of displacement of water is increased in the ratio of the sine of inclination. In one instance where the depth was five feet, the anterior wave was three feet above the level of the water, so that the bow was buried in it, and when the vessel stopped the wave moved at eight miles an hour, and though the vessel drew but 20 inches water, her helm was knocked off. This anterior wave moves with a given velocity proportionate to the depth of the fluid, equal, in fact, to the fall of a heavy body through half the fluid. In some cases, the boat being stopped, Mr. Russell had followed the wave for a mile, and found it advance at the same rate. The object then would be to make the centre of the vessel coincide as much as possible with the centre of the wave, thereby diminishing the anterior wave and diminishing the resistance. This wave is at present generated to so enormous an extent that in one case the waves extended to a considerable depth for a mile and a quarter, the depth of the river being increased 1½ foot in a channel of 500 yards. In six or seven feet water the imersion would be three feet more at stem than when the boat was at rest, the progress being doubly impeded by the anterior wave and by the stern depression. The question then was, to what was the wave due? and how was it to be got rid of? In general, the greater the difference between the velocity of the vessel and that of the wave the more the impediment was diminished. The increase of the velocity of the anterior wave relieves the vessel, and this is obtained not by widening but by deepening the channel, while at the same time the velocity of the stern wave is increased, so as to come forward to the centre of the vessel. In one instance a vessel moved at the rate of 4 miles with twenty two strokes a minute, at 6 miles with 35 strokes, and at 5¼ miles with from 60 to 70 strokes. The next great impediment to steam navigation consisted in the formation of lateral currents on the side of the vessel, which having the same direction with the motion of the paddles, had the effect of diminishing the relative difference of the velocity of the paddles and of the fluid, and thus diminished the propelling power of the paddles, the engine being obliged to make an additional number of strokes.   The third evil arose from the stern or posterior wave or surge, by which great injury was done to the banks of the river and to the smaller vessels navigating it.   At an increased velocity this wave rises in a cycloidal form into a breaking surface.   The remedy for these evils was to be found not in widening the river, as generally supposed, nor in giving gradual or gentle slopes to the sides of the channel, but in deepening the river and rendering its sides as nearly vertical as possible, by which the impediments were diminished to a great amount. Mr. Russell had made experiments with different forms of channels ; as, square or rectangular, with perpendicular sides ; angular, the sides sloping to the centre ; and semicircular.   The general result was, that in a rectangular channel the velocity was that due to the fall through half the depth of the channel. Thus the velocity of a wave of one foot was three miles an hour, of one of four feet eight miles, of one of fifteen feet fifteen miles.   In all cases the rectangular channel was found to be the preferable one.   Such a channel would generally be the most expensive, but sometimes, where, as on the Thames, the land adjoining was of high value and gentle slopes to the banks where therefore not attainable, the rectangular would be the cheaper form.

The next wave generated was what Mr. Russell termed the wave " of unequal displacement, " arising solely, it was found, from the form of the vessel.   This wave was seen diverging on both sides of the vessel, from the bow towards the stern, arranged in two straight lines extending to a great distance behind it.   This wave might be greatly diminished, and sometimes almost entirely removed, by giving the lines of displacement a slight concavity towards the stern, the vessel being sharpened out.   When the vessel does not raise the water in given uniform progression, but is so bluff that certain points displace more than others, an anterior wave is formed of excessive displacement, the injury done by which is only inferior to that of the stern surge.

Mr. Fairburn, of Manchester, stated, in reply to a question put by Dr. Lardner, that the results of his experiments corresponded with those obtained by Mr. Russell, and mentioned one instance where, at a velocity of seven miles an hour, the channel being five feet deep, the stern was dragging on the ground.—Mr. Herapath inquired what posterior form of vessel Mr. Russell had found

the best.   Mr. Russell stated that on this point the result of his experiments indicated a form very different from that approved of by naval officers in general.   They preferred a form bluff in front and tapering towards the stern.   Mr. Russell's experiments went to show that this should just be reversed, and he had made sixteen of them at different velocities, from three to fifteen miles an hour. In the navigation of the Clyde, the progress of the formation of vessels had been in accordance with this opinion.   At first they were built very bluff, with their maximum breadth at a distance from the stern of 1-3 of the whole length ; thus a wave of excessive displacement was generated, going off at right angles, and making a break more than was necessary to allow the stern to pass through.   Now the best vessels were built with full sterns and narrow stems, with their maximum breadth at midships.   For working well, however a very deep keel was, he knew, necessary to give the helm full effect.   In answer to the question whether these experiments might be made with model vessels on a small scale, Mr. Russell said that experiments with models were generally very fallacious and complicated, and that his had been made with vessels from 75 to 100 feet long.   When asked whether they were made with or against tide, he replied that the existence of a previous current modified the velocity of the wave, which was to be measured by the velocity of the water, not by the land.—Mr. Wenfall observed that Mr. Russell's statements were corroborated by an observation of his own, that in an instance where the tide rose thirty-six feet, the effect of the lateral waves had been to form a rectangular excavation to four or five feet.

EVENING MEETING, 11TH SEPTEMBER.

Mr. John Taylor read the financial report, from which it appeared, that a sum little short of 1000l. had been expended under the sanction of the Committee of Recommendations in furtherance of scientific inquiries, and that the total amount of the property and funds of the Association had, notwithstanding, increased to 5,284l. 14s. 6d.   He added, that the number of tickets issued at the close of the Bristol meeting, was 1350, and the number already issued in Liverpool, 1420.

SECTION B.—CHEMISTRY AND MINERALOGY.
SECOND SITTING.

Mr. Hartley read a paper, " On the Corroding of Iron by Salt Water."   The object of the paper was to shew that brass protects both bar and cast-iron in a very perfect manner. The brass did not appear to have undergone any action, which, as stated by the President, Dr. Faraday, is rather opposed to received notions of electro chemical action.

Dr. Andrews next read a paper, 'On some Singular Modifications of the Ordinary Action of Nitric Acid on certain Metals.' Bismuth in nitric acid of specific gravity 1.4, was rapidly acted upon, but this action immediately ceased when the bar was touched by platinum. On removing the platinum from the liquor, the bismuth will sometimes begin again to dissolve; at other times, its surface will become covered with a black crust, which is soon removed by the acid; but the metal, though now exhibiting a beautifully-polished surface, is no longer acted upon by the acid, or, at least, is dissolved only with extreme slowness. Thus, a slip of metal, which in its ordinary state will require only a few seconds to complete its solution, will when thus slightly modified, resist, for many hours, the action of the same acid.

Copper and tin present similar phænomena, but zinc, when treated in the same way, has its oxidation and solution not arrested, but merely retarded. Arsenic was found to present a singular anomaly when heated in nitric acid, so as to give rise to effervescence: the contact of the platinum in the usual way did not produce any effect, whereas, when an acidulous solution of silver is used, platinum exercised its usual influence.

In the case of six metals, platinum checks the action of nitric acid, and three of them appear to be brought into a permanently peculiar state, opposed to chemical action. Platinum always separates any film of oxide as its initial function, but after its separation, it exercises a polarizing action, for example, it brings the other metal into a peculiar state, which enables it to resist chemical action.

On the conclusion of this paper, the President drew the attention of the Section to the anology between the facts detailed by Dr. Andrews, and the preservation of iron by brass, as instanced in the communication of Mr. Hartley. In both cases, according to the known laws of electro-chemical action, effects, the very opposite of what are observed should present themselves. The bismuth copper, &c.should oxidize quickest when in contact with the platinum; and if as would seem demonstrated by Mr. Hartley, brass, protects wrought and cast-iron, the brass itself should be acted upon with increased rapidity. The solution of these anomalies, he conceived quite within the range of sci-

ence in its present state, and he urged upon the members of the Section the necessity of studying the phænomena in question, as their explication would constitute a very valuable addition to the existing state of our electrical knowledge.

SECTION C.—GEOLOGY AND GEOGRAPHY—SECOND SITTING.

Mr. Strickland read a memoir on formations of gravel in the counties of Warwick and Worcester. He commenced by pointing out the great variety of gravel which is found in England, and its varied positions, it being found sometimes in the vicinity of the rocks from which it is derived—at others very far removed; in some places regulary stratified—in others forming outlines on the summits of hills. In some parts we find marine organic remains; in others bones of mammalia and lacustrine shells. All these gravel formations are, however, unconformable to the beds on which they rest, and it is difficult to determine their age. The researches of Mr. Murchison were mentioned with great praise, in elucidating many points respecting the gravel of Wales and the adjoining counties; one point established being the exsistence, in former ages, of a marine current, from Cheshire to Gloucestershire, which had brought with it gravel in its course. The gravel formations described by Mr. Strickland, were divisible into two great portions, one being with flints, the other not containing any; and they occured independent of the minor variations of the surface of the country—the one portion, that without flints, being found to the N. W. of of the Warwickshire Avon, while the other portion occurs towards the oolitic hills; although, in all probability, they are of different epochs, it is not possible to determine their relative age, as no superposition has been observed. Along the oolitic hills there is also to deposit of local gravel, similar to beaches of shingle, as explained by Mr. Murchison in his description of certain similar phænomena near Shrewsbury. Mr. Strickland considers those portions of gravel that are spread over these countries as marine drift, and that gravel of a finer description, to which he attaches the name of fluviatile drift, may be observed in valleys, where it accommodates itself to the inequalities of the actual surface. In the marine drift no remains of any but marine animals are to be observed, whereas in the fluviatile we find the exuviæ of mammalia and fresh-water shells.

Mr. Sedgwick observed, that it is difficult to generalize respecting these formations, as they presented so many variations. He had seen gravel on mountains 2,000 feet high. Erratic blocks, he considered, could not be of fluviatile, but of marine origin, and organic remains of large animals were not likely to be abundant in gravel carried by currents of the sea, from the destruction caused by their violent action. Animal remains had been found in the clay gravel of the east of England; but this gravel he conceived as differing from that in other parts of the country—Sir Philip Egerton said, that Mr. Strickland's flintless gravel, occurring to the N. W. of the Avon, could be only a partial formation, as he had observed that in Cheshire the gravel always contained flint. At Cocknell he had obtained two grinders, of an elephant, and many *marine* shells, and many like shells in other places, all of existing species, and occurring often with pieces of rolled coal.—Mr. Phillips stated that one of the questions proposed by the Association, was the determination of the phænomena of the English gravel formations, but to the present time sufficient evidence had not been collected. He alluded to Mr. Murchison's opinions, that a strait formerly divided England from Wales: into this strait gravel might be drifted from both sides; and Mr. Murchison had discovered, in Wales, local covered by erratic gravel. He himself had discovered, in a valley of the Yorkshire Wolds at an elevation of 600 feet, gravel drifted from Cumberland, and containing bones of the elephant. He mentioned, also, the fresh-water gravel formation in the vale of York, in which Mr. Harcourt had caused sinkings to be made, and had found at the depth of 22 feet, the bones of Mammalia along with fresh-water shells. —Mr. De la Beche spoke, also, of the difficulty of the question. On the Blackdown Hills he had observed a peculiar drift; on adjoining hills a drift of a different kind, and in the intervening valleys a mixture of the two, containing the bones of Mammalia. —Mr. Clark also mentioned the difference of the gravel upon the plastic clay and the chalk of Dorsetshire. In that county he had observed two beds of gravel, one overlaying the other.—Mr. Trimmer mentioned the occurrence of marine shells at an elevation of 1,400 feet in Caernarvonshire; also of gravel at a lower elevation on limestone bored by shells.—Mr. Murchison stated his determination of the local gravel in the part of the country which he has termed Siluria; in this drift no shells are to be found. The drift from the north, he conceives, must have been submarine, and that, in all places, it may have unequal distribution, from the unequal elevation of the subjacent land. He alluded to his communication at the Bristol meeting respecting the elevation of Siluria at a different epoch from the other parts of Britain, as proved

by the difference of the gravel formations. —The discussion respecting gravel was closed by Mr. Sedgwick. He had traced the gravel of the central parts of England to its northern sources; and he instanced a singular phenomenon of a mountain, near Buttermere, which appeared to be water-worn by a stream passing over it. The recent elevation of Siluria, he conceived, was proved by the morasses and lakes in its lines of valleys, which valleys, although shaped under the ocean, had been evidently modified by existing waters.

The next paper, brought before the Section was by Mr. Mallet, "On the Mechanism of the Motion of Glaciers." This gentleman pointed out, that many phænomena of these singular masses had been hitherto overlooked; and, although described by many eminent observers, no solution had been given to the question of their movement, but that of their weight, which he showed could have only a partial operation, as they often rest on rugged beds, and these not always of much inclination. He proposed a very ingenious explanation of their movement by means of hydrostatic pressure, arising from the fact of the lower part of the glacier being of a higher temperature than the upper; this causes a melting of the under part, and a consequent raising of the mass in a perpendicular direction to the earth's surface, while its descent was at right angles to the inclined surface—a progressive motion downwards ensued, following the law of the resolution of forces. Mr. Mallet then spoke of certain causes of the rents and fissures in glaciers, these being often convex downwards, owing to the operation taking place in the middle part of the mass, which descends soonest, while the whole is held in its place by the upper and lower extremities; also tubular fissures are formed by blocks of stone, sinking by degrees in the glacier, owing to their higher temperature melting by degrees the surrounding ice. He then alluded to the singular accumulations of detritus on the glaciers, which are locally termed *moraine*, and are formed by *eboulements* in winter, and covered with snow. These Mr. Mallet found to assume linear directions, parallel to the axis of the glacier; and, from the regularity of these arrangements, he conceived it possible to discover the site of old glaciers from the moraine, which had remained on the ground after their destruction.

The Marquis Spineto made a communication respecting the Geology of the Desert between Suez and Cairo. In this Desert travellers have always suffered great inconvenience from the want of water, and this was likely to prove a serious obstacle to the proposed communication by this route to India. In order to overcome the inconvenience, Mr. Briggs, the British Consul, employed a Swiss engineer to bore for water. Mr. Gensberg, the engineer, caused the first boring to be made in the Valley of Kejehe, but being unsuccessful, he transferred his operations to the Valley of Candelli, where water was found in clay underlying a calcareous rock. Considerable ingenuity was shown in the excavation. Besides the usual boring downwards, lateral openings were made to increase the supply of water : borings were made in other situations, and very singular results obtained. A great variety of strata were penetrated, and this variety existed even within a limited distance of superficial extent: thus in one place marine sand was found ; and a little way off, terrestrial or desert sand ; gravel occurred only in one spot. But the most singular geological phænomenon was the existence of granite over clay, in which good water was obtained.

Mr. Horner exhibited to the Section a drawing representing some of the geological phenomena in the neighbourhood of Christiania in Norway, and read a letter from Mr. Lyell in explanation.

. Dr. Traill read a paper " On some points of the Geology of Spain.

SECTION D.—ZOOLOGY AND BOTANY— SECOND SITTING.

Mr. Nevan detailed some experiments on Vegetable Physiology. The experiments were performed on elms, forty years of age, in February 1836.

1. The stem of the tree was denuded, in a circle, of its cortical integument alone, leaving the alburnum beneath uninjured. On the May following the denuded part was filled up by the exudation of bark and wood from the upper surface of the wound, and the tree had not suffered in growth.

2. The bark and *cambium* were removed in the same manner. In August 1837 this tree sickened, and there was no formation of wood or bark in the wounded part. Two developements, however, took place, one above the other, from below ; the former having the appearance of roots, the latter were branches with leaves.

3. The bark and two layers of alburnum were cut away. The tree was at the time unhealthy ; it, however, put forth its leaves on that and the ensuing spring, but shortly after died. No sap was observed above or below the wounded part. Roots were developed from the upper, and branches from the lower part of the section.

4. The bark and six layers of alburnum were taken off. The tree became much less vigorous, but did not die, and otherwise presented the same appearance as the last.

5. The bark and twelve layers of alburnum were stripped. The consequences were again similar to the last two , the alburnum above and below the cut being dry, but an accidental cut that penetrated into the heart-wood exuded sap.

6. This was a repetition of the experiment of Palisot de Beauvais, by cutting away a circular ring of bark around a single branch. The branch continued to grow, and roots sprouted from the under surface of the isolated bark and branch.

7. In this the whole of the wood of the tree was cut away, except four pillars, composed of bark and sap-wood. In this case the sap first appeared from above, descending by the pith, and then from the heart-wood, the alburnum being dry. In this case the sap must have passed up the alburnum, and horizontally through to the heart-wood.

Mr. Nevan inferred from these experiments—1. That the life of the tree does not depend on the liber or cambium. 2. A descent of sap takes place before the developement of leaves. 3. That new matter arises from below ; which had not previously been allowed. He thought there were two distinct principles in the tree,—one, the ascending, or leaf principle ; the other, the descending, or root principle. Mr. Nevan had also performed some experiments on the conversion of roots into branches, and came to the conclusion, that buds or branches might be developed from any part of the root above its extreme end, from which point it was impossible for buds to be developed.

Professor Lindley remarked that these experiments confirmed entirely the theory of the structure of wood adopted by Du Petit Thouars. He did not think that the existence of any new principle could be inferred from the experiments. In the seventh experiment, the horizontal circulation of the sap was proved, and confirmed the accuracy of Hall's experiment of cutting a tree nearly through on alternate sides, when the sap still ascended.

SECTION E.—ANATOMY AND MEDICINE— SECOND SITTING.

Dr. Holland read a paper " On the cause of Death from a blow on the Stomach, with remarks on the means best calculated to restore animation, suspended by such accident."

The occurence of death from a blow on the stomach has never received any full or satisfactory consideration. The fatal result is referred by the writer to the sudden propulsion of arterial fluid into the left ventricle, and not, as has always been considered, to any injury or impression made on the nervous system

Dr. Copland required an explanation of three questions Had Dr. Holland observed the morbid appearances after death from blows of the stomach ? 2ndly. Is it possible to produce the retrograde motion of the blood from the part of the artery impinged, to the heart, without rupturing the semilunar valves? 3rd. Had Dr. Holland much experience of the treatment?

Dr. Holland knew that his views admitted of discussion and of objection, since they differed so widely from the received notions. He had only observed one case, and it was fatal. The post mortem examination showed a florid appearance of the mucous membrane of the stomach, especially at the pit, not unlike what is observed during digestion. The blood was fluid. With regard to the rupture of the valves, he could present no facts ; but, in his opinion, the valves would not be seriously injured, and failure in resuscitation could not be attributable to the state of the valves.—Dr. Copland thought retrogradation of the blood's current, as mentioned by Dr. Holland, could not take place without a rupture of the valves, or even of the heart itself. The heart could be injured in these cases physically, from the diaphragm as well as tho vessels; but, in considering this kind of death, we are not to attribute its cause to any part of the body singly, but to take a comprehensive view, and to take in the whole collectively.—Dr. Johnson had had his attention directed to this subject from an early age. At school there was a boy a great pugilist, who, in his rencontres, gave what he called his *heart-ing*, meaning a blow over the region of the heart. The first and principal effects were a sudden suspension of respiration, which was relieved and followed by gasping; the heart, oppressed, did not cease its action, for, if it did, *deliquium animi* would ensue: the pain was very peculiar. He agreed with Dr. Copland as to the cause of death in these cases, and could not conceive that a forcible impression of the aorta could throw the blood back, and force the valves; for in dead bodies this was difficult, though the vales were then flaccid, and here it was said to occur to the living—being still more difficult.—Sir James Murray had seen two cases of suspended animation from blows on the stomach ; one recovered, and the other died. The remedy he should recommend would be to throw a bucket of cold water over the body ; gasping would ensue, and respiration follow. He could not agree with Dr. Holland, more especially when he considered the slight influence the small quantity of forced blood would exert. A space of the artery, equal at most to about two inches, would be struck—the blood contained in one inch would be distributed downwards through the iliac arteries to the extremities, where space enough was found ; and the other inch of blood sent upwards, would find a much greater space through all the vessels of the chest and upper extremities. He would not deny that an inch of blood above the healthy quantity, suddenly propelled into the heart might injure that organ, but thought there was not enough to injure the heart and vessels, as they must be, from sudden violent blows on the stomach.—Dr. Williams had not read any author who gave a satisfactory account of the effects of blows on the stomach, but he agreed in opinion with Dr. Copland. He had paid particular attention to the semilunar valves, and must differ from Dr. Johnson. They are perfectly mechanical, and act in the dead as in the living bodies. They completely stop all entrance to the heart, and must be ruptured for entrance there. Dr. Williams then alluded to death from syncope, by poisons, crushing of the limb, ingestion of cold water,—and concluded by recommending treatment by diffusible stimuli.

SECTION G.—MECHANICAL SCIENCE—
SECOND SITTING.

Mr. J. I. Hawkins laid before the meeting the first *marble* bust produced by Mr. Cheverton from the machine invented by Mr. C. and himself.[*] The bust is of the height of about six inches. The machine itself he described as a species of engine lathe, in which the bust to be copied, and the block of marble to be sculptured, are placed in a frame capable of almost universal motion; so that the block to be cut, may be applied in all directions to a cutter in the lathe, while all the parts of the model are brought necessarily in contact with an index fixed at such a distance from the cutter, as are the corresponding parts of the model and of the block. Some cutters, he said, were as small as a pin's head, and in many parts of the machinery an error of 1000th part of an inch would be destructive. Mr Hawkins stated that he and Mr. James Watt had both commenced their experiments in 1804,—Mr. Watt having applied himself to medallions, Mr. Hawkins to round figures.

Mr. Fairburn then read a Report on the comparative strength and other properties of cast iron, manufactured by the hot and cold blast.

At a previous meeting of the Association,

[*] The Athenæum erroneously represents this as being "the first perfect specimen wholly finished by the machine." The circumstance which makes it remarkable, does not consist in any superiority which it possesses over Mr. Cheverton's celebrated ivory busts and statues, but simply in its being the first *marble* bust so finished.—ED. M. M.

Mr. Hodgkinson read a Report on the comparative strength and other properties of iron manufactured by the hot and cold blast.—In the prosecution of inquiries since made, it was conceived desirable to subject the metals operated upon to more than one species of strain ; to vary their forms, and, by a series of changes, to elicit their peculiar, as well as comparative, properties. First, they have been drawn asunder by direct tension. Secondly, they have been crushed by direct compression both in short and long specimens (the results of which will be given in a subseqnent paper) ; and, thirdly, they have been subjected to fracture by transverse strain, under various forms of section, and at various temperatures. Ten. bars of hot and cold blast iron were also loaded with different weights, from 112 lbs. to near the breaking point, and left for many months to sustain the load, and to determine the length of time necessary to effect the fracture. The bars thus loaded, are still (with one exception,) bearing the weight, having been suspended upwards of six months, and, from what we can at present perceive, there is every chance of a long and protracted experiment. In making the experiment on transverse strain, a number of models of different sizes and forms were prepared, and the irons, both hot and cold blast, were run into the form of these models ; but as there is usually a slight

deviation in the size of the castings from that of the model, the dimensions of the bars were accurately measured at the place of fracture, and the results reduced, by calculation, to what they would have been if they had been cast the exact size of the model, assuming the strength of rectangular beams to be as the breadth and square of the depth, and the ultimate deflection to be inversely as the depth, the length being constant. In comparing two irons, the greatest care was taken to subject them as nearly as possible to the same treatment.

A series of experiments was also made to determine the strength of hot and cold blast iron at various temperatures, from 32° (the freezing point) to the boiling point ; for this purpose, a cast-iron trough was employed, in which the bars to be broken were placed, and covered with snow or water (which was kept at the proper temperature by a jet of steam), as the case required ; the weights were then gradually laid on until fracture took place.

The strength of bars made red hot was also tried, and, contrary to expectation, they retained their tenacity and power to resist the load to a considerable extent ; the reduction of strength in a bar one inch square, in a range of temperature from 32° to that of redness, was rather more than one-sixth, the deflection being upwards of 1½ inch in a bar 2 feet 3 inches long.

RESULTS.

Carron Iron, No. 2. (Scotch).

Mean ratio of transverse strength, assuming the cold blast iron at 1000 :   979.9
Mean ratio of power to resist impact...................... 1000 : 1038.9

Whence, in the transverse strength of Carron iron, No. 2,, using a variety of forms of section, the strength of the cold blast is to that of the hot blast, as 100 to 98, nearly.

Devon Iron, No. 3.

Mean ratio of strength in sections of various forms (thirteen experiments... } 1000 : 1409
Power to sustain impact.................................... 1000 : 2712

This is an exceedingly hard iron, with a singular appearance, the centre or more granulated parts of the fracture being surrounded with a circle having the appearance of hardened steel.

Buffery, No. I, Staffordshire iron, cold and hot blast.

Mean ratio of breaking weight .... 1000 : 925
Mean ratio of power to resist impact .... 1000 : 965

In the buffery iron, the hot blast manufacture is weaker, whether we view it in its transverse strength, or its power to resist impact.

Coed Talon, No. 2, North Welsh iron.

Mean ratio of strength in a number of experiments............. 1000 : 1014
Mean ratio of power to resist impact .... 1000 : 1219

Modulus of elasticity in pounds for a bar of one inch square.

Cold blast { 14,680,000 } 14,313,500 lbs.
            { 13,947,000 }

Hot blast { 15,810,000 } 14,322,500 lbs.
           { 12,835,000 }

Elselear Cold Blast, No. 1, against Melton Hot Blast, No. 1. (Yorkshire Iron).
Mean ratio of strength .... 1000 : 809
Mean ratio of power to resist impact .... 1000 : 858

The modulus of elasticity in all the irons are computed, but only given in a few cases in the results.

Relative Strength of Hot and Cold Blast Iron, to resist a Transverse Strain at different Degrees of Temperature.

Cold blast 949.6 at 32°.   Hot ditto 919.7, Mean.
Ratio of strength, 1000 : 977.6.
Power to resist impact, 1,000 : 1,039.
Cold blast, 748.1 at 191°.   Hot ditto, 823.6.

In these experiments, it appeared, that the cold blast lost in strength from 32° up to a blood-red, perceptible in the dark as 949.6 to 723.1; whereas, in the hot blast, the strength is not so much impaired, being as 917.7 at the freezing point, and 829.7 when perceptibly red in the dark.

In all former experiments on the transverse strain of cast-iron, it has been assumed, that the elasticity remained perfect up to one-third the breaking weight. In pursuing these experiments, discrepancies were noticed, and results widely different to those generally received were observed. It was found that one-seventh, and, in some cases, one-eighth, the breaking weight was sufficient to produce a permanent set. These facts induced an extended series of experiments, principally to determine what load was necessary to effect a permanent set; and, if such weight, continued for an indefinite time, would break the bar. It became a question of great importance to know, if a weight, having once impaired the elasticity, would or would not, if continued, increase deflection. The inquiry, therefore, was—to what extent can cast-iron be loaded without endangering its security? To solve this question, ten bars of hot and cold blast, differently loaded, were placed upon a frame, to ascertain the amount of deflection at stated periods, and to determine what was necessary to break the bars with their respective loads.

	Inches.
In the cold blast, with a load of 280 lbs., the deflection increased in 103 days from	1.025 to 1.033
Hot blast, ditto ditto	1.173 to 1.197
Cold blast, with a load of 336 lbs., increased in 105 days, from..	1.344 to 1.366
Hot, ditto, from	1.573 to 1.627
Cold, with a load of 392 lbs., increased the deflection in 108 days, from	1.786 to 1.843
Hot, ditto from	1.891 to 1.966

Cold blast, with a load of 448 lbs., continued to increase in deflection, and ultimately broke, after sustaining the weight 35 days. All the bars from the hot blast broke in the act of loading them with the above weight, 448 lbs.

Mr. Fairburn stated, that all the irons were made of the same materials, and under the same circumstances. The irons were of fifty sorts.

Mr. Cottam inquired as to the elastic forces. Dr. Young and Mr. Tredgold had found that the strength of the material would fail if loaded beyond its elastic force: he wished to know whether the loads had been more or less than 850 lbs. to the foot. Mr. Fairburn stated, that some of the loads were more, some less, and that a weight of 280 lbs. produced a permanent set of an inch square bar. The President remarked, that the calculation as to elastic forces was scarcely to be confided in. Mr. Fairburn, in answer to another question, stated, that the hot blast iron was the more flexible and better capable of bearing impact; but that all the results of impact had been taken from calculations founded on cold blast iron. Mr. Fairburn stated, that the crystalline appearance was finer in hot than in cold blast. There were no experiments made on the loss by remelting, and none on wrought-iron,—all on cast iron. In reply to Mr. Cottam, he mentioned, that all the Scotch irons had no cinder; the composition of the others they did not know. Great difficulty had been experienced on this point, because the different manufacturers were unwilling to give information.—Mr. Guest professed on his part the fullest readiness.—Some conversation took place with regard to the peculiarity of appearance in the broken bars. The President remarked, that when a rectangular bar of any substance is exposed either to fracture, or even to temporary deflexion, a similar appearance was found: this was known from the experiments on glass, by polarized light. Mr. Fairburn in assent said the crystals were always more compact in the edge than the centre. Mr. Webster inquired whether the elastic weight was always less than one-third of the breaking weight. Mr. Fairburn said, always, and afterwards replied to a question from Mr. Guest, that the Scotch hot blast iron shewed a greater comparative strength as compared with cold blast, but that they had made no experiments on South Welsh iron. There was a perceptible permanent set from 280 lbs., the experiments being of from five to ten minutes in duration, and it being possible to judge the deflexion to the 1000th part of an inch.—Mr. Webster said it had been found that the first set was owing to the breaking of the first crust, and that beyond the first permanent set up to the elastic limit, the deflexion increases exactly as the weight.

(To be continued).

LIST OF ENGLISH PATENTS GRANTED BETWEEN THE 28th AUGUST AND THE 28th SEPTEMBER, 1837.

William Armstrong, junior, of Hawnes, Bedford, farmer, for improvements in ploughs. August 28 ; six months to specify.

John Joseph Charles Sheridan, of Ironmonger Lane, London, chemist, for improvements in the manufacture of soda. August 31 ; six months.

John Hanson, of Huddersfield, York, leaden pipe manufacturer, and Charles Hanson of the same place, watch-maker, for certain improvements in machinery, or apparatus for making or manufacturing pipes, tubes, and various other articles, from metallic and other substances. August 31 ; six months.

James Neville, of Clap Hall, near Gravesend, Kent, civil engineer, for a certain apparatus or furnace, for economizing fuel, and for more effectually consuming the smoke or gases arising therefrom ; the same being applicable for the generation of steam, and for heating or evaporating fluids. August 31 ; six months.

William James Gifford, Gloucester-place, Middlesex, surgeon, for improvements in paddle-wheels. September 7 ; six months.

Henry Vere Huntley, of Great Russell-street, Middlesex, Lieutenant, R. N. for improvements in apparatus for facilitating the securing of ships masts. September 7 ; six months.

Thomas John Cave, of Rodney-street Pentonville, Middlesex, gent., for a great improvement in the construction of paddle-wheels, applicable to ship's boats, and vessels of all descriptions propelled by steam or other mechanical power. September 14 ; two months.

Edmund Shaw, of Fenchurch-street, London, stationer, for an improvement in the manufacture of paper, by the application of a certain vegetable substance not hitherto used for that purpose, being a communication from a foreigner residing abroad. September 14 ; six months.

Richard Davies, of Newcastle-upon-Tyne, and Robert Chrissop Wilson, of Gateshead, Durham, earthenware manufacturers, for an earthenware tile, slab, or plate. September 14 ; six months.

Nevil Smart, of Bridge Wharf, Hampstead Road, Middlesex, wharfinger, for certain improvements in preparing the materials for making bricks, which improvements are also applicable to other purposes. September 21 ; six months.

Samuel Cowling, of Bowling, Bradford, York, barber, for improvements in raising water, applicable to various purposes. September 21 ; six months

William Joseph Curtis, of Deptford, Kent, engineer, for an improved boiler, or apparatus for generating steam. September 21 ; six months.

William Augus Robertson, of Islington, Middlesex, gent., and Thomas Simmons Mackintosh, of Coleman-street, London, engineer, for certain improvements in steam engines. September 28 ; six months.

LIST OF SCOTCH PATENTS GRANTED BETWEEN THE 22d OCTOBER AND 22d SEPTEMBER, 1837.

Lemuel Wellman Wright, of Sloan Terrace, Chelsea, Middlesex, engineer, for improvements in machinery, or apparatus for bleaching and cleaning linens, cottons, and other fibrous substances. Sealed 28th August 1837 ; four months to specify.

Archibald Francis Richard Rosser, of New Boswell-Court, Middlesex, Esq., in consequence of a communication made to him by a certain foreigner residing abroad, for improvements in preparing manure and in the cultivation of land. Sept. 1.

John George Hartley, of No. 11, Beaumont-row Mile End Road, Middlesex, Esq., for an improved application of levers, for the purpose of multiplying power. September 1.

James Hunter, of Leys Mill, Arbroath, Forfar, mechanic, for a machine for boring or perforating stones and other substances. September 4.

Henry Stephens, of Charlotte-street, Marylebone, gent., and Ebenezer Nash, of Buress-street, Saint George in the East, Middlesex, tallow chandler, for certain improvements in manufacturing colouring matter, and rendering certain colour or colours, applicable to dyeing, staining and writing. Sept. 6.

Thomas Hancock, of Goswell Mews, Goswell Road, Middlesex, water-proof cloth manufacturer, for an improvement or improvements in the process of rendering cloth, and other fabrics, partially, or entirely impervious to air and water, by means of caoutchouc, or Indian rubber. September 8.

Henry Vere Huntley, of Great Russell-street, Middlesex, Lieutenant, R. N. for improvements in apparatus for facilitating the securing of ship's masts. September 14.

NOTES AND NOTICES.

Birmingham Railway.—On Wednesday morning last, the large engines at the engine-house near Chalk Farm, commenced working the trains of carriages on the London and Birmingham Railroad, from Euston Square to the engine-house, a distance of upwards of one mile, by the rope. The distance is performed in three and a half minutes. The rope runs on friction wheels, firmly fixed on the ground. On the 10th of October the line will be opened to Tring, a further distance of eight and a half miles.

Paris and St. Germain Railway.—The returns of a month's traffic on this railway, from August 26, to September 24, are—passengers 205,736, receipts 250,533 francs. The estimated number of persons that travelled between these two places previous to the formation of the railway, was 1,100 a day (see our first article)—this number is increased sixfold by the railway, the daily average being 6,857.

☞ *British and Foreign Patents taken out with economy and despatch ; Specifications, Disclaimers, and Amendments, prepared or revised ; Caveats entered ; and generally every Branch of Patent Business promptly transacted.*

A complete list of Patents from the earliest period (15 Car. II. 1675,) to the present time may be examined. Fee 2s. 6d. ; Clients, gratis.

LONDON : Printed and Published for the Proprietor, by W. A. Robertson, at the Mechanics' Magazine Office, No. 6, Peterborough-court, between 135 and 136, Fleet-street.—Sold by A. & W. Galignani, Rue Vivienne, Paris.

END OF THE TWENTY-SEVENTH VOLUME.

INDEX

TO THE TWENTY-SEVENTH VOLUME.

G G

CPSIA information can be obtained
at www.ICGtesting.com
Printed in the USA
LVOW12*1609020816

498771LV00023B/200/P